Dispute System Design

DISPUTE SYSTEM DESIGN

Preventing, Managing, and Resolving Conflict

Lisa Blomgren Amsler
Janet K. Martinez
Stephanie E. Smith

STANFORD UNIVERSITY PRESS
Stanford, California

Stanford University Press

Stanford, California

Special discounts for bulk quantities of this book are available to corporations, professional associations, and other organizations. For details and discount information, contact the special sales department of Stanford University Press. Tel: (650) 725-0820, Fax: (650) 725-3457

Printed in the United States of America on acid-free, archival-quality paper

Library of Congress Cataloging-in-Publication Data

Names: Amsler, Lisa Blomgren, author. | Martinez, Janet K., author. |
    Smith, Stephanie E., author.
Title: Dispute system design : preventing, managing, and resolving conflict /
    Lisa Blomgren Amsler, Janet K. Martinez, and Stephanie E. Smith.
Description: Stanford, California : Stanford University Press, 2020. | Includes
    bibliographical references and index. Identifiers: LCCN 2019019671 (print) |
    LCCN 2019021740 (ebook) | ISBN 9781503611368 (electronic) |
    ISBN 9780804771764 (cloth : alk. paper)
Subjects: LCSH: Dispute resolution (Law) | Conflict management.
Classification: LCC K2390 (ebook) | LCC K2390 .A97 2020 (print) | DDC 347/.09—dc23
LC record available at https://lccn.loc.gov/2019019671

Cover design: Rob Ehle

Text design: Kevin Barrett Kane

Typeset by Newgen in 11/14 Minion

My deepest love and gratitude for my husband, Jesse Martinez (1941–2014), for sharing with me a life of study and contribution

JGM

To my husband, Terry Amsler, in gratitude for his inspiration, support, and enduring love

LBA

To my husband, Ted Radosevich, for his continuing love and support and for never giving up

SES

CONTENTS

ACKNOWLEDGMENTS

We thank the many wonderful people who have helped us along the way in writing this book.

Janet Martinez
In transitioning from legal practice to academia, I benefited from many colleagues who shaped my thinking about dispute system design (DSD). At Harvard Law School, Abe Chayes and Antonia Handler Chayes introduced me to international dispute resolution; serving as research director for their book, *The New Sovereignty*, opened a window into DSD. Howard Raiffa, Jim Sebenius, and Mike Wheeler and the Negotiation Roundtable at Harvard Business School provided a teaching group with whom to master a rigorous approach to decision analysis and negotiation pedagogy and practice that is fundamental to conflict resolution. Under the tutelage of Larry Susskind at MIT and the Consensus Building Institute, I acquired the intellectual framework and practice opportunities to engage international DSD through the series of policy dialogues on climate change and international trade. My deepest appreciation goes to my doctoral committee—Larry Susskind, Abe Chayes, Kenneth Oye, and Joseph Weiler—for guiding my research through the lenses of international law and policy, political science, and conflict resolution. This work explored the array of processes used by the World Trade Organization to negotiate treaties on trade policy, undertake national policy implementation, and pursue cross-border policy enforcement—what became the inception of my work in DSD. Upon returning to California, I joined Maude Pervere and the Gould Negotiation and Mediation Program teaching team at Stanford Law School, where I began teaching a course in system design with Stephanie Smith, a rich collaboration and friendship that led to this book.

We are grateful to our students, the many JAMS Weinstein International Fellows who resided at Gould, and our many guests who illuminated system design in practice and whose stories are detailed in many cases in this book.

Stephanie E. Smith

My thanks first go to Phil Heymann, with whom I worked at Harvard Law School when I was a student and thereafter at the Department of Justice in Washington, DC. His wisdom on the strengths and weaknesses of the formal legal system, the impact of public policy on the lives of individuals, and the importance of the responsible use of government power first informed my interest in what became known as DSD. I am also indebted to Magistrate Judge Wayne Brazil, who led the Alternative Dispute Resolution program at the U.S. District Court for the Northern District of California, where I served as the first director, and to Steve Toben, with whom I first worked at the William and Flora Hewlett Foundation, as he shaped and guided the grant making that supported the development of the conflict resolution field. In 1997, I joined the Gould Negotiation and Mediation Program at Stanford Law School to teach negotiation. In 2002, Maude Pervere, then the head of the program, approached me about developing a class with her on DSD, building on my experience as the rapporteur for the Blue Ribbon Commission on Kaiser Permanente Arbitration and my work with the Northern District of California court and other courts in a number of countries on alternative dispute resolution and case management. I am grateful for Maude's leadership and her partnership in developing the DSD Analytic Framework that provides the structure for this book.

In 2008, I began teaching the DSD class with Jan Martinez, who contributed her deep expertise in corporate law, policy analysis, and international treaties and organizations to help the framework evolve further. My final thanks go to our students, who have sparked insights and helped us see the benefit of training lawyers and other professionals to see beyond the litigated case to understand the broader system within which conflicts and disputes arise and the many processes that can be used to address them more effectively.

Lisa Blomgren Amsler (Formerly Bingham)

At the University of Connecticut School of Law, my mentor Peter Adomeit taught me about the system of workplace democracy through labor law. Thanks to training by my partners at Shipman and Goodwin, Brian Clemow and Thomas Mooney, I negotiated collective bargaining agreements representing school boards and municipalities, learning about system dynamics in labor relations firsthand.

When I joined the Indiana University O'Neill School of Public and Environmental Affairs faculty, colleagues A. James Barnes, James Perry, Barry Rubin, and Charles Wise mentored my transition to social science and empirical research on dispute systems. I am deeply grateful to the Keller-Runden Endowment for financially supporting this research.

I cofounded the Indiana Conflict Resolution Institute with Rosemary O'Leary, my longtime valued friend and coauthor, who introduced me to environmental conflict resolution and collaborative public management. Many doctoral and other graduate students worked at the institute and contributed to the ideas, the research, and the many coauthored publications on which my contributions to this book are built. I am grateful to Gina Viola Brown, Lisa-Marie Napoli, Tina Nabatchi, and Susan Summers Raines for their leadership in research and the field of dispute resolution and to Casey Brown, Won Kyung Chang, Won Tae Chung, Scott Jackman, Kiwhan Kim, Yuseok Moon, Rebecca Nesbit, and Denise Walker for all their contributions to the institute. Nan Stager kept us grounded in the realities of mediation practice. My coauthors Beth Gazley, David Good, Deanna Malastesta, and Timothy Hedeen helped build on this foundation.

Research can influence the world; it can also change our lives. Colleagues in four different areas of scholarship led me to DSD. My first empirical research addressed mandatory, or adhesive, arbitration; David Lipsky's generous mentorship encouraged this work. A phone call with Cindy Hallberlin started a twelve-year research project on what became the largest employment mediation program in the world, the U.S. Postal Service REDRESS program. I learned about collaborative public management from Rosemary O'Leary and about evaluating environmental resolution from Kirk Emerson. Most recently, Rosemary; Kirk; Tina; my husband, Terry Amsler; and I have had an ongoing, rich conversation about collaborative governance, bringing together this previous work.

Research is a collaborative enterprise. When the Indiana Conflict Resolution Institute applied for general support from the William and Flora Hewlett Foundation, Stephanie Smith became my program officer. Many DSD scholars and practitioners helped inspire this work. I am particularly indebted to Jeanne Brett, Susan Franck, Timothy Hedeen, Christopher Honeyman, Andrea Kupfer Schneider, Jean Sternlight, and Nancy Welsh.

Who Helped Us

We owe many debts of gratitude to our friends, colleagues, students, and family who supported and helped us as we wrote this book. Wayne Brazil, Mariana Hernandez-Crespo Gonstead, Howard Herman, John Lande, Carrie Menkel-

Meadow, Sheila Purcell, Andrea Kupfer Schneider, Ayelet Sela, Donna Shestowsky, Donna Stienstra, and Nancy Welsh gave us feedback on the earliest, roughest drafts of many chapters, and many of them reviewed final chapters years later, all providing invaluable feedback and support throughout this process. We especially appreciate the expertise and substantial contributions on transitional justice by Megan Karsh and on claims facilities by Itay Ravid. Over the course of years, many guests to our DSD class enriched our understanding of system design in practice, including Janet Alexander, Sim Avila, Byron Bland, Dana Curtis, Terry Demchak, Howard Gadlin, Barry Goldstein, William Gould, Deborah Hensler, Howard Herman, Megan Karsh, Malka Kopell, David Kovick, Sheila Kuehl, Grande Lum, Francis McGovern, Martha McKee, Carrie Menkel-Meadow, Andrew Olejnik, Sharon Oxborough, Sheila Purcell, David Rasch, Colin Rule, P. D. Villarreal, Mary Walker, Mayu Watanabe, Ellen Waxman, and Glenn Wong. We thank Jay Folberg, Jonathan Raab, Amy Schmitz, and Larry Susskind for sharing their expertise. We also appreciate the contributions from participants at a special session of the Stanford Law Faculty Lunch series and over the years in the Ostrom Workshop Colloquium series, including Elinor Ostrom. We are deeply grateful to the research assistants and fellows who helped with literature review and general research support: Kyle Amsler, Gilat Bachar, Loic Coutelier, Amanda Cravens, David DeCarlo, Laura Love, Adam Rachlis, and Noah Susskind. Many law students checked citations and references for accuracy, including Alexander Avtgis, Aurea Fuentes, Peter John, Susanna Foxworthy Scott, Purva Sethi, and Thibault Vieilledent. As we completed a draft of the manuscript, the Vincent and Elinor Ostrom Workshop on Political Theory and Policy Analysis did us a wonderful service by hosting a manuscript review event. Invited guests, Indiana University faculty affiliated with the workshop, and doctoral students each reviewed part of the manuscript and gave us helpful comments and suggestions. This is a marvelous tradition, one especially valuable for this book, because we want it to work for people in as many disciplines as possible. The workshop is interdisciplinary. Mariana Hernandez-Crespo Gonstead and Nancy Welsh were our outside guests. They have been amazingly generous with their time on this project over the years. The majority of participants were from disciplines other than law. We are grateful to Michael McGinnis and Gayle Higgins for organizing this event and to Burnell Fischer, Dan Cole, and James Walker, who also served as moderators. We thank the many people who reviewed chapters, including Stefan Carpenter, Dan Cole, Trish Gibson, Victor Quintanilla, Kenneth Richards, Travis Selmier, Joseph Stahlman, and Keith Taylor. Special thanks go to Carrie Menkel-Meadow and the two other, anonymous, peer reviewers of the manuscript. The expert assistance from Sonia Moss from the Stanford Law Library was indispensable.

We have great appreciation for those who helped us produce the manuscript: Lois Shea, our editor for the first manuscript; Elisabeth Andrews, who brought our three voices and styles into one coherent book; Cynthia Yaudes, our citation editor; AnaMaria Ponce, our administrative support throughout the years; and Eun Sze, our skilled and stalwart production chief in the home stretch. In addition, our thanks go to Kate Wahl, Michelle Lipinski, and their team at Stanford University Press.

And finally, our profound thanks go to our families—Terry, Daniel, Ned, Kyle, Greg, Olivia, Teal, Jesse, Serena, Noelle, Ted, Matt, and Pete—without whose support this book could not have been completed.

INTRODUCTION

AS OUR GLOBAL SOCIETY BECOMES increasingly connected, we face challenges that demand creativity and innovation, from access to justice in local courts to consumer recourse in an online market and from international trade policies to the management of environmental resources. Such challenges inevitably engender conflict as we seek to effectively interact in society and govern ourselves. We need systems that empower people to manage conflict in ways that enable them to tackle challenges together. How do we design systems for managing conflict? What is most fair? What provides meaningful justice? Who has control over the final design? How do systems vary and why? What is most effective? These are the central problems that dispute system design seeks to address. Accordingly, this book is about creating processes and structures that enable people to have access to voice and justice.

The phrase "dispute system design" (DSD) applies to both the product of design (the noun *DSD*) and the activity of designing a system for preventing, managing, and resolving conflicts and legally framed disputes (the verb *to do DSD*). DSD covers systems within all types of organizations: business firms, nonprofit organizations, international and transnational bodies, systems that entail conflict in governance, and public agencies or organizations. It also covers systems designed by groups of people who form social associations or organizations by reason of proximity, shared religion or ethnicity, professional affiliation, or other shared interests in community.

This book provides both a general introduction to DSD practice and a collection of cases that illustrate how DSD applies in specific arenas of conflict. In the first unit of the book, "Foundations of System Design," the six chapters describe broadly applicable bedrock concepts. The second unit of the book, "Case

Applications," comprises chapters with case examples that explore DSD across a range of contexts and experiences. Chapters 7 through 18 contain discussion questions that relate to challenges in each system. The case chapters are clustered into four parts: Part I, "Public and Community Justice"; Part II, "Conflict Within and Beyond Organizations"; Part III, "International and Comparative Systems"; and Part IV, "Multijurisdictional and Complex Systems."

The first unit of the book provides a basic introduction and substantive information for understanding how a dispute system is built. Chapter 1 presents an overview of the DSD field and discusses the multifaceted concept of justice. Chapter 2 provides a DSD Analytic Framework for understanding different systems. Chapter 3 describes the array of processes used in constructing a DSD. Chapter 4 presents essential tasks and skills needed for the design process, and Chapter 5 discusses DSD evaluation and assessment using social science tools. Chapter 6 explores DSD ethics and principles of practice. These six chapters provide core information that applies to the full range of DSD contexts.

The balance of the book consists of case chapters examining specific systems within a particular substantive context or at a defined scale, whether organizational, local, regional, national, or international. These chapters illustrate how to use the foundations to analyze the DSD context, identify strategic choices, assess how the design might affect the outcome, and consider how well a particular system addresses the goals of the respective parties, users, and society. Paired with the foundations, each case chapter can stand independently of the others and be read or taught in any order.

Part I focuses on the systems people encounter where they live when conflict involves broadly applicable rules such as law, neighborhood social norms, and religious or ethical codes. Chapter 7, on court programs, explores judicial systems in multiple countries and courts of different jurisdictions. Chapter 8, on claims facilities, examines systems created in the shadow of courts to manage mass torts or other collective, large-scale litigation. Chapter 9, on communities and justice, addresses community mediation centers, schools, religious institutions, and indigenous peoples' systems of justice.

Part II examines private, nonprofit, and public sector organizations and systems. Within organizations, it explores the fundamental relationship between employer and employee, beginning with Chapter 10, on labor relations, and moving to Chapter 11, on managing conflict in employment, which investigates systems apart from labor relations. Chapter 12, on arbitration in consumer and employment designs, bridges systems inside and outside organizations by examining how arbitrators address both employment conflict and organizations' conflict with consumers, contractors, and other organizations. Chapter 13, on commercial disputes, focuses on systems for disputes between businesses and their partners, suppliers, and government agencies, and Chapter 14, on consumer disputes, looks at disputes between organizations and those who consume their products or services.

Part III brings the discussion to a national and international level. Chapter 15, on transitional justice, addresses systems for countries emerging from war or authoritarian rule. Chapter 16, on international dispute resolution, examines systems aimed at disputes that cross national boundaries, including investment treaties and international arbitration courts.

Part IV addresses systems entailing networks, collaborative public management, and collaborative governance. Chapter 17, on designing systems for collaborative governance, provides an overview of the range of system designs across the policy continuum, including the legislative, executive, and judicial powers of government in a nation, state, province, or municipality. Chapter 18, on designing dispute systems for the environment, illustrates how wickedly complex problems of public policy—like managing a limited water supply or cleaning up a massive toxic waste spill—can involve DSD across the governance continuum.[1]

DSD is a new field, emerging as a synthesis of ideas and skills from a number of professional fields. This is the first book to cover DSD across such an extensive range of contexts across diverse academic disciplines. While each chapter references core scholarship on each topic, the relevant literature is both broad and interdisciplinary. For example, court systems and claims facilities are the subject of legal scholarship. Systems in collective bargaining are covered in labor and industrial relations. Social psychology, conflict management, and human resources literature in business and nonprofit management address employment systems. Transitional justice is a subject of many fields, including law, political science, and sociology. Systems for managing conflict over land use and the environment relate to environmental economics and science, public policy, planning, and public administration. These are a few specific examples; many chapters cross disciplines. This book thus brings multiple academic perspectives to bear on the field of DSD. An in-depth review of each academic literature is beyond the scope of this book. However, readers can use this volume to facilitate deeper inquiry and make connections across the disciplines.

This book is intended for anyone who is interested in the theory or practice of DSD; who uses or wants to understand negotiation, mediation, arbitration, adjudication, or other dispute resolution processes; or who designs or improves existing processes and systems. It aims to do the following:

- Provide a comprehensive introduction to an emerging body of practice and expertise
- Help readers understand the contexts in which conflict arises
- Help readers identify the strategic advantages and disadvantages posed by different processes, structures, and systems
- Present a practical framework for analyzing available options to prevent, manage, and resolve that conflict

DSD is a catalyst for innovation—private, public, nonprofit, and civic—that can shape how we interact globally, promote participatory processes that can lead to integration across difference and boundaries, and help an increasingly interconnected world address the question of "power over" versus "power with" others.[2] Designing is about creating. Accordingly, this is a practical book for empowering those who want to design systems that are fair and just.

FOUNDATIONS OF SYSTEM DESIGN

1   WHAT IS DISPUTE SYSTEM DESIGN?

DISPUTE SYSTEM DESIGN (DSD) is the applied art and science of designing the means to prevent, manage, and resolve[1] streams of disputes or conflict. Consider the following examples:

- *Employment discrimination.* Faced with many discrimination lawsuits by employees and significant employee turnover, a corporate general counsel and the director of human resources are tasked by senior management with proposing ways to decrease the number of disputes and reduce turnover. Which structures and processes should they consider—an ombuds office? In-house mediation? Arbitration?
- *Consumers in the global marketplace.* Customers around the world are buying products online but often have no cost-effective recourse when those products fail to arrive or are defective. Businesses selling these products and their country representatives decide to work with a United Nations committee to develop a dispute resolution system. What combination of international and domestic processes would facilitate cross-border e-commerce and protect consumers? Who should decide—consumer protection agencies? Merchants? Consumers?
- *Courts and access to justice.* Seeking to improve service to the public and efficiency, judges ask a court's staff to propose additional dispute resolution processes to supplement the court's trial option and integrate them for maximum effectiveness. How will effectiveness be measured? Which processes should they offer and for which types of cases? Who should provide the service and who will pay for it? How does the answer change, if at all, for mass torts like those involving medical devices, such as the Dalkon

Shield intrauterine device, asbestos-related injuries, or catastrophic oil spills, such as from the Deepwater Horizon in the Gulf of Mexico?

- *Rebuilding after war.* The leaders of a war-devastated country and other concerned nations struggle with how to adjudicate war crimes, seek justice, unite the country, and prevent future violence. Which processes will they employ—trials, truth commissions, reparations, memorials? Who will fund these efforts?

In each example, a lawyer, businessperson, nonprofit manager, or public official (working alone or with others) must address not just a single dispute but a stream of disputes over time. In each of these very different contexts, people are challenged to do DSD; through DSD, people have created institutions for managing human conflict across cultures and contexts.

The purpose of this book is to provide the analytic tools to help design better processes and structures to address a wide variety of conflicts and disputes more fairly and effectively. However, this book is not only about techniques for engineering DSD; it addresses not just how to do it but also why to do it and how to do it well. This chapter provides a brief chronology of DSD as a field, introduces key terms, and takes a close look at the ultimate aim of DSD: justice.

Origins in Alternative Dispute Resolution

A dispute, conflict, issue, or case submitted to any institution for managing conflict exists in the context of a system of rules, processes, steps, and forums.[2] Dispute resolution exists around the world and is evident throughout history; its processes are not new but, rather, traditional in every culture, through the informal work of village elders, commercial experts, and religious leaders and more formally in courts and tribunals.[3] Beginning in the twentieth century, labor relations provided models for resolving conflict outside government through private justice systems that include negotiation, mediation, and arbitration.

Mary Parker Follett, an early twentieth-century scholar of organizations, administration, labor relations, and political science, developed modern alternative dispute resolution theory in the United States by grounding her research on conflict and its management.[4] Subsequent research in organizational theory,[5] law,[6] economics,[7] human resources management,[8] organizational development,[9] political science,[10] public affairs,[11] and especially social psychology[12] have advanced theory and practice.

Dispute resolution scholars and practitioners advocated institutionalizing processes either outside government or in relation to it as society's way of enhancing community, problem-solving capacity, and justice. Over the last forty years, this movement was labeled alternative dispute resolution (ADR), in contrast to trial. ADR is now commonly understood as appropriate dispute resolution.[13] The ADR movement gave rise to community mediation centers funded in part by the U.S. Department of Justice to address social unrest during the 1960s.[14] In 1976, at the Roscoe Pound Conference on the Causes of Popular Dissatisfaction with the Administration of Justice, Frank Sander suggested innovations that led to the idea of a multidoor courthouse, one that would offer diverse processes depending on the case at hand.[15] During the 1970s and 1980s, the business community expanded the use of ADR to reduce transaction costs in addressing conflict in commercial dealings.[16] In the 1990s, ADR became institutionalized in many judicial systems, both state[17] and federal in the United States[18] and increasingly in Europe and other countries, including South Africa and Australia.[19] ADR also was institutionalized in U.S. federal agencies in 1990[20] and across the European Union in 2011.[21] A wide range of civic and philanthropic organizations have supported the use of ADR,[22] all of which has contributed to the development of process options in DSD.

DSD focuses on identifying the optimal options for preventing, managing, or resolving a specific kind of dispute. These options include both newer and traditional designs. Litigation and adjudication occur in courts and administrative agencies; these too are DSDs and are evolving with the advent of collaborative lawyering and problem-solving courts. Ongoing innovations include partnering, regulatory negotiation, organizational ombuds, and online processes and platforms.

Key Terms Used in DSD

The following are key terms used in the dispute resolution field, many of which arise from ADR (for additional terminology and definitions of process building blocks, see Chapter 3).

- *Conflict.* Divergence that exists when interacting parties (individuals or groups) are divided by apparently incompatible interests or are in competition for scarce resources; broader than the term "dispute."
- *Conflict assessment.* A process of analysis used primarily in multiparty public policy or environmental mediation or facilitation in which the third party identifies stakeholders, interests, and issues, prepares a report, and with feedback from participants, suggests a process for the participants to address the conflict.

- *Conflict stream assessment (CSA).* A process of analysis that in this book refers specifically to an early effort to identify stakeholders, issues, interests, and the nature of disputes and how they are handled; determine the stakeholders' willingness to offer input into DSD; and recommend a process for engagement in system design.
- *Convener.* Person or group who conducts the conflict stream assessment or brings people together for a public, private, or official purpose.
- *Decision maker.* Persons or entity, sometimes several, with authority to commission, approve, fund, and implement a DSD.
- *Designer.* An individual or team, internal or external to the organization of interest, that designs or redesigns its dispute system.
- *Dispute.* Manifest disagreement expressed through language or actions; narrower than the term "conflict."
- *Disputant.* One of two or more persons or entities engaged in a dispute.
- *Dispute stream.* Category of disputes that arise in a particular organization or context.
- *Evaluation.* Systematic empirical research on the implementation, function, and outcomes of a DSD.
- *Interests.* Basic human, social, or economic needs or concerns.
- *Litigant.* A complainant or respondent in a court case (also called a party or disputant).
- *Party.* Any person, group, or organization that is an essential actor in a dispute (including in a court case).
- *Stakeholders.* People, groups, and organizations that create, host, use, or are affected by a DSD.
- *Third party or third-party neutral.* One who is not a disputant, is impartial[23] as to the outcome, and attempts to assist the parties to resolve a dispute. The neutral may facilitate a negotiation among the disputing parties as a mediator, decide the outcome on the issues as an arbitrator or judge, or otherwise serve as a facilitator or decision maker in the processes described in Chapter 3.
- *Users.* The people and organizations that use one or more processes in the DSD.

DSD Within and Beyond Organizations

Throughout history humans have developed systems for managing conflict, but the modern language for DSD emerged from labor-management relations[24] more than thirty years ago as a way to think about improving how organizations, their employees, and other stakeholders address disputes. At the same time, scholars discussed conflict management related to human resources management and non-union employment conflict.[25] "Conflict" is the broader term, encompassing arenas within which disputes occur. Scholars from diverse disciplines—for instance, anthropology, psychology, sociology, law, and economics—have studied the causes and responses to conflict and developed a discipline of conflict analysis.[26]

Now, DSD most often occurs within or in relation to an organization, whether a private company, public agency, international institution, or nonprofit entity. A systems approach to problem definition and resolution of a stream of similar disputes has emerged in, for example, engineering, social science, and natural science[27] but has become notably prominent in organizational development.[28] Historically, organizations only *reacted* to conflict—they did not systematically plan how to manage it.[29] However, organizations became dissatisfied with time-consuming and costly disputing processes that did not produce satisfactory outcomes.

In its initial usage, DSD applied to systems for managing explicit, or "ripe," disputes,[30] such as when unions submit breach of contract claims to a grievance procedure culminating in the quasi-judicial forum of labor arbitration. William Ury, Jeanne Brett, and Stephen Goldberg examined how to improve this system in collective bargaining by inserting a new, mediation step (a third party who helps disputants negotiate) before arbitration (a private adjudication).[31] Would this addition change the dynamics of the system? Would it help parties resolve disputes faster and save money by reducing cases requiring a costly outside arbitrator? They found that providing mediation in unionized coal mines within twenty-four hours of a grievance both resolved disputes more quickly and produced substantial participant satisfaction with the mediation process and outcome.[32]

Grievance mediation as a process focuses on interests (basic human, social, or economic needs and concerns). Ury, Brett, and Goldberg recommended that systems focus on interests instead of rights or power to address conflict.[33] Rights-based dispute resolution requires a neutral third party to apply agreed-on rules from law, policy, or contract to a set of facts to determine who wins. It includes arbitration, administrative adjudication, or a court trial. Power-based processes use dominance in physical force or financial resources to impose an outcome—for example, strikes and lockouts in collective bargaining. Ury, Brett, and Goldberg suggested that a healthy system should use rights-based approaches (such as arbitration or litigation for law or contract) only as a fallback when disputants reach impasse; generally, parties should not resort to power (use of force or strikes).

Subsequent practitioners applied organizational development theories to DSD,[34] advocating more integrated conflict management systems that provide multiple points of entry to conflict resolution methods for an array of disputants with diverse complaints about the organization. Some recommended a key role for an ombuds or administrator outside the usual management hierarchy, but with a direct link to upper management, who has the authority to select staff and manage the ombuds office budget and operations.[35] Organizational DSDs can take a myriad of forms, including a multistep procedure culminating in mediation or arbitration or both, ombuds[36] programs giving disputants different process choices, or simply a single-step binding arbitration. A groundbreaking national study on Fortune 1,000 companies' use of ADR produced a framework for analyzing an organization's environmental factors and motivations that together give rise to a conflict management strategy.[37] The researchers recommend that organizations employ a wide variety of internal methods such as ombuds, peer mediators, resolution facilitators, hotlines, and peer panels.[38]

Dispute resolution scholars and practitioners have also applied DSD beyond the workplace and organizations. Conflict management or dispute resolution programs apply to courts (see Chapter 7), employment (see Chapter 11), education (see Chapter 9), the environment (see Chapter 18), community mediation (see Chapter 9), family and domestic relations (see Chapter 7), and victim-offender mediation or restorative justice (see Chapter 9). They exist in settings ranging from federal, state, and local governments to regional, international, and transnational entities, as well as private and nonprofit organizations.[39] From its early focus on ripe disputes, DSD has increasingly looked to prevent and manage conflict at its formative stages, thereby moving upstream. For example, upon starting a complex construction project, the parties, in a process called partnering, often commit to the principles of their working relationship and procedures for resolving issues that arise (see the example of the Big Dig construction project in Boston in Chapter 13). DSD also occurs during the creation of new entities (e.g., joint ventures) and treaty regimes, as the contracting parties try to anticipate the types of disputes that may arise and create structures and processes for prospective conflicts.

While system designs vary widely, research is just beginning on why designs take certain forms in specific substantive and institutional contexts and which designs are most effective. The case studies in Parts I, II, III, and IV illustrate these systems.

Guiding Principles

While not specifically using the terms of system design, Jeffrey Cruikshank and Lawrence Susskind of the MIT-Harvard Public Disputes Program propose fairness, efficiency, stability, and wisdom as criteria to measure the outcomes of dispute settlement.[40] In their view, fairness incorporates notions of procedure (participation in a legitimate process) as well as outcomes. Efficiency relates to time and personal and financial expense; they argue disputants can trade efficiency off against fairness. Wisdom relates to both fairness and stability: were the right people and adequate information considered in order to achieve a practical and implementable result? While focused on individual disputes, these measures can also apply to dispute streams.

Ury, Brett, and Goldberg specify principles for designing an organization's system for handling employment disputes as well as criteria for comparing process options. They recommend starting with interest-based, lower-cost processes, moving to rights-based, more costly ones only as needed, while providing adequate resources and support for all processes. The rationale for these principles is to minimize transaction costs (time, money, emotional energy), increase disputants' satisfaction with the process and outcome, enhance relationships among the disputants, and reduce recurrence of the disputes.[41]

Cathy A. Costantino and Christina Sickles Merchant focus on principles for organizational systems to determine whether designers can tailor some form of ADR to a specific category of disputes. They seek to ascertain whether prevention (not just dispute resolution) is available, the system is accessible with minimal bureaucracy and maximal choice over the processes and selection of third parties, and the organization supports the DSD. In evaluation, they find that higher-quality systems are more efficient (in terms of cost and time) and lead to more satisfaction with the process, outcome, and ongoing relationship between disputants. They include in the notion of effectiveness the durability of the resolution, the nature of the outcome (quantity and character of dispute recurrence), and the effect on the organizational environment.[42]

DSD scholars consistently refer to fairness and disputants' satisfaction with process and outcome.[43] The quality of a system might be judged by whether it conforms with or diverges from legal and societal norms. Experts often address the importance of justice or fairness in a system. We synthesize these overlapping ideas into a list of key guiding principles:

DSD GUIDING PRINCIPLES
- Create a DSD that is fair and just.
- Consider efficiency for the institution and participants.
- Engage stakeholders—including users—in design and implementation.

- Consider and seek prevention.
- Provide multiple and appropriate interest-based and rights-based process options.
- Ensure users flexibility in choice and sequence of process options.
- Match the design to the available resources, including training and support.
- Train and educate system providers, users, and other stakeholders.
- Make the DSD accountable through transparency and evaluation, with appropriate concern for privacy, to improve it continuously.

Many scholars refer to fairness and justice as essential principles for a system handling conflict; however, there are many ways to define what these concepts mean.

The Overarching Goal of DSD: To Deliver Justice

In developing a DSD to resolve a stream of similar disputes, what should be a dominant concern and primary goal? This book's premise is that any dispute system should aim to achieve some measure of justice. Designers, whether lawyers,[44] consultants,[45] or scholars of institutional design,[46] serve as architects of social structures that provide legal, political, economic, and social order.[47] Some stakeholders may primarily seek objectives such as economic efficiency. DSD can help humans work together by resolving disputes through negotiation and communication. Scholarship on behavioral economics suggests that economic efficiency, standing alone, cannot provide an adequate framework for analyzing how humans can prevent, manage, or resolve conflict.[48] Moreover, effective DSD can produce an appropriately balanced and fair system using available resources, provided a measure of justice remains its lodestar.

Contemporary leading philosophers have commented on the role of justice in shaping society. Amartya Sen departs from the definition of justice as the design of ideal social arrangements and institutions, arguing instead for defining justice in terms of "the lives that people manage—or do not manage—to live," or "a realized actuality."[49] Michael Sandel suggests there have been three approaches to justice: (1) maximizing utility or welfare (utilitarian, or the greatest happiness for the greatest number); (2) respecting freedom of choice, either libertarian (the actual choices people make in a free market) or liberal egalitarian (hypothetical choices people would make in an original position of equality); and (3) cultivating virtue and reasoning about the common good, which is his preferred approach.[50] Both scholars recognize how individual human values and contexts (e.g., political, religious, cultural) and their diversity inform how we define justice; both scholars incorporate people's voice in democracy. Thus, these philosophers suggest justice takes form in a DSD when participants and stakeholders cultivate virtue and reason together to shape resolutions for the common good on the basis of their lived reality. DSD forms—and how they reflect measures of justice—will consequently vary.

This section reviews definitions of justice and how researchers use them in assessing the success and accountability of DSDs. Justice is not simply what a court in a given jurisdiction would order or require. The term "justice" takes on many meanings in philosophy, jurisprudence, organizational behavior, social psychology, codes of ethics, and human norms for fairness.[51] These definitions fall loosely into five families: outcomes (e.g., substantive, distributive, utilitarian, and social justice); process (e.g., voice and procedural justice); organizations (e.g., organizational, interactional, informational, and interpersonal justice); community (e.g., corrective, retributive, deterrent, restorative, transitional, communitarian, and communicative justice); and formal justice, personal justice, and injustice. While these categories simplify the array of definitions, they are not mutually exclusive. A brief survey of research findings related to each type of justice in DSD program evaluation follows.

Outcomes in Substantive, Distributive, Allocative, Utilitarian, and Social Justice

Substantive and distributive justice tend to reflect the justice of an outcome produced by a decision process. Aristotle argued it was distributive justice when the state distributed money, honors, and other things of value.[52] John Rawls distinguished among substantive justice (the assignment of fundamental rights and duties and the division of advantages from social cooperation),[53] formal justice (the regularity of a process),[54] social justice (basic structures of society and arrangement of major social institutions into one scheme of cooperation),[55] distributive justice (distribution of advantages in a society),[56] and allocative justice (distributive justice that occurs when a given collection of goods is to be divided among definite individuals with known desires and needs and the individuals did not produce the goods).[57] He observes that justice becomes efficiency unless equality is preferred and that this view of distributive justice is related to classical utilitarianism, as in "the greatest good for the greatest number."[58] Rawls argues for "justice as fairness."[59] Starting from a social system of equal citizenship and varying levels of income and wealth, he argues that inequality is justified only by improving the situation of the least advantaged person in a situation in which no one knows whether she will be the least advantaged person.[60]

In social science, distributive justice has roots in social equity theory.[61] The theory posits that social behavior occurs in response to the distribution of outcomes. An allocation is equitable when outcomes are proportional to the contributions of group members.[62] Thus, in research on a DSD involving mediation, distributive justice suggests that satisfaction is a function of outcome, specifically the content of a settlement. In theory, participants are more satisfied when they believe that the settlement is fair and favorable. A substantial body of empirical research supports the distributive justice model as an explanation of satisfaction with outcomes.[63]

Egalitarian justice entails distributions that compensate people for undeserved inequalities—for example, by reason of birth.[64] One example is consent decree DSDs providing for affirmative action to compensate for historic discrimination based on race, ethnicity, or gender. DSDs providing for class-wide reparations or mass tort claims can also be viewed as examples of egalitarian justice.[65] In contrast, restitutionary justice imposes strict liability for harm caused as a form of distributive justice on the basis of public policy grounds to reduce risk.[66]

Processes in Procedural Justice

Procedural justice has different meanings in jurisprudence and social psychology. Within the fields of philosophy and jurisprudence, it is a method of arriving at distributive justice—seen, for example, in the fair-division rule that the person who cuts the cake must take the last piece[67] or a rule for distributing goods based on random procedures such as odds, dice, or gambling.[68] In contrast, "imperfect procedural justice" refers to the inevitable human error factor in trials, such as the problem of false convictions of innocent people in criminal trials.[69] Two fundamental principles make a procedure fair: participation and accuracy.[70] Procedural justice as due process has been used, for example, to evaluate the World Trade Organization's Dispute Settlement Procedure.[71]

Within social psychology and organizational behavior, procedural justice and its cousin, organizational justice, are the primary frames through which sponsors or decision makers evaluate DSDs. Most studies take the form of comparative, subjective judgments of fairness and satisfaction based on interviews or surveys of participants and their representatives.[72] Unlike pure procedural justice in law, procedural justice in these fields refers to individual participant perceptions of fairness of the rules and procedures used to resolve conflict;[73] participants' perceptions of fairness in allocation outcomes are substantially affected by factors other than whether they won or lost.[74] In contrast to distributive justice, which suggests that satisfaction is a function of outcome, procedural justice views satisfaction as a function of process (the steps taken to reach the decision). People value participation in the life of their group and their status as members. How other group members treat them in conflict shapes perceptions of procedural justice. When the group's procedures are in accord with participants' fundamental values, like participation, dignity, and respect, they perceive procedural justice.[75]

Procedural justice shapes DSDs in courts and adjudicatory processes.[76] Among its traditional principles are impartiality, opportunity to be heard, legal grounds for decisions,[77] neutrality of the process and decision maker,[78] treatment of the participants with dignity and respect,[79] and the trustworthiness of the decision-making authority.[80] In mass claims DSDs, Kenneth Feinberg developed a reputation as trustworthy in his administration of the compensation fund created for victims of 9/11;[81] later he was given $20 billion by British Petroleum to distribute to victims of the BP oil spill in the Gulf of Mexico, and General Motors hired him to design a system for compensation for injuries from an automobile defect. In general, research suggests that if organizational processes and procedures are perceived to be fair, participants will be more satisfied,[82] more willing to accept the resolution of that procedure, and more likely to form positive attitudes about the organization.[83] However, in some contexts, substantive justice may take priority. In prisons, those incarcerated have different experiences of procedural versus substantive justice; scholars in 2018 challenged the accepted theories of procedural justice, finding that the high stakes in prison grievance systems and the power of institutional context shape attitudes about fairness and justice.[84] These differences make substantive justice dominant.

Interactional, Informational, and Interpersonal Justice

Beginning in the 1980s, researchers in social psychology, organizational behavior, and industrial relations adapted procedural justice to the context of internal and external conflict related to employment in organizations. They developed the notion of interactional justice, or the quality of interpersonal treatment received during the enactment of organizational procedures,[85] focusing on aspects of interactions that are not prescribed by procedures.[86] Research has identified two components of interactional justice: interpersonal justice and informational justice.[87] These two components overlap, but empirical research suggests that they should be considered separately because each has differential and independent effects on perceptions of justice.[88]

Informational justice focuses on communication regarding procedures. In employment DSDs, research suggests that employees' perceptions of informational justice are enhanced if the employer explains the procedures for determining outcomes,[89] because such explanations enable employees to evaluate the structural aspects of the process and their enactment.[90] However, to perceive explanations as fair, employees must recognize them as sincere, communicated without ulterior motives,[91] based on sound reasoning with relevant information, and determined by legitimate (layoffs based on seniority) rather than arbitrary (lottery) factors.[92] This concept differs from the jurisprudence of procedural justice in law, which includes random procedures such as noted above.

Interpersonal justice reflects the degree to which authorities treat people with politeness, dignity, and respect. Interpersonal justice can alter reactions to decisions because people feel better about an unfavorable outcome when authorities treat them with sensitivity.[93] Interpersonal treatment is, for example, interpersonal communication; truthfulness, respect, propriety of questions, and justification; and honesty, courtesy, timely feedback, and respect for rights.[94]

Community and Justice in Corrective, Retributive, Deterrent, Restorative, Transitional, Communitarian, and Communicative Justice

All varieties of justice ultimately concern how humans function in a community. Judges engage in corrective justice when they issue penalties to take away gains and restore equality. Corrective justice assumes an existing structure of legal rights and is useful for both tort[95] and criminal justice, which in turn concerns retributive and deterrent justice.[96] Deterrence rests on the notion that severe penalties are justified if they reduce the overall incidence of crime.[97] Retributive justice enables vengeance or punishment by society in lieu of individual vengeance; it applies to both criminal and tort law.[98] DSDs include criminal justice systems and plea bargaining in the shadow of the criminal trial.[99]

Restorative justice offers an alternative to deterrence and retribution.[100] Drawing on religious traditions advocating atonement, forgiveness, and compassion,[101] restorative justice seeks to promote reconciliation between victim and offender and to reintegrate the offender into the community.[102] For example, it could allow a homeowner and a juvenile who damaged the property to work out repairs. John Braithwaite observes that "restorative justice requires us to think holistically about legal justice and social justice rather than to regard legal justice and social justice as quite separate things, best delivered by separate institutions."[103] DSDs entailing restorative justice include "victim-offender mediation, family group conferencing, peacemaking circles, community reparative boards, and victim impact panels."[104]

Transitional justice is a contested field; in one view, it describes the process of establishing rule of law and democracy in a postconflict society (for a deeper discussion, see Chapter 15).[105] It includes DSDs for different purposes. For example, it might promote national reconciliation using historical inquiries, reparations, selective justice or prosecution, amnesties, administrative measures to redistribute power, and constitutional reform. One goal might be to help the community "to reconstitute the collective across potentially divisive racial, ethnic, and religious lines."[106] A growing literature examines the DSDs of truth and reconciliation commissions, with South Africa's as a leading example.

Communicative justice is idealized speech or undistorted communication.[107] This conception of justice aims to achieve distributive justice through a dialogic process involving neutrality and participation in rational discourse about political legitimacy.[108] For example, an upstream DSD could address conflict over policy involving deliberative democracy[109] by randomly assigning small groups of people to tables to discuss a city budget and recommend allocations. Such public-policy dispute resolution in legislative and quasi-legislative activity allows stakeholders to identify preferences, set priorities, and make policy choices.[110] Communicative and dialogic justice and restorative justice share the central concept of discourse as a process for arriving at just outcomes;[111] for example, a circle of Native American leaders will deliberate on how to resolve an issue facing the tribe. Scholars advocate communicative justice through discourse as a means of self-determination and democracy.[112]

Formal Justice, Personal Justice, and Injustice

These three concepts provide a lens through which to examine dysfunction in DSD. Formal justice has two, related definitions: (1) reasonable rule, equal treatment, public justice, and a procedure to establish the facts[113] and (2) regularity, treating similar cases similarly, implementing the rule of law in legal institutions, and impartial and consistent administration of law and institutions.[114] Court-connected mediation DSDs have been critiqued as lacking sufficient formal justice by failing to provide an adequate fact- and law-based process,[115] because mediation can be interest based rather than focused on only objective measures of right and wrong. Mediation and most commercial arbitration programs do not create rules of law or binding precedent; they are forms of private dispute resolution and private law. In DSDs like consumer, employment, and labor arbitration, arbitrators do not establish precedent binding on other arbitrators;[116] arguably, this is informal justice.

Personal justice is determined by an individual. It can take the form of corruption, such as a judge or arbitrator resolving a dispute on the basis of her personal or economic stake as a relative, investor, or other interested party. A second form involves resolving a dispute on the basis of not rules but the personal characteristics of the disputants—for example, race, sex, ethnicity, age, disability, gender, or sexual preference.[117] Last, the judge or arbitrator may resolve a dispute ad hoc using a general standard and not a specific rule.[118] Conversely, injustice refers to inequalities "not to the benefit of all."[119] Personal justice can be injustice.

ADR proponents advocate for certain DSDs specifically because there is broader discretion over standards as a form of personal justice; arbitration allows the parties to craft their own justice (rules by contract), and mediation allows them to decide an outcome (voluntary settlement) that suits their specific needs and context.

Control over DSD and Stakeholder Power

These fundamental concepts of justice and fairness are vital to understanding the DSD field because the power to design dispute systems is not equally distributed. Control over DSD derives from law and contract and stems from both legal and economic power. Designers exercise that power directly if they have final decision authority within an organization; they exercise it indirectly when they act as agents reporting to decision makers in an organization. For example, federal courts control design for their systems under the Alternative Dispute Resolution Act of 1998.[120] They administer court-connected DSDs for disputes on their dockets; the courts themselves are not disputants but instead are third parties. Federal courts have convened DSD advisory groups of representatives of the plaintiff and defense bar, but courts retain the final power over DSD.

The parties to a dispute sometimes have reasonably equal bargaining power, which enables them to negotiate systems for their own benefit through arm's-length contracts. For example, two Fortune 500 companies may negotiate DSDs that both companies agree to use within their supply chain or other commercial contracts. Labor unions and management negotiate DSDs in their collective bargaining agreements through grievance procedures.[121] In these cases, both law and economic power give multiple parties shared control over DSD.

In the United States, the existing legal framework also gives companies and other organizations the power to design systems for those with little economic or bargaining power, such as their employees and consumers. Companies and organizations can impose DSDs through adhesion contracts (legally binding agreements that are not negotiated and that favor the asymmetrically powerful party). An example is an arbitration clause in a mortgage on a trailer home that requires disputants to travel a thousand miles from their home for a hearing. This unequal power can give rise to ethical abuses—for instance, if a corporation internally manages its binding arbitration program to disadvantage its employees or customers.

We argue here that system participants as stakeholders should have not only a voice in design but also a choice of options, depending on culture and context. People who do not trust systems that others design may choose not to use them. They may also take collective action in response to an imbalance in power over the system, as this century has shown with groups including Black Lives Matter (racial justice), Never Again/Not One More (gun control), and MeToo (sexual harassment and sexual violence). While decision makers may approve a DSD, system participants decide when or whether to use it, and "they are among the most important decision makers in conflict management."[122]

Conclusion

This chapter introduces DSD origins, defines key terms, reviews the general principles of DSD, discusses the centrality of fairness and justice in a system, and describes the many different conceptions of justice. Last, it raises the question of who controls DSD. The power to control the design and execution of a dispute system can determine its fairness and justice in both the process and the outcome. The DSD Analytic Framework, introduced in the next chapter, provides questions to help identify which stakeholders have what powers in the processes and outcomes of DSD. Remaining chapters in the "Foundations of System Design" unit map the many processes and structures in DSDs, describe and illustrate the design process itself, provide tools for assessing and evaluating a DSD's success, and consider the ethical challenges designers face in this field. The case chapters in Parts I, II, III, and IV of the second unit provide opportunities to consider who—a third party, the disputants themselves, or only one disputant—controls the shapes specific DSDs have taken, how they have been implemented, and what conception of fairness and justice they reflect.

2 ANALYTIC FRAMEWORK FOR DISPUTE SYSTEM DESIGN

OVER THE LAST THIRTY YEARS, DSD scholars and practitioners have suggested principles for design practice, as Chapter 1 reviews. Authors have proffered many of these principles as best practices or even proposed them as ethical guidelines; some frame principles as criteria to judge or measure the quality of an organizational system's outcomes. The field requires a more structured approach to DSD. To develop effective DSDs that are tailored to their dispute streams, stakeholders, culture, and contexts, designers need a "framework and conceptual map."[1] This chapter presents an analytic framework for interrogating an existing or prospective system for preventing, managing, or resolving disputes. To place this framework in its larger context, the following section briefly reviews frameworks as components of institutional analysis.

Frameworks in Institutional Analysis

The late Elinor Ostrom, the first woman Nobel laureate in Economics, observed that "the terms—framework, theory, and model—are all used almost interchangeably by diverse social scientists."[2] She instead characterized these terms as nested concepts, moving from the most general to the most detailed assumptions an analyst makes. At the broadest level, "a general framework helps to identify the elements (and the relationship among these elements) that one needs to consider for institutional analysis" and organizes "diagnostic and prescriptive inquiry."[3] A framework provides the most general set of variables for analyzing many kinds of settings. In contrast to a general framework, a theory relates to one or more elements within a framework, permitting the analyst to ask certain questions and to make and test working assumptions. For example, in DSD, procedural justice is a theory in social psychology that enables social scientists to make working assumptions about how processes and structures affect perceptions of fairness (see Chapter 5). At the most detailed level, a model makes "precise assumptions about a limited set of parameters and variables."[4] For example, Robert Axelrod used game theory to test precise assumptions about how different negotiation strategies (cooperate or defect) would operate in a prisoner's dilemma exercise, establishing in certain experiments that cooperating first and punishing defection was the most successful approach.[5]

Ostrom and her colleagues and students at the Indiana School developed the Institutional Analysis and Development framework, which is broadly applicable to institutions of governance. Her focus was on collective action related to common-pool resources like water and land.[6] For the framework, she sought a set of universal building blocks with which to examine action arenas or action situations, which may be nested.[7] For example, any individual case within a DSD may represent an action arena. Ostrom explained that within the arena are participants and an action situation, which interact. The Institutional Analysis and Development framework contains seven clusters of variables that characterize the action arena: "(1) participants (who may be either single individuals or corporate actors), (2) positions, (3) potential outcomes, (4) action-outcome linkages, (5) the control that participants exercise, (6) types of information generated, and (7) the costs and benefits assigned to actions and outcomes."[8] Ostrom's framework treats rules and law as independent (exogenous) variables that shape what can happen in the action arena.[9] Ostrom's other independent variables are physical and biological conditions and attributes of the community.[10]

Research varies with academic discipline and whether a framework, theory, or model is considered. Depending on the specific research question, a researcher may use what Ostrom terms independent variables as dependent (endogenous) variables; a dependent variable is one you expect to change. For example, the Federal Arbitration Act and the U.S. Supreme Court's case law interpreting this legislation together act as independent variables shaping the action arena for adhesive and forced (previously called mandatory) consumer or employment arbitration in the United States (see Chapter 12). These laws allow companies to write and enforce arbitration clauses that prevent employees or consumers from joining class actions (a form of adjudication that qualifies as an action-outcome linkage).

In comparison, Lauren Edelman uses sociological theories and models to interrogate how employers interpret and respond to broad and ambiguous legal mandates regarding employment discrimination at the workplace.[11] Edelman examines how human action through company agents shapes the meaning of law and how employers implement internal DSDs that address workplace harassment or discipline. In this analysis, law is an endogenous variable. At issue is its effectiveness from a policy standpoint in preventing and remedying employment discrimination given how those with the power to do so interpret and enforce it.

Because this chapter starts at the framework level to examine DSDs as institutions, it treats law as exogenous, or independent. It is very important for scholars to challenge law's efficacy from a policy standpoint by examining not only its verbal structure but also law's actual function in terms of how humans interpret the words and how this interaction shapes behavior. Scholars in many disciplines use theories and models to do this work (see Chapter 5).

Institutional design is a broad field, the comprehensive review of which is outside the scope of this book.[12] While Ostrom does not specifically address DSD, her work relates broadly to organizations as institutions.[13] Chapter 5 explores how to evaluate a dispute system using variables like those in the Institutional Analysis and Development framework as well as theories and models within a framework. The next section provides an analytic framework specific to DSD.

Analytic Framework for DSD

The framework presented here is intended to structure analysis of DSD—in short, to elicit the information that a designer, analyst, or user needs.[14] It serves as a quick reference, containing key questions relating to each element of design:

DSD ANALYTIC FRAMEWORK

1. Goals
   a. What do the system's decision makers seek to accomplish?
   b. Which types of conflict does the system seek to address?
2. Stakeholders
   a. Who are the stakeholders?
   b. What is their relative power?
   c. What are their interests, and how are their interests represented in the system?
3. Context and culture
   a. How does the context of the DSD affect its viability and success?
   b. What aspects of culture (organizational, social, national, economic, or other) affect the system?
   c. What are the norms for communication and conflict management?
4. Processes and structure
   a. Which processes are used to prevent, manage, and resolve disputes?

     b. If there is more than one process, are processes linked or integrated?

     c. What are the incentives and disincentives for using the system?

     d. What is the dispute system's interaction with the formal legal system?

5. Resources

     a. What financial resources support the system?

     b. What human resources support the system?

6. Success, accountability, and learning

     a. How transparent is the system?

     b. Does the system include monitoring, learning, and evaluation components?

     c. Is the system successful?

Goals

In designing or redesigning a system, it is important to determine and articulate the system's goals and values at the very outset of the design process. Does a company seek to manage litigation risk or increase employee retention? Does a juvenile court seek to reconcile a victim and offender? If there are multiple goals, what are the priorities among them? Clarifying goals helps determine whether the design should include only one process (such as mediation or arbitration) or provide for more process options.

Decision makers, who determine goals, can be one or more persons or entities with the authority to commission, approve, and implement the design. Decision makers may be individuals, such as a CEO who has the power to approve a final design, or groups, such as an advisory panel or stakeholder group with the power to create all or part of the design process or approve the outcome, or both. The designer is the person or group that creates or refines the dispute system. The designer is also the keeper of the guiding principles for design; his or her role is to encourage the use of these principles in the design process. Because the emerging field of DSD is interdisciplinary, designers may be lawyers or come from other professional or academic disciplines, including management, organizational development, social psychology, labor and employment relations, diplomacy, or international development.

The decision maker and the designer might be the same or different people or groups. Designers might be employees of the organization or entity that will host the DSD or might be contractors, consultants, or others outside the organization. There are advantages and disadvantages to both choices. People from inside the organization know its culture and past practice. They know the personalities of people responsible for managing key offices. They may have the best insight on incentives, disincentives, costs, and benefits of the existing system. However, they are also accustomed to the status quo; they may resist change or feel threatened by it. An outside consultant may have broader knowledge of the possible alternative models and may bring to the organization new ideas for changing the incentive structure. She does not have the baggage or history associated with managers of key offices. By adopting a facilitative process, she may be able to enlist help from people within the organization. However, the outsider faces a steep learning curve in understanding the organization.

A system designer must understand which stages and types of conflict the system seeks to address and what the system's decision maker intends to accomplish through this design. A DSD within an organization may address one, a few, or many categories of disputes or broader conflict. For instance, a company could design a system intended to resolve only internal employee disputes. Alternatively, the company could design a system that addresses disputes with external actors such as customers, partners, or suppliers. For example, General Electric instituted an early dispute resolution system prescribing a protocol on how, when, and by whom disputes between GE and its customer or contractor would be assessed and handled.[15]

Some categories of disputes are subject to legal constraints that limit design choices. In the United States, collective bargaining agreements usually have a defined grievance procedure that employees must use for certain disputes. Statutes mandate certain procedures for specific categories of disputes, such as claims for discrimination or workers' compensation. Public employee systems or special education disputes are subject to due process limits under the U.S. Constitution. It may be challenging to create and effectively integrate new design options alongside existing mandated or historical processes.

Goals that are often identified for DSDs include the following:

- *Conflict prevention, conflict management, dispute resolution.* Is the decision maker focused narrowly on dispute resolution, such as settlement alternatives for litigated cases? Or does he want to prevent conflicts and manage them at an earlier stage, before litigation is threatened or filed?
- *Efficiency, resource savings.* Does the organization want to save time, and if so, whose time? Is minimization of cost a goal? If so, whose cost? An organization could seek to address certain types of conflict and disputes to enhance employee morale and reduce turnover, reduce litigation costs, or avoid adverse publicity. An organization might try to shift costs and resource expenditures onto the other party or parties to discourage them

from pursuing a claim. For example, arbitration clauses that prohibit class action arbitration against companies can make it costlier for individual consumers to pursue small claims against those companies.

- *Relationships.* Do decision makers seek to transform or restructure relationships? They might address disputants within the organization (such as managers and employees) or between insiders and outsiders (for instance, between partners in a joint venture, two neighboring countries, or a business and its customers).

- *Safety.* Is there a desire to prevent violence or damage to property—or to prevent further violence or damage if an incident has already occurred? For example, some designs address potential workplace violence. In this context, the goals of protecting the community might be in tension with the goal of keeping confidential the mental health status of individuals.[16]

- *System operation.* Decision makers might try to enhance system accessibility or decrease caseload. If some categories of conflict are not being addressed, or groups of employees are not using a system, a company may seek to redesign the system to make it more welcoming and to increase usage rates. A company could also try to address conflict earlier to decrease the number of lawsuits filed against the company. The U.S. Postal Service, for instance, used mediation within two to four weeks of an employee filing a discrimination complaint to encourage employees to resolve disputes before litigation (see Chapter 11).

- *Public recognition.* Designers may seek to protect privacy for an organization, its clients, or its employees. Other goals might be providing public vindication of a claimant's rights or creating precedent for future cases. Parties often choose arbitration and mediation to keep outcomes (and sometimes disputes) from public view. While trial results are public (except in very rare instances), arbitration, mediation, fact-finding, and other processes can be either confidential or public, depending on the design and parties' agreements. Important public policy questions may arise, for instance, if private parties—such as the plaintiffs and defendants in a stream of product liability cases—seek confidential processes that keep the public uninformed about a defective and potentially harmful product.

- *Substantive outcomes.* Decision makers may seek to achieve just outcomes, which raises questions of defining "justice."[17] Do they seek fairness of process or of outcome? What is their underlying assumption about justice in the system? Some systems, like the September 11th Victim Compensation Fund, distribute financial assets and seek to achieve some form of distributive justice (see Chapter 8).[18] Some systems emphasize opportunities for complainants to be heard in order to enhance procedural justice. (The September 11th fund tried to achieve both.) In the arbitration process to distribute the proceeds of the Dalkon Shield tort claim facility, individuals harmed by the product (a contraceptive intrauterine device) were given an opportunity to tell their stories to trained arbitrators who awarded damages on the basis of an injury grid. In another example, the Truth and Reconciliation Commission that followed apartheid in South Africa sought to restore and rebalance relationships among victims, the community, and offenders through processes aimed at restorative justice.

- *Reputation (of individuals or organizations).* A business that loses a highly publicized product liability lawsuit may redesign its product and create a consumer complaint resolution process to identify future product defects earlier and help resurrect its reputation. Kaiser Permanente sought to restore its credibility with the patients in its health maintenance organization by improving the speed and transparency of its arbitration system (see Chapters 4 and 14). Other companies have been proactive in issuing public apologies in addition to payment of damages in order to restore credibility and consumer confidence after release of a harmful product.[19]

- *Compliance.* Among decision makers who seek greater compliance with applicable laws and rules, sanctions for noncompliance can be emphasized to deter future failures or the capacity to comply can be enhanced (or both). A corporation that has been sanctioned under federal securities laws may create a system to ensure that whistleblowers can report possible future violations without fear of retribution.

- *Satisfaction.* Whom does the decision maker seek to satisfy—all stakeholders or only some? Does it seek more durable resolutions? The more satisfactory the resolutions, the more durable they are likely to be, because satisfied disputants are less likely to thwart or ignore a previous agreement.

- *Organizational improvement.* Is there a desire to identify and correct institutional weaknesses or injustices? A health care provider may hope not only to decrease the number of medical malpractice lawsuits but also to reduce its level of medical errors (whether or not lawsuits are filed). A company might devise a system to help retain female employees who are leaving in disproportionate numbers because of hostile working conditions.

As discussed above, the decision maker who controls system design has the power to define the system's goals and priorities. However, from a normative standpoint, the issue of control over DSD raises questions of fairness and justice. First, whom does the decision maker represent? Is the decision-making body one party to the disputes in the stream (e.g., a company adopting mandatory arbitration for consumer or employment disputes), both parties to disputes (labor and management), or a third party (court or agency)? Is there an effort to share this power or provide opportunities for stakeholder voice? Second, what form or conception of justice does the system expressly or impliedly incorporate as a goal? The trade-offs required among competing goals may affect the quality of the resulting system. For instance, a significant tension can exist between the goals of efficiency and fairness or justice. Efforts to radically expedite resolution while minimizing costs could result in a system that lacks procedural or substantive fairness. Which would be the more appropriate process in the context of juvenile justice: prioritizing punishment by emphasizing jail time and compensation (retributive justice)? Or seeking to avoid criminalizing a youth, exploring ways—perhaps through mediation between the victim and the offender—that the youth pays a penalty but is also reconciled with the victim and the community (restorative justice)? In assessing the trade-offs among goals, the designer can help the decision maker consider the DSD guiding principles in Chapter 1.

Stakeholders

The second framework element is identification of stakeholders and analysis of their relationships and power. Stakeholders include the people and organizations that create, host, use, and are affected by a DSD. In addition to the immediate parties in conflict, stakeholders can be individuals or entities that are subsidiary to or constituents of those parties, as well as others directly or indirectly affected by the outcome of the dispute. For instance, in a system to allocate financial compensation among claimants injured by a toxic spill, stakeholders would include those injured individuals as well as the companies responsible for the spill, their insurers, counsel for the parties, and perhaps government entities and other groups and advocates for the environment within the broader community where the spill occurred.

The designer might use a multistakeholder process to design or assess the new system. For example, through passage of the Civil Justice Reform Act, the U.S. Congress decreed that all ninety-four federal district courts create and confer with a multistakeholder advisory group in considering ways to reduce cost and delay.[20]

Stakeholders should be involved in the design stage of a DSD through some variant of a conflict stream assessment, discussed in Chapter 4. Diverse stakeholders might influence and be influenced by the system. The more engaged these stakeholders are, and the more deliberative their role in helping select the scope of coverage and establish priorities among possible goals, the more likely it is that the subsequent DSD will be responsive to their needs and expectations. The design will need to assess multiple goals and priorities and make trade-offs among them. The more that stakeholders, including users, are involved in the dispute system's design and continuous improvement, the more likely it will be sustainable in the long term.

Context and Culture

Context is the circumstance or situation in which a system is diagnosed and designed. Jennifer Lynch described the catalysts (five Cs) that often trigger organizational system design: *compliance* with legislation or policy (e.g., the U.S. Administrative Dispute Resolution Act of 1996); *cost* of grievance, litigation, and settlement to spur experimentation with mediation or arbitration; *crisis* in the media, negligent act, or fraud (e.g., the Kaiser case described in Chapters 4 and 14); *competition* within an industry or among professional firms (e.g., GE early case assessment in Chapter 13); and *cultural transformation* to align a firm with its constituents (e.g., the transformation of dispute handling by the U.S. Postal Service in Chapter 11).[21]

   "Culture" refers to patterns of being, perceiving, believing, behaving, and sense-making shared by a group of people.[22] Culture is commonly viewed as arising within national, regional, or religious contexts but can also develop across a profession, a community, or a corporation or other organization. In the relationship between culture and conflict, disputants—individuals, firms, or countries—respond to conflict in a number of ways. Individuals have different conflict management styles; moreover, institutions and organizations may develop particular conflict management approaches. Countries and social groups are influenced by their own cultural understandings and approaches to conflict.

People and Organizational Culture

One framework for understanding people's response to conflict is the "dual concern" model illustrating how people attempt to balance concern for self with concern for others.[23] Individuals tend to choose from or exhibit one of four basic strategies—yielding, problem-solving, contending, or avoiding. "Yielding" is lowering one's own aspirations and settling for less than one would have liked. "Problem-solving" is pursuing an alternative that attempts to satisfy the interests of both sides. "Contending" is trying to impose one's preferred solution on the other party. "Avoiding" is not engaging in the conflict at all.[24]

While these are strategies an individual person may choose, organizations as collections of people may develop their own distinct cultures regarding conflict. These cultures can in turn influence what strategies people and stakeholders choose to use and can shape dispute resolution procedures and their results.[25] Organizational culture consists of patterns of meaning and identity in an organization, which can take the form of communication, symbols, beliefs, language, rules, artifacts, values, or assumptions. For example, a start-up organization may foster an entrepreneurial spirit wherein individual creative effort is highly rewarded. However, if problems arise, this organizational culture may discourage collaborative problem-solving. It is important to align processes to prevent, manage, and resolve disputes with an organization's culture.[26]

David Lipsky, Ronald Seeber, and Richard Fincher[27] developed a framework for analyzing these organizational-level choices for conflict management. They identified independent variables and grouped them into environmental factors and organizational motivations that together give rise to a conflict management strategy to contend, settle, or prevent workplace conflict. The environmental factors include market competition, government regulation, litigation trends, legal and tort reform, statutory and court mandates, and unionization. The organizational motivations include organizational culture, management commitment, the champion's role,[28] the organization's exposure profile, and a precipitating event.

Corinne Bendersky[29] analyzed a human resources department's unsuccessful attempt to reduce the number of equal employment opportunity claims alleging discriminatory promotion decisions within the company. The new policy offered employees confidential counseling on how to address promotions with their supervisor, with an option to use outside mediation services. The effort failed on two counts. Employees were not consulted in the design stage; thus, the process did not reflect their needs or concerns. In addition, company management generally discouraged employees from seeking help in dealing with problems, thereby sending a mixed message. Employees felt that their only options were to directly negotiate with their supervisor (the subject of their complaint), leave the company, or file a legal action. Use of the counseling or mediation services was not seen as a viable option. That cultural disconnect undermined the human resources department's good intentions to prevent and resolve employee promotion disputes.

Culture in a National and International Context

Jeanne Brett offers an iceberg metaphor for approaching cultural differences: visible above the waterline are behaviors and institutions; immediately below the surface are knowledge structures, values, beliefs, and norms; in the murky depths are fundamental assumptions.[30] Behaviors include ritual greetings like exchange of business cards, bows, cheek kissing, or handshakes. Institutions may be legal, economic, political, social (e.g., village elders), or religious.[31] Less visible are the values, beliefs, and norms that call for cultural fluency on factors that influence how people communicate and navigate conflict. Many of these values and norms lie on a spectrum. For example, where do information-sharing norms and values fall in relation to transparency versus privacy? Is time approached in a more flexible manner or are schedules strictly observed? Where does the culture fall in terms of formality versus informality, direct or indirect communication, and individualist or collectivist social values? Cross-cultural data on these values produce general prototypes, and it is important not to stereotype any individual negotiator. People from collectivist societies tend to prefer nonconfrontational procedures in the context of their own societies and be less inclined toward direct competition and problem-solving, whereas people from more individualist societies are seen as more willing to use these latter approaches.[32] In an organizational culture, is management more hierarchical or more lateral? Is decision-making more top down or does it seek consensus? Do the goals of dispute resolution emphasize reaching agreement or improving relationships?

Hierarchical societies have deference patterns that are absent in egalitarian cultures.[33] Another dimension of difference is beliefs or expectations about the behaviors of others based on shared knowledge of conventions, rules, and context. For example, some cultures are quick to trust, assuming they can trust until the other side proves otherwise; other cultures tend to exhibit slow trust, requiring time to build strong relationships before they trust the other side.[34] Norms include conventions of communication. Some cultures use indirect communication, relying on high context because they already share a social context, while other cultures use direct communication (low context) because they share a vocabulary. Brett cautions avoidance of stereotypes and places prototypes on a bell curve of variation. In the tails of the distribution, people from different cultures may overlap.

Culture affects how people perceive fairness regarding how disputes are handled. For example, in some cultures, people value confidentiality, while in others people may expect a more public and transparent process. Parties might have different priorities regarding individual versus collective social interest, direct or circumspect communication styles, and the importance of long-term relationships—all of which inform how they share information and whether they use and expect a more competitive or cooperative approach to disputes.[35] No particular characteristics are objectively preferable, but behavior misaligned with expectations might confound effective communication and impede dispute resolution.[36]

Any individual will be an amalgam of his or her many cultures, which may include nation, religion, gender, educational experience, family context, and professional training.[37] One can design a strategy or process more attuned to the parties' preferences by monitoring one's own words and actions and the meaning one intends, as well as the other parties' words and actions;[38] checking one's assumptions; and deliberately seeking to understand the disputants' cultural contexts and perspectives. The resulting design may help bridge those differences within an organization or a society.

Processes and Structure

Process options and structure constitute the fourth framework element. For existing systems, which processes are used to prevent, manage, and resolve conflicts and disputes?[39] (Chapter 3 identifies and discusses these building blocks.) How are those processes defined, and how do they interrelate within the context of the institution? It might be useful to consider how the system has evolved, how external systems (including the formal legal system) reinforce or constrain it, and what creates incentives and disincentives for its use.

Many different types of processes can be used to prevent, manage, and resolve conflict. Some organizations offer one formal process, such as mediation or arbitration, while others develop a range of processes for one or more types of disputes. If multiple options are offered, those options may be linked or they may exist as discrete, unlinked processes that evolved—perhaps not strategically—in different parts of the organization. Whether linked or discrete, the available processes may have different incentives (e.g., financial, timing) that encourage or discourage use by different stakeholders.

An organization's freedom to design its internal processes for conflict prevention, management, learning, and resolution may be constrained by courts, legislatures, or administrative bodies. Laws and institutional policies require human resources specialists to report certain kinds of known or suspected crimes or risks, for example. Existing law may prohibit or require use of certain processes or specific due process elements. Once designed, an organization's dispute system may be challenged in a court or legislative body if some stakeholders believe its processes run afoul of legal or other societal norms. For example, binding arbitration clauses in adhesion contracts generated decades of litigation in the United States regarding whether such processes should be legally prohibited (see Chapter 12).

A DSD is usually strengthened by multiple options. Some of them should be interest based. A designer should identify disputants' respective interests, which encompass fundamental human needs like security, economic well-being, belonging, recognition, and autonomy. Those interests, in turn, reflect economic, relational, political, and social values.[40] The designer should assess alternative strategies to satisfy those interests and generate options to achieve them.[41]

William Ury, Jeanne Brett, and Stephen Goldberg[42] suggested that dispute systems vary on the basis of whether they reconcile the parties' interests, determine who is right, or establish who is most powerful. The authors argued that processes primarily oriented toward interests are more likely to lead to results with long-term sustainability than rights- or power-based methods and to yield the highest satisfaction with outcome, contribute to the development of better relationships, and therefore help prevent recurrence of the dispute.[43] However, exploring interests may require a significant investment of time. Ury, Brett, and Goldberg advised low-cost, transparent, rights-based procedures (like arbitration) as backups if interest-based approaches are unsuccessful. Sometimes, therefore, a DSD might offer a system of sequential process options—for example, disputants commit to try negotiation, then mediation when negotiation fails to produce agreement, then arbitration if mediation fails as well.

Interest-based processes focus on a basic range of human, economic, and social needs and concerns. Rights-based dispute resolution requires a neutral third party to apply agreed-on rules from law, policy, or contract to a set of facts to determine who wins. Rights-based processes include binding and nonbinding arbitration and the traditional court trial in the justice system. Power-based processes use dominance in physical force or financial resources to impose an outcome; for example, strikes and lockouts are power tactics in the collective bargaining system for managing industrial conflict.

To the extent feasible within the context, the system should be responsive, focus on interests, start with lower-cost options, and aim to address conflict broadly. "Responsive" here means sensitive to basic human needs and interests. Low-cost (wherein "cost" includes financial, temporal, and emotional elements) system arrangements move from prevention to low-cost management, to low-cost resolution processes. A comprehensive system is available to all and open to the broadest scope of coverage that can be managed with the available resources. The broader the scope, the more likely stakeholders will be to engage the system when a dispute is burgeoning—at the grievance or conflict stage—and thus allow it to function as a preventive system as well as one that resolves conflict. Designers may need to balance the scope with resource constraints and efficiency in DSD;

efficiency should also be understood in terms of the costs and benefits of preven-tion relative to resolution.

Social psychologists John Thibaut and Laurens Walker studied process choice, specifically as related to satisfaction and perceived fairness in allocation disputes.[44] They found that factors other than whether the individual has won substantially affected satisfaction and perceived fairness. While distributive justice suggests that party satisfaction is a function of outcome or the decision, the researchers found that satisfaction is also a function of the process or the steps taken to reach the outcome. Tom Tyler and E. Allan Lind theorized that procedural justice follows when procedures align with the fundamental values of the group and the individ-ual.[45] People are social animals who value participation in the life of their group; voice in decision-making reflects their membership in the group and status as members of it. When users choose their own process, they are more likely to be satisfied with both the process and its outcome.[46]

Disputants have different preferences for procedures—such as negotiation, mediation, and arbitration—depending on circumstances. When there is signifi-cant time pressure, disputants may prefer arbitration, which can result in speed-ier outcomes; however, people in close relationships tend to reject arbitration, presumably because of its more coercive and adversarial features.[47] User control over process choice is also a factor increasing the likelihood that the system is fair and unbiased. Within a design, control over process choice allows disputants to select those processes they perceive to be in their best interests. If a disputant believes his conflict involves an important issue of public policy, litigation may be the appropriate choice.[48] To deprive users of that choice through adhesive (forced or mandatory) arbitration, for instance, may be procedurally unfair (see Chapter 12). Moreover, the systematic privatization of public law through adhesive arbitration may undermine the enforcement of public rights and the development of precedent; affording a choice of dispute resolution processes conveys respect for individuals' autonomy. Donna Shestowsky found that participants in experiments preferred high disputant control in every area; they wanted a neutral third party's role to be limited to helping them arrive at their own decision.[49]

Resources

The decision maker needs to decide what resources, human and financial, can be committed to DSD implementation and evaluation. Will internal staff design the system, or will the decision maker retain outside consultants or advisors? Even if outside advisors are involved, how much money and staff time will the organization devote to these design processes?

The designer (or a member of the assessment design team) also needs to assess what resources the current system expends for conflict prevention, management, or resolution. On the human resources side, are neutrals in the current system adequately trained to provide high-quality and ethical services? Do other personnel in the system have sufficient skills, training, and supervision?

How will the new or revamped system be financed? Will its funding level be adequate to achieve the stated goals? What impact do the amounts and sources of funding appear to have on the results of the system? For example, Congress passed a bill authorizing the September 11th fund and provided an open-ended budget of taxpayer dollars for it. In contrast, President Barack Obama and representatives of British Petroleum agreed that BP would commit $20 billion to spend on the DSD formed to address claims following the Deepwater Horizon explosion. (The court subsequently administered a separate compensation scheme under which BP paid additional funds.) The DSDs for allocating donations from the general public to victims of the terrorist attacks in Aurora, Colorado, and Boston, Massachusetts, differed from either of these examples because donations were not conditioned on releasing potential defendants from liability. Ensuring adequate resources in complex systems may require making hard decisions that, as noted above, can affect perceptions of fairness, justice, and likelihood of success.

Also central to DSD resource discussions is who pays for the services. A system financed by some but not all the parties might create bias or a perception of bias. For example, the company implicated in an industrial spill might bear the significant expense incurred for a process to address liability, fact-finding, and compensation involving federal and state agencies, residents of the community, and the business itself. While having only one side pay increases the risk of bias, imposing financial costs on lower-income parties may create burdens that effectively deny access. Some ways to ameliorate the real or perceived risk of bias are to emphasize transparency in the process and to emphasize participation in the decision-making.

Systems need to be designed in alignment with available resources—human, organizational, and financial. A program's credibility depends on both top-down and bottom-up support. Top-down support includes adequate financial and human resources, public statements of support from organizational leaders, and use of the program by key stakeholders. Bottom-up social support includes testimonials from satisfied participants, success stories, and word-of-mouth endorsements. Within a business, for instance, support could be moral leadership by managers, education and training of managers and employees on use of the processes, financial support for the operation, and emotional support for users. In a public context, monitoring and periodic review through published reports, hearings, and the media could be valuable for enhancing credibility.

Success, Accountability, and Learning

Success can be defined not only by whether the system achieves its intended goals but also by whether it achieves broader societal goals, including fairness and justice. A system's success is more readily judged if its outcomes are made available to and studied by independent evaluators (see Chapter 5). Unfortunately, barriers such as cost, privacy concerns, and difficulty in collecting data often preclude such meaningful evaluation.

Accountability, a purpose of evaluation, is important in three primary respects. First, evaluation is necessary for system operators to ascertain whether the system is working. Are key stakeholder groups using the system? Are costs in line with projections? Are neutrals delivering high-quality services and upholding ethics rules? Are users satisfied with the options and services? Second, ongoing evaluation identifies opportunities for system improvement. Third, it is important for users to understand how—and how well—the system operates. Transparency increases credibility and therefore participation, encouraging further feedback from participants. However, it may be important to foster transparency on how a system works in general but preserve privacy on the details of specific cases.

Learning refers both to system improvement based on feedback and to stakeholder training and education. The organizational entity's management must be adequately trained in the system's use and efficacy. Public or private users must be informed about its availability. Staff of an organization—at all levels—benefit from education about conflict management and communication. Consumers and other users learn about specific procedures available for resolving disputes. Meanwhile, third-party neutrals learn about the organization and its culture.[50]

System procedures should be transparent and accountable to all stakeholders and provide a fair, just, balanced, unbiased, and effective means for managing conflict and resolving disputes. As noted in the opening to this chapter, systems have traditionally been deemed effective if they achieved the goals of lessening transaction costs, increasing satisfaction with the outcome, building relationships among the disputants, and reducing recurrence of the disputes.[51]

However, evaluations of the processes and outcomes of DSD have been based primarily on employment systems. Governance systems and transitional justice may have a broader and more complex set of goals, such as establishing peace, security, reconciliation, and the rule of law. Chapter 5 explores best practices for how to conduct an evaluation in these many contexts of system design.

Conclusion

This chapter introduces institutional analysis as social science focused on under-standing institutions in terms of their structure and function. The DSD Analytic Framework is provided for analyzing an existing system for preventing, managing, or resolving conflict. Within this context, the role of the designer is revealed in its full complexity. The designer brings unique expertise to analyze and explain key categories of information: goals; stakeholders; context and culture; processes and structures; resources; and success, accountability, and learning. The next chapter examines the many different types of DSD processes and structures.

3   SYSTEM BUILDING BLOCKS

Processes for Preventing, Managing, and Resolving Conflict

DISPUTE SYSTEMS ADDRESS CONFLICT in many contexts. In organizations, they address conflict among people within the organization or with outside partners, consumers, or stakeholders. In countries, systems seek to resolve and prevent ethnic conflict and restore the rule of law. In government, systems manage conflict over public policy among the public, stakeholders, or interest groups. A vast array of process options is available. Which to use depends on the system's goals, stakeholders, context and culture, and resources (as discussed in Chapter 2). This chapter explores how to understand the process choices by their characteristics and goals, as applied in both the private and the public domains. It introduces several ways to organize and characterize the similarities and differences among these processes. An ADR spectrum and a policy design continuum help system designers situate their options in a context.

In addition to selecting which process options to offer in a system, a designer must embed these building blocks in a program or institution, determine whether and how to connect internal processes, and plan how these will interface with any outside processes and providers. People in an organization need to manage the internal structure; doing so may require expanding or creating new work roles. This chapter describes more than thirty processes used in the private, collective bargaining, and public governance domains that prevent, manage, and resolve conflict.

Understanding Process Choices for DSD

The processes described in this chapter encompass different participants, goals, and inputs and achieve different outcomes. Before examining the specific process options, one might usefully consider the value of using a third party (usually without a direct interest in the substantive matter in dispute) who contributes process-management skill, substantive knowledge, or legal expertise. The third party's contributions can range from balancing participation, encouraging communication, or gathering information and promoting its exchange to helping generate options for agreement, providing expert evaluation of facts, or gauging each disputant's likelihood of success. The third party's style may be facilitative, enabling the parties and their agents to engage more productively, or evaluative, rendering a decision on the merits (in an advisory or binding capacity).[1] The third party can contribute to the efficiency of the dispute resolution process, to the parties' satisfaction with the process and outcome, and to the level of justice that results.

The many possible DSD goals, described in Chapter 2, include the importance of efficiency of time and money, quality of the process and outcome, community involvement, and access to justice. Justice, discussed in Chapter 1, is a goal for all processes, although designers, host organizations, and stakeholders often fail to discuss it explicitly. Different processes incorporate different conceptions of fairness and justice;[2] some systems seek to provide procedural justice, while others seek efficiency and distributive justice through prompt final decisions such as on-line arbitration. Some processes seek restorative justice—for example, to reconcile a criminal offender and community through victim-offender mediation. Others seek transitional justice to help a nation restore the rule of law or move toward democracy. One component of justice is who participates in a process and how. Any process has multiple participants, likely consisting of complaining parties (and respondents), legal or other types of agents for the principals, and other parties affected by the dispute. Participation might include the right to speak of one's experience, choose the process for engaging other parties, or decide on the outcome (self-determination)—all of which compose the notion of voice as a factor in procedural justice. Increased opportunity for voice generally increases satisfaction and likelihood of successfully implementing the outcome.

Voice is a fundamental part of belonging to a social group.[3] It may entail basic communication skills, debate, or deliberation as well as negotiation. It is also an essential component of all dispute-handling processes. As discussed in Chapter 5, processes relating to voice evoke strong psychological responses because they address individuals' group standing. Processes relating to voice vary along several dimensions: scope of participation (broad to narrow), goals for the process (prevention to resolution), presence or role of the third party (from facilitating to deciding), nature of the subject matter (power, rights, or interests), informality and formality, and nature of outcomes (nonbinding to binding). For example, the scope of participation can be broad, as general public comment on policy proposals, or narrow, as a divorcing couple in court. The third party may help facilitate discussion among many stakeholders or adjudicate a disagreement between two. Goals can be simple public input on a draft ordinance to reduce the likelihood of later litigation or an agreement resolving conflict between two parents over custody. People may discuss their interests in a proposed highway or advocate their right to compensation for dismissal from employment. Outcomes can range from nonbinding public dialogue to binding arbitral judgments. All the processes in this book involve some component of exercising voice, although process structures differ.

Process Maps

Because the design context may range from a single business or nonprofit organization to global institutions, multiple scholarly literatures inform our discussion. Scholars from different disciplines have proposed structures and maps to describe the evolution and types of conflict, organize the many available processes, and illuminate their similarities and differences. While much academic attention is given to the resolution of disputes, we urge conducting DSD with a broader vision to address preventing, managing, and resolving conflict (including disputes).

It is important to understand how conflict evolves and to analyze the nature of the conflict or dispute and the possible points of intervention. Questions such as why some grievances are ignored but others become disputes, and why some disputes are pursued in court while the vast majority are not, have caught the attention of legal scholars. Marc Galanter describes a legal iceberg.[4] Richard Miller and Austin Sarat[5] describe a "dispute pyramid": a wide bottom of the vast numbers of grievances of perceived incompatibility (conflicts), a smaller layer of overt disputes in the middle, still fewer legal claims toward the top, and only a few actual court cases at the peak. Movement of grievances to the peak of the dispute pyramid depends in part on structural characteristics of the dispute, such as the relationship between the parties, the type of claim, the relation parties have to the legal system, and whether a party has the resources to pursue resolution.

This approach focuses on the evolution of a conflict over time, and it aligns with William Felstiner, Richard Abel, and Austin Sarat's concepts of "naming, blaming, claiming." A conflict becomes visible with perceiving an injury or problem (naming), the problem is then attributed to the fault of another (blaming), and finally the opposing party is confronted and a remedy is sought (claiming).[6] By focusing on the naming phase, before conflict is transformed into a dispute, the adoption of more preventive processes can affect the number and kinds of disputes that flow downstream to the management and perhaps resolution stages.[7]

Table 3.1 Alternative or appropriate dispute resolution spectrum

Negotiation	*Mediation*	*Arbitration*	*Trial*
No third party	Third party (mediator)	Third party (arbitrator)	Third party (judge, jury)
Nonbinding	Nonbinding	Nonbinding or binding	Binding
	Facilitated	Adjudicative	Adjudicative

Alternative or Appropriate Dispute Resolution Spectrum

Table 3.1 maps key categories of dispute resolution processes on a spectrum. This spectrum is a variation of one commonly used in the dispute resolution field that developed from a focus on process options for ripened disputes and cases in litigation.[8] Negotiation gives maximum process and outcome control to the parties, who may or may not be represented by agents or counsel. Mediation is a process in which a third party, the mediator, facilitates the negotiation. In negotiation and mediation there is no resolution unless the parties agree to it. For this reason, these processes are sometimes called nonbinding. On the right of the spectrum are arbitration and trial, in which a third party controls the process and renders a binding or nonbinding decision (though in arbitration, the parties may have had some input in designing the process through contractual negotiation).

This spectrum arrays process options from interest-based processes on the left to rights-based processes on the right. In addition, moving from left to right, the processes

- Shift from nonadjudicative to adjudicative
- Concentrate more control in the hands of the third party
- Become more formal
- Usually become more expensive in terms of time, money, and damage to parties' relationships
- Become less flexible in terms of outcomes

Policy Design Continuum

Dispute processes can also be understood in the context of policy making, implementation, and enforcement. Policy-making processes, whether in the public or private sector, can be divided into upstream, midstream, and downstream stages. An upstream process is intended to facilitate legislative, quasi-legislative, or private policy making on a given issue, integrate stakeholders' interests, or help prevent the emergence of disputes by creating or clarifying rules. Midstream disputes

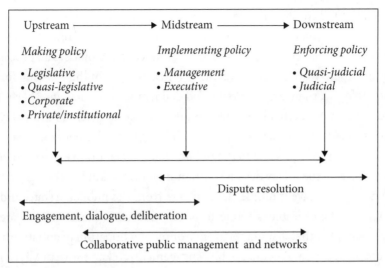

Figure 3.1 Design along the policy continuum

arise from implementing the new policy and call for a different range of dispute management techniques. Downstream processes are oriented to enforcement. (These distinctions are general, however; there can be overlap.)

Figure 3.1 maps different categories of these processes distinguishing upstream, midstream, and downstream phases in the policy design continuum.[9]

In the U.S. government system, the legislative branch makes policy, the executive implements it, and the judicial branch has final enforcement power. For example, Congress made policy through the occupational safety and health law; the Occupational Safety and Health Administration (OSHA) implemented it through rulemaking and inspections; and OSHA, the Occupational Safety and Health Review Commission, and courts enforce it through penalties.

Although this continuum was designed with public sector policy making in mind, it also applies in the private sector. For example, a company's board of directors may make a policy about sexual harassment; management must implement it, perhaps by creating a confidential complaint procedure and a mediation option; and an employee may enforce the policy by filing a complaint with management. Scaling up to a global context, a multinational corporation may make policy by creating an ombuds program that crosses national boundaries; the ombuds may implement a conflict management program for employees of different nationalities and cultures who work together; and the company may enforce rules through employee discipline. Ombuds have established standards of practice[10] and provide a range of services, including conflict coaching and also early neutral evaluation that is informal, off the record, confidential, and offered to one or both parties.[11]

As Figure 3.1 illustrates, the use of dispute resolution, deliberation, and dialogue overlap in the arena of policy development and implementation. In the public sector, the umbrella term "collaborative governance" encompasses all processes as they relate to the work of government.[12] Central to each of the evolving forms of collaborative governance are dialogue and deliberation.[13] In dialogue, participants engage in reasoned exchange of viewpoints, in an atmosphere of mutual respect and civility and in a neutral space or forum, aiming to reach a better mutual under-standing or even consensus.[14] In the public sector, collaborative governance is all forms of voice on the policy design continuum; it involves at least one government actor and may involve multiple stakeholders from the public, private, and non-profit sectors. An example is a long-term environmental cleanup and watershed management plan that disputants to environmental litigation negotiate as part of a consent decree. It might entail public engagement, collaborative public manage-ment of the watershed by stakeholders, and a conflict management procedure. In the private sector, processes for dispute resolution (negotiation, mediation, and arbitration) may involve only private sector actors or any combination of the public, private, and nonprofit sectors and individuals.

While the policy continuum map reflects a linear sequence, in continuing relationships among disputants or business partners, parties may loop back to earlier points on the continuum in a spiral over time. For example, the Supreme Court may signal Congress that it needs to clarify legislation by amendment if it disagrees with the court's interpretation of a statute's language. Congress can amend the statute, the executive branch can implement it, and new litigants can challenge it. This same pattern occurs in collective bargaining as labor and man-agement renegotiate contract language or in supply agreements between business partners that are periodically revised.

DSD Process Building Blocks

The discussion of process building blocks begins with negotiation, the most basic building block for DSD, which crosses the entire design space. Next to follow are third-party processes (both facilitated and adjudicative), specialized collective bargaining processes, and policy-related processes. The chapter closes with new and evolving processes involving technology.

Negotiation, Direct or with Agents

Parties have different degrees of input or control over both process and outcome. Parties negotiating directly have the highest degree of input and control. Parties negotiating with the help of agents and third parties cede to them some input over the process but retain input and control over outcome. Parties may also bring additional people to assist. There is a large literature on negotiation; this chapter introduces terms as they are commonly used in the field.

Assistance can come in many flavors. Principals have decision-making power, while agents negotiate on their behalf. In the United States, lawyers usually negotiate with each other on behalf their respective clients. The clients may be, but usually are not, direct participants in this process. In assisted negotiation, attorney representatives may negotiate in person or through the use of technology, including telephone, video, text-based conferencing, or online exchange.

DIRECT NEGOTIATION. Direct negotiation is an express or implied step in most systems and encompasses direct communication among disputing parties. Direct negotiation has no formal rules or restrictions; parties retain control over how they interact and on what they agree. For example, when one company believes another violated its commercial contract, the parties are likely to communicate and try to resolve the matter before filing a lawsuit. Less than 1 percent of filed civil cases go to trial in the U.S. federal district courts; most civil cases in the United States settle.[15] This statistic demonstrates that most parties continue to negotiate after a case is filed.

Negotiation theory distinguishes interests from positions. Positions are what a party demands. Interests are a deeper expression of what a person or organization cares about, such as needs, concerns, and priorities. For example, an applicant may take the position of demanding a salary of $100,000. His underlying interests might be a desire to live in a given city, pay student debt, support family, and feel respected for education and experience. Negotiation over positions will be more distributive, while negotiation over interests allows for more integrative solutions.

Early negotiation theory focused on positional bargaining and highlighted the advantage of imposing demands and threats while resisting concessions. Game theory developed a highly disciplined, mathematical approach to interactive decision-making based on strict assumptions about information and rational behavior.[16] Later, scholars expanded their focus to include the parties' interests and advanced the notion of a principled approach that would identify and reconcile parties' underlying interests for mutual gain. More recent work recognizes and seeks to integrate both bodies of study through cooperative strategies to create value for all the parties and competitive strategies for each party to claim a greater portion of that value.[17] Behavioral scholars have drawn on cognitive and social psychology to shift the focus from theoretical best outcomes to how people negotiate in practice, especially in terms of communication, trust, relationships, perceptions, and biases.[18]

Research has increased understanding of best practices, necessary skills for effective negotiators, and negotiation strategies most likely to lead to optimal outcomes.[19] Effective interest-based or principled negotiators give in-depth consideration of the issues and relevant norms, necessary and appropriate participants and their goals and interests, and possible alternatives for achieving those goals. They can research barriers to agreement (political, structural, psychological),[20] identify bad faith or hard bargaining,[21] and clarify issues of authority. Negotiation academics recommend that the analysis give thoughtful consideration of the party's best alternative to a negotiated agreement (BATNA),[22] the optimal action that a party can take unilaterally without the other's cooperation or consent. With a litigated commercial dispute, the alternatives may be finding another supplier, declaring bankruptcy, or going to trial. Good negotiators learn how to create value and claim it in the process of exchanging information.[23]

A system design could include training participants in negotiation skills and analysis to help them solve problems and avoid escalation of conflicts into disputes. Some DSDs specify a direct negotiation step before participation in other process options. For instance, in collective bargaining, labor grievance procedures have an informal step to allow the employee and the supervisor to try to work out their differences directly. Likewise, corporate contracts often provide that, upon notice of a dispute, senior executives from both parties agree to use good-faith efforts to negotiate an early resolution before pursuing more formal processes. The pharmaceutical company GlaxoSmithKline developed an early dispute resolution policy that entailed training for all managers in negotiation for early intervention in any disputes.

CONFLICT COACHING. Conflict coaching allows an outside party to assist one of the disputants without the knowledge of the other.[24] The coach helps one disputant think through a conflict analysis and identify positions, interests, BATNA, options, and objective criteria for deciding among options for agreement. Coaches may be professionals or community or family members. A related role is "deal coaching," wherein the coach advises a party in a significant business transaction. Coaching also arises in connection with an ombuds program, which allows employees or consumers to contact a central office in the organization confidentially and choose among direct or assisted negotiation processes.[25]

COLLABORATIVE AND COOPERATIVE LAWYERING. Collaborative lawyering is a process in which disputants agree, in writing, with their counsel and each other to use interest-based negotiation techniques in an effort to settle a dispute without litigation.[26] If the disputants fail to settle, their lawyers are disqualified from representing their clients in litigation. John Lande critiques this provision and urges that parties consider *cooperative* lawyering instead, in which counsel use interest-based bargaining techniques[27] without the disqualification agreement,[28] thus saving the time and expense of bringing in a new set of counsel. Collaborative law is a form of assisted negotiation, but instead of an impartial third party, the disputants use partisan advocates, or agents, whose expertise can improve the effectiveness of the process and help them find mutually acceptable outcomes.

PARTNERING. Direct negotiation as a design step also occurs in partnering in the construction industry—for example, in major public infrastructure projects.[29] The initial phase of partnering is intended to build a strong, collaborative working relationship among contracting parties before disputes arise; it sets up channels of communication (or negotiation) for them to use at the first sign of conflict. Components include retreats, training, planning, and system design for communication processes. In a broader sense, partnering can be a DSD in itself (see Chapter 13).

Facilitated Processes

In facilitated processes, a third party (the neutral)[30] assists the principals (and their counsel or agents) in negotiating a mutually consensual resolution. The neutral has no power to impose an outcome or force a settlement but instead fosters communication and aids in problem solving. If parties reach an agreement, it usually takes the form of a contract that is enforceable in court or a consent decree. In facilitated processes, the parties determine the outcome; in adjudicative processes, the neutral decides. Mediation is the most popular of the facilitated processes.[31] Others are conciliation, early neutral evaluation, and minitrials. These terms are not uniformly defined, and there is considerable local variation in how the neutral carries out her responsibilities in the context of each process.

MEDIATION. Mediation is negotiation assisted by a third party with no decision-making power. The mediator may not impose a solution; she may only assist parties to reach mutually agreeable voluntary settlement.[32] The mediator may provide a safe avenue for communicating interests that the parties are unwilling or unable to share directly. Mediation is generally a confidential process[33] that encourages the parties to explore all possible solutions.[34] The mediator screens the case, explains the mediation process to the parties (e.g., ground rules, opening statements, caucuses, brainstorming), assists them with exchanging information,

helps them brainstorm new ideas to resolve the dispute, and assists them in defining and drafting the agreement.[35]

Mediation is an increasingly common and popular ADR technique. Deciding
which mediator, mediation provider, or mediator panel to use can be a fundamental DSD choice. A DSD may include a mediation process run by the host organization, use an outside provider, or create a hybrid system. Parties may retain an
outside impartial mediator through a government board or panel; a court panel; a
private provider such as the American Arbitration Association,[36] the International
Institute for Conflict Prevention and Resolution,[37] JAMS,[38] or FedArb;[39] or one
of numerous other independent panels. Some U.S. state and federal agencies[40]
have trained in-house neutrals—employees who mediate disputes involving other
employees or members of the public[41]—whereas shared neutrals are employed
in one government agency and cross agency lines to mediate disputes in another
agency.[42] As to impartiality, a key question is whether the neutrals provide full
disclosure and participants give informed consent.

There are a variety of models and contexts for mediation.[43] The choice of mediation model in a DSD can determine disputants' interaction. The generic mediation description given earlier corresponds largely to facilitative mediation,[44]
but mediation models can also be evaluative or transformative, although there is
some controversy associated with these labels.[45] The case chapters in the second
unit of the book discuss empirical research on the effectiveness of mediation
models for particular DSD contexts—for example, facilitative or evaluative mediation in courts (Chapter 7) and transformative mediation in employment settings
(Chapter 11). Mediation also varies considerably in its institutional and national
legal context.[46]

Evaluative Mediation. The evaluative mediator focuses on helping the parties by
assessing their cases' relative strengths and weaknesses and predicting the likely
outcome.[47] Evaluative mediators may begin with all parties (and counsel) present,
but as often they do not have a joint session at all. The mediator may ask for formal
opening statements from each and then conduct one or more private caucuses
with disputants. The mediator focuses on collecting facts, identifying issues, and
analyzing the parties' legal arguments to develop a sense of the case's economic
value. The mediator evaluates who is likely to win and how much (money or
specific rights) they are likely to receive. To encourage the parties to settle, the
mediator will judiciously share this evaluation with each side at strategic moments.
The mediator may propose a settlement. This model also tends to involve a more
directive mediator, one who may pressure the parties to achieve settlement. Attor-

neys sometimes appreciate this approach because it helps them control unrealistic clients and settle cases, especially if the mediator is a retired judge.

Facilitative Mediation. A facilitative mediator will also listen to opening statements and may conduct private caucuses, but he will focus less on disputants' legal positions and more on their underlying needs and how to meet them in an interest-based settlement. For example, when a parent dies, siblings may dispute who is entitled to what portion of the estate, but their interests may also focus on repairing family relationships. Another example is a dispute between two business partners dissolving their firm. Their legal focus may be valuing and dividing the business assets; their deeper interests may involve recognition of contributions to the business, reputation, and respect. The facilitative mediator likely will avoid evaluating the case and instead engage in reality testing to help the parties understand their alternatives to a negotiated settlement and generate ideas for resolving the dispute.

The goal of facilitative and evaluative mediation is to explore whether settlement (defined as reaching an agreement or solving a problem) is possible; a skilled mediator may use both approaches to advance the settlement discussions.

Transformative Mediation. In transformative mediation, the goals of the process are broader than resolving a given dispute. Instead, the parties aim to repair a longer-term relationship using more effective communication.[48] Settlement of a particular dispute is not a goal; the goal is to empower the disputants to engage more productively in a way that allows them to recognize each other's perspective and their own contribution and responsibility for the dispute that led to mediation.

Transformative mediators do not unilaterally structure the process. The mediator will ask the participants how they would like to structure the mediation and, if necessary, will offer them a series of choices or examples. The mediator does not evaluate or offer opinions on the merits of the dispute, pressure participants to settle, or recommend specific settlement terms or options. Instead, the mediator attempts to highlight moments in the discourse when one participant recognizes and acknowledges the perspective of the other.[49]

The example of a boundary dispute between two neighbors provides a means of comparison across mediation styles. A mediator using an evaluative style might focus on fact-finding and applicable real property law to help resolve the dispute. A more facilitative mediator might engage the parties in exploring a range of personal and real property interests. A transformative mediation style would focus on empowering both parties to communicate more effectively on any issues and transform their relationship, with the aim of enabling the parties to more easily resolve whatever issues arise in the future.

New Theories of Mediation. New theories of mediation practice continue to emerge. Psychologists practice *therapeutic mediation* in high-conflict family divorce situations. *Narrative mediation* is an outgrowth of postmodernism and research on how people construct reality in a social context. These models depart from facilitative and evaluative mediation in that settlement is not an object. Instead, the object is deep, mutual understanding through deconstruction of narratives that each disputant has created regarding the conflict.[50] Online mediation entails use of communication technology to offer synchronous and asynchronous communication, using visual and textual modes.

CONCILIATION. In the collective bargaining realm, "conciliation" refers to settlement of labor disputes without a strike—for example, with the assistance of the Federal Mediation and Conciliation Service (29 U.S.C. § 172) or similar state boards.[51] The Equal Employment Opportunity Commission also engages in conciliation after finding reasonable cause in a case of employment discrimination.[52] In international treaties and UN documents, "conciliation" is used for efforts to resolve a dispute between states or between states and investors, generally with the assistance of third parties such as an impartial commission or senior official lending its good offices.[53] Conciliation is also used in civil law jurisdictions, particularly in family and labor disputes. In some countries, "conciliation" is used interchangeably with "mediation," sometimes referring to more directive and evaluative mediation forms.

Adjudicative Processes

Adjudicative processes involve an adversarial presentation of evidence by the parties (or their agents) to a third party who assesses evidence and renders an opinion on facts, rights, or outcomes. Some adjudicative processes are advisory, while others produce binding outcomes. In summary jury trials, the jury is the decision maker. However, in most adjudicative processes, the decision maker is some type of arbitrator, administrative law judge, or court judge.[54]

COURT ADJUDICATION. Civil and criminal adjudication is a process for resolving disputes through the judiciary. This type of adjudication is the most rights-based approach to dispute resolution. In the United States, this process takes its most adversarial form through lawyers arguing the strengths of their cases to the judge or jury as decision makers. The U.S. judicial process also provides for extensive discovery, including interrogatories and depositions (written and oral questioning) of parties and witnesses. In other common law jurisdictions (i.e., the United Kingdom and the former British colonies of India, Australia, New Zealand, and parts of Canada), this adversarial process takes a less extreme form. In Europe, Asia, and other former European colonies in Latin America and Africa, litigation follows civil code traditions in which the lawyers' role is to assist the court in finding the truth and reaching the correct decision.[55]

EARLY NEUTRAL EVALUATION. In early neutral evaluation (ENE) and some variations (often labeled case evaluation), neutrals perform a nonbinding service either through courts or as private providers.[56] This impartial third party with substantive expertise listens to each side present its interests and positions along with a summary of its evidence. The evaluator gives the parties and their counsel a preliminary opinion on the merits of the dispute; the process operates as a reality check.[57] The evaluation is confidential, advisory only, and generally not admissible at trial. The purpose of this process is to foster further, more realistic negotiation and narrow the issues for trial if the case does not settle. It can also allow the parties to design or limit the discovery process. In DSD parlance, this step is a loop back to negotiation.[58] The early neutral evaluator usually does not mediate the dispute but returns the parties to their own negotiation.[59]

MINITRIALS. Minitrials can help resolve litigation over complex commercial disputes.[60] Each party is represented by counsel and often by a senior executive (e.g., CEO) of the relevant company with authority to settle the dispute on the spot. The parties hire a neutral with substantive expertise and high prestige—for example, a retired federal court judge—to supervise the process and answer questions of procedure. The parties' lawyers present abbreviated versions of their evidence and arguments, usually directing each presentation to the CEO of the opposing party. Unlike a trial, they generally present evidence in summary form, not through testimony. Afterward, the CEOs attempt to negotiate a settlement of the dispute, usually excusing their lawyers. However, this process differs from ENE in that the neutral will not give an opinion on the likely outcome of the dispute; occasionally, if the parties reach an impasse in the minitrial, they may ask the neutral to become an evaluator.

SUMMARY JURY TRIALS. Summary jury trials are only rarely used to resolve complex civil litigation. In a summary jury trial, the parties impanel an actual jury, the members of which usually believe they are participating in an actual trial. However, the parties present condensed versions of the evidence. The jury deliberates, and makes findings of fact and liability, after which the judge releases the jury. The parties use the jury's findings to negotiate a settlement. The parties are not bound by the jury's findings; the findings are merely advisory (though the jury may believe otherwise). Summary jury trials, too, are a loop back to negotiation.[61]

ARBITRATION. Arbitration is an ancient practice, dating back at least as far as Roman law and the medieval merchant courts.[62] Parties hire a neutral to serve as a private judge to decide their dispute.[63] Discovery is available, including documents and witnesses, but is subject to the parties' agreement or the rules of the administrating body. Arbitration hearings typically follow the adjudicatory model. The parties make opening statements. The party with the burden of proof (generally a civil preponderance-of-the-evidence test) presents its case; witnesses are subject to cross-examination. The other party presents its rebuttal. The parties may make closing statements or submit written briefs.

Arbitration differs from adjudication in court. First, arbitration is a confidential proceeding and is not subject to public disclosure unless agreed to by the parties. Arbitrators are private judges not accountable to the public in most instances. Usually, the parties select arbitrators for their subject matter expertise, such as in labor, construction, family, real estate, intellectual property, general commercial, securities, or specialized consumer disputes.[64] Hearings are often held in conference rooms. It is common for parties to have representatives in arbitration (either nonlawyers in labor matters or lawyers in commercial or consumer matters). There may be no record of the hearing except perhaps a tape recording. Arbitrators need not strictly follow the rules of evidence used in a court of law. Arbitration may be binding or nonbinding and contractual, ad hoc, or judicial. Most commonly, parties agree in advance to arbitrate disputes arising under a contract, but it is also possible to submit a dispute to arbitration ad hoc after it has arisen. Cases may be decided by one arbitrator or a panel, often of three arbitrators.

Binding Arbitration. Binding arbitration produces an award that the winning party may enforce in court and convert into a court judgment. A key distinguishing feature is the very limited scope of judicial review. Awards will be vacated only if procured by corruption, fraud, or undue means; if there was evident partiality or corruption in an arbitrator; if there was misconduct in refusing to postpone the hearing or refusing to hear evidence pertinent and material to the controversy; or if the arbitrator exceeds her powers or so imperfectly executes them that a mutual, final, and definite award on the subject matter was not made.[65]

Advisory Arbitration. Nonbinding, or advisory, arbitration produces an award that is advisory only and is a loop back to negotiation if the parties choose not to accept it. The question of judicial review arises only in binding arbitration; in all other models in which the award is advisory, parties can simply reject it. In labor relations, about 10 percent of all grievance procedures have advisory arbitration as a final step for grievances over breach of contract. Generally, the parties abide by the terms of the arbitration award; it has great moral force and suasion. However, management may be unwilling to delegate full authority to the arbitrator.

Many courts have adopted nonbinding arbitration to provide a more expedited process or to reduce crowded dockets. In some courts, for some categories of cases, this court-annexed arbitration is a mandatory step before trial. Nonbinding arbitration can serve as a reality check for parties, but it lacks finality. If parties reject the award and litigate, they may spend more in transaction costs than they would have without the interim step. Some critics suggest that mandatory nonbinding arbitration in effect limits access to courts by imposing additional costs on those who can least afford them.[66]

Expedited Arbitration. In expedited arbitration, the hearing is usually scheduled within weeks of the demand, there are no written briefs, and the arbitrator must render an award on an abbreviated time schedule, usually two weeks (although sometimes the parties will ask the arbitrator to render an award from the bench). The arbitrator's decision, or award, may be reasoned or not and is not necessarily public, except if enforced in a court of law.

Collective Bargaining Processes

Collective bargaining may be the birthplace of modern DSD. This category of DSD is discussed in greater detail in Chapter 10; its processes are outlined here.

RIGHTS COMPARED WITH INTEREST ARBITRATION. Rights arbitration is the *retrospective* adjudication of who is entitled to what under an existing contract that one side claims the other violated. It may also be arbitration of statutory rights, as when employer and employee agree to submit a discrimination claim under an existing statute to an arbitrator.

In interest arbitration, the arbitrator determines *prospectively* who will be entitled to what under some future contract[67]—for example, baseball arbitration over future salaries.[68] The arbitrator takes evidence to determine the parties' interests and evaluate how to combine them to structure their future relationship; the arbitrator might write a contract for the parties. Rights arbitration is quasi-adjudicative and interest arbitration is quasi-legislative.

GRIEVANCE, LABOR, AND EMPLOYMENT ARBITRATION. Labor arbitration encompasses grievance arbitration and includes arbitration designed through a collective bargaining agreement.[69] Grievance arbitration in labor contracts is rights arbitration over a claim of breach of contract. It directly substitutes for state or federal court litigation over the meaning of the collective bargaining agreement as a contract. There are two categories of grievances: discipline and contract interpretation. In the former, when management seeks to dismiss, suspend, or discipline an employee, management has the burden of proof to show facts justifying the action, generally to a just cause standard. In the latter, when the union claims that management misinterpreted or misapplied the contract, the union has the burden of proof. Labor arbitration as a system of industrial justice has been very successful in providing a relatively quick, inexpensive means of reaching final decisions in contract disputes.

In contrast, employment arbitration is a form of commercial rights arbitration without collective bargaining or union representation. In recent decades in the United States, it has been imposed on employees through adhesive contract clauses (called forced and, previously, mandatory arbitration) in a job application or personnel manual without direct negotiation.[70] In a related process, companies impose arbitration on consumers through an adhesive clause in a warranty or credit card agreement.

FACT-FINDING. In labor relations, "fact-finding" is a term of art for nonbinding interest arbitration, usually in the public sector. The arbitrator is called a fact-finder. She listens to presentations of evidence and argument on each disputed clause or article in a proposed new or successor collective bargaining agreement, then evaluates the evidence and issues an award, often called a report, in which she proposes specific contract language or benefits on each disputed issue and explains her rationale. The parties generally are not bound by the report unless they fail to reject it within a certain period specified in the state labor relations statute. Usually, parties reject it as a matter of course but use it to return to the bargaining table and cut a deal that differs from what the fact-finder proposed. Often, the parties request mediation for this round of negotiations. In other words, fact-finding is yet another loop back to negotiation.

"Fact-finding" can also refer to a joint process undertaken as part of a facilitation or mediation before trial; representatives of the stakeholders work together to determine a series of factual findings relevant to the dispute.[71] In an international context, fact-finding is the gathering of immediate, credible, firsthand information generated using sound methodology by impartial fact-finders; it may be undertaken by an official state investigating authority or a nongovernmental organization. "Facts" and "truth" have varied meanings, taking into consideration legal truth, personal or narrative truth, social or dialogical truth, or healing or restorative truth, each of which may serve different goals. As an example, the South African Truth and Reconciliation Commission distinguished factual and objective information from personal, dialogic, or restorative truths.[72]

Another variety of fact-finding allows the neutral to determine the disputed facts of a case so that the parties may jointly use these facts to negotiate a settlement. This process entails presentations of evidence to a subject matter expert, who may have highly technical scientific or engineering knowledge. The parties are usually bound by the fact-finder's decision. This process is particularly useful in environmental and public policy disputes in which the parties may disagree about policy analysis evidence or about scientific reports of risk or toxicity.[73]

Hybrid Processes

Some processes are combined, integrated, and adapted. ENE, minitrial, summary jury trial, and nonbinding arbitration are hybrid processes because they combine aspects of the core third-party dispute resolution processes of mediation, binding arbitration, and trial. Another hybrid is *mediation-arbitration* (med-arb), in which a third-party neutral first mediates the dispute, and then, if mediation fails, the same person arbitrates it. It does not represent pure mediation, because the mediator has the power to compel acquiescence of the parties. It ensures finality and is efficient in its use of neutrals; the arbitrator already knows a great deal about the case from the mediation. Its disadvantage is that the parties may not confide their bottom-line demand or offer or other sensitive information (e.g., BATNA) to the mediator for fear he will use it against them in the later arbitration. This concern may interfere with voluntary settlement. *Arbitration-mediation* (arb-med), another hybrid, allows the third party to conduct an arbitration hearing, reach a decision, seal it in envelopes for the parties, and then conduct mediation. If mediation reaches impasse, the third party delivers the arbitration award to the disputants, but if the parties settle in mediation, the award is destroyed.[74]

Building Blocks for Policy Design

Collaborative governance includes deliberative democracy[75] and participatory democracy, which use large-scale interactive processes to address broader social and political conflict upstream. These processes are amenable to system design, entail various institutions, and encompass many process variations. Many organizations and citizen groups have pressed for more public participation, or participatory governance, in the policy process.[76] This movement seeks more citizen deliberation, dialogue, and shared decision-making[77] at the level of public policy in local, state, national, and even international governance. It also takes advantage of new technologies for communication and includes e-democracy and e-government.

As shown in Figure 3.1, several processes are used in the upstream, midstream, and downstream phases of collaborative governance. Some of these processes, such as convening, facilitation, and consensus building, are also used in private sector settings. Larger public engagement processes may also be used in the private sector, such as in the development of corporate social responsibility policy or the engagement of an international nonprofit with local community partners,[78] but these examples are exceptions in the realm of private sector policy making. For this reason, the following discussion of the policy building blocks focuses on applications in the public sector.

Public Engagement Using Dialogue and Deliberation

Public engagement processes using dialogue and deliberation engage the diffuse or general public in addition to or sometimes in lieu of stakeholders.[79] There are many models of practice. As an example, Everyday Democracy produces materials for citizens engaging in dialogue on issues such as civil rights, criminal justice, diversity, education, student success, growth and sprawl, and immigration.[80] They help organize a representative and diverse cross section of a community for dialogue. After small groups work in parallel, they converge to share ideas for solving problems in ways that will benefit the entire community.

In a different model, deliberative polling,[81] a random sample of the public has access to policy experts and an opportunity to deliberate with others. Before deliberation begins and again at the end, organizers conduct surveys to assess participant views. The results of the process can provide decision makers with

a statistically significant, representative account of citizens' preferences after dialogue. Empirical research in the 2010s has documented that opinions change
after deliberation, illustrating that point-in-time opinion polls in the absence of
complete information are unreliable as measures of citizen preferences.

Other than three minutes at the microphone or New England town hall meetings, the process most commonly used at the local government level is the Kettering Foundation's National Issues Forums.[82] Organizers hold large-scale citizen
meetings with small groups for structured discussions of policy choices such as
urban sprawl and sustainable development. The foundation provides a briefing
booklet for each issue with nonpartisan information that helps participants better
understand the costs, benefits, impacts, and consequences of policy approaches.
This model addresses local ordinances and policy choices or problems such as racial or ethnic conflict within a city. These processes help people clarify their policy
preferences to themselves, give them better understanding of the preferences of
others, and permit those with extreme views to moderate them.

The model of citizen juries allows governments to convene a public group for
legislative purposes, applying the jury model used for fact-finding in a judicial
or court setting instead to a policy-making context. In Denmark, the citizen jury
allows a representative group of citizens to participate in the legislative process,
addressing complex matters of technology policy, such as genetically modified
plants or organisms. Expert fact-finders may be called on to provide comprehensive information about a technical issue. The jury may question them; it need not
reach consensus but can attempt to arrive at decisions through voting. The jury
makes policy makers better informed about public opinion on the intersection
between technical policy issues and human values. Similarly, in planning cells and
consensus conferences, citizens deliberate to reach consensus on a policy issue.[83]

Multiparty and Public Policy Processes
and Collaborative Public Management

In the public sector, stakeholders may implement policy through what the public
administration literature calls "collaborative public management": an alternative
to command-and-control bureaucratic action in government.[84]

CONVENING. As a discrete third-party process, convening in the public sector
involves complex multiparty negotiations concerning issues of public policy,
public-private developments, or science—for example, in environmental conflict
resolution. In the private sector, it has a broader and more general meaning. The
convener is an impartial third party who identifies stakeholders in the dispute,

helps identify the issues, determines appropriate representatives for the negotiation, assesses whether there is a reasonable likelihood of reaching agreement in a timely manner, identifies resources that may be necessary to conduct the process, and recommends whether to go forward with the negotiation.[85] This process is called a conflict assessment. This book uses the term "conflict stream assessment" to describe the initial stage of DSD (see Chapter 4), one in which the convener or designer collects information about the potential users and categories of disputes to be managed, prevented, or resolved.

FACILITATION. Public processes use facilitation in many ways. City councils have used facilitation for setting agendas and goals and in budget deliberations with public participation.[86] The facilitator chairs all meetings as well as any working groups and orchestrates discussion by asking problem-solving questions in an effort to help the parties identify underlying shared interests and brainstorm possible ideas for settlement (defined as reaching an agreement or solving a problem). In general, a facilitator is less directive than a facilitative or evaluative mediator, instead making it possible for the parties to conduct discussions on complex issues.

CONSENSUS BUILDING. Another term for facilitation or mediation with multiple stakeholders and complex issues is "consensus building." Such facilitation uses interest-based negotiation techniques to attempt to reach consensus.[87] Consensus building is both an inclusive process and a mode of decision-making. As a decision rule, consensus may be defined as unanimity or as best efforts to achieve unanimity. Some argue that consensus building is the best option for decision-making in multimember public councils, boards, or commissions. Environmental conflict resolution often uses consensus building.[88]

NEGOTIATED RULEMAKING, OR REGULATORY NEGOTIATION. Facilitation is a process common to negotiated rulemaking and to complex environmental or public disputes.[89] Regulatory negotiation (reg-neg) has been adopted by many U.S. regulatory agencies. Rather than issue draft regulations and invite comment, an agency invites stakeholders to participate directly in drafting the regulations with the expectation that the stakeholder group will propose regulations they can support (as close to unanimously as possible). The agency then aims to adopt the recommendations.[90]

These are just a few of the many processes for large-group dialogue and deliberation.[91] Within these processes, third-party neutrals and facilitators may use negotiation, mediation, and other dispute resolution approaches, described earlier in this chapter.

New and Evolving Processes and Structures: Online Dispute Resolution

Online dispute resolution is the use of information and communication technology to resolve disputes. It encompasses a broad array of tools and mechanisms that differ from off-line processes in efficiency and kind, and it includes e-filing and case flow management, automated and assisted negotiation, online ADR and court processes,[92] and assisted decision-making using algorithms.[93] Legal technology spans advances in provider platforms, legal chatbots, artificial intelligence applied to legal regulation, and predictive analytics.[94] Online dispute resolution has many examples of innovation. The online sales platform eBay offers consumers online options to resolve a seller-buyer dispute, ranging from diagnosing the problem and facilitating negotiation between the parties to providing third-party assistance or a decision rendered by a third party (see Chapter 14). The Ohio Board of Tax Appeals offers an online diagnostic process for a taxpayer to input relevant data and assess the probability of a successful appeal through use of big data.[95]

Ayelet Sela traces the interdisciplinary nature and evolution of online dispute resolution, engaging not only legal procedure and infrastructure but also computer science, psychology, business (customer redress), engineering, and medicine.[96] The emergence of the block chain and design of smart contracts implies another avenue for online dispute resolution.[97] Sela examines the differences in the types of processes that parties experience in online mediation and arbitration versus their in-person equivalents, finding that disputants prefer software when the decision control remains with the parties but prefer human intervention when the decision control transfers to a third-party arbitrator. These observations reflect both the degree of autonomy possible with online dispute resolution and the expectations that disputants bring to their experience.[98]

In *Digital Justice*, Ethan Katsh and Orna Rabinovich-Einy trace the trajectory of access to justice and how technological tools contribute to preventing and resolving disputes. Their analysis highlights three major historical shifts: from offline face-to-face interaction to online interaction, from use of third-party neutrals to use of technology as a "fourth party," and from small data to big data.[99] These shifts offer opportunities for increased access to justice but come with risks in terms of accountability, privacy, and transparency.[100] The International Council of Online Dispute Resolution is undertaking an international effort to examine principles for online dispute resolution design from which international standards can emerge to guide practice.[101] The potential applications of online dispute resolution are vast and therefore are addressed in multiple chapters in this book (Chapters 7, 14, and 16).

Conclusion

This survey of process building blocks provides a typology for understanding and organizing the many process choices available to designers. It is important to remember that this survey is, of necessity, incomplete. People continue to create new ways to communicate about and deal with conflict. Succeeding chapters examine how to choose among processes, array them in sequence, and assess or evaluate how they function in context. In addition to choosing which processes to include in a DSD, the designer must place the processes within the organizational structure and determine who will manage and play the roles in their implementation. Processes may be housed in different units of an organization. DSD principles recommend that processes be offered in a coherent, integrated way that educates users about options and offers choice. Examples of process structures are discussed in the case chapters in the second unit.

4   SYSTEM DESIGN PRACTICE

THE DSD GUIDING PRINCIPLES described in Chapter 1 and the DSD Analytic Framework in Chapter 2 help potential designers understand a system as it exists and guide them in designing a new or improved system. The building blocks presented in Chapter 3 capture the many different structures and processes that a system can contain. But how can designers apply these concepts in approaching the design process? How do system designers work with people in a specific organization to choose the best processes for a particular context? What skills does a good designer need?

This chapter begins with ideal qualities of designers, then delves into the process by which they design.

The Professional Designer

No governing body licenses or certifies dispute system designers, yet designers should possess special knowledge, skills, and expertise. A system designer may be an independent person or firm (a nondisputant), a person internal to an organization that is a disputant, or a multiperson team. Perspectives and responsibilities will vary accordingly. In organizational development terms, the designer serves as an intervener who catalyzes energy and change, educates the organization about the stakeholders and conflict techniques, tailors and facilitates a process suitable to the prospective participants and situation, and serves as a role model.[1]

Designers (or members of the design team) need to possess strong interviewing, listening, and communication skills, in writing as well as when presenting to and interacting with people. The designer must have knowledge of the process options under consideration, as well as the related ethical standards and best practices. A designer may need a wide range of specialized knowledge and skills to proceed with all phases of design: assessment, design process, design implementation, and evaluation. For example, someone experienced in court management could assist a court seeking to integrate new process options to the management of its case docket; likewise, someone with expertise in environmental engineering or policy making could be needed to advise on handling claims related to a Superfund site cleanup.

A designer or design team's ideal knowledge and abilities align closely with the DSD principles and Analytic Framework outlined in Chapters 1 and 2, respectively. Again, these qualities are optimal (to the extent relevant for a particular DSD context) and may be contributed by multiple persons. Designer knowledge, abilities, and skills include the following:

KNOWLEDGE
- Organizational (or institutional or bureaucratic) development, psychology, human resources management
- Design and practice of workplace training, including adult learning theory
- Conflict theory
- Social science theory to evaluate how a system (and the organization within which it is embedded) functions
- Relevant laws and regulation
- Processes and structures through which people and stakeholders might prevent, manage, and resolve conflicts (see Chapter 3)

SKILLS AND ABILITIES
- Ability to analyze an existing system and its goals, stakeholders, context and culture, processes and structure, resources, and outcomes
- Capacity to identify the stakeholders and assess the stream of conflict, its sources, and its dynamics within the existing system
- Interpersonal skills to actively listen to and engage stakeholders and, where appropriate, the broader public to ensure a set of processes that solicit and incorporate diverse perspectives[2]
- Assessment methodology—for example, statistics, interview protocols, surveys, focus groups
- Thorough grounding in the sources of ethics for shaping, implementing, and operating the resulting system and its constituent processes and structures[3]

Conflict Stream Assessment

Expanding on the theory and practice of conflict assessments,[4] this chapter introduces conflict stream assessment (CSA) and discusses its essential content. A CSA[5]

Who Are Designers? Some Examples

- Cathy Costantino, counsel for the Federal Deposit Insurance Corporation, is a lawyer, mediator, and conflict management systems designer.[6]

- Ken Feinberg, a former trial counsel and public servant, has designed many claims facilities, including for the Agent Orange, September 11, Deepwater Horizon, and Las Vegas mass tragedies (see Chapter 8).

- Chelsea Mauldin, Public Policy Lab, is a social scientist specializing in public sector innovation.[7]

- The Stanford Legal Design Program applies design thinking to community-led system design for public clients such as in revision of the guardianship process for the California Judicial Council.[8]

- Morrison and Foerster, a San Francisco–based law firm, has produced a handbook for designing claims facilities for natural disasters.[9]

is an early effort to identify stakeholders, issues, interests, the nature of conflicts (some of which may become disputes) and how they are handled; determine the stakeholders' willingness to offer input into DSD; and recommend a process for engagement in system design. Each stakeholder will have a perspective on and expectation of the process. Because DSD addresses not just one but rather a series or stream of conflicts, a CSA is used to determine which parties and conflict issues are or will be coming to the system and why. This section reviews the scope, process, and product of CSA and summarizes the steps involved. The model is presented in the context of a business, nonprofit, or government agency with significant resources to devote to the design process; however, designers can streamline and adapt its concepts to any design situation. With even a modest investment of time, human, and financial resources, a designer-assessor can interview a representative group of parties and stakeholders to ascertain the key issues and their willingness to participate in a design.

A convener may organize and lead the effort to commence the assessment and design process and advise on selecting an assessor.[10] The assessor may be internal or external. Because independence and objectivity can be essential to the

CSA's impact and credibility, an internal assessor may prompt concerns among stakeholders regarding confidentiality and potential bias. In practice, however, budget or temporal constraints or the need for internal organizational expertise may prevent the use of an outside consultant.

The assessor has a range of choices on how to structure the assessment. A CSA might proceed with the following steps.[11]

EXAMPLE STEPS FOR CONDUCTING A CONFLICT STREAM ASSESSMENT

- The decision maker consults with the convener to select the assessor. The convener may be the decision maker if the focus is on the stream of disputes within a specific organization; if decision-maker bias is a concern, the convener may be another party with an interest, broad access, and resources (e.g., a government agency or community organization).
- The convener introduces the assessor to the potential stakeholders.[12]
- The assessor develops a confidential interview protocol with questions on the history of conflict, stream of disputes, and dispute handling within the organization or institution, what issues are important and why, what other individuals or organizations have an interest in the situation, what the key interests and concerns are, and whether the interviewee would be willing to engage in a consensus-building process.
- The assessor consults with the convener to identify the first round of stakeholders.
- The assessor schedules the interviews (and offers confidentiality, if necessary) and uses these contacts to identify additional stakeholders for interviews.
- The assessor drafts a report summarizing findings of essential facts and history, areas of agreement and disagreement, issues in common and in contention as viewed by each stakeholder group, feasibility of proceeding with a design process, and willingness of prospective stakeholders to participate.
- The assessor circulates the draft report to interviewed stakeholders. The assessor summarizes the range of opinions but does not attribute specific opinions to individuals. The assessor asks interviewees to confirm accuracy of their input.
- If the assessor recommends—and the designer concurs—proceeding with DSD, the assessor will propose a design process with a specific set of goals, issues to discuss, participants to include for balance, a time and topic schedule for meetings, necessary documents or data sources, joint fact-finding processes,[13] and a format for report writing.

- The assessor may propose ground rules for the design decision-making that include roles and responsibilities of participants, cost allocation, interaction with media, use of working groups, and how to prepare, circulate, and review documents.

A CSA will benefit from the assessor using qualitative field research methods from social science. A neutral outsider conducts confidential stakeholder interviews either in person or by telephone, video conference, or written survey. Often, focus groups with key stakeholders provide input to the CSA. The assessor can identify stakeholders through snowball sampling (asking interviewees whom else to consult) or use of a representative sample.[14] A less formal sample may risk omitting relevant voices or causing the assessor to reach a skewed conclusion. The assessor can use a multistakeholder committee with representatives of key groups to provide formality and accountability in overseeing the assessment.

The CSA is a model for the subsequent design process and should provide sufficient information for consideration of the six DSD Analytic Framework elements described in Chapter 2. The CSA report should thoroughly describe the kinds of disputes to be addressed, stakeholders in these disputes and what issues are important to them, the processes currently in place, stakeholders' usage or avoidance of current processes, and the institutional, financial, and human resources available. The report should examine stakeholders' competence to use the system, organizational and legal constraints, and opportunities for improving the system. Additionally, the report should include an analysis of any data that exist to examine the current system's efficiency and quality of outcomes. For an existing system, the assessor should determine which stakeholders chose or designed it and why. Stakeholders should have an opportunity to comment on the draft report for accuracy and completeness.

Thus, the designer undertakes a CSA to understand the scope of conflict the system could address. The CSA then forms the basis for recommending both a design process and design components. The process of assessment offers benefits in at least four ways: (1) it provides an impartial *map* of the conflict structure, (2) it *educates* stakeholders about what it takes to collaborate on addressing the conflict, (3) it builds a working *relationship* between the stakeholders and the assessor or designer, and (4) it develops a sense of *ownership* among the stakeholders for handling the dispute stream ahead.

A CSA requires the designer to gather information about (1) the sources for conflict that make their way into the stream, (2) how the conflict may evolve from an unperceived harm into a dispute and claim,[15] (3) how context and culture influence the incidence of conflict, and (4) the opportunities that exist for changing the dynamic. The following questions are examples of what can be answered through strategies such as background research, surveys, and interviews.

SAMPLE INTERVIEW PROTOCOL FOR A CONFLICT STREAM ASSESSMENT

1. What are the sources of conflict? How do they give rise to disputes?
   - What categories of stakeholders have an interest in the conflicts and disputes that form the stream?
   - Who are the affected parties, and are they individuals or organizations?
   - Who is eligible as a claimant or decision maker?
   - What issues are important to these stakeholders?
   - Do issues involve values, relationships, structure, data, or interests?[16]
   - Are there recurring disputes? Or were the disputes triggered by a singular event or condition?
   - What is the cultural context of the conflict and how diverse are individual stakeholders' cultures?
   - What is the institutional or organizational culture for managing conflict?
   - Do the cultures emphasize interests, rights, or power?
2. What are the conflict and dispute dynamics?
   - What is the intensity of the conflict—is it early or small, or is it advanced or severe?
   - How do disputes evolve over time in the conflict stream?
   - What is the time frame of the dispute stream, and how urgent is a dispute's resolution?
   - At what point in the stream might disputants have an incentive to negotiate?
   - How and when does urgency to resolve a dispute contrast with strategic advantage for one or more stakeholders through delay?
   - Who has relative power? From what sources?
   - Is essential information broadly known or asymmetrically controlled?
   - What are the parties' and stakeholders' alternative strategies for achieving their respective interests?
   - What is the role of publicity, public scrutiny, and public relations?
   - Are there evidentiary (proof) issues?
   - How do the cultures shape attitudes, tactics, and stakeholder conflict management styles?
3. Where are there structural or organizational opportunities for preventing, learning from, managing, or resolving conflict?

- How does the volume of disputes in relation to the availability of re-
  sources (time or money) affect design decisions?
- How have these kinds of disputes been handled and resolved in the past
  (in this and other forums)?
- What flexibility is there to resolve the disputes; are there organizational,
  legal, economic, or other constraints?
- What are the stakeholders' best alternatives to a negotiated agreement?[17]
  What are the costs, uncertainties, and preferences associated with
  them? Who stands to gain or lose from a change in the status quo?
- What are the relationships in play (past, present, and future)?
- Are disputants able to compromise, or do principles or precedent con-
  strain them?

The decision maker generally determines the scope of the CSA and who will participate. The designer can serve as a voice for unrepresented stakeholders and recommend a broader assessment, but the decision maker will need to balance such considerations against other needs and available resources.[18] In a crisis, decision makers may focus narrowly on the "hot topic."[19] Furthermore, the scope of the CSA may differ from that of the design. A broad CSA of a company might identify conflict internally among employees and externally with suppliers and consumers, but the decision maker might choose to focus the DSD only on employee conflict.

Conducting a DSD Process

The CSA phase should provide a comprehensive picture of how the organization currently handles conflict, how stakeholders view existing procedures in terms of process and outcome, what other procedures might better meet stakeholders' interests, what existing and additional resources and skills would be required to design a system, and whether stakeholders are willing to engage in a design process. If the decision maker in consultation with stakeholders decides to go forward with a DSD process, here are next steps.

DSD PROCESS STEPS

1. Establish a stakeholder-driven design team.
2. Develop a vision for system goals shared by stakeholders and users.
3. Use participatory and collaborative processes to engage stakeholders
   and users, identify and prioritize user options, and solicit feedback on a
   draft DSD.
4. Implement the final DSD through a continuous cycle of outreach, training, disclosure, evaluation, and feedback.

5. Build a process for evaluating the program and adjusting the DSD on the basis of its performance and evaluation.

The remainder of this chapter illustrates the specific steps of a dispute system redesign using the example of Kaiser Permanente. This case is not intended to serve as an optimal model but rather as a description of a real situation in which Kaiser undertook an integrated assessment and design.[20]

Kaiser Permanente and Its Medical Malpractice Arbitration System

Wilfredo Engalla was a patient whose care was provided by Kaiser Permanente.[21] He had lung cancer and filed a medical malpractice arbitration claim for failure of the doctors to diagnose the cancer earlier. Engalla died 144 days later, the day after a neutral arbitrator was selected but well before the arbitration claim was heard. His estate sued for the right to have the case heard in court, claiming "fraud in the inducement of the arbitration agreement" and unconscionability. In 1997 the California Supreme Court, in *Engalla v. Permanente Medical Group*,[22] found that there was "evidence to support the trial court's initial findings that Kaiser engaged in fraudulent conduct justifying a denial of its petition to compel arbitration," but "questions of fact remain to be resolved by the trial court."[23] The California Supreme Court's opinion cited independent analysis of data collected from 1984 to 1986 to highlight how Kaiser's arbitration system had fallen short of its stated goals in several critical respects: speed, cost effectiveness, and fairness. Faced with fallout from the Engalla opinion, Kaiser looked to improve the system quickly. In addition to the pressure and publicity of the pending case, another likely concern for Kaiser management was discussion in the California legislature of limiting consumer binding arbitration in health care.[24]

Importantly, fairness and by implication some form of justice were important factors in shaping Kaiser's system redesign. With this background, the section describes each design step and how Kaiser engaged in the process.

1. Establish a stakeholder-driven design team. The best way to ensure that a DSD meets stakeholders' and users' needs is to involve them in the process of creating it, managing its implementation, and evaluating its success. The assessor, convener, or designer (or some combination of these actors) might propose the design team. The team should ensure stakeholder input for both policy decisions and implementation.

In the design phase, the design team translates the CSA into an action plan. The design team clarifies the goals of the design, including the range and scope of conflicts to be addressed, who will use the system, who will manage it and with what resources, how the system fits into the formal and informal fabric of the organization and formal legal options, and how stakeholders will define system success. Typical design team tasks are the following:

- Confirm the goals for the DSD (as determined during the CSA stage) with the decision maker and representative stakeholders, including the categories of conflicts and disputes to be addressed and the resources available for design and implementation.
- Examine whether the DSD goals align with the organization's incentive structure, culture, and values.
- Specify how stakeholders fit within the organizational structure and their roles and responsibilities for the design and implementation process.
- Compare the dispute processes under consideration to current procedures and their sequence, cost, and impact.
- Develop the DSD planning strategy (with a pilot if feasible), applying the DSD guiding principles described in Chapter 1.[25]
- Identify information to collect from operation of the system and determine who (e.g., users, the public) will have access to the data.
- Determine or review the training needed to institute the pilot for users, managers, and neutrals, among others.
- Determine or review the communication plan.
- Following implementation, evaluate the system against the goals identified in the design (see Chapter 5).[26]

Kaiser Design Team

In the uncertain and pressured context of the Kaiser case, management needed to decide quickly what the process scope of the redesign would be—whether to focus on the existing arbitration system or consider additional disputing processes; who would take the lead in redesigning the system; what resources, both human and financial, would be devoted to the project; and how quickly these changes needed to occur. Given the lack of confidence in Kaiser's arbitration program demonstrated by the court, as well as the accusations by the Engalla family and others that Kaiser intentionally delayed arbitrations for its own benefit, Kaiser chose to create and fund a three-person advisory panel of outside experts with a rapporteur to help organize, shape, and document the process and recommendations. The Blue Ribbon Panel consisted of Eugene Lynch, a retired federal judge and an arbitrator and mediator for JAMS (formerly Judicial Arbitration and Mediation Services), a private provider of ADR services; Sandra Hernández, a physician and the executive director of the San Francisco Foundation; and Phillip L. Isenberg, an attorney and retired member of the California State Assembly. Stephanie Smith, coauthor of this book, was named the rapporteur. Kaiser management instructed the Blue Ribbon Panel to suggest improvements to Kaiser's arbitration process "in order to provide an arbitration system that is sensitive to the members and fair to all parties involved."[27]

2. Develop a vision for system goals shared by stakeholders and users. To understand the system in context, the design team needs a broad understanding of the organization's structure and culture. Cathy Costantino and Christina Merchant have discussed extensively how organizations function, learn, perform, and change, whether those organizations are corporations, government agencies, schools, nations, nonprofits, courts, or universities. In Costantino and Merchant's view, conflict subsystems function better when they are integrated with an organization's overall operation rather than isolated within the legal or human resources department. They argue that changing technical systems alone is inadequate; designers must adapt social systems as well.[28] The best way to understand the system in context is to engage stakeholders and users in identifying how the organization needs to change to prevent, manage, and resolve conflict effectively. This effort requires substantial stakeholder and user engagement during the consideration and decision-making stage.

3. Use participatory and collaborative processes to engage stakeholders and users, identify and prioritize user options, and solicit feedback on a draft DSD. To achieve buy-in and optimize implementation, the design team should work collaboratively with stakeholders and users throughout the design process. Chapter 3 describes collaborative and participatory techniques, both face-to-face and online, that practitioners have developed to brainstorm, generate ideas, select and refine the best ideas, and build consensus. Techniques can include surveys, small-group dialogues, focus groups, larger-scale forums, online voting, blogs, and collaborative internal wiki websites.

Kaiser Assessment and Design Process

The Blue Ribbon Panel met once a week for three months. Representatives of stakeholder groups[29] and experts on health care, arbitration, and ADR were invited to make presentations and discuss potential system designs. Panel members and the rapporteur also conducted research and interviews and obtained written reports. In total, the panel received information from over seventy-five individuals. The Blue Ribbon Panel's recommendations included the following:[30]

- Appointment of an independent administrator to manage the Kaiser arbitration process
- A permanent stakeholder advisory committee made up of volunteers
- A clear statement of goals and communication of these goals to stakeholders
- A more expedited and efficient process—including calendar benchmarks for case management events and completion of cases
- Encouragement of early settlement discussions
- Expansion of the pool of arbitrators
- Regular data collection on system performance and outcomes
- External audits and evaluation of the new process
- Written, reasoned decisions by arbitrators
- Information about the potential arbitrators and their prior rulings made available to all parties at the time of arbitrator selection

Several items beyond the core arbitration issues were also in the recommendations, such as creation of a mediation program and institution of an ombuds position.

4. Implement the final DSD through a continuous cycle of outreach, training, disclosure, evaluation, and feedback. For a system to function, it must provide adequate motivation, training, and resources. To improve how disputes are handled, it must allow consultation before use and evaluation and feedback afterward.[31] John Conbere surveyed the literature on DSD theory and practice and found that major authors agreed on the need to support users with coaching, an ombuds, or a third party to help users understand process choices.[32] They stressed that designers must integrate the DSD with its host organization and seek backing from the organization's leadership, as well as support for the disputants and training for the providers. Moreover, effective implementation uses internal and external publicity (employee briefings, press releases, video, newsletters, system champion's reports), informational materials, point people as resources, goal setting, outreach, intake, and monitoring.[33]

Mindful of available resources, the design team must establish procedures for case selection and handling (ideally starting with a DSD pilot) and define roles and responsibilities for managers and service providers and specifications for how users of the DSD will access the system. The team should devise a communication plan as part of the training and education of stakeholders and neutrals, and it should include information in handbooks, protocols, and other disseminated materials.

Kaiser Design Implementation

Kaiser published the Blue Ribbon Panel report and, over time, adopted almost all the panel's key recommendations.[34] Kaiser created an advisory group representing the key stakeholder groups[35] and, to run the revamped arbitration system, contracted with an outside attorney to create the Office of the Independent Administrator, located outside Kaiser but funded by the company. The office's protocols and rules were developed in collaboration with the advisory group and Kaiser and were posted online.

   5. *Build a process for adjusting the DSD based on evaluation.* An oversight body composed of stakeholder representatives should be built into any DSD and tasked with monitoring, evaluation, and system improvement. As discussed in Chapter 5, criteria for evaluating dispute systems are transaction costs, relationships among the disputants, recurrence of the disputes,[36] efficiency in time and cost, durability of resolution, effect on the organizational environment, and satisfaction with the process, relationships, and outcome.[37] The continuous collection of data helps the designers and managers assess whether the DSD is functioning as intended and its goals are being met. Such data collection must include objective statistics, such as use and outcomes, and feedback from stakeholders on how the procedures are working.

   Any DSD generates potentially confidential information, so it is necessary to develop a clear plan for information management that has policies regarding information collection, protection, access privileges, distribution, and destruction, as well as a policy for handling security breaches. Continual data collection can help provide objective accounts of a program's function and point to ways to improve it. Stakeholder feedback is essential to a program's success, because it encourages ownership and, if positive, encourages others to use the program. Objective data about program outcomes can also help create internal support for allocating monetary and human resources to the system.

Kaiser Monitoring Program and Evaluation

The annual reports published by the Office of the Independent Administrator indicate substantial progress in satisfying the key goals of the redesign, including reduction in the time to arbitration and expansion of both the number of arbitrators and the availability of information about them. The office's activities were substantially more transparent than the previous arbitration process, and ample data on arbitration cases were made available on its website. Early annual reports tracked the progress of each recommendation, and an independent audit of the office was conducted in its fifth year, as proposed by the panel.[38] However, in the first several years after the Office of the Independent Administrator was established, Kaiser took no action on several of the panel's recommendations, including those proposing mediation and an ombuds office. Kaiser subsequently created a hybrid of these two process options within its system, as described in Chapter 14.

Conclusion

This chapter puts the system design approach of the DSD Analytic Framework into practice. A skillful designer or design team is able to identify and engage the full set of stakeholders, probe for their priority interests, and assess the culture and context of the situation. The CSA both serves as a model for communication and engagement and generates ideas for processes to pilot and monitor in order to launch a system and adjust as needed. The next chapter focuses more deeply on planning for and conducting an evaluation of the system over time.

5   ACCOUNTABILITY

Evaluating Dispute System Design

THIS BOOK LOOKS SYSTEMATICALLY at the institutions used to prevent, manage, and resolve conflict. DSDs are dynamic, not static. Viewed over time, they produce a pattern of outcomes. As systems evolve, outcomes may change. Evaluating systems requires periodic assessment to measure whether these outcomes are achieving goals that designers intended and whether the system is fair and just. The guiding principles for DSD discussed in Chapter 1 provide ways for thinking about the relationship between goals and outcomes.

A critical component of a comprehensive DSD is accountability through program evaluation, providing transparency and information to stakeholders—individuals and organizations that create, host, use, and are affected by a DSD. Sharing information on how a system functions can engender trust in it, which can in turn enhance its use. Evaluation also provides a feedback loop for improving the system. Without a comprehensive, longitudinal view of the system and its outcomes, it is hard to justify continuing investment of resources in a DSD.

This chapter first addresses accountability in a system. It revisits the conceptual question raised in Chapter 1: To what extent should, or can, DSDs be evaluated on norms of fairness or their capacity to deliver some form of justice? The second part of the chapter explains the functional steps of program evaluation in relation to the original conflict stream assessment (see Chapter 4). Last, researchers usually examine disputant perceptions and outcomes in a DSD aimed at resolving ripe disputes, not how the DSD functions upstream in preventing or managing conflict. The concluding section briefly offers some ideas extending evaluation to new, broader designs.

This chapter introduces accountability and evaluation; these structures and skills, like DSD itself, must fit within a context and culture.[1] Case chapters in this volume review more quantitative and qualitative empirical studies on specific contexts, such as courts (Chapter 7),[2] agencies (Chapter 17),[3] arbitration in domestic or international[4] settings (Chapter 12), and the environment (Chapter 18). Chapter 17 introduces accountability and evaluation in large-scale collaborative governance designs.

Accountability Forums: Justice and Fairness

Accountability, a component of the DSD Analytic Framework discussed in Chapter 2, has two broad, complementary meanings as adapted to DSD.[5] First, it is a means or procedure to facilitate a relationship between the responsible person giving an explanation or account to her superior, an oversight body, or forum. Second, organizations hosting a DSD and its program managers owe a duty of accountability to stakeholders and participants; accountability is a benefit or end in itself.

Public administration scholars describe accountability as comprising six promises of means and ends that public officials implicitly make in managing programs.[6] Three promises are of instrumental value (means): control (inputs), ethical behavior or choices (processes), and performance (outcomes). Three promises are of intrinsic value (ends): integrity (inputs), legitimacy (processes), and justice (outcomes).

Table 5.1 applies these promises to system design.[7] The first column illustrates means designers use as inputs to the system to carry out instrumental promises of control over the system, ethical behavior or choices within the system, and the system's performance. The second column illustrates substantive intrinsic promises that the system will operate with integrity, legitimacy, and justice. Ethics (Chapter 6) illustrate the intrinsic promise of integrity, but for them to be effective, system managers must enforce them, reflected in the instrumental promise of ethical behaviors or choices. Evaluation, management, and measurement reflect the instrumental promise of system performance, the subject of this chapter.

Chapter 1 introduces how theorists have defined "justice" in dozens of ways related to fairness or equity across fields of literature including jurisprudence, philosophy, social psychology, sociology, economics, and political science. While these categories to some degree overlap, they relate to (1) the outcomes of the process (distributive and substantive justice), (2) party voice and control over process (procedural justice), (3) impacts on organizations and organizational values (organizational justice), or (4) impacts on communities (transitional, restorative, and communitarian justice).[8] For accountability theory, varieties of justice provide norms of fairness or equity that stakeholders, participants, and

Table 5.1 Promises of accountability in DSD

	Instrumental promise	*Intrinsic promise*
Inputs	Control • Standing to use the system • Multiple access points to system • Selection of looping back and looping forward resolution processes • Selection of third-party neutral	Integrity • Protection against retaliation • Policies guaranteeing privacy and confidentiality • Codes of ethics for ombuds, mediators, arbitrators, or neutrals • Transparency of the system processes and outcomes in the aggregate
Processes	Ethical behavior/choices • Training programs • Clear rules and processes • Investigations • Enforcing ethics code for ombuds, mediators, arbitrators, or neutrals	Legitimacy • Voice in design phase • Oversight body composed of key stakeholders • Peer review • Options for appeal outside line of supervision • External impartial third parties
Outcomes	Performance • Evaluations of system processes and outcomes • Performance management • Performance measurement	Justice • Procedural or organizational justice in ombuds, mediation, arbitration, litigation, or other processes • Distributive justice consistent with rule of law and goals of design

Source: Lisa Blomgren Amsler and Jessica Sherrod, "Accountability Forums and Dispute System Design," *Public Performance Management Review* 40, no. 3 (2017): 538.

designers may identify as goals in the DSD Analytic Framework (see Chapter 2); they are the fundamental standards for the success of a system. They also provide concepts to incorporate into measures for an evaluation. However, with the exception of procedural, organizational, and restorative justice, designers and evaluators rarely discuss these many differing conceptions of justice. Best practice suggests they should.

Melvin Dubnick and H. George Frederickson explain that, in accountability, the "promise of justice/equity assumes the opportunity to seek justice in light of some claimed act or possible act will result in justice or fairness."[9] It takes place in judicial settings with due process guaranteeing just treatment.[10] The accountability promise of justice has both intrinsic and instrumental value. Access to impartial arenas reflects justice as a process to challenge and judge an abuse of authority; receiving fairness or equity from the forum reflects justice as an outcome. Chapter 3 illustrates judicial and quasi-judicial processes downstream on the policy continuum. In DSD, these processes can take many forms, from the formal trial court or administrative agency adjudication to the less formal ADR forums like mediation and arbitration. They also include upstream forums for public dialogue on policy. DSD focuses on more than a single case; it entails designing and evaluating the forum for a stream of cases within a system, as Chapter 4 discusses. Across the policy continuum, these DSDs provide forums of accountability for those who manage them.

Evaluation in DSD: Variables and Indicators

Program evaluators use empirical methods and tools to assess behavior within a system to learn how the system's design functions on chosen criteria. This analysis applies empirical social science theories about institutions to generate research questions.[11] To implement accountability and justice, designers need to analyze a DSD as an institution that an internal or external team can evaluate. Any evaluation design requires an indicator in which change is expected (a dependent variable) and a basis for comparison (one or more independent variables). Scholarship from various disciplines can provide these tools.

Fairness and Satisfaction

The broad empirical literature on DSD contains studies of all varieties of justice.[12] For indicators of procedural or distributive justice, some procedural justice studies use questions about a participant's judgments of fairness of the process or outcome.[13] Researchers have used questions about perceptions of fairness of process and a participant's satisfaction with outcome in an action arena within a DSD.[14] While a participant's answers about satisfaction may sometimes correlate with those about fairness, different information may drive these judgments—for example, whether the outcome is better or worse than someone else's or than what was expected.[15]

Marc Galanter and Mia Cahill provide a set of arguments for dispute resolution and settlement as alternatives to adjudication in courts that can serve as dependent variables for comparing different DSDs. Their categories are party preference (party pursuit, satisfaction, and needs), cost reduction (party savings), court or forum efficiency (saving courts' time and resources), superior outcome (golden mean, superior knowledge of facts and parties' preferences, normative richness, inventiveness, compliance, personal transformation of the participants), and superior general effects (deterrence, moral education, mobilization and demobilization of future legal actors, and precedent and patterning in which settlements send signals about legal standards, practices, and expectations).[16] For example, a comparison of systems could ask which is more efficient or satisfying for the participants. However, this set does not expressly refer to justice. Instead, many of the arguments relate to the administration of justice; this observation is particularly true of the cost-reduction arguments.[17] Judith Resnik suggests that, in court-based ADR, evaluators should consider the volume of court ADR rule-making and the privatization of court-based interactions, under which criteria courts have adopted rules to foster contract formation and reduced public access to information about regulation of ADR.[18]

Ostrom and Institutional Analysis and Development: The Case as an Action Arena

To evaluate and thus hold accountable a specific system, the late Nobel laureate and political economist Elinor Ostrom provides a useful construct for analysis of independent variables in a DSD: the action arena.[19] Any individual case within a DSD represents an action arena. Within the arena are participants and an action situation, which interact. Seven clusters of variables characterize the action arena:

> (1) The set of participants [single individuals or corporate actors], (2) the positions to be filled by participants, (3) the potential outcomes, (4) the set of allowable actions and the function that maps actions into realized outcomes [action-outcome linkages], (5) the control that an individual has in regard to this function, (6) the information available to participants about actions and outcomes and their linkages, and (7) the costs and benefits—which serve as incentives and deterrents—assigned to actions and outcomes.[20]

The action arena is nested in institutions and shaped by external, or exogenous, variables that include rules, biophysical and material conditions, and attributes of community. These external variables can shape what happens in an individual case in the stream of cases identified in a conflict stream assessment; for example, the rules and policy establishing the DSD shape which outcomes are possible. If the DSD entails mediation, a voluntary settlement is a possible outcome. If it entails binding arbitration, a third-party decision is a possible outcome. Ostrom's categories for analyzing the action arena for each case provide ways to identify independent variables for evaluation of the DSD and what happens when evaluators aggregate multiple cases in the conflict stream. DSDs depend on their national legal and cultural context; countries regulate dispute resolution in varying ways that can shape what happens in the action arena.[21]

Structural Features of DSD as Independent Variables in Evaluation

Typically, evaluations examine whether a DSD's components produce the desired outcome. The DSD's components are the structural features that qualify as what social scientists call independent variables. These structural features include the context for DSD, the system's process elements, and its administration. They vary widely across institutions.

PARTICIPANTS, POSITIONS, CONTROL, AND CONTEXT FOR DSD. DSDs are often nested in other institutions. An employee grievance procedure may be nested in a private company; a mediation program may be in a court. As Ostrom asks of any action arena, what are the participants and their roles? Elements of context for DSD are sector or setting for the program (public, private, or nonprofit); overall DSD (integrated conflict management system, silo or stovepipe program, ombuds program, outside contractor); subject matter of the conflicts, disputes, or cases over which the system has jurisdiction;[22] and participants eligible or required to use the system (and their roles and demographics).[23]

POTENTIAL OUTCOMES AND ACTION-OUTCOME LINKAGES. The DSD is an institution with rules that structure what can happen in the action arena. These rules define the allowable actions and their linkage to outcomes, the range of potential outcomes, accessible information, and costs and benefits. In DSD, they might be the following:

- Nature of the process or intervention (e.g., training, facilitation, consensus building, summary jury trial,[24] or nonbinding or binding arbitration)
- Nature, training, qualifications, and demographics of the neutrals[25]
- Sequence of processes or interventions, if more than one
- Within intervention, the model of practice (if mediation, evaluative, facilitative, or transformative; if arbitration, rights or interests, last-best offer, issue by issue, etc.)
- Other structural elements of the process (e.g., decision standard in arbitration)
- Timing of the intervention (before complaint is filed, immediately thereafter, after discovery or information gathering, or the eve of an administrative hearing or trial)
- Whether the intervention is voluntary, opt out, or mandatory
- Presence or absence of procedural safeguards like a due process protocol or the right to counsel
- Other due process protections (discovery, location of process, availability of class actions, availability of written opinion or decision)

ADMINISTRATION OF THE SYSTEM: PARTICIPANT CONTROL, ACCESSIBLE INFORMATION, AND COSTS AND BENEFITS. Control over the system's design, evaluation, management, and administration shapes what happens in the action arena. With respect to level of self-determination or control that disputants have as to DSD and its processes and outcomes, who makes decisions? Both parties together, one party unilaterally, or a third party for them? Who pays for the neutrals, and what is the nature of their financial or professional incentive structure?[26] Who pays for the costs of administration, filing fees, hearing fees, hearing space? How is transparency and accountability ensured through an evaluation system? What structural support and institutionalization is provided with respect to conflict management programs or efforts to implement the design?

RULES AS EXOGENOUS VARIABLES. Each of these categories of rules entails a structural element of the DSD. Moreover, each must be embodied in a contract, policy, guideline, regulation, statute, or other form of rule. For example, an arbitration clause might provide that the loser pays for all the administrative costs and arbitrator fees in the case. This cost shifting creates an economic disincentive to use the system. Each element might give rise to a separate question or series of questions: Why did you choose that element? What is its purpose? What effect do you expect it to produce? Why is that effect desirable? What is your overarching goal?

Practical Program Evaluation

Program evaluation stems from scholarship in public policy analysis and administration. It can include applied field research and quasi-experiments. Joseph Wholey, Harry Hatry, and Kathryn Newcomber define program evaluation as "the systematic assessment of program results and, to the extent feasible, systematic assessment of the extent to which the program caused those results."[27] They define a program as "a set of resources and activities directed toward one or more common goals, typically under the direction of a single manager or management team."[28] DSDs either arise ad hoc, evolve, or are created through a planning process (that ideally is inclusive). This inclusive and participatory design for evaluation should be developed at the DSD's inception—not after a crisis or court challenge.

The steps for evaluating a DSD resemble the steps for DSD and conflict stream assessment presented in Chapter 4, because designing the evaluation is a component of designing the system itself:

1. Identify and recruit stakeholders to participate in design of the evaluation process.
2. Identify the questions the evaluation must answer.
3. Identify the information that will answer the questions.

4. Structure a process to collect that information.
5. Structure a method to analyze and compile the information.
6. Report results to stakeholders.
7. In consultation with stakeholders, use results to improve both the design and the evaluation.

The process for designing the evaluation is as important as the process for designing the system as a whole. Evaluation requires resources. As designers, stakeholders, and host institutions consider these steps, it is critical to identify and allocate those resources. Following these steps, designers and evaluators can provide a continuous feedback loop to improve DSDs over time.

Identify and Recruit Stakeholders to Participate in Designing the Evaluation

An organization may choose to use an evaluator from inside its ranks or who is an outside consultant. Evaluators should engage stakeholders in a broadly participatory way to help design the evaluation as part of the initial system design. Chapter 2 addresses how to identify stakeholders. They are not the same as the general public for the purposes of evaluation design; they are people, associations, or organizations that may use the system, provide resources for it, or have a stake in how it functions. They have different perspectives on a system and varied insights; they are also a source for creativity in determining how best—practically and cost effectively—to collect data. This design step may involve focus groups, surveys, or online brainstorming to identify what should be measured and how. As with the DSD, the evaluation requires consensus on goals; consensus on criteria for the system's success; stakeholder buy-in for collecting data; ways to decentralize data collection, use, analysis, and transparency; and dissemination of results.

Stakeholder buy-in is essential. People in organizations tend to do only what gets measured and reported. Measurement creates incentives and disincentives; it can also create unintended consequences. Consequently, evaluation is a highly sensitive and political issue.

Stakeholders and participants can make meaningful contributions to DSD because their perceptions of a process and their resulting preferences may evolve. Donna Shestowsky and Jeanne Brett have researched disputant preferences for different aspects of procedures in courts before and after experiencing them. They suggest that procedural preferences before experiencing a process may be shaped by insufficient information and experience.[29] Disputants preferred adjudicative

---

When Employees Sabotage a Cost-Benefit Evaluation

A federal agency had a system for handling employment discrimination complaints in which some employees worked full-time conducting investigations and administering case files for adjudicatory informal and formal hearings. The agency decided to test a new DSD in which outside mediators handled the discrimination complaints. The agency hired new staff to administer the mediation program because current employees lacked mediation and interest-based negotiation skills. The agency wanted a cost-benefit analysis comparing the new program with the old one. Naturally, employees in the old program feared losing their jobs. As a result, they sabotaged data collection for the cost-benefit analysis and it failed. Through a participatory design process, however, an organization might be able to address similar concerns up front and allay fears—for example, by offering retraining and transfers for these employees.

---

processes before they experienced them but facilitative and mediated processes once they had more experience.[30]

Identify the Questions the Evaluation Must Answer

Chapter 2 outlines how to identify a DSD's goals; the evaluators determine whether the system has achieved these goals. The literature on justice can help define standards of fairness in evaluating the DSD. From stakeholders' perspectives, how critical is some form of justice as the system's goal? Does the design incorporate a broad array of stakeholder goals or only the (institutional) designer's perspective? Ostrom recognizes social norms as standards of fairness in an institution.[31] Who has control over the DSD, and are their goals driving the evaluation? Is a corporate designer focused solely on managing financial risk from litigation, or does the organization seek to achieve voice for employees to foster perceptions of fairness?

What evaluators measure may or may not reflect notions of justice. For example, if a system aims to reduce the time a case spends on a court's docket, designers might expect fewer days from filing a complaint to closing the case. This expectation reflects the court's goal of efficiency and budget savings. In comparison, focusing on reducing litigants' transaction costs in court might reflect concerns for substantive or distributive justice. If an organization's goal is to improve the way that supervisors and employees communicate in a conflict, evaluators might expect that supervisors and employees will make more use of active listening skills. This measure might relate to organizational justice, which includes a component of interpersonal justice. These two examples reflect different goals and require different evaluation designs, although both require collecting data before and after the organization implements a new DSD.

Identify the Information That Will Answer the Questions

To answer the questions, evaluators look for change coded in certain information as a function of the structural elements of the DSD. For example, to measure improved speed for resolving cases, one can count the days from filing to case closure. To measure whether employees and supervisors are learning better communication skills, one can conduct surveys asking about whether one party listened, understood, or acknowledged the other party's viewpoint. This information can take the form of indicators (dependent variables in social science parlance). There can be great variety in the indicators, or information, that designers might use to answer these questions and the ease with which they can obtain the information.

The following variables are commonly used in both qualitative and quantitative evaluation research:

- Settlement rates
- Case flow rates
- Time on the docket or time to settlement
- Perceptions of or satisfaction with process, neutral, or outcome (sometimes called micro justice)
- Transaction costs savings
- Party success in the process (sometimes called distributive justice) or overall patterns of outcomes from the process (sometimes called macro justice)
- Change in the relationships among the parties
- For workplace systems, employee turnover and retention rates, absenteeism, productivity, or employee citizenship behaviors
- Voluntary compliance with the outcome or noncompliance, recidivism[32]

Dispute resolution is fundamentally about human communication; evaluating DSD involves considering how goals, context and culture, processes and structure (including rules), and resources affect that human communication across streams of disputes. To get the most useful information for evaluating the system, it is important to balance both the human interaction and the system dynamics—that is, to use qualitative and quantitative data.[33]

The literature on DSD evaluation is still relatively new. Certain DSDs present complex evaluation challenges. For example, how might one evaluate a design for a multioption, multidoor courthouse with several goals? The system might involve settlement conferences, private ADR, victim-offender reconciliation, and nonbinding arbitration. Interest-based processes like mediation have goals that differ from rights-based processes like arbitration. In a design for transitional justice, how and with what indicators might one evaluate the success of a truth and reconciliation commission? One might measure change using indicators at a societal level: voter turnout, civil conflict as reflected in case filings in courts, and crime rates.

Structure a Process to Collect That Information

Common data collection methods are mail or online surveys; in-person, online, or telephone interviews; examination of archival records, case files, or datasets; and sometimes observational data. Information may be quantitative or qualitative. Quantitative information includes analysis of numbers or frequencies of an event; qualitative information includes analysis of text,[34] speech, or descriptions of observed behavior. Information may come from a number of sources; most commonly, it comes from the DSD host and government, business, and public records and from the neutrals, the disputants themselves, their representatives, and other stakeholders.

There are obstacles to meaningful evaluation—and to rigorous empirical research on DSDs—imposed by traditions of confidentiality. Most mediation or arbitration occurs under a confidentiality agreement; usually, parties will not agree to publish settlements and awards. Researchers must demonstrate a willingness to respect confidentiality and develop data collection plans in collaboration with the host organization or the third-party service provider that manages a roster of mediators or arbitrators. Since mediators and arbitrators are reluctant to introduce observers into the delicate interpersonal dynamics of a dispute, data collection methods are often limited to surveys and archival data; nevertheless, some researchers have done observational studies (see Chapter 9).

Survey and interview methods present their own problems because of low response rates or biased sample selection. To use many of the tools of statistics, social scientists need a random sample. Selection bias may occur when disputants have a choice of which dispute process to use. For example, providing a process by random assignment to only some disputants in courts is rarely feasible; it might not be perceived as fair. Therefore, a researcher may have samples of disputants

Evidence of How a System Affects Organizational Culture

In the employment arena, researchers use procedural and organizational justice to assess how giving people voice may contribute to higher satisfaction with the process or outcome of a workplace conflict management procedure. Indicators are judgments of satisfaction or fairness with variables of participation, information, treatment with respect, impartiality of mediators or arbitrators, overall outcome, and speed of outcome. Chapter 11 describes how the U.S. Postal Service used this frame to examine the impact of a national mediation program for employee complaints of sex, race, age, disability, and other forms of discrimination. Through surveys administered at the end of each mediation session and sent to an independent outside evaluator, the USPS found that employees and supervisors were equally satisfied with the process and the mediators. Employees were more willing to use this voluntary program that they perceived as fair. By tracking case filing rates over time before and after the program was implemented in each geographic area, the USPS found both informal and formal complaint rates dropped. This suggested that over time and with experience, disputants learned to resolve their own disputes by reaching voluntary settlements before the mediation session.

who use mediation and those who choose not to, but these are not random categories. Similarly, using a pilot site and a control site to structure a study in a court or agency is rarely possible, although this approach is certainly desirable. To use a before-and-after design, the evaluator must become involved with an organization early in the development of a dispute resolution program; the evaluator must collect baseline data before the host implements the program and then collect data over a prolonged period after implementation. Together, these constraints limit what researchers have learned about DSD.

Another challenge to effective evaluation is the reliability of the people doing the data collection, particularly when a DSD host may be adding to existing workloads by assigning data collection tasks. In courts, getting information directly from litigants rather than their lawyers is often difficult. While it cannot address all these challenges, an inclusive and participatory stakeholder process for designing the evaluation is key to making useful information accessible.

Structure How to Analyze the Information

To answer questions in a meaningful evaluation, researchers expect to see change in one or more of the indicators (e.g., settlement rates, case flow rates, time on the docket, satisfaction with outcome). This analysis requires that evaluators identify baseline conditions and when and how they might expect to see change. Common dimensions of comparison in DSD might include pilot sites and control sites (with and without the intervention, respectively), before and after implementation of a DSD, or time series (change over time) with repeated measurements. Meaningful evaluation also requires that researchers rule out other causes for the change that are unrelated to the structural elements of the DSD (called exogenous variables in social science).

Such analysis requires the tools of statistics. Descriptive statistics are ways to summarize characteristics of information or data. These calculations include means (averages), medians, percentages, or frequencies. For example, an evaluator can describe the percentages of men and women disputants, the demographics of people who use the system, the average frequency of settlement in a mediation process, and the average number of days it takes to resolve a dispute. However, descriptive statistics cannot say anything about whether a new DSD is better than a preceding system. For that analysis, evaluators need to be able to compare the new system with the previous DSD in a way that rules out chance differences.

Analytic statistics test for significant differences in the indicator along the chosen dimension of comparison; significant differences are those that are not simply attributable to chance.[35] Evaluators can use descriptive statistics for any collected data.[36] To generate enough usable data and have the capacity to judge the impact of changes in the DSD itself, it is preferable to institute continuous longitudinal data collection as part of any DSD's evaluation design.

Report Results to Stakeholders

For stakeholders to trust—and use—a dispute system, they need information about its efficacy. Whether private or public, a DSD addresses conflict among people. Social psychology explains how people experience these systems through control,[37] group value,[38] and fairness heuristic theories.[39] Each of these theories requires that people have information about the process and outcome. Further literature on trust emphasizes the importance of making information about a system available. Trust is both belief in a person and a willingness to act on what that person says or does.[40] Trust is confident positive expectations regarding another as a function of relationship. The more multifaceted the relations and the more interactions that occur in a wide array of settings, the more complex the relationship and the greater opportunities there are to develop trust. Similarly, scholarship identifies elements that build trust in organizations and agencies.[41] Legitimacy is also related to trust.

If people do not trust a system, they will not use it (unless they have no choice; some systems are mandatory, as described in Chapter 12 on arbitration).[42] For these reasons, it is important for the host of a DSD to report the results of any evaluation to the stakeholders and participants. Reports can take many forms: organization newsletters, descriptive results like averages of satisfaction with process, and outcome published online. Outside evaluators can publish reports in academic journals or professional outlets or present reports at public conferences. Managers can report results directly at staff meetings, or top management can reward managers on the basis of voluntary participation in the system and share participation rates with all in the organization. Managers should report DSD evaluation data regularly, at a minimum annually.

Use Results to Improve the DSD in Consultation with Stakeholders

Evaluation can and should lead to improvements in a system. If evaluators collect data continuously over time, designers can examine how changes in the system affect its function. This data creates a feedback loop for improving the design. Consider, for example, a classic study of auto lemon law arbitration in New Jersey.[43] The state trial court's DSD contained a structural element that required disputants to enter into nonbinding arbitration six months after the plaintiff filed the complaint. The court maintained longitudinal and continuous data on the days each case spent on the docket before and after the program's implementation. Designers had expected the program to decrease the average amount of time that cases spent on the docket. The reverse happened; the wait time on the docket increased. Researchers theorized that the six-month rule created a deadline effect, inducing lawyers to delay bilateral settlement negotiations until the eve of arbitration. This result suggests that eliminating a fixed deadline for arbitration might in turn reduce the time to disposition. Longitudinal data collection would permit researchers to test the change.

Evaluation can provide the information that stakeholders need to decide whether they want to participate in the system—if they have a choice and the system is voluntary. Not all systems are; for example, the criminal justice system is not voluntary for the defendant once the prosecutor exercises discretion to try the case. Adhesive arbitration may be forced (sometimes called mandatory), but data on outcomes may convince a complainant not to engage because the odds of losing are so high. On the other hand, if the employer's goal is for employees to voluntarily use the system, data showing that both employees and supervisors are satisfied with its fairness might provide an incentive to opt in. Evaluation can thus provide the information for stakeholders to determine what outcomes the system is producing, whether it is fair, and how to improve the system.[44]

Evaluating Prevention and Management of Conflict

The frontier of evaluation research entails measuring prevention and management systems or components of systems. In the transitional justice setting, it is difficult to measure whether a design prevents future conflict. In an employment example, the USPS collected data on the percentage of cases disputants resolved on their own before getting to mediation but after a complaint was filed. They inferred that higher early resolution and fewer complaints and appeals suggested that the system helped both prevent and better manage conflict. The USPS considered this trend as evidence of moving conflict management upstream. Another USPS metric was the participation rate, or how many employees who had filed a complaint voluntarily chose to use mediation; managers in a facility with a 75 percent participation rate received a favorable employment evaluation, regardless of settlements. At a broader scale, the concept of moving conflict management upstream can be relevant to issues of national policy.[45] Design and evaluation concepts apply to upstream processes like public engagement, but these processes are largely outside the scope of this book. Upstream, midstream, and downstream conflict management are discussed further in Chapter 17.

The DSD field needs new and better methodologies to evaluate the prevention and management of conflict, not only its resolution. Evaluation of prevention and management is more challenging than evaluating disputes in an ongoing stream. Evaluators can compare the number of complaints filed before and after an organization implements a new DSD; if complaint filing drops, that may signal success.[46] However, what if complaint filing rates are steady in a system that has not changed? How does one know when conflict is prevented? Evaluators must consider a DSD's reporting structures, questions concerning confidentiality and zero tolerance policies, mandatory reporting, and record keeping. Do these deter people from coming forward with concerns? It is also important to evaluate how DSDs evolve over time, expanding types of disputes or geography—for example, through a merger or acquisition—and how these changes affect whether the DSD is sustainable. Collecting consistent data on citizenship behaviors like attendance, productivity, employee morale, and other indicators of organizational culture may allow researchers to infer indirectly whether a DSD is contributing to prevention and management of conflict.

Conclusion

Here are some questions to consider:

- How does control over DSD relate to control over its evaluation?
- What impact does control over DSD have on what research questions and what independent and dependent variables evaluators include in their data collection and analysis?
- Why might evaluators choose *not* to collect certain data?

These questions relate to the DSD Analytic Framework: What are the goals of a dispute system? What makes it fair? Which conception of justice is implicit in the design? If, after consultation with a wide array of stakeholders, a system design identifies, incorporates, and articulates concrete notions of justice into its goals, there is a greater likelihood of higher satisfaction and institutional legitimacy in the long term. Certain varieties of justice may be easier to evaluate than others; certain stakeholders' perceptions and expectations of justice may be easier to address than others. However, the fundamental purpose of a design is to deliver some form of justice; making this purpose explicit through evaluation will improve the system. If there is no significant difference in average outcomes between court adjudication and ADR,[47] arguably the systems provide roughly equivalent distributive justice, which is evidence designers can use for guidance.

To build the field of DSD, it is important that the results of evaluation are widely disseminated among all stakeholders. Sharing these results will enhance the reputation of a system. This publicity will, in turn, provide a feedback loop that builds participation in the system—and participation is the ultimate measure of a system's success. Sharing rigorous evaluation results will help build the social science of DSD and improve the delivery of justice.

ETHICS IN SYSTEM DESIGN

DEFINING ETHICS or even best practices in a field as new and varied as DSD is challenging. Designers function in a dizzying array of organizational contexts, from corporations to multinational treaty structures, and from courts to international agencies. The individual designer can also be found in a wide variety of roles: as the employee of the designing entity, a consultant to a decision maker, an official of an international organization, or a government employee. Designers hail from many fields and professions, including law, social sciences, management, technology, city planning, and environmental consulting—all of which have their own professional cultures and some of which have their own formal codes of ethics. All questions of ethics ask us to probe our sense of fairness and justice, in their many meanings and sometimes tensions and conflicts.

Ethical complexity is also found in the widely varying scope of DSD projects. Some designers are asked to deal narrowly with mature, legally framed disputes involving relatively well-defined processes, such as mediation and arbitration. Others work on DSDs to prevent and manage a broader array of conflicts (and sometimes disputes) within one corporation or government agency. A third realm involves systems for broader, multiparty disputes, such as environmental public policy matters or human rights violations.[1] Although very different, these contexts raise overlapping sets of ethical concerns.

A further set of questions involves culture. Should answers to ethical questions or best practices change in different cultures or countries? Many ethics sources stem from work in a single national setting, the United States. However, DSD encompasses transnational, international, and multicultural applications.

Ethical guidance can take the form of proposed minimum standards, best-practice guidelines, or at its most developed, enforceable codes of ethics. In its current formative period, DSD is not yet a fully defined profession (and may never reach that level because of its diverse roles, contexts, and scope). Carrie Menkel-Meadow concludes that, while there are many ethics issues to be explored, it is too early to propose a formal, broad code of ethics for DSD.[2]

Rather than proposing such a code, this chapter identifies some of the many ethical questions that arise in DSD and provides perspective on how to address them, exploring sources for DSD ethics, key issues, how a design's cultures and context may affect a designer's choices, how ethical dilemmas may arise in the design setting through goal conflicts with the client or employer, and how the designer might address and minimize the number of those ethical dilemmas. Many of these ethical issues align with the DSD principles introduced in Chapter 1. In exploring these ethical questions for the designer, this chapter touches on the ethics of individual processes, especially mediation and arbitration, which may be part of the designed system. These process ethics are important for two reasons: a competent designer must be able to design ethical processes as part of any DSD and process ethics are more developed and serve as a source for some of the standards proposed for DSD ethics frameworks.

Sources for DSD Ethics

This discussion draws on ethics and standards developed in other ADR professional contexts related to DSD, including those for institutional providers of dispute resolution services, internal conflict management systems in the workplace, the ombuds profession, and the legal profession. Provider organizations—for example, courts, public agencies, and private providers such as the American Arbitration Association (AAA) and JAMS, formerly the Judicial Arbitration and Mediation Services—handle streams of cases, usually from multiple sources.[3] The primary ADR processes they offer are mediation and arbitration, though some also offer conflict management services.[4] These providers are usually third-party designers, meaning they design systems for the disputants but are not disputants themselves. However, they become joint designers when they engage in multi-party processes to create or monitor DSDs. In 2002, a multistakeholder task force convened by Georgetown Law School and the Center for Public Resources (CPR)[5] issued "Principles for ADR Provider Organizations" (CPR-Georgetown principles), the first major general guidelines for ADR provider organizations.[6] These principles are not law or otherwise binding, but third-party and other providers may implement them voluntarily.

Another set of ethical norms comes from the realm of integrated conflict management systems (ICMS), which looks beyond legally framed disputes to help organizations build capacity to prevent and address conflict. A committee of the ADR in the Workplace Initiative of the Society of Professionals in Dispute Resolution (now the Association for Conflict Resolution) prepared guidelines for designing and implementing such workplace systems (ICMS guidelines).[7]

An important source of guidance will be ethics codes that emerge from the online dispute resolution (ODR) sector involving use of information and communication technology. With recognition of technology as the fourth party[8] and the provider of the technology as the fifth party[9] in ODR, ethical standards relevant for these new dimensions of dispute resolution are only beginning to be shaped. Susan Nauss Exon has proposed that effectively addressing the obligations of the fourth and fifth parties will require developing a separate set of standards that can be cross-referenced with the long-standing model standards for in-person dispute resolution processes.[10]

Key Ethical Issues

Each designer must address and resolve specific ethical issues for each design context. These issues include party self-determination; legal rights and representation; the special case of binding arbitration; confidentiality and privacy; costs, payment structures, and efficiency; competence; and independence, neutrality, and impartiality.

Party Self-Determination

Self-determination in DSD refers to a party's control of the process for handling a dispute and its outcome. Support of party self-determination is a core value in the DSD field and underlies such DSD guiding principles as engaging stakeholders in design and implementation of the DSD, training them to use the system and its processes, considering multiple process options, and allowing users flexibility in the choice and sequencing of those options. The DSD principle of promoting transparency and evaluation of programs also supports self-determination by informing users of what works and what does not so they can make better choices and push for improvements.

Party self-determination is a cornerstone of mediation.[11] The broadly applicable "Model Standards of Conduct for Mediators"—jointly developed by the American Arbitration Association, the American Bar Association, and the Association for Conflict Resolution—state that party self-determination involves "coming to a voluntary, uncoerced decision in which each party makes free and informed choices as to process and outcome."[12] However, even within the relatively mature field of mediation, the definition of "self-determination"

> **Discussion Questions**
>
> In designing a court-connected ADR program, you are considering having the judge recommend that parties try mediation. Would this recommendation constitute coercion, thereby undercutting self-determination, or is it justified to help overcome the barriers to resolution in the adversary litigation process? Could the judge's wording of this recommendation affect your answer to this question?

is disputed. The debate regarding transformative, facilitative, and evaluative mediation models often addresses concerns over how a mediator should perform services within a given case. Should the mediator attempt to engender empowerment and recognition among the parties?[13] Does the mediator usurp party self-determination when he gives an opinion regarding the likely outcome of a case in court,[14] or might an expert opinion on the law or likelihood of prevailing at trial be important, and even essential, for the parties to make an informed decision?

Self-determination is also related to questions of power, addressed by provisions for protection of less powerful parties, including party capacity to participate, protection from violence, and the presence of legal representation or other support.[15] In the realm of ODR, power imbalances could arise from "available bandwidth, language fluency, comfort with technology, typing speed, and more."[16]

These values are reinforced in related professional codes. The ICMS guidelines from the Society of Professionals in Dispute Resolution identify principles "critical to the fairness of processes within a system and to the system as a whole," including voluntariness, diversity and accessibility, prohibition of reprisal and retaliation, respect for the role of collective bargaining agents, and nonpreclusion of statutory and workplace rights.[17] Support for multiple process options is also reflected in professional guidance from other ADR sectors, such as encouragement from the International Ombudsman Association in its "IOA Best Practices" guidance for ombuds to support development of multiple process options, both rights-based and interest-based, within organizations.[18]

Legal Rights and Representation

One benefit of ADR processes is the ability of participants to design an outcome that meets their interests that a court could not necessarily order. However, measuring a possible consensual outcome against the alternatives may require parties to understand whether they have a legal claim, and if so, how it would likely resolve in court. How should the designer think about the role of the law and lawyers in the DSD process and the ADR processes that will be part of the eventual design?

The DSD Analytic Framework stresses the need to understand how a DSD meshes with the legal system. Whatever processes are created must, at a minimum, be able to withstand a court challenge. But should the system require or recommend that disputants have counsel or at least legal information? Does the answer depend on the context and the stage of the conflict? Is legal advice more important in a court setting, in which the conflict has matured into a legally framed dispute with the trial option clear and present? Is legal advice less critical in some workplace settings, in which some conflicts will not have legal bases, though others will?

The "Model Standards of Conduct for Mediators" does not mention counsel specifically but notes that in some cases a mediator "should make the parties aware of the importance of consulting other professionals to help them make informed choices."[19] The "Model Standards of Practice for Family and Divorce Mediation," however, provides more detailed protections and obligations, including that the mediator "should recommend that the participants obtain independent legal representation before concluding an agreement."[20]

The ICMS guidelines identify protection of legal rights as essential to a fair DSD, stating that the "design and operation of the system must not undermine statutory or constitutional workplace rights." The guidelines add that in the collective bargaining setting, the "design, implementation, and operation of an integrated conflict management system must not undermine the contractual and legal rights of exclusive bargaining representatives."[21] Regarding general designer obligations, Menkel-Meadow writes that designers must "know what participants' legal rights are (and what they might be giving up or waiving to participate in a particular system)."[22]

Discussion Question

You are designing a process for landlord-tenant disputes that will be staffed by volunteers with interest-based skills but without legal knowledge. If the tenants do not have legal counsel, have you created a fair process?

The Special Case of Binding Arbitration

Most dispute resolution process options, such as mediation, are nonbinding unless parties reach a consensual agreement at the end of the process. In the binding arbitration field,[23] general ethics codes usually do not address self-determination (a party's control over the process and outcome of handling a dispute), presumably because of the traditional assumption that a contract is sufficient evidence of party consent and, therefore, of self-determination.

Issues of party self-determination have been extremely controversial in cases of predispute binding arbitration clauses in consumer, health care, and employment agreements—contexts in which arm's-length bargaining is absent. Binding arbitration precludes use of trial courts and therefore raises significant questions of fairness. The current state of the law in the United States is that the stronger contracting party may require the weaker contracting party to participate in arbitration of any disputes arising out of the contract through an adhesive clause, provided that clause meets the standards for enforcing a contract in that jurisdiction. Defenses against enforcing the contract include duress, unconscionability, fraud, and to a limited extent, public policy.[24] In this context, if the weaker party proceeds with the economic relationship (e.g., employment, medical treatment, purchase of consumer goods or services), the weaker party is generally deemed to have consented to the clause. This is "consent" as a legal concept.[25] Many disgruntled would-be litigants would assert forcefully that it is not voluntary consent or self-determination as a subjective, psychological, or commonly understood concept (see Chapter 12).

Some companies operate dispute resolution systems in which they control the major design choices and are parties to the disputes; these can be understood as one-party designs. These companies operate internal processes to address conflicts or disputes with customers or employees; in this capacity, they can also be considered ADR provider organizations. The most controversial subset is those companies that operate internal, binding arbitration processes that preclude parties from taking their cases to court.[26] A series of well-publicized cases led to growing criticism of the unfairness of some providers' systems—both internal systems and those operated by private providers (see Chapter 12). Courts applied existing case law to clarify the definition of arbitrator under the Federal Arbitration Act.[27] An apparent third-party provider may be operating a de facto one-party system if it administers cases under a program primarily designed by one disputant to handle a stream of its own disputes.

Spurred by public outcry and political pressures, working groups with representatives from external providers, the plaintiffs' bar, the defense bar, consumer groups, and professional associations of mediators and arbitrators developed guidelines to improve the fairness of these adhesive and forced arbitration systems. These protocols added new elements of transparency and due process that were closer to public justice standards. The Due Process Protocol for Mediation and Arbitration of Statutory Disputes Arising out of the Employment Relationship attempts to guarantee employees some due process safeguards, such as the right to counsel, discovery, information about arbitrators' records, a role in selecting the arbitrator, allocation of arbitration fees, and a reasoned award.[28] The American Arbitration Association enforces the employment protocol by screening each document describing an employer's program and working with employers to bring them into compliance. Similarly, protocols for health care and consumer dispute resolution attempt to provide standards for system design through self-regulation. However, since none of the protocols have the force of law, they impose no real limit on an institutional player that decides to opt out and set up its own panel or contractual relationship with a noncompliant third-party provider.

Some one-party providers have established their own, higher ethical standards. Responding to harsh criticism by the California Supreme Court of the fairness of the adhesive and forced arbitration system operated by Kaiser Permanente for medical malpractice disputes with its members,[29] the health maintenance organization substantially redesigned its process, adding numerous due process provisions, expanding the pool of arbitrators, increasing disclosure of arbitrators' past awards, and requiring written findings in support of those awards. It also moved administration of these cases outside Kaiser to a third-party provider overseen by a multistakeholder body that issues an annual assessment of the program.[30]

In the 2010s, some companies determined that adhesive and forced arbitration is unethical for certain categories of cases, specifically claims of sexual assault or harassment. For example, for these claims, Uber announced it would make arbitration voluntary for customers, employees, and contractors and would provide voluntary mediation as an alternative.[31]

Confidentiality and Privacy

Confidentiality and privacy are strong values in the ethics of ADR processes. In mediation, protection of these values can encourage candor among participants, a core tenet of the process. Parties, especially commercial entities, may select arbitration to keep conflicts out of the public eye (which supports their private self-determination). Confidentiality may come into conflict with other values, such as the public interest in knowledge of wrongdoing, as in the case of product liability or patterns of harassment or discrimination.

The CPR-Georgetown principles acknowledge the many levels and sources of confidentiality norms in different contexts by stating that providers "should take all reasonable steps to protect the level of confidentiality agreed to by the parties, established by the organization or the neutral, or set by applicable law or contract."[32] Provider rules sometimes echo codes for individual mediators on exceptions such as prevention of violence.[33] Some court rules acknowledge a broader range of situations in which mediation confidentiality may be breached in the interests of justice.[34]

Some providers also make a limited confidentiality exception for program research and evaluation. Certain court programs make explicit provisions for data collection,[35] while other provider guidelines acknowledge the ethical propriety of research and evaluation if the identities of participants are protected.[36] Ways to resolve this tension include aggregating data to avoid revealing confidential information and redacting party names from arbitration awards in order to make them available to future parties seeking to understand an arbitrator's track record. This balancing act is captured in the DSD guiding principles in Chapter 1 as the urging to "make the DSD accountable through transparency and evaluation, with appropriate concern for privacy."

Confidentiality is also important to consider in the role of an ombuds in a dispute system. Because an ombuds is an employee of an institution, it is important to ensure that the confidentiality and privacy of those who use the services of the ombuds will be respected. The "IOA Code of Ethics" states, "The Ombudsman holds all communications with those seeking assistance in strict confidence, and does not disclose confidential communications unless given permission to do so. The only exception to this privilege of confidentiality is where there appears to be imminent risk of serious harm."[37] The potential for abuse is clear. An ombuds could purport to be helping an employee but instead reveal confidences to the employer or to a court.[38]

How much confidentiality a designer can promise participants in a DSD process may also pose an ethical quandary. A legal privilege has been upheld for ombuds in some cases and jurisdictions.[39] No such privilege or immunity for designers of DSD processes has been established.

Privacy issues in ODR are of special concern, because online communications in the course of dispute resolution processes are recorded and transmitted. Use of online communications in DSDs may require special protocols and assurances regarding access to data and length and form of data retention.[40]

Cost, Payment Structures, and Efficiency

A number of ethics concerns relate to questions of cost, efficiency, and financial incentives for neutrals participating in a dispute resolution system. Timeliness and efficiency of processes are important fairness considerations in all dispute resolution procedures. In addition to the specific provisions in the due process protocols noted above, the CPR-Georgetown principles identify "reasonable time limits" as among the "key *indicia* of fair and impartial processes and forums."[41]

In creating a DSD, the designer should always design the system with the budget in mind. A program with multiple processes and outside neutrals will fail in a small organization with a limited budget.[42] ADR process guidelines urge that the cost to users be kept as low as possible while maintaining quality. A thorny issue is who pays. Professional code and best practice are conflicted on the issues of ability to pay for a process and ability to pay for counsel. The employment proto-col recommends equal division and payment of arbitrator fees, if possible.[43] The "Model Standards of Conduct for Mediators" states that a mediator "may accept unequal fee payments from the parties" but cautions that "a mediator should not allow such a fee arrangement to adversely impact the mediator's ability to conduct the mediation in an impartial manner."[44] The "Reporter's Notes" to the model standards refers to this unequal payment as a "significant, controversial practice" in private sector mediation but concedes that in some sectors, this is a "reality of contemporary practice" in which all parties are comfortable with the arrangement. Although disapproving of the practice, it recognizes that "some argue that parties would not have access to the benefits of mediation if such fee payment arrangements were not available."[45]

Ethical codes for dispute resolution processes also address other ways that financial arrangements can create bias and otherwise affect the fairness or per-ception of fairness of outcomes. The Ethical Standards for Mediators, which are part of California's Rules of Court, prohibit making the mediator's compensa-tion contingent on the amount of the settlement to avoid creating an incentive for the mediator to pressure parties to settle or consciously or unconsciously work to maximize the settlement payout.[46] "The Code of Ethics for Arbitrators in

Discussion Questions

To reduce the costs to patients, health care and insurance provider Kaiser Permanente restructured its arbitration program to allow use of one arbitra-tor rather than a panel of three if the patient in the dispute preferred that. If Kaiser still wanted a three-person panel, it would pick up the cost of addi-tional arbitrators. How well does this rule address the core problem? What other solutions might address the problem more effectively?

Commercial Disputes," developed by the American Arbitration Association and the American Bar Association, admonishes arbitrators not to increase their rate of compensation during the course of an arbitration proceeding "absent extraordinary circumstances."[47] Incentives to neutrals to resolve a high percentage of cases could lead them, intentionally or otherwise, to place inappropriate pressure on parties to resolve their disputes. Again, this tension exposes the possible opposition between two positive goals—here efficiency and self-determination—that may affect justice.

An organization may choose in its DSD to send a stream of cases to an outside provider of ADR services. This outsourcing can lead to a perceived lack of independence and impartiality of the service provider, a perception that is due to the provider's potential financial dependence on the client.[48] Research has demonstrated that some arbitration awards showed a "repeat player effect," disproportionately favoring the party that was an ongoing client of the ADR provider.[49] To address this issue, the CPR-Georgetown principles state that the provider should disclose "any interests or relationships" likely to affect its "impartiality or independence" or that might reasonably create an appearance of bias. This provision specifically requires disclosure of financial relationships, including contractual or de facto streams of referrals and any funding relationship between a party and the provider.[50] In 2009, the attorney general of Minnesota took action against the National Arbitration Forum, a third-party provider of arbitration and mediation services, for conflicts of interest and consumer fraud because of its lack of independence from the debt-collection industry. In response to the action, the National Arbitration Forum agreed to cease handling consumer arbitration cases.[51]

The Trans Atlantic Consumer Dialogue has issued guidelines for ODR systems designed to help resolve disputes related to online commerce. These guidelines closely track the issues and guidance of codes for more traditional dispute resolution systems:

> ADR systems should be independent. They should be operated by reputable third parties, which could include government, nonprofit organizations, for-profit entities that are not directly involved in the disputes, or any combination thereof. If ADR systems are offered by trade associations or other industry groups, they should be separate and independent, and operate in consultation with consumer organizations. ADR personnel should have no direct interests in the disputes or the parties involved. If funding for ADR systems comes from the business sector, that commitment should be honored regardless of the decisions that are rendered.[52]

A DSD created with more processes, and processes with more procedural steps, will take more time and cost more money. Use of such a system could cost parties more than the value of their claim.[53] A major challenge for designers can be determining the appropriate trade-off between process and cost. When might saving money create unfairness and injustice? When might a proliferation of process choices create costs for the parties that decrease usage or otherwise cause unfairness or injustice?

Competence

Chapter 4 explores the wide range of skills, qualifications, and training a designer needs to be competent across the range of contexts within which she functions. Among these skills are assessment, problem identification, process knowledge, cultural insight, and organizational expertise. At a minimum, the designer should have knowledge of the possible process options under consideration and the ethical standards and best practices for those options.

The skills needed may vary depending on the work context and scope of the design task. A human resources professional asked to improve an internal corporate grievance system faces a context and set of demands different from those of a UN employee working with local political factions and interested superpowers on creating transitional justice mechanisms following a war. The designer is always working within an organization or structure and may be able to assemble the additional personnel with needed skills from within that organization.

Independence, Neutrality, and Impartiality

Independent and impartial neutrals are critical to both mediation and arbitration.[54] Codes describe this requirement as "freedom from favoritism, bias or prejudice"[55] and avoidance of "impropriety or the appearance of impropriety."[56]

Discussion Question

You are working with a public agency to establish criteria for mediators to serve in its new program. One person has suggested that all mediators must be experienced and must demonstrate at least an 80 percent settlement rate. Are these criteria acceptable for promoting efficiency and identifying "successful" mediators, or are they unacceptable because they may reward the mediator for coercion of one party?

Rules and laws in this area rely on disclosures and possible waiver of any disclosed conflicts by the parties.[57] Conflicts can arise from business, financial, or personal relationships—past, present, or future—with parties, counsel, witnesses, or other stakeholders.[58]

As a designer, in what sense can you be independent and neutral? If you are an employee or contractor, you have contractual obligations to the client and are paid by the client, itself a conflict of interest. The ombuds profession provides some helpful perspective. An ombuds is an employee of the organization who deals with a wide array of upstream conflicts as well as some legally framed disputes, all embedded within the culture and complexity of a private or public enterprise. Many of the rules in the "IOA Code of Ethics" aim to provide as much independence and protection as possible for a neutral who is paid by an entity that may be a party to the conflicts and disputes in question.[59] The code of ethics states, "The Ombudsman, as a designated neutral, remains unaligned and impartial. The Ombudsman does not engage in any situation which could create a conflict of interest."[60]

The International Ombudsman Association guidelines provide a detailed set of recommendations to protect the ombuds, including that the ombuds report directly to "the highest level of the organization . . . in a manner independent of ordinary line and staff functions" and "be protected from retaliation (such as of elimination of the office or the Ombudsman, or reduction of the Ombudsman budget or other resources) by any person who may be the subject of a complaint or inquiry."[61]

Cathy Costantino has posed a set of fundamental questions regarding what it means to be neutral as a designer. She notes that a designer is hired to apply expertise, to have an opinion, and therefore cannot and should not be neutral on all matters. Is it the designer's obligation to provide the fairest DSD process, she asks, or to produce the fairest outcome?[62] Which is more important, procedural or substantive justice?

Ethics Considerations in a Cultural Context

The DSD guiding principles outlined in Chapter 1 urge creating a design that is fair and just within the context, including concepts of culture. The ethics rules and frameworks described in this chapter, for ADR processes and system designers, were developed primarily from experience in the United States. How might these rules and best practice frameworks need to be amended or left more flexible to allow for cultural differences? How applicable are these concepts to other jurisdictions and cultures? Ethicists might ask, to what degree are DSD ethics standards universal and to what extent is a more culturally adapted approach appropriate?[63]

Cultural issues are sometimes addressed in ethical codes for dispute resolution processes in the United States. Arbitration guidelines are largely silent on these issues, while mediation and conflict management guidelines are generally more cognizant of them. The ICMS guidelines for the workplace context note the desirability of "diversity in the corps of neutrals" and need for "legitimate, inviting, and accessible" systems.[64] Ethics standards for family law mediation are more specific, stating that a qualified family law mediator should "be able to recognize the impact of culture and diversity"[65] and that such a mediator "should be sensitive to the impact of culture and religion on parenting philosophy and other decisions."[66]

How well do these codes and best practices work when extended to designing systems for international organizations and contexts? National contexts vary both in culture and in the legal and institutional framework for mediation.[67] Some but not all the emerging international codes and guidelines address cultural issues. The "European Code of Conduct for Mediators," issued by the European Commission, makes no reference to cultural sensitivity and competency.[68] In contrast, the World Bank handbook for assessment and implementation of commercial mediation discusses the importance of cultural sensitivity in depth.[69]

These questions become particularly relevant when considering the potential clash of culture, law, and tradition when a designer from one country works on rule of law or transitional justice design in another country. Transnational mediation organizations are beginning to tackle these issues. The International Mediation Institute has established criteria to certify mediators in a set of standards and skills for "intercultural competence."[70] The World Bank's commercial mediation handbook identifies key topics for assessing whether a commercial mediation program should be introduced in a given country, including the culture of dispute resolution, litigiousness, social acceptance of the settlement, rate of settlement within and outside courts, trust in the court system and judiciary, perceived and real corruption, approach to legal and judicial reform, economic and social background, and legal and cultural background of the region.[71]

This list hints at the array of thorny questions faced in cross-cultural systems design. How should a designer approach conflicts between individual and communitarian standards? Should the ideal of the independent, unbiased neutral be applied in societies with long-standing traditions of elders or other respected members of the community resolving disputes? Even if a more independent third party were desired by the parties, what can be done in small communities in which citizens may be connected in complex ways that make U.S. standards of indepen-

dence infeasible? How should the designer address the tensions between traditional justice systems, which may be biased against women or minority groups yet
perhaps satisfactory to local citizens, and formal systems based on international
human rights models? Is it the designer's job to reflect the values of the system's
users or to try to change the culture? When these conflicts arise, who decides?
Some of these challenges in designing international dispute systems are addressed
in more depth in Chapter 15 and Chapter 16.

Operationalizing Ethics for Designers

Once you determine your ethics and values framework, how do you operation-
alize it and avoid unethical behavior? Many of these issues arise in the context of
possible goal conflicts with the client. Options for addressing them may depend
on the designer-client relationship.

An external designer needs to navigate a set of foundational questions: Who is
the client? What is the designer's relationship to the client? What are the client's
goals? Are these goals ones the designer can support?[72] External designers should
answer these questions at the contracting stage. They should learn the context
and challenges in the organization, including the history of past design efforts,
and require the potential client to be as clear as possible about goals. In return,
the designer needs to be clear about his role, values, and expectations.[73]

For an employee, rather than an outside contractor, the context is likely to
be more constrained. Many employees will perform some aspect of a designer's
role without seeing themselves as designers within the DSD field. Employees
are contractually bound to do as the employer wishes, within legal and ethical
bounds. If an employee finds her ethics or values to be in conflict with those of
her employer, she may be able to persuade her superiors to support her position
by citing external ethical codes and norms or relevant legal obligations.

Members of other professions that have their own ethical codes may be bound
to those codes in their roles as designers. As legal ethicists have chronicled, lawyers
have struggled to clarify how their ethical obligations to clients—which are built
on assumptions of representation in an adversary process—translate to obligations as a mediator, serving as a neutral between parties.[74] What are the ethical
obligations of a designer with contractual obligations to a client to that client and
to the other stakeholders in the DSD process?[75]

Designers also need to determine what they will *not* do in a particular design
context. Carrie Menkel-Meadow recommends "[being] sure, as much as . . . [pos-
sible], that a system of dispute resolution does not systematically discriminate
against or harm particular individuals." She cautions against becoming a "'tool' of

a client or organization or government that wants to use process design to achieve inappropriate or illegitimate ends." She describes circumstances in which she declined to be a DSD consultant for a company whose main goal was to quash a union and cites another case in which a client offered a dispute resolution process to its non-U.S. employees that appeared to offer a benefit, but in which judgments in favor of employees were unenforceable.[76]

The dictum to engage all stakeholders in a DSD process does not address how competing interests will be resolved in the system. All stakeholders do not have equivalent power. Encouragement to support bottom-up rather than top-down processes implies that the designer may have a role in rebalancing power in the organization in some way.[77] As in the mediation field, there will be those who argue that such a role is ethically mandated in order to promote justice and others who argue that it is and should be outside the purview of the designer. Howard Gadlin, former ombuds at the National Institutes of Health and University of California at Los Angeles, has written about the potential of management to use DSD to manipulate or chill claims of employees or consumers.[78]

Reasonable people may differ on the appropriate ethical stance in a given circumstance. For instance, assume that a designer has helped create a mediation process for employees of a company that results in fewer employee lawsuits. Has the designer improved fairness and justice by providing a process that is faster and more cost efficient for all parties (including the employer) and that better meets the needs of claimants? Or has she been party to suppressing important civil rights claims that will never make it to court to vindicate employees' rights? In a given case, some of these questions might be answered in part through social science research and understanding the specifics of the systems in question. To some degree, however, the answers turn on competing goals, which reflect competing values.

Another set of questions concerns possible differences between the system as designed and the system as implemented. Some commentators urge that designers take responsibility for implementation and do their best to ensure that there will be evaluation, competence, and fairness in system administration and even outcomes. Internal designers may (or may not) have the continuity and authority to oversee these efforts; outside designers can raise these issues, but their contracts may end well before the implementation phase begins. Commentators have also highlighted the possible ethical questions when organizations hire multiple designers over time. Are they hiring a series of designers to try to continue to improve their systems, or are they engaging in "designer shopping" until management gets an answer it likes?[79]

Conclusion

The DSD field is still very young. Increasing documentation and analysis of DSD experience are providing a richer discussion of possible ethical standards, but many questions remain. Given the large range of design contexts, both public and private, it may be impossible to create rules to cover all situations without diluting the proscriptions so much as to render them useless. A consistent piece of advice, echoing the core ethic of the medical profession, is to "do no harm."[80] Most system changes will, however, benefit some and burden others. While there may never be a unified set of ethical precepts for the whole DSD field, more focused ethical guidance may emerge around specific roles, contexts, and practice areas. The case chapters in the second unit continue to explore issues of ethics, best practices, and values, addressing in more detail the questions and dilemmas that arise in the wide panoply of DSD contexts.

CASE APPLICATIONS

PART I

PUBLIC AND COMMUNITY JUSTICE

7 COURT PROGRAMS

IMAGINE YOU ARE THE CHIEF JUDGE of a trial court in internal turmoil. A group of your judges wants to introduce ADR options, such as mediation and early neutral evaluation, in civil cases. They believe that ADR can reduce cost and delay and give parties more creative and satisfying outcomes. A second group of judges opposes all ADR, believing that courts were created to provide justice through a public trial process and that anything else dilutes that mission and undermines core values. A final group of your colleagues favors adding ADR processes but only if they save the court significant time and money.[1]

You want your court to deliver justice and provide service to litigants at a reasonable cost. You are also mindful that your state legislature may cut the judiciary's budget in the next few years. The lowest-cost alternative would be to require all cases to go to private mediators or evaluators, which might have the additional benefit of reducing your court's heavy, and growing, caseload. Would such a plan be fair? What alternatives might be better? Will the resistant judges join the effort or at least not undermine it? How will you decide which strategy to pursue? Who else should be involved in making this decision?

Issues to consider are as follows.

- What is the proper role of courts? Should they only litigate cases, or should they more broadly assist the public in managing and resolving its disputes?
- How should courts resolve the tension between efficiency and quality?
- What are the special challenges of DSD in addressing criminal cases?
- How can courts better use and integrate online dispute resolution tools and platforms?

- How do the answers to these questions change, if at all, when applied to countries with widely varying national, local, and legal cultures?

History and Context of Alternative Dispute Resolution and Other Design Innovations in U.S. Courts

In the United States, courts have expanded from primarily providing trials to offering a wider range of formal and informal conflict resolution processes.[2] At first glance, a court seems an unlikely place for dispute system innovation, given the centrality of the trial in the United States as a rights-based option to determine facts, resolve disputes, interpret the law, and create precedent—yet courts themselves were a design innovation, a rule-based structure created to reduce violence and self-help as means of resolving disputes in society.[3]

As the legal historian Lawrence Friedman has documented, by the beginning of the twentieth century American courts faced acute problems of "complexity, waste, and injustice," exemplified by "the astonishing number of reported cases that turned not on the merits of the case, but on tiny points of procedure or pleading."[4] Efforts at procedural reform culminated in 1938 with major changes in the Federal Rules of Civil Procedure (FRCP), design innovations to allow more parties to access the courts through simplified "notice" pleading.[5] The designers of the FRCP also introduced new procedures intended to reveal the facts more expeditiously and at lower cost, including requiring parties to share key information through the discovery process.[6] Under FRCP Rule 16, judges were given new discretion to manage their cases, including encouraging settlement discussions.[7]

Beginning in the 1970s, an increasing number of judges and scholars in the United States questioned the efficiency and efficacy of the trial-based system. Though designed to decrease cost and adversariness while expediting getting to the truth, the discovery process had become another slow and costly battleground.[8] Critics of the courts' civil litigation processes pointed to the impact of cost and delay on litigants and the court, the toll of the adversarial process on business and personal relationships, and the failure of the courts' rights-based processes and limited remedial options to address the underlying issues that activated disputes.

Frank E. A. Sander, at the Pound Conference in 1976, introduced the powerful idea that courts could offer more process options to better address these interests, a concept that came to be known as the multidoor courthouse.[9] While U.S. courts were already taking steps to encourage settlement, and in many jurisdictions judges were serving as settlement facilitators, these conversations spurred experimentation in design that became a trend toward broader incorporation of ADR in U.S. courts. Every U.S. federal district court now authorizes ADR in some form, and more than one-third authorize multiple process options.[10] The National Center for State Courts reports that "every state now has some type of court-connected ADR at some level—but rarely statewide."[11] ADR has also become a significant part of U.S. rule of law development assistance to other countries.[12]

New ideas were also advanced concerning how courts might work with other institutional actors to address societal problems through means other than traditional trial and incarceration. New community justice mechanisms, including community mediation, were developed starting in the 1960s (see Chapter 9). Neighborhood disputes were referred to these processes by courts or sought out directly by community members, aiming to avoid litigation and in some cases to focus on restorative rather than retributive justice.[13]

These developments were followed by experiments with problem-solving courts, also called specialized or specialty courts, which connected the judge with broader social and medical expertise and services in order to address underlying and chronic causes of conflict.[14] Following the opening of the first drug court in Miami, Florida, in 1989,[15] courts across the United States and internationally began developing problem-solving courts, which now include community courts, domestic violence courts, youth courts, veterans courts, and DUI (drunk driving) courts.[16]

Case Examples from Federal and State Courts in the United States
Civil Cases in the U.S. District Court for the Northern District of California

In 1990, Congress passed the Civil Justice Reform Act, which encouraged experimentation in ADR and case management in all federal trial courts.[17] Under the reform act, the U.S. District Court for the Northern District of California was designated one of five "demonstration districts" directed to "experiment with various methods of reducing cost and delay in civil litigation, including alternative dispute resolution."[18] The court was well positioned for this designation because it already offered several ADR processes under Chief Judge Robert Peckham's leadership: nonbinding arbitration, early neutral evaluation (ENE),[19] and judicially hosted settlement conferences. ENE was first conceived in this court; to develop it, the court used a variant of a conflict stream assessment (see Chapter 4) by convening a multistakeholder group of attorneys from different practice areas who represented public and private clients as well as plaintiffs and defendants from various types of cases. Wayne Brazil, then a professor at Hastings College of the Law, led the process, reporting to and consulting with Chief Judge Peckham.

This group became the design team, investigating multiple process options. The court piloted and evaluated the ENE process, and given the pilot's success,[20] the judges decided to expand the ENE program court-wide.[21]

While some courts' primary goal in using ADR is to reduce caseload, the Northern District of California court had made clear that its chief goal was to provide additional, high-quality process options to better meet the needs of litigants. Brazil, who subsequently was appointed a magistrate judge, became the judicial officer who guided and supervised the court's ADR program in this period. Commenting on the high cost of litigation and the few cases that reached trial (or even had significant contact with a judge),[22] he concluded that "free or low cost ADR programs represent one of the very few means through which courts can provide any meaningful service to many litigants."[23]

The Civil Justice Reform Act mandated its own multistakeholder process, another variant on conflict stream assessment. The act required creation of an advisory group including representatives from the bar and litigants.[24] Following broad consultation with key stakeholder groups, including the judges, the clerk of the court, the court's ADR staff,[25] and the advisory group, the court decided to maintain its array of existing ADR options and add mediation. This addition provided an interest-based option with the potential to enable parties to preserve their relationship; create a broader, more creative array of settlement options than the court could order; reach more durable solutions; and reduce cost and delay.

The court then faced a set of important policy questions and design challenges in how best to determine which cases would be paired with which processes. The questions included the following:

- What role should be played by parties, their counsel, the judge, and the court ADR administrators in deciding whether to use ADR, and if it is, which process and when?
- To what degree should the court encourage or require use of an ADR option?
- Should certain cases be exempt from particular or all ADR options?
- Who should provide the ADR services, and what qualifications should they have?
- Who should pay for these new services, and what should they cost?

The court's solution, the Multi-option Pilot Program,[26] required counsel to discuss the court's ADR options with clients and confer with opposing counsel to select a process option.[27] If the parties failed to agree or opted against ADR, the new rules required counsel[28] to participate in an ADR phone conference with the court's ADR staff. These calls provided individualized attention, educating and advising counsel on the potential benefits and costs of the ADR options. If the parties still could not agree on an option or if they agreed that no option was appropriate, the ADR administrator would either recommend an ADR process to the judge or recommend that no ADR was appropriate at that time. The goal was to educate and engage all key stakeholders to determine which ADR process, if any, was most appropriate.

Although the Multi-option Pilot Program presumed that an ADR option would be used early in the life of every case, judges could approve requests for delaying ADR or exempting the case. This approach reflected an effort to balance the court's goals of encouraging parties to use helpful processes without pressuring or requiring parties to participate in a program that could, in some cases, be a waste of time and money.[29] The court's website, information booklet, and ADR staff helped the parties and counsel compare the processes in terms of likely party satisfaction; flexibility, control, and participation; improved case management; improved understanding of the case; and potential to reduce hostility between parties.

Two major staffing models are most used in court ADR programs. Courts with a staff-neutral model employ trained court staff to serve as ADR neutrals; this model is used in some federal circuit courts of appeal and a smaller number of federal district courts. Largely because of cost considerations, however, many courts use a panel model, relying on private practitioners to serve as ADR neutrals on a court-administered or court-sponsored panel.[30] Although Congress provided limited funds for additional court staff under the Civil Justice Reform Act, the funding was not sufficient to hire enough staff to serve as neutrals in a significant number of cases. Because of these resource constraints and the court's deep commitment to the quality of the neutrals, the Northern District of California court used staff resources to screen, recruit, train, and supervise panels of private neutrals for the mediation, ENE, and arbitration programs.[31] When time permitted, the court's ADR staff attorneys also mediated cases.

Compensation was handled differently for different ADR processes. The court, pursuant to a statute that predated the reform act, provided very modest compensation for arbitrators. Judges handling settlement conferences received no compensation beyond their normal salaries. No other public funds were available to pay mediators or ENE neutrals. As a result, mediators and ENE evaluators volunteered their preparation time and first four hours of meetings. After this point, if the parties chose to continue the session, the evaluator or mediator could charge for his services.[32] These new rules reflected a compromise between the desire to offer a free public service, in the same manner as trials and judicially hosted settlement conferences, and the acknowledgment that skilled ADR professionals provide a valuable service. It was also unreasonable and unrealistic to expect the most highly skilled attorneys[33] to fully donate the significant time necessary to provide high-quality services for the expanding caseload.[34]

The pilot program proved to be a beneficial first step in dispute system redesign because it allowed experimentation and refinement of the model, created allies of the pilot judges, improved the skills and confidence of the ADR neutrals, and increased the comfort level and competence of counsel representing the parties. The pilot program was evaluated, pursuant to the act's mandate, by the Federal Judicial Center, the research arm of the federal courts. The study, led by Donna Stienstra of the center, reported that over 60 percent of counsel believed that use of the court's ADR options had reduced time to disposition and the cost of their cases, with median cost savings per party estimated at $25,000. Eighty-one percent of attorneys were satisfied with case outcome and 98 percent "thought the procedures used in the ADR process were somewhat or very fair."[35] In 1999, the court refined the model and expanded the program court-wide.[36]

Family Law Cases in the Courts of San Mateo County, California

San Mateo County, California, also created a multioption ADR program. This state court offered ADR programs, including mediation and arbitration options, for eight distinct types of cases, including family law cases. The San Mateo court program shared elements with that of the Northern District of California court but was distinct in several ways, such as in its family law focus, the high percentage of parties not represented by counsel, its more diverse funding base, and its multistakeholder management committees with representation from the court and the bar.

As in the Northern District of California court, the San Mateo court was dedicated to giving parties more process choices, but it explicitly acknowledged the desire to help both the court and the parties save time and money. It also recognized the very high priority that families in difficult transitions place on resolving disputes quickly and in a manner best suited to help their children.

The San Mateo court tapped stakeholder groups to help design its programs and created ongoing, multistakeholder groups to advise and monitor the programs. One committee provided oversight on all eight San Mateo court ADR programs. This committee's members included the court's presiding judge and chief executive, the executive director of the Peninsula Conflict Resolution Center (a community mediation nonprofit), and representatives from the San Mateo Bar Association's board of directors, the plaintiffs' bar, the defense bar, and nonattorney members and representatives from the court's ADR program staff. Other stakeholder committees of attorneys, judges, and court staff monitored and advised each of the other ADR programs. Advisors to the family law program were judges and representatives from legal aid, the court's ADR staff, the family law section of the local bar association, referring agencies, and other specialists as needed.

The court's family law ADR program began in 1996 as a project of the local bar association, which provided referrals to a panel of private attorney mediators and arbitrators.[37] In 2000, the program was reorganized and moved to the court, and a coordinating attorney was subsequently hired to expand and manage it. The program offered both mediation and arbitration to litigants, including those without counsel. The court had an extensive education and outreach program, including meetings with judges and court staff, access to digital and print resources, and educational programs for attorneys. Judges could recommend that parties meet with court ADR staff to consider whether to choose ADR. Sheila Purcell, director of the program from 1996 to 2012, refers to the court's philosophy as "mandatory education, voluntary mediation."[38]

The San Mateo court assembled an innovative array of funding sources to support the program. As in the Northern District of California court, the San Mateo court began with a small pilot program. Because of that program's success in civil cases, court resources were obtained to hire a staff person to coordinate the new family law ADR program.[39] The bar continued to provide financial and human resources to support the program. Attorney mediators agreed to charge only one hundred dollars (fifty dollars per person) for the first ninety minutes of mediation (well below market rates), with the option of conducting additional sessions at the mediators' regular hourly rates.

This program offered both mediation and binding arbitration. Though the use of binding arbitration is somewhat rare in family law cases and can be challenging for cases with self-represented parties, Purcell reports that binding arbitration was chosen by the parties in approximately 10 percent of cases in 2008 and can be very effective in "pots and pans cases," in which parties are seeking a quick resolution to disputes over small property items.[40]

The U.S. economic crisis of 2008 took its toll on the California state budget and court ADR programs. Of the nearly 300 referrals to the San Mateo family law program in 2009, 149 developed into active cases, with approximately half mediated by private neutrals and the other half by the attorney mediator, who is also the program manager, on-site at the court. Budget cuts, reorganizations, and staff reductions of 60 percent in 2009 and 2010 prompted the staff mediator to suspend on-site mediation and recruit a court-administered volunteer panel to pick up some of the caseload. Referrals to the program dropped as administrative support shrank, to 167 referrals in fiscal year 2010 with 65 cases being assigned to either the private panel or to the limited on-site program with a new group of volunteers.[41]

Some have questioned whether mediation should ever be used in cases with a history or threat of domestic violence. This is a very real concern and an area of controversy.[42] The San Mateo court's family law ADR program created the Domestic Violence Screening and Assessment Procedure to determine whether cases were appropriate for ADR. The assessment included searches of the court's criminal database, telephone interviews with parties to determine the history and nature of the domestic violence or fears of abuse, and review of the family court file for allegations or protective orders.[43] Staff asked questions to determine how recent the abuse or threats were, the nature and extent of any physical violence, how the couple historically handled conflict, the presence of weapons, and whether the parties felt comfortable meeting together off-site (if applicable). On the basis of this assessment, staff might offer referrals to collateral agencies or process protections or might decline to accept referral to the ADR program.

The San Mateo family ADR programs were evaluated through questionnaires to lawyers, mediators and arbitrators, and parties to disputes. A court-conducted study of cases from July 2007 through July 2008 revealed that 81 percent of cases achieved some resolution through use of an ADR process; parties estimated that ADR reduced court time for all cases and reduced costs for 97 percent. Both parties and attorneys showed high levels of satisfaction with the process. Even with this high success rate, subsequent resource cuts required significant program reductions.[44]

Criminal Cases at the Red Hook Community Justice Center, Brooklyn, New York City

In 1992, the Brooklyn neighborhood of Red Hook was devastated by the death of a beloved elementary school principal caught in the crossfire of a drug gang shootout. The neighborhood was struggling with a high level of crime and the crack epidemic of that era. The tragedy motivated Brooklyn District Attorney Charles Hynes, joined by New York's chief judge, Judith Kaye, to lead a process to create a new approach to address public safety in Red Hook.[45]

Hynes and Kaye turned to the Center for Court Innovation, a nonprofit research and policy-advising entity for the New York state courts, to guide the design process.[46] This public-private partnership had been instrumental in developing the successful Midtown Community Court in New York City in 1993 to better address "quality of life" crimes, such as prostitution, graffiti tagging, and low-level drug possession.[47] Midtown, the first community court in the United States, employed restitution, community service, drug treatment, and other techniques and succeeded in reducing some categories of crime while increasing case efficiency and generating more positive public opinion in the then very high-crime Times Square area.

In Red Hook, the broad initial DSD goals were "improving the safety of the neighborhood and enhancing the legitimacy of the justice system in the eyes of local residents."[48] The designers sought to incorporate community ideas but were also committed to situating the resulting programs within the New York City court system.[49] Greg Berman and Aubrey Fox of the Center for Court Innovation described the final DSD goals as (1) promoting accountability (all offenders receiving some sanction), (2) repairing conditions of disorder (such as fixing broken windows and painting out graffiti), (3) solving underlying problems (such as providing drug treatment), (4) engaging the community, and (5) making justice visible (by locating the court and support services in the Red Hook neighborhood).[50]

The design process took six years. Government stakeholders included prosecutors, police, judges, and court staff. Community stakeholders included community organizations, nonprofit groups, and the residents of Red Hook. Berman and Fox describe neighborhood outreach as including "focus groups held at the local library with community leaders, social service providers, young people, and single mothers—a wide variety of informants that went beyond the 'usual suspects' of established local leaders."[51] In addition to "dozens of individual interviews," the designers sponsored bus trips to the Midtown Community Court, attended community meetings "held at precinct councils, PTAs, civic associations, tenant groups, and local churches," and "convened town-hall-style meetings that attracted hundreds of participants."[52]

The design process resulted in the opening of the Red Hook Community Justice Center, the first multijurisdictional court in the United States, in 2002. The center, housed in a former Catholic school, combined court services with enhanced community services, such as drug treatment referrals and mediation,[53] and support services, such as GED classes, youth development programs, and job training, which were also made available to the broader community.

Rather than adding processes to a traditional court model, the Red Hook experiment created a new structure, changing the role of the judge from solely an arbiter of legal status to the leader of an interdisciplinary, problem-solving team integrating court and social services. The court's emphasis was on avoiding jail sentences, where appropriate, in favor of sanctions that benefited the defendant and the community through community service as restitution and through treatment to address underlying problems, such as drug addiction and mental illness.

Monitoring and evaluation were embedded in the program design. The center received regular input from the Community Advisory Board, comprising more than three dozen members, including "tenant leaders, clergy and civic leaders, as well as representatives from local institutions like the schools and the police."[54] External evaluators have found substantial positive impacts that include reduction in recidivism and reduction in crime,[55] a more positive view of the court by community members, and significant hours of service devoted to community improvement.[56]

Court Alternative Dispute Resolution Outside the United States

The movement to include multiple dispute resolution options in U.S. courts emerged in a specific context: U.S. courts were well developed and well funded but were criticized for cost, delay, limited remedial options, and damage to parties from the adversarial model. Likewise, distinct historical, political, legal, and social contexts in other countries affect the goals, options, and choices designers make worldwide regarding court ADR.

The goals of DSD in justice systems can go beyond the just resolution of disputes to encompass broader goals of economic development, empowerment of the poor, and good governance. International development funders, such as the World Bank and U.S. Agency for International Development, have supported expanding ADR mechanisms in some countries as a means of increasing access to justice.[57] In countries where formal court systems are expensive, difficult to access, and plagued by corruption, some commentators urge greater use of informal dispute resolution mechanisms in conjunction with efforts to bolster the formal justice system and create more inclusive and responsive governance systems.[58] However, in courts suffering from corruption, the addition of court-connected confidential settlement processes may provide more venues for injustice away from the public eye.

Specific local challenges call for tailored, creative solutions. Each setting requires careful assessment of goals and process choices.[59]

The United Kingdom, Italy, and the European Union Directive on Mediation

Mediation continues to spread through Europe, but the regulatory structures, degree of usage, and connection to courts vary enormously across countries.

In civil law countries, growth in the use of mediation in legal cases has been, overall, slower and more uneven than in common law countries.[60] Nadja Alexander explains that Anglo-American common law courts generally have more authority and flexibility to write their own court rules, which more easily allows court-by-court experimentation.[61] She notes, however, that cost and delay are less of a problem in many civil law countries and that the established presence of judicial settlement and case management in civil law courts may have slowed acceptance of mediation.[62] Alexander also observes that, unlike those in the United States, lawyers in most civil law countries initially resisted mediation, allowing psychologists and other professionals outside the legal field to begin "to carve a niche for themselves as mediators of disputes (particularly in family, community and victim-offender matters) well before the legal profession became involved."[63]

In 2008, the European Parliament issued a Directive on Mediation requiring EU member states (with the exception of Denmark) to develop legal frameworks to offer mediation for cross-border commercial and some civil matters, including certain family and labor law cases.[64] The directive's goals included increasing access to justice by encouraging mediation and "ensuring a balanced relationship between mediation and judicial proceedings."[65] The directive applies to cases of party-initiated voluntary private mediation and to "cases where a court refers parties to mediation or in which national law prescribes mediation."[66]

A 2014 study on the directive, commissioned by the European Parliament, reported on the wide variation in mediation uptake across the European Union. The study estimated that only the United Kingdom, Netherlands, Italy, and Germany were holding over ten thousand mediations per year, and thirteen of the twenty-eight countries covered by the directive were holding fewer than five hundred per year.[67]

In the United Kingdom, mediation and conciliation in family, neighborhood, and consumer cases was well established for several decades before the EU directive.[68] Leadership on ADR expansion into commercial cases in the United Kingdom had come from a coalition of powerful stakeholders: lawyers involved in commercial litigation, the courts (including the Commercial Court), the Lord Chancellor's Department (which oversees the courts), the Department of Trade and Industry, and some academics.[69] Interest in ADR expanded significantly as a result of Lord Woolf's 1995 and 1996 *Access to Justice* reports and subsequent civil procedure legislation.[70] Surveys of the public in that period revealed high levels of dissatisfaction with the civil justice system, which was seen as too slow, too complicated, unwelcoming, and dated.[71] Following Lord Woolf's reports, a slate of reforms went into effect that simplified procedures (to achieve reductions in cost and delay), made judicial case management more active, and implemented ADR. A new civil procedure act passed in 1997.[72]

There is no national law in the United Kingdom that controls and regulates mediation practice, so the practice varies by type of court and jurisdiction. Mediation is voluntary, though the courts can encourage its use and impose sanctions for a party's "unreasonable" refusal to participate.[73] Mediation is administered primarily by private providers, such as the Centre for Effective Dispute Resolution for commercial cases and the ADR Group for family law and commercial cases.[74] In contrast to the United States, private providers in the United Kingdom lead in design of the procedural rules, screening and training of neutrals, and quality control.[75] A Centre for Effective Dispute Resolution study identified eight thousand mediations of commercial and civil matters in 2012.[76] Because this public-private model of ADR was already so advanced in the United Kingdom, the directive did not bring about major changes.

In contrast, mediation was not used in Italy as a form of ADR by the general public before 2008.[77] Italy had a strong culture of supporting litigation among members of the legal profession and the public, despite substantial delays,[78] and Italian lawyers, who are powerful stakeholders, viewed mediation as a significant threat to their livelihoods.[79] Following issuance of the directive, Italy passed legislation that led to a requirement that certain categories of civil cases try mediation before court action. In protest, attorneys went on strike, and a leading association of lawyers successfully challenged the constitutionality of the new requirements, thereby halting virtually all mediations in the country, including private, consensual mediations.[80] A modified law, passed in 2013, created a four-year experiment in which certain commercial and civil cases (approximately 8 percent of all civil cases) required an initial, low-cost mediation session.[81] Under the law, judges have the power to order parties into mediation at any point in the life of the case.[82] The law also provides financial incentives to parties who resolve a case in mediation and financial penalties for lawyers who fail to educate their parties regarding mediation.[83]

A 2016 research report commissioned by the European Parliament concluded that "in the majority of the Member States mediation is on average still used in less than 1% of the cases in court."[84] A 2016 progress report from the European Commission concluded that the directive had helped increase the use of mediation in domestic cases in some countries, but a lack of awareness and information presented barriers to greater use in at least ten countries. The report made recommendations, such as education of litigants, creation of financial incentives for mediation, and development of a better database on the use of mediation. To address resource needs, the European Commission committed to continue to cofinance certain mediation-related efforts and raised the possibility of financially supporting a "stakeholder-driven development of European-wide quality standards for the provision of mediation services."[85] To encourage the use of mediation in courts in the European Union, a 2018 report recommended adoption of a model of "required mediation with easy opt-out," which has substantially increased mediation usage and settlement in the categories of court cases in Italy in which it is used.[86]

Bhutan

Unlike most European nations, many countries have long-established, informal, community-based processes that remain the norm for conflict resolution. In these countries, rights-based courts are the alternative, and less frequently used, form of dispute resolution. Such is the case in the small Himalayan country of Bhutan, which is experiencing a huge political shift as it evolves from an absolute monarchy to a constitutional monarchy with an elected parliament.

With approximately 750,000 citizens, many living in remote villages, Bhutan held its first national elections in 2008 under a new constitution and subsequent general elections in 2013 and 2018. Bhutan has representatives from all branches of government working together to design a dispute resolution system with the goals of building trust in the judiciary and advancing the rule of law. The system is intended to enhance the quality of traditional community-based processes and link them to the courts.[87] The courts have also described their goals as encompassing national and Buddhist religious values of compassion and peaceful coexistence and promotion of the government's policy of gross national happiness.[88]

Historically, mediation in Bhutan has been conducted by community leaders, elders, and monks. Many mediations have been conducted by *gups*, well-respected, locally elected county heads; their deputies, known as *mangmis*; and village representatives known as *tshogpas*. Because *gups* are being required to take on more administrative duties, their availability for mediation is constrained.[89] There is also a perceived need to provide court processes or other options when a *gup*, *mangmi*, or *tshogpa* has a conflict of interest in a particular case.

Bhutan has approximately two hundred lawyers, very few of whom are in private practice. Almost all are employed by the government in a range of judicial, administrative, policy, and legal capacities. To bridge the traditional, interest-based community processes with the formal, rights-based courts, judges are educating the public about the new laws via radio and personal appearances. Judges have also begun conducting mediation training programs throughout the country to increase *mangmis'* mediation skills, regularize mediation models, and educate these officials about the developing substantive law.[90] Program design in Bhutan will need to continue to evolve as its government systems and economy develop.

Key Framework Issues in Court DSD

Goals

In ADR design, a court may prioritize service to litigants, including reducing cost and delay and providing more individualized, less adversarial, and more creative procedures and outcomes than a trial can offer. The court may also seek to help litigants preserve or repair relationships, especially in cases involving child custody, business partnerships, and other contexts in which parties may need to work together after the lawsuit ends. Many courts choose to add ADR options wholly or in part to reduce the cases on their dockets. These widely varying goals raise fundamental questions about the purpose of courts and judges in a society.[91]

An important question for a court dispute system designer is which, if any, cases to exclude from an ADR program. The U.S. District Court for the Northern District of California excluded self-represented parties[92] from automatic inclusion in the multioption program to decrease the risk of coercion to settle and ensure that all parties had the advice of counsel on the legal merits of their cases during private ADR processes.[93] However, increasing recognition of how the traditional trial-based court system fails to meet the needs of self-represented parties has led to an increase in ADR programs for this growing clientele. As of 2011, at least twenty-one federal district courts allowed some self-represented parties to participate in court-connected mediation.[94]

Discussion Questions

With problem-solving courts, a designer faces a very broad list of goals. Possible goals are reducing caseload, promoting peaceful community relations, addressing community health challenges such as drug addiction and mental illness, engaging youth, and combating unemployment. How many goals can and should a court tackle and with what priorities? When engaging multiple stakeholders with differing interests and levels of power, which actors are and which should be most influential in determining the court's goals?[95]

Processes and Structure

Courts that add one or more ADR options must determine how to best integrate these options with each other and with traditional court activities. Judicially hosted settlement conferences, whether conducted in a facilitative, evaluative, or hybrid model, are also ADR options but may not be considered as such because they are traditionally conducted by judges and often predate the development of other ADR options.

The Red Hook Community Justice Center is one example of a specialty or problem-solving court integrating many new structures, processes, and procedures. These new court structures are not categorized as ADR programs but often include ADR processes, such as mediation and other assisted negotiation models, and incorporate some of the philosophies that gave rise to ADR and community justice programs, such as restorative justice and therapeutic jurisprudence.[96]

Developments in online dispute resolution (ODR) offer new tools and opportunities to improve the quality and efficiency of court processes, both traditional and ADR, including increasing the use of online filing, enabling counsel and the public to get more information through online sources, and providing phone and video conferencing. Almost all U.S. circuit courts of appeal have conducted

Examples of Specializations for Problem-Solving Courts

- Community courts (for quality-of-life crimes)
- Dependency (child welfare)
- Domestic violence
- Drug treatment (adult and juvenile)
- DUI/DWI (driving under the influence or while intoxicated)
- Family treatment or unified family (domestic violence, substance abuse)
- Homeless
- Juveniles
- Mental health
- Opioid intervention
- Prostitution/human trafficking intervention
- Reentry (of the formerly incarcerated back into the community)
- Teens/youth
- Tribal healing-to-wellness programs
- Veterans[97]

Discussion Question

In courts covering large geographic areas, the cost and time to travel is prohibitive for some parties. Some courts rely largely or exclusively on telephone
conferences to conduct mediation sessions. What are the benefits and disadvantages of this form of ODR in court-connected mediation?

---

mediations by phone, with the Fourth Circuit U.S. Court of Appeals conducting
over 95 percent of mediations by telephone in 2013.[98]

Ethan Katsh and Orna Rabinovich-Einy note that courts and administrative
tribunals are experimenting with new models from private sector ODR applications such as those at eBay and PayPal.[99] In Canada, the British Columbia Civil
Resolution Tribunal has established a multistage ODR process for small claims
and certain condominium cases.[100] The first level of interactive, online engagement provides problem diagnosis and interpretation of the facts of the dispute in
a legal context. If this does not resolve the case, the parties move through stages
of a possible negotiation option, followed by facilitation, and finally adjudication,
all conducted online, by phone, or through videoconference.[101] Other court ODR
innovations, addressing case types like family law, small claims, traffic violations,
and cases with self-represented parties, have been tested or are being implemented
in the United Kingdom, the Netherlands, and U.S. states, including Ohio and
Michigan.[102]

Interaction with the Legal System

In designing any dispute resolution system, the designer must be cognizant of how
that system will interact with the formal legal system and whether the courts will
permit such a program if it is challenged. These questions take an interesting twist
when a court itself is creating the dispute resolution options. An obvious threshold
question is whether the ADR processes themselves are permissible under the law.
Binding arbitration, for instance, could not be imposed by a court in the United
States, because it would deny parties their constitutional right to trial.

What about the legality of a court encouraging or requiring parties to use other,
nonbinding ADR procedures? Appellate cases in different U.S. jurisdictions have
held that a judge cannot mandate participation in a summary jury trial against the
wishes of the parties[103] but can require parties to try mediation.[104] The Alternative
Dispute Resolution Act of 1998 requires every federal district court to offer at least

Discussion Questions

Some commentators express concern about the decline in the percentage of cases filed in U.S. courts going to trial. What is the ideal percentage of cases or types of cases that should go to trial? What factors would you consider in trying to answer this question?

one ADR option and authorizes judges to mandate participation in mediation and ENE.[105] Other court opinions have addressed the enforceability of good-faith participation requirements.[106]

Another potential conflict exists between the mediation norm of protecting confidentiality and the courts' need to determine facts. Judges may override mediation confidentiality protection when a conflicting public policy objective is deemed overriding.[107] The Uniform Mediation Act, adopted by twelve jurisdictions,[108] has confidentiality exceptions for criminal activity or mediator misconduct.[109] Many codes, model standards, and court ADR rules explicitly provide confidentiality exceptions to prevent violence[110] or to investigate impropriety by the mediator.[111]

Problem-solving courts have reported many positive outcomes, but both ends of the political spectrum have raised concerns regarding a potential abandonment of accountability on the one hand and disproportionately intrusive interventions on the other.[112] Defense attorneys have questioned whether these new courts create inappropriate pressure on defendants to plead guilty in order to obtain services and whether they deny defendants the benefit of the full legal defense they would receive at trial.[113] An additional critique connects some of the early community courts to the broken-windows strategy, as implemented under New York City Police Chief William Bratton and Mayor Rudolph Giuliani in the 1990s.[114] This attempt to reduce crime by substantially increasing arrests for low-level offenses is now criticized by some as ineffective and a contributor to overpolicing and harassment of communities of color.[115]

Resources

Elements in the DSD Analytic Framework interact and can be interdependent, perhaps none more so than resources. For example, a decrease in court resources may increase pressure on a court to narrow its broader public service goals to focus on court efficiency. Such a choice could lead to pressure to settle cases, which may undercut party self-determination, party satisfaction, and the delivery of justice. These pressures may also create ethical dilemmas for court administrators and ADR neutrals.

Public court funding is limited, and allocating those resources to processes other than traditional trial-related activities can be controversial. However, shifting the costs of court-sponsored ADR programs to litigants can present questions of fairness, because of the financial burden on the parties and the risk of bias if only one party pays the provider. Self-represented parties are particularly vulnerable. Insufficient resources challenge a court's ability to provide high-quality services, including training, monitoring, and evaluation of ADR process providers.

Significant reductions to court budgets in the United States since 2007 have had a dramatic impact on court ADR programs.[116] Drastic budget cuts to the state courts in California in 2009 resulted in staffing cuts in San Mateo County that affected the level of referrals and the work of the ADR program's important multistakeholder committees. The system adapted to diminished staff resources by using the stakeholder groups as an on-call support base for consultations on policy, procedures, and program monitoring.[117] In the Northern District of California court program, federal budget cuts eliminated in 2018 most of the previously required early phone conferences between counsel in a case and a member of the ADR legal staff.[118]

The Red Hook court has been supported by a mix of public funding (from several levels of government), nonprofit foundation funding, and AmeriCorps staff.[119] As with any design innovation, these specially funded programs must demonstrate their worth, often within a short time, to compete successfully for public resources.

Evaluation

Court ADR programs are notoriously difficult to evaluate. Different court programs are motivated by different goals, which may not be fully specified at the outset of new programming. Measuring efficiency in cost or time (for parties and the court) and tracking user satisfaction (of parties or counsel) requires surveys.

Understanding settlement rates can be difficult, because many courts fail to track key data on how cases resolve and whether ADR options were employed. Harder still to assess are more qualitative program goals such as rebuilding the parties' relationship and enabling them to reach creative outcomes a court could not order.

As discussed in Chapter 5, meaningful evaluation of court programs is also challenging because of the wide range of variables. For courts with ADR programs, these variables include the number of ADR processes offered, types of cases eligible for each process, the definition of mediation and other ADR processes, the number of processes a given case may encounter, and the wide range of actual practice within each process offered. For specialty courts, the greater number and complexity of goals increases the assessment challenge.

Differences in local legal cultures and program design elements—such as referral structures, training of neutrals, and education of counsel, parties, and judges—make efforts to compare programs more challenging. Individual court cases have their own many variables of the subject matter and complexity of the case, the contentiousness of counsel, the relationships between or among the parties, and more. Effective evaluations of such programs are sophisticated and expensive, with few courts having sufficient resources to conduct thorough long-term analyses. The Northern District of California and San Mateo programs demonstrated high satisfaction rates and savings of cost and time for parties. However, given the wide array of contexts, designs, process definitions, and data-collection methods, it is not surprising that surveys of court programs around the United States have shown widely varying outcomes.[120] These challenges have resulted in broad variability in study quality and a general call for more and better data collection and evaluation.[121]

Because of courts' interest in reducing the number of cases on their dockets, settlement rates are often used as a key measure of success for court ADR programs. The risk of this approach is that it can create an incentive for the court and its mediators to coerce parties into settlement, regardless of procedural or substantive fairness. Even if settlement is the goal, it is often difficult to know which one or more of the activities in the life of a case—or which characteristics of the ADR program—contributed to its settlement.[122]

A critique of many of the earlier court ADR studies is that they paid scant if any attention to the wide range of activity being labeled mediation. Under the Civil Justice Reform Act, Congress tasked the RAND Corporation with evaluating a cross section of courts paired with so-called comparison courts.[123] In contrast to the Federal Judicial Center studies, RAND's results showed no savings of time or money[124] and generated substantial controversy. Although the pairs of courts were deemed similar by the study's designers, they were viewed by some commentators as "quite different, geographically, culturally and in terms of their caseloads."[125] The results were also questioned because the court programs being studied were "moving targets," changing their programs to respond to the legislation over the course of the study.[126]

New research is focusing on what actually takes place within the many processes labeled mediation and on participants' satisfaction with the process and outcome. ADR programs in the Maryland state courts have been evaluated in a series of studies led by Lorig Charkoudian. In a study of day-of-trial mediations in civil cases in the district courts, the researchers observed the mediations and recorded and coded mediator and participant behaviors. The evaluators categorized the styles used by the mediators in this program as (1) *reflecting* (articulating what the participants' expressed, focusing on their interests and emotions), (2) *eliciting* (asking participants for their ideas on solutions and following up on those ideas), and (3) *offering opinions and solutions* (mediators' own opinions and proposed solutions).[127] Of the three strategies, only the elicitive strategy had a positive effect on reaching an agreement.[128] The evaluation also found that while caucusing had no statistical impact on reaching a settlement, the greater the amount of time spent in caucus, the more likely the case would return to court within a year for enforcement action.[129] Another promising research development is Donna Shestowsky's direct study of litigants' perceptions of different dispute resolution options over the life of a case, which will provide knowledge to enhance the quality of future court DSD.[130]

Evaluation of new court structures, such as Red Hook's problem-solving court, reflects the challenge of measuring conflict prevention. This objective seeks better outcomes for the community as well as for individual perpetrators and victims. Program designers seek to achieve not only retributive justice but also procedural and sometimes therapeutic or restorative justice. A comprehensive evaluation of Red Hook noted the program's success in enhancing procedural justice and cited this increase as the likely contributor to the positive findings of reduced recidivism in adult criminal cases[131] and increased community approval of the courts.[132]

All courts should commit the necessary resources to collect data that will allow effective internal and external evaluation. Best practices include coding case data in the internal court system, such as the type and time of ADR referral, the processes to which the case was referred, the outcome of these processes, the type of case, and whether parties were represented. Following the ADR process, the parties, counsel, and neutral should be surveyed.[133]

Conclusion

Court program innovations are institutionalized in federal and state courts in the United States and are expanding internationally. New process options have led to new designs and reconsideration of the court's role in democratic governance, including the strengthening of connections between courts and the communities they serve. In response to societal changes and the unanticipated effects of court rules and changing legal culture, courts continue to innovate, creating and amending procedural rules and process options to try to improve the delivery of justice.

Effective application of the DSD Analytic Framework elements can help create systems that provide maximum benefit to users in these sensitive contexts, but this application will require clarity of goals, deep cultural and historic knowledge of local dispute resolution systems, and the willingness and ability to evaluate and adapt as societies and technologies continue to evolve.

FOLLOWING THE 2013 BOSTON MARATHON attack, One Fund Boston was founded to collect private donations to compensate those injured. That experience prompted interest in the idea of a national compassion fund. Such a fund would serve as a centralized facility for nonnatural disasters, as a counterpart to the International Red Cross, which aids victims of natural disasters.[1] Imagine that you are a partner with a firm that specializes in nonprofit organizations. Will you advocate creating this fund or suggest that victims use the traditional tort mechanism? If you opt for a fund, how might you approach its design? Should there be different categories of circumstances covered? Who would finance the administration of the fund and its compensation payments? Would claimants be entitled to opt out of the fund and use regular courts?

"Claims resolution facility" is a term used to describe entities like this hypothetical fund that are organized to process and compensate mass injury claims.[2] A facility may derive from a range of circumstantial and legal triggers. A natural disaster like Hurricane Katrina, an act of terror like the Boston Marathon bombing, a defective product like asbestos—each demands a means to achieve justice. Claims facilities are often used as an alternative or a supplement to the standard litigation civil action (usually tort proceedings) to determine liability, establish a compensation mechanism, and compensate those injured.

Issues to consider are as follows.

- What are the range of triggers for claims facilities? Does it matter whether it is a natural or human-caused disaster? Should different types of human-caused disasters be distinguished (for example, terrorist vs. corporate-negligence-driven disasters)?

- How might the source of resources—government, donations, private firms (single or many, deep pockets or bankrupt)—affect the goals and process?
- How does one balance efficiency with equity in administration and compensation design?

The Traditional Court-Based Tort Mechanism and the Challenge of Mass Torts

At its most basic, tort law "consists of the rules governing civil suits for injuries caused by wrongs to others" and is as varied as the human activity that might cause risk of injury.[3] Most frequently, individuals file tort lawsuits against entities that have harmed them. Plaintiffs can seek a remedy for either economic (medical bills, future earnings) or noneconomic losses (pain and suffering). In tort claims, the court (judge or jury) determines liability and a defendant (and its insurer) that is held liable bears the cost. If the magnitude of the claim exceeds the defendant's assets, recovery is limited to the defendant's bankrupt estate. An administrator appointed by the court determines how to distribute the funds.

For over thirty years, the American tort system has been broadly criticized for its awards (considered by some too parsimonious and by others too profligate), the volatility of judgments, the enormous costs, the slow pace of proceedings, and the adversarial structure.[4] Before the 1970s, most tort claims were filed by an individual or a few individuals against a specific tortfeasor (the actor alleged to be responsible for the plaintiff's harms). During the 1970s and particularly the 1980s, however, mass tort litigation emerged, in which "hundreds of thousands of people sued scores of corporations for losses due to injuries or diseases that they attributed to catastrophic events, pharmaceutical products, medical devices or toxic substances."[5] Three main differences distinguish mass torts from individual tort claims: the large number of claims associated with a single litigation, the congruence of actors and issues within a litigation (such as public interest lawyers acting as private attorneys general), and the interdependency of claim values.[6]

Private Tortfeasor Responsibility

Mass tort litigation cases have added complexity to an already stressed civil justice system, with courts struggling to resolve cases fairly and efficiently. Some strategies adopted to address these problems are managing cases at their pretrial stages, in hopes of reducing duplicative activities and transaction costs, and formal or informal aggregative or collective procedures.[7] One highly contested formal option is filing class actions, governed in federal cases by Rule 23.[8] Although class action may serve some efficiency purposes, scholars argue this tool has been largely

rejected by key courts, which refuse to recognize mass tort claims to fulfill the
conditions of that rule,[9] and lawyers, who claim that using class actions will affect
individual lawyer-client relationships.[10] Moreover, this mechanism is criticized
as inequitable for subjecting all individuals to uniform class treatment.[11] Courts
adopted a more informal means of collective disposition through negotiated settlements. Unfortunately, even the most creative and innovative judicial solutions
adopted by courts were unable to address the challenges of the asbestos and
the Dalkon Shield cases, leading to the adoption of court-administrated claim
facilities.[12]

Asbestos

Asbestos is a naturally occurring substance of fibrous threads that are resistant to
heat, fire, and chemicals. Thus, asbestos was widely used by industry for insulation
and protection. The Environmental Protection Agency (EPA)[13] deemed asbestos
to be carcinogenic in 1970, and since then nearly a million claimants have filed
suit against 8,400 business entities in arguably the longest-running mass tort
in U.S. history.[14] Starting with the U.S. Court of Appeals for the Fifth Circuit
decision that manufacturers could be held liable for injuries caused by asbestos
exposure,[15] a barrage of litigation ensued, causing chaos and consternation among
civil courts, insurance companies, corporations, lawyers, and plaintiffs.[16] Asbes-
tosis and mesothelioma can be caused by a single asbestos fiber, and the latency
period preceding symptoms can exceed a decade. Thus, it can be very difficult,
and even impossible, for a claimant to prove that a specific party is responsible
for his injury—a problem that has been called the "indeterminate defendant."[17]
Although courts initially aimed to handle asbestos cases on an individual basis,
claims exponentially increased and courts turned to aggregative procedures.[18]

On the one hand, parties, and to some extent also judges, were eager to avoid
trials on the merits and, on the other hand, parties were not willing to settle
without at least a trial date (as a form of leverage).[19] Numerous judicial initiatives,
attempting to lower transaction costs, ranged from a coercive judicial consolidation to reach settlements based on administrative schedules to a computer-
driven model to generate case values, transforming asbestos litigation into a de
facto quasi-administrative regime.[20] Bankruptcy proceedings of the liable asbestos
manufacturers became a dominant venue for resolving asbestos claims, typically
involving "valuation of present and future asbestos claims against a bankrupt
defendant . . . and then a reorganization plan" to compensate claimants from the
defendant's assets through creation of an administrative claims facility.[21] However,
some funds were exhausted before fully compensating victims.

Another approach attempted to collaboratively create trusts outside the bankruptcy courts as a way to reach a global class action settlement. One such fund was established by a consortium of defendants (the Center for Claims Resolution settlement); a separate attempt was made to settle all litigation against Fibreboard, a major defendant.[22] These two alternative trusts were not approved by the U.S. Supreme Court because of their failure to provide protection for the individuals who did not consent to them, resulting in a termination of all attempts to reach global settlements through class action litigation in the asbestos case.[23] Other out-of-litigation solutions were also attempted, such as adopting a consolidated manufacturer and insurer process, administered by an independent firm, the Center for Public Resources. Using expedited class action rules, the center provided three-arbitrator panels that devised a strict allocation formula under the aegis of the bankruptcy court.

More than $250 billion has now been spent on litigation over nearly fifty years.[24] The mass harm represented by the asbestos cases spurred attempts to achieve greater efficiency through consolidation, aggregated lawsuits, group settlement conferences, group trials, and group settlement contracts. Unfortunately, these attempts have had limited success, are fraught with exorbitant administrative costs, result in deadlocks among parties and counsel, and give inconsistent compensation to victims. Deborah Hensler comments that such aggregation benefits some but disadvantages others and that the courts should have usefully developed rules and practices that align with the realities of such litigation.[25]

Dalkon Shield

The Dalkon Shield cases began in 1971 with women who had suffered injury from the eponymous intrauterine birth control device manufactured by A. H. Robins Company. By 1985, Robins had disposed of more than nine thousand tort claims, with five thousand more pending in federal and state courts. At this stage Robins had paid approximately $530 million in punitive and compensatory damages. Thus, the traditional tort mechanism was able to provide remedies to a meaningful number of claimants. Challenges began on August 1985, when Robins filed a petition for bankruptcy.[26] Under the umbrella of the bankruptcy court, Robins attempted to reach a "global peace" settlement for all present and future victims. Two decisions were made: establishing a "bar date" after which claims could not be submitted and establishing a "closed fund" for compensation. Some claimants feared the fund would be inadequate and suggested that either Robins should be sold to produce revenue or an unrestricted fund should be created. The court responded by appointing an expert to devise a mechanism through which claims could be evaluated, but the lengthy process prevented full consideration of individual plaintiffs' cases.[27]

The final aggregated amount was decided by the court after a long process of hearings and expert testimonies, allowing Robins to form the Dalkon Shield Claimants Trust[28] and an in-house claims resolution facility that assumed the responsibility of Robins and its successors for Dalkon Shield personal injury claims. The facility aimed to deal with the science of causality, the responsibility of specific defendants, options to reach a comprehensive aggregate settlement, and a distribution mechanism.[29] The court determined that plaintiffs could recover damages on the basis of the defendants' market share, because a handful of companies accounted for a majority of the market and had collaborated on the manufacture of the product. Claimants were given three payment options, representing "a trade-off between speed and level of recovery, on the one hand, and evidentiary requirements and evaluation of individual factors, on the other." Option 1, a flat amount calculated according to a schedule of benefits, handled nearly half the claims in a few months; Option 2 aimed to resolve the bulk of the remaining Dalkon Shield claims, and its amount varied by type and extent of injury while minimizing administrative expenses. The most difficult and complex claims were expected to pursue a traditional litigation style as Option 3. The process in Option 3 was designed to be adversarial, with a right to trial if a settlement could not be reached. The options provided some tailoring of process to the claim and aspired to address concerns over the dehumanization of the legal process.

Criticisms of the options were that less educated or unrepresented claimants might choose Option 1 regardless of an individual claim's merit[30] and that many

Health Courts

As a senior health policy staffer for the Senate Committee on Health, Education, Labor, and Pensions, you have been asked to analyze the revival of a bill to pilot design of health courts. Such specialized courts, which have been adopted in several states, constitute a tort replacement regime to shift the venue from medical malpractice cases filed in common law courts (based on findings of fault and damages) to adjudication in specialized, dedicated tribunals and "expedite, simplify, and rationalize compensation decisions."[31] What other goals might you consider, and how would you measure success? What legal arguments are likely to be raised? What kind of design process would you recommend? What qualifications for an expert neutral?

Opioid Epidemic

Over three hundred thousand lives have been lost to the opioid epidemic between 2000 and 2017. Early lawsuits against opioid manufacturers were personal injury claims brought on behalf of persons with addiction who overdosed. In January 2018, Judge Dan Aaron Polster of the U.S. District Court of the Northern District of Ohio remarked, "We don't need briefs and we don't need trials." The litigation has now reached 1,548 federal court cases, brought on behalf of 400 cities and counties; 77 tribes, hospitals, and union benefit funds; and millions of people. Another 332 cases have been filed in state courts. Judge Polster has brought his long experience with multidistrict litigation to bear and assigned three special masters to work in parallel, but these cases appear to be the most complex litigation our courts have faced.

Judge Polster does not want to just move money around. He says, "What we've got to do is dramatically reduce the number of pills that are out there and make sure that the pills that are out there are being used properly."[32] Given the complexity of law, the many parties (individual, corporate, government agencies, local cities and towns, physicians, hospitals), and public policy, what steps might be undertaken, and by whom, to address this "behemoth" issue?[33]

plaintiffs perceived the process as hostile to them.[34] Carrie Menkel-Meadow, an arbitrator in the Dalkon Shield process, noted that "some claimants will not feel good about the justice system, no matter what the financial outcome, unless they have a chance to tell their story, report their pain, and in some cases, confront some representative of the company that wronged them."[35] Indeed, although the trust attempted to communicate directly with claimants through newsletters and informational meetings, there was little opportunity for the claimants to achieve meaning making by expressing their own perspectives.[36]

Deepwater Horizon

On April 20, 2010, a blowout and fire on the oil rig Deepwater Horizon, leased by BP, a British company, caused the largest-ever oil spill in U.S. waters. BP immediately agreed with the U.S. government to establish a Gulf Spill Independent Claims Fund in the amount of $20 billion and an environmental cleanup fund of $1 billion; BP appointed Kenneth Feinberg as the independent administrator (the Gulf Coast Claim Facility, or GCCF). The facility—created by agreement, not by a court or federal legislation—was established to offer a faster and more predictable outcome for potential claimants compared with those affected by the *Exxon Valdez* spill of 1989.[37]

As described in the press, "The administration and BP got together . . . and decided, both, that coming up with a guaranteed sum to pay eligible claims was a creative alternative to years and years of protracted litigation."[38] The purposes of the fund were therefore clear—to avoid court time and expense, uncertainty, and legal fees. All claims previously filed in court against BP were transferred to the GCCF. The first phase, aimed at Gulf residents and businesses, allowed those who claimed injury from the spill to apply for emergency payments, requiring only that the claimant submit by November 23, 2010, a claim with documentation of prespill income. Those claiming the emergency payment were not required to waive their right to sue[39] and could reapply for losses every month until the program concluded.[40]

The second and final phase of the claims process, which began after emergency claims filing closed, was planned for three years. Individuals could claim for full-review final payment, interim payment, or quick final payment.[41] Those who chose full review could submit proof for past and future damages and seek a lump-sum final payment but gave up the right to sue BP and other companies involved in the spill (although they could decline the final offer). Those choosing to receive interim payment could claim only past damages and had to provide documentation of loss. They were not required to sign a release of claims and could reapply every quarter. Quick payments supplied $5,000 for individuals and $25,000 for businesses but required claimants to sign a release and waive the right to sue BP in the future. Only those who received compensation as part of the first emergency phase were eligible to submit either interim payment claims or quick payment final claims. A limited appeals process featured a GCCF panel of judges selected by the chancellor of the law school at Louisiana State University (Jack Weiss). In sharp contrast to the tort class actions of asbestos and Dalkon Shield, the court oversight of claim administration was waived in favor of a private facility manager.

BP has paid $8.2 billion to individuals and businesses. The press praised the fund as "a remarkably effective alternative to the cumbersome way damages are usually meted out after a corporate accident. . . . The whole point of the Gulf Coast fund is to keep cases out of court; in return for compensation . . . the victims get monetary damages, just as they would if they won a court case, but without the expense of a lawsuit."[42] However, the BP fund was also criticized for its vague legality, its questionable valuation mechanisms, and its overall lack of transparency.[43]

Ultimately, BP's aspiration to minimize litigation in civil courts was only partially successful. In August 2010, actions related to the spill were transferred to Judge Carl Barbier in the U.S. District Court for the Eastern District of Louisiana for consolidated pretrial proceedings. By June 2, 2011, the litigation—originating in different districts—consisted of hundreds of cases and over a hundred thousand claimants.[44] A few dozen of the claims asked for a judicial regulation of the GCCF. BP attempted to push back against regulation of the fund, but in February 2011, the court partially granted the request to supervise communications.[45]

One of the most significant elements of the court's decision was that "while Feinberg and the GCCF were independent of BP with regard to the evaluation and payment of claims" they were not fully independent. The court ordered BP, Feinberg, and the fund not to present Feinberg and the fund as fully independent or neutral and not to contact represented claimants or provide legal advice to unrepresented claimants. They were also asked to clearly express claimants' rights both to file claims in lieu of accepting a final payment and to get advice from counsel before reaching settlements. Moreover, the dissatisfaction of claimants and the government's growing concern with the fund caused Attorney General Eric Holder to investigate the facility. Findings were announced in June 2012, declaring that the GCCF's assessment procedures often underevaluated the damages.[46] Before the investigation report was submitted, BP and plaintiffs' lawyers announced the end of the Gulf Spill fund process under Feinberg. A new fund was administered by the court, with the goal of making settlement more appealing to more people.

The Deepwater Horizon Court-Supervised Settlement Program now administers the procedure for medical claims and economic and property damages claims.[47] Subsequent legal rulings concern BP's liability for damage and injuries, with further decisions expected on penalties due under the Clean Water Act.[48] According to the information provided at the website of Deepwater Horizon Claims Center, 405,266 economic and property damage claims were filed and 184,552 payments of $12 billion were made by mid-2019.[49]

This experience highlights the important role of the court—and the transparency, independence, and legitimacy it represents—in designing a mechanism that falls somewhere between the strictly legal process of the *Exxon Valdez* and the not-quite-independent BP-Feinberg GCCF. For example, Lawrence Susskind recommended paying Feinberg's firm through a panel of stakeholder representatives who could verify that Feinberg was doing what he agreed to do.[50] The administrative feasibility of the GCCF addressed the *Exxon Valdez* problems but did not outweigh the loss of the court's legitimacy.[51]

Jack Weinstein, after years of teaching, serving as legal advisor to public agencies, and presiding as judge in every kind of judicial matter, reflected on the difference between tort law as oriented to individuals and in the case of mass disasters. The goal in the individual tort case is to achieve justice; in the mass tort case, the court aims to deliver mass justice through adapted case management, either with class action or consolidation case process. But this shift from the individual to the mass comes at a high cost, resulting in less justice to the individual and to society, and with significant loss of efficiency and increase in ethical concerns.[52] Carrie Menkel-Meadow, who served as a lawyer and as a neutral in tort cases handled by Weinstein, took on the challenge of how to preserve individual justice in the mass context by examining the fairness of outcomes and the procedural protections. Among her recommendations were to undertake special scrutiny of who participates and to design more varied processes to enhance parties' satisfaction.[53] The following case illustrates how Menkel-Meadow's approach has been implemented.

Fortune 500 Race Discrimination

A race discrimination class action was filed against a Fortune 500 company. In 2013, a U.S. district court approved a settlement of $160 million to be distributed to class members. The distribution was administered by a special master, Lynn P. Cohn, working with a federal court, who designed a combination of conflict resolution techniques to assess damages.[54] This claims facility in effect acted as an ADR provider by establishing a panel of neutrals who underwent training and then conducted hearings. Class members had two options for relief: file either a simple claim form or a detailed claim form to request payment from the settlement fund. The simple claim form contained three brief questions on length of service, status, and time in class period, and payment was made within a month of submission due date, without any individualized review. The detailed claim form had about fifty questions, conveyed the right for an individualized assessment by a neutral, and was eligible for a claim against the $25 million extraordinary fund, but a claimant who filed it also retained the right to elect an expedited monetary award according to the simple form calculation. All interviews took place during a three-month period in 2014 in Chicago, via in-person conference or videoconference. The process was characterized by the highly intense emotions of many claimants. Neither defendants nor their counsel participated in the hearings. The special master had responsibility to ensure the fairness and consistency of awards.

The special master concluded that the process used could serve as a model for settlements for a certified class under Federal Rules of Civil Procedure 23(c)(4) (or any settlement involving a large number of plaintiffs), subject to consideration of the time and cost to handle the individualized assessments. The opportunity for claimants to be heard by an experienced neutral in a nonadversarial setting that emphasized fairness and consistency proved successful to the plaintiffs and neutrals in this case. The absence of the defendant and counsel in the hearings relaxed the adversarial tone experienced in litigation, or even in mediation and arbitration; however, the overall fairness may be balanced by the court's role in establishing the class and the settlement fund. This case demonstrates how a flexible process design with options for voice, control, and efficiency, plus careful oversight of the settlement parameters, can deliver justice to the satisfaction of both the parties and the court institution.

Natural Disasters

Claims facilities for natural disasters draw on public funds to compensate those affected. Victims of natural disasters may attribute partial responsibility to public agencies for failing to take adequate prevention measures. The primary goal may be efficient disaster relief and horizontal equity (those similarly situated receive similar compensation). In such cases, the public expects speed in eligibility determination and distribution and minimized expense in administering public resources. Nevertheless, the challenge of coordinating federal, state, and local agencies can pose significant barriers to responding with sufficient speed. Moreover, if significant human error is at issue and damages are severe, expectations for justice will encompass not only distributive but also procedural and retributive elements, which approximate a tort framework and include opportunities for voice and acknowledgment.[55]

Hurricane Katrina

On August 29, 2005, Hurricane Katrina struck the Mississippi Gulf Coast, causing one of the worst natural disasters in the history of the United States. Coastal flooding extended into Alabama, levee failures led to severe flood damage in New Orleans and surrounding areas, and wind damaged residential and commercial buildings throughout Louisiana and Mississippi. Nearly 1,700 lives were lost, 800,000 people were displaced, and estimated economic losses exceeded $125 billion.[56] In New Orleans, thousands of people took shelter in the Superdome stadium, where supplies were scant and conditions deteriorated rapidly. It took the Federal Emergency Management Agency (FEMA) five days to get water to the Superdome.[57]

President George W. Bush declared it a disaster relief area on September 14.[58] To provide efficient relief equitably among recipients, the U.S. Senate approved nearly $60 billion in federal aid to state and local governments through the Robert T. Stafford Disaster Relief and Emergency Assistance Act (Stafford Act).[59] The act allows payment of up to $25,000 to any individual or household for repairing damaged property; the Small Business Administration offered loans of up to $200,000 to homeowners for repairs to damaged primary residences and up to $1.5 million for business property, machinery, and inventory. By April 2006, some $88 billion in federal aid was allocated for relief, recovery, and rebuilding and another $20 billion requested to help victims of Hurricanes Katrina and Rita (which hit the area less than a month later). Distributions were made by administrative agencies according to regulated standards.

In such circumstances, the most efficient solution is arguably to give the same flat award to every claimant (who can prove residence in the affected area). An equitable solution would require each claimant to provide proof of the losses to support compensation. However, the more rigorous the procedure for determining eligibility, causation, and damages becomes, the more inefficient it renders the process. Moreover, equitability is undermined by excessively long procedures. At some point, justice delayed becomes justice denied.[60]

A second issue is bureaucratic competence and capacity. In the case of Katrina, FEMA took the lead on investigating and managing compensation, but it was poorly operated. Scholars observe that public sector agencies make suboptimal decisions "by not using principles of benefit-cost analysis when making their decisions as to whether to protect an area as illustrated by the Corps of Engineers decision not to strengthen the New Orleans levees."[61] When Hurricane Harvey hit Houston, Texas, in 2017, FEMA had significantly improved its operations and coordination with state and local agencies to provide assistance. Nevertheless, greater investment in prevention infrastructure like seawalls and dams may be a cost-effective measure.

Manitoba Floods

The 2011 floods in Manitoba, Canada, highlighted the complexity of victims' perceptions of causation and fairness during natural disasters and the implications for design of a compensation scheme. Historic flows of many rivers and creeks of the Assiniboine River systems resulted in flooding of fields and cities. The Manitoban government opened a portage to divert the water, an action that arguably

San Diego Wildfires

In 2007, wildfires tore through San Diego County. Fourteen people were killed, 160 others were injured, and 1 million people were evacuated. The major contributing factors were drought in Southern California, hot weather, and Santa Ana winds. Nearly a million acres burned.

More than two thousand law suits were filed against San Diego Gas & Electric (for sparks from transmission lines) by more than five thousand plaintiffs. Parties included individuals, the City of San Diego, the County of San Diego, Cal Fire, the San Diego County Parks and Recreation Department, and multiple insurance carriers and underwriters.

Consider the DSD Analytic Framework, and sketch out the potential goals and processes you would consider in designing a system for this situation.[62]

aggravated the situation. Over seven thousand people were evacuated and over Can\$1.2 billion was paid out by the province. Lindy Rouillard-Labbe conducted an extensive study of the victims' experience with that compensation process.[63] She found that Manitobans attributed over 75 percent responsibility to the government for failure to prevent the disaster. The severity of the damages and perception of human responsibility created an expectation for compensation (both damages and need for retribution) and for voice and acknowledgment. A tort framework that tracked damages was considered more fair than a fixed-amount reimbursement. Those who attributed the catastrophe to nature had lower expectations of both economic and noneconomic awards from the process.[64]

Terrorist Acts
September 11th Victim Compensation Fund
Following the terrorist-related aircraft crashes of September 11, 2001, Congress adopted the Air Transportation Safety and System Stabilization Act (ATSSSA) to preserve the viability of the U.S. air transportation system and establish the September 11th Victim Compensation Fund (VCF) to compensate any individual who was injured or killed. This bill was deemed imperative to save the airlines,[65] because the threat of lawsuits, coupled with an unstable economy, made it impossible for airlines to borrow the necessary operating capital to remain in business.

The fund incorporated both a bailout for the airline industry and an alternative to the tort litigation system for victim's families. Kenneth Feinberg was appointed special master by U.S. Attorney General John Ashcroft and given wide discretion on design of the fund procedures. The VCF was freestanding, with no limits on its administration or individual payments. The goal was to provide fair repayment for the sudden loss of a loved one and some degree of justice for that loss. Unlike the BP fund he would administer ten years later, this fund gave Feinberg full responsibility for determining what was fair and just.[66] In both cases, court procedures were initially bypassed: with 9/11, the responsible party was known but infeasible to prosecute; with BP, the responsible party admitted liability and volunteered compensation. With 9/11, an individual hearing process was offered; with BP, beyond lost lives, property damage made up the bulk of the claims, which were submitted under an evidentiary process.

Feinberg was directed by ATSSSA's section 405 to "determine . . . the extent of the harm to the claimant, including any economic and noneconomic losses" and set the amount of compensation "based on the harm to the claimant, the facts of the claim, and the individual circumstances of the claimant."[67] The statute covered only claims for physical harm or death, not for property damage. Economic losses were determined by the victim's lost income from 9/11 through his or her expected retirement.[68] Noneconomic losses were set at fixed amounts for all victims: $250,000 for all victims and $50,000 (later raised to $100,000) for a victim's surviving spouse and each surviving child. Losses were reduced by certain collateral sources of compensation (life insurance, pension funds, death benefits programs, and any government payment on account of death but not personal savings, investments, or other assets).

Janet Alexander has posed questions on procedural design in the context of the VCF: What is the purpose of a compensation program? What values should the program embody? Why should eligible claimants be treated differently from apparently similarly situated persons? Why are existing procedural institutions inadequate to compensate these persons?[69] Alexander argues that the design was unsatisfactory.

> First, no real thought was given to procedural design. The drafters, in a tearing hurry and with many other large and urgent matters to think about, took the simplest procedural form that was ready to hand. . . . The central purpose of the Act was not to compensate victims but to keep the airlines running by, among other things, protecting them from going broke paying tort judgments.[70]

George L. Priest adds his own criticism by comparing the VCF with the social norms for dealing with the consequences of unintended losses: tort law, private market insurance, government insurance, and government welfare. In each of these four options, there is a rationale for award (and limits) relative to the loss. While Priest finds no specific fault with Feinberg's method or outcomes, he states that the fund had no coherent rationale or ethic of restraint and that the definition of awards was entirely dependent on Feinberg.[71] Priest also expresses some concerns regarding Feinberg's use of grids and caps, award limits, methodology and evidence for future income, application of the collateral source rule (regarding life insurance), and the ineligibility of other terrorist attacks.

Feinberg met with nearly a thousand families. In the end, 7,403 claims were filed, and 5,560 of these received over $7 billion, averaging $1.2 million, with no legal fees or taxes. In March 2009, thirty families (3 percent of the total victims) opted out and filed suit against the Port Authority of New York and New Jersey, architects, Motorola, and the airlines. It is difficult to assess whether using the facility reduced the overall compensation provided for victims. First, the data that exist are imprecise, though they reveal that settlement in litigated claims was around $5 million each, much higher than the fund's $1.2 million average. Second, it is unclear how to measure the economic effect of the procedural route, which saved the claimants from going to trial. As Gillian Hadfield notes in one of the few studies evaluating victims' views on the process, those opting for litigation were motivated primarily by nonmonetary gains of the litigation process—namely, the opportunity to obtain information, force accountability, and prompt responsive change through litigation.[72]

In retrospect, Feinberg concluded that the VCF was very successful under the circumstances but that he would not hold it out as a standard model for no-fault public compensation. The several success factors he highlighted seem relevant to other circumstances. Claimants were treated fairly and with respect, dignity, and compassion. Participation was very high. There was a focus on consistency and transparency and on narrowing the gap between higher- and lower-recovery claimants. Distribution was unskewed, despite an economic remedy based on future earnings. Administration was efficient; the VCF had 450 employees and only 1.2 percent of its expenses were administrative. The review process featured a high level of information disclosure and opportunity for claimants to tell their stories and achieve a level of closure. Significantly, the congressional body was able to preserve the airlines, which was the primary motivation of the ATSSSA.[73] Scholars do not dismiss Feinberg's take on his own creation but are puzzled by the disparity between Feinberg's satisfaction with the VCF and his claim that it should not be used as a future model.[74]

The VCF was "closed in 2004, having paid over $7.049 billion to surviving personal representatives of 2,880 people who died in the attacks and to 2,680 claimants who were injured in the attacks or the rescue efforts . . . thereafter."

President Obama signed into law the James Zadroga 9/11 Health and Compensation Act of 2010, under which the World Trade Center Health Program was established; later the act was reauthorized for another five years, until 2020. On July 29, 2019, President Donald Trump signed into law a renamed Never Forget the Heroes Act.[75]

One Fund Boston

On April 15, 2013, an explosion during the Boston Marathon killed three people and injured over two hundred. The perpetrators were quickly identified, but there was no public source of compensation for the deaths and injuries. Instead, the Commonwealth of Massachusetts and City of Boston retained the law firm of Goodwin Proctor to organize One Fund Boston as a nonprofit organization.[76] Governor Deval Patrick and Mayor Thomas Menino urged the public to make donations on the NPR radio program *Talk of the Nation* and through social media.[77] Kenneth Feinberg was invited to serve as administrator of the fund with a "mission to distribute the funds fairly, reasonably and as quickly as possible."[78]

Feinberg's initial draft of the payment protocol was shared at public meetings over two days in Boston; feedback resulted in a change to also compensate people who received outpatient emergency treatment but no overnight hospital care.[79] Eligible claimants were those with claims for death and physical injury that resulted in amputation of a limb, hospitalization for one or more nights, or treatment on an emergency outpatient basis at one of the Boston area hospitals. There was no adjustment for economic loss or emotional distress. Feinberg chose a hospital visit as a proxy for eligibility, because the claimant pool could have otherwise included everyone at the marathon (and even beyond). Further, his protocol avoided in-depth, fact-specific, and time-consuming administration. Claimants could submit a personal statement and could request a meeting with Feinberg (meetings were held between June 15 and 25, 2013). Claims were accepted for one month (May 15 through June 15, 2013); payments commenced on June 30, 2013. Table 8.1 lists the initial claimant payments as of June 28, 2013.

As Table 8.1 reveals, approximately $61 million was distributed in the first seventy-five days to the families of the four deceased (including the police officer shot by the perpetrators of the bombing) and more than two hundred other individuals. The payments were a charity gift without a liability waiver (adopting a different approach to that of the 9/11 VCF, in which accepting payment meant waiving the right to sue in court). An advisory panel of survivors was formed to guide distribution of the remaining funds.[80] In July 2015, the fund completed its distribution of over $80 million to over two hundred victims and their families.

Table 8.1   Payments to victims of the 2013 Boston Marathon bombing

Injury	Number of victims	Allocation per victim
Death claims	4	$2,195,000
Amputation of two limbs	2	$2,195,000
Amputation of one limb	14	$1,195,000
Hospital overnights		
32 or more	10	$948,300
24–31	5	$735,000
16–23	5	$580,000
8–15	15	$480,000
3–7	16	$275,000
1–2	18	$125,000
Outpatient ER treatment patients	143	$8,000
Total	232	$60,952,000

Source: City of Boston, "One Fund Boston Administrator Ken Feinberg Distributes Nearly $61 Million Among 232 Eligible Claimants," July 1, 2013, http://www.cityofboston.gov/news/default .aspx?id=6211.

An additional $1.5 million was set aside to "continue to provide personalized care and support."[81]

From a structural perspective, plaintiff counsel to those injured faced uncertain terrain on sources of compensation for their clients. The One Fund Boston was limited (although vastly more generous than funds organized for the tragedies at Virginia Tech or Aurora, Colorado).[82] The terrorists' family was poor, the organization that ran the marathon had capped liability, and government officials had sovereign immunity,[83] so lawyers considered other possible defendants to sue in civil court, like the makers of the pressure cookers and ball bearings used in the explosive device. The Massachusetts Bar Association called on Massachusetts Attorney General Martha Coakley to give victims and other people injured in the bombing a chance to appeal the One Fund Boston's awards or at least to apply for some of the subsequent donations. Feinberg responded, "I must say the goal here, to distribute $60 million in roughly 60 days at no cost to the claimants, with 100 percent of the $60 million going to the victims, requires rough justice. . . . We cannot start evaluating individual claims and individual circumstances without slowing down the process, at great cost, to evaluate medical records."[84] Efficiency dominated the compensation process, with equity paying an obvious price. Future research evaluating the victims' perceptions of the process could shed light on the desirability of such trade-offs.

Israeli Policy—Hostile Actions Casualties

In contrast to the United States, where injuries from terrorist acts may or may not be compensated, Israel's Benefits for Victims of Hostilities Law, 5730-1970), establishes the rights of casualties of "Hostile Actions" and their family members to monetary remuneration and other benefits, including monthly payments, rehabilitation, annual grants, and lump-sum grants. "Hostile harm" is defined by law and generally refers to a harm caused by enemy troops of a state or entity hostile to Israel, so long as the act leading to harm stems from the Israeli-Palestine conflict or is executed by a terrorist organization. The National Insurance Institute of Israel is the administrative body responsible for receiving the requests for benefits and deciding on the amounts and benefits provided. Legal proceedings—first before an administrative committee and later before labor courts—can be taken if disagreement as to entitlement or benefits amount arises. This mechanism assumes the Israeli state bears the responsibility to compensate victims and family members of all acts caused by hostile states or terror organizations and that no other entity will compensate victims for their loss. Despite the broad state responsibility for the compensation, the insurance institute was criticized for its bureaucratic processes. Note that Israel's Property Tax and Compensation Fund Law (15 L.S.I. 101 [1960/61]) separately provides compensation for terrorism-caused property damage.[85] Considering the contrasting compensation policies of Israel and the United States, how would you advise another country to frame and decide among available options?

Key Framework Issues in Claims Facilities

The formation of a claims facility is often determined by the nature of the triggering event and its associated paradigm for determining liability and distribution.[86] In the case of a natural disaster, such as Hurricane Katrina, the model is primarily a welfare design, to provide a social safety net to ensure basic needs are met in a time of crisis. The government is the likely administrator and funder. In contrast, if a disaster is reasonably anticipated, some degree of preventive land use policy or insurance may ameliorate the damage of future events. Whether before or after the event, it is the taxpayers (local or national) who bear the burden.

Salient factors and claimant priorities are different under a tort model, in which a court can determine the responsible party, assess damages to compensate the victims, and punish the defendants to deter future bad behavior. Claims facilities are one means of attempting to improve administrative feasibility in mass tort situations. Menkel-Meadow highlights significant factors in claims facility design as including the "nature of the injuries, whether [injuries manifest in] death, long-term disability, latency, medical monitoring, loss of consortium, etc.; the science of causation; the relative number of defendants; the depth of the defendant's pockets; the numbers of claimants; and the fee structures of their lawyers."[87] Another important factor may be the opportunity of the injured to tell her story to an authority, have her damages and injuries acknowledged, and confront the wrongdoer.

Terror attacks complicate the picture, because these are public disasters with low predictability and, although manmade events, are generally not caused by parties that can realistically be sued for damages. This circumstance calls for the adoption of a mechanism similar to the natural disaster paradigm. In these cases, there may not be resources to compensate the injured. The victims of the USS *Cole*, 1993 World Trade Center, and Oklahoma City attacks received no compensation. In contrast, Congress authorized $6 billion (taxpayer funds) for payment to the families who lost their loved ones on 9/11 to forestall mass litigation that could have put the airline industry out of business. The compensation for victims of the Boston Marathon came from private donations.

The stakeholders and parties of a claims facility include individuals, businesses, insurers, government agencies, counsel, the media and the public, and the facility's organizer—whether a court, legislature or executive agency, nonprofit or private entity. Often the tort model of determining liability, assessing damages, and providing compensation is employed; the more the facility involves the court, the more transparency is expected and the more legitimacy is accorded.[88] If an individual is appointed administrator, he may have the flexibility to decide the procedural and substantive criteria for claimant eligibility and compensation and the fund's accountability with regard to the parties and the public. Such flexibility may be cause for concern if the decision-making criteria are not transparent, as some perceived in the GCCF fund.[89]

Goals

In most cases, there are multiple desirable goals, and the facility administrator will need to determine the priorities of the stakeholders and assess the trade-offs among them. The primary tension is among administrative feasibility, efficiency, and equity. Equity calls for fair compensation (claimant eligibility and compensation criteria), a fair process by an independent neutral administrator, and a balance of privacy and transparency. Efficiency calls for low transaction costs for claimant and administrator, ease of filing a claim (but without fraud), concern for the number of claimants (trying to include only those eligible), speed of process, and finality of the process (as opposed to right of appeal within the administrative process or to a court).[90]

Who decides among these tensions? Francis McGovern notes the challenges faced by administrators and believes systems operate best when the court and a neutral claims administrator cooperate. "The more available the data about the potential ramifications of resolving a tension one way or another, the more ex ante, rather than ex post, those tensions are resolved, the more transparent the decision-making process can be. And the more considered the expectations of the parties and the more accountable the implementer, the more likely the design of the distribution process could approximate a second-generation dispute system design."[91]

The identity of the facility designer, her relationship and engagement with the stakeholders, and the resources available for the design process and claimant distribution will significantly shape implementation of the priority goals for the system. Kenneth Feinberg, whose experience designing and administering claims facilities spans nearly five decades and a diverse array of circumstances, highlights three elements critical to design: substantive criteria on which claimants are eligible for relief, procedural criteria for filing a claim, and practical mechanics for processing claims.[92]

Processes and Structure

The processes described in this chapter are both facilitative and evaluative. Administrators sought to balance privacy with transparency. Legitimacy derives from a fair neutral, fair process, and fair outcome, most often rendered by a court. Substantive due process covers (where applicable) a determination of liability, eligibility, and payment criteria. Procedural due process aims for accessibility and transparency of claim filing, efficient claims handling (speed of process and finality, minimized transaction costs for claimant and administrator), and a respectful claimant experience (e.g., choice of process, opportunity to be heard, and opportunity to confront the wrongdoer).

Claims facilities for resolution of dispute streams are provoked by urgent, unanticipated events. However, lessons from one experience can inform system design structure or options for future prevention through public policy around natural disasters and possibly tort reform. Optimally, one would compare factors contributing to equity (fair outcomes, eligibility, and payment criteria) and

Las Vegas Shooting

Following the Las Vegas shooting of October 1, 2017, the Las Vegas Victims Fund gathered $31.4 million from private contributions and distributed it to over 500 claimants, in three categories: families of the 58 killed or with permanent brain or physical injuries, those injured and admitted to hospitals before October 10, and those injured and treated before October 10. Kenneth Feinberg collaborated with the National Center for Victims of Crime in administration of the process, which was completed in March 2018, in accordance with their highest priority: "collecting and distributing money as soon as possible."[93] In addition to the distribution, a number of fee-only financial advisors from across the country volunteered to offer free financial advice to recipients of fund payouts, coordinated by the Las Vegas Survivors Project at the Investor Protection Clinic at the William S. Boyd School of Law at the University of Nevada at Las Vegas. What distinguishes this process design, and what lessons might be usefully drawn?

fair process (transparency, independent neutral, and sources of legitimacy) to capture the metrics of substantive or procedural justice and administrative due process.[94]

Evaluation

System design for claims facilities would benefit from more empirical research on stakeholder perspectives (equal treatment, satisfaction, perception of fairness, claims administrator neutral and stable) and observed characteristics (percentage of claimant participation, finality, objective and transparent decision-making criteria, administrative costs, processing time, fraud prevented), supplemented with process tracing of how the system was designed, by whom, and according to what goals.

Conclusion

Claims facilities are an effort to provide justice on a large scale. Key takeaways from scholarship[95] and the administrative structures used in these cases include the following:

- If a tort action is the trigger, more coordination between the relevant court and administrator is critical to demonstrate legitimacy of the process and outcomes; claim consolidation and aggregation may ease the administrative pressure.

- The greater the number of claimants, the more important the transparency of the structure and process for setting claim eligibility and payment criteria.

- The longer the claim period and the smaller the compensation fund, the more likely that claimants will opt for efficient administration over customized amounts.

- The more complex the injury and damage, the more likely that claimants will benefit from process options: quick, fast, and accessible (without counsel) may be preferred by many. Claimants with more evidence and time may prefer a more tailored process.

- Whether a tort, a terrorist event, or a natural disaster with some human culpability (e.g., a government agency with jurisdiction to help prevent the disaster), claimants may deeply value an opportunity to express their losses, be acknowledged by someone in authority, or confront the responsible party—even if that expression does not yield higher compensation.

9   COMMUNITIES AND JUSTICE

A FOURTEEN-YEAR-OLD TRESPASSES on private property and spray-paints graffiti on a single-family home. The boy lives in a nearby low-income housing development; his single mother recently took a night-shift job, and he has been home alone at night. The resident, an older woman living alone, is alarmed and calls 911. The police arrive and detain the boy, and the case is referred to juvenile court. The boy admits to the trespassing and vandalism, his first offense. How can the juvenile court judge address this problem? Or consider this situation: A dog is territorial and has a loud bark; the person next door works the night shift and sleeps (or tries to) during the day. After many complaints, the two neighbors almost come to blows. Does this case belong in court?

Communities can form their own justice systems outside the traditional state-operated civil and criminal courts. The term "community," which usually refers to groups of people living in proximity, can also apply to people with shared characteristics or interests (retired, monastic, academic, scientific) or to people or countries that share a common history or social, economic, political, or policy preferences.[1] Community dispute systems handle conflicts among family members, neighbors, or within or among businesses or nonprofit organizations. These systems predate more formal structures; people have long used decentralized village practices involving elders and respected local residents for resolving conflict—for example, over property or grazing rights. Communities create systems outside of, substituting for, or augmenting formal legal structures that both build and enforce the ties of social capital, including trust and cooperation.[2]

Issues to consider are as follows.

- How can community mediation be used to pursue reconciliation through restorative justice rather than retributive or deterrent justice through punishment or damages?
- How do some fields of business use DSD to settle disputes within their communities?
- What can DSD offer communities of residents looking to address entrenched problems like homelessness and unmet mental health needs?

Community Mediation

Community mediation was practiced in traditional societies around the globe long before its current Western models.[3] To address disputes over mates, family, property, status, and land, people living in social groups have sought intervenors to help resolve conflict without resort to violence. Examples are the Bushmen of the Kalahari's small-scale and large-group intervenors, Hawaiian Islanders using a spiritual leader to bring together a family, and the Kpelle of Liberia using neighbors and family members in a moot court for small matters not fitted to traditional courts. In modern cities, the Yoruba of Nigeria use a lineage head or elder to mediate and arbitrate; China has a two-thousand-year Confucian tradition of mediators.[4]

In the United States, an eruption of violence and civil unrest in urban centers led to distrust of traditional civil and criminal justice; community mediation originated in the social and political movements of the 1960s to provide residents with the means to resolve their own disputes.[5] Two streams of community mediation emerged: neighborhood justice centers to divert minor civil and criminal matters from the courts, and local organizations to empower and mobilize communities to take control of decision-making, develop leadership, and reduce tensions.[6] These efforts received support from both philanthropists and the overloaded judiciary. Community mediation programs comprise a range of community-based services and activities outside or straddling the perimeters of the formal legal system;[7] the majority offer some type of family mediation, school based or peer mediation, facilitation of public meetings, training and conflict coaching, and restorative justice programs.

By providing an alternative to the state-run system, the original community mediation designers like Ray Shonholtz of Community Boards in San Francisco, California, sought to empower a community to define and determine justice itself and create a system appropriate to its conflicts. Community Boards developed some of the earliest materials for peer mediation in schools and assisted communities in developing these programs.[8] While Community Boards was successful in training mediators and assisting other organizations and the public schools with conflict resolution programs, some criticized Community Boards for failing to prove it had an impact on conflict in the broader community.

Principally using trained volunteers, community mediation programs handle tens of thousands of conflicts per year in the United States.[9] The National Association for Community Mediation offers an overarching definition for the practice:

> Community mediation offers constructive processes for resolving differences and conflicts between individuals, groups, and organizations. It is an alternative to avoidance, destructive confrontation, prolonged litigation or violence. It gives people in conflict an opportunity to take responsibility for the resolution of their dispute and control of the outcome. Community mediation is designed to preserve individual interests while strengthening relationships and building connections between people and groups, and to create processes that make communities work for all of us.[10]

Most programs (85 percent) are run by private (nonprofit or for-profit) organizations; the rest are agencies of local government associated with the judiciary, prosecutors, and probation offices.[11]

Community mediation generally encompasses an array of community-based services and activities aimed at resolving disputes. Typical among them are neighbor-to-neighbor, family, landlord-tenant, youth and juvenile misconduct, petty crime, property crime, small claims, and minor business disputes. (Rarely will domestic violence be pursued through community mediation; such practice is controversial and potentially inappropriate.) Community disputes reflect the friction of humans living in proximity, such as neighbor disputes over noise, pets, parking, and trees or yard care; vandalism, public safety, threats, fights, and other public nuisance; roommate and household disturbances; youth behavior; shoplifting; and other civil or low-level criminal matters. These disputes might otherwise involve police, small claims court, housing court, drug court, or other courts of special jurisdiction. Community mediation allows people to use conflict settlement services for disputes with other local residents outside (or at the perimeters of) the formal legal system.[12] The following sections apply the DSD Analytic Framework to community systems.

Goals

Rather than the retribution or deterrence of criminal justice, community mediation programs may seek to achieve restorative, communitarian, or communicative justice (see Chapter 1). All these forms of justice can be observed in the earliest known practices of community conflict resolution.

Programs using restorative justice seek to heal the rift in a community created by criminal conduct. These efforts can include mediation after a conviction to help offenders understand the impact of their actions on victims, help victims come to terms with the offense and reconcile with offenders, and help both parties reintegrate into the community.[13] Community mediation programs sometimes include victim-offender mediation (VOM, previously called victim-offender reconciliation programs, or VORP).[14]

Programs using communitarian or communicative justice provide community dialogue and deliberation. They may work with local government in upstream DSDs involving deliberative democracy and public-policy dispute resolution.[15] Studies indicate that some community mediation programs in the United States offer services to promote dialogue on important issues of public policy.[16] For example, the Participatory Budgeting Project works with communities to engage the public in allocating local government resources.[17] Communicative, dialogic, and restorative justice share the core idea that discourse is a process through which people may achieve justice,[18] self-determination, and democracy.[19]

The immediate goals of community mediation programs are generally divided into two categories: fair and efficient resolution of disputes and empowering individuals and communities. The first includes diverting cases from the court, providing more efficient and accessible services, reducing case processing costs, improving the image of the justice system, providing a better quality of justice based on the community's own values, and for some cases providing a more appropriate or effective process.[20] The second includes decentralizing control of decision-making, building capacity in community leadership and responsibility, and reducing community tensions.[21]

Stakeholders

The principal stakeholders in community mediation should be the members of the community, which is usually geographically defined. Other stakeholders are funders, such as community foundations, courts, probation offices, prosecutors' offices, counties, local businesses, and charities such as United Way. Stakeholder representatives may serve on the community mediation center's board of directors. A more diverse board of directors in terms of demographics and representativeness of sectors of the community will generally be more successful in building caseload.[22] Stakeholders such as management, staff, and volunteers tend to be highly motivated by and committed to the underlying theory of social justice that inspires community mediation. Disputants are also stakeholders; they may become volunteers within an organization that has assisted them in resolving a dispute.

Funders have substantial power and include referral services like courts. Disputants have less power but do have leverage because community mediation organizations need cases to justify their existence to funders. Ideally, community mediation centers use participatory design processes to engage the public and incorporate their values and sense of justice.

Context and Culture

Community mediation, or consensus-based conflict management, has a long global history. It exists in Native American tribes,[23] among the Maori in New Zealand, in African villages, and across communities in Korea, China, Indonesia, Malaysia, and elsewhere in Asia[24] and Latin America.[25] Increasingly, commentators urge that the former colonial powers and international global governance organizations recognize the legitimacy of justice and conflict resolution systems of indigenous peoples.[26]

For example, Native American and First Nations communities use traditional peacemaking: nonadversarial approaches of conciliation to restore peace and harmony.[27] The "peacemaker" term, which refers both to leaders who play important roles in resolving conflict among tribes and to Peacemaker Courts, dates back to the Iroquois (Haudenosaunee) Peacemaker Deganawida. As the architect of the Iroquois Confederacy that predated North American colonization, he is historically credited with spreading peacemaking practices across the Iroquois, Huron, Mohawk, Seneca, Cayuga, and Oneida tribes.[28] The Seneca Peacemaker Court, established in 1848, hears cases involving Senecas, their families, other residents in their community and outlying areas, and others domiciled on their territory. The Peacemaker Court hears all civil actions, including domestic relations, child welfare, land disputes, and environmental issues. Such disputes may be child protection services and orders of protection as well as restraining orders. Its goal is to maintain children within Seneca Nation boundaries and provide a fair hearing to any person who wishes one nation in accordance with the Seneca Nation Constitution and its laws, ordinances, customs, and traditions.

Religious communities also provide alternative justice systems.[29] For example, in Pakistan and Afghanistan, people practice Sharia law under Islam and religious authorities; this system of quasi-judicial decision-making uses forms analogous to arbitration and processes for divorce outside the state-run civil justice system. Orthodox Judaism provides an alternative forum for family, contractual, and commercial disputes among businesspeople in their faith community. In many religious communities, a design is imposed on the congregation as part of the hierarchical organization of the religious tradition; for example, the Catholic Church exists as a quasi-state actor through the pope and Vatican.

All these cultural contexts shape the nature of processes and how they are practiced. In Asia, the term "mediation" may refer to a practice that people in the United States would describe as med-arb (mediation-arbitration); the community elders provide guidance and exercise more directive persuasion by pressing parties to accept a particular resolution.[30] These contexts also shape legal and human rights—for example, through significant gender differences under religious authorities.

Institutions may also represent culture and context. Communities may form within a particular arena of commercial activity; these commercial systems often use arbitration to settle disputes. Institutions of higher education have developed mediation programs for students, staff, faculty, and members of the community.[31]

Processes and Structure

Community mediation programs may be community based, sponsored by the justice system, hosted by a nonprofit, or supported by some combination of these. To prevent, manage, and resolve disputes, community mediation centers provide services such as conflict coaching, varieties of mediation, conciliation (by phone or visits), victim-offender mediation or reconciliation, school-based conflict resolution, public meeting facilitation, and skills training in communication, facilitation, and negotiation.[32] Mediation designs vary from a single mediator to a co-mediation model of two mediators or a dispute panel (usually of community members).[33] Mediators may be volunteers, employees of the center, or outside contractors. Mediation models may be facilitative, evaluative, or transformative. Mediation may be voluntary or through mandatory court referral. Usually, the mediation occurs at the center's office, in a community setting like a public library or church, or in small claims court. System designs may provide referral to a rights-based alternative either through a peer advisory panel or private advisors or through binding arbitration. Disputants may resort to courts should mediation fail or be deemed inappropriate.

The formal legal system will often preempt community mediation if a claimant resorts to court first—for example, when a victim of theft reports it to police. There are exceptions for religious organizations: The First Amendment's free-exercise clause may create a zone of protection from external interference—for example, in financial relations. Native American systems of justice and traditional courts provide an alternative to the Anglo-American judicial tradition for culturally

informed understanding of marriage and other relationships.[34] Sometimes disputants may not share the cultural values of the larger community, yet a community
mediation program will allow them to design their own justice. For example, in
religious systems that do not recognize a woman's rights separate from those of
her husband, a community justice system may engage women volunteers in a
co-mediation model to provide more voice to women reluctant to go to court.
Generally, U.S. designs avoid mediating domestic violence cases; better training in
police departments is increasing appropriate judicial intervention in these cases.

In criminal cases, one incentive to avoid the formal public criminal justice
system is to prevent disproportionate punishments. With the escalation of sentences and one-third of African American men in the United States spending
some time in prison,[35] in some states community justice may be the only way to
avoid a third strike with its life sentence. Community mediation provides a design with the values of the neighborhood; it allows neighbors to implement local
justice. VOM as part of the design is a process that provides interested victims,
primarily of property crimes and minor assaults, the opportunity to meet to address the juvenile or adult offender. VOM programs provide "resources, training,
and technical assistance in VOM, conferencing, circles, and related restorative
justice practices."[36] Ideally, it provides a safe and structured setting in which the
community can hold the offender directly accountable while assisting the victim.[37]

A VOM program may be part of a larger, more comprehensive community
mediation center or may be a specialized program. VOM programs vary in their
relation to the criminal justice system; they may be offered through a diversion
program (after an offender is charged but before adjudication), after adjudication
but before sentencing, or after final disposition and sentencing. For lesser crimes,
a few programs take cases before any resort to criminal trial court proceedings.
Programs are generally voluntary for victims. Consider these questions:

- Do neighborhood justice centers that operate primarily through court
  referrals provide real justice or only "shadow justice"?
- Do they enforce legal rights or undermine them through informal
  processes?

While most VOM programs focus on juveniles, some include adults. VOM has
begun to be used for cases in which the defendant is guilty of serious violence such
as homicide. Because the criminal justice system provides a punishment but not a
structure through which a victim can reconcile with a defendant, advocates argue
that VOM provides a meaningful alternative to or supplement for existing criminal justice; critics counter that it undermines legal rights through informalism.[38]

Community mediation programs collaborate with the traditional justice system by providing mediation services at the courthouse, particularly in small claims matters. Lawyers who are aspiring mediators also seek mediation experience through these programs and court-sponsored small claims mediation programs not affiliated with a community mediation center.

Resources

Community mediation centers are most often organized as nonprofits but may in some cases be embedded as an office or program within a government entity. An ongoing challenge for community mediation is inadequate resources. Resources shape design for both centers and parties; centers obtain resources through donations, fees for services, and contracts.

National organizations such as professional associations for mediators, arbitrators, and lawyers can assist with design, training, standards of practice, and limited grant making.[39] States may provide support by diverting funds from court filing fees or other budget sources to support community mediation programs (as California, Michigan, New York, and Oregon have done).[40] Other financial resources come from community foundations, donations from local businesses or the chamber of commerce, the United Way, and private charitable donations from the community.

Typically, community mediation centers serve underprivileged communities, so civil cases are likely to involve low monetary value such as interpersonal disputes among neighbors, juvenile vandalism, or domestic and family conflict (but generally not domestic violence). Centers may charge fees per case on a sliding scale. Mediation saves the disputants transaction costs in court. Whether the dispute is civil or criminal, disputants may not have the resources to obtain private legal counsel to successfully navigate the complexities of the law. Although disputants may be legally entitled to a public defender in criminal cases, these programs are so underfunded and overloaded with cases that critics claim they do not provide competent representation in many instances.

To survive financially, most community mediation centers in the United States have entered into a contractual referral relationship with the formal legal system, including courts, probation offices, prosecutors' offices, and municipal government; some argue this may co-opt the center, undermining its original purpose.[41] A contract may involve civil, criminal, juvenile, family, or other courts of limited jurisdiction. A national study of community mediation centers found that 50 percent of the centers have formal contracts with courts of law to manage case referrals and program services, 35 percent have contracts with public schools,

27 percent with police or probation departments, 24 percent with health and human services agencies, and 20 percent with other nonprofit organizations.[42] Sometimes VOM programs involving juvenile or adult criminal matters receive support from U.S. Department of Justice block grants.

Community mediation depends on substantial collaboration across organizational and sectoral boundaries. Human resources include the board of directors and volunteers, with some limited paid management and staff usually operating on a shoestring budget. These programs rely on a diverse set of public and private partners for case referrals, funding, and logistical support. Local higher education institutions may provide student interns and professional volunteers. Community mediation programs also manage extensive networks of informal interorganizational relationships to share information, clients, staff, and volunteers.[43]

Success and Accountability

Like other ADR programs, the typical measures for community mediation's success are dispute resolution rates; satisfaction with the mediation process, mediator capacities or behaviors, and outcomes; fairness; durability of resolutions; cost and time efficiencies; and impacts on volunteers and communities. Most efforts to measure the effectiveness of community mediation programs address only limited goals and appear only in the unpublished evaluation reports rather than published academic scholarship.[44] Research on agreement rates, cost efficiency, and time efficiency can capture how efficiently mediation programs dispose cases, but it fails to shed light on other valuable aspects of mediation, such as the restoration of relationships between disputants and the practices of accepting others' values and perspectives. Whether mediation programs improve a community's capacity for resolving problems is an intractable question to answer.[45]

Looking at the research on mediation more broadly, we see that evaluators generally measure the success of mediation by the proportion of cases that reach agreement; many studies have reported that more than two-thirds and up to 81 percent of cases referred to community mediation concluded in full or partial agreements.[46] If the center has resources to collect data (and most do not), researchers assess participants' evaluation of mediation programs, the durability of agreements reached, and the cost and time efficiency in cases referred to mediation. Regardless of disputants' positions and results, participants have consistently shown high levels of satisfaction with the mediation process, which range from over two-thirds to 95 percent satisfied. Notably, satisfaction levels with the court process are much lower.[47] Similarly, there were higher average levels of satisfaction with specific mediators (ranging from 88 percent to 100 percent) contrasted to that with judges (ranging from 44 percent to 64 percent). More participants were satisfied with the outcome of mediation (between 73 and 86 percent) than with judge outcomes (between 33 and 67 percent). The great majority of mediation participants found mediation to be a fair process and generally fairer than the court process.[48] A body of research on VOM in particular demonstrates positive contributions to reduction of recidivism.[49]

Studies conducting follow-up interviews with disputants who concluded cases with mediation agreements in small claims courts report that mediation programs produce durable agreements that parties implement and that these agreements reduce the occurrence of new disputes among the same parties.[50] Parties were almost twice as likely to implement and comply with mediated settlements as court judgments.[51] In addition, compared with court processing, mediation produced lower average costs and shorter duration in case processing.[52] However, other goals of community mediation—specifically the nature of programs as community programs rather than simply alternatives to the court system—have received less attention. For example, a study of the diversity of boards of directors examines its impact on case referrals,[53] but little is known about the extent to which board composition represents all the voices in a community. Neither has research compared the nature and extent of collaborative or interagency activity in communities that have community mediation programs with that of communities without such programs. While research shows community mediation programs can provide services like facilitating participatory decision-making, it is unclear what impact such services have on the community.

Community mediation in nonprofit programs is generally not very transparent. As is true of ADR more broadly, mediation settlements are generally not public decisions; mediation is confidential. Moreover, mediation usually produces no precedent; although arbitration awards might produce precedent, they, too, are generally confidential. Moreover, most community mediation centers handle few arbitration cases. More research is needed to evaluate programs and outcomes and provide guidance for best practices.

Business Communities

Some business communities use consensus in decision-making to achieve stability and predictability in long-term business relationships. The diamond and cotton industries provide examples of democratically designed systems in which the contracting parties have opted out of both the traditional civil justice system and third-party ADR providers.[54]

The New York Diamond Dealers Club (DDC) is a private organization with more than two thousand members.[55] Membership provides standing in the world diamond community and is available only to those with certain minimum experience. Comprising authorized bulk purchasers of rough diamonds—manufacturers, wholesalers, and brokers in the U.S. diamond industry—the DDC elects representatives to its board of directors. Lisa Bernstein describes its dispute system as "an elaborate, internal set of rules, complete with distinctive institutions and sanctions, to handle disputes among industry members."[56] This private arbitration system uses mandatory, prearbitration conciliation; Bernstein reported that, as of 1992, approximately 85 percent of the 150 disputes submitted annually settled in conciliation, a settlement rate similar to most court programs. The DDC uses procedural rules for arbitration "structured to give the parties control over the dispute resolution process and to create financial incentives to settle."[57] While DDC members are obligated to use the system, it is sufficiently well designed that nonmembers voluntarily use it to avoid the transaction and reputation costs incurred by using the courts.[58]

The system's first step is a fact-finding by the DDC's floor committee of club members elected to two-year terms. If the committee determines there was a material issue of fact, the dispute goes before the board of arbitrators (again consisting of members elected to two-year terms). Proceedings and awards are confidential, and the arbitration fee is small. The arbitrators allocate fees and expenses of arbitration and can decide to refund the fee. Parties can appeal to a five-arbitrator board of elected members who have not heard the original case. The filing fee for an appeal is three times the amount of the initial fee, and members deposit funds or security to cover any judgment. Parties also have the right to counsel.[59]

The DCC can refuse to arbitrate claims outside the diamond business, claims involving nonmembers, or claims implicating "complicated statutory rights."[60] Moreover, the DCC may refuse to arbitrate on grounds of forum non conveniens if the claim is burdensome or inconvenient. If the DCC declines to arbitrate, the parties could resort to court.[61] The representative structure of the DDC permits those affected by its DSD to influence the design's structure, with the resulting process being fairer and more balanced.

The cotton industry has also negotiated use of arbitration in a private justice system, replacing the public legal system with a venerable system of private commercial law. It handles disputes over raw and manufactured cotton products and shipping. This system is governed by trade rules and arbitration provisions built into contracts for the purchase and sale of cotton between merchants or between merchants and mills. Professional associations within the industry operate through a democratic structure that represents members' interests. There are two main sources of arbitration services in the industry: the Board of Appeals created by the American Cotton Shippers Association and the American Textile Manufacturers Institute, primarily for disputes between merchants and mills, and the Memphis Cotton Exchange Arbitration Tribunal, created primarily for disputes between merchants.[62]

Both tribunals are the result of a quasi-legislative process among the members of the respective professional associations. Members of these associations agree, as a condition of membership, to submit disputes to arbitration and to build arbitration into their contracts. Participation in this system is not mandatory, and contracting parties need not be members of these associations and they remain free to negotiate other terms.

The influence of mutual control over DSD is evident in the procedural rules for these arbitral bodies. For example, the Board of Appeals consists of one arbitrator each, appointed by the president of each, of the two collaborating professional associations, the cotton shippers and the textile manufacturers, on the basis of the appointees' industry experience and reputation for fairness and integrity.[63] The board conducts a paper review of the briefs and documentary evidence, with the parties' identities redacted from all documents. The anonymity is intended to control arbitrator bias toward anyone, although the board does know whether each party is a merchant or mill. Public circulation of the board's written opinions, which include the names of the arbitrators, discourages board members from systematically favoring one industry segment over the other; disputants could observe any pattern and choose arbitration under other industry auspices.[64]

The Memphis Cotton Exchange panel has seven arbitrators, appointed annually by its board.[65] The panel holds oral hearings and permits cross-examination of witnesses but does not publish its opinions. There is a norm of consensus decision-making; from 1944 to 1991, only four of ninety-two decisions were not unanimous. The seven-member constitution of the panel may also constrain arbitrator bias.[66] Both arbitration bodies permit limited discovery and representation by counsel.

One of the reasons the cotton industry system succeeds is that the parties have negotiated detailed, standard, bright-line rules for inclusion in their contracts.[67] Bernstein states that this private legal system works "extraordinarily well," resolves disputes "expeditiously and inexpensively," and keeps transaction costs, error costs, legal system costs, and collection costs low.[68] It also yields an internal body of written decisions that reflect coherent jurisprudence. Decisions are respected and are implemented promptly and voluntarily.

The Nation's Peacemaker

The federal government through the Department of Justice provides support to communities in conflict via its Community Relations Service.[69] The department considers the Community Relations Service its "peacemaker," stating that the service, created by the Civil Rights Act of 1964, "works with all parties, including State and local units of government, private and public organizations, and civil rights groups, and community leaders," to resolve "conflicts and tensions arising from differences of race, color, national origin, gender, gender identity, sexual orientation, religion, and disability."[70] With a cadre of experienced mediators, the Community Relations Service provides conciliation services to assist in reaching mutual understandings and agreements as alternatives to violence in a community. For example, it worked with Martin Luther King and city officials in Selma, Alabama, during the 1965 march protesting voting rights abuse; a day after police beat nonviolent protesters on the bridge into Selma, mediators brokered a compromise allowing a peaceful protest. More recently, it provided on-site coaching and facilitation for community groups in Ferguson, Missouri, when massive community protest erupted after a police officer shot an unarmed black teenager.[71]

Community Public Engagement

Many community mediation centers are leading public dialogue and engagement processes. One example is the Community Justice and Mediation Center in Monroe County, Indiana, which had a contract with the city of Bloomington to address homelessness and public health issues.[72] Bloomington is a small city with about 80,000 residents (of which 48,000 are students at a large public university), located in a county with 130,000 residents. Like many communities, in the decade after the Great Recession, Bloomington witnessed a significant increase in people experiencing homelessness, substance or alcohol abuse and addiction problems, and mental health needs. Businesses and members of the public expressed concerns about safety and public health.

An invited steering committee (of Community Justice and Mediation Center staff, volunteers, board members, and community, local government, and business representatives) collaboratively designed and carried out a three-stage process to address these concerns. Related to the mayor's Downtown Safety, Civility, and Justice Project, the process combined stakeholder dialogues with public engagement. Stage 1 entailed seven different focus groups: people experiencing homelessness, patrons of local businesses downtown, service provider organizations, businesses that were members of the chamber of commerce, the justice system, nonprofits, and city and county local government. Facilitators conducted a storyboarding process with participants in groups of 12 to 18 people (108 total) and a large group discussion that generated key themes for focus.[73]

The community appeared to be operating and supporting a multicounty, regional system to address a geographically large problem related to homelessness and substance abuse. State agency policies did not support mental health services, and state allocations were insufficient. The Bloomington community had insufficient resources; it required more organized collaboration across the public, private, and nonprofit sectors; the faith-based community; and the university. Participants also identified an organized, systematic panhandling group located at specific locations in town, independent from individual, peaceful panhandlers, with high traffic in these locations disproportionately affecting public perceptions of safety and civility. Participants reported public health problems due to human waste and substance abuse paraphernalia in parks, trails, downtown alleys, and the public library.

In stage 2, delegates from stage 1 participated in a large-group representative stakeholder dialogue (thirty-one people); each small-group table mixed representatives from across the focus groups and brainstormed solutions to the problems discussed in stage 1. Attendees voted on and prioritized the most promising ideas, such as building a public bathroom downtown; addressing housing needs, substance addiction, and abuse; establishing a work-release program; and tasking key stakeholders (university, city, county, state, federal agencies, out-of-town business owners, service organizations) to collaborate to address the problems.

In stage 3, the public was invited to city hall for small-group deliberations on proposed solutions from stage 2. The resulting report went to a task force appointed by the mayor, which adopted its findings. In the time since this process concluded, the community and local government have taken steps to implement recommendations. They have opened a detox center, are planning construction of public bathrooms, developed a work release center, created a new city web portal for collaboration, and are organizing and supporting public events in the parks to foster more positive interaction between the general public and people experiencing homelessness or other needs. There is ongoing dialogue among organizations that participated in the public engagement process. This example illustrates how community mediation centers can provide the civic infrastructure and intervenors to address large-scale conflict over policy and assist communities with public engagement in decision-making.[74]

Mediation and Conflict in a Community's Schools

The heart of any community is its children and the institutions that help families raise and educate them. Community mediation centers provide conflict resolution education to enable schools to implement peer mediation programs,[75] offer restorative circle processes in lieu of adjudicative disciplinary processes resulting in suspension or expulsion,[76] and otherwise foster problem-solving skills in the curriculum and administration.

Public schools are also a highly regulated, rights-based environment, which provides an intersection among community mediation programs, school administration, state departments of education enforcing state and federal regulations, and national law. In the United States, students with disabilities have federal legal rights to a free, appropriate public education; to resolve conflicts among students, their parents, and school administrators, there is a legislated dispute resolution process with mediation, complaints to the state agency, and a due process hearing.[77] For the school community, national legislation mandates providing an interest-based process, mediation, for families and school administrators.

However, Nancy Welsh explains that law does not dictate key elements of the system design—specifically whether the mediator practices facilitative, evaluative, or transformative mediation; she conducted in-depth qualitative interviews with real disputants before and after mediation to assess their views and experience. She found disputants valued mediation both for procedural justice and the resolution it provides, including mediator interventions that were facilitative, evaluative, or transformative.[78] Her colleague in this research, Grace D'Olo, found that the state agency's training and evaluation for mediators gradually reflected an institutional bias that influenced mediators to move from a facilitative to a more efficiency-oriented evaluative model to settle cases and reduce the number of due process hearings.[79]

This example illustrates how what happens in the mediation action arena can be shaped by law and rules as independent variables.[80] Here, Congress (a third party) dictated the mediation design by law; however, that law gave state agencies control over how to implement the mediation design.[81] State agencies are responsible for the special education budget in collaboration with public school districts. While it might appear that the state agency is a neutral third party in relation to parents and school administrators, in fact it has an interest in containing costs of educational services. In keeping with Elinor Ostrom's metaphor of institutions as nested, Amy Cohen suggests that we consider analytic scale in DSD, or "how we conceptualize levels of social organization (individuals, groups, institutions, corporations, communities, societies, states)."[82] This also illustrates how a network of institutions and intergovernmental relationships can shape how a community addresses conflict (see Chapter 17).

Conclusion

Community mediation has developed as a field with distinct values and a coherent vision. Hundreds of mediation programs across the United States hear and resolve thousands of varied disputes. Programs have trained thousands of community residents in conflict resolution and provided a volunteer service system. However, the field faces continuing challenges, including loss of a community responsibility focus and community-building values, views, and practices. It risks loss of its volunteer service system perspective, less independence and more co-optation, reduced availability of funding, and less responsiveness to the diverse needs of mediation participants.[83]

Conflict is a natural and ubiquitous aspect of the human condition. This chapter offers one snapshot showing some of the ways different communities have come together to design and implement systems to manage conflict. This arena of DSD reflects both long-standing cultural traditions worldwide and contemporary efforts to design innovative and flexible systems.

PART II

CONFLICT WITHIN AND BEYOND ORGANIZATIONS

10   LABOR RELATIONS

The Birthplace of Dispute System Design

A LARGE LOCAL FOOD CO-OP evolved from a community-run organization to one with a board of directors that effectively delegated all power to a single general manager. The board's role was to review compliance reports from the general manager. Despite many reports and consistent board findings that the co-op was in compliance with policies, major violations emerged. No grievances advanced beyond an initial human resources screen, employees did not receive annual reviews that were a condition of receiving a raise, the vast majority of employees were stuck at minimum wage, and co-op food prices were so high that employees could not afford to shop there. After failed efforts to seek redress from the general manager and the board, employees filed a petition for a union election. As this dispute became public, member-owners showed up at board meetings in large numbers to protest the board's failure to honor collectivist values. They threatened to boycott the co-op unless the board agreed to be neutral in the election. After hiring a labor lawyer who advised union avoidance (union busting), the general manager backed down and agreed to neutrality. Employees voted by an overwhelming majority (over 80 percent) for union representation. Why did employees choose to unionize?

Issues to consider are as follows.

- How are contemporary employment practices changing DSD is labor relations? Can collectively bargained DSDs withstand the economic forces changing the workplace?
- How can we approach collective bargaining through the DSD Analytic Framework?

- How is the public sector form distinct from private sector forms of DSD in collective bargaining?

DSD in Collective Bargaining: The Evolving Workplace

Much of the early DSD literature stems from U.S. labor relations. Before the 1800s, employers set terms and conditions of employment with individual employees under master and servant law in bonded servitude (indentured servants for a period of years).[1] Guilds evolved as precursors of labor unions; however, U.S. courts developed the doctrine of employment at will, under which employee or employer could terminate the relationship for any reason at any time. In the 1800s during industrialization, workers began to unionize.[2] A period of widespread industrial violence against workers followed, during which hostile courts issued injunctions against strikes and refused to enforce arbitration clauses in collective bargaining agreements. Congress created a DSD, the Federal Mediation and Conciliation Service, focused on mediation and grievance arbitration.

Later, in 1935, Congress passed the Wagner Act, or National Labor Relations Act,[3] which protects private sector employees' right to form, join, or assist a union or engage in concerted activity for mutual aid and protection.[4] Administered by a federal agency (the National Labor Relations Board),[5] the act obligates management to recognize and bargain in good faith with the union that a majority of employees elect. Bargaining culminates in a collective bargaining agreement (a contract).[6] The War Labor Board, a DSD created by executive order, sustained in a 1942 statute, and dissolved in 1945, served as the impetus for growth in labor dispute resolution. Through mediation and interest arbitration, the board had the power to settle negotiation impasses and stop strikes. Through rights-based grievance arbitration, it addressed claims of breach of contract.[7] In 1947, Congress passed the Labor-Management Relations Act, or Taft-Hartley Act, which governs the activities of labor unions;[8] it created a framework for judicial review of collective bargaining agreements in its Section 301. These statutes created institutional infrastructure within which private U.S. labor relations DSDs are nested. The Wagner Act and its amendments through the Labor-Management Relations Act mandate good-faith bargaining on wages (salaries, hourly rates), hours (schedules and overtime), and terms and conditions of employment (management rights, no-strike clauses, sick leave, vacation, reductions in force). Mandatory subjects of bargaining also include how to resolve grievances, grievance mediation, and binding or advisory arbitration. Effectively, U.S. labor law mandates collaborative DSD at the firm or industry association level. The negotiating parties themselves design the paradigmatic private justice system: grievance arbitration.[9]

The U.S. Supreme Court shaped a national policy in support of labor arbitration to solve labor disputes through three cases known as the Steelworkers Trilogy.[10] One issue was arbitrability: when is something subject to arbitration and who decides, the court or the arbitrator?[11] In *United Steelworkers v. American Mfg. Co.*,[12] the court held that when a contract has an arbitration clause and a no-strike clause, all grievances must be submitted to the arbitrator unless they are expressly excluded by the contract.[13] In *United Steelworkers v. Warrior & Gulf Navigation Co.*,[14] it held that courts should not prevent arbitration unless it can be said with positive assurance that the contract does not cover the dispute; doubts are resolved in favor of coverage.[15] Last, in *United Steelworkers v. Enterprise Wheel & Car Corp.*,[16] the Supreme Court held that courts generally will defer questions on arbitrability to the arbitrator. The arbitration award need only "draw its essence from the collective bargaining agreement."[17] Together, these rulings achieved a national policy supporting labor arbitration; courts will rarely overturn a labor arbitration award.[18]

However, the unionization rate in U.S. private sector employment has dropped below 7 percent. Political attacks on employees' right to organize and engage in collective bargaining have weakened rules intended to protect labor rights. Business interests argue they face global competition from countries with much lower wage structures, such as China, which has no tradition of or legal infrastructure supporting collective bargaining. Income inequality in the United States is worse than it was before the Great Depression. How should those responsible for DSD shape it within this modern context for conflict between labor and management?

Systems in Private Sector Labor Relations

This section applies the DSD Analytic Framework (Chapter 2) to traditional labor relations in the private sector. The next section examines public sector collective bargaining.

Goals

In labor relations, the major parties to a DSD—labor and management—have both shared and conflicting goals, which are similar across national boundaries. Unions are political entities with a policy agenda; they are also membership organizations with a duty to provide services. They may operate at the national, state, or local level. As political entities, they may seek to influence the legislative agenda and provide policy-relevant research in support of workers. As service entities providing representation, unions seek the best collective bargaining agreement for employees in order to earn union dues revenues and membership support.

Negotiation success aids reelection to their state or federal labor board certification as exclusive bargaining representative. Unions also seek to meet their legal duty of fair representation of individual employees in grievance handling and negotiation; if they fail, they may face liability, weakened power, and a challenge in elections to leadership roles in the union or by a rival union.

Private sector management, in contrast, seeks to minimize labor costs and maximize profit for the board of directors and shareholders. Labor and management may also have shared goals. Both may seek a desirable place for people to work. Both seek competitive salaries to attract the best talent. Moreover, both may seek an efficient and effective way to address workplace conflict to save money and time. These priorities require nuanced choices regarding DSD, depending on whether management wants to avoid unionization or complement existing collective bargaining.[19] There is great variation in organizational cultures for managing conflict at the workplace; both union and nonunion firms value legal advantages and efficiency as benefits of ADR.[20] However, one factor influencing management's choice is the priority it places on improving and controlling workplace relationships.[21]

David Lipsky, Ronald Seeber, and Richard Fincher[22] report the 1997 results of their unique longitudinal survey on Fortune 1,000 union and nonunion companies' use of dispute resolution (mediation, ombuds, fact-finding, peer review, arbitration, minitrials, mediation or arbitration, and in-house grievance procedures). The authors identify two categories of independent variables that shape organizational conflict management choices: environmental factors and organizational motivations. Environmental factors include market competition, government regulation, litigation trends, legal and tort reform, statutory and court mandates, and unionization. Organizational motivations include organizational culture, management commitment to ADR, the champion's role in promoting it, the organization's exposure profile, and a precipitating event. Company conflict management strategies take three forms: to contend, to settle disputes, or to prevent conflict. Contending may be a scorched-earth approach using litigation to suppress workplace conflict or bust a union.

Stakeholders

Stakeholders are labor, management, and their respective constituencies: individual employees; other unions; union affiliates at the local, state, and national levels; union executive leadership; union stewards; management; human resources; in-house counsel and outside counsel; the corporate board of directors; and shareholders. Stakeholder interests are represented directly or indirectly through a representative at the bargaining table and in the grievance procedure. For example, employees facing discipline have a right to a union representative.

Beyond this immediate circle of players and parties to the contract, another circle of interested stakeholders contains other members of the industry through an industry council, multiemployer bargaining association, or professional association. It could also include consumers, taxpayers, and the broader public affected by a strike or labor-management unrest.

Management and labor have distinct powers. Private sector management can usually move the work to another country, shut down the plant, or declare bankruptcy to relieve itself from contract obligations. Depending on economic circumstances, this is substantial power. If management claims financial exigency, it must share private financial information with the union for bargaining purposes; it may prefer to keep this information confidential. Unions, in contrast, have the power to strike, picket, boycott, and generate political support. However, right-to-work statutes weaken the capacity of unions to organize and maintain representation by banning mandatory withholding of union dues from paychecks. Unions work through the AFL-CIO and national affiliates to strengthen labor law.

Management has an additional form of power; it can categorize people doing work as either employees or independent contractors. Consider these questions:

- How does independent contractor status affect a worker's ability to control the design of and participation in a DSD?
- What alternatives do independent contractors have to resolve conflict at or about work?
- How does the widespread disruption of industries through technology (e.g., from working out of a call center to making calls from a worker's home as piece work, or from driving taxis to driving for Uber or Lyft) affect how stakeholders manage conflict?

Context and Culture

The bargaining relationship at a given workplace is nested within its national legal framework. Cultural differences in degrees of hierarchy or egalitarianism, individualism or collectivism, and direct or indirect communication practices shape traditions for resolving workplace conflict. In the United States, while its strong culture of individualism has strengthened individual employee rights through legislation such as the Civil Rights Act of 1964 and the Occupational Safety and Health Act, its weak culture of collectivism has undermined labor unions. In contrast, France experiences national strikes through unions with a stronger capacity for collective action, and German unions have greater voice in policy and the workplace.[23]

Processes and Structure

There are three important nested layers of structures and processes in labor DSD: the legal framework within which collective bargaining occurs, the process for resolving disputes in negotiation over the future contract's contents, and the DSD the parties produce through bargaining to resolve disputes over the existing contract's language. This section addresses the legal framework and grievance arbitration, which is the most common collectively bargained DSD embedded in a contract.

Labor law mandates shared control over DSD, and a grievance procedure is a mandatory subject of bargaining.[24] The procedure allows parties to quickly settle conflicts over contract interpretation and address new and unanticipated issues without resorting to court.[25] Generally, the contract defines what constitutes a grievance or case; the grievance alleges management has committed some breach, violation, misinterpretation, or misapplication of language in contract.[26] Grievance procedures usually cover contractual provisions on mandatory subjects, such as wages, hours, overtime, the grievance procedure, management rights, no-strike clauses, leave, vacations, benefits, seniority, reduction in force, vacancy postings and promotion, discharge and discipline, and job classifications, and sometimes they cover discrimination clauses, workplace safety and health, and subcontracting. The definition of a grievance may also include disputes that arise during the term of a contract but are not mentioned in its language—for example, plant closings, bankruptcy, or charges of unfair labor practice over unilateral changes in terms or conditions of employment (e.g., changing the provider of a health care plan).

Grievance procedures typically consist of several steps progressing to higher levels of management and ending in arbitration subject to limited judicial review. The common progression is informal step, first formal written step, appeal to higher management, and grievance mediation or arbitration using inside or outside neutrals. The informal step usually requires the employee, sometimes with the union steward, to discuss the grievance with the immediate or first-line supervisor and seek to resolve the dispute as early or quickly as possible. The parties settle many grievances at this early step. Traditional management information systems rarely record these resolutions, so it is difficult to measure the true extent of grievances.

If the employee and supervisor cannot resolve the dispute informally, then the grievant must submit a grievance in writing. Parties' positions tend to harden once a grievance becomes formal. Usually, there are time limits within which employees must act relative to the occurrence that gave rise to the grievance or when the employee knew or should have known of the event. For example, an employee should have known about a policy from the date of notice. The first-line supervisor must issue a formal written response within the negotiated time limit. Some contracts provide that if the management representative fails to respond in a timely fashion, the grievance is deemed denied; others provide that it is deemed granted. If the employee or union is dissatisfied with the first-step response, the grievance may move to step two, appeal.

At step two, the grievant generally presents the dispute to officials higher in the organization. In the private sector, the grievance might move from the immediate supervisor to a plant manager. Officials hear the complaint and render a written decision. The employee or union may still appeal, generally within a stricter and shorter time frame.

A complaint may reach higher steps because it has precedent-setting ramifications, major cost implications, or broad application within the firm's operation.[27] Top management and top union representatives participate. Again, the responding official renders a written decision within a limited time. Since the next appeal is usually arbitration, this is often the step at which parties call in legal counsel or regional union business representatives to attempt to settle the dispute. The union typically has the sole prerogative to determine which grievances go to arbitration and has an internal union grievance committee for making these decisions.

The final step in the grievance process is usually rights-based arbitration,[28] which evolved in response to judicial hostility to unions' claims of breach of contract. Arbitration awards (of which about 10 percent are published) now provide the common law of the workplace,[29] specifically guidance and persuasive precedent for similar disputes about contract interpretation[30] and discipline[31] in other workplaces. The Federal Arbitration Act in 1925[32] and state adoption of the Uniform Arbitration Act beginning in 1955[33] forced courts to defer to private systems in commercial settings. Under these laws, there is limited scope for judicial review of binding arbitration. Grounds include fraud, collusion, undue influence, an incomplete or imperfect award, or an award outside the scope of the submission. A more detailed discussion appears in Chapter 11.

The arbitrator, a neutral third party, conducts a quasi-judicial informal hearing, receives evidence from labor and management, and renders a decision, called the arbitration award.[34] The great majority of contracts provide that the award is final and binding.[35] The union's right to representation includes the right to information reasonably necessary to represent employee interests in the grievance process.

However, there is generally no formal discovery or transcript of the hearing or witnesses' testimony. While there is direct examination and cross-examination, there are generally no limits on the scope of cross-examination. Labor arbitrators generally do not strictly enforce rules of evidence (like the hearsay rule) absent the parties' agreement.

Usually, parties select a single arbitrator by naming a permanent umpire or a third-party service provider in the contract, such as the American Arbitration Association or Federal Mediation and Conciliation Service. Sometimes, the parties use a tripartite panel, consisting of one management arbitrator, one union arbitrator, and a neutral. The parties often equally split the cost of arbitration: arbitrator fees, transcripts, and hearing administrator costs. Each party bears its own attorneys' fees, but sometimes a loser-pays clause shifts costs for the arbitrator to the losing party or authorizes the arbitrator to apportion costs.

The National Academy of Arbitrators is the leading policy-making professional organization of labor arbitrators.[36] It emerged as an outgrowth of the National War Labor Board's support for the labor arbitrator profession. In the last two decades, there has been some criticism of "creeping legalism" in labor arbitration through instances of increased delay, use of transcripts and posthearing briefs, and additional study and hearing days among arbitrators.[37] However, with shared power over DSD, labor arbitration generally is perceived as cost effective, fair and balanced, and a good system for substantive dispute resolution.

Designs vary. A minority of contracts specify grievance mediation as a final step before arbitration.[38] Some programs provide for a single outside mediator; some provide for union-management pairs or peer mediation by employees. A minority of contracts feature peer dispute panels as a final step before arbitration. These hybrid structures act as both mediators and nonbinding arbitrators and may save money and keep conflict management in-house.

Resources

The parties to any dispute have different levels of financial resources to support the system. Unions collect membership dues to cover the costs of collective bargaining and grievance administration. Companies earn profits. The human resources supporting the system are the union's administrative hierarchy and its legal and advocacy support staff. Management usually has a human resources management staff and in-house labor relations staff, but often management contracts this work to outside labor relations counsel.

Generally, a grievance procedure exists alongside other employment dispute resolution processes, such as employee assistance plans, hotlines, and internal procedures or external agency processes for addressing discrimination, sexual harassment, workers' compensation, unemployment compensation, and Social Security disability.

Success, Accountability, and Learning

Most grievance procedures do not contain an evaluation component. Service providers like the American Arbitration Association regularly report either voluntarily or pursuant to state law the percentage of arbitration cases that labor or management wins. Companies will publish awards if both parties consent. There is, however, extensive research literature in the fields of industrial relations and human resources management on voice and grievance systems that provides general lessons for DSD.[39] The "exit, voice, and loyalty" theory suggests that voice provides an alternative to leaving a company: the existence of a grievance procedure may contribute to greater organizational loyalty by providing an avenue for employees to be heard, although research results are mixed.[40]

Case Examples in the Private Sector

The private and public sectors differ significantly, according to Elinor Ostrom's description of rules-in-form (on paper) and rules-in-use.[41] Not only do laws differ, but norms (rules or strategies) differ. To illustrate this, examples follow from both sectors.

Private Sector Designs: FirstGroup

FirstGroup, a British transportation conglomerate, expanded into the United States through acquisitions. The acquisition of Laidlaw International in 2007 included sixty thousand yellow school buses serving 1,500 school districts in many states. Unions organized some of the acquired facilities and met over the next few years. FirstGroup's Corporate Social Responsibility policy specified that employees have freedom to associate and collectively bargain. When unfair labor practice charges were made against FirstGroup, it adopted a freedom of association policy and appointed a third-party neutral expert in labor disputes.[42] The policy aimed to protect the rights of employees to speak and associate with each other as part of a union organizing campaign.

In late 2007, Moir Lockhead, CEO of FirstGroup, invited William Gould to serve as independent monitor of FirstGroup's freedom of association policy in the United States. FirstGroup disseminated information about its program through announcements, a letter to employees, bulletin boards, an internet-based training program for managers, a paycheck insert, a DVD training module, and a website featuring relevant forms. The monitor program's goal was to resolve freedom of association complaints, reduce obstacles to free and fair union elections, resolve disputes more quickly, and apply standards more rigorous than those of the National Labor Relations Act.[43]

Unfair labor practice claims can lag in litigation for years. Unions are likely to pursue alternative strategies, including corporate campaigns of public pressure on employers to cease antiunion efforts. The monitor program investigated complaints and reported findings to the company and the complaining party within sixty days of the complaint. The independent monitor would appoint an investigator, gather information, conduct interviews, and prepare a preliminary report. Upon finding a violation of the freedom of association policy, the monitor made recommendations for company action that the company could accept, adopt, reject, or modify.

Over three years, the independent monitor reviewed 372 alleged violations of the policy and issued 143 written reports. Of the alleged violations, 32 were withdrawn and 72 found to be outside the program's jurisdiction. Slightly over half the complaints were filed by employees, the rest by unions. The independent monitor found 67 freedom of association policy violations and made 152 recommendations. The company adopted 51 percent of those recommendations, modified 15 percent, and rejected 33 percent.

The independent monitor program was efficient: on average, complaints were investigated and reports issued within forty-five days. The program was voluntary, emphasized transparency, was accessible to employees, and provided more expansive association rights than the National Labor Relations Act. However, the program had been designed and adopted unilaterally by the company, and some felt that it undermined the representation of employees and was not uniformly supported by senior management. Further, employees and unions felt that the meaning of the policy was unclear and could be misinterpreted.

Overall, the independent monitor program met FirstGroup's need to resolve union organizing disputes. The monitor was distinct from an arbitrator and functioned "more like a 'standing neutral' who is limited to making recommendations to resolve disputes." Clearly, the program process was faster than an administrative proceeding with a formal hearing. "For this reason," Gould concluded, "the FirstGroup IM [independent monitor] Program could be a model for companies with union organizing disputes to adopt."[44]

Private Sector Designs: Grievance Mediation in the Coal Mining Industry

The coal mining industry was one of the first in the private sector to employ grievance mediation to resolve disputes.[45] In the 1970s, labor and management had long-term bargaining relationships in the bituminous coal industry but suffered an eruption of wildcat strikes. One study of the coal mining industry's historically high strike rates found that strikes were more frequent in mines where supervisors were perceived as ineffective at handling grievances or where issues could not be resolved locally between employees and supervisors.[46]

Substantial process delays led both parties to become dissatisfied with the operation of grievance arbitration.[47] Small conflicts—for example, over the theft of steel-toed work boots—escalated into wildcat strikes, which shut down the mine and violated the contract's no-strike clause. Management had the power to stop wildcat strikes by pursuing litigation and obtaining court injunctions ordering employees back to work, but this process was time consuming and antagonistic. The strikes were costing workers, management, and owners money.

In a grievance mediation experiment, outside mediators were on call to address grievances in the mines within twenty-four hours of a grievance. In the experiment, William Ury, a National Academy professional arbitrator and labor mediator with substantial credibility, served as the first grievance mediator. Subsequently, other outside mediators were trained to facilitate conversations among the disputants rather than conduct hearings. If the parties reached impasse, the mediator provided labor and management a nonbinding opinion on the likely outcome should the dispute go to arbitration. In their design of the mediation experiment, Ury, Jeanne Brett, and Stephen Goldberg used an evaluative mediation model, finding that the incidence of wildcat strikes declined after the grievance mediation step was implemented at the immediate supervisor level. Participant surveys showed that parties were highly satisfied with the process, labor and management being equally satisfied, although labor was slightly less satisfied than management with the outcomes.[48]

In the literature, many benefits are ascribed to grievance mediation: parties perceive it as less costly and time consuming than arbitration, it facilitates interest-based rather than rights-based bargaining, neither party relinquishes decision control, it is less formal than arbitration, the mediator acts as a facilitator to reach agreement, and it supports mutual learning. Goldberg conducted longitudinal research on grievance mediation in several settings—from coal mines to manufacturing industries[49]—and found that grievance mediation was interest based, not rights based. Of nearly 3,400 cases between 1980 and 2003, 86 percent settled; of these settlements, half were compromises. Grievance mediation averaged 43.5 days to complete, compared with 473 days for arbitration. Unions and management were highly satisfied with the process (68 percent and 89 percent, respectively). The grievant was less so (47 percent). In interviews of twenty-eight union and twenty-three management representatives, 83 percent said they were more able to resolve grievances through mediation than through arbitration. Respondents reported that the mediation process trained managers to look at all sides of an issue; parties learned communication skills and settled cases earlier in the process.[50] Furthermore, comparisons of third-party neutral interventions in the field of labor relations found higher satisfaction with mediation than arbitration.[51]

Systems in Public Sector Labor Relations

Public employment was initially a patronage-spoils system that transitioned to merit-based appointment and civil service systems.[52] Following the broad adoption of collective bargaining in the private sector in the 1950s, Congress and states extended collective bargaining rights to federal, state, and local government employees, although bargaining laws generally prohibited strikes.[53] Federal and state bargaining laws govern federal civilian and state employees as well as municipal employees such as teachers, police officers, and firefighters. Public sector designs differ in some significant ways from those in the private sector; statutes and case law may limit parties' design choices and narrow the scope of bargaining,[54] rendering certain issues that would be mandatory subjects of bargaining in the private sector to be instead permissive (optional) or illegal (prohibited) topics in the public sector. For example, school hours are usually not a mandatory subject of bargaining in public education. State law may exclude work hours for teachers from the scope of bargaining and limit the range of grievances subject to a grievance-arbitration procedure.

The DSD Analytic Framework and Public Sector Labor Relations

GOALS. Stakeholders in the public and private sectors share many goals for labor costs, wages and benefits, and job security. However, the public sector is much more extensively unionized than the private sector. Public sector employers wish to minimize labor costs to reduce demand on the tax base to maintain political support among residents while providing the expected level of public services. In the public sector, management can contract out public services to the private sector, which has become more common in the last several decades. In contrast to the private sector, labor has more direct political power at all levels of the public sector. Furthermore, public employees are a political constituency active in elections, so the appearance of fairness to employees is an independent political concern.

STAKEHOLDERS. In the public sector, stakeholders vary with the level of jurisdiction (municipal, state, or federal). They include all three branches of government: legislative controls the budget, executive implements policy and manages work, and judicial provides oversight and hires public employees to run the courts. Each government organization is nested in other levels of government and may have network or intergovernmental relationships or collaborative public management relationships with other organizations or agencies in the public, private, and nonprofit sectors.[55] Potentially, any partners or contractors in public work are stakeholders.

A central concern is taxpayers, a powerful stakeholder group who ultimately pay the costs of any contract. Taxpayer groups' influence on bargaining may vary with their distance from the relevant public services and public employees. For example, taxpayer impact will be greater at the local level of government and more attenuated at the national level.

CONTEXT AND CULTURE. Scholars of public administration and management have uncovered a substantial public service motivation within public sector agencies and organizations. The construct has six dimensions: attraction to public policy making, commitment to the public interest, civic duty, social justice, self-sacrifice, and compassion.[56] In an organization populated by people with high public service motivation, the context and culture may be very different from that of the private sector, with resultant effects on public sector bargaining.

Labor and management are locked in a place-based relationship. Management can privatize work or contract it out (hiring a sanitation service, for example, and closing down the sanitation department). However, its power is limited in that it cannot usually relocate work offshore. Labor can mobilize members to influence elections, but union power is limited in that public employees cannot usually strike and ultimately are subject to public budgetary constraints and public law. The collective resources are limited to tax revenues and public goodwill.

STRUCTURES AND PROCESSES. The chief difference between public and private sector dispute resolution is that public employees generally do not have the right to strike.[57] Public employees collectively bargain over new contracts under the aegis of varying state and federal laws. Thus, while private sector designs focus on resolving grievances during the life of a contract, public sector designs also focus on resolving bargaining disputes that reach impasse during the formation of a contract. Legislatures are third parties that design public processes for labor and management to settle bargaining disputes over the substance of contractual terms like wages, hours, and conditions of employment. These designs include creating agencies, state boards of mediation and arbitration, and public employee relations boards.

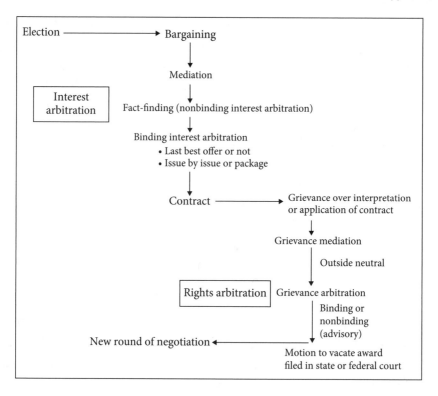

Figure 10.1 Labor dispute resolution processes

To substitute for the right to strike, many states' laws provide for interest arbitration to resolve bargaining impasses over the collective bargaining agreement.[58] Interest arbitration creates a contract, whereas in rights arbitration (grievance arbitration), the arbitrator interprets and enforces an existing contract. Figure 10.1 illustrates the nested dynamic of public sector DSDs.

Structural elements include a time frame mandated by statute, mediation, nonbinding fact-finding, and sometimes binding interest arbitration. These vary widely from state to state. Interest arbitration can take the form of last-best-offer arbitration or broader authority to the arbitrator to craft a compromise, either issue by issue or in an entire contract package. These processes are rarely used in the private sector (except in baseball salary arbitration). Statutes usually establish a decision standard and criteria for arbitrators to apply when evaluating evidence, arguments, and offers for parts of a new contract. Criteria may be the cost of living, the community's tax base or ability to pay, and data on prevailing wages in nearby communities.

Public sector collective bargaining agreements, like their private sector counterparts, have grievance procedures culminating in binding grievance arbitration.

As a result of laws removing subjects from the scope of bargaining, the parties may negotiate a two-tiered grievance definition that permits a grievant to use the lower steps of the procedure but not arbitration. For example, a two-tiered definition might allow an employee to raise any concern regarding management policies through the internal steps but submit only a claim of breach of contract to arbitration. The grievance might move from an immediate supervisor to a department head or from a school principal to the superintendent of schools. It might include a step involving an elected or appointed public agency, such as a board of police commissioners, school board, city council, personnel board, or other public body. Larger employers like the U.S. Postal Service establish their own panels. Some public sector employers have access to state panels such as a state board of mediation and arbitration.

RESOURCES. All unions rely on dues paid by members to fund services for collective bargaining and grievance arbitration. Previously in the public sector, unions could require nonmembers to pay a share of dues related to the costs of representation, called agency service fees. Overruling a long-standing precedent, the U.S. Supreme Court held in 2018 that public sector employees who are not union members have First and Fourteenth Amendment rights that forbid unions from collecting agency service fees through a mandatory payroll deduction.[59]

What impact does the Supreme Court's decision have on grievance-arbitration procedures as DSDs? Consider these questions:

- What if some employees pay for union services and others do not? What impact will that have on the DSD?
- How does the Supreme Court's decision affect the dynamics of negotiation?

SUCCESS, ACCOUNTABILITY, AND LEARNING. Public organizations are more transparent and accountable than private organizations. Data are available on the number of grievances brought to arbitration in some major public organizations like the USPS. Unlike the private sector, public agencies are subject to state and federal freedom of information acts and sunshine laws that require them to provide more transparency in the form of data and records. State and federal agencies may also have statutes both authorizing and requiring the use of dispute resolution. Such statutes have spurred innovations such as shared neutrals programs, in which agencies trade employees who act as mediators. For example, in the public sector, the American Postal Workers Union and the USPS used a co-mediation model in which internal mediators, who were USPS employees, mediated grievances in union-management pairs.[60]

Leading empirical assessments of interest arbitration have found the process effective as a means of resolving public sector collective bargaining disputes. In New York, a law provides mandatory interest arbitration for police and firefighters; researchers compared cases from the first three years immediately after its passage with cases from 1995 to 2007, finding that the period after its passage saw no strikes, a decline in dependence on arbitration, and highly effective mediation.[61] Contrary to stated fears, there was no "chilling or narcotic effect" (negative impact) on voluntary negotiated settlement; the parties did not appear to disproportionately rely on interest arbitration in lieu of bargaining. Moreover, negotiated and arbitrated salary rates were essentially equal.[62] Compared with the private sector, public sector employees tend to win grievance cases more frequently, fewer cases result in long suspensions, and fewer suspension and reprimand cases reach arbitration.[63]

Case Examples in the Public Sector

In the public sector, government may shape DSD through law that varies from jurisdiction to jurisdiction, from the national, state, or provincial to the local levels of government. The following are only two examples of many different DSDs.

Teacher Bargaining and Impasse Resolution in Connecticut

The statutory process for resolving collective bargaining contract impasses for teachers in Connecticut[64] was created by a third party, not by the disputants. The elected Connecticut General Assembly passed and the governor signed legislation creating the DSD. The system, administered by the executive branch, is an effort to balance the interests of labor and management and is also structured to reflect public and taxpayer interests in costs, quality, and children's educational experiences.[65]

The statute mandates deadlines for stages of collective bargaining, aligned with the school district's budget calendar. The parties bargain, mediate, and then enter binding interest arbitration. The statute mandates issue-by-issue last-best-offer binding interest arbitration using either a single mutually agreed neutral arbitrator or a panel of three arbitrators. Two are party arbitrators chosen by each side to advocate for them during deliberations, and the third is a neutral arbitrator chosen by the party arbitrators. Disputants' legal counsel or advocates submit evidence and testimony in support of their final offer on each contract issue. The design also includes decision standards for the arbitrators, who must weigh the evidence in light of these standards to select one party's offer on each issue; they cannot craft a compromise.[66] The arbitrators assemble a complete contract by ruling on each disputed issue and combining it with those issues the parties had reached agreement on before the arbitration.

The standard of review is also noteworthy. The arbitrators issue a binding arbitration award that is subject to judicial review on the grounds listed in the Connecticut Administrative Procedure Act.[67] These standards differ from the grounds for judicial review of arbitration awards under the Federal Arbitration Act or Uniform Arbitration Act.[68] Essentially, it is easier to overturn a binding interest arbitration award creating a collective bargaining agreement than it is to overturn a grievance-arbitration award arising under that contract's grievance procedures.

This system provides an alternative to the exercise of power in impasses that arise in collective bargaining. Teachers do not have the right to strike, but they have a fair and balanced alternative if labor and management fail to reach agreement. However, the system may chill collective bargaining by allowing elected officials to dodge decisions that might be politically unpopular, such as raising public employee salaries. Similarly, it permits labor leadership to dodge decisions cutting public employee salaries and benefits that its own membership might have voted against if members had the power to ratify the interest arbitration award. A wave of state legislation has cut back the scope of mandatory bargaining, eliminating interest arbitration for some state and local employees and giving employers new powers to reject collective bargaining agreements in cases of fiscal emergency. Some states have even repealed collective bargaining for state employees.[69] Nonetheless, systems like these persist in some states.

Labor-Management Cooperation in Resolving Federal Sector Grievances

Congress enacted legislation in 1978 empowering the Federal Mediation and Conciliation Service to assist labor and management by encouraging and supporting joint labor-management activities. These activities, conducted by committees organized at the plant, area, and industry level, are designed to improve labor-management relationships, job security, and organizational effectiveness.[70] Although the federal mediation guidelines[71] specify that a labor-management committee is no substitute for the grievance procedure, the goal of a labor-management committee is to improve lines of communication and workplace climate. In theory, this cooperation can help labor-management relations by involving employees in solving problems, reducing absenteeism and turnover, improving morale, making better use of employee skills and knowledge, and reducing costs.[72] Design elements include statement of purpose and commitment to the committee;

specifications for structure and size; procedure for sharing agendas and minutes; time, place, duration, and frequency of meetings; and selection of permanent members and rotating at-large members.[73] The Federal Mediation and Conciliation Service funds proposals for topics such as use of employee health care plans and apprenticeship in the automotive industry and construction.[74]

In the early 1990s, a large federal civilian employer created an innovative labor-management committee as a formal final step in the grievance procedure before binding arbitration.[75] The Resolution Committee comprised six members, three from labor union leadership and three from management. The committee heard evidence regarding grievances, then engaged in a form of mediation. If there was no agreed settlement, the committee sought to reach a binding decision through consensus. If no consensus could be reached, the union could take the case forward to arbitration. The committee decided cases such as violations of a no-smoking policy, absence without leave in serious weather conditions, misuse of government funds for purchase of personal items, and disciplinary actions.

Seven years in, a focus group of representatives from labor and management discussed their experience with the Resolution Committee. Generally, focus group participants felt the committee had played a valid role as a step in the negoti- ated grievance procedure. The committee's key goals, they said, were identifying problems and necessary modifications to the contract, encouraging decisions at a lower level, and improving union-management-employee understanding of labor-management issues. There was broad support among participants to continue the committee. However, the committee had process problems of in- consistency, scheduling, and confusion in the hearing process due to unknown rules, delays, poor communication, limited feedback, poor documentation of outcomes, closed findings, and difficulty training people to present cases. Recom- mendations from the focus group were that the committee provide feedback to the organization on employment relations issues, ensure a fast turnaround time, publish data on results, improve processes, and disseminate information on the process and lessons learned.

Focus group members also discussed relations among Resolution Committee members. Interactions were sometimes polarized, strategic, and reflected conflict- ing interests. Some members felt that union members discussed and predecided cases, that there were off-the-record deals, and that the outcome was oriented toward concession and compromise. Some felt managers were not well prepared and were intimidated by union leadership. All felt there should be true team op- erations using an interest-based approach toward common goals, perhaps using a secret ballot, to achieve high-quality, ethical, and informed decisions. Focus group participants agreed that the committee had too much on its plate, should be contract based, and should limit its jurisdiction to resolution of disputes and not policy making. They sought training for committee members, who rotated regularly, and noted that the committee needed management's support for implementing and enforcing outcomes.

This case illustrates design issues in a quasi-legislative group process with decision makers aligned with both partisan sides. After implementing most of the focus group's suggestions, this homegrown DSD, built without outside consultants, continued to function reasonably well for more than a decade.

Conclusion

The field of labor relations was the founding discipline for DSD; it provided models for using mediation, interest arbitration, rights arbitration, and consensus building to handle an ongoing stream of disputes, particularly between unions and management. However, in 2017 only 10.6 percent of all employees (private and public) in the United States were union members; this is one of the lowest union density rates among Organization for Economic Cooperation and Development countries.[76] Most U.S. unionized employees work in the public sector: 33.9 percent of public sector employees are unionized compared with just 6.4 percent in the private sector.[77] There is room for considerably more innovation in DSDs for these contexts.

The first two decades of the twenty-first century have seen dramatic changes in the structure of employment, becoming what has been called "the fissured workplace."[78] Large firms have shed traditional employment, particularly in noncore aspects like cleaning, maintenance, human resources, and other service areas. Instead, they have contracted out this work to smaller companies that are in fierce price competition with each other. This dynamic has suppressed wages, contributing to the dramatic escalation in U.S. income inequality,[79] uncertainty, and decreased opportunity.[80] These small contractors do not provide the job security, wages, or benefits of traditional employment.

There has also been tremendous growth in work provided by disruptive businesses like Uber, Lyft, and Airbnb. These companies are creating new business models by attracting people to what is labeled as self-employment, although these businesses control virtually all aspects of the work through standards and conditions of membership. A nascent labor movement to find ways to unionize these workers is underway but faces challenges in the common law definition of "employee" implicitly incorporated into the National Labor Relations Act, which lacks a specific definition of the term. Some scholars urge shared capitalism and a move to employee ownership of enterprise.[81]

There are economic incentives that explain why firms organize themselves as they currently do.[82] However, we may find that the income inequality and uncertainty that current conditions produce give rise to instability and protest on a large scale. New forms of collectivism will be needed.[83] Labor and employment relations scholars are looking at reinventing collective bargaining through mass participation in strikes, bargaining for the common good and good of communities, setting minimum wage at the state and local government levels, campaigning for a domestic workers bill of rights, worker-driven social responsibility, and an increase in labor standards across global supply chains.[84]

IN 1994, THE U.S. POSTAL SERVICE had a significant problem on its hands. Employees filed 25,000 discrimination complaints against the USPS each year, and half of them proceeded to a formal administrative hearing. How could an organization with offices and employees dispersed throughout the country handle complaints at this scale?

As union membership has declined, and with it access to the traditional collectively bargained grievance procedure, employers and consultants experimented with designs for organizational justice. The phrase "dispute system design" emerged from labor-management relations,[1] while business scholars concurrently wrote about "conflict management" for conflict in human resources related to nonunion employment.[2] Conflict management systems in employment vary from those with a broad scope (e.g., organizational ombuds offices and integrated conflict management systems) to those narrowly targeted at one category of claims (e.g., mediation for allegations of employment discrimination or a grievance procedure used for complaints of sexual harassment). Some systems cover claims by both employees (that the employer violated a right or interest) and employers (that the employee owes the employer repayment of unearned commissions or advances of salary). The field of employment DSD includes conflict management, a phrase that characterizes the broad scholarly literature in organizational behavior and social psychology that addresses human interactions within an organization. With the right system for resolving disputes, conflict can actually build social capital at work, enhancing good workplace citizenship behaviors and improving organizational efficiency and effectiveness.

Issues to consider are as follows.

- How do employment DSDs vary across the dimensions of the DSD Analytic Framework, such as goals, stakeholders, and processes?
- How can different features of a workplace dispute resolution system be used to improve outcomes?
- What role does voice at the workplace play in a design's success and the delivery of organizational justice?

The DSD Analytic Framework in Nonunion Employment

The great majority of U.S. private sector employees (over 93 percent) and a substantial majority of public sector employees (over 64 percent) are not covered by a union contract or grievance procedure.[3] The United States has the second-lowest union membership of major countries in the Organization for Economic Cooperation and Development (although there has been a decline in union density among almost all OECD countries over the first two decades of the twenty-first century,[4] and other countries like China have few legal protections for organized labor).[5] Within a given organization, there may be no union, or one subset of employees may belong to a bargaining unit covered by a collective agreement but most others do not. Moreover, an increasing proportion of the U.S. workforce earns a living outside a recognized or traditional employment relationship as temporary employees, independent contractors, or subcontractors of independent contractors.[6]

Goals

Employment disputes historically involve conflict arising out of an employment relationship. Goals of DSDs vary from the broad intent to prevent, manage, and resolve conflict to narrow goals of minimizing or avoiding risk and liability.[7] For conflict management in employment, organizational justice is a major goal of DSD.[8] A variant of procedural justice, organizational justice is about an employee's opportunity to exercise voice about some decision or event in the organization. It also includes interactional justice and reflects how a manager treats the employee. Employees who experience greater organizational justice are better organizational citizens—they tend to be absent from work less and more loyal to their place of employment.[9] Conflict management scholarship also addresses exit, voice, and loyalty theory (the notion that employees have a choice to leave the organization, exercise voice about their concerns and can contest decisions, or remain loyal and accept the status quo for some period).[10] Conflict management goals are efficiency (effective use of scarce resources), equity (fairness and justice), and voice (participation in design and operation);[11] scholars recommend a pluralist approach to balance common and conflicting interests to achieve these goals in conflict management.[12] Organizational justice and DSD provide avenues for voice and equity.

While dispute or conflict resolution scholars view conflict as a constructive force,[13] human resources (HR) managers, responsible for recruitment, productivity, and retention, may seek to move conflict management upstream to avoid or curtail conflict.[14] For an HR department, a healthy conflict management culture helps employees, coworkers, and supervisors address their differences before rather than after a complaint is made. Related goals include improving morale, performance, and employee citizenship behaviors (attendance, teamwork,[15] productivity, commitment), and protecting the employer's image. Good conflict management through voice is a feature of high-performance work systems,[16] which in turn correlate with better firm-level outcomes.[17]

In contrast, generally the goal of in-house counsel is to manage and avoid risk by structuring processes to reduce the likelihood of financial liability in the event of litigation (without regard to ongoing HR management).[18] These two internal stakeholders may have conflicting goals because they focus on different ends of a spectrum, with HR looking at conflict management upstream before a formal complaint while the law department focuses on dispute resolution afterward.[19] However, both sets of internal stakeholders share goals of reducing complaints, transaction costs, and litigation costs in the interest of efficiency.

With respect to the pursuit of justice in terms of legal rights, Lauren Edelman unpacks how employers interpret and respond to broad and ambiguous legal mandates regarding employment discrimination at the workplace.[20] She demonstrates how company agents shape the meaning of law and dilute rights. Employers implement internal DSDs that ostensibly address workplace harassment or discipline. Edelman questions, however, how effective these systems are in preventing and remedying employment discrimination given the structure allocating the power to interpret and enforce the law to organizational leadership.[21]

Stakeholders

There are internal and external stakeholders in employment systems, which may differ among private, public, and nonprofit organizations. Internal stakeholders include management, employees, and their representatives. Within management, stakeholders are the chief executive officer, highest managers, in-house law department, outside counsel, HR department, risk management officers, labor relations manager, front-line or low-level supervisors, and other staff. Outside management, internal stakeholders are both union employees (if any; see Chapter 10) and non-union employees, professionals, and staff. They also are temporary employees, and individual independent contractors who operate under direct and close control (and therefore likely do not qualify legally as independent contractors).

External stakeholders include governing bodies, consumers, contractors or partners, constituents, and beneficiaries. Among these stakeholders are the board of directors, board of trustees, or elected public sector board, council, or commission. In all sectors, members of the public as consumers of products or services are stakeholders. In the private sector, they are shareholders of stock in the company. In the public sector, stakeholders are taxpayers and parents and students in the public schools. Nonprofit organizations have beneficiaries of charitable services; all sectors have contractors, suppliers, and other business partners. More distantly, stakeholders may include industry associations and other similar entities to which organizations might look for best practices or models[22] or with which they may share legislative agendas. For example, the U.S. Chamber of Commerce's legislative agenda is to maintain predispute adhesive mandatory arbitration programs for both employment and consumer claims in the face of repeated bills in Congress to prohibit these programs[23] (see Chapter 12).

Stakeholders have different levels of power in DSD. Unlike employers in union workplaces, where labor and management share control over DSD on mandatory subjects of bargaining, employers in nonunion workplaces have almost complete control. However, employees may have market power, which varies with demand for their services or skills and economic conditions. How stakeholders' interests are represented in the system varies with the organization's conflict management culture. In a nonunion environment, if the organization's primary concern is managing risk, there is usually little express representation of employee interests.

In high-performance work systems, in which organizations seek to prevent and manage conflict, the design process may be more inclusive.[24] Designers may use focus groups and organizational development practices to identify interests of all stakeholders.[25] Workers may find ways to shape the system through collective action. For example, Google workers walked out in protest of developing artificial intelligence for military uses. Managers and workers in high-tech industries provided support for people making claims of sexual harassment as part of the MeToo movement, even though many of them had previously been bystanders to the harassment. People outside the Black Lives Matter movement, protesting police violence against African Americans, and the Never Again movement, advocating for more effective gun control, act as affinity groups. Shareholders and consumers can also play this role of pressuring organizations to develop fairer dispute resolution practices.

Context and Culture

The context for employment dispute systems depends on the location of the workplace, which in turn may determine the national and organizational culture within which employment occurs. In the United States, the employment relationship is highly regulated and varies across the private, nonprofit, and public sectors. An internal organizational employment DSD is nested in external government agencies exercising oversight over employment policy arenas. Moreover, the external agency is nested within the executive branch of the government and the legal framework. Employment policy is thus politicized, reflecting competition between employees and company interest groups for favorable legislation.

Typical federally regulated claims are wage and hour violations, occupational safety disputes, discrimination claims (e.g., race, sex, age, disability), whistleblower retaliation, unfair labor practice charges for violation of federal labor law, pension benefit regulation, and regulation of other benefit statutes (e.g., protecting leave of absence for childbirth or family health care). State-regulated claims include wrongful discharge (a state law tort), workers' compensation, unemployment compensation, negligent supervision (resulting in employee violence at the workplace), and breach of an individual contract. For disputes regarding individual statutory employee rights, an employee might first seek relief through processes internal to the organization; if this attempt fails, the employee might seek redress externally through an administrative agency. Conflict may also arise from alleged violations of administrative policies on performance evaluation, supervision, or assignment of duties, communication problems in the chain of command, or discord among coworkers. These types of claims would likely remain internal to the organization.

For example, in the United States a private sector employee could claim discrimination through a state's fair employment practices agency or the Equal Employment Opportunity Commission, file a tort claim for wrongful discharge in state court, or claim federal whistleblower protection. In the public sector, employees may appeal to an external civil service review board or teacher tenure system. The National Labor Relations Board and state boards of labor relations all protect employees from dismissal in retaliation for collective union, or what is called "protected concerted activity," subject to administrative appeals in federal or state court. In other countries with more collectivist cultures, the workplace may reflect less structured practices. In a community with traditional community mediation, people may appeal to elders rather than challenge superiors at work.

In the workplace, cultural and experiential differences may give rise to conflict arising from implicit bias based on race, ethnicity, gender, disability, and age.[26] Implicit bias entails unconscious or unintentional discrimination. Elayne Greenberg has proposed a multi-intervention reconciliation-focused dispute resolution system design that incorporates the values of peace reconciliation related to restorative justice, entails training in implicit bias to foster mutual understanding, and includes mediation.[27]

Processes and Structure

Important structural features in employment DSD are the nature or sequence of interventions, employee due process protections, whether use of the DSD is voluntary or mandatory, timing, and the quality and characteristics of mediators, arbitrators, or other neutrals. Employment designs use many different interventions or combinations of processes, such as conflict coaching, interest-based negotiation, early neutral assessment, fact-finding, peer panels, mediation, and binding or advisory rights or interest arbitration. These processes may be nested in an ombuds program or integrated conflict management system, or they may exist independently and in parallel. For example, the USPS uses union grievance-arbitration systems, employee assistance plans (with coaching and referral to outside psychological and social services), an HR system for investigating workplace injury for a quasi-judicial workers' compensation claim, a nonunion administrative grievance process with mediation for those employees not covered by a union contract, a confidential sexual harassment grievance procedure, and a hotline or other confidential whistleblower procedure. Halliburton (formerly Brown and Root), a large nonunion construction company, has an adhesive, or mandatory, binding arbitration provision for dismissal cases *after* mediation.[28]

Sometimes dispute resolution programs exist in a silo, as an isolated program with dedicated staff within the organization. Alternatively, an employer with unilateral control over design may insert a predispute mandatory arbitration clause in its personnel manual[29] as its only dispute resolution program. Within the dispute resolution system, the boundaries of subsystems depend on whether the workplace is solely nonunion or the subsystems coexist with a union grievance procedure.[30] Solicitation of grievances can be a mandatory subject of bargaining. However, as discussed in Chapter 10, current federal labor law allows employees to file individual discrimination complaints independently from the union grievance procedure; the law is in flux, and individual rights may be subject to negotiated waiver.[31]

Corinne Bendersky suggests that a system is complementary when its individual components interact to mitigate the limitations of a single component.[32]

One design brings together the subsystems in a single point of reference: the ombuds office.[33] The ombuds program at the Massachusetts Institute of Technology is considered a model. The office provides a confidential, independent, neutral channel of communication for all MIT employees. The ombuds listens and provides information about MIT policies, employee options, and where employees should file formal claims, if necessary. The ombuds provides informal, confidential, voluntary dispute resolution services but does not investigate, arbitrate, or adjudicate claims.

The incentives and disincentives for using a system depend on its structure. Halliburton established an early program viewed by many as a forward-looking model, despite its predispute binding arbitration provision.[34] Created by the company's law department after considering comments from employees and managers, the system's internal elements were an open door policy, listening, discussion of options (or conflict coaching), internal mediation, internal fact-finding, and an informal ombuds who reported to HR. Managers were given conflict management training. An employee with a substantive legal claim had external options for dispute resolution, including mediation and arbitration. Halliburton provided up to $2,500 reimbursement for an employee's attorneys' fees, making arbitration more accessible. This provision is noteworthy because in many predispute mandatory binding arbitration plans not only do employers not provide employees with financial resources for legal assistance but they use cost shifting as a strategy to avoid risk and suppress claims. For example, companies might require that employees pay for certain costs of binding arbitration, such as filing fees, hearing room fees, arbitrator fees, or even the employer's attorney's fees if the employee loses. The risk of these costs creates a disincentive for an employee to file a claim.

The employer's internal system will interact with external federal and state structures according to its design. For example, if the employer has a voluntary mediation program, that will not supplant the formal legal system (it will merely supplement or precede it). However, an employer's predispute binding arbitration program may effectively bar access to the formal legal system, including access to a civil trial, a class action, or even the court of public opinion; it will also dramatically reduce the scope of judicial review in any subsequent appeal.

Resources
The financial resources that support the system depend on who pays for the system and its goals. A company's HR department may support a dispute resolution system through programs like ombuds, inside peer mediation, or inside peer panels. As Halliburton and the USPS do, companies may provide conflict management skills training for managers and supervisors, pay for outside mediators

and arbitrators, and subsidize employee attorney's fees. Alternatively, the employer may contract out its program through external mandatory binding arbitration administered by a third-party dispute resolution service provider. The American Arbitration Association is such a service provider, and it enforces the Due Process Protocol for Mediation and Arbitration of Statutory Disputes Arising out of the Employment Relationship, which suggests that employer and employee should share in payment for the arbitrator. However, courts have recognized that arbitrator fees may be so prohibitive that they effectively deny employees access to justice.

Success, Accountability, and Learning

William Ury, Jeanne Brett, and Stephen Goldberg suggest four criteria by which to judge the success of a workplace DSD: transaction costs, satisfaction with outcomes, effect on the relationship, and recurrence.[35] Generally, companies in the private sector are not transparent about dispute resolution. There is reason for this: employment disputes can hurt a company's reputation. Employers seek to avoid class action litigation. The State of California has mandated disclosure of employment arbitration data, but the mandate has met with mixed success. Public sector systems are governed by state and federal freedom of information acts and are much more transparent, but even these data are exempt from disclosure if they qualify as personnel files or other information that, if disclosed, would amount to an invasion of privacy.

When external public agencies invest taxpayer dollars in DSDs, evaluation helps provide accountability to the public. For example, in 1995, the Massachusetts Commission Against Discrimination agreed to adopt a protocol for resolving discrimination claims through mediation and arbitration.[36] This voluntary, fee-for-service ADR program required parties to have legal representation.[37] Mediators used facilitative and directive strategies.[38] In 2000, Thomas Kochan, Brenda Lautsch, and Corinne Bendersky published the results of a three-year study of the program.[39] The study compared ninety-five mediation cases using the new protocol with fifty-six traditional cases and concluded that the program showed promise;[40] for example, 63 percent of those who chose mediation reached a settlement compared with 21 percent for those in the traditional process.[41] Participants expressed a higher degree of satisfaction with the process than with the outcomes: 63 percent of claimants and 77 percent of supervisors said they would use mediation again, while 50 percent of claimants and 68 percent of the supervisors were satisfied with the outcomes.[42]

Unfortunately, very few employer systems incorporate evaluation components. Employers give priority to using resources to run the system; it is rare for them to invest in evaluation. When intervening to examine the DSD and evaluation system, dispute resolution professionals need to seek out information by asking questions like the following.

- What are the DSD's reporting structures? Is reporting mandatory?
- Who or what office maintains records?
- How does the system protect confidentiality? Are surveys confidential?
- How does the system assess trust and use by those whom it should reach?
- Is there zero tolerance for threats, violence, and racial, religious, ethnic, or gender-based slurs?
- Do conflict management professionals engage in reflective practice—that is, is self-evaluation taking place?
- In large organizations with multiple geographic locations, how do conflict managers coordinate and maintain consistent norms and practices?
- What happens to the DSD when organizations merge or change?

The conversation about justice (see Chapter 1) also seems absent from much of the work on DSD and organizational conflict management. Organizational justice researchers have identified four factors of organizational justice—distributive, procedural, informational, and interpersonal dimensions—to explain perceptions of fairness with organizational processes.[43] However, much organizational justice research looks at the relation between a disputant and a neutral or higher-level decision maker, not at the relation to the other disputant.[44]

The following case study about equal employment opportunity mediation at the USPS examines a system design that encompassed the most comprehensive empirical evaluation ever conducted at the time (1994–2006), and one that explored dimensions of organizational justice. Although the USPS is a unionized public employer, equal employment opportunity claims are not subject to collective bargaining, and the mediation system it implemented functions as a useful model for nonunion environments.

Mediation System Case Study: The USPS REDRESS Program
The USPS Resolve Employment Disputes, Reach Equitable Solutions Swiftly (REDRESS) program shows how mediation can help manage workplace conflict in a large, unionized organization. The program had its limits: it applied only to complaints of discrimination, not workplace conflict generally. Nevertheless, by 2000, REDRESS was the world's largest employment mediation program. The twelve-year research collaboration between the USPS and Indiana University's O'Neill School of Public and Environmental Affairs gave the field of conflict

management its most comprehensive quantitative evaluation of an employment mediation program's organizational impact, key results of which we discuss in this case study.

The Analytic Framework and the REDRESS Program

USPS STAKEHOLDERS AND CONTEXT. Since the Postal Reorganization Act of 1970, the USPS has supported itself through the sale of postal products like postage stamps. As an establishment that serves every community in the United States and reaches internationally, its external stakeholders include the broadly conceived public. The USPS is also a large, civilian, unionized employer. The National Labor Relations Board, which primarily oversees private sector labor relations, has jurisdiction over the USPS, which has at least seven collective bargaining units. Thus, its internal stakeholders include employees, their elected representatives and union leadership, managers in each region and function, senior leadership and board of governors, the Postal Regulatory Commission, and contractors. The REDRESS program was not part of the collective bargaining process and provides a DSD model that applies equally to a nonunion employer.

At the inception of its mediation program in 1994, the USPS had over eight hundred thousand employees and was one of the world's largest civilian employers. The USPS created REDRESS for individual employee complaints of discrimination arising under federal equal employment opportunity laws, including Title VII of the Civil Rights Act of 1964,[45] the Americans with Disabilities Act,[46] and the Age Discrimination in Employment Act.[47] Under relevant law pertaining to federal employers, the USPS addressed equal employment opportunity complaints internally for the first two stages: inquiring into an informal complaint and investigating a formal complaint. Thereafter, in accordance with law and regulation, the case went to the Equal Employment Opportunity Commission. Equal employment opportunity complaints were not subject to mandatory bargaining in labor relations;[48] employees subject to a collective bargaining agreement could pursue a claim outside the negotiated grievance-arbitration procedure. Title VII provided a conciliation procedure. Thus, in 1994, the USPS had a legal right to unilaterally structure a voluntary dispute resolution program for these complaints.

GOALS TO ADDRESS A MASSIVE STREAM OF DISPUTES. When the USPS conceived REDRESS, equal employment opportunity complaints were growing. Processing time had increased, but the capacity of Equal Employment Opportunity Commission staff to handle cases had not. In 1994, employees filed almost 25,000 complaints alleging discrimination; by 1997, complaints approached 28,000 annually.[49] Of the

34,262 federal sector equal employment opportunity cases for fiscal year 1997, a total of 13,549—over 39 percent—involved the USPS.[50]

POSTAL SERVICE DESIGNS, STRUCTURE, AND RESOURCES. The USPS began a giant experiment, possible only because it was large and had consistent working conditions at each of its more than 31,000 locations in the United States. Multiple locations allowed for natural quasi experiments. Moreover, during the design period from 1994 to 2000, the economics of the USPS were relatively stable (unlike the financial stress faced by the agency now, when electronic communication has significantly eroded income from first-class mail). The prospect of transaction cost savings through better conflict management in such a large organization justified the resources that it devoted to this new system.

The USPS initially adopted mediation effective in autumn 1994 as part of a negotiated settlement to a class action discrimination suit in the Panhandle of Florida. Union leaders, employee lawyers, and the USPS Law Department represented internal stakeholders in settlement negotiations. In this and subsequent design changes, the USPS consulted with internal stakeholders and focus groups. However, it never negotiated with unions over the structure and content of REDRESS; with seven different bargaining units, doing so would have been difficult. Thus, the USPS exercised effective unilateral control over DSD for REDRESS. However, that control was constrained by law; the USPS could not mandate that all equal employment opportunity complainants use ADR. Thus, it had to design a program that employees would want to use. The design elements are as follows.[51]

- To be eligible, an employee must file an informal complaint of discrimination in employment with the USPS equal employment opportunity office.
- ADR equal employment opportunity specialists offer mediation to almost all complainants, with limited exceptions.
- Mediation is voluntary for the complainant.
- Mediation is mandatory for the respondent supervisor, who is an agent of the USPS as employer.
- Program administrators schedule a mediation session promptly, generally within a month of a request.
- If complainants choose to bring a representative, they may bring anyone, whether lawyer, union representative, coworker, friend, or family member.
- The respondent is accompanied by, or has immediate access to, a management representative with authority to authorize a settlement.

- Mediation sessions occur in a private location at the workplace during working time for which the USPS pays participant employees.
- If the employee is a member of a bargaining unit, the employee's union has the right to review the settlement to ensure that it is consistent with the contract.
- During the Indiana University evaluation, the mediator distributed exit surveys and completed a report.

EXPERIMENTAL PHASES. The REDRESS program moved through three phases. During the early pilot phase of the program, starting in 1994, the USPS used facilitative, outside neutral mediators trained by the Justice Center of Atlanta. Indiana University researchers found that participants, both supervisors and employees, said that they listened to each other in the facilitative mediation.[52] This occurrence was a significant change in the culture for managing conflict. In a separate study, the researchers also found that employees and supervisors were highly and similarly satisfied with the Justice Center's facilitative mediation process and its mediators.[53] This was important to the USPS as an organization because it provided outside validation that employees and supervisors judged the system to be fair. Although employees were statistically significantly less satisfied than supervisors with outcomes, this result was consistent with both common sense and with the procedural justice literature. Complainants' expectations are disappointed, while respondents are relieved the case is resolved.

In the second REDRESS phase, between 1994 and 1997, the USPS experimented with two program designs to determine whether using federal employees as mediators was feasible. One pilot tried exchanging employees trained as mediators with the Veterans Affairs Administration but failed for lack of use. A second pilot used USPS employees as inside neutral mediators, providing them with Justice Center training in the facilitative style. One DSD in upstate New York used both inside and outside neutral programs. However, there was selection bias: equal employment opportunity ADR specialists referred cases to inside neutrals if they felt settlement was likely.

Evaluators found that disputants were more satisfied with outside mediators than with inside mediators.[54] One possible explanation is perceived bias: as fellow employees, inside mediators were more subject to USPS control. Another possible explanation is that they were less skilled. However, the selection bias by equal employment opportunity ADR specialists meant the insiders had easier cases; moreover, they knew the USPS as an organization far better than any outsider could. One important design feature is that employees did not have a choice between inside and outside neutral designs. In contrast, an ombuds program uses conflict coaching to help employees determine the best way to proceed. Instead, the USPS implemented inside and outside neutral designs in different geographic locations to allow for a natural experiment. If employees had been permitted to choose, there might not have been a difference in satisfaction; they might have been predisposed to be satisfied with their choices.

In the third and final phase, starting in 1998, the USPS leadership rolled out the REDRESS program nationally, taking it from twenty-five cities to every zip code in the country. This policy decision dictated a single, national, consistent DSD. To pursue its goal of moving conflict management upstream and fostering individual learning of better communication skills, the USPS adopted the transformative mediation model nationwide. Robert A. Baruch Bush and Joseph P. Folger first published *The Promise of Mediation* in 1994, advocating for a different model of practice, transformative mediation.[55] They describe "evaluative mediators" as subject matter experts who provide an opinion on the substantive, legal merits of a discrimination complaint. These mediators are termed "directive" in that they press disputants in mediation to settle. Bush and Folger describe "facilitative mediators" as those who use interest-based negotiation, ask problem-solving questions, brainstorm solutions, and use reality-testing techniques. Indicators of success are resolution, implementation of agreements, satisfaction, and progress in understanding how the conflict occurred.[56] While both types of mediators use active listening and communication skills, including reframing, Bush and Folger see the primary goal of both evaluative, or directive, and facilitative mediators as settlement. This model, as described by Bush and Folger, involves mediators seeking to foster communication between disputants, empower them, and help them recognize each other's perspectives. Empowerment and recognition might naturally lead to settlement, but settlement is not the primary goal. Transformative mediators help disputants identify resources and information they need to make decisions. They do not evaluate the merits of a claim or its legal strengths and weaknesses or give an opinion on the likely outcome before an administrative law judge or in court.

Transformative mediators are ethically prohibited from opining on the merits of a claim, even when the parties ask them to. In selecting its mediators, since mediators were not expected to evaluate cases on their legal merits, the USPS sought not only lawyers but also mediators from the fields of psychology, counseling, and social work, as well as teachers, academics, HR professionals, and retirees from those professions. Mediators were trained for free in exchange for mediating one case pro bono. Equal employment opportunity ADR specialists observed mediators to ensure that they practiced in the transformative model. The eventual mediator roster reached 1,500 experienced mediators; 44 percent were women and 17 percent were minorities. In a sample of 671 active mediators, 570 were Caucasian, 77 were African American, 4 were Asian American, 3 were Native American, and 17 were Latino, making up the most demographically diverse mediator roster of its time.

SUCCESS, ACCOUNTABILITY, AND EVALUATION. The USPS and Indiana University collaboratively designed a system for continuous data collection that became part of each design experiment and ultimately part of the national program. That system had the following components:

- Mediators distributed a confidential exit survey to each participant and her representative. There were no identifying numbers on the survey.
- The exit survey contained the zip code of the mediation; procedural and organizational justice items measuring satisfaction with process, mediator, and outcome; an item about whether there was full, partial, or no resolution; and later transformative indicators. It contained no demographic information because of concerns about discovery for use in class action litigation.
- Participants were invited to complete the exit surveys on work time and mail them to the university, in stamped, addressed envelopes.
- As a condition of getting paid, the mediator completed a report on who attended the mediation; whether there was a full, partial, or no settlement; and how many exit surveys were distributed.

USPS program managers used the basic descriptive satisfaction data to manage program performance and consistency. By the time the national program was fully implemented, the USPS was conducting about 15,000 REDRESS mediation cases a year. Generally, each mediation session had four participants (two disputants, each with a representative). Eventually, by the close of 2006 when data collection ceased, the exit survey database had over 270,000 surveys. For the final national REDRESS DSD, Indiana University redesigned the exit survey to add indicators intended to capture elements of the transformative mediation model such as empowerment, recognition, and directive or evaluative mediators.[57] Researchers used the exit survey dataset to examine a series of organizational justice questions.

The national model using transformative mediation generally produced the same pattern of procedural justice results as the facilitative style.[58] Specifically, in analysis of over 81,000 exit surveys completed between 1998 and 2003 (the transformative period), both employees and supervisors were equally and highly satisfied with the mediation process.[59]

EVALUATING SYSTEMIC IMPACT ON THE USPS AS AN ORGANIZATION. The USPS mediation program was successful by many measures. By 2006 USPS internal data, controlled for changes in the size of the workforce, suggested that informal equal employment opportunity complaint filings had dropped 30 percent since their peak before the USPS implemented REDRESS nationally in 1997. Moreover, there was a change in the composition of the complainant pool. By 2006, the complaints were coming from 40 percent fewer people, meaning that the people filing complaints were more likely to be repeat filers. Researchers also found that implementation of the mediation program correlated with a substantial drop (more than 25 percent) in formal complaints.[60] This trend suggested that mediation had a positive impact on the USPS system for addressing complaints of discrimination, in that complaints were resolved through mediation at the informal stage and did not reach the formal stage. Additionally, the rate at which disputants resolved their own cases—after mediation had been scheduled but before it took place—gradually increased from 2 percent to 14 percent, indicating a broader shift in the organizational culture toward conflict resolution.

Lessons Learned About Conflict Management and Organizational Justice
Procedural and organizational justice provided the primary frame for the Indiana University evaluation of REDRESS. Most work on organizational justice explains perceptions of fairness in a two-way relationship, in which one decision maker (a supervisor or management) holds authority and control over a subordinate (an employee or workforce). Most organizational justice research involves an employee and a supervisor, with the supervisor acting as an authority figure and an agent for the organization responsible for implementing policies or making decisions. This is not the same role that an outside mediator plays in a workplace. A mediator does not apply organizational policies or decide disputes as a management step in a grievance procedure. A mediator attempts to help parties communicate. The REDRESS program provided a new test for organizational justice, highlighting the importance of communication between the disputants themselves.[61]

The USPS did not examine distributive justice in terms of systematic patterns in the outcomes of mediation. The median distributive economic value of settlements reported in exit surveys was zero; about a third of the settlements contained commitments to communicate in future with mutual respect. Other substantive outcomes were retrospective granting of leave, providing access to overtime, opportunities for details (a temporary transfer) to higher-rated positions, and adjustments in discipline. Some complainants observed in the exit surveys that they wanted supervisors punished for their behavior; however, REDRESS was not designed to provide retributive or deterrent justice for poor behavior at the workplace. It was an effort to restore relations in the workplace community, one mediation case at a time. One important finding from the REDRESS research is that cases were more likely to reach settlement when employees and supervisors reported that they listened to each other during transformative mediation. This insight is useful for designing employment conflict management systems, because it suggests that transformative mediation may foster settlement better than evaluative mediation.

Moreover, the findings suggest the need to adjust the determinants of organizational justice when designing conflict management programs. Particularly in transformative mediation, disputants' satisfaction with their own interactions (disputant-disputant) in theory should be an important factor in perceptions of organizational justice, but the triadic structure of mediation suggests a need to adapt organizational justice scales and measures. Voice matters; providing people with the opportunity to have their voices heard in a safe environment and permitting disputants to discuss their differences can have a positive impact on organizations.

Ombuds Programs

The USPS program is a standalone equal employment opportunity mediation program. In contrast, a workplace ombuds is a neutral operating inside and on an organization's payroll to assist other employees, stakeholders, or customers as an information resource, channel of communications, complaint handler, and dispute resolver.[62] An ombuds office generally offers both formal and informal methods of conflict resolution, can handle numerous and varied organizational conflicts, and offers flexible design to fit the organization.[63] It may offer conflict coaching, counseling, hotlines, open doors, mediation, peer panels, fact-finding, and arbitration, among other processes.

One study found that federal workplace ombuds offices are most effective when the equal employment opportunity office has too many complaints that are not related to equal employment opportunity, the employee assistance plan is receiving workplace complaints outside its mandate, personnel-related offices are not working together, employee morale is low, there is poor employee-management communication, significant workplace issues emerge and surprise management, there are poor labor-management relations, or there are frequent employee claims of retaliation.[64]

Ombuds exist in the public and private sectors[65] and have a professional association and code of ethics.[66] Ombuds programs have increased, particularly in multinational corporations and organizations that operate across cultures (e.g., the World Bank).[67] Employers may distort the ombuds title in unilaterally adopted nonunion arbitration programs. For example, one employer had its ombuds represent employees as their advocate in arbitration and select the arbitrator on behalf of both parties. This resulted in the repeated selection of the same arbitrator, who always ruled for management.[68] This structure, in which the ombuds departs from a neutral role, gives at least the appearance of a conflict of interest.

The champions of integrated conflict management system design first emerged from the ombuds profession. Mary Rowe long served as organizational ombuds for MIT and over time developed a perspective on how the myriad complaint streams in a major university might be able to function in parallel and in coordination.[69] She found that people wanted options and choices and that these preferences were well matched with the university's policy of providing redundancy in resources and structures for addressing problems. She developed ideas about how to design the dispute system, beginning with the characteristics of the complainants and including stakeholder input. She asserts that an effective system requires core values of fairness, voice, and freedom from reprisal for using the system; many options for resolving conflict; multiple access points; an organizational ombuds outside line and staff reporting structures; wide scope; and continuous improvement.

Best Practices Reports

As theories about integrated conflict management systems emerged, practitioners in the conflict resolution field began to work on a set of best practices and presented them in two reports from committees of the Society for Professionals in Dispute Resolution (which has since merged into the Association for Conflict Resolution). One key difference between these reports and the Due Process Protocol for Mediation and Arbitration of Statutory Disputes Arising out of the Employment Relationship, a protocol adopted by professional associations, concerns voluntariness, or consent. The authors of the best practices reports on integrated conflict management systems urge that all use of ADR be truly voluntary, that it not be imposed on an unwilling participant.[70] Conversely, the employment protocol did not take a position on mandatory ADR processes and thus, by default, allows them.

Some of the best practices in integrated conflict management system design are encouraging employees and managers to voice concerns and constructive dissent early, integrating collaborative problem-solving approaches into the culture of the organization, encouraging direct negotiation among the parties in a dispute, and aligning conflict management practices with each other and the mission, vision, and values of the organization. The work that emerged from the ombuds field and the best practices reports has identified five essential characteristics of integrated conflict management systems:

- Options for addressing all types of problems that are available to all people in the workplace, including employees, supervisors, professionals, and managers
- A culture that welcomes dissent and encourages resolution of conflict at the lowest level through direct negotiation
- Multiple access points and persons who are easily identified as knowledgeable and trustworthy for approaching with advice about a conflict or the system
- Multiple options for addressing conflicts, including rights-based and interest-based processes
- A systemic structure that coordinates and supports the multiple access points and multiple options and integrates effective conflict management practices into daily organizational operations[71]

These characteristics help promote a workplace climate in which disputes are constructively addressed and resolved.

Conclusion

The USPS created REDRESS in a unique set of circumstances, but the model is easily transferable to other settings.[72] Voluntary employment mediation can contribute to organizational health by providing opportunities for multiple forms of justice, including procedural justice, organizational justice, and distributive justice. In the increasingly diverse globalized workplace, DSD can incorporate training in implicit bias to foster mutual cross-cultural understanding. These programs can provide an opportunity for voice, allow people to feel treated with respect, and permit disputants to reconcile. Organizations can use mediation to correct a wrong in a way that provides disputants with what they want and need rather than what a court determines they are entitled to receive. This capacity fosters individual disputant self-determination and restores the relationship between coworkers and between disputants and the organization.

To provide such benefits, mediation programs need to avoid both the appearance and reality of pro-employer bias. In the United States, employers—in the absence of a union—have almost complete control over the design of a dispute system. The temptation to design a system that maximizes employer benefit and minimizes risk can easily result in a system that is skewed in the employer's favor. Effective systems require structures that provide checks and balances. In RE-DRESS, the USPS tried to achieve this balance by using transformative mediation. Because mediators could not evaluate the merits or strengths and weaknesses of cases, the USPS kept the focus in the mediation session on empowering the disputants and helping them understand each other's views and perspectives on the conflict.

The shift from collective bargaining rights to individual employee rights has brought with it the need for new systems of employee voice to manage workplace conflict. Interest-based processes like training and employment mediation can serve a key role in these new systems by yielding lasting solutions to workplace conflict. Chapter 12 examines the most common rights-based alternative, adhesive, or forced, employment arbitration.

12 ARBITRATION IN CONSUMER AND EMPLOYMENT DESIGNS

IMAGINE A CONSUMER who buys a new computer by mail order. He opens the warranty information and learns that, by virtue of the purchase, he is bound by an arbitration clause. The clause requires that he arbitrate in Chicago—but he lives in another part of the country—if he thinks the company has violated its warranty. Further, he must file a claim with the International Chamber of Commerce located in Paris, France, which has a nonrefundable $2,000 initial filing fee. This fee is more than twice the cost of the computer. What if the clause also provided that the loser pay the arbitrator fees and the company's legal fees? Financially, what makes more sense if the computer fails? Should the consumer go to arbitration over the warranty violation or give up and buy a new computer from a different company?

Another example involves employment. Imagine an eighteen-year-old woman who waits on tables. She experiences what she describes as repeated sexual harassment by her supervisor at the restaurant. She has no union. She tries to file a discrimination complaint but learns that she is bound by an arbitration clause. The arbitrators who will decide the case are managers of other restaurants in the same chain.[1] The arbitration clause bars her from seeking redress directly in court or joining a class action with other women. These examples are adapted from real cases.[2]

Issues to consider are as follows.

- What are the baseline considerations for arbitration system design?
- How do strategic choices contrast with ethical considerations?
- What are the implications of adhesive arbitration for fairness and justice?

This chapter focuses on forms of arbitration in the private sector that have become increasingly common in the United States, although not permitted in many other national legal systems.[3] U.S. employers and businesses adopt mandatory, or adhesive, binding arbitration clauses to manage the risk of perceived extreme jury awards, or what business interests characterize as abusive class action litigation.[4] Corporate organizations generally have the power, as an economically stronger repeat player, to impose these arbitration clauses on the weaker, usually one-shot player.[5] These clauses appear frequently as a condition of some economic relationship, such as employment, consumer purchases, or health care.[6] Arbitration clauses may embody a complete DSD that stands alone; alternatively, they may be a final step in a more comprehensive design that is part of an ombuds program or a grievance procedure with conflict coaching and mediation before arbitration.

Arbitration is a fast-evolving and highly controversial area of law[7] and DSD practice[8] in the United States. As commerce and consumer transactions become increasingly global,[9] international stakeholders are working on new systems to address related disputes, explored further with respect to online dispute resolution in Chapter 14.[10] Reconciling differing national legal frameworks for DSD in this globalized economy remains a challenge for designers. Scholars in the European Union proposed system design for consumer-to-business dispute resolution using such processes as conciliation, adjudication, arbitration, and ombuds under a broad EU directive.[11]

The U.S. Legal Framework for Arbitration Systems
In the nineteenth century, private justice systems arose in the United States in the shadow of the courts.[12] Both or all parties negotiated arbitration clauses in their labor relations or commercial contracts or adopted them ad hoc. One way to analyze the current legal framework for arbitration as system design is through Elinor Ostrom's Institutional Analysis and Development (IAD) framework regarding the impact of rules on systems.[13] The framework aids in understanding the "nested" nature of conflict resolution institutions.[14] As discussed in Chapter 10 with respect to the emergence of collective bargaining, the New Deal Congress passed the National Labor Relations Act in 1935.[15] The U.S. Supreme Court shaped a national policy in support of labor arbitration to solve labor disputes through three cases known as the Steelworkers Trilogy.[16] The basic holdings are that when a contract has an arbitration clause and a no-strike clause, parties must submit all grievances to the arbitrator,[17] courts should not prevent arbitration unless it can be said with positive assurance that the contract does not cover the dispute. Doubts are resolved in favor of coverage,[18] and courts generally will defer questions on arbitrability to the arbitrator.[19] Through this national policy supporting labor arbitration, courts

will rarely overturn a labor arbitration award,[20] except that unionized employees cannot be forced to arbitrate equal employment opportunity claims under civil rights statutes.[21] This legal framework applies only to unionized employees.

During the same era, private justice systems arose in the commercial arena. Courts were hostile to arbitration, refusing to enforce clauses that were perceived as ousting courts of jurisdiction.[22] To address this problem, Congress passed the Federal Arbitration Act (FAA)[23] in 1925.[24] Under the original legislative intent of the FAA,[25] the statute primarily protected commercial arbitration from the courts. It has not been substantially amended in decades.[26] Key provisions include the definition of commerce under 9 U.S.C. § 1, which courts had originally interpreted to exclude employees in interstate commerce,[27] and the enforcement of arbitration contracts under 9 U.S.C. § 2, which protects arbitration clauses by making them valid, irrevocable, and enforceable (unless they are voidable on the same grounds as any other contract).[28] Perhaps most troublesome, another contested and actively litigated provision defines the grounds for overturning or vacating an arbitration award: 9 U.S.C. § 10. This provision does not permit courts to overturn arbitration awards on the basis of an error of law, such as when an arbitrator mistakenly applies the law.[29]

What is the impact of the FAA standard for judicial review in contrast to other standards? It certainly departs from de novo review on questions of law.[30] The FAA standard is far more deferential to an arbitrator than appellate review of findings of fact in courts. It also dramatically differs from the scope of review found in the Administrative Procedure Act, 5 U.S.C. § 706, which permits courts to correct violations of the Constitution and errors of law.[31] In other words, if an employment discrimination case is heard by an administrative law judge under Equal Employment Opportunity Commission jurisdiction, a court is free to overturn that decision if there is an error of law, but courts will not overturn arbitration awards on the same grounds under the FAA. Generally, once an arbitrator issues a binding arbitration award, the burden and standard of proof for the person challenging the award are so high as to discourage an attempt to overturn the award.

Some commercial DSDs have collective choice rules, including DSDs in the diamond[32] and cotton[33] industries. These are robust in the sense that each is enduring, stable, adaptive, and participatory. Both the diamond and cotton industry DSDs use a private democratic structure that selects arbitrators from among the members. The DSDs are subject to monitoring by that membership association, which is self-governing. Their members choose the design, adopt it through their associations' constitutions and bylaws, and participate in the design either as disputants, decision makers, or arbitrators in their own private justice systems.[34]

However, in 1991 the U.S. Supreme Court dramatically altered the direction of case law under the FAA in *Gilmer v. Interstate/Johnson Lane Corp.*;[35] for the first time it enforced an adhesive arbitration clause in an Age Discrimination in Employment Act claim. The clause was in a Securities and Exchange Commission registration form that a securities industry employee had signed as a condition of employment.[36] This instance was the first case of what is now called adhesive, mandatory, or forced arbitration in employment.

In adhesive arbitration, there is no collective choice. A single disputant with superior economic power has taken unilateral control over designing a dispute system for future conflicts to which it will be a party. It uses its one-party control to impose the system as a condition of the economic relationship, whether that is employer–employee or seller–buyer. Moreover, designers may choose DSDs that effectively restrict recourse to the public civil justice system, because arbitration DSDs are nested in a legal framework for arbitration in interstate commerce under the FAA.

Some scholars argue that the case precedents on labor arbitration and commercial arbitration are converging.[37] Critics of this trend state that employees and consumers lack meaningful access to justice under this form of arbitration.[38] Other commentators counter that transaction costs preclude meaningful access to legal counsel and courts even absent adhesive arbitration clauses.[39]

**One-Party Control over DSD in Arbitration
over Consumer and Employment Claims**

In his classic article on the quality of settlement, Marc Galanter argued that all dispute resolution occurs in the shadow of the civil justice system.[40] His examples demonstrate the concept of reservation price, or the lowest or least advantageous agreement that a party will accept. A party offered anything worse than her reservation price will implement her best alternative to a negotiated agreement (BATNA) and walk away from the negotiation.[41] Galanter examines transaction costs for each of two litigating parties and demonstrates that the settlement range[42] is often produced by a combination of differences in parties' estimates of the outcome in court and the known costs of pursuing litigation. Sometimes the settlement range is entirely a function of transaction costs.[43] In the civil justice system, lawyers estimate outcomes on the basis of substantive legal knowledge and an understanding of how the relevant court system functions in a particular jurisdiction, including the reasonably foreseeable costs of litigation.[44]

Control over DSD allows a disputant to change the formula. When one party designs an adhesive arbitration system, the other party finds herself bargaining in a different shadow. This imbalance can alter the case's settlement range to such an extent that, in some circumstances, it may be more cost effective for the plaintiff to abandon the claim. This outcome, of course, is the designer's strategic goal. Parties define their reservation prices by considering alternatives to negotiation; the best of these alternatives, or BATNA, shapes the reservation price.[45] Often, the BATNA is litigation,[46] or it may be dropping the claim or waiving it. In some cases, it becomes the WATNA, or worst alternative to a negotiated agreement.

Negotiating settlement in the shadow of an adhesive arbitration clause changes the BATNA from litigation to arbitration. Negotiation scholars observe that changing the alternatives to a negotiated agreement can have a powerful effect on the bargaining set.[47] Worsening the other side's alternatives and improving one's own is an effective bargaining strategy.[48] While much arbitration data is confidential and unavailable, some studies have provided information on how different systems function.[49] Studies indicate that a repeat-player effect exists in adhesive arbitration, meaning organizations in control of DSD who arbitrate repeatedly in a pool of cases have superior outcomes and win rates (scholars disagree on explanations for the effect).[50]

Practitioners and stakeholder professional associations have adopted protocols to provide guidance on design features that are essential for a fair system: the Due Process Protocol for Mediation and Arbitration of Statutory Disputes Arising out of the Employment Relationship (employment protocol)[51] and the Consumer Due Process Protocol (consumer protocol).[52] Both are voluntary; they are essentially self-regulatory standards for third-party providers of mediation and arbitration services. Both protocols provide employees or consumers with some limited due process in arbitration. Protocol subscribers refuse to participate in an arbitration case unless it complies with the relevant protocol's protections.[53]

The protocols, however, lack the force of law. "Due process" is, of course, a term of art borrowed from the Constitution. Courts have defined it to include notice, reasonable discovery of relevant evidence, an opportunity to be heard, the ability to confront and cross-examine witnesses, the right to have counsel or a representative, an impartial hearing officer, a record of the proceedings, and a reasoned decision explaining what evidence persuaded the decision maker.[54] What due process the Constitution requires for government action will vary with the nature of the protected interest at stake, the risk of error, and the nature of the public interest. Technically, the Constitution's due process clauses do not apply to the private sector. However, most procedural safeguards are available during the typical labor arbitration. Both protocols require these basic safeguards.[55] The consumer protocol also requires that consumers retain access to small claims court and that arbitration occur in a reasonably convenient location. But not being law and absent consent, the protocols do not bind the parties.

By generally enforcing adhesive arbitration clauses in standard-form contracts under the FAA, courts have opened the doors to institutional experimentation in designing dispute systems that minimize the settlement value of claims.[56] Such enforcement allows one party to experiment with all the DSD elements that have not yet been held unconscionable or otherwise unenforceable. The decisions available to the more powerful party are numerous and include time limits for filing; whether a third-party administrator will be required or the arbitration will be nonadministered; whether a panel or individual arbitrator will hear the case; the method to select the arbitrators; the location of the arbitration hearing; the apportionment of filing fees, arbitrator fees, and disputants' attorneys' fees; the extent of discovery available during the process; the substantive standard the arbitrator must apply; the scope of the arbitration itself; the extent of confidentiality of the process, award, or outcome; the remedies available; the availability of class action relief; the availability of written, reasoned decisions; the standard of review for errors of law; and whether the award can establish new legal precedent.[57]

Law and Design Choices in Arbitration System Designs

One can view the evolving U.S. case law under the FAA through the lens of DSD choices. In drafting an arbitration clause and deciding on the rules, the designer must consider many questions:

- Who is the arbitrator? What qualifications, experience, or panel membership are requisite?
- How many arbitrators? One, three, or some other number?
- Who selects the arbitrator? How is the selection process structured?
- Will the arbitration clause discuss costs or be silent? Will it specify which party pays for the arbitrator, the hearing room, and the administrative, filing, and expert fees?
- What is the power of the arbitrator to interpret the contract?
- What discretion, if any, will the arbitrator have to consider contract defenses like unconscionability?
- What power over procedural decisions will the arbitrator have?
- Will the clause place limitations on the type or extent of available remedies? What weight, if any, will the arbitrator give remedy-stripping provisions? Will the clause afford the arbitrator any discretion in interpreting these provisions?

- Will the clause eliminate class actions in court, in arbitration, or both?
- Which jurisdiction's law will apply? Put differently, what is the choice of law decision?
- Will the clause truncate the applicable statute of limitations?
- Will the clause allow the arbitrator to decide which due process protections will apply?
- What rules of evidence will apply?
- Will claims for injunctive relief or summary judgment be available?
- Will the clause afford an appeal to a second arbitral body?

These questions arise in litigated cases and settings.[58] When only one of the disputants controls the design choice, each design question becomes an important strategic consideration.[59] A brief review of federal case law follows.

Issues arise regarding arbitrator powers over questions of contract formation and scope, such as whether the arbitrator can determine meaning and validity of the contract as a whole, including the arbitration clause. Grounds for invalidating contracts are fraud, duress, and unconscionability. Do these grounds have to pertain to the arbitration clause specifically? What if the claim is that the whole contract is invalid on these grounds? In *Prima Paint Corp. v. Flood & Conklin Mfg. Co.*,[60] a claim arose regarding fraud in the inducement as to the contract as a whole; the Supreme Court held this was a question for the arbitrator,[61] while fraud in the inducement of the arbitration clause alone would have been for a court to decide.[62] In *Buckeye Check Cashing Inc. v. Cardegna*,[63] consumers claimed in state court that a contract containing an arbitration clause was, as a whole, usurious and violated state civil and criminal law; the court applied the *Prima Paint* rule and compelled arbitration.[64] The decision on whether the contract was enforceable was left to the arbitrator.[65] Because an error of law is not grounds for vacating an arbitration award, this precedent permits corporate designers effectively to escape public law on consumer protection.

Questions on the validity and scope of the arbitration clause concern substantive arbitrability, or whether the parties agreed to arbitrate the subject matter.[66] Who decides such questions, a court or an arbitrator? In theory, a court should decide; the Supreme Court held that courts must decide the threshold question of whether the FAA applies to a given contract.[67] In *Granite Rock Co. v. International Brotherhood of Teamsters*,[68] the Supreme Court confirmed that courts should decide whether the parties actually agreed to arbitrate and whether the arbitration clause itself covers the subject matter.[69]

The designer, however, may determine whether to give the arbitrator the power to decide questions of procedural arbitrability, contract defenses, what remedies are available, or whether to prohibit class actions.[70] The designer may delegate questions of procedural arbitrability to the arbitrator, such as whether claims are time barred and whether there was adequate notice, laches, or estoppel.[71] The designer may also delegate to the arbitrator questions of unconscionability as to the arbitration agreement.[72] Should the arbitrator decide contract defenses to the arbitration clause? Should a designer use the arbitration clause to give maximum decision power to the arbitrator?[73]

What about the ability of the designer to limit the availability of remedies, such as punitive damages?[74] In *PacifiCare Health Systems, Inc. v. Book*,[75] the arbitration clause prohibited punitive damages, but the federal racketeering statute allowed them. The Supreme Court held that the arbitrator needed to interpret whether the contract allowed the claimants to vindicate their rights given its limitation on damages.[76]

It is now clear in the United States that designers may draft an arbitration clause so as to prohibit access either to a class action in court or to class arbitration. In *AT&T Mobility LLC v. Concepcion*,[77] plaintiffs bought a cell phone from AT&T; the transaction included an adhesive arbitration clause that precluded class arbitration. The California Supreme Court had previously ruled that class action waivers in consumer arbitration agreements were unconscionable. The plaintiffs brought suit in federal district court; their case was consolidated with a class action. AT&T moved to compel arbitration, but the lower courts refused to grant the motion on the grounds that a class action waiver in an arbitration clause was unconscionable under California law. On appeal, the U.S. Supreme Court held that the FAA preempted California's law. It held that California's rules effectively fashioned class arbitration and violated the policy of the FAA.[78] In effect, the decision may mean a designer can compel a consumer to arbitrate a claim individually, even if the claim is small and the costs of arbitration may preclude meaningful recovery.[79] In *Epic Systems Corp. v. Lewis*, the Supreme Court held that employers can ban class actions through mandatory arbitration clauses and that the FAA prevails over wage and hour and collective bargaining laws.[80]

The designer may also give an arbitrator the power to control discovery and limit it to a reasonable amount different from what a court would permit.[81] Arbitrators may have power to subpoena witnesses and documents but maintain less power than courts over such third parties. What if court discovery might prove that there is a class of similar litigants? What about discovery to prove adverse impact on a class? A designer is able to truncate discovery expeditions early in the choices made; thus, limits on discovery are a strategic design choice.

"Vacatur" is the term of art for a court vacating or overturning an arbitration award. What if the designer tries to change the scope of judicial review for an arbitration award? What if he tries to change the scope of review by expanding it? Can designers expand the scope of review beyond the grounds in the FAA? For example, the arbitration clause could provide for vacatur if "the arbitrator's conclusions of law are erroneous."[82] The Supreme Court held in *Hall Street Associates v. Mattel*[83] that under the FAA, the language of sections 10 and 11 provide the "exclusive regimes for review" of an arbitration award.[84] It is likely a court may not overturn a commercial arbitration award on public policy grounds or for manifest disregard of the law.[85]

Design choices may include choice of law, meaning what state's or country's law governs the transaction.[86] A key strategic advantage in mandatory arbitration is a designer's ability to shift costs onto the other disputant.[87] In *Green Tree Financial Corp.-Ala. v. Randolph*,[88] the Supreme Court held that an arbitration agreement that was silent on who paid filing fees, arbitrator fees, and other costs was nevertheless enforceable. Who has the burden of proof as to costs?[89] The Supreme Court recognized that substantial costs might preclude a claimant from vindicating federal statutory rights but observed the record was silent as to costs and placed the burden on the complainant, a purchaser of a mobile home, to prove them. Costs are a critical question because they may mean the difference between an adequate or accessible forum. Before a case is arbitrated, how is it possible to know and prove costs? The court did not address how prohibitive costs must be before it will intervene. This issue raises strategic design choices. What does the designer advise about arbitrator fees, administrative fees, location of process, attorneys' fees, experts, or the cost of the hearing room?

Strategy in Arbitration System Design

When making strategic choices among competing design elements in an arbitration system,[90] the designer might be tempted to think about the following questions. Whether these are the right questions to ask from an ethical standpoint is a separate discussion, addressed in Chapter 6 and in the coming pages.

- *What is the likelihood that a litigant can successfully challenge an arbitration clause?* If the odds are in the employer or company's favor, the incentive to manage litigation risk might suggest using an adhesive, or mandatory, arbitration clause.
- *What resources does it take to mount and defend such a challenge?* Some corporations take a scorched-earth approach to conflict management, meaning they litigate regardless of costs.[91]
- *What is the state of the law on arbitration clauses? How many disputants will realize some aspect of the design is unenforceable?* Given the limited

review courts give arbitration awards, cases like the examples at the opening of this chapter have required litigants to take a case to a federal court
of appeals; few are able to do so.

- *What is the company's cost-benefit analysis for taking risks with question-
  able, but not yet illegal, design choices?*[92] While an employer or a seller of
  consumer goods may ultimately both lose and set a new arbitration law
  precedent down the road, Galanter suggests that repeat players are willing
  to take such risks in order to shape the rules of the game.[93]

The discussion of ethics in Chapter 6 suggests that the preceding questions may
not be the right ones for a designer to ask. Instead, the designer should return to
the DSD Analytic Framework (Chapter 2). What are, or rather, what should be the
sponsor's goals for the system? Who are the stakeholders?[94] What will employees
and consumers conclude if they learn the company has intentionally sought to
implement a system that tips the balance in its favor when conflicts arise?[95] In light
of these questions, what is the current legal framework for binding arbitration
when the designer undertakes the project, and how would the structures and
processes relate to the judicial system?[96] In good faith, what is the fair answer on
unresolved legal issues?[97]

When Is the Relationship Between a Third-Party Alternative Dispute Resolution Service Provider and One of the Disputants *Too Close*?

The National Arbitration Forum (NAF) advocated and helped design a
binding arbitration system for banks to incorporate into credit card agreements for collection disputes on debt.[98] The design provided collection
services to banks through an independent company in which NAF held stock
through affiliation with a hedge fund. The company sent arbitration notices
as postcards through the mail. NAF arbitrators ruled in favor of the bank in
the event of a default. Banks prevailed in over 99.8 percent of the cases. From
the banks' perspective, this system was economically efficient and low risk; it
was unlikely a consumer would challenge it because the amounts in question
would generally not justify the expense of a court case. However, ultimately,
attorneys general in several states charged NAF with fraudulent consumer
practices; Minnesota's attorney general prevailed in a settlement in which
NAF terminated the system.[99]

For example, Congress has considered legislation banning predispute adhesive arbitration clauses.[100] The Consumer Financial Protection Bureau was a product of the Dodd-Frank Act and efforts to regulate the financial industry after the 2008 financial crisis.[101] Dodd-Frank banned the use of mandatory arbitration in mortgage and home equity loan contracts;[102] the bureau adopted regulations to prohibit mandatory arbitration clauses in mortgage documents.[103] The bureau's mission calls for studying the use of mandatory, or adhesive, arbitration in credit card and consumer debt agreements.[104] It maintains a database of credit card agreements, some of which have arbitration clauses.[105] A 2013 study by the Consumer Financial Protection Bureau found significant growth in use of adhesive arbitration.[106] In light of this trend, it may be more fair to offer a predispute clause with an opt-out period or a postdispute clause. In each case, an employee or consumer has a choice to agree or not to arbitration, whether before or after the dispute arises.

Consumers have also taken collective action through nongovernmental agencies to attack the business model and reputation of a company on the basis of its business practices.[107] As companies increasingly operate globally and adopt corporate social responsibility policies, they may wish to consider the impact of business practices in connection with drafting adhesive arbitration clauses.

Scholars have proposed alternative approaches to the current U.S. Supreme Court jurisprudence. Thomas Stipanowich suggests a new analogue to the Good Housekeeping Seal of Approval in the form of an arbitration fairness index.[108] An independent entity using standards for measuring an arbitration DSD might rate clauses on their fairness as a means to empower the market to address abuses. Stipanowich suggests rating programs on five categories of program elements: "(1) Meaningful Consent, Clarity, and Transparency; (2) Independent and Balanced Administration; (3) Quality and Suitability of Arbitrators; (4) Fair Hearings; and (5) Fair Outcomes."[109] Corporations that earned the index's seal of approval might find a market advantage among consumers and potential employees. Companies that received negative ratings might experience public pressure. Employees and consumers could make more informed choices.

Nancy Welsh suggests that the Supreme Court is in effect creating a national small claims apparatus through arbitration. Welsh offers a creative approach for the courts inspired by the Employee Retirement Income Security Act (ERISA).[110] Using the ERISA by analogy and borrowing from the ERISA cases, particularly *Metropolitan Life Insurance Co. v. Glenn*,[111] she suggests courts might consider a fiduciary duty similar to what employee benefit program administrators owe to beneficiaries.[112] Courts could exercise appropriate supervision to control arbitration's potential for structural bias by imposing a similar fiduciary duty toward claimants on the designers and supervisors of company arbitration plans. She suggests that the Supreme Court may be able to maintain a deferential standard of judicial review for arbitral awards while also considering the severity of structural bias in the mandatory predispute arbitration context. She argues that if the severity of structural bias is named as a relevant factor for courts to consider, it would open the door for plaintiffs to demand discovery regarding all the indicators of structural bias. She points to the impact of discovery in ERISA cases and potentially in mandatory predispute arbitration cases[113] and shows that discovery is one way to transparency.[114] Discovery could bring to light all the design choices that result in structural bias.

What is the empirical impact of design choices?[115] Is there a way to build a transparent evaluation system to assess the fairness and effectiveness of the resulting system? Is there an ongoing way to collect and share data with stakeholders and users to assure them of the system's balance? For example, expansions in the availability of information online may suggest efficient ways for employees and consumers to share knowledge or for organizations to leverage the comments of employees and consumers to build databases on systems.[116] In effect, employees and consumers may increasingly crowdsource and share information using social media.

Conclusion

Dispute systems using adhesive arbitration clauses have generated substantial policy debate in the United States,[117] with commentators arguing they are unconstitutional and eviscerate public law.[118] They also depart from common legal practices in other countries. The UN Commission on International Trade Law, UNCITRAL, has a working group that seeks to establish an online dispute resolution framework to resolve cross-border e-commerce disputes that involve economically modest claims.[119] In the United States, several legal and extralegal remedies have been proposed to limit or counterbalance the observed or potential bias of mandatory arbitration clauses toward the companies designing the systems, ranging from consumer watchdog schemes to new Supreme Court approaches. The MeToo movement has illustrated collective action efforts to empower victims of sexual harassment; mass mobilization has attracted substantial media attention and led to high-profile cases and resignations of the accused offenders. Despite such trends, however, mandatory arbitration clauses still further disempower vulnerable persons and suppress the advancement of legal precedent.[120]

13   COMMERCIAL DISPUTES

A COMPANY SETTING OUT TO BUILD a new airport for a municipality, on a multibillion-dollar budget with hundreds of subcontractors and serving a population of thousands, would do well to consider how to manage disputes before any arise. It is clearly in the interest of both the contractor and the client to manage a project within its budget and complete it on time with working relationships intact. What dispute resolution processes can best serve these goals?

This chapter examines the handling of dispute streams in the commercial domain. Organizations encounter a wide array of disputes, internally with and among employees (Chapters 10 and 11), externally with customers (Chapter 14), and in relationships with suppliers, venture partners, and government agencies, which are the topic of this chapter.

Issues to consider are as follows.

- What unique DSD contexts do business-to-business relationships present?
- What role does ADR currently play in large organizations such as corporations and the federal government?
- What are the benefits of early case assessment and dispute resolution in contrast to downstream approaches?

Process Choice and Stakeholder-Lawyers

Organizations vary in their handling of disputes and in their perspective on goals, process, and the role of the stakeholder-lawyer. A corporation's profit goal may be in direct tension with the economic interests of its customer, supplier, or even partner. A government agency may have objectives that are in tension with its operational, regulatory, or enforcement mandate, such as consistency or compliance with regulatory standards. Disputes between organizations may be provoked by different organizational or cultural values, relationships gone off track, changes in the competitive market, lack of accurate data, or misaligned interests.[1] Mapping the parties' common, conflicting, and independent goals should be part of a negotiating process to reach the agreement that forms the basis for the parties' relationship. Once the goals of commercial parties are clarified, there are a wide range of processes for dealing with problems that develop in practice, both early in the relationship before disputes arise and later when they emerge.

Two avenues for processing disputes arise in the context of a business organization. In one, the parties voluntarily choose to engage with one another at the outset and thus have an opportunity to clarify expectations over the term of their relationship. In such cases, a conflict stream assessment (see Chapter 4) can be performed upstream to determine the nature of disputes likely to arise and how and when intervention should occur—that is, whether to intervene earlier (prevention) or later (resolution) in the dispute life cycle. Dominant processes for resolving business disputes are negotiation and litigation. Given increasingly global and complex supply chains, the location of the parties and the attendant cultural norms will be relevant. Litigation in the United States is distinct in terms of its professional judiciary, use of juries, high cost of discovery, risk of punitive and pain and suffering damages, and contingency fees for lawyers; it is a thoroughly rights-based process. The cost of litigation in the United States increases incentives to explore alternative, interest-based processes, perhaps more so than in other countries.

Contractual arrangements are the provenance of lawyers, with both inside counsel and outside firms advising each party. This layer of legal expertise may enhance or obfuscate the parties' business goals and may amplify or diminish the emotional aspects of business relationships. Lawyers involved early in the parties' relationship are better able to anticipate the kinds of problems that are likely to arise and tailor the process choices to prevent, manage, and resolve them. Lawyers engage through several modes: as counsel, both in-house and in firms; through professional legal and dispute resolution organizations, such as the American Bar Association and the Center for Public Resources; and through the local norms of the courts.

Examples from the Commercial Domain

Three examples of the numerous approaches to commercial DSD are discussed here. The first has a long history integrating the prevention, management, and resolution of disputes in the construction industry, particularly public infrastructure projects. The second examines corporate dispute streams through use of early case assessment and early dispute resolution policies. The third considers the federal government's procurement procedures. Less developed, but on the horizon, is a fourth example: the role of technology in affecting disputes and addressing them.

Construction Project Dispute Management

The construction industry traditionally employs three distinct DSD processes: partnering, dispute boards, and construction arbitration. In construction disputes, there are two primary parties—the contractor and the client—as well as a network of other possible parties (subcontractors) and stakeholders (local and national authorities, environmental and other interest groups, and the general public). In most instances, the primary parties select the process. Partnering and dispute boards are selected before a project begins, to address disputes that subsequently arise during the course of a construction project; construction arbitration may be selected by the parties either before or after initiation of a project.

Partnering, in which the contractor and client collaborate as equals in establishing the business objectives and partnering principles for project management, evolved in response to adversarial and expensive construction litigation, which tended to result in poor performance, time delays, cost increases, and poor quality of workmanship.[2] Parties may conduct training sessions together to establish their working relationship and optimize performance in terms of cost, time, quality, buildability, fitness for purpose, and other success criteria and to articulate steps for preventing disputes or resolving them as they arise.[3] Industry experience with partnering has been positive overall, with a high percentage of cases enjoying cost savings, on-time completion, lower inspection costs, and high levels of party satisfaction.[4]

A second process for handling construction disputes is the formation of dispute review boards. The neutral may offer expert opinions, mediate, offer nonbinding or binding advice, or adjudicate. Dispute review or resolution (nonbinding) boards and dispute adjudication (binding) boards usually consist of three to five experts who follow a project from its inception. Such boards are used worldwide in major infrastructure projects. In some cases, a dispute resolution advisor performs on-site visits and conducts meetings so that disputes are less likely to occur or to escalate. Experience in the United Kingdom (where dispute boards are mandatory) with the International Federation of Consulting Engineers and with World Bank projects has led to the use of such boards increasingly becoming standard industry practice. Key factors that contribute to satisfaction are the timing of the neutral's engagement, the neutral's knowledge of a particular project, and the opportunity to use a process selected by the parties (rather than one imposed by law). Generally, facilitative interventions are better received during the project, because they engage the interests of all disputing parties and their inputs on resolution; evaluative adjudication is more suited to payment issues in which the neutral considers all the salient facts and makes a decision on what she considers a just outcome.[5]

A third approach for construction dispute resolution is the more formal process of construction arbitration. The American Arbitration Association, the primary provider of commercial and construction dispute resolution services, developed construction industry arbitration rules with three different paths for cases of different sizes. The fast-track path covers cases with claims of less than $100,000 and emphasizes speed and simplicity with accelerated timetables, expedited arbitrator appointment, limited information exchange, and streamlined hearings. The standard-track path is aimed at cases with claims up to $1 million and focuses on arbitrators with clearly articulated authority, expedited proceedings, and a concise written breakdown of the award. The large-and-complex-track path is for cases with claims of more than $1 million and employs an elite panel of neutrals, special supplementary hearing procedures, and arbitrator-supervised discovery.[6] The American Arbitration Association has sought to maximize the flexibility of its arbitration procedures and customize the process to the needs of the cases. Further, the association pruned its roster of construction arbitrators to enhance quality of neutrals and maintains a multidisciplinary list of arbitrators with legal, design and engineering, and construction expertise.

Of these processes, partnering agreements take effect soonest. To anticipate and prevent disputes, the contracting partners become acquainted with their respective executives and managers and agree on processes for exchanging information and keeping current on the project's progress. They may also undergo joint training on interest-based negotiation. The intent of partnering is to identify tensions before disputes emerge and escalate. Dispute review boards may also be agreed on before commencement of a project and take a nonbinding (review) or binding (adjudication) approach. Once it is in place, the board stands ready to provide expertise for timely resolution. A dispute advisor can also monitor issues and tensions before they escalate.

The stakes are sufficiently high in public infrastructure construction projects for the parties to give significant thought to DSD. The parties' goals are usually aligned—everyone wants the project done well, on time and on budget, with working relationships intact—which creates incentive to negotiate terms for preventing, managing, and resolving disputes. The parties have the authority to control that design, thus tailoring the procedure and role of dispute handler. Most parties are familiar with the baseline provisions offered by professional associations and will form contracts. If other parties or nonparty stakeholders are involved, then other processes (e.g., public agency hearings, court litigation) may operate in tandem with the specialized construction dispute system processes.

The Big Dig in Boston, Massachusetts,[7] provides an illustrative example of a construction project DSD. Officially the Boston Central Artery/Harbor Tunnel project, the Big Dig was the largest urban transportation project in U.S. history. It cost $14.5 billion and involved seventy-five primary construction contracts with hundreds of subcontracts. The project started in 1991 and was substantially completed in 2005. It comprised design and construction of major tunnels, highway interchanges, and a fourteen-lane river crossing—all through, over, and under a major American city. The project was built under the auspices of the Massachusetts Highway Department, a state agency. The Federal Highway Administration, the major funder of the project, was involved in overseeing its design and execution.

Massachusetts Highway Department planners recognized the potential benefit of a well-designed dispute resolution process to handle claims faster and less expensively than through court proceedings while providing for technically sound solutions.[8] Secondary goals were flexibility and control over conflicts and preservation of the client-contractor relationships. The key elements of the system were partnering retreats, a multilevel issue resolution process, dispute review boards, and mediation. The general design of the system was in the hands of the highway department planners, with assistance from a management consultant (a joint venture of Bechtel Corporation and Parsons Brinckerhoff Company).

PARTNERING RETREATS. The objectives of the partnering sessions were to prevent disputes, involve stakeholders, and design multiple dispute resolution processes. Initially, only contractors whose contracts were for more than $1 million and at least one year were involved in these retreats. After some successful sessions, other stakeholders (design contractors, internal partnerships, subcontractors, and other engineers) were invited to join in. The facilitators stressed the value of teamwork, attempting to focus all parties on common goals rather than self-interest. The purpose was to encourage cooperative behavior among the different actors. In over seventy partnership retreats, facilitators guided groups of stakeholders toward a mutual orientation and team goals, such as a safe working environment and meeting budget and schedule goals.

MULTILEVEL ISSUE RESOLUTION. Multilevel procedures were introduced to encourage early negotiated resolution and early dispute management. During the partnering retreats each team committed to a resolution model of defined levels of escalated procedures for resolving disputes (which were deliberately referred to as "issues" instead of "claims" or "conflicts"). For each resolution level, the parties specified participants (field engineers to project manager) who would be most affected and familiar with the problem and time parameters (three hours to two weeks). The issue would move through all levels before it could be submitted to the dispute review board and subsequently become a claim.

DISPUTE REVIEW BOARDS. The system provided for early intervention by dispute review boards before full-fledged claims developed and moved into administrative review, arbitration, or litigation. Each contract of more than $20 million had a separate board; more than forty boards were established. Representatives from each side of a dispute suggested three potential members, from which the other side chose one. Those two members, working together, chose a third member. Their task was to resolve claims and discuss potential problems. Each board was free to design its procedures but received a suggested protocol drafted by the planners. Board members had at least ten years' experience in construction or engineering and could serve on multiple dispute review boards.

A claimant referring a claim to the dispute review board presented a statement of position with supporting documentation. The board members asked questions of the parties and witnesses to understand the factual and technical specifics. The board could make site visits to identify and handle potential disputes. The board was empowered to render a written set of findings and a legal advisory opinion. The detailed assessment of the board was anticipated to play a strong role in moving the parties to resolution, and the costs of dispute review boards were borne by both disputing parties.

MEDIATION. Last, the planners provided for the possibility of informal mediation at any stage of a dispute, using outside neutrals. (Later on, a flood of claims resulted in adjusting this mediation process.)

The Big Dig dispute system was designed in line with DSD principles, with multiple process levels that included both interest-based and rights-based options. Measured against its set goals, the system was successful as a filtering process that reduced the number of cases going to arbitration or trial. The participation in the partnering process was high, which likely led to early handling of issues before they became disputes. By 1999, some six thousand issues had been raised, half of which were resolved through the issue resolution process, with no contract claim filed in court. Over the life of the project, twenty-eight formal claims were referred to the dispute review boards, which conducted thirty advisory hearings. Mediation was used on six contracts, and in three contracts parties litigated over nine claims. Whereas relatively simple conflicts were resolved early on, the resolution of a significant number of complex claims was left to the end of the contract.

The low number of conflicts brought before and resolved by the dispute review boards can be attributed both to the effectiveness of a teamwork atmosphere fostered during the partnering retreats and, unfortunately, to weaknesses in the dispute review board design.[9] Dispute resolution experts criticized the extended resolution process for having too many layers, an adversarial tone with lawyers, time-consuming preparation for hearings, and dispute review board decisions lacking clarity and credibility. The system was developed by the planners, without input from many other stakeholders, and was not equipped to handle the high number of complex claims.[10]

Corporate Dispute-Handling Policy: Early Case Assessment and Early Dispute Resolution

John Schulman, executive vice president and general counsel for Warner Bros. Entertainment, notes, "I have a lot of sayings using the 'C' word. We don't want claims to turn into cases, or cases to turn into causes, or causes to turn into calamities."[11] He articulated well the theory behind early dispute handling. A focus on upstream intervention has been the practice of corporations like General Electric and other members of the International Institute for Conflict Prevention and Resolution (CPR) for many years.[12] This section describes the specific experience of GE during the 1990s and more recent corporate practice to prevent, manage, and resolve disputes.

In 1995, P. D. Villarreal, counsel for litigation and legal policy at GE, was faced with mushrooming litigation and a mandate to apply the Six Sigma Quality Initiative to his litigation department. Six Sigma is a management approach for achieving a defect-free manufacturing process 99.9 percent of the time. Litigation management was considered part of the manufacturing process and so needed to be defined, measured, analyzed, improved, and controlled.[13] GE was a founding member of CPR, a nonprofit association of corporate, law firm, and individual members that promoted ADR for litigated cases, and thus nominally supported use of ADR.[14]

In general, Six Sigma required that the litigation department reduce defects in its legal procedures. GE's lawyers needed to think from the company's point of view by quantifying standards of satisfaction. GE's goals were the following:

- Quick resolution of disputes
- Inexpensive resolution of disputes
- Minimal waste of executive and management time
- Reduced damage to important business relationships
- Minimized uncertainty of results

These goals expanded beyond efficient handling of specific disputes to preventing and managing conflict at earlier stages. Stakeholders were not only executives, shareholders, and employees but also GE's inside and outside counsel, vendors, customers, and partners. Overall, GE sought increases in efficiency and relationship preservation to maximize its profits.

GE's early dispute resolution program resulted. Once a business unit identified a significant dispute, over a period of sixty to ninety days in-house counsel prepared an early case assessment and management plan. The assessment included reviews of the industry and corporate context, analysis of the facts and law, damage (best and worst case scenarios), important principles and precedents, use of a judge or other neutral, venue and jurisdiction, opposing counsel, legal fees through stages of defense, and noneconomic costs and benefits. The preliminary dispute management plan included ADR and litigation.

At the first stage, designated Level 1, the business personnel closest to the dispute initiated informal, business-to-business discussions. If those discussions were unsuccessful, the case would move to Level 2, and a GE dispute resolution team, of an attorney and manager, would work with the other party through an external, third-party neutral (mediator or arbitrator) to resolve the dispute. (Employment and product disputes followed separate processes.) At Level 3, management might elect to try a case for reasons of principle, precedent, or cost effectiveness or because settlement at earlier levels was unsuccessful.

GE also employed an early warning system to identify litigation trends at the earliest stage and an after-action review by management and litigation counsel of lessons learned from each case that recommended actions to prevent or mitigate future problems. Thus, GE created a structure of linked processes to constitute a more integrated conflict management system (Table 13.1).[15]

The early dispute resolution program required significant investment in training for management and legal counsel to synchronize the complex corporate bureaucracy. A pilot project was instituted in GE's airline engine division. Offering mediation, arbitration, and a grievance procedure, the program successfully prevented any division cases going to trial. Direct savings were in

Table 13.1 GE prevention, management, and resolution processes

Prevention processes	Management processes	Resolution processes
Early warning system to identify litigation trends	Level 1: Informal business discussion and direct negotiation	Level 2: Mediation or arbitration
After-action review: lessons learned to mitigate future problems		Level 3: Adjudication

the many millions of dollars; total savings were likely far greater when taking management time saving and preservation of key business relationships into consideration.[16]

GE's Six Sigma approach helped redefine corporate legal counsel's objective from winning lawsuits to preventing and managing conflicts more efficiently. Early dispute resolution has since become fundamental to best-practice business problem-solving at multinational corporations, including Motorola, Shell Oil, DuPont, and GlaxoSmithKline. Corporate adoption of early dispute resolution required two fundamental shifts: anticipating and preventing disputes and moving from rights-based to interest-based processes. To use early dispute resolution, a company would need to determine threshold factors for applying early case assessment, such as a claim for more than a certain dollar value and whether injunctive relief, reputational harm, or a troubling precedent would significantly disrupt business operations. In its efforts, GE worked closely with its outside counsel, who needed to broaden their skill sets to assist in this expanded role of process counselor and advisor.

Villarreal subsequently designed a similar early stage system with Glaxo-SmithKline. Glaxo's Master Program emphasizes a conflict management process designed to facilitate more informed and expedited decision-making at the early stages of a dispute.[17] Delayed dispute resolution costs money, reputation, and relationships, and the program's goal is to ensure capacity for both legal counsel and the business to manage disputes on a proactive, systematic basis.

GlaxoSmithKline's program has two components: early case assessment and early dispute resolution. Early case assessment is mandatory for significant disputes that involve another business, government entity, or individual and in which there is potential for financial exposure over $1 million, significant injunctive relief, reputational harm, or precedent. As soon as a dispute comes to light, the involved GlaxoSmithKline business manager contacts the legal department, which identifies key facts, issues, business concerns, and amount at risk; Glaxo-SmithKline's objectives; what constitutes a good resolution; and the best way to achieve that resolution at the earliest possible time. The business manager and the designated dispute resolution professional attorney engage outside counsel, analyze and collect data, and develop timing and parameters for resolution in an early case assessment report. A litigation risk assessment is completed as applicable.

The early dispute resolution process calls for transforming the goals developed in the early case assessment report into action: direct negotiation begins in which the GlaxoSmithKline manager talks with the other disputant, facilitated negotiation (mediation) occurs in which an intermediary assists the parties, and then arbitration (private adjudication) takes place if the parties agree to have a neutral decide the outcome and be bound by that decision.

GlaxoSmithKline's implementation of its Master Program has involved education and internal training sessions for its legal and business managers, a webpage, and an online toolkit. Its contracts with researchers and distributors include dispute resolution provisions, and the company provides negotiation training to all its executives worldwide. The strategy has allowed the company to focus on core business functions, save money and time, avoid escalation of disputes, preserve relationships, and allow more creativity in resolving disputes.

The approaches taken by General Electric and GlaxoSmithKline are expanding throughout the corporate world.[18]

The CPR has an Early Case Assessment Toolkit available on its website,[19] and with the Centre for Effective Dispute Resolution, launched the "21st Century

Monsanto's Road Map to Relationship-Based Conflict Resolution

Monsanto, an international agricultural conglomerate, faced investors who were troubled by the company's significant litigation load. Conflicts not only threatened litigation but also diminished a core business asset: its business and commercial relationships, both existing and prospective. Monsanto and DuPont, one of its significant business partners, announced a far-reaching collaborative licensing agreement built on principles of "civil competition" and structured litigation—including executive negotiation, mediation, and efficient arbitration.[20] What factors would foster a corporation's commitment to and capacity for adopting such a holistic, collaborative licensing arrangement like Monsanto's, and what obstacles might exist? How might one evaluate the program's effectiveness?

CPR's "21st Century Pledge"

Our company believes the costs, delay and damage to relationships resulting from adversarial litigation practices have risen to levels that are unsustainable in the present day global business arena. Alternative dispute resolution (ADR) practices developed over the last 30 years have encouraged more cost-effective and collaborative solutions.

Nevertheless, we recognize innovation and advancement need to continue.

We believe it is a priority to explore the use of cost-efficient, sustainable, dispute resolution.

We believe that our businesses can and should engage in a systematic and collaborative approach to dispute management and resolution with domestic and global customers, suppliers, partners and competitors.

We believe that outside counsel can be an integral part of our dispute management team and law firms schooled in ADR can better serve our legal needs.

We believe that disputes can be resolved using ADR methods so that the outcome enhances both the company's short and long term well-being, as well as sustaining its vital business relationships.

In recognition of the foregoing, we subscribe to the following statement of principle on behalf of our company and its global subsidiaries.

Our company pledges to commit its resources to manage and resolve disputes through negotiation, mediation and other ADR processes when appropriate, with a view to establishing and practicing global, sustainable dispute management and resolution processes.[21]

Pledge" to use corporate ADR in the United States and United Kingdom (see the box with this title).[22] The aim of the pledge is to influence behavior through public commitment to this standard of dispute handling.

CPR anticipated that by taking this pledge, signatories would communicate to their stakeholders and shareholders their commitment to a proactive, systemic approach to dispute handling. Moreover, as major corporate clients increasingly seek outside counsel with this expanded systems-design skill set, successful law firms will be those that can respond to clients' growing need for full-spectrum representation.[23]

Alternative Dispute Resolution in Federal Procurement

While beholden to Congress and taxpayers instead of shareholders and investors, the federal government's procurement contracts make up a significant portion of national commerce. As in the construction and corporate examples, federal government has also adopted statutory, regulatory, and policy initiatives using a range of ADR techniques to resolve a wide variety of contractual, labor, and regulatory disputes. The Administrative Dispute Resolution Act of 1996 amended the Contract Disputes Act of 1978 to require that contracting officers and contractors provide a written explanation whenever they declined a request for ADR.[24] President Bill Clinton established the Interagency Alternative Dispute Resolution Working Group to assist the federal government in operating more efficiently and, when possible, to foster prevention and resolution of disputes. The memorandum directed the interagency group to further advance the use of ADR, training on use of ADR, procedures to obtain the use of neutrals on an expedited basis, and record keeping to evaluate ADR benefits.[25]

The military, in particular the U.S. Department of the Navy, has been on the forefront of ADR procedure development. Secretary of the Navy John Lehman established ADR for the acquisition community in 1986,[26] issuing Instruction on Use and Development of ADR to resolve disputes and conflicts as early, inexpensively, and quickly as possible and at the lowest possible organizational level. He also directed the ADR program to conduct periodic reviews.

ADR in the navy is a continuum of the process options of partnering, conciliation, facilitation, mediation, ombuds, fact-finding, minitrials, neutral evaluation, and arbitration or any combination thereof[27] and interest-based negotiation and judicial settlement. Conflicts brought to the navy's ADR procedures could be workplace, environmental, contract, and personnel (both navy and civilian). The navy hosts a video on the experience of various stakeholders with the ADR program's mediation process.[28]

Contracting and DSD

Underlying any business relationship is a voluntary—implied or explicit—agreement on its terms. Customers enter a website or a brick-and-mortar store and offer payment for performance of a service or delivery of a product. Partners negotiate the terms of a joint venture. Suppliers specify conditions for provision of a product or services. Significant agreements are negotiated and formalized in a written contract. Contract law scholars Robert Scott and George Triantis of Stanford Law School[29] discuss a theory of contract design that balances the efficiency of investment at the front end (time to negotiate precise rather than vague terms) and back end (enforcement or litigation). This theory argues that the parties try to anticipate whether transaction costs will be greater during contract negotiation or in later litigation.

One common contract provision concerns how disputes will be handled. Dispute resolution clauses range from a single sentence (e.g., "the parties will use all reasonable efforts to resolve disputes that arise") to multiple pages on the prospective processes and providers. Parties tend to be cooperative during the initial phase of contract negotiation, making this stage an agreeable setting for anticipating the kinds of issues that are likely to arise and providing a suitable process for resolution.

Standardized arbitration clauses have been used for decades, as well as forum selection, choice of law, and other procedural terms. More recently, multistep clause drafting allows sequential stages of dispute resolution in consensual (negotiation, mediation) and adjudicatory processes (arbitration or litigation).[30] John Lande has long advocated planned early dispute resolution, to parallel the thoughtful strategic planning that business executives readily invest in.[31]

Thomas Stipanowich, of Pepperdine University's Straus Institute for Dispute Resolution, and Ryan Lamare conducted an empirical study of corporate counsel at Fortune 1,000 companies on their experience with ADR.[32] A comparison of their 1997 and 2011 surveys shows that the more recent respondents used arbitration less frequently, but virtually every corporate counsel used mediation. Corporate counsel are increasingly involved in control of the dispute management process, such as early case assessment and selection of neutrals.[33] Most often, use of ADR is triggered by contract dispute clauses.[34]

In drafting dispute provisions, parties choose the process that will best meet their underlying goals. Periods of negotiation or mediation would be favored if the parties' goals are to maintain their relationship and maintain control over the process and outcome. The importance of privacy, the desire for a court to decide a remedy, and litigation costs are also factors to be considered in process choice. Arbitration might be attractive to parties wishing to select a neutral with substantive expertise; design customized, expedited procedures; and maintain privacy of the proceedings and outcome.[35]

A multistep clause provides a sequence of processes. Timing (how long to attempt resolution through each process), what circumstances trigger use of each process, the availability of provisional remedies, and conditions for enforcement can be tailored to the parties' needs. It may be important to specify schedules; who does what, where; how information is exchanged; and degrees of confidentiality. The detail required may depend on the parties' performance and breaches of agreement, the parties' priorities, and how urgent parties deem the need for consensus (e.g., before or after a business deal is executed).[36]

CPR's leadership and members have devoted extensive expertise to outlining the role a corporate law department can play in designing a dispute management system tailored to its client and the given stream of disputes. They emphasize the importance of creating a core group of senior legal and business executives, conducting a pilot program, providing training tailored to the corporate culture, and ensuring a systematic analysis of covered cases, access to a full spectrum of processes, effective ADR advocacy strategies, and evaluation of practice success.[37]

In 2016–2017, the Global Pound Conference[38] sponsored a series of forty events bringing together stakeholders in dispute resolution: commercial parties, lawyers, dispute resolution providers, and influencers. Four questions were posed and responses collected:

- *What do parties want, need, and expect with regard to access to justice and dispute resolution systems?* Parties focus on money or a particular legal outcome and look to legal counsel to lead them to efficient and predictable results.
- *How is the market currently addressing those needs and expectations?* Providers tend to focus on parties' interests, the rule of law, and general principles of fairness, with significant value placed on face-saving, control over outcomes, and cost efficiency. Mediation was considered the most effective ADR process, but adjudicative processes were supported by roughly half the attendees.
- *How can dispute resolution be improved?* More emphasis on predispute processes, such as mediation, arbitration, and hybrids, all with court encouragement. Lawyers were deemed most resistant to change.
- *What action items should be considered and by whom?* Education was identified as the key action item, with the government, arbitrators, and judges as the chief actors.[39]

The surveys conducted as part of the conference series uncovered methods for improving commercial dispute resolution, such as drafting predispute clauses as an early, deliberate exercise rather than a last-minute boilerplate insertion; exploring how a conflict specialist (as part of upper management) could integrate dispute handling across an organization; and cooperating with experienced litigation counsel to select the processes that balance legal costs, the likely outcome, and efficiency.[40]

For cross-border commercial disputes, commercial arbitration and enforcement under the New York Convention took many years to become a standard. Similarly, mediation of cross-border disputes is gradually gaining ground with parties and counsel, especially after adoption of the 2008 European Directive on Mediation and the more recent United Nations Convention on International Settlement Agreements Resulting from Mediation, which opened for signature August 1, 2019.[41]

Smart contracts built on the blockchain are an emerging domain.[42] Two implications flow from this technological advance: the contracts are a different kind of agreement that crafts legal commitments in computer code, and use of online dispute resolution may offer comparative benefits—and even feasibility—over traditional process options.[43] Sagewise is one of several start-up companies whose platform provides solutions for prospective smart contract disputes.

Conclusion

Since medieval merchant courts, the commercial sector has valued an expert and expedited approach to resolving disputes. In modern times, contracting parties increasingly take a pragmatic approach to anticipate and prevent disputes and facilitate resolution. The parties' goals are not only to achieve a certain outcome but to minimize waste of executives' time, expense, and damage to the business relationship and productivity overall. A diverse range of processes have been employed, both interest based and rights based, often in parallel. Most notably, more emphasis is placed upstream, on preventive efforts (like partnering in the construction industry) rather than solely reacting postdispute in the courts. Part of this change is due to court ADR policies (see Chapter 7), part to a pragmatic handling of claims before they become expensive lawsuits, and part to industry organizations like CPR urging members to use early assessment tools. The best lawyers counsel their clients during the underlying business negotiation to anticipate how claims may arise and plan for how best to prevent and resolve them.

14 CONSUMER DISPUTES

A CANCER PATIENT DIES while awaiting review of his medical malpractice claim; his family sues. Thousands of homeowners struggle to renegotiate with their lenders during the Great Recession. Customers of a major online retailer search for redress when purchased products do not arrive or are defective. These examples illustrate some of the ways that individuals may be in conflict with a firm or organization over the provision of services or products. The consumer domain overlaps in context with the commercial, public, and employment arenas discussed elsewhere in this volume, but the consumer domain features unique relationships between disputants, some of which occur largely in cyberspace.

Issues to consider are as follows.

- Usually, a consumer dispute is between an individual and an organization, with the attendant power imbalance based on the latter's greater experience, information, and resources. A dispute may involve a single incident for the consumer, but the organization or firm likely faces a string of incidents over time with various disputants. How does that influence consumer DSD?
- How does the time frame of the potential intervention—upstream (predispute) or downstream (postdispute)—affect consumer DSD?
- What tensions exist around balancing efficiency (time and expense for the consumer, business, and dispute system provider) and fairness of process and outcome?[1]

We use three primary case examples to illustrate these issues. *Engalla v. Permanente Medical Group*, a medical malpractice dispute, was also discussed in Chapter 4. Following a California Supreme Court ruling on the serious inadequacies of

Kaiser Permanente's claim handling process, Kaiser sought to improve operation of its predispute mandatory arbitration process for medical malpractice claims. The second case examines mortgage foreclosure mediation between borrowers and mortgage lenders in five states. During mortgage foreclosures, mediation may be offered after foreclosure proceedings commence and thus is postdispute, or downstream in the dispute cycle. The third case examines the online auction site eBay and its process innovation of online dispute resolution that addresses issues before they become full-blown disputes and provides access to diagnosis, direct negotiation, assisted negotiation, mediation, and arbitration through online forums.

Kaiser Permanente Health System

Wilfredo Engalla had lung cancer and sought treatment from his health provider, Kaiser Permanente. Caregivers failed to diagnose and treat his condition in a timely manner, and Engalla's only recourse under his insurance plan was to file an arbitration claim. When Engalla died before his arbitration hearing, his estate filed an action in California superior court for the right to have the case heard in court.[2] Kaiser formed its Blue Ribbon Panel, whose charge was to suggest improvements to Kaiser's arbitration process, "in order to provide an arbitration system that is sensitive to the members and fair to all parties involved."[3] The panel made recommendations, listed in Chapter 4.

The Office of the Independent Administrator, established in 1999 to handle claims against Kaiser, issues annual reports on its goals of providing arbitration that is fair, timely, costs less than litigation, and protects the privacy of the parties. The report for 2018 highlighted the following:

- In 2018, the office received 606 demands, a decrease of 81 from the prior year, in all regions (Northern California, Southern California, and San Diego).
- Most (95 percent) cases involved allegations of medical malpractice.
- In approximately 32 percent of the cases, the claimants did not have attorneys.
- It took an average of sixty-three days to select an arbitrator for a case; cases closed, on average, in twelve months. For cases before a neutral arbitrator, hearings completed, on average, in less than twenty-two months.
- The Office of the Independent Administrator had a pool of 225 neutral arbitrators; 41 percent were retired judges. More than half the arbitrators served on a case.

- Of all cases, 76 percent closed through action by the parties (settlement, withdrawal, or abandonment), while the other 24 percent were decided by the neutral arbitrator (after a hearing, summary judgment, or dismissal). All cases that went to hearing were heard by a single arbitrator.
- Almost half (48 percent) of the claimants received some compensation, either when the cases settled (46 percent) or when successful after hearing (2 percent). The range of award was $4,500 to $3,469,778.
- With the consent of claimants, Kaiser paid the neutral arbitrators' fees in 93 percent of the cases closed. Hourly rates charged by neutral arbitrators averaged $524. For the 528 cases that closed and for which information was available to the Office of the Independent Administrator, the average fee charged by neutral arbitrators was $7,160.
- Parties who responded to Office of the Independent Administrator questionnaires expressed satisfaction with the neutral arbitrators and would recommend them to others, giving an average rating of 4.5 on a 5-point scale.[4]
- The arbitration system administered by Office of the Independent Administrator was better than, or the same as, going to court, according to 96 percent of the responding parties and attorneys, and 4 percent reported that it was worse.[5]

The Kaiser Arbitration Oversight Board—comprising stakeholder members from the public, employers (who make Kaiser Health Care available to their employees), labor, plaintiff bar, defense bar, physicians, hospital staff, and Kaiser Health Plan members—reviewed the 2018 annual report and used the following measures to evaluate the system: independent administration, rules, oversight, accessibility, fairly selected and qualified arbitrators, timeliness, performance measures, evaluation, cost effectiveness, convenience, clarity, audit, transparency, cultural sensitivity, and continuous improvement.[6]

Several years after the Office of the Independent Administrator was established, Kaiser took action on the panel's recommendations regarding mediation and an ombuds office by creating a hybrid process: a health care ombuds-mediator, which is now available in California.[7] This neutral party is made available at the health facility point of care when a patient raises a concern. The neutral does not advocate for the specific interests or concerns of the organization, the patient, or the provider; rather, she advocates for a fair process.[8] The ombuds-mediator can informally investigate the complaint and facilitate communication among those affected—members of the medical care team, the health care provider staff, the patient, and the patient's family. His goal is to improve satisfaction of the provider and its staff and the patient as well as patient safety. The ombuds-mediator can be flexible in developing a resolution that addresses both patient and provider perspectives in a respectful manner that helps overcome earlier mistrusts and fears. The process also flags warnings on emerging issues and provides feedback to senior management while maintaining individual confidentiality.

In Kaiser's experience, patients and families harmed by unanticipated outcomes "have the same basic trio of needs: honesty and information in real time, close to the event; an acknowledgement of their pain and suffering and an apology if warranted; and an assurance that what happened to them won't happen to someone else."[9]

More broadly, mediation offers an effective setting for meeting these needs because it centers on the patient, involves deliberate listening, and generates information from all parties to address their respective needs, allowing for apology without assigning liability. Crucially, what is said in mediation is confidential and cannot be used in court (or arbitration). Dealing with disclosure of medical errors and adverse events calls for a commitment to thoroughness and transparency in the culture of the hospital; interest-based mediation can offer an important policy option. Chris Stern Hyman and colleagues authored a study examining the potential for mediation to improve patient care.[10] The study used structured interviews of participants and mediators in thirty-one mediated malpractice lawsuits involving eleven nonprofit hospitals. The study measured perceptions of the process and mediation's effects on settlement, expenses, apology, satisfaction, and information exchange. Both plaintiff and defense attorneys were satisfied with the process, as were plaintiffs, hospital representatives, and insurers. Changes in hospitals' practices or policies to improve patient safety were identified. However, this study also demonstrates that major challenges stand in the way of achieving mediation's full benefits; absence of physician participation minimized the chances that mediated discussion of adverse events and medical errors could lead to improved quality of care.

The Medical Ombuds/Mediator program at the National Naval Medical Center in Bethesda, Maryland, offers another example of enabling providers and patients to resolve conflicts in a nonadversarial way.[11] Three success factors consistently noted were improved communication "premised on honesty, transparency, and compassion"; an "integrated conflict management system supported internally by the institution"; and "neutral, independent, and confidential conflict management experts" supported by training and coaching.[12]

Change of this sort will require medical leaders, hospital administrators, and malpractice insurers to approach medical errors and adverse events as learning opportunities and to retain lawyers who embrace mediation as an opportunity to solve problems, show compassion, and improve care.[13] As noted by Viggo Boserup and colleagues of the American Bar Association Health Law Section,

> When given the opportunity, people who have experienced an unanticipated outcome of a medical procedure tell the mediator that they want information. They desire to learn what happened, why it happened, who was responsible, and what might be done to make them whole. They also want to know what can be done to keep it from happening again so that the patient/patient's family can be assured that the perceived injury was not in vain. . . . The point is not that compensation, typically money, does not matter; rather, it is that a patient who feels injured often has needs that money alone cannot satisfy.[14]

Patients with medical injuries are now being offered communication-and-resolution programs. Research on these patients' experience reveals encouraging results. Patients were most satisfied when communications were empathetic and nonadversarial. "Patients and families expressed a strong need to be heard and expected the attending physician to listen without interrupting during conversations about the event . . . and strongly desired to know what the hospital did to prevent recurrences of the event."[15]

Since the *Engalla* case, Kaiser's dispute-handling goals have been to offer a timely, cost-efficient, confidential, and fair process. While the arbitral process is mandatory predispute, its transparency of neutrals, due process, and outcomes have contributed to its fairness. Alan Morrison of George Washington University Law School evaluated Kaiser's system on the basis of its goals "to provide a fair, timely and low-cost arbitration system that respects the privacy of the parties." Morrison noted the necessary trade-offs among the system's goals and concluded,

> Although I am an arbitration skeptic, the Kaiser Permanente arbitration system is almost certainly less expensive for claimants and faster than court litigation, and neither its speed nor its low cost seems to interfere with a claimant's ability to present his or her case fully. On the output side, the results seem reasonably just, and there is no evidence that claimants would be happier (and win more often and/or obtain larger verdicts) in the civil justice system, in the same time frames and at the same costs. It also appears that, for small and medium size claims, Kaiser Permanente's arbitration program makes it more

possible for them to be brought there than in court. The loss of a public trial before a jury is a negative, but whether it outweighs the positives is a question that will not be answered in the same way by everyone. What can be said is that Kaiser Permanente's arbitration system has a number of very positive aspects to it, and almost no obvious negatives beyond constraining the choice of forum, which suggests that it deserves further study.[16]

The addition of the option for a health care ombuds-mediator offers an even more timely, confidential, and flexible means for all affected parties to resolve issues as soon and as inexpensively as possible.[17]

The University of Florida Health system incorporated a mandatory presuit mediation agreement into its informed consent process. Data drawn from the program's first eight years, 2008–2015, demonstrated a reduction in economic and noneconomic costs of traditional litigation. Success was measured by number of claims resolved relative to the total claims mediated through the program (nearly 70 percent), the time from claim to resolution (reduced from five years for a litigated case to an average of six months), and legal expenses for each settled claim (reduced 87 percent from national average). The positive results were attributed to the Florida mediation infrastructure of mediator certification, standards of professional conduct, and a mediator disciplinary process to enforce those standards. Further, early nonevaluative mediation intervention contributes to benefits beyond compensation, including enhanced patient understanding of what happened and what will be done to reduce recurrence, improved patient safety, and a rebuilt patient-provider relationship.[18]

Mortgage Foreclosure Mediation
Before the foreclosure crisis that culminated in 2008, people borrowed money from their local savings and loan provider to purchase a home. If any problems

---

Discussion Question

A complex form of medical conflict relates to the advances of medical technology. Consider a country that has highly sophisticated genetic treatments for diseases, such that patients will come from around the world for care. What kind of health care ombuds-mediator option would make sense in this cross-cultural situation of hospital, physician, and patient?

arose, the borrower could deal with this local financial institution. Starting in the 1990s, mortgages were securitized, or bundled with other mortgages in a secondary mortgage market. Borrowers no longer had a direct relationship with their lenders; rather, they dealt with a loan servicer.

In Arizona, Florida, Illinois, Nevada, and Wisconsin, mediation programs were designed to address the overwhelming numbers of home foreclosures that followed the Great Recession. States each regulate the foreclosure process differently. A basic procedural distinction is whether the state follows a judicial or nonjudicial foreclosure process. A judicial foreclosure process requires that the lender give notice to the borrower upon default, after which the lender files with a court the notice of foreclosure on the mortgaged property. A nonjudicial foreclosure state has no centralized foreclosure process; rather, the lender files the notice of foreclosure with the borrower and can proceed to take possession of, and sell, the mortgaged property.[19]

Arizona

Arizona allows both judicial and nonjudicial foreclosures. In early 2010, foreclosures in Arizona were double the national rate.[20] A basic frustration among homeowners was their inability to have a meaningful discussion with the entities that owned or serviced their mortgages. The U.S. Bankruptcy Court for the District of Arizona created a foreclosure mediation pilot program for homeowners who filed in bankruptcy court to halt foreclosure proceedings. Distinct from other programs, this pilot program provided an impartial forum, not one advocating for homeowners to remain in their homes. The core problem targeted by the pilot was communication between homeowners and lenders. Lenders wanted an impartial program (one not geared to punish them for the foreclosure crisis); homeowners wanted lenders to commit to good-faith participation. The court could direct or either party could elect for the case to go to mediation. Mediators were selected on the basis of their financial, real estate, and mediation expertise.

Within fourteen days of a mediation order, a telephone conference (with counsel or pro se) was arranged to schedule the mediation and information exchange. As of December 2012, the pilot had forty-six mediation orders and had completed twenty-eight mediations, of which 53 percent were settled. Another 7 percent of mediated cases settled after the mediation conference, and in 11 percent of the cases negotiations were continued. Key lessons learned were the importance of stakeholder participation in design of the program; impartiality of mediation to facilitate communication, understanding, and resolution development; neutrals' expertise; opportunity for information exchange; and case screening by judges.[21]

Florida

Florida is among the most developed states in its mediation practice and regulation. As of 2008, the Florida Supreme Court had certified nearly six thousand mediators, the Office of the State Courts Administrator had a state office of dispute resolution, and a state-wide system of mediation program administrators was in each of the twenty judicial circuits. Nevertheless, that preparedness and enthusiasm for mediation services did not translate into successful mediation during the foreclosure crisis.

When foreclosure filings increased fivefold in two years, the Florida Supreme Court created the Task Force on Residential Mortgage Foreclosure Cases.[22] However, few mortgage foreclosure cases were referred by trial judges to mediation. Reasons included the power disparity between parties and a strong judicial sentiment that these cases were inappropriate for mediation. Further, court rules on funding and appearances were exacerbated by the lack of administrative staff to handle the cases, lack of financial resources by homeowners to pay for mediation, and lack of willingness of plaintiffs-lenders to engage in negotiations.

After an administrative order to guide mediation design was implemented in the circuit courts,[23] borrowers' contacts about mediation increased, yet relatively few cases that were eligible for mediation settled. Foreclosure cases were deemed successful if they resulted in loan modification, short sale, or transfer of deed (to mortgage holder) in lieu of foreclosure. It remained difficult to notify borrowers of the mediation option, there was a perception that the process was biased toward bankers, and only cases that could not be settled ended up in court (and thus eligible to be referred to mediation.) As of December 2011, the administrative order authorizing mediation was rescinded.[24] Despite significant support by the judicial leadership and mediation profession, the Florida foreclosure experience was a very disappointing one.

Illinois

Resolution Systems Institute (RSI), a Chicago-based nonprofit, undertook a years-long evaluation of foreclosure mediation at six different programs in Illinois. The programs all had goals to increase borrower understanding, facilitate communication among parties, and keep parties accountable through the process. RSI's assessment of the programs identified four elements that correlated with the more successful of the six programs:

- Simple entry requirements for borrowers
- An ongoing focus on keeping cases moving forward

- Provision of financial counseling and legal services to borrowers
- Continual monitoring of program performance and use of monitoring data to improve program functioning[25]

Nevada

In 2009, the Nevada legislature adopted the Foreclosure Mediation Act that created the State of Nevada Foreclosure Mediation Program to provide "homeowners and lenders with an opportunity to discuss alternatives to foreclosure" and help keep families in their homes (placing more emphasis on homeowner advocacy than on neutral facilitation of borrowers and lenders). The guiding principles for the program are respect, equity, accountability, and sensitivity.[26] An advisory committee[27] was formed to recommend rules and evaluate the effectiveness, operation, policies, and practices of the program. The program allows homeowners to participate in foreclosure mediation after the filing of a notice of default by a lender or trustee and requires creditors to bring certain documentation. Since October 2013, homeowners have been automatically referred into foreclosure mediation after the lender files the default notice. More than 12,000 mediations were conducted between 2009 and 2011, of which 88 percent resulted in no foreclosure. Of those nonforeclosure cases, 46 percent resulted in loan modification agreements that allowed homeowners to remain in their homes. During Nevada's fiscal year 2013, 1,411 mediations were held; 31 percent reached agreement. About half the homeowners whose cases reached agreement were able to remain in their homes.

Wisconsin

Wisconsin is a judicial foreclosure state, which requires any foreclosure action to be processed through a court. Milwaukee's mayor convened the Milwaukee Foreclosure Partnership Initiative in September 2009; the initiative's steering committee, comprising stakeholders, suggested creating a mediation option for homeowners and lenders.[28] The process for notifying homeowners of the mediation option entails attaching a notice and the mediation request form, on pink paper, to each foreclosure summons filed in court. Applications for mediation can be submitted by mail, email, or fax; the court summons provides information on applying for mediation. A response from the lender's counsel is due within seven days. If the parties agree to mediate, each pays a hundred-dollar fee and completes a financial questionnaire before the mediation session. Mediation sessions are one or two hours long; the homeowner, lender's counsel, and mediator appear in person, and the loan servicer (located anywhere in country, but at a desk with access to computer files) appears by phone. Housing counselors sometimes attend to support the homeowner.[29]

About 20 percent of homeowners in Milwaukee who receive a foreclosure summons request mediation. In evaluating the Milwaukee experience, Andrea Schneider of Marquette Law School and Natalie Fleury highlight the care given to encouraging participation, making key loan information available when needed, suiting the process to the situation, and giving the process credibility (mediator impartiality and homeowner representation) to get good results (for borrower and lender). A satisfaction survey, administered to borrowers, lenders' counsel, and borrowers' counsel immediately after the mediation session, found that process satisfaction, outcome satisfaction, and mediator performance were rated positive or very positive, at 94.9 percent. Two additional factors that were rated positively were fluidity (ability of process to adapt over time) and permeability (extension of the program beyond the Milwaukee community).[30]

Lydia Nussbaum undertook an extensive evaluation of nearly twenty mediation programs (including Arizona, Florida, Illinois, Nevada, and Wisconsin mediation programs). From this review, she drew a preliminary set of best practices: borrowers benefit more when screened and referred to programs by housing counselors who can help access the necessary information and educate parties on options for resolution; programs are more effective with participation of a trained third-party facilitator as well as the homeowner, lender representative, housing counselor (e.g., Department of Housing and Urban Development–approved housing counseling organizations), and legal assistance.[31] Other key elements are judicial oversight and sanctions and adequate resources to fund the program and compensate the mediators and the housing and legal counselors. Funds come from borrower and homeowner contributions and government funding.

Nussbaum notes the potential for achieving efficiency and a meaningful opportunity for informed negotiation between the parties:

> By introducing facilitated negotiation as a compulsory step in foreclosure proceedings, [foreclosure ADR] programs reconstruct important aspects of the borrower-lender relationship lost by securitization. Specifically, they establish clear lines of communication and require the third-party loan servicer to behave as a traditional lender might, assessing whether foreclosure in fact makes the most financial sense for investors or whether an alternative might yield a greater return on the investment.[32]

Comparison of the five programs reveals the range of approaches taken. All had a multistakeholder advisory body. The goals varied between providing a neutral forum for communicative justice between lender and homeowner (Arizona and Milwaukee) and promoting social justice to enable homeowners to stay in their homes (Florida and Nevada). The processes varied as well: court-screened and court-ordered mediation (Arizona and Florida) or homeowner-elected mediation (Nevada and Milwaukee); judicial foreclosure (Milwaukee) and nonjudicial foreclosure (Arizona and Nevada). Florida used extensive existing mediation infrastructure through its court system but mandated a uniform model and preexisting procedural court rules that confounded access and use. Mediators in Florida were certified through the court's procedural rules, in Milwaukee were certified by the Marquette Law School, and in Nevada were assigned by judges in the U.S. Bankruptcy Court. Most foreclosure mediation programs focus at the downstream stage of dispute handling: after a borrower has fallen behind on the mortgage payments, the lender has initiated foreclosure proceedings, and the case is under the jurisdiction of the local or bankruptcy court. A more integrated system might offer financial literacy training to prospective homeowners to reduce the risk of foreclosure or early warning information sessions for homeowners finding themselves unable to meet their obligations, plus a clearly outlined communication process between borrowers and lenders. Processes like these have been launched by the U.S. Consumer Financial Protection Bureau.[33]

eBay

Since 1995, online platforms that facilitate commercial and personal transactions have proliferated. Emblematic of this revolution is eBay, the leading online auction website, which employs over 14,000 people and has more than 182 million active buyers. As of 2018, over $21 billion in gross merchandise value was traded on

---

Discussion Question

The broad reach of the mortgage crisis previews another crosscutting financial crisis, that of student debt and default. A 2018 U.S. Department of Education report notes that "at nearly $1.4 trillion in loans outstanding, student debt is now the second-largest source of household debt (after housing) . . . [yet] the main problem is not high levels of debt per student, but rather the low earnings of dropout and for-profit [college] students."[34] What design approach that addresses upstream and downstream factors might be considered?

eBay. Although less than 1 percent of these transactions generate problems, the problems that do arise are not easily resolved by traditional litigation because of geography and procedural requirements.[35]

From its inception in 1995, eBay founder Pierre Omidyar articulated an umbrella of good-faith business guidelines and anticipated the importance of creating informational processes to clarify communication and resolve misunderstandings before online transactions became disputes. The case of eBay presents two types of innovation: online techniques that can substitute for face-to-face and telephonic commercial interactions and an integrated structure of online processes for resolving disputes. eBay's system demonstrates how online interactions have the capacity for increased transparency (of information and access) and accountability.

eBay's goal is to maximize the potential for online businesses to thrive. Such business depends on buyers receiving the goods they intend to purchase and on sellers receiving payment, both in a timely manner. Thus, eBay has been willing to commit financial and personnel resources to provide a dispute resolution system that reflects goals of accessibility, low cost, efficiency, privacy, voluntariness, and independence—all in the interest of increasing business profits and maintaining trust in the online marketplace. Potential stakeholders include individual and corporate business buyers and sellers; repeat and one-time traders; eBay's management, employees, shareholders, and directors; third-party vendors (e.g., escrow services); mediators; insurance appraisal companies; and other online commerce platforms.

Multiple processes are integrated in eBay's online platform. Disputants have different types of preventive, management, and resolution mechanisms available to them. Bulletin boards, which are public online websites, are available for trading questions, opinions, and socializing. The "eBay Community" web page provides hundreds of expert community members to identify, address, and resolve issues. The company's web page "Feedback Forum" describes its rating system, which allows buyers and sellers to comment on transactions and create a reputation. This automated process allows buyers to get information—for example, on a merchant's service or product—and set reasonable expectations for delivery and quality criteria. After a transaction, eBay buyers can submit a positive, neutral, or negative rating of the seller and a comment. If a seller receives too many negative ratings in too short a time, that seller's account will be suspended. The "Seller Ratings" web page enables detailed, anonymous buyer feedback, with financial incentives for good performance and penalties (such as being thrown off the site) for bad. eBay sellers can also leave a positive feedback rating and comment on buyers.

The company's "Resolution Center" provides an online hub where users can see all their transactional problems in one place, communicate with their transaction partners, and track problems to resolution. Through direct negotiation, parties can communicate via an internet forum to describe problems and possibly agree on resolution.[36] Approximately 60 percent of filed disputes are resolved at this stage, at no charge. Additional software-assisted processes act as a progressive filter to resolve disputes; mediation, evaluation, and arbitration are available if direct negotiation does not lead to successful resolution.

The eBay processes are not exclusive but rather offered as an accessible alternative or supplement to other consumer complaint processes, such as credit card chargebacks, small claims court, the federal Consumer Financial Protection Bureau, and the FBI's Internet Crime Complaint Center. By making its information and resolution processes accessible online and by integrating automated enforcement of outcomes, eBay has provided temporal and financial incentives for its customers to use these internal processes.

A key feature of the eBay dispute settlement system is that it functions in the same technological domain as the underlying business transactions. eBay has engaged stakeholders by encouraging continual buyer and seller feedback. An evaluation process has led to design improvements in this structure of integrated processes. Inadequate information is at the heart of most disputes, whose resolution is vastly facilitated by new internet-enabled processes. As noted above, a majority of disputes are resolved amicably through the information exchange facilitated by direct negotiation online, which enhances eBay's reputation.[37]

These online dispute handling processes have expanded since eBay's design, both in scope of application and in geography, within the business-to-consumer domain and beyond.[38] Amy Schmitz, a leading scholar in consumer rights, and Colin Rule, former director of eBay's dispute resolution program and founder of Modria, an online business-to-consumer platform developer, have examined these online processes from the perspective of the business and the consumer with the ultimate goal of providing fast and easy access to achieve fair and consistent redress. In *The New Handshake*,[39] they identify key factors for optimal business-to-consumer redress design that enable every customer issue to be resolved satisfactorily as easily, quickly, securely, and fairly as possible—and cement consumers' trust in and loyalty to the merchant. The authors underscore how the interests of consumers, businesses, and regulatory authorities converge.

The European Union has taken the lead in regulatory policy for online dispute resolution (ODR). Pablo Cortés tracks the EU experience with its Directive on Alternative Dispute Resolution for Consumers and the Regulation on Online

Dispute Resolution for Consumers (the latter entered into effect in 2015).[40] Now, all EU member states must ensure that consumer complaints can be resolved online by nationally certified ADR entities. The Directive on Alternative Dispute Resolution does not make participation compulsory but requires all EU national governments to ensure availability of certified providers that meet the procedural standards in the directive—for example, process complaints online, be free or low cost to the consumer, be independent, resolve disputes within a specified period, be transparent in publishing annual activity reports, and be fair and legal.[41]

On the international front, Working Group III of the UN Commission on International Trade Law (UNCITRAL) undertook a multiyear effort around use of ODR and issued technical notes in April 2017. As noted in the preamble, "Online dispute resolution can assist the parties in resolving the dispute in a simple, fast, flexible and secure manner, without the need for physical presence at a meeting or hearing." The technical notes set forth an approach to ODR system design that encompasses negotiation, facilitated settlement, and a final-stage decision and embodies "principles of impartiality, independence, efficiency, effectiveness, due process, fairness, accountability and transparency."[42]

The design and implementation of ODR is expanding beyond ecommerce to courts,[43] administrative tribunals, and private firms worldwide, and it is raising questions about the relationship between private and public justice[44] and whether international performance and ethical standards could or should be established. The International Council on Online Dispute Resolution was formed to explore such standards in conjunction with the American National Standards Institute and offer ODR training and certification. Motivating principles for such standards are that they be accessible, accountable, competent, confidential, equal, fair and

---

Discussion Questions

An emerging issue in the online world is that of cyberbullying, which is not so much a conflict to be resolved as a victim-offender situation in which online platforms are used in ways that lead to harm—emotional, psychological, physical, or financial. One example of a platform for online harassment is Twitter. What possible goals would motivate development of a DSD system? Would the designer differentiate among kinds of claims or claimants? Who are the stakeholders? What combination of processes would advance those stakeholders' goals?[45]

impartial, legal, secure, and transparent. Converting these principles into operational metrics through a multistakeholder, global process would contribute to an upstream literacy around the standards and their implementation.[46]

Conclusion

Consumers of products and services generate a category of disputes distinct from many others. These disputes reflect tensions between individual and organizational entities: corporations have more power and resources (economic, human, and legal) than individual consumers. Corporations have experience handling disputes and often have the ability to unilaterally establish the dispute resolution process before disputes arise. Further, businesses and consumers have different goals: companies tend to emphasize efficiency and reputation, while consumers seek a fair process for voicing concerns and achieving just outcomes.

In Kaiser Permanente's process, the contractually mandated arbitration procedure for medical malpractice complaints was strengthened by the guidance of a multistakeholder advisory group, neutral arbitrators, transparent operational statistics, and a complementary process of ombuds-mediation available from the time of medical service to sort out any surprises or misunderstandings during treatment. Similarly, mortgage foreclosure programs tended to be more successful—whether mediation was ordered by the court or elected by the parties—if they were designed by a multistakeholder group and oriented to ensure an expert neutral could guide discussion between an informed lender and homeowner to explore alternatives to foreclosure. The eBay system provides the broadest array of process choice, with multiple preventive and management options available predispute, as well as a progressive series of postdispute processes, from diagnosis and direct negotiation to mediation to arbitration.

The range of current and emerging information and communication technology, along with big data and artificial intelligence, will continue to pose challenges to fairness, security, and regulation. Ongoing events in the sports, elder care, financial, and medical fields have highlighted concerns about mandatory predispute arbitration that preclude the consumer from bringing a claim to court. So far, the U.S. Supreme Court has upheld predispute arbitration provisions pursuant to the Federal Arbitration Act.[47] Efforts are underway in several fora to regulate such mandatory arbitration provisions in the context of consumers. The Consumer Financial Protection Bureau issued regulations pursuant to the Dodd-Frank Wall Street Reform and Consumer Protection Act. The bureau's rule would not have barred predispute arbitration clauses outright but would have prohibited banks and other consumer financial companies from including mandatory arbitration clauses that block group lawsuits in any new contract after the compliance date. The rule would have required more transparency regarding arbitration, to help the bureau and others better monitor such arbitrations for procedural fairness, and provided an incentive for businesses more broadly to comply with the law.[48] The Arbitration Fairness Act of 2018 (S.2591) submitted to the 115th Congress would prohibit predispute agreements that require arbitration in employment, consumer, antitrust, or civil rights disputes but would allow postdispute agreements to arbitrate. These regulatory and legislative efforts have not gone very far, but the issues will certainly remain prominent in commercial, financial, consumer, and regulatory affairs.

PART III

INTERNATIONAL AND COMPARATIVE SYSTEMS

IMAGINE A NATION EMBROILED in a horrific civil war for ten years. Over half a million civilians were killed and another estimated half a million were injured or raped. The country's infrastructure lies in ruins and much of the countryside is without electricity or running water. It has now been four months since rebel and government forces finally laid down their arms. The United Nations just passed a resolution changing its mission in the nation from peacekeeping to aiding with the transition. You are a senior program director on the UN transition team. Your job is to conduct a comprehensive needs assessment and propose a multifaceted conflict resolution system that addresses the country's many needs and enables it to move forward in peace.

Where do you start? Many are calling for those who committed atrocities during the war to be brought to justice, but the courthouse has been destroyed, some of the accused are children who were fighting for the rebels against their will, and the mastermind of the rebel's entire strategy is outside your geographic jurisdiction. You have a number of options you could propose, from trials against perpetrators to development projects to rebuild devastated communities to reintegration programs for former child soldiers. What should you prioritize? Who must be involved in the decision-making process? How do you ensure that whatever you propose is actually feasible?

The concept of transitional justice focuses on seeking accountability for the crimes of war, often centering on retributive justice: bringing perpetrators to trial. The possible goals of transitional justice extend beyond punishment, however, to include reconciliation, psychological healing, and good government to support a stable, just society. After a war or the collapse of an authoritarian regime, societies struggle with how to address mass human rights violations perpetrated against the population while trying to establish order and rebuild the nation. Processes include exposing the truth, holding perpetrators accountable, providing reparations for victims, and reforming the state institutions that failed to prevent and may have actively participated in atrocities. This is an extremely complicated undertaking. Following a period of violent conflict, passions run high and people with varying degrees of culpability may remain in positions of power.

Issues to consider are as follows.

- What are the appropriate goals for transitional justice and who should decide?
- Is it possible to identify one set of standards or even define "best practices" for transitional justice, or is each case unique?
- In the rapidly evolving transitional context, with limited resources, how should the designers prioritize and sequence the timing of transitional justice processes with other postconflict security, development, governance, and infrastructure needs?
- In evaluating the success of a transitional justice design, should the outcome be measured against an ideal or against what was possible under the circumstances, within real-world constraints?

Culture and context matter enormously in transitional justice because designers work within a rapidly changing society that is emerging from trauma. The needs of a particular country will depend on its history and culture as well as the evolving political, economic, and societal context. The design process must begin promptly and adapt in a swiftly changing environment, often with very limited resources and many stakeholders. There will also be many designers, who may include peace negotiators (who may address transitional justice issues in a peace agreement), government officials, UN representatives, officials from countries providing foreign aid, and experts in international criminal law and transitional justice.

Key Concepts and Process Categories

Accountability

Acts of mass violence are planned, organized, and carried out by numerous individuals. Transitioning out of a period of violence requires identifying those responsible and holding them accountable for their actions. The purpose of creating accountability is to restore order, provide some sense of justice to victims and survivors, and send the message that one cannot commit acts of violence with impunity.

The need for accountability is often addressed by a trial process. In the transitional justice context, such trials have been held by courts at the local, national, or international level, through special tribunals or the International Criminal Court, or through some combination of these venues. The International Criminal Court is intended to complement existing national judicial systems and may therefore exercise its jurisdiction only when certain conditions are met, such as when national courts are unwilling or unable to prosecute.[1]

Prosecutions alone, however, cannot provide sufficient justice for survivors. Even well-funded court systems like the International Criminal Court have financial, timing, and human resources constraints, and domestic courts are often weakened or even destroyed during conflict. As a result, trials often focus only on those most responsible for the conflict: the planners and organizers. In cases where implementers are prosecuted, it is usually only the most senior-ranking soldiers or militants. Those who carry out the murders, kidnaps, and rapes are rarely brought to trial. Designers of transitional justice processes often try to address this "impunity gap"[2] by supplementing criminal trials with other transitional justice mechanisms such as reparations and community or traditional justice measures. The design aspects of accountability measures thus vary considerably among cases, as seen in the examples of Rwanda and East Timor.

Rwanda faced the aftermath of a civil war and genocide that killed an estimated eight hundred thousand people—over a tenth of the country's population and three-quarters of ethnic Tutsis.[3] With very limited resources and an urgent need to address many thousands of perpetrators,[4] Rwanda and the international community created a multitiered set of processes geared to the types and severity of alleged crimes. A special international tribunal prosecuted those accused of leading the genocide, and the Rwandan courts prosecuted the next tier of defendants. The *gacaca* courts, a quasi-judicial form based on a traditional justice process, were created to address and reintegrate the lower-level perpetrators at the village level.[5]

Following a period of colonial domination by Portugal, East Timor (now the nation of Timor-Leste) was brutally occupied by Indonesia from 1975 to 1999. A referendum in favor of independence resulted in mass violence instigated by Indonesia and allied militias, halted by the intervention of international forces. It is estimated that more than one-quarter of the East Timorese population died at the hands of the occupying Indonesians and allied Timorese militias. The UN intervened, establishing the UN Transitional Administration in East Timor in

1999, which became the stand-in sovereign for the devastated East Timorese state, exercising legislative, judicial, and executive authority.

The UN established a special judicial process to investigate serious crimes committed during the conflict but was stymied by a lack of cooperation from Indonesia, which refused to contribute to investigations or make accused Indonesian perpetrators available for trial. In addition, Timorese state institutions suffered from a lack of political will and judicial capacity to conduct investigations and prosecutions. Timor-Leste has had marginally more success with its nonjudicial transitional justice efforts, which included the Commission for Reception, Truth, and Reconciliation.[6]

Accountability sometimes fails because of grants of amnesty. Amnesties may be granted in peace accords to incentivize combatants[7] to stop fighting or on case-by-case bases to encourage midlevel perpetrators to turn in more responsible individuals. International law and norms have developed to try to prohibit blanket and unconditional amnesties and amnesty for serious international crimes such as genocide, crimes against humanity, and war crimes. The UN has established clear guidelines for its representatives, indicating that they may not encourage or condone such amnesties.[8] The jurisprudence of the Inter-American Court of Human Rights has declared amnesties for human rights violations to be illegal, though these rulings have met resistance from some nations.[9] Even when amnesties are granted, the passage of time and changing political context may result in subsequent prosecutions.[10]

Another significant development regarding accountability for mass crimes is the increasing recognition of universal jurisdiction, which allows national authorities of any state to investigate and prosecute perpetrators of serious international crimes even if they were committed in another country. The doctrine is based on the notion that some crimes are of such exceptional gravity that they affect the fundamental interests of the entire international community. Judge Baltasar Garzon of Spain asserted the universal jurisdiction doctrine to seek the extradition of former Chilean dictator Augusto Pinochet from London, where he was receiving medical treatment.[11] The number of countries applying the principle in practice is increasing but remains low, and some countries, including the United States, do not allow cases to be brought in their courts under a theory of universal jurisdiction.[12]

Truth Seeking and Truth Telling

Truth-seeking processes assist postconflict and transitional societies investigating past human rights violations and are undertaken by truth commissions, truth and reconciliation commissions, commissions of inquiry, or other similar enterprises. As described in UN guidance, "Truth commissions are non-judicial or quasi-judicial investigative bodies, which map patterns of past violence, and unearth the causes and consequences of these destructive events."[13]

Some truth commissions have reconciliation as an explicit goal. Reconciliation is defined by the International Center for Transitional Justice as

> a complex set of processes that involve building or rebuilding relationships, often in the aftermath of massive and widespread human rights violations. It can occur at the individual, interpersonal, socio-political, and institutional levels and be described as "thin" if it is based on coexistence with little or no trust, respect, and shared values, or "thick" if it is based on the restoration of dignity, reversing structural causes of marginalization and discrimination, and restoring victims to their position as rights bearers and citizens.[14]

South Africa and Chile took different approaches to truth finding, tailored to their individual contexts, while both had reconciliation as a goal.

Nelson Mandela was released from prison in South Africa in 1990 after serving twenty-seven years as a political prisoner. He was elected president of the country four years later. His election was a historic triumph of justice over oppression, yet South Africa still faced the hard questions of how to achieve accountability and move forward after the violence and economic injustices of apartheid. With the support of the international community, South Africa instituted processes to that end, the most famous of which was its Truth and Reconciliation Commission. The commission heard testimony from over twenty-one thousand victims and witnesses, two thousand of whom spoke at public hearings.[15] Broad media coverage of the commission's proceedings provided transparency and public education about the process and its progress. The commission had three committees: the Human Rights Violations Committee (which conducted the public hearings), the Amnesty Committee, and the Reparations and Rehabilitation Committee.[16] Though widely considered one of the most successful transitional justice mechanisms to date, some have criticized the South African commission for its generous grants of amnesty and for looking at only individual instances of violence carried out within the apartheid era and not the systemic injustices of apartheid.

In Chile, General Augusto Pinochet ruled with a brutal hand for seventeen years and was responsible for killing and torturing thousands of citizens. When new president Patricio Aylwin took office in 1990, he faced substantial political constraints in seeking justice. A broad amnesty, granted by the Chilean military to itself in 1978, prevented prosecution of most human rights crimes, and the

The Greensboro Truth and Community Reconciliation Project

In 1979, clashes between anti–Ku Klux Klan demonstrators and supporters of the Klan and the American Nazi Party in Greensboro, North Carolina, resulted in the death of five demonstrators. Police were accused of failing to prevent the violence or alert protesters to the danger despite prior knowledge that violence was likely. Two subsequent criminal trials resulted in acquittals by all-white juries, though some police, Klan, and Nazi Party members were found civilly liable. The Greensboro Truth and Community Reconciliation Project was convened in 2004 to "examine the 'context, causes, sequence and consequences'" of these events and "make recommendations for community healing around the tragedy."[17] How is a truth commission held decades after the events in question different from one convened soon after violent events? How would the culture and context of a truth commission in this city in the United States differ from commissions in other cities and countries?

country's constitution had been amended to allow Pinochet and the military to maintain substantial political influence. President Aylwin established a National Commission on Truth and Reconciliation through presidential decree that addressed only loss of lives.[18] By 2003, the passage of time had created more political space, enabling President Ricardo Lagos to establish the National Commission on Political Imprisonment and Torture to address a broader set of victims, estimated by some to be in the hundreds of thousands.[19]

Reparations

Reparations seek to recognize and address the harms suffered by victims. In their simplest form, reparations are payments or actions made by perpetrators to their victims as a form of redress. Under international law, "reparation must, as far as possible, wipe out all the consequences of the illegal act and re-establish the situation which would, in all probability, have existed if that act had not been committed."[20]

Reparations can take many forms, including direct compensatory payments to victims and their families; services and support such as education, medical care, and employment; and actions such as apology and memorialization.[21] The South African Truth and Reconciliation Commission recommended a reparations package of $600 million in direct payments to a projected twenty-five thousand victims, though the government and donors failed to assemble such funds.[22] The findings of the Chilean National Commission on Truth and Reconciliation in 1991 led to government pension payments to families of the killed and disappeared that reached an annual peak of almost $16 million.[23] Surviving victims of torture and imprisonment in Chile, estimated at between fifty thousand and two hundred thousand, were excluded from the mandate of this commission but were covered by the subsequent National Commission on Political Imprisonment and Torture. In 2005 Chile began awarding pension, health, housing, and other benefits to tens of thousands of survivors of political imprisonment.[24]

Reparations may also be awarded en masse to large groups of victims. The Extraordinary Chambers in the Courts of Cambodia, also called the Khmer Rouge Tribunal, was established in 2003 and became fully operational in 2007.[25] It was created to try the most senior leaders of the Khmer Rouge regime, which tortured, starved, and killed as many as two million Cambodians in the 1970s. Millions more were forced into labor camps, dispossessed of their property, and separated from loved ones. The tribunal's primary purpose was to hear evidence against senior officials and determine their guilt, but it had a secondary duty of awarding "collective and moral reparations" to victims in the event of convictions.[26] The tribunal interpreted this mandate to mean that it could award only nonmonetary reparations such as educational programs and memorials to be built on behalf of victims who had been admitted as parties to the proceedings. It refused to award individual monetary payments to victims and was heavily criticized for refusing to investigate whether the accused had assets that could pay for any of the awards.[27] Victims ultimately had to raise funds via representatives to receive any of the benefits of the reparations projects endorsed by the court.[28]

Security and Institutional Reform

During conflicts, public institutions such as the police, military, and judiciary may be used as vehicles of repression and systemic abuse of citizens' rights. Some of the primary mechanisms for prevention and management of future destructive conflict are strengthening existing government institutions and building new ones. Well-functioning, noncorrupt, law-abiding public servants and institutions—police, prosecutors, courts, and other government agencies—are critical to maintaining peace and protecting citizens' rights. Decision makers must determine which institutions require reform and in what order, which actors were responsible for the failures of the institutions during the conflict and whether they must be dismissed from their roles, and how to integrate former combatants into the new, postconflict society.

Vetting and purging are common transitional justice measures employed by countries transitioning to peace. While there is some disagreement in the field about the exact definitions of these and related terms, "vetting" is usually defined as assessing an individual's responsibility for human rights abuses caused during the conflict and suitability for public employment in the future. "Purging" and "summary dismissal" refer to the firing en masse from public employment anyone affiliated with a group or political party deemed accountable for abuses during the conflict.[29]

Disarmament, demobilization, and reintegration (DDR) of soldiers, including the creation of jobs to transition them to civilian life, is important for preventing recurrence of violent conflict or conversion of armed combatants into criminal networks. First instituted in 1989 in connection with the UN Observer Group in Central America, DDR programs are increasingly part of peace negotiations and postconflict peace-building processes around the world.[30] Though DDR programs are critical to stopping violence, their results, such as the possibility that payments to ex-combatants are more generous than compensation to victims, may conflict with other transitional justice goals.

Application of the Analytic Framework

Goals

The many designers in a state in transition will have numerous goals. A key designer is usually the new government, working in an unstable political environment, with varying degrees of coordination with international and local actors—other states, international and regional bodies, and civil society.[31] The system designer in a postconflict setting must determine the time period of conflict and the types of crimes that the new procedures will address. In countries that experience waves of violence, the selected time frame may have significant political ramifications, perhaps focusing on the actions of one group but not another. Covering longer periods will also incur higher costs. South Africa chose the period from March 1, 1960, to May 10, 1994. The first date marked the banning of political organizations, severe oppression of those fighting apartheid, and a massacre.[32] Some argued for expanding the time parameters, and one suggestion was that the commission's review should begin with the first arrival of white settlers in 1652.[33]

While justice is a central goal of any transitional system, the designers must identify which of the many forms of justice are desired.[34] As described above, goals of transitional justice systems may include punishment of perpetrators and avoiding impunity; truth telling and determination of facts; reconciliation, healing, and forgiveness; economic repair and reparations; and peace or preventing recurrence of violence.

To achieve these ends, designers may embed them within broader governance goals, such as rule of law and democracy building. Rule of law and democracy have been explicit, or at least implicit, goals in many Western-funded transitional justice efforts.[35] These goals have been praised for serving as a vehicle for spreading international norms, including human rights, and providing a structure for economic development. This "rule of law paradigm," with its focus on building state institutions, has also been criticized—for example, for failing to provide access to justice for the poor.[36] In many cases, the judiciary and the legal sector have been destroyed or corrupted or were complicit in human rights abuses, and overhauling these institutions is necessary to establishing accountability and preventing future violations. The challenge is to design institutions and processes that will meet these goals in the local and national contexts and be sustainable.

One process may target multiple goals. The South African Truth and Reconciliation Commission had among its aims "to establish the truth in relation to past events as well as the motives for and circumstances in which gross violations of human rights have occurred," "to make findings known in order to prevent a repetition of such acts," "to pursue national unity," "to obtain understanding but not vengeance," and "to advance reconciliation and reconstruction."[37] By offering the possibility of amnesty in return for truthful confession, the commission hoped to reveal the facts of past atrocities while also achieving a measure of justice.

Some goals may be in tension with each other.

JUSTICE VERSUS PEACE. Should amnesty ever be granted to war criminals to achieve a peace agreement? Peace negotiators may perceive granting amnesty to a heinous leader as the only way to stop the bloodshed, but human rights advocates argue forcefully for the primacy of prosecution to achieve justice.[38] Failure to punish perpetrators may allow them to rise again with an insurgent force or to devolve into criminal networks that can also debilitate a postconflict society. Failure to punish may also increase the risk of vigilantism, as victims of past crimes take justice into their own hands.

Andrea Kupfer Schneider sees the justice versus peace question as a false dichotomy, contending that in most situations of gross human rights violations, both peace and justice are necessary for a country to be able to move forward.[39] She cites the war crimes tribunal in Japan after World War II as providing justice but not peace or reconciliation with Korea and China and other neighbors, leaving tensions that still reverberate many decades later.[40] Schneider points to the amnesties in Chile, Guatemala, and Argentina as examples of peace without justice, though she notes that some of those nations "have started to revisit those decisions and to prosecute."[41] Mark Freeman of the Institute for Integrated Transitions urges a "fundamental reframing of the debate on amnesty." He perceives a debate between "competing conceptions of justice," with those who "privilege the human dignity and interests of victims of past abuse" by opposing amnesties on one side and those who "privilege the dignity and interests of victims of verifiable current abuse and inevitable future abuse" by seeking to end violence through amnesty on the other.[42]

JUSTICE VERSUS RECONCILIATION. While prosecutions can succeed in punishing perpetrators (providing retributive justice), they can also inflame partisan passions, making reconciliation (and restorative justice) more difficult. The issue is particularly fraught when reconciliation means forgetting to some and, to others, means directly addressing the harm. Even a single individual may initially need to repress the traumatic experience but later want to air it or vice versa. The tension between justice and reconciliation is particularly charged in countries such as Rwanda where victims and their families must learn to live side by side with perpetrators.

TRUTH VERSUS JUSTICE. To defend themselves in criminal proceedings, perpetrators may deny their abuses; victims and their family members may never learn the truth of what occurred. The threat of prosecution may keep other perpetrators underground and the truth of certain crimes perpetually hidden.

In an individual case, choosing one option, such as amnesty, may preclude other options, such as trial. However, sometimes these process choices are not sharp dichotomies but rather sequencing issues. Which actions does a country take now rather than later? Which cases will be directed to one process versus another? The views of transitional justice experts have evolved from framing transitional justice in these sharp dichotomies toward a greater understanding of the relationship and interdependence among the different transitional justice mechanisms. In the 1980s and early 1990s, there was prominent debate between those who prioritized the goal of punishing human rights violators to avoid impunity and those who called for some flexibility in light of the needs and constraints of the context.[43] Decades later, some of the staunchest advocates for the primacy of prosecution have evolved in their thinking, seeing the value of an integrated, comprehensive approach, including truth processes, that lifts up the voices and preferences of victims.[44]

TRANSITIONAL JUSTICE IN A SYSTEMS CONTEXT. Countries dealing with human rights violators will be grappling simultaneously with a much larger array of governance and state-building tasks that need to be addressed successfully for a postconflict society to stabilize and thrive. Transitional justice activities are nested within multiple layers of other governance, political, and economic systems.

In 2002, the Center for Strategic and International Studies and the Association of the United States Army developed a typology of issues that need to be addressed after violent conflict.[45] Scores of essential tasks were identified and clustered into four categories: security, justice and reconciliation, social and economic well-being, and governance and participation. Without security mechanisms that enforce the cessation—or at least significant diminution—of violence, most other goals cannot be met. Without the creation of stable and legitimate government systems and economic opportunity, violence may recur. Successful designers must understand how their tasks fit and will function in this broader, evolving, interconnected system. As the authors of the resulting report noted, "Countries emerge from conflict under differing and unique conditions. Therefore, the priority, precedence, timing, appropriateness, and execution of tasks will vary from case to case."[46]

Stakeholders

All citizens are stakeholders, groups of whom will have differing interests depending on the context of the conflict. Representatives from the combatant groups following war will be key stakeholders. Subgroups of victims could include women, ethnic or religious minorities, or youths—if, for instance, children were abducted and forced to become soldiers or women were systematically raped as a weapon of war. Representation is particularly challenging in the transitional justice context, because of the likely weakness of civil society and absence of organized, representative political parties or advocacy groups.

Neighboring countries, regional actors, and sometimes superpowers will have an interest in the conflict, as will countries that become donors or contribute troops to peacekeeping and peace-building efforts. Such efforts may be implemented through multinational bodies such as the UN, European Union, or African Union, which may have their own institutional interests and constraints. Additional stakeholders may be national and international media; historians, anthropologists, archivists, and sociologists; national and international nongovernmental organizations, particularly those focused on human rights; and legal representatives of stakeholders. If the voices of key stakeholders are not heard and their needs not addressed, systems can lack fundamental fairness and the seeds of future conflict may be sown.

The South African government created a multistakeholder process to help design their transitional justice system, engaging citizens, representatives from major political parties, local and international academics, and experts with experience in truth commissions. Two international conferences, civil society input at public hearings, and a robust debate in the South African Parliament resulted in the legislation that created the South African Truth and Reconciliation Commission.[47]

The Cambodian tribunal also innovated in engaging stakeholders. The Extraordinary Chambers in the Courts of Cambodia was the first international tribunal to create a mechanism for recognizing victims as official parties to the proceedings, ostensibly with many of the same rights as the prosecution. This meant that individuals who suffered as a result of crimes for which the Khmer Rouge leaders were being tried could apply to be recognized as civil parties at the court. This recognition would afford the possibility of testifying and the opportunity to seek reparations in the event of a conviction. The development was a significant advance for victims' rights in transitional justice. The reality of representing thousands of individual survivors with their personal stories and grievances was not, however, sufficiently considered in the design phase, and victims' role and voice became smaller as proceedings progressed.

While there is agreement that more should be done to raise up the voices of victims, achieving this goal poses many questions. Who represents the victims? They may be diverse in many ways, including how they suffered, the feature that they feel most defines their victimhood, and their geographic location. The special needs of women are still insufficiently addressed in transitional justice mechanisms, though attention to this critical area continues to grow. Diane Orentlicher praises the international tribunals for Rwanda and the former Yugoslavia for prosecutions that "brought crimes of sexual violence—mostly ignored in postwar prosecutions—out of the proverbial shadows."[48] The Sierra Leone Truth and Reconciliation Commission structured attention to these issues by dedicating one day a week to testimony from female victims of sexual abuse, presented in both private and public sessions.[49]

In postwar peace processes and agreements, a primary goal is to stop the killing, so attention must understandably focus on combatants, who are primarily men.[50] Increasingly, there is pressure to add more women, and more attention to the experiences and needs of women, in peace processes and transitions. In 2000, the UN Security Council passed Resolution 1325, which condemns the use of sexual violence against women and girls as a weapon of war, calls for greater protections of women and girls from gender-based violence, and promotes more participation of women at all levels of peacemaking and peacekeeping processes.[51]

The 2015 UN Sustainable Development Goals also address the importance of including women's perspectives and leadership in peace and security decisions.[52]

Context and Culture

Transitional justice and related rule of law efforts have too often been dominated by a top-down change strategy, with the United States and other international donors aiming to replicate a Western-derived model.[53] The limitation of this strategy, for transitional justice and for rule of law efforts more broadly, is that it often attempts to impose a rigid template without sufficient sensitivity to local history, culture, capacity, and conditions. A contributor to some of the disappointing outcomes of transitional justice efforts to date has been the failure of the most powerful stakeholders—often international donor states and organizations—to obtain meaningful input from less powerful, local stakeholders, who must live with the new system and will determine its success or failure. Ruti Teitel, who coined the term "transitional justice" in the late 1980s, critiques what she calls the "bureaucratic model" of transitional justice work, in which international nongovernmental organizations and public agencies aim to develop "a global answer" such as "best practices," which they apply across countries and contexts without being "sufficiently informed by local politics."[54]

There is an evolving consensus that local actors should not only have a significant role but should, when possible, take the lead in postconflict transitions.[55] James Michel, former longtime senior administrator for the U.S. Agency for International Development, spent many years working to advance rule of law as an international development funder. He writes, "Experience has demonstrated that working on the basis of an existing system, one rooted in local needs, values, and customs, is the most likely way to achieve a sustainable, desirable result. The alternative of trying to introduce an alien system, no matter how well designed from a developed-country perspective, is rarely a path to success."[56]

This desire informed the creation of hybrid tribunals, such as Sierra Leone's Special Court and the Extraordinary Chambers in the Courts of Cambodia, in which every function of the court has international and national counterparts. The reality, however, is that coordination and communication between the nationals and internationals is often missing at best and contentious at worst.

Context is critical. In South Africa, the Truth and Reconciliation Commission was an explicit compromise by the democratically elected government to forgo a measure of justice to achieve peace. Richard Goldstone, a former justice of the Constitutional Court of South Africa, stated, "If the [African National Congress] had insisted on Nuremberg-style trials for the leaders of the former apartheid government, there would have been no peaceful transition to democracy, and if the former government had insisted on blanket amnesty then, similarly, the negotiations would have broken down. A bloody revolution sooner rather than later would have been inevitable."[57] South Africa's choice was shaped by the values of its designers and its citizens, including their religious values. In contrast, Neil Kritz uses the example of a proposed compensation scheme for Rwanda, based on that of Chile, to highlight the risk of grafting a program from one country onto another nation with very different economic and political realities. Chile "had a very narrowly defined class of eligible beneficiaries and a fairly healthy economy," while in Rwanda, "the exact opposite exist[ed]: a massive class of beneficiaries and a non-existent economy."[58]

Timing is also critical; what is impossible at one moment may be possible later. In Chile, prosecution was not possible in 1990. The context continued to evolve, and the country was later able to indict and convict hundreds of officials for human rights violations.[59]

Processes and Structure

Another set of challenges facing designers is determining which transitional justice processes are for prevention, which are for management, and which are for resolution. A trial is a dispute resolution process. Is it also designed to—or is it likely to—prevent future conflict? Reconciliation processes may be intended to create and restore relationships to prevent future conflicts and decrease the likelihood of violence. Do they also, in some sense, resolve disputes? DSD principles argue for using multiple process options to address the needs of multiple stakeholders and achieve stated goals.

TRIALS. A trial process is usually central to a transitional justice design, for punishing past crimes and trying to deter future violence. The structure and forms of this adjudicatory process can vary. Who will be the judges? Will they come from inside the country, outside the country, or both? Following the violence, is there national capacity to operate a court that will have credibility with all sides of the conflict? Does the country have sufficient resources to operate the court, or will it require ongoing international resources?

East Timor's Special Panels for Serious Crimes, a hybrid tribunal of local and international jurists, was created to address the highest-level perpetrators, with lesser crimes assigned to the local courts.[60] This panel, based in the Dili District Court, resulted in some trials and convictions but was criticized on many grounds, including severe lack of resources and staff training, ineffective case management, inadequate legal representation for defendants, and lack of political will by the UN and the Timorese government.[61] Another key impediment to success was the political context and power imbalance between Timor-Leste and Indonesia. In many transitional justice settings, the key combatants on both sides of the conflict reside in one country. In East Timor, the principal perpetrators of war crimes were across the border in Indonesia and outside the jurisdiction of Timorese courts, hobbling the new country's capacity to achieve satisfactory retributive justice.[62]

The International Criminal Tribunal for Rwanda was sited in Arusha, Tanzania, a neutral venue but far from the location of the atrocities. This court has been praised for fighting impunity, advancing the goals of due process, and developing important international law principles. However, it has been criticized for its inaccessibility to Rwandan citizens and failure to adequately include victims in its process.[63]

TRUTH COMMISSIONS. Truth commissions serve many purposes—enabling victims to tell their stories in their own words, revealing previously denied truths, undercutting official denials, and in some cases providing the basis for reconciliation as well as future prosecutions and remedies. The UN notes that "core activities usually include collecting statements from victims and witnesses, conducting thematic research, including gender and children analysis of violations including their causes and consequences, organizing public hearings and other awareness programs, and publishing a final report outlining findings and recommendations."[64]

CUSTOMARY, OR TRADITIONAL, JUSTICE PROCESSES. Every society has formal and informal processes for addressing disputes. In countries in transition, customary, or traditional, justice processes may conflict with international human rights

Discussion Questions

In truth commission processes, should perpetrators of human rights violations be named? Naming perpetrators would help fulfill the important goals of truth finding and truth telling. But is it fair to publicly label individuals as violators of human rights when they are not able to defend themselves, as they could do in criminal trials? If you favor disclosure, would your answer change if the safety and security of witnesses and commission staff—or alleged perpetrators—were threatened by disclosure?[65]

norms—for example, by discriminating against women or denying due process. Historically, the international community has often endeavored to wipe away the traditional processes and replace them with Western models that meet those human rights standards. The rule of law paradigm initially ignored local and customary law, assuming that the Western human-rights-oriented legal model would be successfully introduced and displace local practices. The failure of this strategy to achieve the anticipated success has led to increasing recognition of legal pluralism, the existence of formal and informal legal systems in a society and how they interact.

For example, judges in the Rwandan government chose to revive and adapt a traditional process—the *gacaca*—to address the goals of justice and reconciliation for midlevel and lower-level offenders.[66] The judges were local citizens, not required to be trained in law, who were elected by the local communities. The *gacaca* courts were authorized to mete out penalties determined by the seriousness of the charges, with reduction in penalties given for those who confessed.[67] The process was created in response to the crisis of over a hundred thousand prisoners awaiting trial in a country with a judicial system that had been devastated by the war.[68] Laura Grenfell says of the tensions in the *gacaca* process, "On the one hand, the use of these hybrid local courts represents an affirmation of local norms of dispute resolution; it also assists Rwanda in building a legal culture and encouraging large-scale participation in a state institution, both important aspects of the rule of law. On the other hand, the *gacaca* system potentially violates international legal standards."[69]

In East Timor, a broad consultative process resulted in creation of the Commission for Reception, Truth, and Reconciliation, a mechanism that drew from Timorese customary justice processes but respected human rights. The stated goals of this process were truth seeking, reconciliation, rehabilitation of victims, and recommendations (for, e.g., prosecutions and reparations).[70] Although the process has been criticized, a significant majority of participants are reported to have viewed their experiences as a success.[71]

INSTITUTIONAL AND GOVERNANCE REFORM. In its inception, the field of transitional justice focused on human rights and the primary goal of punishing wrongdoers and avoiding impunity. Addressing these goals may require significant governance reform, including vetting of public employees and security sector training for police and the national army to avoid impunity in the future. How vetting—and purging of current personnel—are implemented will have significant implications for the risk of future violence and the ability of a society to reintegrate following war. For example, after the fall of Saddam Hussein in the Iraq War, Great Britain,

---

Discussion Questions

You are running a program to disarm, demobilize, and reintegrate former combatants and are considering making cash payments to ex-combatants to motivate them to disarm and to help them transition back into civilian life. What are the pros and cons of providing cash assistance? If you provide such assistance, how will you define "ex-combatant"? Will you include only those who took up arms or also those who supported the fighters? What proof would you require to identify eligible ex-combatants? How should the amount paid to ex-combatants relate, if at all, to the amount paid to their victims in reparations?

---

a U.S. ally, recommended removal of around five thousand Baath Party members from government positions. The United States chose to purge to a deeper level, removing around thirty thousand government employees. This intensive purging contributed to the growth of the violent insurgency and resulted in a loss of expertise that could have aided in reestablishing delivery of government services in postwar Iraq.[72]

HISTORY AND EDUCATION. Conflicts both reflect and generate contested stories of a society's past, sustaining historical grievances while blaming and demonizing the "other." Hopes for a peaceful future rest on creating and sustaining a new story that can support coexistence. Truth commissions and trials may illuminate the multiple perspectives on the truth and permit that new collective narrative to emerge. A major challenge in a transition is determining how to teach children about their past and present to shape a nonviolent future. Curricula may include civics and human rights as well as difficult history, which will inevitably be shaped by politics and the views of multiple internal and external stakeholders.[73]

REPARATIONS. The evolution of reparations provides another example of the complex, systemic nature of DSD in the transitional justice context. The initial intent of reparations was to aid individual victims with cash payments, benefits, and services. With more experience in a wider range of contexts, transitional justice practitioners are increasingly exploring community or collective remedies when defined groups have been affected, such as the destruction of whole villages or when the resources are not sufficient to make significant payment to each victim.[74]

In some cases, these collective efforts have been criticized for appearing indistinguishable from economic development and failing to adequately recognize the specific damages caused by war.[75]

Victims can seek reparations in cases before the International Criminal Court.[76] Its Trust Fund for Victims is designed "to implement reparations awards ordered by the Court, and to provide humanitarian assistance to victims in situations before the Court."[77] The Inter-American Court of Human Rights has also issued reparations orders covering a vast array of remedies. In addition to ordering money to victims and provision of education, the court has ordered human rights training for police, government officials, and even the general public and directed law and policy changes of prison reform and new protections for criminal defendants.[78] The court has also ordered community-wide remedies. In Guatemala, the court ordered the government to provide "medical personnel for a health center, food security programs, improved streets, supply of water, drainage and sewers, and improved schooling facilities" for resettled victims who had fled a massacre.[79]

Resources

Countries emerging from war or otherwise undergoing massive transition are usually devastated economically. Multinational and bilateral donors usually bear the cost burden of transitional justice mechanisms.[80] In the area of transitional justice, and development in fragile states more broadly, donor countries sometimes commit to give aid and then fail to follow through, decreasing the chances for success.[81]

The priorities of the powerful stakeholders that are providing major funds will affect process priorities. The International Criminal Tribunal for Rwanda cost the international community around $2 billion.[82] The International Criminal Court has cost over $1 billion and as of 2017 has convicted at best a handful of people for war crimes or crimes against humanity.[83] The substantial resources devoted to the international tribunals and International Criminal Court reflect the priorities of key donors in the international community for retributive justice and for developing important international legal norms. A major policy challenge for system designers in transitional country settings is to decide which goals should take priority and when and how to allocate limited resources accordingly across short-term and longer-term needs, within and beyond the justice sector.

Success, Accountability, and Learning

Success in transitional justice can be extremely difficult to measure. If the stated goal is solely the punishment of war criminals, a key measure will be the number of trials and convictions. When the goals are reconciliation and prevention of future violence, the metrics are much more difficult and the time line for determining success becomes long. The easiest data to collect from a court or a truth and reconciliation commission are quantitative, such as number of victims testifying, number of convictions, or the amount of damages or types of remedies ordered. Such data do not capture the quality of the processes and may fail to track key information, such as the effectiveness of implementation. How soon after beginning to institute changes is it appropriate to expect success? Transitional justice mechanisms seek to change not just rules and structures but entire cultures and societal behaviors. As a study of Liberia noted, "It is quite likely that the meaningful metric for significance in change will actually be generational."[84]

Often, the goals of a transitional justice DSD are not agreed on and clarified at the outset of design. Colleen Duggan has noted that this failure of designers to clearly define goals at the beginning of a project means that "it is often the evaluator who must articulate or reconstruct the theory of change (often *ex post*) prior to beginning work."[85] Even when goals are clear, they may conflict with each other, further challenging the evaluator. The study in Liberia identified citizens' goals and priorities for justice systems as affordability, accessibility, and timeliness.[86] These researchers also found that the Liberian citizens preferred the goals of restorative justice and social reconciliation rather than the goals of individual rights and punitive sanctions that were promoted by the formal justice system and most Western donors.[87]

Designers and evaluators also need to identify the appropriate reference point for success. Should a system be measured against an ideal, such as full compliance with international human rights norms? Or should progress be compared with what existed in the past? Would the best analysis examine how the outcome compares with the best of what was possible under the circumstances, a standard of pragmatism that will always be subject to debate? Duggan notes that additional measurement challenges are absent or insufficient baseline data, the failure to address local context, and the need to develop new methodologies, including better collaboration between social science research and development evaluation.[88]

Perceptions of success can change with time. The South African process received substantial praise initially, though criticism has since increased. Supporters praise the Truth and Reconciliation Commission's achievements in revealing new facts to the public; aiming to promote restorative, not retributive, justice; and working to foster a culture of human rights in South Africa.[89] James Gibson defined four components of the goal of reconciliation in South Africa: interracial reconciliation, political tolerance, support for the principles (abstract and applied) of human rights, and legitimacy of South Africa's new political institutions.[90] His research found some evidence that South Africans who accepted the truth as produced by the commission were more likely to support the rule of law, but he found significant racial differences in those perceptions.[91] The South African process has failed to deliver justice in the form of promised economic development, land redistribution, and other reparations. Nonetheless, for many, the fact that South Africa has not slid back into war meets the primary criterion of success.

Conclusion

The field of transitional justice was established in response to a sense of collective global failure to prevent major atrocities. Designs have varied in their goals, applications, and quality. Each transitional justice design has benefited from those that have gone before, and international laws and norms have progressed accordingly.

Design of transitional justice systems and, more broadly, postconflict governance has evolved and will continue to evolve. The designers of the South African Truth and Reconciliation Commission examined and learned from earlier transitional justice efforts, especially those in Chile and Argentina.[92] The South African process has been a model for many subsequent efforts. Context and culture are, however, central to transitional justice efforts, and the variations in factors such as history, culture, politics, relative power of stakeholders, and levels of human and financial resources necessitate that each case receive individual analysis.

Designers in transitional settings will need to focus on what is most likely to bring about long-term, sustainable change in each case. Transitional legal systems will need to incorporate both formal and informal mechanisms in a way that will increase justice over time. Amplifying local voices and the views of others knowledgeable about the transitioning society, its history, and its lived experience will increase the likelihood of success.

When does a transition end? When, if ever, is a sufficient level of justice achieved? The sense of injustice and the demand for reparations can endure long past the formal end of a war. In the United States, President Ronald Reagan signed the Civil Liberties Act of 1988,[93] providing apology and reparation payments to survivors of Japanese internment camps in the United States in World War II. More than 150 years after the end of the U.S. Civil War, local, state, and federal government officials are grappling with demands for removal of Confederate statues and memorials,[94] and powerful arguments are being advanced for the appropriateness of reparations to African American descendants of slaves in the United States.[95]

Successful transitional justice demands systemic thinking, including more co-operation, knowledge sharing, and integration among practitioners and scholars from different fields. Legal and government specialists will need to work with other experts, including development professionals, sociologists, and political scientists. All these contributors must be able to cut across disciplinary silos to develop integrated transitional justice plans and adapt those plans as circumstances change. Further research on the effectiveness of the many transitional justice mechanisms will provide improved guidance to system designers on how best to positively influence these important and difficult cases that affect many millions of lives.

16   INTERNATIONAL DISPUTE RESOLUTION

CONSIDER A EUROPEAN pharmaceutical company that has invested in an African country (host nation) by forming a research-and-development operation to exploit a naturally occurring plant product with medicinal potential. There is an existing investment treaty between the relevant European and African countries. After some period of operation in the host country, the pharmaceutical firm claims that the host country has breached that treaty by changing its regulations to limit conversion and transfer of domestic profits. To whom does the firm appeal? What processes are in place to resolve this type of cross-border dispute? What are the potential remedies and how can they be enforced?

In the domain of international disputes, cross-border DSD involves a tremendous diversity of goals, stakeholders, and processes, coupled with constraints on enforcement. This chapter discusses DSD for four types of cases: sports, foreign investments, international trade, and cross-border e-commerce.

Issues to consider are as follows.

- What types of organizations provide cross-border DSD?
- What are the shared or conflicting goals among parties in cross-border disputes?
- Can greater upstream focus (policy making) improve downstream dispute resolution? How do public and private options relate?

Table 16.1 summarizes the four types of international disputes discussed in this chapter. While this set of dispute types is not exhaustive, these four systems illustrate variation in the goals (compliance, expedited decisions, transparency), parties (individuals, firms, states, organizations), issues (sports, trade in products and services across borders, foreign investments, and online commerce), and

Table 16.1 Examples of international disputes

Institutional auspice or category	Issues	Parties	Processes
Court of Arbitration for Sport	Sport-related disputes	Athlete, club, commercial sponsor, sport federation or organization	Arbitration; mediation
Bilateral investment treaties	Foreign investments	Nation-states, private firm investors	Negotiation/consultation; arbitration
World Trade Organization	International treaty-based organization dealing with rules of trade for goods and services	Member states	Negotiation; conciliation; arbitration; appellate court review
United Nations Commission on International Trade Law	Cross-border e-commerce transactions	Individual consumers, business firms	Conciliation; mediation; arbitration

processes (direct negotiation, consultation, mediation, arbitration, and court) of international dispute resolution. The Court of Arbitration for Sport primarily uses arbitration with athletes, clubs, and international sports organizations. Bilateral investment treaties usually involve arbitration between investor firms and host nations. The World Trade Organization contemplates negotiation as well as facilitated and adjudicated processes between member nations; the United Nations Commission on International Trade Law recognizes a shift in the process domain from in person and in writing to online facilitated and evaluative processes to handle cross-border e-commerce disputes.

Court of Arbitration for Sport

The Court of Arbitration for Sport (CAS) was created in 1984 (and reformed in 1994) to provide a customized, expert, and flexible procedure to hear and decide sports-related disputes at minimal time and expense. The CAS is recognized internationally as a credible forum for handling sports-related disputes related to Olympic and non-Olympic sports, football (soccer) issues, doping infractions, and international commercial contracts.[1]

CAS arbitrators come from over a hundred countries, are appointed for four-year terms, and have specialized knowledge of arbitration and sports law. In the nearly three hundred commercial and disciplinary cases it adjudicates every year,[2] the CAS uses several types of procedures. Its ordinary arbitration procedure is used for international commercial arbitration cases in the first instance in disputes over licensing, sponsorship contracts, media, broadcasting, and more. The appeals arbitration procedure governs appeals against decisions of sports bodies (the majority of cases) in football transfer (or trade), compensation disputes, and disciplinary sanctions for antidoping violations. An ad hoc division is set up onsite during Olympic and other major sporting events, with a panel of arbitrators on call to hear disputes and render decisions within twenty-four hours of filing. Mediation is available to all parties before arbitration begins. The CAS also provides a consultation procedure to render advisory opinions.

Parties must consent to CAS arbitration. For appeals to sport body decisions, the consent may be according to the regulations of the sport body, a specific arbitration agreement, or an athlete's signed entry form for a sport event. Some question whether the athlete's consent is freely given, in that failure to sign an entry form would bar the athlete from competing. However, the Swiss Federal Tribunal has held that the need for a quick and uniform dispute resolution system in international sports prevails over the right of an athlete to have his case adjudicated by ordinary courts.[3]

The arbitral seat for all CAS procedures is Lausanne, Switzerland. CAS arbitrations are governed by the Swiss Act on Private International Law, which helps ensure procedural consistency and predictability. The rules and regulations of the sports organization that issued the challenged decision constitute the applicable law. The Swiss Federal Tribunal has a role in review and enforcement of CAS awards. Under Articles 184 and 185 of the Swiss Act on Private International Law, the court at the arbitral seat may assist in taking of evidence and has jurisdiction if judicial assistance is required. Although infrequently used, the Swiss courts play a useful role—for instance, if disciplinary hearings give rise to criminal proceedings such as for spot fixing and match fixing. However, sports governing bodies are highly resistant to attempts to infringe on their autonomy.[4]

Nearly half of CAS cases originate from the Fédération Internationale de Football Association; a third of the cases relate to doping violations.[5] About 90 percent of the CAS caseload falls under the appeals arbitration division. Appeals are heard by a panel of 3 arbitrators selected from a roster of 386 from 107 nations who have legal training, recognized competence in sports law and international arbitration, a knowledge of sport in general, and command of at least one CAS working language. Whereas the ad hoc tribunals render decisions within twenty-four hours of appeals, so that events may continue on schedule, in other CAS appellant arbitration cases an athlete has twenty-one days from receipt of decision to appeal and another ten days to file her brief. The respondent has twenty days from the appeal brief to file an answer. The panel decides whether to hold a hearing (usually lasting less than one day), and the award is issued within three months. The parties may agree to expedite procedural times.

In addition to speed, another key factor for the CAS is cost. The CAS may arrange legal aid to persons without sufficient financial means. Costs of arbitration are usually borne by the losing party, as is reimbursement of some portion of the prevailing party's legal fees, with discretion according to the parties' circumstances. Transparency is also highly valued. The CAS publishes the awards issued in appeal proceedings. Any challenge to a CAS award is submitted to the Swiss Federal Tribunal. CAS cases and challenges have increased significantly in recent years—from fewer than 50 cases filed in 1986, to 298 in 2010, to 498 in 2015[6]—putting more pressure on the system's capacity. CAS awards can be enforced under the New York Convention on the Recognition and Enforcement of Foreign Arbitral Awards,[7] but usually sports organizations in appeal cases have internal procedures for ensuring compliance with decisions rendered.

The CAS system involves individual athletes, sport clubs, federations, and sponsors and offers facilitative and adjudicative processes to settle disputes among them, integrating with the Swiss Tribunal court for specified functions. Given the goals of expeditious decisions, uniformly rendered, at minimal cost to the athlete, the CAS appears to be successful.

Bilateral Investment Treaties

Firms use foreign direct investment to better access foreign markets, natural resources, and local labor, thus advancing global trade. Foreign direct investment

International Parental Abduction

An interpersonal dispute that spans nations is a cross-border parental abduction. These disputes endanger a child's safety and security, pose questions of jurisdiction, and raise difficult decisions for courts to resolve. Federal ministries and national and local agencies do sometimes collaborate, such that federal and local courts and families consider whether mediation might benefit all affected parties. Who would design, implement, and evaluate such a system?[8]

currently exceeds $25 trillion globally, which surpasses trade in goods and services. The World Bank states a global goal to promote international investment and, as a means to do so, to foster confidence in the international investment dispute resolution process.[9] A key objective is to protect cross-border investments, both from political risks in the host country—primarily expropriation, adverse regulatory changes, transfer, and convertibility restrictions—and from breach of contract. The host countries, in turn, are seeking to uphold their domestic sovereignty over commercial activities within their borders.

International investment agreements are commitments between states concerning the treatment of investors and investments, with a mechanism for enforcement of those commitments.[10] One type of international investment agreement is a bilateral or multilateral investment treaty. Nearly 2,400 bilateral investment treaties were in force worldwide as of 2019.[11] The motivating rationale of these treaties is that increased investment (both foreign and domestic) leads to increased prosperity; more favorable business conditions encourage investment relationships by increasing predictability and decreasing risk.[12]

International investment agreements have dispute resolution mechanisms, of which the most frequently used is international investor-state arbitration. An injured investor can sue the host state for damages arising from a violation of the correspondent treaty obligations. The International Convention on the Settlement of Investment Disputes is the setting of many such disputes, which usually involve an investor bringing a claim against a host developing country, often involving oil, gas, mining, electric power, or energy. Two or three cases are filed with the convention per month. Within a bilateral investment treaty terms and conditions are arbitral (and rarely, conciliation) provisions, which provide the requisite consent by both parties to submit any dispute to arbitration. While an individual dispute award is applicable only to the specific parties without having binding precedent for others, interested actors (including executives, bankers, lawyers, government ministers, and public citizens) pay close attention to these cases and their implications for future investment arrangements. The decision-making processes of the International Convention on the Settlement of Investment Disputes derive from Article 33 of the United Nations Charter, which states that "a contracting state has an obligation to seek peaceful solutions to disputes and engage in good faith negotiation."[13] The original goals for the dispute resolution processes were to provide a neutral venue for international conflict, enhance good governance and rule of law in developing countries, and increase the effectiveness and efficiency of developing countries' domestic courts.

In state-to-state bilateral investment treaty disputes, processes usually include negotiation, consultation, and diplomacy, as well as arbitration conducted within the International Centre for Trade and Sustainable Development or another forum. State-state arbitration is a public process and as such is the most important process to protect treaty norms. Arbitration involves a tribunal of three arbitrators: one selected by each state party, who jointly select the third. The tribunal renders a decision by majority; the decision is binding and final.

Investor-state bilateral investment treaty disputes are more prevalent than state-to-state cases. Processes for resolution include negotiation and consultation for some defined period (usually six months); because this process is usually confidential,[14] available data on its use are limited. As mentioned, although a given case decision is binding only on the parties, it has implications for bilateral investment treaty rule and norm development.[15] However, in the international forum, it is unusual to grant an individual the ability to compel a state to appear before the tribunal.

Investors, states, and related stakeholders have examined the investment arbitration regime on coherence and consistency across outcomes, efficiency, and legitimacy. Arbitral panels are not bound to follow the precedent of a prior tribunal's decision, and thus awards interpret the same treaty provisions inconsistently. The consequential lack of predictability undermines enforcement of a coherent DSD. Efficiency issues also arise on several fronts. As the number of cases administered increases, so does time to reach judgment (some taking three to four years), despite their reputed design as "swifter, cheaper, more flexible and more familiar for economic operators" than domestic alternatives in the host country.[16]

In terms of legitimacy, the scholarship presents an array of perspectives. In the strictly rights-based dimension, investment dispute procedures need to withstand both substantive and procedural scrutiny to possess legal legitimacy. Laurence Helfer and Anne-Marie Slaughter of Harvard Law School analyzed in detail the qualities of effective supranational adjudication; they found that authoritative, impartial tribunals that issue final rulings have the most legitimacy.[17] Academic scholars and political leaders have questioned the fairness and democratic accountability of investor-state arbitration with respect to bias in favor of corporate investors, conflict of interest among arbitrators, and corporate investment rights without corresponding responsibilities for labor standards and environmental harm.[18] This tension reflects the public-private hybrid nature of investor-state disputes. On the one hand is the public's right to have input into matters of public interest, such as the governance, health, land use, and resources of their country;

on the other hand is an expectation of confidentiality based on private commercial dealings, which are usually confidential to the contracting parties.[19]

Mariana Hernandez-Crespo Gonstead has focused extensively on the system design challenges of investment treaties in Latin America.[20] She expands the policy goal of legitimacy to provide an integrated decision-making process for optimal investment stability. At a micro level, negotiation of sustainable investment agreements would benefit from engaging the local stakeholders with participation as an instrumental goal to collaborative governance; at a macro level, building capacity and integrity in the justice system would enhance dispute handling through court, as well as strengthen ADR options.

Despite numerous calls for an overhaul of the investment arbitration system,[21] many experts advocate for adapting the current system to enhance public accountability. In 2014, the Mauritius Convention was adopted with Transparency Rules to enhance disclosure of arbitral proceedings and accept amicus curiae briefs. Among the proposals are increasing use of conciliation, strengthening the legal consistency of awards through appellate review, strengthening domestic courts, and even forming a permanent international court.[22] From a structural perspective, there are concerns about the unequal bargaining power between investors and host states, both ex ante and ex post.

On the process options, arbitration and conciliation are both available, but the latter is used only rarely. Antonio Parra, the first deputy-general of the International Convention on the Settlement of Investment Disputes, notes the "desire of parties to engage in third-party dispute settlement procedures only if they produce a definitive outcome to the 'nature of bureaucracies, governmental and corporate, to prefer to shift [to an arbitral tribunal responsibility for the terms of settlement] rather than to assume responsibility' themselves, as they would in a conciliation. However, the potential benefits of mediation and conciliation are well recognized."[23]

Much of the discussion on bilateral investment treaties is focused on stronger downstream enforcement processes that incur high costs (fees and time), to the detriment of both the investor and the host country. An upstream approach to foreign investment could be made more robust through due diligence research and analysis (by both parties) before the investment decision, secured by investment insurance; further, the parties could devote more effort to laying the groundwork for implementation as well as adaptation to changing circumstances. These steps could increase the likelihood of preserving the working relationship between the investor and host nation and enhance benefits for workers and local communities.[24] As with public construction projects, described in Chapter 13, investor-state transactions represent enormous investments by both parties, thus warranting a more deliberate process design. Something akin to the partnering and standing dispute boards of construction might offer useful lessons for consideration.

World Trade Organization

The World Trade Organization (WTO) now hosts one of the most frequently used international dispute settlement processes in the world.[25] The WTO and its antecedent, the General Agreement on Tariffs and Trade (GATT), have been resolving international trade disputes for over seventy years. At the end of World War II, as part of the Bretton Woods negotiations on international commercial and financial institutions, twenty-three countries drafted the GATT treaty to govern trading relations. The GATT's primary purpose was to reduce trade barriers that would impede the free movement of goods and services across borders. The GATT comprises a complex set of reciprocal trade commitments among the contracting parties, along with rules to minimize government actions that limit the importation of products. Parties to the GATT are obligated to limit tariffs, avoid discrimination among nations, avoid discrimination between domestically produced and imported goods, and avoid the use of quotas and other restrictions on imports.

Following the Bretton Woods agreement, for over forty years the GATT's signatories conducted nine negotiating rounds to expand the treaty's scope of coverage. The Uruguay Round of Multilateral Trade Negotiations (1986 to 1994) was not simply a revision of the original GATT treaty but a fully reconceived institutional structure plus an elaborate series of rules and remedies, all adopted by consensus as a single undertaking.[26] The designers of the new trade agreements, the WTO, were the more than 130 member countries who signed the agreements in 1994. They put in place a network of decision-making processes that correspond to different dimensions of conflict. The literature on WTO dispute settlement focuses on the Understanding on Rules and Procedures Governing the Settlement of Disputes, adopted as part of the Uruguay Round, which resolves disputes at the policy enforcement level. The dispute settlement understanding sets forth specific steps for pursuing trade disputes through a series of four processes: formal consultation, panel review, appellate review, and implementation of the recommendations for compliance. The decision makers are appointed trade-expert panelists, appellate judges, and all WTO members sitting as the dispute settlement body.

In addition to this policy enforcement process, the WTO also engages in policy making and policy implementation. In these three phases of WTO activity, as with most international organizations, the primary stakeholders are the member nations and their constituent ministries, legislatures, citizens, industry, and non-governmental organizations. At the policy-making level, WTO member-countries' delegations participate in ministerial conferences every two years. The primary process used in this phase is direct formal and informal negotiation among the countries to compose an agenda of items to be regulated by new policy measures.

Once the agenda is created, trade negotiation committees endeavor to integrate a package of provisions into an agreement that can achieve consensual support. However, intense conflict to the point of impasse has arisen over the course of the Doha Round since 2001[27] among the now more than 160 member countries over the scope of new rules—for example, those on agricultural subsidies. In past rounds of negotiation, the Green Room—the "friends of the chair" of the negotiating committee—often formed the coalition with the most leverage, while a crosscutting coalition of middle-sized countries bridged the gaps to achieve consensus. Winfried Lang, the former ambassador for Austria to the WTO, describes the negotiation thus:

> Because consensus is not unanimity but the construction of a coalition that agrees surrounded by a group that is willing to go along, power is the way in which consensual coalitions are created. Proximity of parties on issues and differentiation of coalitions among various types account for the types of power available and are applicable to building winning coalitions.[28]

Between these policy-making negotiations and the policy enforcement of the dispute settlement understanding lies policy implementation, wherein each WTO member must translate the international rules adopted in each trade negotiating round into implementing legislation. The Trade Policy Review Mechanism assists members in adhering to the WTO rules through mandated periodic country reviews. The WTO staff conducts an in-depth analysis of a country's legal, economic, and political systems. The report is distributed to all WTO members, who then have an opportunity to ask representatives from the reviewed country questions about its policies. Conflicts can arise over whether the reviewed country has implemented its WTO obligations effectively in national policy and, if not, what remedies are recommended.

Thus, the key stakeholders—the WTO member-country delegates—wear different hats: as formal negotiators in the ministerial conferences to make international trade policy, as the trade policy review body to determine whether countries have appropriately implemented WTO policy, and as the dispute settlement body to determine whether a specific country has complied with its obligations to a trading partner.

In policy making, the scope of the goals is broadest—security and predictability in multilateral trade relations—and the process requires achievement of consensus for adoption. The extended struggles of the most recent negotiations, the Doha Round, begun in 2001 and still ongoing in 2019, reflect the overwhelming procedural and substantive complexity of multiparty negotiations, which are significantly impaired by the power dynamics between large developing nations (e.g., Brazil and India), China, and large developed-country parties (e.g., the European Union and the United States). Countries with relatively less power cannot impose consensus, but they can block it.

In policy implementation, the goal is more focused: fact-finding and capacity building to enable countries' adoption of already-committed-to trade measures. The process is regularized, applied to all member countries, and less dominated by individual members. Problems that surface at this stage can serve as an early warning, enabling conflict prevention. This process is a partially rights-driven (mandated by WTO rules) consultation on the interests of the target country, its trading partners, and the WTO as an institution.

In policy enforcement, the goal is to preserve the rights and obligations of member countries, with the subsidiary objectives of solving trade disputes while maintaining institutional integrity. This process is primarily rights driven, but power (the resources to prosecute or defend) is a significant factor.[29] Between 1995 and 2003, nearly two-thirds of disputes filed in the WTO were resolved before submission of arguments to the arbitration panel. Similarly, as of "January 2008, only about 136 of the nearly 369 cases filed had reached the full panel process. Most of the rest have either been notified as settled . . . or remain in a prolonged consultation."[30] This tendency to negotiate once the panel is established suggests that while the legal process provides an important opportunity for public notice, the processes of mutual or facilitated consultations can achieve satisfactory resolution relative to the parties' expected outcomes from arbitration. The dispute settlement body is currently reviewing a framework of twelve issues: mutually agreed solutions, third-party rights, strictly confidential information, sequencing, postretaliation issues, transparency and amicus curiae briefs, time frames, remand, panel composition, flexibility and member control, effective compliance, and development country interests (including special and differential treatment).[31]

Given the features of these three phases, a shift by the WTO to increased emphasis on the policy implementation phase could offer benefits on several fronts: the transaction costs are moderate, relative to the high costs for all countries to engage in policy making and policy enforcement; satisfaction with outcome and processes is likely to be higher with policy implementation to the extent that parties retain relatively more control; and the effect on relationships is positive, which suggests that, among the process options, a higher emphasis on policy implementation—a rights-interest hybrid—would advance the overall goals of the WTO. Systemically, policy implementation relieves pressure on the policy-making process with more practice-based information and alleviates stress on policy enforcement by anticipating and potentially resolving problems before concrete disputes emerge.

In terms of best practices, process models from other sectors could be constructively applied in this setting. In the enforcement phase, for instance, negotiation, conciliation, and mediation are not fully used. As did ADR in the District Court for the Northern District of California in Chapter 7, a pilot program that offers interests-rights hybrids might open the door to less costly dispute resolution. The operating committees and the Trade Policy Review Mechanism audits clearly uncover conflicts in their early stages, but at present the WTO lacks a companion process with third-party neutrals to enhance the WTO's transparency, accountability, and compliance short of full adjudication. Large industrial countries appear to have sufficient resources and commercial familiarity with domestic ADR processes to pilot such options.

United Nations Commission for International Trade Law

If a person buys a pair of leather boots directly from an online vendor in Buenos Aires and the boots fail to arrive, are not as described, or are damaged, the buyer's only option to dispute the charges may be to fly to Argentina and file a claim there. To resolve such low-value, cross-border e-commerce disputes,[32] the United Nations Commission on International Trade Law (UNCITRAL), created in 1966 to facilitate foreign trade, has worked over several years to develop its technical guidelines for an online dispute resolution (ODR) framework. Legal disparities across borders require expert advice to explore and navigate dispute-handling options, any of which would increase the transaction costs of international dealings.

E-commerce and accompanying online disputes have penetrated domestic marketplaces throughout most of the world.[33] Merchants' and consumers' uncertainty about what forum and law would apply in a dispute spurred the EU ODR Directive. Because limited access to justice and ensuing lack of trust in the e-commerce system diminish trade growth, experts in law, commerce, dispute resolution, and online technology speculate that if an effective dispute resolution system were in place, both merchants and consumers would flock to new cross-border opportunities. An effective system would ideally promote a harmonized legal standard of practice, due process, and quick, efficient, enforceable access to justice.[34]

UNCITRAL convened an ODR colloquium in 2010[35] as a first step toward creating a cross-border ODR system for e-commerce. Speakers at the colloquium confirmed that disputes arising from low-value e-commerce transactions could annually amount to substantial sums. Other than credit card chargeback protection, which is not available in most countries, few if any legal redress mechanisms are currently available, leaving a wide legal gap in the online marketplace. Several experts argued that the rapidly developing online marketplace and emerging new payment structures require correspondingly progressive ADR systems. Speakers also recommended that any set of rules accommodate transactions made over mobile phones, possibly using mobile payment options, as well as other e-commerce platforms. Finally, given the nature of the online marketplace, speakers asserted that there was no reason to distinguish between business-to-business and business-to-consumer transactions in developing model ODR rules and processes for low-value transactions.

Shortly after the colloquium, state delegates[36] to UNCITRAL overwhelmingly supported the creation of a working group to establish an ODR framework to resolve high-volume, low-value e-commerce disputes. Specifically, the Working Group III mandate included a four-part framework: procedural rules, substantive rules and legal principles, guidelines for neutrals and standards for ODR providers, and an enforcement protocol.[37] It is anticipated that independent ODR providers will provide their services in accordance with the framework, as opposed to UNCITRAL or national government agencies. Assuming integrity of the system as to the rules and regulation of neutrals and providers, practical issues of language, cost, and usability by consumers remain.[38]

Such an ODR process would differ from existing redress options in two distinct ways: it would sit outside the payment channels, and claimants would lose their rights to seek redress in court. Proponents point to several advantages: arbitration is necessary to ensure enforcement in a cross-border context, the process must be binding predispute or else sellers will not participate postdispute, and blacklists and trustmarks will help sellers comply with the awards. Vikki Rogers expands:

> We are looking to accommodate three needs: buyers looking for cheaper buying options, sellers looking to expand markets, and states wanting to protect their citizens' rights—in some cases constitutionally protected rights. Insisting on a binding arbitration system makes it very difficult to accommodate these three interests and can hinder, rather than encourage, cross-border e-commerce.[39]

UNCITRAL issued "Technical Notes on Online Dispute Resolution," a product of deliberation by over sixty member states and numerous international organizations.[40] The technical notes, while nonbinding, reflect principles of impartiality, independence, efficiency, effectiveness, due process, fairness, accountability, and transparency. An ODR (technology-aided) process may consist of three stages: negotiation, facilitated settlement, and evaluation or adjudication.

Building on UNCITRAL's efforts, the Asia-Pacific Economic Conference is developing a cooperative ODR framework for business-to-business harmonization of relevant ODR laws through international instruments. It is focusing especially on small and medium enterprises, for which neither court nor arbitration are feasible options. If, as UNCITRAL notes, "ODR can assist the parties in resolving the dispute in a simple, fast, flexible and secure manner, without the need for physical presence at a meeting or hearing,"[41] it is in the interest of businesses to use this resource.

In a parallel and complementary approach, the International Council on Online Dispute Resolution formed in 2017 to engage its global members—individuals, firms, dispute resolution providers, and official agencies—in developing principles around use of ODR, certification, and training of providers. The principles, intended to inform international performance standards, include accessibility,

---

International Mediation Enforcement

The New York Convention on the Recognition and Enforcement of Foreign Arbitral Awards has been the gold standard for international commercial disputes. The convention, signed by 150-plus countries, provides that any arbitral award may be enforced in a court of a signatory country. Mediation has no such enforcement mechanisms. As an alternative to arbitration, mediation offers advantages of flexibility, shorter time, and lower expense, but the resulting settlement agreement has lacked the enforcement tool of the New York Convention. UNCITRAL's Working Group II commenced work in 2015 to address this mediation enforcement gap and issued the Singapore Convention on Mediation in June 2018; it was adopted by the UN General Assembly in fall of 2018 and opened for signature in Singapore on August 1, 2019.[42] What does this experience suggest in terms of goals and the design process in an international context?[43]

accountability, competence, confidentiality, equality, fairness, impartiality, neutrality, security, legality, and transparency.[44]

Conclusion

The international dispute resolution mechanisms described in this chapter reflect a great diversity of goals, stakeholders, legal systems, and cultures. Of these, two have multilateral structures—the CAS and the WTO. Bilateral investment treaties are bilateral by definition; UNCITRAL contemplates a hybrid: bilateral agreements between merchants and customers, combined with a multilateral agreement under which national governments, domestic consumer agencies, ODR providers, and merchants agree to a system of opt-in processes that would be available across borders.

No one country can unilaterally impose a design goal or structure on another—it must be negotiated to become an accepted norm to have any chance of broad compliance and enforcement. Most of the goals discussed in the DSD Analytic Framework of Chapter 2 are pertinent: conflict prevention, management, and resolution; efficient administration and participation; maintenance of relationships; just and legitimate outcomes; and institutional reputation. Achieving a measure of all these goals takes broad participation and thus time.

The canonical sequence of methods recognized by international law for the peaceful settlement of disputes starts with negotiation, followed by a stepladder of facilitated (conciliation and mediation) and adjudicated (or arbitrated) processes.[45] Very few disputes are resolved by the International Court of Justice, because countries resist waiving their national sovereignty. Instead, institutionalized negotiation, at its best, offers transparency and broad participation (tempered by political power), a preferable alternative to the more adversarial processes. With specialized arbitration, the opportunity to select expert neutrals in a regulated process has proved effective and satisfactory in many instances, including CAS, WTO, and cross-border business-to-business disputes at the International Chamber of Commerce in Paris and Singapore International Arbitration Center.[46]

International dispute resolution processes have both upstream and downstream components. Given the severity of relinquishing sovereignty to an extraterritorial downstream process, there may be reasons to focus more on addressing issues upstream and midstream. These issues are situated within a broader context: the tension between public and private interests. Historically, courts were viewed as public forums with public officials publicly deciding cases on the basis of public law. In contrast, using contemporary private mechanisms, disputants select experts to render decisions according to preferred standards in a more informal and confidential venue. This shift from public to private has occurred in both the domestic and the international arenas. Deborah Hensler reviews this "blurring boundary" and considers the relative benefits: "What do we lose and what do we gain when public dispute resolution becomes private, and private decision-makers acquire the ability to resolve disputes with significant public policy consequences?"[47] Hensler raises concerns on the diminished legitimacy of government and due process that privatized processes pose. While transparency is a hallmark of public processes, some private processes are also pushing for more transparency. In the international domain, there is an even stronger tension between the private and public interests. In investor-state disputes, when negotiating with large multinational corporations state actors have significant interests in protecting their sovereignty, yet they owe their citizens a level of public responsibility. From UNCITRAL's Working Group II emerged the Mauritius Convention, which adopts transparency rules, including open hearings, published awards, and amicus briefs.[48]

Conflict that arises internationally spans two-party to multiparty and is multi-issue, multisector (public, private, nonprofit), lengthy, and in the public and private domains. Similarly, process options designed by governments and private firms and organizations offer choices on who decides (public officials or private experts), on what basis (law or contract), and under what rules (public or private). Despite the complex challenges posed, the international field offers opportunities to deliberate and test those systems on measures of fairness and justice suitable to the stakeholders.

PART IV

MULTIJURISDICTIONAL AND COMPLEX SYSTEMS

17 COLLABORATIVE GOVERNANCE AND DISPUTE SYSTEM DESIGN

SOUTH AFRICA'S TRUTH and Reconciliation Commission fused traditional legislative, executive, and judicial governance structures with a DSD for addressing conflict. The commission's purpose was procedural and restorative justice, enabling people to exercise voice in a way that would foster transition from apartheid to South Africa's new democracy (see Chapter 15). The commission's DSD integrated the participation of all three branches of government and civil society. The commission's enabling statute defined the conditions of amnesty and applied those conditions to crimes committed during apartheid for a defined and limited time.[1] It also created a quasi-judicial institution empowered to hold public hearings.[2] With a DSD for public engagement, the commission invited the public to participate in these hearings through committees, direct testimony, public access, and broadcasts.[3] Its design was both substantive (conditions of amnesty) and procedural (transparency as a means of reconciliation). Some view the Truth and Reconciliation Commission as a successful DSD,[4] yet it was also an important part of a peaceful transition in governance, illustrating collaborative governance through a DSD that incorporated public engagement and restorative justice processes in collaboration with civil society.

Most literature on DSD refers to systems for preventing, managing, and resolving conflict in organizations. It is important to recognize, however, that these designs are also nested in a context that is itself an institution: a society that governs itself.[5] Governance is the means to reconcile differences in policy priorities, goals, and interests among residents; stakeholders in the public, private, and nonprofit sectors; and branches of government. Elinor Ostrom observes that institutions create rules in the sense of regulations; these shape what happens in an action arena.[6] DSD therefore applies not only to courts and organizational grievance procedures but equally to systems for governance and particularly to systems that use collaboration and consensus building. Collaborative governance is in this sense a form of public sector DSD. Governance scales from local to state or provincial to national[7] and international. Chapter 9 examines a local community example of collaborative governance using focus groups, representative stakeholder dialogues, and public engagement, but dispute resolution practitioners have long used dialogue and mediation skills to address difficult and controversial large-scale public discussions.[8]

This chapter introduces collaborative governance and applies the DSD Analytic Framework (Chapter 2) to public engagement, deliberative democracy, collaborative public management, and networks. It examines three examples: a large-scale energy infrastructure project licensed by a U.S. public agency, negotiated rulemaking, and participatory budgeting. It also introduces accountability and evaluation in large-scale collaborative governance designs.

Issues to consider are as follows.

- How can DSD foster collaborative governance at different points along the policy continuum?
- What are the benefits of deliberative democracy, and what processes encourage it?
- How can the DSD Analytic Framework guide assessment of collaborative governance needs and models?

Collaborative Governance

This chapter takes the normative position that governance should afford people democratic practice, voice in decisions that affect them, security and human rights within the rule of law,[9] transparency, and appropriate forms of justice. Definitions of governance vary widely[10]—for example, it is "organized efforts to manage the course of events in a social system" and "how people exercise power to achieve the ends they desire."[11] Governance also is "theories and issues of social coordination and the nature of all patterns of rule," with contemporary definitions placing less emphasis "on hierarchy and the state, and more on markets and networks."[12] There are three distinctive features of modern governance: it is hybrid,[13] is multi-jurisdictional, and has plural stakeholders who operate in networks.[14] The "new governance" entails policy tools that involve privatization of previously public work and devolution of responsibility from unitary bureaucracies to networks and contractors.[15] In the twenty-first century, DSD examples are designing new national constitutions and national and international initiatives aimed at reforming corrupt or failed states or addressing the needs for governance of nonstate actors who seek to achieve an independent state. Theories of institutional design in political economy explain governance designs.[16]

The Policy Continuum for Governance

Governance interventions, such as DSD, are nested in institutions across the entire policy continuum of the legislative, executive, and judicial branches of government. The policy continuum consists of stages in a continuous and dynamic cycle. The stages of policy making identify policy problems, identify approaches or tools for solving the policy problems,[17] set priorities among these approaches or tools, select from among the priorities, draft proposed legislation, enact legislation, identify policy problems left for the executive to resolve within the boundaries of the legislation, identify approaches or tools for regulations and other management strategies, set priorities for and select tools and strategies, draft proposed regulations, enact regulations, implement regulations (e.g., project or program management, permits), enforce law through executive agency adjudication, and enforce law through litigation within the jurisdiction of the judicial power.[18]

Collaborative governance (introduced in Chapter 3) is increasingly necessary for solving "wicked" problems—those too complex for a single agency to resolve using command and control approaches.[19] Designing governance in the modern world means more than simply creating a constitution that establishes branches of government, even if these branches have well-functioning public agencies and institutions. Governance necessarily entails a complex dance with public, private, or nonprofit stakeholders[20]—and with the public more generally[21]—to make, implement, and enforce policy and law.[22] This undertaking involves collaboration between the public and stakeholders[23] in decision-making across the entire policy continuum through public engagement,[24] dialogue and deliberation (or deliberative democracy),[25] collaborative public or network management, and ADR.

Upstream in policy formation, collaborative governance entails dialogue and deliberation, or deliberative democracy,[26] in contrast with the traditional adversarial processes of governance, which usually center on debate. Deliberative democracy uses a variety of models and techniques for engaging the public and stakeholders.[27] Midstream in policy implementation, collaborative public management involves agencies and stakeholder organizations from the public,[28] private, and nonprofit sectors cooperating in networks through arrangements or policy tools that include contracts and public-private partnerships.[29] Downstream, collaborative governance uses ADR in quasi-judicial or judicial contexts within or independent of government.[30]

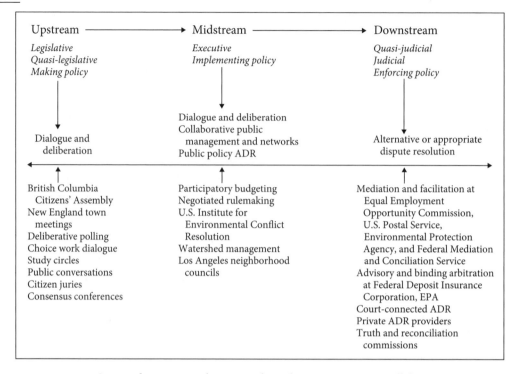

Figure 17.1   System design examples across the policy continuum in collaborative governance

Voice processes in collaborative governance allow people to engage in creating, implementing, and enforcing public policy and law as part of the work of legislative, executive, and judicial branches of government on this continuum. Figure 17.1 builds on Figure 3.1, providing real-world examples of collaborative governance mechanisms along the continuum.

Public Engagement: Dialogue, Deliberation, and Deliberative Democracy

Political theorists have an ongoing debate over the function, structure, and contributions of public deliberation in governance.[31] In theory, many diverse voices provide government with better and more complete information on which to base decisions, making collaborative governance more efficient than hierarchical decision-making.[32] Deliberative democracy is valuable instrumentally to build consensus, determine the truth, raise awareness of public policy issues, improve public decision-making, and enhance the legitimacy of government.[33] Jürgen Habermas observed that those with shared class interests in the bourgeois public sphere could benefit from use of reason in a rational or critical debate on matters of common concern.[34] However, theorists have criticized the lack of inclusiveness within many deliberative democracy efforts—the control over the agenda by elites and the reasons they give for that control—as disadvantaging nonelites, and others have criticized the exclusion of other modes of communication through emotion, storytelling, and compassion as relevant to matters of public concern. Framing deliberation around the common good may discourage collective action like traditional bargaining for issues like fair distribution;[35] conservatives may use public deliberation to suppress or discourage collective action.

In discussing these competing views and models, terminological clarity is warranted.[36] Deliberative democracy may engage the "public" (the broad and general populace), "citizens" (eligible voters), "residents" (inhabitants of a particular locale such as a housing subdivision or building), or "community" (members of a particular neighborhood or area). The commonly used term "stakeholders" (individuals who have a vested interest in an issue by virtue of their professional role or involvement in a formal group or organization) has become more controversial because of its history as reflecting settlers who staked a claim in land on which Native Americans or First Peoples lived and from which they were displaced. Critics suggest the terms "parties" or "disputants," but these terms evoke adjudicated claims. Some scholars prefer "engagement" or "involvement" (which are general terms for assembling individuals to address an issue), "public participation" (which is a legal term of art), "collaboration" (which generally refers to multiple organizations or a network addressing an issue), and "deliberation" or "deliberative" (which refers to a specific mode of reasoned communication during engagement).

While some scholars advocate for reaching consensus as a goal of public deliberation,[37] others now define full deliberation as "a careful examination of a problem or issue, the identification of possible solutions, the establishment or reaffirmation of evaluative criteria, and the use of these criteria in identifying an optimal solution."[38] Empirical research suggests that practitioners' norms for deliberative process are participant satisfaction, group productivity, a positive atmosphere, making progress, good emotional interaction and reason giving, common good viewed as common ground, and the free flow of ideas. Inequality is an obstacle to deliberation.[39]

There is a broad academic and practitioner literature on public engagement in fields like public administration, public policy, political science, planning, law, and conflict resolution.[40] Models for public engagement vary widely, from the classic "three minutes at the microphone" widely adopted in public hearings at the community level to increasingly deliberative forms in which people in groups of eight to ten engage in a facilitated conversation and generate ideas to approach a specific policy problem.[41] Models differ along dimensions that are similar to those in the DSD Analytic Framework (Chapter 2): general purpose and specific goals, participation mechanism and methodology, size and participant selection, participant recruitment and preparation, communication mode and plan, locus of action, connection to the policy process and specificity of recommendations, and recurrence and iteration.[42]

Informed participation is key to deliberative democracy. One model for encouraging informed participation is the Kettering Foundation's National Issues Forum,[43] which produces issue booklets with background information to brief participants before they deliberate on a public problem like urban sprawl in planning. Another model is deliberative polling, which provides participants with experts they can query to deepen discussion on an issue.[44]

AmericaSpeaks offers a historical example; this nongovernmental organization (NGO) piloted large-scale deliberative forums. (Lack of resources forced it to close, which is a major problem in DSD of collaborative governance.) Funded by sponsors, it convened a process to determine how to redevelop Ground Zero, the site of the former World Trade Center that was leveled by the 9/11 terrorist attacks in 2001. The process, "Listening to the City," engaged a demographically representative sample of the New York City electorate, other residents, and undocumented workers (over 4,500 people) for a full day of dialogue and deliberation.[45] Tables, each with a professional facilitator, of ten to twelve people deliberated while connected online to screens and a theme team at a computer bank. They voted on ideas using handheld keypad devices to record their preferences and demographic information. By the end of the daylong process, the AmericaSpeaks theme team had analyzed the data and prepared a written report for decision makers and participants.

Collaborative Public Management and Networks

The field of public administration has examined collaboration among organizations and networks using many terms: new governance, collaborative governance,[46] and collaborative public management. Networks consist of organizations from the public, private, or nonprofit sectors that work together to share information or achieve some common goal. Some scholars frame "new governance" in the examination of tools, such as tax incentives, contracts privatizing services, and partnership agreements. These tools create some structures for collaboration, such as contracts to perform certain public services. Broader conceptions of new or collaborative governance include the practices and processes through which the public and stakeholders participate in the work of government.[47] These practices and processes too are part of design and structure.[48] Increasingly, collaborative governance provides the structures for global governance, in light of hybrid organizations, NGOs, and interaction across national boundaries.[49]

Collaborative structures form in so many types of settings as to raise questions. For example, collaboration occurs within and across organizations and within and across sectors. How do networks of agencies—for example, federal agencies coordinating on environmental conflict resolution—compare with networks of public, private, and nonprofit organizations, such as watershed management networks with local, regional, state, federal, nonprofit, and other members? Among the many dimensions of variation in collaborative management and networks are shared and divergent goals, public participation, controversy, professional facilitation, and structures.

SHARED AND DIVERGENT GOALS. Collaboration can occur among like-minded, or homogeneous, partners. Environmental groups may form a coalition; yet in a collaborative effort, these groups may work with private sector polluters; local, regional, state, or federal government agencies; and citizens with varied concerns. Participants may have both shared and divergent goals. In planning and land use, for example, fifty-nine municipal authorities collaborated in Hamilton County, Ohio, to develop a plan for growth and development, and they reached unanimous agreement on its outlines. In the Florida Everglades, stakeholders collaborated to resolve a conflict over the science of restoring the watershed and how to foster and measure progress.[50]

PUBLIC PARTICIPATION. Collaboration also occurs both with and without broader public participation. Emergency management planning in New Orleans before Hurricane Katrina involved representatives of local, state, and federal government and was largely limited to professionals.[51] Such lack of public participation engendered substantial criticism. Planning for recovery from Katrina now involves collaboration of local, state, and federal agencies and a series of large-scale, high-profile public forums in addition to participation of elected officials.

CONTROVERSY. Collaboration can address highly contentious issues or topics that are not very controversial. Environmental conflict resolution (addressed in more detail in Chapter 18) involves multiparty negotiation and mediation concerning conflict over air, water, or land; natural resource allocation and development; and land use development.[52] Documented cases from less contentious settings include emergence of regional, voluntary service coordination and collaboration among local governments[53] and local neighborhood councils collaborating with city service agencies to enhance communication and responsiveness.[54]

PROFESSIONAL FACILITATION. Collaboration sometimes features professional facilitators or mediators. Facilitated or mediated collaboration has occurred at many highly polluted sites; parties are local, regional, state, and federal government; Native American tribes; nonprofit organizations; environmental advocacy groups; and groups of local residents. Other facilitated or mediated collaborations have concerned food safety, HIV/AIDS treatment, urban air quality, and dam decommissioning. In watershed management, while some groups have used professional facilitators, others have avoided this practice.[55]

STRUCTURES. Collaboration yields different organizational structures and designs. Networks themselves are intentional structures of collaboration, though in practice networks are not always labeled as such (nor do they necessarily label themselves as engaging in collaborative public management). Design incorporates network decision rules or ground rules such as consensus, aggregation of votes for majority or supermajority rule, and behavioral norms such as principled or interest-based negotiation and conflict. Collaborative network design also includes systems for resolving conflict within the network, systematic incorporation of the public's voice through civic engagement, and means for transparency in communicating the work of collaboration. Design issues also consider the relationship of collaboration to accountability structures. Networks need to identify the new contribution, product, or output expected from collaboration and align accountability structures accordingly. They need to build data collection on direct measures of collaborative behaviors and actions.

Adapting the DSD Analytic Framework to Collaborative Governance

Most of this book examines the DSD Analytic Framework for institutions that resolve conflict downstream through forms of dispute resolution.[56] However, DSD applies to designs for deliberation and conflict over public decisions, including making policy upstream and implementing policy midstream on the continuum. This section examines collaborative governance and the DSD Analytic Framework.

Purposes and Goals

Collaborative governance entails DSD for a public purpose, as part of public decision-making. Goals may be social justice and equity. John Rawls describes social justice as encompassing the basic structures of society and arrangement of major social institutions into one scheme of cooperation. The substantive justice produced by a DSD corresponds to the underlying substantive law defining rights and obligations. Public policy goals in law may include fundamental public values[57] such as protection of human and civil rights,[58] protection of property,[59] physical security,[60] and satisfaction of basic needs for food, water, shelter, and health care.[61] Collaboration in governance also entails procedural justice: public voice, participation, and transparency.[62] The democratic merit of collaborative governance is seen in inclusiveness, representativeness, impartiality, transparency, deliberativeness, lawfulness, and empowerment.[63] Goals and ethics for community disputes entailing large-scale protest or racial or ethnic conflict should encompass how the process promotes "core values of freedom, justice, and proportional empowerment."[64]

Public and Stakeholders

For democratic governance, legitimacy and effectiveness depend on the participation of the public and stakeholders. Collaborative governance can include the broadest scope of stakeholders within and outside government, such as the public; transnational, national, state, regional, and local government agencies; indigenous peoples; civil society; nonprofit organizations; and businesses.[65] DSD can strengthen their role. In public engagement, models vary from open invitation of the diffuse public to representative samples and random samples. With the diffuse public comes the risk of self-selection bias; participants tend to be disproportionately higher income, white, and well educated. To increase the diversity and representativeness of a deliberative public forum, it may be necessary to schedule the event outside normal working hours, provide food or childcare, conduct broad outreach, and address cultural differences among members and groups of the public.

Convening participants in collaboration or multiparty negotiation requires a different process to identify the context, stakeholders, resource needs, obstacles, and guidelines for leadership.[66] This process identifies who is affected by the issues, who will need to implement an agreement, and who could block its implementation. The convener will interview these key groups in a conflict assessment (see Chapter 4). Often the participants are agents representing stakeholder interests who must deal with technical complexity, missing parties, and determining common interests or common ground on behalf of others.[67] Among their duties are ensuring they have clarity on their organization's interests, obtaining information on technical issues, ensuring their constituents share an understanding of the problem, and addressing divergent interests and disagreements between the principal and agent.

Context and Culture

In collaborative governance, "context" and "culture" refer to the national, state, regional, local, social, cultural, and institutional context[68] for governance (see Chapter 3). Governance systems vary with both the formal constitutional structure for government and the stability of the nation-state or community within which collaborative governance is designed. To increase participation, designers may reach out to immigrant or minority communities through media outlets like newspapers and radio stations for minority-language communities or through meetings with local community, neighborhood, religious, or labor leaders. Context and culture also inform sensitivity to participants' sense of safety and willingness to participate in a public meeting. Beyond outreach to bring in participants, designers must make the event itself accessible by addressing barriers related to physical mobility, income, family needs, and language. For example, one nonprofit provided simultaneous translation equipment to municipalities for public meetings after some residents objected to spending public funds to make meetings accessible to attendees who did not speak English.[69]

The organization Partners for Democratic Change builds local capacity in developing countries by setting up nongovernmental organizations in countries. Each member organization is led and staffed by people from its nation.[70] Each member determines its mission on the basis of what its country needs. The Slovakia affiliate worked to build cooperative conflict management skills by training leaders from the nongovernmental organization, local government, and private sectors; training trainers to provide a multiplier effect; applying conflict management processes such as mediation, facilitation, and consensus building; and promoting public policy supporting mediation.[71] Partners Slovakia also developed conciliation commissions to assist ethnic communities with conflict management and reconciliation.[72] In contrast, Partners Morocco focused on leadership training for women.

Processes and Structure

Designing collaborative governance involves shaping both procedural and substantive structures. Procedures are *how* government takes action; substance is *what* action it takes. For example, transparency is a procedural choice. Freedom of information laws, public records, open access to government meetings, and management choices like the Open Government Initiative all provide transparency.[73] Substance refers to the decisions and actions that transparency reveals (and potentially influences). While sunshine is the great sanitizer of public corruption, there is tension between transparency and the necessary confidentiality for effective negotiation and mediation. Collaborative governance entails processes of multiparty negotiation, facilitation, mediation, and consensus building[74] and sometimes fact-finding[75] and adjudicative processes for impasse resolution.[76]

CONFLICT OR ISSUES ASSESSMENT. Multiparty negotiation processes require a conflict or issues assessment.[77] Experts recommend an impartial third-party intervenor or convener for this task, as now codified in the U.S. Negotiated Rulemaking Act.[78] The convener explains her role and authority, then begins information gathering by identifying the necessary parties. These are the parties that can stop a settlement or its implementation. One method is snowball sampling (asking key people who should participate, then asking those they suggest, and so on, until the same group of names recurs). Another is convening a small group of key parties to discuss additional invitees. Conveners may conduct interviews that range from brief discussions to in-person and in-depth meetings using mediator skills such as active and reflective listening and open-ended questions. They may use a formal interview protocol and assurances of confidentiality. Critical information to gather is history; key issues for the present and future; the parties' interests; ideas for solutions; negotiable and nonnegotiable points; perceptions and reactions; barriers to interventions using negotiation, mediation, and consensus building; and the likelihood that parties can reach a settlement.[79] The convener writes an analysis for the parties and proposes a process design, goals, an agenda, selection of stakeholder representatives, and a time frame for suggested process stages; the parties receive a draft or final written report on which the convener may invite feedback.

CONSENSUS BUILDING. Consensus is the objective of most multiparty processes. Although it is defined as "unanimous concurrence" under the Negotiated Rulemaking Act, in practice it is not necessarily unanimity but rather general agreement that participants can live with and support the outcomes of the process. Lawrence Susskind, a founder of public policy consensus-building research and practice, and Jeffrey Cruikshank[80] provide an overview of process elements for consensus building: meeting with a convener as the leader and having an assessment by a neutral; assigning roles and responsibilities, with a facilitator as an insider or outsider who notes, reports, and checks in with constituents; facilitating group problem-solving by venting, sharing interests, inventing, delaying commitments, packaging, and brainstorming; reaching agreement by consensus—not by voting but asking instead, "Can you live with this?"—and asking open-ended "why" questions if not; and holding people to their commitments with flexibility for the unexpected. As these principles illustrate, consensus building requires a complex set of professional skills from impartial third-party conveners, facilitators, and mediators.

Resources

Available resources depend on the scope and context of the design, which in the arena of governance, law, and policy can be tremendously broad. For example, global governance structures like the United Nations or European Union may provide logistical support or funding for dialogues to assist with postconflict reconstruction after a civil war.[81] The public sector resources in a country may be constrained by the political and economic context. Given fiscal limitations, local, state, and federal public agencies cannot often devote resources to in-person public engagement or public policy dispute resolution and collaboration. Online dialogues and brainstorming, which may be less resource intensive, allow the public to post ideas and comment or vote on proposals.[82] Under the U.S. Open Government Initiative, federal agencies have implemented online designs to allow the public to comment on and participate in policy making and implementation.[83]

Accountability, Success, and Learning

The question for evaluation is what and how to measure with respect to *good* governance, because the theory behind collaborative governance is that governance will improve.[84] Often, the underlying premise of international initiatives is that good governance can help produce the rule of law. The World Bank identifies six dimensions of good governance in its Worldwide Governance Indicators: voice and accountability; political stability and the absence of violence; government effectiveness; regulatory quality; rule of law; and control of corruption.[85] In an empirical study of transitions from dictatorship to democracy, nonviolent civic forces (people power) played a key role in achieving freedom; there was comparatively little effect for top-down transitions led by elites; and cohesive nonviolent civic coalitions were the most important factor contributing to a transition.[86] This indicates that public engagement and consensus building may be the most effective approaches to wicked problems. Research on consensus building's effectiveness is still in its early stages, because it requires complexity science in a context requiring confidentiality, which makes data collection difficult.[87] However, as communication and technology improve, and as the tools of big data become more accessible for public decision-making, researchers may be able to better measure the impact of public engagement and consensus building on measures of good governance.[88]

Upstream and Downstream in a Public Agency: Large-Scale Energy Infrastructure

One illustration of the many types of collaborative governance designs is licensing of energy infrastructure such as gas and energy transmission lines and hydroelectric dams. These licensing systems may explicitly encompass both upstream and downstream applications. The U.S. Federal Energy Regulatory Commission has extensive experience with involving stakeholders in these licensing programs. In a prefiling process, applicants must identify and engage stakeholders that may be a federal, state, or multistate, tribal, or local agency; an affected nongovernmental organization; or interested persons (such as citizens along the likely transmission line path). This preapplication process of engaging stakeholders both disseminates information about the proposed project to stakeholders and offers them a reasonable opportunity to present their views and recommendations with respect to the need for and impact of a facility covered by the permit application. Usual practice is to hold open houses at strategic geographic locations along the proposed route or in the dam's area with informal workshops, formal transcribed testimonials, and information booths. Once a party files a formal application, the Federal Energy Regulatory Commission begins a legally mandated process; to participate, stakeholders must formally file a motion.

Drawing on years of experience with these processes, Lawrence Susskind[89] and Jonathan Raab[90] have developed principles for licensing and siting large-scale energy infrastructure that call on consensus building:

1. Initiate stakeholder involvement as early as possible and set realistic but firm timetables.
2. Ensure broad representation of legitimate stakeholder groups (including government agencies and, for site-specific projects, citizen groups).
3. Seek consensus, and consider using a professional neutral to facilitate collaborative decision-making.
4. Do not exclude contentious issues; instead seek ways to address negative aspects of any proposal (including compensation, contingent agreements).
5. Consider incorporating alternative siting processes (such as voluntary processes, preapproval, competitive solicitations).

6. Structure stakeholder involvement processes to supplement but not supplant the formal backstop process while modifying formal processes to
   better accommodate consensus-building opportunities.[91]

Although this example of an integrated design for governance is for a specific
policy arena (energy), the six principles have broad application.

Negotiated Rulemaking as Collaborative Governance

Negotiated rulemaking is a collaborative process in which stakeholders meet with
the help of a facilitator to reach agreement on the substance and language of draft
government regulations. Under the federal Negotiated Rulemaking Act, which has
inspired similar legislation in some states, a convener examines the likelihood that
a representative group of stakeholders might reach consensus within a reasonable
period on draft language for a regulation. If the group can, the agency publishes
notice of its intent to form a negotiated rulemaking committee. Once formed,
the committee includes an agency representative and uses a facilitator to help it
develop ground rules and conduct meetings. If the committee reaches consensus
on draft regulations, the agency must submit the committee's recommendations
to the statutory rulemaking process under the Administrative Procedure Act,
which allows for public notice and a period to comment. However, the agency
may change the final regulatory language.

The choice of stakeholder representatives for the committee is critical. For
example, if a negotiated rulemaking committee is formed to draft agricultural
regulations and fails to include as representatives relevant growers with different
interests, this omission may jeopardize the committee's success. Scholars disagree
on the efficacy of negotiated rulemaking; while one scholar suggests it lacks value
because it is as time consuming as traditional informal rulemaking, others indicate that matters submitted to negotiated rulemaking resolve issues that might
otherwise might have led to litigation challenging final regulations.[92]

Participatory Budgeting

Beyond administrative procedure statutes requiring agencies to provide opportunities for public participation, governments increasingly recognize the need for
broader and more meaningful public engagement. Participatory budgeting is one
engagement process that offers benefits for agencies and community members. In
an era of declining fiscal resources, participatory budgeting allows a community
to help elected officials set priorities for how to use tax dollars. Residents identify

their preferences through surveys or interactive public processes like deliberative polling, in which residents exchange with each other and experts information about the sources for and demands on public revenue.[93]

Participatory budgeting is gaining popularity as a design that gives residents some control over spending decisions about discretionary budget dollars that

Participatory Budgeting as Collaborative Governance

Porto Alegre, Brazil, is one of the earliest examples of a successful participatory budgeting process.[94] Established in 1989 as part of the municipal budget cycle, the process by 2000 had over twenty thousand people who participated in deciding how to distribute a $160 million budget. A significant number of the participants were poor and historically marginalized from politics and governance. What distinguished Porto Alegre's DSD was its complex institutional design, which allowed it to become embedded in city management as part of a continuing process. The DSD entailed large-scale, open regional assemblies at which residents took part in holding the administration to account, voting on neighborhood and regional priorities for infrastructure investment (e.g., sanitation, road paving, health care), and electing citizens to the sixteen regional budget forums and the Council of the Participatory Budget.[95] The sixteen large forums were distributed over the city's neighborhoods. The elected delegates, proportionate to the voters in that neighborhood, participated in regional budget forums in which they voted on and prioritized demands from the assemblies. They also negotiated with city agencies and monitored how well they implemented projects. Meetings were open to the public to provide transparency. Because issues extended beyond neighborhood boundaries, another structural design piece was citywide thematic assemblies to deliberate on issues like environment, health, and education. To accommodate this participation in governance, the city established new administrative structures such as a centralized planning service to work with the budget priorities and a community relations department to mobilize participants. Participatory budgeting resulted in redistributing revenues to the poorest neighborhoods in the city to provide basic infrastructure, with near completion of projects involving sewage, water, and municipal public education.

can be used for projects to benefit their neighborhoods. However, participatory budgeting generally addresses only a small part of a community's budget. Moreover, the question remains whether communities can sustain and institutionalize this approach.

Conclusion

At each stage in the policy process, there is an opportunity for DSD that fosters the voice of the public and stakeholders and provides for collaborative governance. However, the complexity of policy dynamics is such that the impact of an isolated intervention may be dwarfed by that of other forces. Research shows that formal institutions are necessary but not sufficient to achieve the rule of law; informal institutions, such as voluntary networks, are essential for enduring transformation.[96] Collaborative governance provides a way to design bottom-up, participatory, democratic practice in decision-making on public policy.

Chapter 12 addresses how mandatory arbitration may suppress legitimate claims arising out of social movements such as MeToo and Black Lives Matter. DSDs in collaborative governance may provide more large-scale and effective designs for deliberating over the systemic sexism and racism that gave rise to these movements. Professionals in the fields of dispute resolution and public engagement may bring together their related skill sets to forge innovative designs.

To achieve good governance, designers can use collaborative governance and structure DSD across the policy continuum in a way that causes the three branches of government to reinforce the interventions and each other. Designers must consider not only formal but also informal institutional arrangements in the context of social norms, history, and culture. However, DSD also requires a pragmatic willingness to identify metrics and indicators of success for the system and measure its performance in light of its goals. Empirically evaluating design efforts and adjusting designs in response to these results is a final and critical piece of DSD;[97] it permits repeated democratic experimentalism over time to design good governance.

18 DESIGNING DISPUTE SYSTEMS FOR THE ENVIRONMENT

CONSIDER GROUNDWATER, a significant source of water for agricultural and municipal use all over the world. This resource is subject to an array of legal, political, economic, environmental, social, cultural, and moral claims.[1] Disputes over groundwater can involve a plethora of parties from the public, private, and nonprofit sectors. How can these parties best address this type of multisectoral conflict, which has become known as a "wicked problem?"[2]

Environmental conflict resolution (ECR) concerns such fundamental and ongoing differences among disputants regarding values and behavior[3] as they relate to actual or potential disputes involving the environment (air, water, soil, flora, and fauna), natural resources, or public lands.[4] These conflicts involve multiple parties in a decision-making process who disagree about issues traceable to an action or policy that has potential environmental impacts.[5]

Issues to consider are as follows.

- Who determines how to prevent, manage, or resolve conflicts over environmental resource use?
- What processes are used to make decisions under often uncertain conditions, and with what information?
- How are ECR outcomes measured for success?

In this chapter, we discuss what distinguishes environmental disputes from other conflicts, examining how such conflicts have multiplied with increasing knowledge about environmental impacts and with changing values and institutions. The analysis of two cases illustrates both upstream and downstream system design. The downstream case is drawn from a community in Maine that struggled to address a seeming increase in cancer incidence that some residents suspected was correlated with the local paper mill (although the mill was in compliance with applicable regulations). The upstream case involves implementation of California's Marine Life Protection Act to designate reserve, conservation, and recreational areas along its coast.

The Analytic Framework and Environmental Conflict

What distinguishes environmental conflict from many other types of disputes is that a single ECR case can serve as a dispute system unto itself. ECR processes often involve multiple interim decisions as more information comes available (for example, in response to ongoing monitoring of a contaminant in water or air). The ECR process thus functions over time as a system for resolving a series of disputes. Instead of treating the case as the unit of measurement, it becomes possible to take measurements of diverse indicators across participants and at multiple points in time. However, the question of context remains: If ECR is not a case but a system, how is it organized and how can data be captured to evaluate the system?[6]

Goals

Environmental disputes can be classified as upstream (planning or policy making), midstream (policy implementation), or downstream (compliance and enforcement). For example, upstream environmental conflicts can involve the creation of government policy at the national, regional, state, or local level, such as environmental or natural resource policy, health or safety policy, and education policy. Midstream environmental conflicts might concern the ways lands are used, the allocation or distribution of natural resources, the siting of industrial or other large facilities, or the granting of environmental permits. Downstream, environmental conflicts may center on the prevention, cleanup, and consequences of water, air, or soil pollution. Environmental conflicts can also be categorized by their scope. For example, policy-level disputes pertain to *general* classes of resources, locations, or situations, while site-specific disputes involve *particular* natural resources, locations, or situations.[7]

A policy-level dispute is normally an upstream dispute, whereas a site-specific dispute is usually a midstream or downstream dispute. In both settings, the dispute often emerges from differences in values and worldviews, conflicting interests, and the uncertainty that surrounds the distributional consequences, risks, and outcomes of environmental courses of action.[8] In addition, popular attitudes and political culture, technology, laws and political interests, economics, and religion—especially as they relate to Native American culture and the often disparate

Sustainable Groundwater Management

An example of an issue that spans upstream, midstream, and downstream conflict is groundwater management in California. State legislation and its implementation in over a hundred separate groundwater basins in severe or moderate overdraft, through designation of groundwater sustainability agencies and design of groundwater sustainability plans, requires reconciling the goals of multiple levels and types of stakeholders. Doing so in a time of severe drought and limited public resources poses a significant challenge to system design.[9] How might a basin undertake a conflict stream assessment? Who might convene the assessment and the subsequent DSD? What processes might stakeholders (farmers, municipalities, tribes, environmental advocates, etc.) consider?

cultures of developing countries and the developed world—can trigger environmental conflicts.[10]

In ECR as in most conflict contexts, procedural justice can be a goal, aiming to afford the public and stakeholders voice. However, goals also include *environmental justice*,[11] or the principle that "people should neither experience disproportionate environmental burdens nor be excluded from the decision-making processes that produce them."[12] Environmental justice advocates have argued for more participatory decision-making, particularly by those historically affected by environmental burdens, which in the United States include low-income communities, minority ethnic groups, and Native Americans.[13] Globally, environmental justice encompasses climate change and is sometimes framed as the Global North versus the Global South, the toxic waste trade, or developed versus developing countries.[14] ECR can include environmental justice through global treaties with embedded DSDs for managing conflict over public goods like the sea[15] and the ozone layer.

Stakeholders

Given the breadth of contextual issues, a host of government, public, and private interests have a potential stake in environmental conflicts. Elected and appointed government officials at the local, county, state, and federal levels in the United States are usually involved in environmental conflicts because many of these conflicts arise from the formation or implementation of legislation and policies.

Often government officials represent agencies that differ in their mandate (e.g., Department of Interior versus Environmental Protection Agency), branch of government (e.g., legislative versus executive branch), or function (regulation making versus enforcement), or represent different departments or subdivisions within an agency (e.g., the Bureau of Land Management and the Fish and Wildlife Service in the Department of Interior), or even represent different branches of government (e.g., officials in Congress and officials from an administrative agency such as the Department of Agriculture).[16] These examples span federal jurisdiction and their layers of state and local agencies.

The numerous public interests represented in environmental conflicts can be community residents, Native American tribes, environmental interest groups, and public interest law firms. Private interests also play a large role in environmental conflicts. Siting facilities, pollution abatement issues, and the granting of permits all engage industry, commercial, and other business interests in environmental conflicts. Frequently these government, public, and private interests also need and use the services of scientific, research, and technical consultants, adding to the number of stakeholders involved.

Context and Culture

With respect to context, the triggering event is critical. For example, people may discover an environmental harm, such as a hazardous substance, at a Superfund site. A legislative body or regulatory agency may initiate proceedings around management of a resource, which may be spurred by either an upstream phase like policy making or a downstream phase like civil enforcement. In either case, multiple stakeholders will likely be involved, which introduces a diversity of cultures and values (e.g., organizational, racial, religious, economic) to a complex set of scientific and policy issues. This multitude of stakeholders and cultures makes process design especially important in terms of voice, transparency, and degree of formality in decision-making.

For example, Congress founded the U.S. Institute for Environmental Conflict Resolution, a federal agency providing mediation services in multiparty disputes involving natural resources, and located it in the Southwest, in part because of extensive water and natural resource conflict that crosses not only state and municipal lines but also Native American sovereign nations' boundaries. To address the unique historical and cultural context of these conflicts, the institute created a roster of Native American leaders trained in mediation and collaborative governance techniques.[17] The roster also lists mediators who can address conflict that crosses national boundaries with Mexico and Canada. Native American culture historically views natural resources not as assets for humans to mine or sell but as part of the earth not subject to ownership. Environmental conflict in this context can take on spiritual dimensions and trigger disputes over deeply held cultural values.

Processes and Structure

Many environmental conflicts are submitted to the courts, which are structured to focus on a legal question and compliance with a given statute or regulation. As the Harvard University labor economist and former secretary of labor John Dunlop observes,

> The regulatory process encourages conflict, rather than acting to reconcile opposing interests. Moreover, there is a sense that it is wrong for the regulatory agency to try to bring parties together and develop consensus. Reliance on public and highly formal proceedings makes the development of consensus extremely difficult, if not impossible. And unless this consensus can be developed, neither party has any stake in the promulgated rule. Thus both are free to complain that it is biased, stupid, or misguided. Moreover, each side is free to continue the controversy in the form of endless petitions for review, clarification, and litigation before the agency and the courts. Nothing is ever settled because true settlement can come only through agreement, consent, or acquiescence.[18]

Lawrence S. Bacow and Michael Wheeler of MIT further describe shortfalls of litigation and the benefits of negotiation as an alternative process.[19] However, the court has distinct advantages in the empowerment it offers parties, its degree of leverage, its provision of public education, and its transparency, whereas the challenge of an assisted negotiation or ECR is considering whom to include in the negotiation, what incentives will induce parties' engagement, how to garner sufficient data and technical expertise to inform the process, whether a neutral third party should be engaged, and how the process will be funded and the agreement enforced.

ECR consists of a set of techniques, processes, and roles that enable parties (and a range of other stakeholders) in a dispute to reach agreement, usually with the help of one or more third-party neutrals. Despite the variance in ECR techniques and processes, researchers have identified five characteristics shared by most forms of ECR (except binding arbitration):

- Participation is voluntary for all participants.
- The parties or their representatives are able to participate directly in the processes.

- Any and all participants have the option to withdraw from the ECR process and seek a resolution through a more formal process, such as litigation.
- The third-party neutral does not have independent, formal authority to impose an outcome but rather helps the parties reach their own agreement.
- The parties agree to the outcome or resolution of the dispute. The purpose of the process is to help parties reach their own solutions, which requires their consent to the decision or recommendation.[20]

It is possible to arrange ECR processes along a continuum from less formal, interest-based negotiation or consensus-based techniques to more formal, adjudicatory arrangements. Consensus-based techniques aim to achieve full support, or what all (not just a majority) can accept, for the outcome or decision.[21] Defining consensus as "unanimous concurrence," the Negotiated Rulemaking Acts of 1990 and 1996—adopted to encourage federal agencies to negotiate with interest groups on a proposed administrative rule—allow for consensus to be redefined as a majority decision but only if all parties agree to this redefinition at the outset of a given negotiated rulemaking activity.[22] Consensus-based techniques are generally used for upstream disputes, whereas quasi-adjudicatory processes are generally used for downstream disputes when the priority goal shifts from participation to reaching a determination. Chapter 3 describes many of these processes in more detail.

ECR processes are based on negotiation. Negotiation can be relatively cooperative, as it is when both sides seek a solution that is mutually beneficial (commonly called interest-based or principled negotiation), or it can be confrontational (commonly called win-lose or adversarial negotiation) when each side seeks to prevail over the other.[23] The motivation for parties and stakeholders to engage in a consensus-based process depends on the probability of reaching certain outcomes through an alternative process of litigation or regulation.

Consensus-based or consensus-building processes (described in more detail in Chapter 17) comprise collaborative decision-making techniques in which a third-party neutral such as a facilitator or mediator assists diverse or competing interest groups in reaching an agreement on a site-specific or policy-level environmental conflict.[24] These processes are used to foster dialogue, clarify areas of agreement and disagreement, improve the information on which a decision is based, and resolve controversial issues in ways that all stakeholders find acceptable.[25] Consensus building, usually used for upstream disputes, typically involves informal, structured, face-to-face interaction among representatives of different stakeholder groups with different viewpoints. The goals are to promote early participation by the affected stakeholders, produce sensible and stable policies or decisions that have a strong and wide base of support, and reduce the likelihood of subsequent disagreements or legal challenges. The most common consensus-based processes used in environmental conflicts are conflict assessment (or convening), facilitation, mediation, conciliation, negotiated rulemaking, and policy dialogues.

In most ECR cases, a mediator uses a facilitative, directive, or evaluative mediation style. In facilitative mediation, mediators are less likely to provide direct advice, propose solutions, or predict outcomes and more likely to assist the parties in identifying and merging interests by establishing an atmosphere that allows parties to communicate more effectively about their interests and options.[26] Conversely, in directive mediation, the mediator diagnoses the problem and tries to persuade the parties to accept a reasonable solution.[27] In evaluative mediation, the mediator gives the parties an expert opinion on the merits of the dispute[28] to help the parties understand the strengths and weaknesses of their cases, provides guidance about the likely outcome in court, and suggests appropriate grounds for settling.

Key to handling environmental conflict is understanding the nested systems and complexity in organizational, community, and natural resource systems.[29]

Lake Tahoe Watershed

Chapter 17 discusses collaboration in the context of public management as another lens through which to study environmental conflict. One much-researched type of collaborative public management connected to the environment is watershed management,[30] such as that of Lake Tahoe, which crosses multiple municipal and two state boundaries (California and Nevada). Lake Tahoe's watershed management system brings together representatives of state agencies, municipalities, recreational users, property owners, businesses (for example, the casino industry from Nevada and skiing resorts in California), and environmental advocacy groups. Over the years, stakeholders have balanced development with protecting the legendary clarity of the water by using facilitators to run ongoing, regularly scheduled discussions.

Resources

Environmental DSD relies on substantial funding by federal, state, regional, and local government. Philanthropic institutions are also funding experiments in collaborative governance, including forums for public deliberation, community problem-solving, and multistakeholder dispute resolution.[31] Members of the public and stakeholders use public interest law firms to threaten or pursue environmental litigation, sometimes recovering substantial costs and attorneys' fees; for example, the Sierra Club may be a litigant or a participant in mediation or negotiated rulemaking. These private attorneys general may augment or complement the government's resources for environmental enforcement.[32] Residents may provide resources through volunteer work on cleanup, monitoring conditions, and ensuring implementation of an agreement.

Success and Accountability

The work of Elinor Ostrom, particularly her Institutional Analysis and Development framework, provides a substantial body of empirical research assessing how humans can develop collaborative systems to manage common-pool resources like water, fisheries, forests, and grazing land that include components like a conflict resolution system.[33] In comparison, ECR research has focused on using program evaluation to examine how mediation and facilitation can resolve conflict. Individual case studies reveal that ECR techniques have been successfully used in both site-specific and policy-level disputes involving a wide variety of issues.[34] Yet for decades, judging their overall success was difficult because there was little systematic and empirical research using rigorous research designs to assess ECR.[35] The Institute for Environmental Conflict Resolution developed an evaluation model shared across selected state and federal agencies. The model examined whether outcomes reached agreement, the quality of agreement, and whether working relationships among the parties improved, finding that effective engagement by the affected parties in the ECR process substantially contributed to all three outcomes. Other significant factors were involvement of appropriate parties, the skills and practices of ECR mediators and facilitators, and incorporation of relevant and high-quality information.[36] Kirk Emerson (the founding director of the institute) and Tina Nabatchi developed this work to model collaborative governance regimes, referring to the structure of the collaborative process itself in a multistakeholder case.[37] They propose evaluating the productivity of collaborative governance regimes by examining performance levels (actions, outcomes, and adaptation) using units of analysis (participant organizations, collaborative governance regime, and target goals). Their performance matrix has nine dimensions, arranged three by three.[38] The frontier of ECR research remains as establishing whether a collaborative process has measurable positive impacts on air, earth, or water.

Lawrence Susskind and colleagues combined the results of empirical studies with their own experiences and the views of mediators and participants to develop recommendations for when ECR is most and least helpful. ECR is most helpful for the following:

- Each participant views the outcome as very important.
- The issues are relatively clear.
- The relevant laws are flexible enough to permit a negotiated settlement.
- ECR is started at an early stage of conflict, before going to public hearings.
- The actual decision makers are willing to participate or formally designate representatives.
- There is no inherent danger to the safety of the participants.

ECR should not be used for the following:

- Public health or safety requires that action be taken immediately.
- Precedent setting is important.
- Participants do not recognize the other side's rights.
- The party providing financial support insists on complete control over the process.
- The process is being used to delay real action or create an illusion that something is being done.[39]

ECR has been used in land use disputes involving commercial development, housing, facility siting, and transportation; natural resource use or management involving fisheries, timber, and mining; water resources issues such as water quality, flood protection, and water use; air quality issues such as pollution, odor, and acid rain; and issues related to toxics such as chemical regulation, asbestos removal, and waste cleanup policies.[40]

The complexity of environmental conflicts can make the application of ECR techniques challenging. These complexities can include multiple forums for decision-making, interorganizational as opposed to interpersonal conflicts, multiple parties, multiple issues, technical complexity and scientific uncertainty, unequal power and resources, and public and political arenas for problem-solving.[41] An additional challenge is the accountability of the mediator not only to all parties at the table but also to those who are not present but may be affected by the outcome or the precedent set.[42]

Cases in Maine and California, respectively, provide examples of downstream policy compliance and upstream policy development.

Maine Public Health Mystery

Four towns in a valley along the Swift and Androscoggin Rivers of Maine were experiencing what they believed were unusually high rates of cancer in the early 1990s, and residents questioned whether the local paper mill was responsible.[43] One-third of the valley's workforce was employed by the mill. The mill and its predecessors had operated in the valley for more than a century, and the relationship between the business and residents had been largely positive until a series of strikes in the 1980s, followed by increasing environmental concerns.

The mill's application for a license to increase its emissions led to a confrontation with local residents. The Maine Department of Environmental Protection faced a dilemma: the mill was in compliance with federal and state statutes, with emissions well under the Clean Air Act's allowable ceilings for criteria pollutants such as sulfur dioxide, nitrous oxide, and particulate matter. Recent technological improvements at the mill had substantially lowered pollutant levels. However, air monitoring around the mill revealed levels of toxics exceeding state health guidelines. Did the mill cause increased rates of cancer? The lack of sufficient data made it difficult to answer this question.

Dennis Kechel, director of Maine's Bureau of Air Quality Control, decided that because the situation did not call for regulatory action he would organize a consensus-building process. The Northern Oxford County Coalition (NOCC) was formed. Its twenty-five members were citizens of the affected towns (including employees of the mill), health care providers, small-business owners, mill managers, local and state elected officials (some from the Maine legislature), and representatives of state and federal agencies responsible for protecting health and the environment. After four facilitated multistakeholder meetings in 1994, with an Environmental Protection Agency grant of $80,000, participants still had not reached agreement on how to proceed. Despite shared frustration about air quality and public health, factual information was lacking and opinions differed on how to structure the participation and agenda for further meetings.

The EPA approached the Consensus Building Institute, a nonprofit provider of nonpartisan facilitation services, to help broker a solution. The institute offered to work with the coalition on a pro bono basis for the first year so that the EPA grant could be used to support whatever substantive fact-finding the coalition decided to undertake.[44] While dissension remained, participants agreed that NOCC's first task would be to "'put on the table' all the existing studies about air quality and public health, so everyone could review them together."[45] The goal was not yet defined, but a process was launched.

Process and Goals

The Consensus Building Institute conducted a stakeholder analysis, interviewing forty-eight stakeholders and identifying eight stakeholder groups: state and federal agencies, local government, small and large businesses, organized labor, interested citizens, health care providers, environmental advocacy groups, and state nongovernmental organizations concerned about public health and the environment. The report recommended expanding membership of the NOCC to include local health care providers and concerned citizens and adding a summer retreat to develop a work plan.

The assessment laid a foundation for collaborative dialogue by gathering concerns: some people were most concerned with cancer rates, others with respiratory illnesses, and others with pollution prevention. Within and across the stakeholder groups there was no agreement on whether the four-town area had elevated cancer rates. Overall, those interviewed voiced a common interest in enhancing the public health of the valley. On the basis of Consensus Building Institute recommendations, the NOCC prepared three framework agreements to guide the work: ground rules, an overarching mission, and a detailed work plan.

GROUND RULES. Three categories of ground rules were established: communication protocol, member roles and responsibilities, and decision-making. Early on, members sought substantive discussion rather than consideration of ground rules; once discussions ensued, the value of rules became apparent. Members proposed a timeout provision when discussion became heated and a "disagreement list" for contentious issues to be addressed later.

MISSION STATEMENT. Strong differences emerged on defining the problem to be addressed: some wanted to focus on cancer rates and the mill's emissions, others on the lack of public education on the dangers of smoke and pollution from businesses, vehicles, and households. All cared about improving the quality of life in the valley and gaining a clear understanding—based in scientific fact—about public health and air quality. They eventually reached consensus on a mission statement: "The NOCC has been established to improve the quality of life in the valley by protecting and promoting public health and enhancing air quality."[46]

WORK PLAN. The members revised the stakeholder assessment to consider what questions the coalition should ask during a joint fact-finding process. They contacted experts in epidemiology, toxicology, and air monitoring to explore how to answer questions about cancer rates, how to find data, and how long it would take to analyze it. The NOCC anticipated the study would take three months to complete; it took eight. The NOCC members had underestimated how long it would take to develop a work style, review complex technical information, interview experts and agencies, and revise research questions. The search for an independent expert to analyze the data whom all parties could agree on was also more time intensive than expected.

The resulting study report showed that rates for all cancers combined for both males and females in the four-town area were indeed elevated when compared with the rest of Maine. Yet another struggle was how to interpret and report the data. Nine of the ten members of the technical subcommittee charged with interpreting the findings agreed; the lone dissenting member attached a letter enumerating his concerns. While disappointed by the inability to reach unanimity, all members recognized the great effort that went into preparing a credible and thorough report. NOCC members were able to gather and analyze empirical data on cancer and draw their own conclusions. For the first time, the community had concrete, credible information on cancer rates. Committee members recognized significant value in the insights they gained by their own investigation and by involving a technical expert who understood the role he should play in a community-based consensus building process.[47]

Resources
Initially, the residents expected the Maine Department of Environmental Protection to act to address cancer rates and air pollution. The EPA's financial support made the community problem-solving process feasible, helped bring people to the table, and was responsive to resident concerns in providing additional resources for fact-finding. While the mill could have contributed financially, such support may have threatened the perceived legitimacy of the process. Other local institutions lacked the means to provide funding. Concerned citizens—who devoted their time to twice-monthly meetings, plus preparation time, for two years—provided the bulk of the human resources.

Success and Accountability
The Consensus Building Institute summary report highlighted what the NOCC accomplished. It:

- Designed a study to investigate cancer rates in the valley
- Initiated a community-wide radon-testing program that tested four hundred homes
- Worked with agencies to evaluate recent air-monitoring data and to design a continuing air-monitoring program
- Held a public forum on dioxin and pollution prevention
- Wrote an action plan with numerous recommendations and distributed it as a community newsletter
- Organized a new Healthy Communities coalition to continue the NOCC's work[48]

Compiling and issuing the final report was important in itself. Working with a community education specialist, NOCC members formed a drafting subcommittee that reviewed the initial draft prepared by the Consensus Building Institute. In the fall of 1997, NOCC mailed its twelve-page newsletter to more than seven thousand households and held a press conference[49] on how the valley's quality of life could be measured and improved. The release of the report and continuation of the NOCC's efforts as a Healthy Communities group affirm the NOCC's value and effectiveness.

Charles Sabel, a political economist commenting on the NOCC experience, noted that "the stakeholder analysis is at the heart of this new kind of public problem solving precisely because it creates a setting in which the definition of the problem to be solved can be elaborated even as the circle of those who can or should contribute to its solution is (re)drawn, and vice versa. Contrast this with the normal procedure of representative democracy, in which the legislature, representing the citizens, defines the problem and delegates its solution to an administrative agency."[50] Further, the investment in the stakeholder analysis builds a foundation for subsequent conflict resolution on the presenting problem, as well as models an approach for other issues in the community.

California Marine Life Protection Act

The California legislature passed the Marine Life Protection Act (MLPA) in 1999 to design a coherent and scientifically rational network of marine protected areas (MPAs) to preserve the state's coastal marine life and habitats. The MLPA Initiative, a public-private partnership, was established to implement this legislation in a "public process of unparalleled transparency."[51] The initiative was phased over four regions, each of which had a regional stakeholder group, a science advisory team that developed detailed decision criteria for designing MPAs, and a governor-appointed blue-ribbon task force to oversee the process and provide recommendations to the Fish and Game Commission. Initiative staff (facilitator, outreach coordinator, GIS technicians) supported the process.[52] Following the pilot region of the Central Coast, the next region was the North Central Coast (extending 173 miles, from Point Arena to Pigeon Point), the focus of this case study.

Goals

The MLPA statute set out the goals of protecting marine life, habitats, heritage, and ecosystems; improving educational and recreational opportunities; ensuring that MPAs are designed and managed as a network; and ensuring that MPAs have clearly defined objectives, effective management measures, and adequate enforcement and are based on sound scientific guidelines.[53] The MLPA Initiative focused on two equally valuable products: a high-quality process and MPA alternatives that would garner support and recommendation from the blue-ribbon task force.

Structure of Stakeholder Process

Participants in the MLPA Initiative included the task force and its contract staff, the science advisory team, the Fish and Game Department, the initiative team, and the forty-five-member regional stakeholder group. The stakeholders were nominated according to specific criteria, then interviewed and selected. The regional stakeholder group met over nearly a year: as a full group for fifteen days, plus work group sessions and select task force, science advisory team, and Fish and Game Commission meetings. The regional stakeholder group developed regional goals and objectives to guide planning and forwarded these to the task force for approval, then it subdivided into three cross-interest work groups to generate specific recommendations.

The task force was a key innovation for MPA design and public decision-making. It was a buffer for the commission, overseer of stakeholder design of MPA alternatives, decision maker on MPA recommendations to the commission, and public forum for identifying and framing key policy issues. The task force operated under close public scrutiny in a context with intense and contentious values of conservation, recreation, and access. The task force fostered a transparent, open, and secure atmosphere for members who committed substantial time and resources to the process. A critical factor was an early meeting between the task force and the regional stakeholder group to clarify roles, objectives, responsibilities, processes, and expectations about the relationship. The task force did not meet again formally with the regional stakeholder group until its final decision meeting, at which time the group explained its proposals for protected areas that satisfied science advisory team criteria and reflected balancing of consumptive and conservation interests.

Resources
Adequate public and private funding was provided to support the process. An additional component was a geospatial decision support tool, MarineMap.

Success and Accountability
In his evaluation of the North Central Coast MLPA Initiative, Jonathan Raab used an online survey, review of documents, and interviews with participants. Raab observed,

> There is value in the complex and occasionally inefficient process of MPA development. It would be understandable for private sector funders to expect a certain amount of efficiency, with the potential for future cost savings, based on the experience of two study regions. One candidate may be decision support tools like Doris [a web-based application decision support tool for planning marine protected areas] and Marine Map. Experience and efficiency may also lead to cost savings in terms of basic meeting planning and preparation for the [science advisory team, regional stakeholder group, and blue-ribbon task force]. However, efficiency in stakeholder decision-making is a different matter, primarily because each study region and its stakeholders and public are essentially new. The Initiative's success to this point can be attributed in significant part to the resources available for high-quality public process. To the extent cost-saving is a goal for funders, any cuts should be balanced carefully against the benefits of a well-funded, high-quality, and robust public process.[54]

Comparing Two ECR Approaches
The Maine and California cases share many characteristics, with some interesting distinctions. The California MLPA defined the goals and process in legislation. With a sophisticated decision-making structure for regions, bodies, and working groups, the goal was to design a high-quality process and produce policy recommendations. In contrast, the Maine NOCC struggled to identify its priority goal until members went through a conflict assessment and designed a process for joint fact-finding.

In both cases, the stakeholder representation was extensive across public, private, and nonprofit groups, which incorporated diverse viewpoints and built legitimacy. Both efforts involved capable neutral facilitators and experts who led the groups through fact-finding, analysis, interpretation, and options for action. The MLPA had an additional element of using technology, the MarineMap decision support tool,[55] to integrate several measures to show their effect. The contextual trigger for the NOCC was public concern that cancer rates were unusually high, so the downstream focus was on fact-finding and resolution; however, through the fact-finding process, the goal shifted to one of public health in the community. In Maine, the community culture comprised a mix of residents (many of whom were employees of the paper mill), a major employer (in compliance with applicable laws), and local, state, and federal agencies, each of which had different motivations and perspectives. The MLPA process, on the other hand, was launched by the state legislation that set forth structural process and participation guidelines for engaging diverse private, commercial, public, and personal interests.

Resources were quite limited for the NOCC community, and thus the effort relied on a significant contribution of time from participants. Modest public funding supported the expert information development. The MLPA was a more formal process, adequately funded by both public and private sources. The Maine community achieved a significant, concrete result in its final report and continued with a community improvement coalition. The MLPA had a more formal, independent evaluation but also very positive results.

Conclusion

ECR is by its nature context specific and will demand careful consideration of the components of the DSD Analytic Framework (see Chapter 2). The wide variety of stakeholders engaged in environmental disputes means that some are likely to hold competing beliefs regarding the purpose and preservation of environmental resources. Fact-finding processes are therefore paramount and can benefit from both qualified experts and data visualization tools that can help nonexperts better understand the issues and their implications. As the two examples illustrate, the process by which communities pursue solutions is critical to arriving at decisions that are perceived by stakeholders as credible, fair, and effective.

CONCLUSION

THIS BOOK PROVIDES the analytic tools to help design better processes and structures to address a wide variety of conflicts and disputes more fairly and effectively. It describes not only techniques for engineering DSD but also why to do DSD and how to do it well by integrating knowledge across many different academic disciplines. Consequently, this book provides a foundation for students, scholars, and practitioners in business, law, and public affairs to build on in differing contexts for DSD.

What emerges from the "Foundations of System Design" and "Case Applications" units is the importance of recognizing human dignity by delivering justice while balancing competing considerations: interests and rights, equity and efficiency, voice and administrative feasibility, and prevention and enforcement. These competing considerations implicate the individual versus the institution and their relative power in and over DSD. Who has what control over DSD and over process and outcome in its constituent parts?

One influential strand of thought prioritizes free markets and individual freedoms as organizing principles for society. Immediately after World War II, Milton Friedman led a wholesale strategy of political economy to undo the New Deal that President Franklin D. Roosevelt had put in place to recover from the Great Depression. As described by Larry Kramer, Friedman's followers successfully lobbied to change law and policy to a focus on an individual's freedom of choice to maximize utility; a nation's measure of success as national wealth and the utility its individual members value; and limited government to establish and protect free markets as the best means possible for rational, self-interested individuals to maximize aggregate wealth.[1] This frame does not include the interests of society, as a collective entity, in the commons or public good; indeed, it excludes anything not reducible to economic value.

However, human dignity is a fundamental interest for society as a collective. In conflict, an individual actor is not alone. Frances Moore Lappé and Adam Eichen point out that the insufficiently regulated free market system concentrates wealth in a few hands, shrinking the number of people who have economic power to exercise freedom of choice to maximize their utility.[2] Extreme income inequality correlates historically with social unrest. Amartya Sen argues for defining justice in terms of "the lives that people manage—or do not manage—to live," or "a realized actuality."[3] Michael Sandel defines justice as "cultivating virtue and reasoning about the common good."[4] This book addresses society's interest in recognizing both the dignity of the individual in conflict and the collective, shared interests in fair and just systems for preventing, managing, and resolving disputes. If well designed, dispute systems provide a means for people to step out of pure (and not always entirely rational) self-interest and instead to cultivate virtue and reasoning about the common good as it relates to conflict.

Using the DSD Analytic Framework presented in Chapter 2, this conclusion examines how the competing considerations of interests and rights, equity and efficiency, voice and administrative feasibility, and prevention and enforcement manifest in actual practice given stakeholders' relative power to control DSD.

Goals

What do the system's decision makers seek to accomplish, and which types of conflicts does the system seek to address?

Chapter 2 describes a cornucopia of goals that stakeholders might value, including justice (in a public, private, and community sense; see Chapter 1), fair outcomes and process, efficiency in time and cost for users and administrators, party self-determination, voice, legal compliance, relationships, reputation, and quality of process experience. Throughout the case chapters, goal-setting features prominently. Key issues are who decides the priority among goals and with what trade-offs, and who evaluates how well those goals were achieved. Decision makers may be individuals, an advisory panel, or a stakeholder group, drawn from a range of professional disciplines. The designer may be internal or external and may be an individual or part of a team. The more—and more representative—input the designer gathers, the better the DSD is likely to satisfy its users and operators. The goal-setting process is valuable for focusing the effort, creating a collaborative learning environment, exploring upstream interventions to prevent disputes, and providing a benchmark for evaluation. Grappling with and being clear about goals for a DSD, their relative priority and trade-offs, and how they can be met and measured, is the most important element in real-world DSD.

Stakeholders

Who are the stakeholders, what are their respective interests, and what is their relative power?

Stakeholders are the people and organizations that create, host, use, and are affected by a DSD. This element involves identifying affected stakeholders, their respective interests, and how to engage them in the design process in a meaningful way. In almost half the case chapters (those concerning consumers, commercial disputes, transitional justice, international disputes, and environmental disputes), stakeholder issues are prominent, mostly because of the complexity of the relationships among the relevant actors. With respect to claims facilities (Chapter 8), the crisis context combines with many affected stakeholders (injured parties, those potentially liable, their respective counsel, public and private interests, court and out-of-court neutral administrators) to heighten the strain on balancing efficiency and equity. In Chapter 11, the asymmetric power of employers and employees—nested within an industry and its geographic and organizational culture, involving long-term relationships and reputation—increases the number and profile of stakeholders. Community disputes (Chapter 9), transitional justice (Chapter 15), and environmental disputes (Chapter 18) have not only many diverse stakeholders but also increasingly high stakes and consequences and interdependent public and private interests. The more complex the array of public rights and private interests, the more time needed to educate participants and the greater the need for structure and facilitators to manage the process in a transparent, fair, and efficient manner. As is evident with the cases in the community and environmental dispute chapters, the presence of a stakeholder advisory group (or at least a conflict stream assessment that interviews representative stakeholders) has a significant effect on the robustness of the DSD and its subsequent implementation success. The examples in the transitional justice chapter demonstrate how the multiplicity of funders, stakeholders, and power centers makes collaboration and coordination even more difficult, challenging policy making, policy implementation, and administrative feasibility.

Control over DSD—over the elements in the DSD Analytic Framework—is a form of power. The appendix illustrates how the power to control DSD varies in different systems—from one party asymmetrically in control in adhesive and forced or mandatory employment or consumer arbitration in the United States to two or more parties negotiating system design in labor relations or commerce, to third-party control in courts, administrative agencies, or community mediation. The appendix also illustrates how public, private, and nonprofit parties may exercise power and control over DSD, with examples from case chapters to illustrate the systems. Power is in part a function of law and rules. These structures may give or deny public or private organizations specific authority to design and mandate use of certain processes in a system. Private companies can negotiate arbitration contracts with commercial or business partners or mandate consumer or employment arbitration under the Federal Arbitration Act; federal agencies cannot mandate arbitration under the Administrative Dispute Resolution Act. Federal courts can mandate participation in ADR programs under the Alternative Dispute Resolution Act of 1998. Stakeholders' relative economic power may also shape the choice of system (e.g., between courts and community mediation or a developing country abandoning a claim under investment treaty arbitration). Collective action may also give people power through civil disobedience.

Stakeholder analysis encompasses understanding the existing formal and informal systems; what power public, private, and nonprofit organizations and membership associations have; what economic and political incentives or disincentives they have; and what interests (in the language of interest-based negotiation) may influence how they exercise their power.

Context and Culture

How do the context and culture affect the systems' viability and success?

Context and culture encompass the specific situation, cultural norms, and expectations surrounding the DSD. If the context is one of crisis, as with many claims facilities, then public pressure for administrative efficiency, equity, and transparency is high. With courts (Chapter 7), the context may be case management overload or a desire for an interest-based process like mediation, with pressure to increase efficiency or provide alternative process options (or both). In collective bargaining (Chapter 10), there are layers of stakeholders not only within an organization but also among counsel, government, industry, and geographic culture. In employment (Chapter 11), the employers carry more power, but a crisis like the MeToo movement to expose sexual harassment can shift that balance. With consumers (Chapter 14), the asymmetric character of repeat-player merchants and individual consumers led to the prevalence of adhesive and forced arbitration precluding class actions. Community disputes (Chapter 9), especially when combined with issues of race and violence, call for more broad-based public and private engagement, education, and intervention to address current incidents and prevent future conflict. Transitional justice (Chapter 15) poses an especially difficult situation postviolence with political, economic, and social chaos in which the legal infrastructure may have been destroyed.

Organizational, social, and national culture add another layer to the DSD environment. An industry culture may tend toward hierarchy in traditional management-employee style or be more egalitarian in a new entrepreneurial start-up; a country with a history of democracy may be more supportive of stake-holder engagement in public decision-making. A nation with homogeneous ethnicity may have less experience and comfort with diversity and communication across different ethnicities. A culture that esteems the opportunity to appear in court may differ in its judicial design from one that prioritizes peace and harmony in the community. The variation in these situations, cultures, and stakeholders poses significant challenges for the designer and decision maker and points to the importance of a transparent process and extensive assessment for voice of stakeholders' priority interests.

Processes and Structure

Which processes are used to prevent, manage, and resolve disputes; how are processes linked or integrated; what are the incentives for use; and how do these processes interact with the formal legal system?

Chapters 3 and 4 discuss the process building blocks available and how a designer can assess the goals and resources of the parties and stakeholders in proposing one or more complementary processes to fit their needs. Those processes range from involving two or more parties (with or without counsel) negotiating directly over their engagement and decision-making to two or more disputants using a third-party neutral to facilitate, mediate, or adjudicate their dispute—and can include any combination of such processes in sequence or parallel.

The use of multiple processes is expanding in the private and public sectors. Stakeholders choose different combinations of process characteristics: a focus on interests versus rights, direct negotiation or use of a third-party neutral, facilitated (mediation) or evaluative (court or arbitration), binding or nonbinding, final or subject to appeal, confidential versus public, oriented to prevention or enforcement, and oriented upstream to policy making or downstream to enforcement. Courts have expanded from focusing primarily on offering trials to providing an array of adjudicative and facilitated options to meet the needs of litigants. In several arenas, the opportunity for voice is especially crucial. New processes, using technology and online options, may increase capacity for dispute diagnosis, fact-finding, and negotiation, as well as facilitated and adjudicative options. Having flexible process options (both rights-based and interest-based choices) is important yet subject to the resource capacity to implement the DSD. In the public policy arena, the more complex the case, as with governance and environment, the more likely the public will seek to participate or raise concerns. Upstream interventions that take advantage of deliberative democracy may reap better outcomes.

Resources

What financial and human resources support the system?

Sufficient resources are essential to implementation and effectiveness. The most thoughtful, sophisticated DSD will fail if there is inadequate attention to training of providers, education of users, and financing of the operation. At the inception of the design process, engagement of an independent designer or design team may be optimal but not financially feasible, in which case the internal designer will need to be especially careful about transparency of the decision-making process; the same holds for any process that is funded by one stakeholder. For some processes, such as the one that assisted victims of the 2013 bombing of the Boston Marathon, the designer, who also serves as the third-party neutral, contributes professional services, and the compensation for victims comes from private donations. Courts facing budget cutbacks may be pressured to increase efficiency of case management and settlement and to reduce process options that provide parties more self-determination and satisfaction. Under these circumstances, evaluation of DSD success will be essential. Technological process options may help address some challenges; new online court processes in the United Kingdom and British Columbia will provide opportunities to test this approach.

Success, Accountability, and Learning

How transparent is the system; does it include monitoring, learning and adapting, and evaluation components; and is it successful?

Success derives from both whether the system achieves its intended goals and whether it achieves the broader societal goals of fairness and justice. Evaluation is fundamental to determine whether the DSD is working—are key stakeholders using the system? Are users satisfied that the neutrals provide high-quality services? Are potential improvements to the DSD tracked and adopted? Is the DSD transparent in its operation and results?

Accountability relates to how well the DSD operates; accountability is both instrumental (enhances the means to achieve the goals, as with control, ethical behavior, and performance) and intrinsic (directly valuable to the users, as with integrity, legitimacy, and justice). Ideally, DSDs are evaluated independently, but this effort may be constrained by limited resources. At the least, data gathering and disclosure on measures of efficiency (transaction costs), user satisfaction on relevant dimensions, and actual outcomes will enable the designer and decision makers to create a baseline from which to measure progress and yield opportunities for improvement. Additional measures, like the parties' relationship post-dispute and recurrence of the disputes, can provide valuable information.[5]

The field of DSD requires careful study of how systems function in achieving their goals, including justice and fairness. The more familiar scholars and practitioners become with the concepts of DSD and the more precise the goal definition, the more—and more sophisticated—will be the data available to systematically study DSDs and therefrom to prevent, manage, and resolve conflict more effectively.

Final Thoughts

DSD has expanded well beyond its birthplace in the dispute resolution field. DSD concepts are connecting with and informed by law, industrial relations, business, psychology, political science, public affairs, economics, anthropology, sociology, organizational development, biology, engineering, technology, and other fields. Insights are being shaped by practitioners and theorists in the public and private sectors (nonprofit and for profit), some described in the case chapters of this book. We hope that the stories told and the analysis provided in this book will be helpful to academics, practitioners, policy makers, teachers, and students as they strive to provide ever better ways to address conflict constructively.

People share an interest in recognizing the dignity of the individual in conflict and the collective, shared interests in fair and just systems for preventing, managing, and resolving disputes. DSD, guided by sound principles and the DSD Analytic Framework, can provide a means for people from varying perspectives and backgrounds to cultivate virtue and reasoning about both the individual and the common good.

APPENDIX: POWER AS CONTROL IN DISPUTE SYSTEMS

	Control at the individual case level	
Control of the overall system design	Disputants control outcome in a single case	Third party controls outcome in a single case
All parties (disputants)	Ad hoc mediation, or ad hoc early neutral evaluation (ENE), nonbinding arbitration and evaluative processes • Collective bargaining • Federal Mediation and Conciliation Service • CPR Institute for Fortune 1,000	Ad hoc or negotiated binding arbitration, med-arb and arb-med • Union grievance procedure • Bilateral investment treaty arbitration • Some mass claim systems
One party	Mediation or nonbinding processes • Ombuds programs • USPS REDRESS mediation of equal employment opportunity cases	Binding arbitration • Adhesive (forced) employment arbitration • Adhesive (forced) consumer arbitration
Third party	Court or administrative agency ADR programs • Courts of general or limited jurisdiction, problem-solving courts (mediation, ENE, summary jury trials, nonbinding arbitration or other nonbinding processes) • Equal Employment Opportunity Commission mediation Community mediation • Victim-offender reconciliation • Neighborhood justice	Court or administrative adjudication • Consent decrees • Truth and reconciliation commissions Legislation mandating binding arbitration • September 11th Victim Compensation Fund • Amateur Sports Act Olympic arbitration • State auto lemon laws

NOTES

Introduction

1. "Wicked" problems are described in Horst W. J. Rittel and Melvin M. Webber, "Dilemmas in General Theory of Planning," *Policy Sciences* 4 (1973): 155–69.

2. Mariana Hernandez-Crespo Gonstead stresses the need to distinguish "power over" and "power with," particularly in system design. "Power with" views all parties as contributors, prioritizing the relationship, incentives, and rewards. In contrast, "power over" emphasizes unilateral control, viewing parties as competitors. See Mariana Hernandez-Crespo Gonstead, "A New Dance on the Global Stage: Introducing a Cultural Value–Based Toolbox to Optimize Problem-Solving, Innovation, and Growth," *Ohio State Journal on Dispute Resolution* 34 (forthcoming).

Chapter 1

1. The phrase "prevent, manage, and resolve" is shorthand for a wide array of actions in relation to conflicts and disputes, including anticipate, identify, prevent, assess, manage, learn from, follow up on, and resolve. In this book, the term "managing" indicates not suppression of conflict but constructively dealing with and learning from conflict.

2. Lisa Blomgren Bingham, "Designing Justice: Legal Institutions and Other Systems for Managing Conflict," *Ohio State Journal on Dispute Resolution* 24, no. 1 (2008): 1–51.

3. See Jerome Barrett, with Joseph Barrett, *A History of Alternative Dispute Resolution: The Story of a Political, Cultural and Social Movement* (San Francisco, CA: Jossey-Bass, 2004). Mediation and arbitration were used by the Mari Kingdom (Syria) with other kingdoms in 1800 BC.

4. For an excellent brief history of the conflict resolution literature, see Carrie Menkel-Meadow, "Roots and Inspirations: A Brief History of the Foundations of Dispute Resolution," in *The Handbook of Dispute Resolution*, ed. Michael Moffitt and Robert Bordone (San Francisco, CA: Jossey-Bass, 2005), 13–31.

5. Lewis Coser, *The Functions of Social Conflict* (New York: Free Press, 1956); Kurt Lewin, *Group Decision and Social Change* (New York: Holt, Rinehart and Winston, 1952); Morton Deutsch, *The Resolution of Conflict: Constructive and Destructive Processes* (New Haven, CT:

Yale University Press, 1973); Lon L. Fuller, *The Morality of Law* (New Haven, CT: Yale University Press, 1964).

6. Frank Sander and Stephen Goldberg, "Fitting the Forum to the Fuss: A User-Friendly Guide to Selecting an ADR Procedure," *Negotiation Journal* 10 (1994): 49–68; Carrie Menkel-Meadow, "Mothers and Fathers of Invention: The Intellectual Founders of ADR," *Ohio State Journal on Dispute Resolution* 16 (2000): 1–37, reprinted with additional essays in Carrie Menkel-Meadow, *Dispute Processing and Conflict Resolution* (Burlington, VT: Ashgate and Dartmouth, 2003); Robert Bordone and Michael Moffitt, eds., *The Conflict Resolution Handbook* (San Francisco, CA: Jossey-Bass, 2005).

7. Thomas C. Schelling, *The Strategy of Conflict* (Cambridge, MA: Harvard University Press, 1960); Richard E. Walton and Robert B. McKersie, *A Behavioral Theory of Labor Negotiations* (New York: McGraw-Hill, 1965).

8. See, for example, David B. Lipsky, Ronald L. Seeber, and Richard D. Fincher, *Emerging Systems for Managing Workplace Conflict: Lessons from American Corporations for Managers and Dispute Resolution Professionals* (San Francisco, CA: Jossey-Bass, 2003).

9. See, for example, Cathy A. Costantino and Christina Sickles Merchant, *Designing Conflict Management Systems: A Guide to Creating Productive and Healthy Organizations* (San Francisco, CA: Jossey-Bass, 1996).

10. Elinor Ostrom, *Understanding Institutional Diversity* (Princeton, NJ: Princeton University Press, 2005).

11. Robert Agranoff and Michael McGuire, *Collaborative Public Management: New Strategies for Local Governments* (Washington, DC: Georgetown University Press, 2003); Barbara Gray, *Collaborating: Finding Common Ground for Multiparty Problems* (San Francisco, CA: Jossey-Bass, 1989); Jeffrey Cruikshank and Lawrence Susskind, *Breaking the Impasse: Consensual Approaches to Resolving Public Disputes* (New York: Basic Books, 1987).

12. See Kenneth J. Arrow, Robert H. Mnookin, Lee Ross, Amos Tversky, and Robert B. Wilson, *Barriers to Conflict Resolution* (New York: W. W. Norton, 1995); Kenneth Kressel, Dean G. Pruitt, and associates, *Mediation Research: The Process and Effectiveness of Third-Party Intervention* (San Francisco, CA: Jossey-Bass, 1989); Dean G. Pruitt, Jeffrey Rubin, and Sung Hee Kim, *Social Conflict: Escalation, Stalemate, and Settlement* (Boston, MA: McGraw-Hill, 2004); Richard Birke and Craig Fox, "Psychological Principles in Negotiating Civil Settlements," *Harvard Negotiation Law Review* 14 (1999): 1–28; Donna Shestowsky, "The Psychology of Interpersonal Persuasion: Lessons for the Advanced Negotiator," in *The Negotiator's Fieldbook*, ed. Christopher Honeyman and Andrea Schneider (Washington, DC: American Bar Association, 2006), 361–70; and Max H. Bazerman and Margaret A. Neale, *Negotiating Rationally* (New York: Free Press, 1992).

13. Recognition that trial is but one of many available processes, and in fact one of the least used, has led to more common use of "ADR" (alternative dispute resolution) to mean "appropriate" dispute resolution, encompassing the full range of available processes.

14. See, for example, the website of the National Association for Community Mediation, which was founded to support the maintenance and growth of community-based mediation programs, at https://www.nafcm.org.

15. Frank E. A. Sander, "Varieties of Dispute Processing," in *The Pound Conference: Perspectives on Justice in the Future*, ed. A. Leo Levin and Russell R. Wheeler (St. Paul, MN: West, 1979), 65–87; Lara Traum and Brian Farkas, "The History and Legacy of the Pound Conferences," *Cardozo Journal of Dispute Resolution* 18, no. 3 (2017): 677–98. See, generally, "Jed D. Melnick Symposium: The Pound Conferences;

Where Do We Come From? What Are We? Where Are We Going?," *Cardozo Journal of Dispute Resolution* 18, no. 3 (2017): 513–698.

16. Major ADR providers handling commercial cases include the American Arbitration Association (https://www.adr.org); the International Institute for Conflict Prevention and Resolution (https://www.cpradr.org); and JAMS (https://www.jamsadr.com).

17. The National Center for State Courts collaborates with the Conference of Chief Justices and the Conference of State Court Administrators to support state court administration and leadership, including regarding ADR program development and management. See the organization's website, at https://www.ncsc.org.

18. The Federal Judicial Center, the research and education agency of the U.S. federal courts, conducts research and offers training on ADR program development and management. See its website, at https://www.fjc.gov.

19. Nadja Alexander, ed., *International Comparative Mediation: Legal Perspectives* (The Hague, Netherlands: Kluwer International, 2009).

20. Lisa Blomgren Bingham and Charles R. Wise, "The Administrative Dispute Resolution Act of 1990: How Do We Evaluate Its Success?," *Journal of Public Administration, Research and Theory* 6 (1996): 383–414; Jeffrey M. Senger, *Federal Dispute Resolution: Using ADR with the United States Government* (San Francisco, CA: Jossey-Bass, 2003). See also the website of the Interagency Alternative Dispute Resolution Working Group, at https://www.adr.gov.

21. The European Parliament adopted in 2008 Directive 2008/52/EC on certain aspects of mediation in civil and commercial matters. See "Mediation in Civil and Commercial Matters," Eur-Lex, August 17, 2015, http://europa.eu/legislation_summaries/justice_freedom_security/judicial_cooperation_in_civil_matters/l33251_en.htm.

22. The William and Flora Hewlett Foundation made contributions that were central to the development of ADR in the United States. For the history of this program, see David Kovick, "The Hewlett Foundation's Conflict Resolution Program: Twenty Years of Field-Building, 1984–2004," May 2005, https://www.hewlett.org/wp-content/uploads/2016/08/HewlettConflictResolutionProgram.pdf. For a summary of research gaps Hewlett identified upon completion of its funding program, see Robert A. Baruch Bush and Lisa Blomgren Bingham, "Knowledge Gaps: The Final Conference of the Hewlett ADR Theory Centers," *Conflict Resolution Quarterly* 23, no. 1 (2005): 99–122.

23. The terms "neutral" and "impartial" are subject to debate in the dispute resolution field. Some third-party dispute resolvers are embedded in an organization, community, or field (e.g., community elders or religious leaders); the notion of neutrality or impartiality may not apply in some cultures or contexts. Bernard Mayer provides another perspective, describing the third party in a given matter as located at a point on a continuum between neutrality and advocacy, depending on the parties' preferences. Bernard S. Mayer, *Beyond Neutrality: Confronting the Crisis in Conflict Resolution* (San Francisco, CA: Jossey-Bass, 2004), 116.

24. William L. Ury, Jeanne M. Brett, and Stephen B. Goldberg, *Getting Disputes Resolved: Designing Systems to Cut the Cost of Conflict* (San Francisco, CA: Jossey-Bass, 1988).

25. David W. Ewing, *Justice on the Job: Resolving Grievances in the Non-union Workplace* (Cambridge, MA: Harvard Business School Press, 1989); Douglas C. McCabe, *Corporate Nonunion Complaint Procedures and Systems: A Strategic Human Resources Management Analysis* (New York: Praeger, 1988); M. Afzalur Rahim, *Managing Conflict in Organizations*, 4th ed. (London: Routledge Taylor and Francis, 2017).

26. The extensive work on the study of conflict and conflict analysis is beyond the scope of this book. Dispute system designers must understand both constructive and destructive forces and how direct and third-party interests are advanced or curtailed by conflict. The following offer references to start that study: Kevin Avruch, *Encyclopedia of Cultural Anthropology* (New York: Henry Holt, 1996); Morton Deutsch, Peter T. Coleman, and Eric C. Marcus, eds., *The Handbook of Conflict Resolution*, 3rd ed. (San Francisco, CA: Jossey-Bass, 2014); Lewis Coser, *The Functions of Social Conflict* (New York: Free Press, 1956); Morton Deutsch, *The Resolution of Conflict: Constructive and Destructive Processes* (New Haven, CT: Yale University Press, 1973); Gary T. Furlong, *The Conflict Resolution Toolbox: Models and Maps for Analyzing, Diagnosing and Resolving Conflict* (Mississauga, ON: Wiley, 2005); Louis Kriesberg, *Constructive Conflicts: From Escalation to Resolution*, 2nd ed. (New York: Rowman and Littlefield, 2003); John Paul Lederach, *The Little Book of Conflict Transformation* (Intercourse, PA: Good Books, 2003); A. H. Maslow, "A Theory of Human Motivation," *Psychological Review* 50 (1943): 370–96; Lynn Mather, "Disputes, Social Construction and Transformation," in *International Encyclopedia of the Social and Behavioral Sciences*, ed. Neil J. Smelser and Paul B. Baltes (Amsterdam: Elsevier, 2001), 3772–76; Bernard Mayer, *The Dynamics of Conflict Resolution: A Practitioner's Guide* (San Francisco, CA: Jossey-Bass, 2000); Christopher Moore, *The Mediation Process: Practical Strategies for Resolving Conflict*, 4th ed. (San Francisco, CA: Jossey-Bass, 2014); and Dean G. Pruitt, Jeffrey Rubin, and Sung Hee Kim, *Social Conflict: Escalation, Stalemate, and Settlement* (Boston, MA: McGraw-Hill, 2004).

27. Ludwig von Bertalanffy, "An Outline of General Systems Theory," *British Journal for the Philosophy of Science* 1 (1950): 134–65; Francis Fukiyama, *Political Order and Political Decay* (London: Farrar, Straus and Giroux, 2014); E. O. Wilson, *Biophilia* (Cambridge, MA: Harvard University Press, 1984).

28. Lewin, *Group Decision and Social Change*. Kurt Lewin is the father of organizational development with action research around the three phases of change: unfreeze, change, and refreeze. D. L. Bradford and W. W. Burke, *Organizational Development* (San Francisco, CA: Pfeiffer, 2005). For more on organizational learning and systems thinking, see Peter Senge, *The Fifth Discipline: The Art and Practice of the Learning Organization* (New York: Doubleday, 1990).

29. Lipsky, Seeber, and Fincher, *Emerging Systems for Managing Workplace Conflict*.

30. For a discussion of "ripeness," see I. William Zartman and Maureen Berman, *The Practical Negotiator* (New Haven, CT: Yale University Press, 1982).

31. Ury, Brett, and Goldberg, *Getting Disputes Resolved*, 41–64.

32. Jeanne M. Brett and Stephen B. Goldberg, "Grievance Mediation in the Coal Industry: A Field Experiment," *ILR Review* 37, no. 1 (1983): 49–69.

33. Ury, Brett, and Goldberg, *Getting Disputes Resolved*.

34. Costantino and Merchant, *Designing Conflict Management Systems*. For more on the private sector, see Karl Slaikeu and Ralph H. Hasson, *Controlling the Costs of Conflict: How to Design a System for Your Organization* (San Francisco, CA: Jossey-Bass, 1998). Particularly instructive is Marvin Weisbord's six-box model, which focuses on an organization's effectiveness and viability by examining its purpose, structure, relationships, reward system, and alignment of people, structure, and purpose. See Marvin R. Weisbord, "Organizational Diagnosis: Six Places to Look for Trouble With or Without a Theory," *Group and Organization Studies* 1, no. 4 (1976): 430–47.

35. Mary P. Rowe, "Disputes and Conflicts Inside Organizations," *Negotiation Journal* 5, no. 2 (1989): 149–57; Jennifer Lynch, "Beyond ADR: A Systems Approach to Conflict Management," *Negotiation Journal* 17, no. 3 (2001): 207–16; Society for Professionals in Dispute Resolution, "Designing Integrated Conflict Management Systems: Guidelines for Practitioners and Decision Makers in Organizations," January 1, 2001, http://digitalcommons .ilr.cornell.edu/icrpubs/2; Costantino and Merchant, *Designing Conflict Management Systems*. For more recent work, see Mary Rowe, "An Organizational Ombuds Office in a System for Dealing with Conflict and Learning from Conflict," *Harvard Negotiation Law Review* 14 (2009): 279–89.

36. See International Ombudsman Association, "IOA Standards of Practice," October 2009, https://www.ombudsassociation.org/ assets/docs/IOA_Standards_of_Practice_Oct09 .pdf; and Mary P. Rowe, "The Ombudsperson's Role in a Dispute Resolution System," *Negotiation Journal* 7 (1991): 353–72.

37. David Lipsky and Ronald L. Seeber, "In Search of Control: The Corporate Embrace of ADR," *University of Pennsylvania Journal of Labor and Employment Law* 1 (1998): 133–57.

38. Lipsky, Seeber, and Fincher, *Emerging Systems for Managing Workplace Conflict.*

39. For review articles on field studies and evaluation of the uses of mediation and DSD in the contexts of employment, education, criminal justice, the environmental, family disputes, civil litigation in courts, and community disputes, see Tricia S. Jones, ed., "Conflict Resolution in the Field: Special Symposium," special issue, *Conflict Resolution Quarterly* 22, no. 1 (2004): 1–320. This special issue was commissioned with general support to Indiana University by the William and Flora Hewlett Foundation.

40. Cruikshank and Susskind, *Breaking the Impasse,* 21–32.

41. Ury, Brett, and Goldberg, *Getting Disputes Resolved,* 11–13.

42. Costantino and Merchant, *Designing Management Systems,* 168–89.

43. For additional views on principles of design, see Khalil Shariff, "Designing Institutions to Manage Conflict: Principles for the Problem Solving Organization," *Harvard Negotiation Law Review* 8 (2003): 133–57; and Cathy Costantino, "Second Generation Organizational Conflict Management Systems Design: A Practitioner's Perspective on Emerging Issues," *Harvard Negotiation Law Review* 14 (2009): 81–100. See also John Conbere, "Theory Building for Conflict Management System Design," *Conflict Resolution Quarterly* 19 (2001): 215, 228. Conbere reviews this literature for units of analysis for the emerging field of DSD. Strictly speaking, these have not been tested empirically and found to be superior strategies. Future design efforts might usefully research traditional measures of transaction costs, organizational development, or procedural justice, which would yield a more robust theory of system design. Two symposia on DSD in 2008 stimulated significant scholarship: Ohio State University's St. Moritz School of Law hosted "The Second Generation of Dispute System Design: Reoccurring Problems and Potential Solutions" on January 24, 2008, from which volume 2008 of the *Ohio State Journal on Dispute Resolution* published several articles; Harvard Law School hosted "Dispute System Design Across Contexts and Continents" on March 7, 2008, from which volume 14 (2009) of the *Harvard Negotiation Law Review* published articles.

44. Lon L. Fuller, "The Lawyer as an Architect of Social Structures," in *The Principles of Social Order: Selected Essays of Lon L. Fuller,* ed. Kenneth I. Winston (Durham, NC: Duke University Press, 1981), 264–70.

45. See, for example, Costantino and Merchant, *Designing Conflict Management Systems.*

46. Neil MacCormick, *Institutions of Law: An Essay in Legal Theory* (Oxford: Oxford University Press, 2008); Glen Morgan, John L. Campbell, Colin Crouch, Ove Kaj Pedersen, and Richard Whitley, *The Oxford Handbook of Comparative Institutional Analysis* (Oxford: Oxford University Press, 2010); Ostrom, *Understanding Institutional Diversity*.

47. Fuller, *Morality of Law*, 264–65.

48. Russell B. Korobkin and Thomas S. Ulen, "Law and Behavioral Science: Removing the Rationality Assumption from Law and Economics," *California Law Review* 88, no. 4 (2000): 1051–144; Richard H. Thaler and Cass Sunstein, *Nudge: Improving Decisions About Health, Wealth, and Happiness* (New York: Penguin Books, 2009).

49. Amartya Sen, *The Idea of Justice* (Cambridge, MA: Belknap Press, 2009), 18.

50. Michael J. Sandel, *Justice: What's the Right Thing to Do* (New York: Farrar, Straus and Giroux, 2009), 260. Sandel concludes, "A just society can't be achieved simply by maximizing utility or by securing freedom of choice. To achieve a just society, we must reason together about the meaning of the good life, and to create a public culture hospitable to the disagreements that will inevitably arise" (261).

51. Bingham, "Designing Justice."

52. Richard A. Posner, *The Problems of Jurisprudence* (Cambridge, MA: Harvard University Press, 1990), 339.

53. John Rawls, *A Theory of Justice* (Cambridge, MA: Belknap Press, 1971), 58.

54. Ibid., 59.

55. Ibid., 54.

56. Ibid., 88.

57. Ibid.

58. Ibid., 88.

59. Ibid. For the argument for a common-sense notion of fairness as the guide for mediators in thinking about justice in mediation, see Jonathan M. Hyman, "Swimming in the Deep End: Dealing with Justice in Mediation," *Cardozo Journal of Conflict Resolution* 6, no. 1 (2004): 19–56.

60. Rawls, *A Theory of Justice*, 89.

61. This discussion of justice in social psychology and organizational behavior is drawn from Lisa Blomgren Bingham, "When We Hold No Truths to Be Self-Evident: Truth, Belief, Trust, and the Decline in Trials," *Journal of Dispute Resolution*, 2006, 131.

62. John W. Thibaut and Laurens Walker, *Procedural Justice* (Mahwah, NJ: Lawrence Erlbaum, 1975), 122–24.

63. Dean G. Pruitt, *Negotiation Behavior* (New York: Academic Press, 1981); Howard Raiffa, *The Art and Science of Negotiation* (Cambridge, MA: Belknap Press, 1982); Jeffrey Rubin and Bert R. Brown, *The Social Psychology of Bargaining and Negotiation* (New York: Academic Press, 1975).

64. Rawls, *A Theory of Justice*, 100; Posner, *The Problems of Jurisprudence*, 318.

65. Francis E. McGovern, "The What and Why of Claims Resolution Facilities," *Stanford Law Review* 57 (2004–2005): 1361–89.

66. Posner, *The Problems of Jurisprudence*, 324–27.

67. Rawls, *A Theory of Justice*, 86; Raiffa, *The Art and Science of Negotiation*, 288.

68. Joseph B. Stulberg, "Mediation and Justice: What Standards Govern?," *Cardozo Journal of Conflict Resolution* 6 (2005): 213–45, esp. 214–15; Joseph Stulberg, "Procedural Justice, Legitimacy, and the Effective Rule of Law," *Crime and Justice* 30 (2003): 283–357.

69. Rawls, *A Theory of Justice*, 85.

70. Lawrence B. Solum, "Procedural Justice," *Southern California Law Review* 78 (2004): 181, 192–224.

71. John P. Gaffney, "Due Process in the World Trade Organization: The Need for Procedural Justice in the Dispute Settlement System," *American University International Law Review* 14 (1999): 1195–221.

72. For an illustration of survey questions used in interview protocol to compare bilateral settlement, arbitration, and trial, see E. Allan Lind et al., "In the Eye of the Beholder: Tort Litigants' Evaluations of Their Experiences in the Civil Justice System," *Law and Society Review* 24 (1990): 991–96.

73. William G. Austin and Joyce M. Tobiasen, "Legal Justice and the Psychology of Conflict Resolution," in *The Sense of Injustice: Social Psychological Perspectives*, ed. Robert G. Folger (Boston, MA: Springer, 1984), 122.

74. Thibaut and Walker, *Procedural Justice*; John Thibaut and Laurens Walker, "A Theory of Procedure," *California Law Review* 66 (1978): 541–67.

75. Lind et al., "In the Eye of the Beholder."

76. For excellent syntheses of the procedural justice literature as applied to court-connected dispute resolution, see Donna Shestowsky, "Disputants' Preferences for Court-Connected Dispute Resolution Procedures: Why We Should Care and Why We Know So Little," *Ohio State Journal on Dispute Resolution* 23 (2008): 549–626; and Donna Shestowsky, "Misjudging: Implications for Dispute Resolution," *Nevada Law Journal* 7 (2007): 487–99.

77. Michael D. Bayles, *Procedural Justice: Allocating to Individuals* (Boston, MA: Kluwer Academic, 1990), 19–85.

78. Lind et al., "In the Eye of the Beholder," 20.

79. Robert J. Bies and Joseph S. Moag, "Interactional Justice: Communication Criteria of Fairness," in *Research on Negotiation in Organizations*, ed. Roy J. Lewicki, Robert J. Bies, and Blair H. Sheppard (Newton, MA: JAI Press, 1986), 43–55; Lind et al., "In the Eye of the Beholder."

80. Lind et al., "In the Eye of the Beholder."

81. Tracy Hresko, "Restoration and Relief: Procedural Justice and the September 11th Victim Compensation Fund," *Gonzaga Law Review* 42 (2007): 95–131.

82. Lind et al., "In the Eye of the Beholder."

83. Ibid. See also Tom R. Tyler, "The Psychology of Legitimacy: A Relational Perspective on Voluntary Deference to Authorities," *Personality and Social Psychology Review* 1, no. 4 (1997): 323–45. Procedural justice has been used to examine DSDs involving courts. See Donna Shestowsky, "The Psychology of Procedural Preference: How Litigants Evaluate Legal Procedures Ex Ante," *Iowa Law Review* 99 (2014): 637–54; Donna Shestowsky, "How Litigants Evaluate the Characteristics of Legal Procedures: A Multi-court Empirical Study," *University of California Davis Law Review* 49 (2016): 793–841; Donna Shestowsky, "When Ignorance Is Not Bliss: An Empirical Study of Litigants' Awareness of Court-Sponsored Alternative Dispute Resolution Programs," *Harvard Negotiation Law Review* 22 (2017): 189–239; and Donna Shestowsky, "Inside the Mind of the Client: An Analysis of Litigants' Decision Criteria for Choosing Procedures," *Conflict Resolution Quarterly* 36, no. 1 (2018): 69–87. For an overview and critique of previous procedural justice studies, see Shestowsky, "Disputants' Preferences for Court-Connected Dispute Resolution Procedures." Procedural justice has been used to examine special education. See Nancy A. Welsh, "Stepping Back Through the Looking Glass: Real Conversations with Real Disputants About Institutionalized Mediation and Its Value," *Ohio State Journal on Dispute Resolution* 19 (2004): 573–678. Procedural justice has been used to examine domestic violence. See Deborah Epstein, "Procedural Justice: Tempering the State's Response to Domestic Violence," *William and Mary Law Review* 43 (2002): 1843–905. Procedural justice has been used to examine criminal sentencing. See Adam Lamparello, "Social Psychology, Legitimacy, and the Ethical Foundations of Judgment: Importing the Procedural Justice Model to Federal Sentencing," *Columbia Human Rights Law Review* 38 (2006): 115–50.

84. Valerie Jenness and Kitty Calavita, "'It Depends on the Outcome': Prisoners, Grievances, and Perceptions of Justice," *Law and Society Review* 52, no. 1 (2018): 41–72.

85. Bies and Moag, "Interactional Justice."

86. For how interactional justice interacts with psychological biases that create impediments to settlement, see Russell Korobkin, "Psychological Impediments to Mediation Success: Theory and Practice," *Ohio State Journal on Dispute Resolution* 21 (2006): 281–338.

87. Robert D. Folger and Russell Cropanzano, *Organizational Justice and Human Resource Management* (Thousand Oaks, CA: Sage, 1998); Tom R. Tyler and Robert J. Bies, "Beyond Formal Procedures: The Interpersonal Context of Procedural Justice," in *Applied Social Psychology and Organizational Settings*, ed. John S. Carroll (Hillsdale, NJ: Lawrence Erlbaum, 1990), 77–98.

88. Jason A. Colquitt, "On the Dimensionality of Organizational Justice: A Construct Validation of a Measure," *Journal of Applied Psychology* 86 (2001): 386–400; Jason A. Colquitt et al., "Justice at the Millennium: A Meta-analytic Review of 25 Years of Organizational Justice Research," *Journal of Applied Psychology* 86 (2001): 425–45.

89. Robert J. Bies, "The Predicament of Injustice: The Management of Moral Outrage," *Research in Organizational Behavior* 9 (1987): 289–319; Robert J. Bies and Debra L. Shapiro, "Voice and Justification: Their Influence on Procedural Fairness Judgments," *Academy of Management Journal* 31 (1988): 676–85; Jerald Greenberg, "Organizational Justice: Yesterday, Today, and Tomorrow," *Journal of Management* 16 (1990): 399–432; Debra L. Shapiro, "Reconciling Theoretical Differences among Procedural Justice Researchers by Re-evaluating What It Means to Have One's Views 'Considered': Implications for Third-Party Managers," in *Justice in the Workplace: Approaching*

Fairness in Human Resource Management, ed. Russell Cropanzano (Hillsdale, NJ: Lawrence Erlbaum, 1993), 51–78.

90. Colquitt et al., "Justice at the Millennium"; Jerald Greenberg, "The Social Side of Fairness: Interpersonal and Informational Classes of Organizational Justice," in Cropanzano, *Justice in the Workplace*, 79–94; Jerald Greenberg, "Using Socially Fair Treatment to Promote Acceptance of a Work Site Smoking Ban," *Journal of Applied Psychology* 79 (1994): 288–97.

91. Robert J. Bies, Debra L. Shapiro, and L. L. Cummings, "Casual Accounts and Managing Organizational Conflict: Is It Enough to Say It's Not My Fault?," *Communication Research* 15, no. 4 (1988): 381–99.

92. Robert Folger, David Rosenfield, and Thomas Robinson, "Relative Deprivation and Procedural Justification," *Journal of Personality and Social Psychology* 45 (1983): 268–73.

93. Colquitt et al., "Justice at the Millennium"; Greenberg, "The Social Side of Fairness"; Greenberg, "Using Socially Fair Treatment to Promote Acceptance of a Work Site Smoking Ban."

94. Bies and Moag, *Interactional Injustice*.

95. For characterization of the tort of retaliatory discharge on the basis of public policy as a judicial exercise in distributive justice better left to legislatures and the tort of abusive discharge as an exercise in corrective justice the courts have overlooked, see Martin H. Malin, "Topic in Jurisprudence: The Distributive and Corrective Justice Concerns in the Debate over Employment-at-Will: Some Preliminary Thoughts," *Chicago-Kent Law Review* 68 (1992): 117–46. For an argument based on corrective justice that tort liability increases risk whether or not harm occurs, see Christopher H. Schroeder, "Corrective Justice and Liability for Increasing Risks," *University of California Los Angeles Law Review* 37 (1990): 439–78.

96. Schroeder, "Corrective Justice and Liability for Increasing Risks," 329.

97. Ibid., 330.

98. Ibid., 330–31.

99. Michael M. O'Hear and Andrea Kupfer Schneider, "Dispute Resolution in Criminal Law: An Introduction to Dispute Resolution in Criminal Law," *Marquette Law Review* 91 (2007): 1–8. For the observation that 95 percent of convictions are obtained by way of guilty plea and an argument for enhanced procedural justice in plea bargaining, see Michael M. O'Hear, "Plea Bargaining and Procedural Justice," *Georgia Law Review* 42 (2007): 409.

100. For an argument against punitive justice and in favor of a system that restores victims, offenders, and communities through atonement, forgiveness, and compassion and in favor of deterrence after restorative justice fails, see John Braithwaite, *Restorative Justice and Responsive Regulation* (New York: Oxford University Press, 2001).

101. Ibid., 1.

102. For a discussion of theories of justice in criminal law, see Erik Luna, "Punishment Theory, Holism, and the Procedural Conception of Restorative Justice," *Utah Law Review* 2003 (2003): 228.

103. For a discussion of the criminal justice system for legal justice and the welfare system for social justice, see John Braithwaite, "Holism, Justice, and Atonement," *Utah Law Review* 2003 (2003): 391.

104. Cynthia Alkon, "The Increased Use of 'Reconciliation' in Criminal Cases in Central Asia: A Sign of Restorative Justice, Reform, or Cause for Concern?," *Pepperdine Dispute Resolution Law Journal* 8 (2007): 67. For work that describes evaluation studies of victim-offender mediation, see Mark S. Umbreit, Robert B. Coates, and Betty Vos, "Victim-Offender Mediation: Three Decades of Practice and Research," *Conflict Resolution Quarterly* 22

(2004): 279–97. For work that describes other models of restorative justice, including family group conferences and peacemaking circles, see Howard Zehr, "Commentary: Restorative Justice: Beyond Victim-Offender Mediation," *Conflict Resolution Quarterly* 22 (2004): 305–16.

105. M. Cherif Bassiouni, ed., *Post-conflict Justice* (Ardsley, NY: Transnational, 2002).

106. Rudi Teitel, *Transitional Justice* (New York: Oxford University Press, 2000), 225.

107. Posner, *The Problems of Jurisprudence*, 338.

108. Ibid., 336.

109. Mariana Hernandez Crespo, "Building the Latin America We Want: Supplementing Representative Democracies with Consensus-Building," *Cardozo Journal of Conflict Resolution* 10 (2009): 425–90.

110. Lisa Blomgren Bingham, "Collaborative Governance: Emerging Practices and the Incomplete Legal Framework for Citizen and Stakeholder Voice," *Journal of Dispute Resolution* 2009, no. 2 (2010): 269–326. See also John Gastil and Peter Levine, eds., *The Deliberative Democracy Handbook: Strategies for Effective Civic Engagement in the Twenty-First Century* (San Francisco, CA: Jossey-Bass, 2005).

111. Bruce P. Archibald, "Let My People Go: Human Capital, Investment and Community Capacity Building via Meta/Regulation in a Deliberative Democracy—a Modest Contribution to Criminal Law and Restorative Justice," *Cardozo Journal of International and Comparative Law* 16, no. 1 (2008): 1–86.

112. Russell A. Miller, "Theoretical Approaches to International Indigenous Rights: Collective Discursive Democracy as the Indigenous Right to Self-Determination," *American Indian Law Review* 31 (2007): 341–62.

113. Posner, *The Problems of Jurisprudence*, 124.

114. Rawls, *A Theory of Justice*, 58–59.

115. Deborah R. Hensler, "Suppose It's Not True: Challenging Mediation Ideology," *Journal of Dispute Resolution* 2002, no. 1 (2002): 96–97. For the argument that the appropriate comparison is not between mediation and trials but between mediation and the litigation process, which usually does not result in a trial, see Chris Guthrie, "Procedural Justice Research and the Paucity of Trials," *Journal of Dispute Resolution* 2002, no. 1 (2002): 127–30.

116. Frank Elkouri and Edna Elkouri, *How Arbitration Works* (Washington, DC: Bureau of National Affairs, 2003).

117. For studies of gender as a characteristic, see Debra J. Mesch, "Arbitration and Gender: An Analysis of Cases Taken to Arbitration in the Public Sector," *Journal of Collective Negotiations in the Public Sector* 24 (1995): 207–18. Mesch suggests that women charged with felonies are treated more leniently than men. For the finding that a cooperative setting empowered men and women to use different approaches to conflict, with men using informal processes and women choosing formal ones, see Elizabeth A. Hoffmann, "Dispute Resolution in a Worker Cooperative: Formal Procedures and Procedural Justice," *Law and Society Review* 39 (2005): 51–82. For a recent comprehensive review of this literature, see Michael Z. Green, "Reconsidering Prejudice in Alternative Dispute Resolution for Black Work Matters," *SMU Law Review* 70, no. 3 (2017): 639–80; and "ADR Symposium," special issue, *SMU Law Review* 70, nos. 3–4 (2017).

118. Posner, *The Problems of Jurisprudence*, 318–19.

119. Rawls, *A Theory of Justice*, 62.

120. Alternative Dispute Resolution Act of 1998, 28 U.S. Code § 651 et seq.

121. See, for example, Walton and McKersie, *A Behavioral Theory of Labor Negotiations*.

122. We thank an anonymous reviewer of this book for this contribution.

Chapter 2

1. Elinor Ostrom, *Understanding Institutional Diversity* (Princeton, NJ: Princeton University Press, 2005), 8.

2. Ibid., 27.

3. Ibid., 28.

4. Ostrom, *Understanding Institutional Diversity*, 28.

5. Robert Axelrod, *The Evolution of Cooperation* (New York: Basic Books, 1984). See also Robert Axelrod, *The Complexity of Cooperation: Agent-Based Models of Competition and Collaboration* (Princeton, NJ: Princeton University Press, 1998).

6. Elinor Ostrom, *Governing the Commons: The Evolution of Institutions for Collective Action* (Cambridge: Cambridge University Press, 1990).

7. Ostrom, *Understanding Institutional Diversity*, 5–8.

8. Ibid., 14.

9. Ibid., 16–22. See, generally, Elizabeth Baldwin, Tingjia Chen, and Daniel Cole, "Institutional Analysis for New Public Governance Scholars," *Public Management Review* 21, no. 6 (2019): 890–917; Daniel H. Cole, "Laws, Norms, and the Institutional Analysis and Development Framework," *Journal of Institutional Economics* 13, no. 4 (2017): 829–47; and Konrad Zweigert and Hein Kötz, *An Introduction to Comparative Law*, 3rd ed. (Oxford: Oxford University Press, 1998).

10. Ostrom, *Understanding Institutional Diversity*, 22–27.

11. Lauren B. Edelman, *Working Law: Courts, Corporations, and Symbolic Civil Rights* (Chicago: University of Chicago Press, 2016).

12. See, generally, Glenn Morgan et al., eds., *The Oxford Handbook of Comparative Institutional Analysis* (Oxford: Oxford University Press, 2010); and Neil MacCormick, *Institutions of Law: An Essay in Legal Theory* (Oxford: Oxford University Press, 2007).

13. Lisa Blomgren Amsler, "The Evolution of Social Norms in Conflict Resolution," *Journal of Natural Resources Policy Research* 6, no. 4 (2014): 285–90.

14. The original version of this framework was developed in 2002 by Maude Pervere and Stephanie Smith in connection with their first class on system design at Stanford Law School. The framework has been further developed and refined by Stephanie Smith and Janet Martinez. It was first published and discussed in Stephanie Smith and Janet Martinez, "An Analytic Framework for Dispute Systems Design," *Harvard Negotiation Law Review* 14 (Winter 2009): 123–69. Since that publication, "culture and context" has been added as an explicit element of the framework.

15. P. D. Villarreal, "Unnecessary Litigation: A System Flaw—GE Launches Zero Defect Campaign," *Metropolitan Corporate Counsel Annual Index* 7, no. 8 (1999): 1–36. See also Chapter 13.

16. Richard V. Denenberg and Mark Braverman, *The Violence-Prone Workplace: A New Approach to Dealing with Hostile, Threatening, and Uncivil Behavior* (Ithaca, NY: Cornell University Press, 1999). See also Washington State Department of Labor and Industries, "Workplace Violence," https://www.lni.wa.gov/Safety/Research/OccHealth/workVio/default.asp#Resources (accessed September 26, 2019).

17. For definitions of "justice," see Chapter 1.

18. Kenneth Feinberg, the special master for the September 11th fund, used an algorithm to calculate compensation for each individual claimant but retained discretion to adjust the amounts to be more fair.

19. Two examples of high-profile corporate apologies for product defects are Johnson and Johnson and Toyota. See Barbara Kellerman, "When Should a Leader Apologize—and When Not?," *Harvard Business Review*, April 2006, https://hbr.org/2006/04/when-should-a-leader-apologize-and-when-not; and Micheline Maynard, "An Apology from Toyota's Leader," *New York Times*, February 24, 2010, https://www.nytimes.com/2010/02/25/business/global/25toyota.html.

20. Civil Justice Reform Act, Pub. L. No. 101-650, § 104, 104 Stat 5089 (1990) (before 1991 amendment).

21. Jennifer F. Lynch, "Beyond ADR: A Systems Approach to Conflict Management," *Negotiation Journal* 17, no. 3 (2001): 207–16, esp. 208, 211.

22. Michelle LeBaron, "The Alchemy of Change: Cultural Fluency in Conflict Resolution," in *The Handbook of Conflict Resolution: Theory and Practice*, 3rd ed., ed. Peter T. Coleman, Morton Deutsch, and Eric C. Marcus (San Francisco, CA: Jossey-Bass, 2014), 581–603; Roy J. Lewicki, Bruce Barry, and David M. Saunders, *Negotiation* (New York: McGraw-Hill, 2005), 441; Jeffrey Z. Rubin and Frank E. A. Sander, "Culture, Negotiation, and the Eye of the Beholder," *Negotiation Journal* 7, no. 3 (1991): 249–63.

23. Dean Pruitt, Jeffrey Z. Rubin, and Sung Hee Kim, *Social Conflict: Escalation, Stalemate, and Settlement*, 3rd ed. (New York: McGraw-Hill, 2004), 37.

24. Ibid., 67.

25. Deborah M. Kolb, *When Talk Works: Profiles of Mediators* (San Francisco, CA: Jossey-Bass, 1994).

26. Cathy A. Costantino and Christina Sickles Merchant, *Designing Conflict Management Systems: A Guide to Creating Productive and Healthy Organizations* (San Francisco, CA: Jossey-Bass, 1995).

27. David B. Lipsky, Ronald L. Seeber, and Richard D. Fincher, *Emerging Systems for Managing Workplace Conflict: Lessons from American Corporations for Managers and Dispute Resolution Professionals* (San Francisco, CA: Jossey-Bass, 2003).

28. Ibid., 225–30. A champion is a senior official or executive who has the authority to set policy and marshal the necessary organizational resources to implement it.

29. Corinne Bendersky, "Culture: The Missing Link in Dispute Systems Design," *Negotiation Journal* 14, no. 4 (1998): 307–11.

30. Jeanne M. Brett, *Negotiating Globally: How to Negotiate Deals, Resolve Disputes, and Make Decisions Across Cultural Boundaries*, 2nd ed. (San Francisco, CA: Jossey-Bass, 2007), 27–52.

31. Ibid., 28–29.

32. Brett, *Negotiating Globally*, 34–37; Max H. Bazerman and Margaret A. Neale, *Negotiating Rationally* (New York: Free Press, 1992); Dean G. Pruitt and Peter J. Carnevale, *Negotiation in Social Conflict* (Ann Arbor, MI: Open University Press, 1993).

33. Brett, *Negotiating Globally*, 37–38.

34. Ibid., 39.

35. Geert Hofstede, *Culture's Consequences: International Differences in Work-Related Values* (Thousand Oaks, CA: Sage, 1980); Edward T. Hall, *Beyond Culture* (New York: Doubleday, 1976). Hofstede describes four key dimensions: power distance, collectivism versus individualism, masculinity versus femininity, and uncertainty avoidance (weak to strong). Hall focuses on four factors: primary interest (the relative importance of relationship or the transaction); communications (indirect, or "high context," or direct, or "low context"); time (punctual or more flexible); and space (more or less personal space, level of formality).

36. Hofstede, *Culture's Consequences*; Shalom H. Schwartz, *Beyond Individualism/Collectivism: New Cultural Dimension of Values* (Thousand Oaks, CA: Sage, 1994); Catherine H. Tinsley, Jared Curhan, and Ro Sung Kwak, "Adopting a Dual Lens Approach for Examining the Dilemma of Differences in International Business Negotiations," *International Negotiations* 4, no. 1 (1999): 5–22; Catherine H. Tinsley, "Models of Conflict Resolution in Japanese, German, and American Cultures," *Journal of Applied Psychology* 83, no. 2 (1998): 316–23.

37. For a series of essays on culture, conflict resolution, and the relationship between and a description of culture as a constituent of human cognition and social action, see Kevin Avruch, *Culture and Conflict Resolution* (Washington, DC: U.S. Institute of Peace, 1998), 4.

38. Jeswald W. Salacuse, *Making Global Deals* (New York: Random House, 1991).

39. In this book, the phrase "prevent, manage, and resolve disputes" is shorthand for a wide array of actions in relation to conflicts and disputes, including anticipate, identify, prevent, assess, manage, learn from, follow up, and resolve.

40. Vindication of rights can also be an interest.

41. The centrality of interests in negotiation is highlighted in Roger Fisher, William L. Ury, and Bruce Patton, *Getting to Yes: Negotiating Agreement Without Giving In*, 3rd ed. (New York: Penguin, 2011); Howard Raiffa, *The Art and Science of Negotiation* (Cambridge, MA: Harvard University Press, 1982); David A. Lax and James K. Sebenius, *The Manager as Negotiator* (New York: Basic Books, 1986); and Robert H. Mnookin, Andrew S. Tulumello, and Scott R. Peppet, *Beyond Winning* (Cambridge, MA: Harvard University Press, 2000). For a discussion on negotiation theory more broadly, see Chapter 3.

42. William L. Ury, Jeanne M. Brett, and Stephen B. Goldberg, *Getting Disputes Resolved: Designing Systems to Cut the Costs of Conflict* (San Francisco, CA: Jossey-Bass, 1988).

43. Ibid., 14.

44. The two first core dimensions of procedural justice—process control and decision control—were first proposed in John Thibaut and Laurens Walker, *Procedural Justice: A Psychological Analysis* (Mahwah, NJ: Lawrence Erlbaum, 1975), 122.

45. Tom R. Tyler, "The Quality of Dispute Resolution Processes and Outcomes: Measurement Problems and Possibilities," *University of Denver Law Review* 66, no. 3 (1989): 419–36; Tom R. Tyler and E. Allan Lind, "Procedural Justice," in *Handbook of Justice Research in Law*, ed. Joseph Sanders and Lee V. Hamilton (Berlin: Springer, 2001), 65–92, esp. 68–69; Tom R. Tyler, "What Is Procedural Justice? Criteria Used by Citizens to Assess the Fairness of Legal Procedures," *Law and Society Review* 22, no. 1 (1988): 128–42.

46. Donna Shestowsky, "When Ignorance Is Not Bliss: An Empirical Study of Litigants' Awareness of Court-Sponsored Alternative Dispute Resolution Programs," *Harvard Negotiation Law Review* 22 (Spring 2017): 189–202.

47. Pruitt, Rubin, and Kim, *Social Conflict*, 25–34.

48. For multiple commentators' views on this topic, see "*Against Settlement*: Twenty-Five Years Later," special issue, *Fordham Law Review* 78, no. 3 (2009), which is dedicated to a symposium held in April 2009 on Owen Fiss's article "Against Settlement," published in the *Yale Law Journal* in 1984.

49. Donna Shestowsky, "Procedural Preferences in Alternative Dispute Resolution: A Closer, Modern Look at an Old Idea," *Psychology, Public Policy, and Law* 10, no. 3 (2004): 211–43.

50. Costantino and Merchant, *Designing Conflict Management Systems*, 142–49. For the extensive implementation rollout of a large system, see Lisa Blomgren Bingham, "Mediation at Work: Transforming Workplace Conflict at the United States Postal Service," October 2003, http://www.businessofgovernment.org/sites/default/files/Mediation.pdf.

51. Ury, Brett, and Goldberg, *Getting Disputes Resolved*, 11–13.

Chapter 3

1. Leonard L. Riskin, "Understanding Mediators' Orientations, Strategies, and Techniques: A Grid for the Perplexed," *Harvard Negotiation Law Review* 7 (1996): 17–30; Leonard L. Riskin, "Decision-Making in Mediation: The New Old Grid and the New New Grid System," *Notre Dame Law Review* 79, no. 1 (2003): 22–23.

2. Lisa Blomgren Bingham, "Designing Justice: Legal Institutions and Other Systems for Managing Conflict," *Ohio State Journal on Dispute Resolution* 24, no. 1 (2008): 1–51.

3. E. Allan Lind and Tom R. Tyler, *The Social Psychology of Procedural Justice* (New York: Plenum, 1988).

4. Marc Galanter, "Why the 'Haves' Come Out Ahead: Speculations on the Limits of Legal Change," *Law and Society Review* 9, no. 1 (1974): 134.

5. Richard E. Miller and Austin Sarat, "Grievances, Claims, and Disputes: Assessing the Adversary Culture," *Law and Society Review* 15, nos. 3–4 (1980–1981): 544.

6. William Felstiner, Richard Abel, and Austin Sarat, "The Emergence and Transformation of Disputes: Naming, Blaming, Claiming," *Law and Society Review* 15, nos. 3–4 (1980–1981): 631–54.

7. Some managers refer to this as moving conflict resolution upstream, to an earlier point in the emergence and transformation of the dispute.

8. This spectrum describes a basic array of process options. For a more detailed

spectrum, see Jay Folberg et al., *Resolving Disputes: Theory, Practice, and Law*, 3rd ed. (New York: Wolters Kluwer, 2016), 6. For an extended discussion on the process array, see Leonard L. Riskin et al., *Dispute Resolution and Lawyers*, 4th ed. (Eagan, MN: West Academic, 2014), 14; and Stephen B. Goldberg et al., *Dispute Resolution*, 5th ed. (New York: Wolters Kluwer, 2007), 4–5.

9. Adapted from Lisa Blomgren Amsler, "Collaborative Governance: Integrating Management, Politics, and Law," *Public Administration Review* 76, no. 5 (2016): 700–711. For a more detailed description of these processes, see Lisa Blomgren Bingham, "Collaborative Governance: Emerging Practices and the Incomplete Legal Framework for Public and Stakeholder Voice," *Journal of Dispute Resolution* 2009, no. 2 (2010): 270–325. See also Lisa Blomgren Bingham, "The Next Generation of Administrative Law: Building the Legal Infrastructure for Collaborative Governance," *Wisconsin Law Review*, no. 2 (2010): 297–356; and Lisa Blomgren Bingham, "Reflections on Designing Governance to Produce the Rule of Law," *Journal of Dispute Resolution* 2011, no. 1 (2011): 67–89.

10. See International Ombudsman Association, "IOA Standards of Practice," October 2009, https://www.ombudsassociation.org/assets/docs/IOA_Standards_of_Practice_Oct09.pdf; and Mary P. Rowe, "The Ombudsperson's Role in a Dispute Resolution System," *Negotiation Journal* 7 (1991): 353–72.

11. Mary P. Rowe, "Disputes and Conflicts Inside Organizations," *Negotiation Journal* 5, no. 2 (1989): 149–57; Jennifer Lynch, "Beyond ADR: A Systems Approach to Conflict Management," *Negotiation Journal* 17, no. 3 (2001): 207–16; Society of Professionals in Dispute Resolution, "Designing Integrated Conflict Management Systems: Guidelines for Practitioners and Decision Makers in Organizations," January 1, 2001, http://digitalcommons.ilr

.cornell.edu/icrpubs/2; Cathy Costantino and Christina Sickles Merchant, *Designing Conflict Management Systems: A Guide to Creating Productive and Healthy Organizations* (San Francisco, CA: Jossey-Bass, 1996). For more recent work, see Mary Rowe, "An Organizational Ombuds Office in a System for Dealing with Conflict and Learning from Conflict," *Harvard Negotiation Law Review* 14 (2009): 279–89.

12. Bingham, "Collaborative Governance."

13. Carolyn J. Lukensmeyer and Steven Brigham, "Taking Democracy to Scale: Large Scale Re-interventions—for Citizens," *Journal of Applied Behavioral Science* 41, no. 1 (2005): 47–60; Lars Hasselblad Torres, *Deliberative Democracy: A Survey of the Field* (Washington, DC: AmericaSpeaks, 2003).

14. Daniel Yankelovich, *The Magic of Dialogue: Transforming Conflict into Cooperation* (New York: Simon and Schuster, 1999).

15. For the twelve months ending March 31, 2019, the percentage of cases going to trial is 0.8 percent. See United States Courts, "Table C-4: U.S. District Courts—Civil Cases Terminated, by Nature of Suit and Action Taken, During the 12-Month Period Ending March 31, 2019," 2019, https://www.uscourts.gov/statistics/table/c-4/federal-judicial-caseload-statistics/2019/03/31. See also Marc Galanter, "The Vanishing Trial: An Examination of Trials and Related Matters in Federal and State Courts," *Journal of Empirical Legal Studies* 1, no. 3 (2004): 459–570; and Samuel Issacharaoff, *Civil Procedure*, 3rd ed. (New York: Foundation Press, Thompson/West, 2012), 28.

16. See John von Neumann and Oskar Morgenstern, *Theory of Games and Economic Behavior* (Princeton, NJ: Princeton University Press, 1944); and Thomas C. Schelling, *The Strategy of Conflict* (Cambridge, MA: Harvard University Press, 1960).

17. See, for example, Richard E. Walton and Robert B. McKersie, *A Behavioral Theory of Labor Negotiations* (New York: McGraw-Hill,

1965); Roger Fisher, William L. Ury, and Bruce Patton, *Getting to Yes: Negotiating Agreement Without Giving In*, 3rd ed. (New York: Penguin, 2011); Howard Raiffa, *The Art and Science of Negotiation* (Cambridge, MA: Harvard University Press, 1982); David A. Lax and James K. Sebenius, *The Manager's Negotiator: Bargaining for Cooperation and Competitive Gain* (New York: Free Press, 1986); Robert H. Mnookin, Scott R. Peppet, and Andrew S. Tulumello, *Beyond Winning: Negotiating to Create Value in Deals and Disputes* (Cambridge, MA: Harvard University Press, 2000); Howard Raiffa, *Negotiation Analysis: The Science and Art of Collaborative Decision Making* (Cambridge, MA: Harvard University Press, 2007); Russell Korobkin, *Negotiation: Theory and Strategy*, 2nd ed. (Austin, TX: Wolters Kluwer, 2009); Roy J. Lewicki, David M. Saunders, and Bruce Barry, *Negotiation*, 7th ed. (New York: McGraw-Hill Higher Education, 2014); Carrie Menkel-Meadow, Andrea K. Schneider, and Lela P. Love, *Negotiation: Processes for Problem-Solving*, 2nd ed. (Danvers, MA: Wolters Kluwer/Aspen, 2014); and David Lax and James K. Sebenius, *3-D Negotiation: Bargaining for Cooperation and Competitive Gain* (Boston, MA: Harvard Business School Press, 2006).

18. See Max H. Bazerman and Margaret A. Neale, *Negotiating Rationally* (New York: Free Press, 1992); and Neil Rackham and John Carlisle, "The Effective Negotiator—Part I: The Behaviour of Successful Negotiators," *Journal of European Industrial Training* 2, no. 6 (1978): 6–11. Cognitive biases include self-serving bias, salient information, anchoring and adjustment, reactive devaluation, framing, attribution, loss aversion, and risk aversion. See Russell B. Korobkin and Thomas S. Ulen, "Law and Behavioral Science: Removing the Rationality Assumption from Law and Economics," *California Law Review* 88, no. 4 (2000): 1051–144; Jennifer K. Robbennolt and Jean R. Sternlight, *Psychology for Lawyers: Understanding the*

Human Factors in Negotiation, Litigation, and Decision Making (Chicago: American Bar Association, 2012); and Leigh L. Thompson and Brian J. Lucas, "Judgmental Biases in Conflict Resolution and How to Overcome Them," in *The Handbook of Conflict Resolution: Theory and Practice*, 3rd ed., ed. Peter T. Coleman, Morton Deutsch, and Eric C. Marcus, 255–82 (San Francisco, CA: Jossey-Bass, 2014).

19. A comprehensive review of the research literature is outside the scope of this book. Efforts to bring together research and practice through individual chapters by leading scholars are reflected in Christopher Honeyman and Andrea Kupfer Schneider, eds., *The Negotiator's Fieldbook: The Desk Reference for the Experienced Negotiator* (Washington, DC: American Bar Association, 2006); and Christopher Honeyman and Andrea Kupfer Schneider, eds., *The Negotiator's Desk Reference*, 2 vols. (Minneapolis, MN: DRI Press, 2017). Efforts to make negotiation teaching materials widely available are found in Christopher Honeyman, James Coben, and Giuseppe De Palo, eds., *Rethinking Negotiation Teaching: Innovations for Context and Culture* (St. Paul, MN: DRI Press, 2009); Christopher Honeyman, James Coben, and Giuseppe De Palo, eds., *Venturing Beyond the Classroom* (St. Paul, MN: DRI Press, 2010); Noam Ebner, James Coben, and Christopher Honeyman, eds., *Assessing Our Students, Assessing Ourselves* (St. Paul, MN: DRI Press, 2012); and Christopher Honeyman, James Coben, and Andrew Wei-Min Lee, eds., *Educating Negotiators for a Connected World* (St. Paul, MN: DRI Press, 2013). See also G. Richard Shell, *Bargaining for Advantage*, 3rd ed. (New York: Penguin, 2018).

20. Robert H. Mnookin, "Why Negotiations Fail: An Exploration of Barriers to the Resolution of Conflict," *Ohio State Journal on Dispute Resolution* 8, no. 2 (1993): 235–49; Kenneth J. Arrow et al., eds., *Barriers to Conflict Resolution* (New York: W. W. Norton, 1995).

21. William Ury, *Getting Past No: Negotiating with Difficult People* (New York: Bantam
Books, 1991).

22. BATNA, as an acronym, was first used
in Roger Fisher and William Ury, *Getting to Yes*
(New York: Penguin, 1981). Subsequent commentators have refined this concept to include
WATNAs (the worst alternative) and MLATAs
(most likely alternative). See also Noah G. Susskind, "Wiggle Room: Rethinking Reservation
Values in Negotiation," *Ohio State Journal on
Dispute Resolution* 26, no. 1 (2011): 79–117. For a
description of some common misconceptions
regarding Fisher and Ury's intended meaning
of BATNA, see Susskind, "Wiggle Room," 89.

23. One study shows that interest-based ne-
gotiation is at least as effective or perhaps more
effective than hard, or competitive, bargaining.
See Andrea Kupfer Schneider, "Shattering
Negotiation Myths: Empirical Evidence on the
Effectiveness of Negotiation Style," *Harvard
Negotiation Law Review* 7 (2002): 143–233.

24. Ross Brinkert and Tricia S. Jones, *Conflict Coaching: Conflict Management Strategies
and Skills for the Individual* (Los Angeles: Sage,
2008).

25. See Chapter 11; Rowe, "An Organizational Ombuds Office in a System for Dealing
with Conflict and Learning from Conflict";
Mary Rowe, "The Ombudsperson's Role in
a Dispute Resolution System," *Negotiation
Journal* 7, no. 4 (1991): 353–72; D. Leah Meltzer,
"The Federal Workplace Ombuds," *Ohio State
Journal on Dispute Resolution* 13, no. 2 (1998):
549–609; and Charles L. Howard, *The Organizational Ombudsman: Origins, Roles, and Operations—a Legal Guide* (Chicago: American Bar
Association, 2010). For information on ombuds
in government organizations in the European
Union, see Gabriele Kucsko-Stadlmayer, "The
Legal Structures of Ombudsman-Institutions
in Europe: Legal Comparative Analysis," in
*European Ombudsman-Institutions: A Com-
parative Legal Analysis Regarding the Multi-*

faceted Realization of an Idea (Vienna: Springer,
2008).

26. John Lande, "Principles for Policymaking About Collaborative Law and Other ADR
Processes," *Ohio State Journal on Dispute Resolution* 22, no. 3 (2007): 619–706, esp. 619. See
also Uniform Law Commission, "Collaborative
Law Act," 2010, https://www.uniformlaws.org/
committees/community-home?CommunityKey
=fdd1de2f-baea-42d3-bc16-a33d74438eaf.

27. John Lande, *Lawyering with Planned
Early Negotiation: How You Can Get Good
Results for Clients and Make Money* (Chicago:
American Bar Association, 2011).

28. John Lande, "Possibilities for Collaborative Law: Ethics and Practice of Lawyer
Disqualification and Process Control in a New
Model of Lawyering," *Ohio State Law Journal*
64, no. 5 (2003): 1315–84.

29. Jeffrey M. Senger, *Federal Dispute Resolution: Using ADR with the United States Government* (San Francisco, CA: Jossey-Bass, 2003).

30. Some argue a neutral should intervene
to aid the weaker party and redress a serious
imbalance of power in the discussions, but
others criticize this approach as undermining
the neutral's impartiality. For more discussion
of ethics in design, see Chapter 6.

31. Jonathan M. Hyman, "Swimming in the
Deep End: Dealing with Justice in Mediation,"
Cardozo Journal of Conflict Resolution 6, no. 1
(2004): 19–56.

32. Christopher W. Moore, *The Mediation
Process: Practical Strategies for Resolving Conflict*, 3rd ed. (San Francisco, CA: Jossey-Bass,
2003).

33. See Uniform Law Commission,
"Uniform Mediation Act," 2003, https://
www.uniformlaws.org/viewdocument/final
-act-no-comments-45?CommunityKey=
45565a5f-0c57-4bba-bbab-fc7de9a59110&tab=
librarydocuments.

34. Mediators usually have a privilege
against being called as a witness in the event

of a legal proceeding, and offers of settlement are often inadmissible as evidence in any event. The specifics of the privilege (for example, whether the parties or the mediator hold it) and its extent varies from state to state because state legislatures may change the language of the model act (see the Uniform Mediation Act). Mediators from the Federal Mediation and Conciliation Service hold the privilege and may invoke it against the parties to a labor dispute. NLRB v. Joseph Macaluso, Inc., 618 F.2d 51 (1980). Parties may enter into a contract providing for confidentiality.

35. See, generally, Sarah R. Cole et al., *Mediation: Law, Policy and Practice* (Eagan, MN: West, 2012). For a discussion of mediation steps and approaches, see Lisa Blomgren Bingham and Rosemary O'Leary, *A Manager's Guide to Resolving Conflict in Collaborative Networks* (Washington, DC: IBM Center for the Business of Government, 2007), 24–26.

36. For more information on the American Arbitration Association, see its website, at https://adr.org.

37. For more information on the International Institute for Conflict Prevention and Resolution (formerly known as the Center for Public Resources), see its website, at https://cpradr.org.

38. For more information on JAMS (formerly known as Judicial Arbitration and Mediation Services), see its website, at https://jamsadr.com.

39. FedArb's panel of neutrals is substantially composed of retired federal judges. See the organization's home page, at https://www.fedarb.com.

40. Lisa B. Bingham and Charles R. Wise, "The Administrative Dispute Resolution Act of 1990: How Do We Evaluate Its Success?," *Journal of Public Administration, Research and Theory* 6, no. 3 (1996): 383–414.

41. *Alternative Dispute Resolution: A Resource Guide* (Washington, DC: U.S. Office of Personnel Management), http://www.au.af.mil/au/awc/awcgate/dispute_resolution/opm_adrguide.pdf (accessed May 20, 2019).

42. Federal Mediation and Conciliation Service, "Shared Neutrals Programs," https://www.fmcs.gov/sharedneutrals (accessed May 20, 2019).

43. Michael L. Moffitt, "Schmediation and the Dimensions of Definition," *Harvard Negotiation Law Review* 10 (2005): 69–102.

44. Riskin, "Understanding Mediators' Orientations, Strategies, and Techniques"; Riskin, "Decisionmaking in Mediation."

45. Moffitt argues that prescriptive definitions out of context do not sufficiently advance our inquiry into how specific mediator practices function. He suggests five key questions to consider about mediation: who is allowed to do it, who should get regulatory benefits, whom the market should turn to for services, what works, and what behavior is appropriate. Moffitt, "Schmediation and the Dimensions of Definition."

46. Jacqueline Nolan-Haley, Ellen E. Deason, and Mariana Hernandez-Crespo Gonstead, *Global Issues in Mediation* (St. Paul, MN: West Academic, 2019).

47. Riskin, "Understanding Mediators' Orientations," 23–32; Riskin, "Decision-Making in Mediation," 11–20.

48. Robert A. Baruch Bush and Joseph P. Folger, *The Promise of Mediation: The Transformative Approach to Conflict*, 2nd ed. (San Francisco, CA: Jossey-Bass, 2004).

49. Ibid.

50. John Winslade and Gerald D. Monk, *Narrative Mediation: A New Approach to Conflict Resolution* (San Francisco, CA: Jossey-Bass, 2000).

51. See, e.g., Mediation and Arbitration Services by State Board of Mediation and Arbitration, Conn. Gen. Stat. § 5-276 (2016).

52. Conciliation: Procedure and Authority, 29 C.F.R. § 1601.24.

53. Lawrence Susskind and Michele Ferenz, "'Good Offices' in a War-Weary World: A Review of the Practice and Promise of Track One and a Half Diplomacy," Harvard Law School Program on Negotiation working paper 01-1, 2001.

54. In the United Kingdom and Australia, the word "adjudication" has come into use in the construction-industry context to describe an abbreviated and simplified hearing as an alternative to litigation, similar to a streamlined construction arbitration in the United States. The term "arbitration" had become associated with more complex procedures in this context, and the parties sought an expedited and simpler forum. Adjudication Society, "About Us," http://www.adjudication.org/about (accessed May 20, 2019); Nadja Alexander, ed., *Global Trends in Mediation*, 2nd ed. (Alphen aan den Rijn, Netherlands: Kluwer International, 2006).

55. James G. Apple and Robert P. Deyling, *A Primer on the Civil-Law System* (Washington, DC: Federal Judicial Center, 1995).

56. For a history and analysis of ENE, see Wayne D. Brazil, *Early Neutral Evaluation* (Chicago: American Bar Association, 2012).

57. See California Courts, "ADR Types and Benefits," https://www.courts.ca.gov/programs -adr.htm (accessed May 20, 2019).

58. William L. Ury, Jeanne M. Brett, and Stephen B. Goldberg, *Getting Disputes Resolved: Designing Systems to Cut the Costs of Conflict* (San Francisco, CA: Jossey-Bass, 1988).

59. Note that in the U.S. District Court for the Northern District of California an evaluator may mediate in some circumstances.

60. For more on minitrial procedures, see International Institute for Conflict Prevention and Resolution, "CPR Minitrial Procedure," https://www.cpradr.org/resource-center/rules/ international-other/mediation/cpr-minitrial -procedure (accessed May 20, 2019).

61. Samuel G. DeSimone, "Summary Jury Trial—Untapped Tool for Effective State Courts," https://njcourts.gov/courts/civil/ cdrappendices.html (accessed May 20, 2019).

62. Amalia D. Kessler, *A Revolution in Commerce: The Parisian Merchant Court and the Rise of Commercial Society in Eighteenth-Century France* (New Haven, CT: Yale University Press, 2007).

63. Thomas E. Carbonneau, *The Law and Practice of Arbitration*, 2nd ed. (Huntington, NY: Juris, 2012); Thomas E. Carbonneau, *Arbitration in a Nutshell*, 3rd ed. (St. Paul, MN: Thomson West, 2012); Alan Miles Reuben, Frank Elkouri, and Edna Asper Elkouri, *How Arbitration Works* (Arlington, VA: Bureau of National Affairs, 2010). One form of arbitration is called private judging, in which parties use court space and resources to conduct the hearing.

64. Peter H. Kaskell and Thomas J. Stipanowich, *Commercial Arbitration at Its Best: Successful Strategies for Business Users; A Report of the CPR Commission on the Future of Arbitration* (Chicago: CPR Institute for Dispute Resolution, 2001).

65. Federal Arbitration Act, 9 U.S.C. § 10. For both labor and commercial arbitration, the Supreme Court has interpreted the Labor-Management Relations Act (29 U.S.C. § 141 et seq.) and Federal Arbitration Act (9 U.S.C. § 1 et seq.) to limit judicial review and enforce a strong policy of deferral to arbitration.

66. Other unintended consequences are possible. One scholar found that mandatory nonbinding arbitration slowed the clearing of a court's docket by diverting cases from bilateral settlement; the parties simply waited until the arbitration before they talked about settling. Robert J. MacCoun, "Unintended Consequences of Court Arbitration: A Cautionary Tale from New Jersey," *Justice System Journal* 14, no. 2 (1991): 229–43.

67. Christine D. Ver Ploeg, "Pay Equity in Interest Arbitration," *William Mitchell Law Review* 27, no. 2 (2000): 811–39.

68. Josh Chetwynd, "Play Ball? An Analysis of Final-Offer Arbitration, Its Use in Major League Baseball and Its Potential Applicability to European Football Wage and Transfer Disputes," *Marquette Sports Law Review* 20, no. 1 (2009): 109–46; Benjamin A. Tulis, "Final-Offer 'Baseball' Arbitration: Context, Mechanics, and Applications," *Seton Hall Journal of Sports and Entertainment Law* 20, no. 1 (2010): 85–130.

69. Brian J. Malloy, "Binding Interest Arbitration in the Public Sector: A 'New' Proposal for California and Beyond," *Hastings Law Journal* 55, no. 1 (2003): 245–69.

70. Edward Brunet et al., *Arbitration Law in America: A Critical Assessment* (Cambridge: Cambridge University Press, 2006).

71. See Lawrence Susskind, Patrick Field, and Mieke van der Wansem, "Integrating Scientific Information, Stakeholder Interests, and Political Concerns in Resource and Environmental Planning and Management," in *Fostering Integration: Concepts and Practices in Resource and Environmental Management*, ed. Kevin S. Hanna and D. Scott Slocombe (Cambridge: Oxford University Press, 2005), 181–203. See also Brian Panka, "Use of Neutral Fact-Finding to Preserve Exclusive Rights and Uphold the Disclosure Purpose of the Patent System," *Journal of Dispute Resolution* 2003, no. 2 (2003): 531–46; and Herman Karl and Lawrence Susskind, "Use of Joint Fact Finding in Science Intensive Policy Disputes, Part I: MIT; Joint Fact Finding in Science Intensive Policy Disputes (Lecture 2 of 2)," Academic Room, http://www.academicroom.com/video/use-joint-fact-finding-science-intensive-policy-disputes-part-i-mit-joint-fact-finding-science-intensive-policy-disputes-0 (accessed May 20, 2019).

72. Alex Boraine, "Truth and Reconciliation in South Africa: The Third Way," in *Truth v. Justice: The Morality of Truth Commissions*, ed. Robert I. Rotberg and Dennis Thompson (Princeton, NJ: Princeton University Press, 2000), 151–53.

73. Peter S. Adler et al., *Managing Scientific and Technical Information in Environmental Cases: Principles and Practices for Mediators and Facilitators* (Tucson, AZ: U.S. Institute for Environmental Conflict Resolution, 1999). This product of a working group of leading environmental mediators and scholars is an invaluable resource.

74. A new hybrid innovation is the Arb-Med-Arb Protocol by the Singapore International Arbitration Center. A dispute is referred to arbitration before mediation commences. If the parties settle in mediation, the agreement is entered as a consent award. Singapore International Arbitration Center, "The Singapore Arb-Med-Arb Clause," http://www.siac.org.sg/model-clauses/the-singapore-arb-med-arb-clause (accessed May 20, 2019).

75. Douglas Henton et al., *Collaborative Governance: A Guide for Grantmakers* (Menlo Park, CA: William and Flora Hewlett Foundation, 2005).

76. John F. Forester, *The Deliberative Practitioner: Encouraging Participatory Planning Processes* (Cambridge, MA: MIT Press, 1999).

77. Tina Nabatchi et al., eds., *Democracy in Motion: Evaluating the Practice and Impact of Deliberative Civic Engagement* (New York: Oxford University Press, 2012).

78. See, for instance, the work of Accountability Counsel, described on its website, at https://accountabilitycounsel.org; and Rachel Cernansky, "It Takes Consultation to Help a Village," *New York Times*, July 17, 2018, https://www.nytimes.com/2018/07/17/opinion/development-aid-liberia.html.

79. Yankelovich, *The Magic of Dialogue.*

80. Everyday Democracy, "About Everyday Democracy," https://www.everyday-democracy.org/about (accessed March 3, 2019); Patrick L. Scully and Martha L. McCoy, "Study Circles: Local Deliberation as the Cornerstone of Deliberative Democracy," in *The Deliberative Democracy Handbook: Strategies for Effective*

Civic Engagement in the 21st Century, ed. John Gastil and Peter Levine (San Francisco, CA: Jossey-Bass, 2005), 199–202.

81. Bruce Ackerman and James S. Fishkin, *Deliberation Day* (New Haven, CT: Yale University Press, 2004); James S. Fishkin, *When the People Speak: Deliberative Democracy and Public Consultation* (Oxford: Oxford University Press, 2009).

82. See the National Issues Forums' website, at https://www.nifi.org/es/home, and the Kettering Foundation's website, at https://www.kettering.org.

83. Lyn Carson and Janette Hartz-Karp, "Adapting and Combining Deliberative Designs: Juries, Polls and Forums," in Gastil and Levine, *The Deliberative Democracy Handbook*, 120.

84. Robert Agranoff and Michael McGuire, *Collaborative Public Management: New Strategies for Local Governments* (Washington, DC: Georgetown University Press, 2003); Lisa Blomgren Bingham and Rosemary O'Leary, *Big Ideas in Collaborative Public Management* (Armonk, NY: M. E. Sharpe, 2008); Rosemary O'Leary and Lisa Blomgren Bingham, *The Collaborative Public Manager* (Washington, DC: Georgetown University Press, 2009); Barbara Gray, *Collaborating: Finding Common Ground for Multiparty Problems* (San Francisco, CA: Jossey-Bass, 1989).

85. The U.S. Negotiated Rulemaking Act defines a convener as "a person who impartially assists an agency in determining whether establishment of a negotiated rulemaking committee is feasible and appropriate in a particular rulemaking." 5 U.S.C. § 562(3). See also David M. Pritzker and Deborah S. Dalton, eds., *The Negotiated Rulemaking Sourcebook* (Washington, DC: Administrative Conference of the United States, 1995).

86. In environmental and public policy negotiation, the facilitator may first assess whether the dispute is "mediable"—that is,

whether there is any prospect of reaching a settlement within a reasonable period of time. Lawrence E. Susskind and Jeffrey L. Cruikshank, *Breaking Robert's Rules: The New Way to Run Your Meeting, Build Consensus, and Get Results* (New York: Oxford University Press, 2006); Lawrence Susskind, Sarah McKearnan, and Jennifer Thomas-Larmer, *The Consensus Building Handbook: A Comprehensive Guide to Reaching Agreement* (Thousand Oaks, CA: Sage, 1999).

87. "Consensus building is a process of seeking unanimous agreement. . . . [It is] a good-faith effort to meet the interests of all stakeholders. Consensus has been reached when everyone agrees they can live with whatever is proposed after every effort has been made to meet the interests of all stakeholding parties." Susskind, McKearnan, and Thomas-Larmer, *The Consensus Building Handbook*, 6–7. They observe, "Most consensus building efforts set out to achieve unanimity . . . but settle for overwhelming agreement that goes as far as possible toward meeting the interests of all stakeholders. . . . It is absolutely crucial that the definition of success be clear at the outset of any consensus building process" (ibid.).

88. Rosemary O'Leary, with Terry Amsler and Malka Kopell, *Environmental Conflict Resolution: Strategies for Environmental Grantmakers* (Menlo Park, CA: William and Flora Hewlett Foundation, 2005).

89. The Negotiated Rulemaking Act defines a facilitator as "a person who impartially aids in the discussions and negotiations among the members of a negotiated rulemaking committee to develop a proposed rule." 5 U.S.C. § 562(4). See also Roger M. Schwarz, *The Skilled Facilitator: A Comprehensive Resource for Consultants, Facilitators, Managers, Trainers, and Coaches*, 2nd ed. (San Francisco, CA: Jossey-Bass, 2002).

90. Lawrence Susskind and Gerard McMahon, "The Theory and Practice of Negotiated

Rulemaking," *Yale Journal on Regulation* 3, no. 1 (1985): 133–48; Cary Coglianese, "Assessing the Advocacy of Negotiated Rulemaking: A Response to Philip Harter," *New York University Environmental Law Journal* 9, no. 2 (2001): 386–447.

91. For resources on the many additional models for large-group dialogue and deliberation, see National Coalition for Dialogue and Deliberation, "Resource Center," http://ncdd.org/rc (accessed September 6, 2019); and Abigail Williamson and Archon Fung, *Mapping Public Deliberation: A Report for the William and Flora Hewlett Foundation* (Cambridge, MA: John F. Kennedy School of Government, 2005).

92. For examples of online courts, see Nicole Wilmet, "Utah Small Claims Court Launches New Online Dispute Resolution Pilot Program," *Just Court ADR*, December 3, 2018, http://blog.aboutrsi.org/2018/pilot-program/utah-small-claims-court-launches-new-online-dispute-resolution-pilot-program; Lord Justice Briggs, "Civil Courts Structure Review: Final Report," July 2016, https://www.judiciary.uk/wp-content/uploads/2016/07/civil-courts-structure-review-final-report-jul-16-final-1.pdf; Hangzhou Internet Court, "The Operation Process," https://www.netcourt.gov.cn/portal/main/en/index.htm (accessed May 20, 2019); and the Civil Resolution Tribunal, "Welcome to the Civil Resolution Tribunal," https://civilresolutionbc.ca (accessed May 20, 2019).

93. See Elayne E. Greenberg and Noam Ebner, "What Dinosaurs Can Teach Lawyers About How to Avoid Extinction in the ODR Evolution," St. John's School of Law Legal Studies Research Paper No. 19-0004, January 17, 2019, https://papers.ssrn.com/sol3/papers.cfm?abstract_id=3317567.

94. See, for example, Adam Liptak, "Sent to Prison by a Software Program's Secret Algorithms," *New York Times*, May 1, 2017, p. A22. Liptak describes a Wisconsin case in which use of probability software to predict a defendant's likelihood of recidivism was upheld.

95. Colin Rule, *Online Dispute Resolution for Business: B2B, E-commerce, Consumer, Employment, Insurance, and Other Commercial Conflicts* (San Francisco, CA: Jossey-Bass, 2002).

96. Ayelet Sela, "The Effect of Online Technologies on Dispute Resolution System Design: Antecedents, Current Trends and Future Directions," *Lewis and Clark Law Review* 21 (2017): 635–83.

97. See Amy J. Schmitz and Colin Rule, "Online Dispute Resolution for Smart Contracts," *Journal of Dispute Resolution* 2019, no. 2 (2019): 103–25.

98. Ayelet Sela, "Can Computers Be Fair? How Automated and Human-Powered Online Dispute Resolution Affect Procedural Justice in Mediation and Arbitration," *Ohio State Journal on Dispute Resolution* 33 (2018): 91–148.

99. Ethan Katsh and Orna Rabinovich-Einy, *Digital Justice: Technology and the Internet of Disputes* (New York: Oxford University Press, 2017).

100. Carrie Menkel-Meadow, "Are There Systemic Ethics Issues in Dispute System Design? And What We Should [Not] Do About It: Lessons from International and Domestic Fronts," *Harvard Negotiation Law Review* 14 (2009): 195–212.

101. See the pending list of seventeen principles at National Center for Technology and Dispute Resolution, "Ethical Principles for ODR," 2016, http://odr.info/ethics-and-odr. See also Leah Wing, "Ethical Principles for Online Dispute Resolution: A GPS Device for the Field," *International Journal of Online Dispute Resolution* 3 (2016): 12–29; Daniel Rainey, "Ethical Principles for ODR," *International Journal of Online Dispute Resolution* 4 (2017): 21–26; and Susan Nauss Exon, "Ethics and Online Dispute Resolution: From Evolution to Revolution," *Ohio State Journal on Dispute Resolution* 32, no. 4 (2017): 609–49.

Chapter 4

1. The leading literature on weaving concepts from organizational development with system design is Cathy A. Costantino and Christina Sickles Merchant, *Designing Conflict Management Systems: A Guide to Creating Productive and Healthy Organizations* (San Francisco, CA: Jossey-Bass, 1996).

2. See, for example, Paul Brest and Linda Hamilton Krieger, *Problem Solving, Decision Making, and Professional Judgment: A Guide for Lawyers and Policymakers* (New York: Oxford University Press, 2010). See also Roger Schwarz, *The Skilled Facilitator: Practical Wisdom for Developing Effective Groups*, 2nd ed. (San Francisco, CA: Jossey-Bass, 2002); and Lawrence Susskind, Sarah McKearnan, and Jennifer Thomas-Larmer, eds., *The Consensus Building Handbook: A Comprehensive Guide to Reaching Agreement* (London: Sage, 1999). The facilitator should foster agenda setting, coordinate fact-finding, identify and synthesize points of agreement and disagreement, engage diverse people and ensure all have voice, and surface underlying issues and concerns. Nancy H. Rogers et al., *Designing Systems and Processes for Managing Disputes*, 2nd ed. (New York: Wolters Kluwer, 2019), chap. 15.

3. See Chapter 6; and Rogers et al., *Designing Systems and Processes for Managing Disputes*, chap. 15.

4. Gerald W. Cormick, "Structuring Issues in Multi-party Public Policy Negotiations," *Negotiation Journal* 5, no. 2 (1989): 125–32; Susskind, McKearnan, and Thomas-Larmer, *Consensus Building Handbook*; Joyce L. Hocker and William W. Wilmot, "Hocker-Wilmot Conflict Assessment Guide," in *Interpersonal Conflict*, 2nd ed., ed. Joyce L. Hocker and William W. Wilmot (Dubuque, IA: William Brown, 1985), 129–56; Paul Wehr, "Conflict Mapping Guide," in *Conflict Regulation* (Boulder, CO: Westview Press, 1979), 18–21.

5. We have created the term "conflict stream assessment" to apply to a stream of disputes in DSD. Related and overlapping terms from other fields are "assessment," "issue assessment," "situation assessment," "stakeholder analysis," and "conflict assessment."

6. See "Cathy A. Costantino," Georgetown Law, https://www.law.georgetown.edu/faculty/cathy-a-costantino (accessed May 20, 2019).

7. See Public Policy Lab, "About Us," http://publicpolicylab.org/about-us (accessed May 20, 2019).

8. Stanford Law School, "Community-Led System Design," https://law.stanford.edu/courses/community-led-system-design (accessed May 20, 2019). The design thinking approach is an interactive, iterative process of inspiration, ideation, and implementation. See Tim Brown, "Design Thinking," *Harvard Business Review* 86, no. 6 (2008): 84; and Victor D. Quintanilla, "Human-Centered Civil Justice Design," *Penn State Law Review* 121, no. 3 (2017): 745–806. See also the Harvard Law School's Negotiation and Mediation Clinical Program, which has led assessment, design, and evaluation efforts in the United States and abroad. Harvard Law School, "Harvard Negotiation and Mediation Clinical Program," http://hls.harvard.edu/dept/clinical/clinics/harvard-negotiation-and-mediation-clinic (accessed May 20, 2019).

9. Morrison and Foerster, "2017–2018 Southern California Wildfires, Mudslides, and Related Disasters Helping Handbook: A Resource for Individuals, Families, and Small Businesses," January 24, 2018, https://www.mofo.com/culture/community/2017-2018-southern-california-disasters.html.

10. Chapter 3 describes a convener's role in conducting a conflict assessment. As distinguished from a CSA, a conflict assessment is an analysis used primarily in multiparty public policy or environmental mediation or facilitation in which the third party identifies

stakeholders, interests, and issues; prepares a report; and with feedback from participants, suggests a process for the participants to address the conflict.

11. These steps are adapted from Susskind, McKearnan, and Thomas-Larner, *Consensus Building Handbook*, 99–136.

12. Costantino and Merchant elaborate on the initial stage of engagement, when advisors recognize the presenting problem and engage an assessor and designer whose values and philosophy match the organization. Costantino and Merchant, *Designing Conflict Management Systems*, 69–85; see also Rogers et al., *Designing Systems and Processes for Managing Disputes*, 49.

13. See the process of joint fact-finding in Chapter 3.

14. Costantino and Merchant, *Designing Conflict Management Systems*, 105–11.

15. See William Felstiner, Richard Abel, and Austin Sarat's concepts of naming, blaming, and claiming in William Felstiner, Richard Abel, and Austin Sarat, "The Emergence and Transformation of Disputes: Naming, Blaming, Claiming," *Law and Society Review* 15, nos. 3–4 (1980–1981): 631–54.

16. Christopher W. Moore, *The Mediation Process: Practical Strategies for Resolving Conflict*, 3rd ed. (San Francisco, CA: Jossey-Bass, 2003), 60.

17. BATNA analysis is a means to compare what resolution can be achieved by a party through negotiation to an alternative strategy—for example, a court trial, delayed resolution, or mediation. See Chapter 3. For the acronym's use, see Roger Fisher, William Ury, and Bruce Patton, *Getting to Yes: Negotiating Agreement Without Giving In*, 3rd ed. (New York: Penguin, 2011), 97.

18. On consensus building and democracy, see Lawrence Susskind, "Deliberative Democracy and Dispute Resolution," *Ohio State Journal on Dispute Resolution* 24, no. 3 (2009): 395–406.

See also the discussion of "activist mediators" in John Forester, *Dealing with Differences: Dramas of Mediating Public Disputes* (New York: Oxford University Press, 2009), 5, 19.

19. See the discussion of the five Cs that may trigger design and implementation of an integrated conflict management system in Jennifer F. Lynch, "Beyond ADR: A Systems Approach to Conflict Management," *Negotiation Journal* 17, no. 3 (2001): 207, 212.

20. For detailed case studies of system design practice, see Rogers et al., *Designing Systems and Processes for Managing Disputes*.

21. This case is also discussed in Chapter 14.

22. Engalla v. Permanente Medical Group, Inc., 64 Cal. Rptr. 2d 845 (1997).

23. Ibid., 848.

24. Excerpted and adapted from Stephanie Smith and Janet Martinez, "An Analytic Framework for Dispute Systems Design," *Harvard Negotiation Law Review* 14 (Winter 2009): 138.

25. In the Kaiser case, there was no pilot phase. The DSD for the U.S. District Court for the Northern District of California did include a pilot, as discussed in Chapter 7.

26. Association for Conflict Resolution, "Report on Competencies in Conflict Management Systems Design," 2000, https://cdn .ymaws.com/acrnet.org/resource/resmgr/docs/ SPIDR_Report_on_Competencies.pdf.

27. See Blue Ribbon Advisory Panel on Kaiser Permanente Arbitration, "The Kaiser Permanente Arbitration System: A Review and Recommendations for Improvement," January 5, 1998, http://www.oia-kaiserarb.com/pdfs/ BRP-Report.pdf.

28. Costantino and Merchant, *Designing Conflict Management Systems*, 28.

29. Stakeholder groups were patients (Kaiser members), employers (whose employees are Kaiser members), Kaiser doctors, Kaiser nurses and other medical staff, Kaiser management, plaintiffs' counsel who represent members in medical malpractice cases, defense counsel

who represent Kaiser in medical malpractice cases, and arbitrators who serve in Kaiser cases, among others. Smith and Martinez, "An Analytic Framework for Dispute Systems Design," 139–40.

30. Blue Ribbon Advisory Panel on Kaiser Permanente Arbitration, "The Kaiser Permanente Arbitration System," 31–45.

31. William L. Ury, Jeanne M. Brett, and Stephen B. Goldberg, *Getting Disputes Resolved: Designing Systems to Cut the Costs of Conflict* (New York: Penguin, 1988), 42–64.

32. John Conbere, "Theory Building for Conflict Management System Design," *Conflict Resolution Quarterly* 19 (2001): 213–36.

33. For example, see the discussion of the U.S. Postal Service REDRESS rollout in Lisa Blomgren Bingham, "Mediation at Work: Transforming Workplace Conflict at the United States Postal Service," October 2003, http://www.businessofgovernment.org/sites/default/files/Mediation.pdf.

34. Some changes were implemented by Kaiser before issuance of the report, such as expedited processes for managing cases in which the claimant is terminal and a process for indigent claimants to obtain relief from payment of some arbitration costs. See Blue

Ribbon Advisory Panel on Kaiser Permanente Arbitration, "The Kaiser Permanente Arbitration System, appendix C.

35. The group was originally the Arbitration Advisory Committee and was later succeeded by the Arbitration Oversight Board.

36. Ury, Brett, and Goldberg, *Getting Disputes Resolved*, 11–13.

37. Costantino and Merchant, *Designing Conflict Management Systems*, 121.

38. The Blue Ribbon Advisory Panel on Kaiser Permanente Arbitration recommended adoption of a mediation program. See Blue Ribbon Advisory Panel on Kaiser Permanente Arbitration, "The Kaiser Permanente Arbitration System: A Review and Recommendations for Improvement," January 5, 1998, http://www.oia-kaiserarb.com/pdfs/BRP-Report.pdf. The Kaiser Arbitration Oversight Board reports annually on the status of Blue Ribbon Panel recommendations and noted Kaiser's creation of an ombuds-mediator position as of December 31, 2018. See Kaiser Arbitration Oversight Board, "Board Comments on the Annual Report for 2018," http://www.oia-kaiserarb.com/pdfs/AOB-Comments.pdf (accessed June 14, 2019).

Chapter 5

1. Mariana H. C. Gonstead, "A New Chapter in Natural Resource-Seeking Investment: Using Shared Decision System Design (SDSD) to Strengthen Investor-State and Community Relationships," *Cardozo Journal of Conflict Resolution* 18 (2017): 551–620.

2. See, for example, Roselle Wissler, "Court-Connected Settlement Procedures: Mediation and Judicial Settlement Conferences," *Ohio State Journal on Dispute Resolution* 26 (2011): 271–325.

3. See, for example, Nancy A. Welsh, "Stepping Back Through the Looking Glass: Real Conversations with Real Disputants About

Institutionalized Mediation and Its Value," *Ohio State Journal on Dispute Resolution* 19, no. 2 (2004): 573–678.

4. Lisa Blomgren Amsler, "Dispute System Design and the Global Pound Conference," *Cardozo Journal of Conflict Resolution* 18 (2017): 621–35.

5. Mark Bovens, "Two Concepts of Accountability: Accountability as a Virtue and as a Mechanism," *West European Politics* 33, no. 5 (2010): 946–67; Mark Bovens and Thomas Schillermans, "Meaningful Accountability," in *The Oxford Handbook of Public Accountability*, ed. Mark Bovens, Robert E. Goodin, and

Thomas Schillermans (Oxford: Oxford University Press, 2014), 673–83.

6. Melvin J. Dubnick and H. George Frederickson, "Accountable Agents: Federal Performance Measurement and Third-Party Government," *Journal of Public Administration Research and Theory* 20, suppl. 1 (2010): 143–59; Melvin J. Dubnick and H. George Frederickson, introduction to *Accountable Governance: Problems and Promises*, ed. Melvin J. Dubnick and H. George Frederickson (Armonk, NY: M. E. Sharpe, 2011): xi–xxx; Melvin J. Dubnick and Kaifeng Yang, "The Pursuit of Accountability: Promise, Problems, and Prospects," in *The State of Public Administration: Issues, Challenges, and Opportunities*, ed. Donald C. Menzel and Harvey L. White (Armonk, NY: M. E. Sharpe, 2011), 171–86.

7. This discussion draws on Lisa Blomgren Amsler and Jessica Sherrod, "Accountability Forums and Dispute System Design," *Public Performance Management Review* 40, no. 3 (2017): 529–50.

8. Lisa Blomgren Bingham, "Designing Justice: Legal Institutions and Other Systems for Managing Conflict," *Ohio State Journal on Dispute Resolution* 24, no. 1 (2008–2009): 1–51.

9. Dubnick and Frederickson, "Accountable Agents," 145–46.

10. Ibid., 145.

11. The field of policy analysis includes evaluation on policies in statutes, regulations, and executive orders and how agencies and courts implement policies through programs. For example, the RAND Institute for Civil Justice evaluated the impact of the Civil Justice Reform Act of 1990 on dispute processing in a sample of federal district court programs. James S. Kakalik et al., *An Evaluation of Mediation and Early Neutral Evaluation Under the Civil Justice Reform Act* (Santa Monica, CA: Rand Institute for Civil Justice, 1996).

12. The discussion in this section first appeared in Bingham, "Designing Justice." For review articles on field studies and evaluation of the uses of mediation and DSD in employment, education, criminal justice, the environment, family disputes, civil litigation in courts, and community disputes, see Tricia S. Jones, ed., "Conflict Resolution in the Field: Special Symposium," special issue, *Conflict Resolution Quarterly* 22, nos. 1–2 (2004): 1–320. For extensive background on DSD efforts in the federal government, see Interagency Alternative Dispute Resolution Working Group, "Federal ADR Programs and Contacts," https://www.adr.gov (accessed May 20, 2019). For evaluation reports reflecting the results of DSD in the federal courts, see the website of the Federal Judicial Center, at https://www.fjc.gov/subject/alternative-dispute-resolution-adr. For similar reports on DSD in state courts, see the website of the National Center for State Courts, at https://www.ncsc.org/Topics/Civil/ADR/Resource-Guide.aspx.

13. Nancy A. Welsh, "Mandatory Predispute Consumer Arbitration, Structural Bias, and Incentivizing Procedural Safeguards," *Southwestern Law Review* 42 (2013): 187–228; Nancy A. Welsh, "Perceptions of Fairness," in *The Negotiator's Fieldbook: The Desk Reference for the Experienced Negotiator*, ed. Andrea Kupfer Schneider and Christopher Honeyman (Washington, DC: American Bar Association, 2006), 165; Kees van den Bos et al., "Evaluating Outcomes by Means of the Fair Process Effect: Evidence for Different Processes in Fairness and Satisfaction Judgments," *Journal of Personality and Social Psychology* 74, no. 6 (1998): 1493–503.

14. E. Allan Lind et al., "In the Eye of the Beholder: Tort Litigants' Evaluations of Their Experiences in the Civil Justice System," *Law and Society Review* 24, no. 4 (1990): 953–96, esp. 992; American Bar Association Section of Dispute Resolution, "Report of the Task Force on Research on Mediator Techniques," June 12, 2017, https://www.americanbar.org/content/

dam/aba/administrative/dispute_resolution/
med_techniques_tf_report.pdf.

15. American Bar Association Section of
Dispute Resolution, "Report of the Task Force
on Research on Mediator Techniques." While
experimental subjects might be satisfied with
their outcomes and while fairness judgments
correlated in some conditions with satisfaction, social judgment comparison points
(others doing the same, worse, or better in the
same process) were more related to fairness
judgments, and outcomes compared with
expectations (outcome as better, the same, or
worse than you expected) were more related to
satisfaction judgments.

16. Marc Galanter and Mia Cahill, "Symposium on Civil Justice Reform: 'Most Cases
Settle'; Judicial Promotion and Regulation of
Settlements," *Stanford Law Review* 46 (1994):
1349–51.

17. It is nevertheless possible to use some
of these arguments as indicators or measures
of the presence of certain forms of justice.
For example, satisfaction measures are often
related to theories of procedural and distributive justice from social psychology. Superior
outcome arguments suggest better distributive
or substantive justice. Arguments for creativity
suggest Pareto optimality as used by Rawls in
his theory of justice as fairness. John Rawls,
A Theory of Justice (Cambridge, MA: Belknap
Press, 1971), 67–69.

18. Judith Resnik, "The Contingency of
Openness in Courts: Changing the Experiences
and Logics of the Public's Role in Court-Based
ADR," *Nevada Law Journal* 15, no. 3 (2015):
1631–88.

19. Elinor Ostrom, *Understanding Institutional Diversity* (Princeton, NJ: Princeton
University Press, 2005).

20. Ibid., 32.

21. Nancy A. Welsh, "Theory and Reality in
Regulating Dispute Resolution," *Dispute Resolution Magazine* 20, no. 4 (2014): 22–25.

22. For neighborhood disputes, see Victoria
Malkin, "Community Courts and the Process
of Accountability: Consensus and Conflict at
the Red Hook Community Justice Center,"
American Criminal Law Review 40 (2003):
1573–94.

23. Michael C. Dorf and Charles F. Sabel,
"Drug Treatment Courts and Emergent Ex-
perimentalists Government," *Vanderbilt Law
Review* 53 (2000): 852–61; John Lande, "Failing
Faith in Litigation? A Survey of Business
Lawyers' and Executives' Opinions," *Harvard
Negotiation Law Review* 3 (1998): 1–70.

24. Donna Shestowsky, "Improving Sum-
mary Jury Trials: Insights from Psychology,"
Ohio State Journal on Dispute Resolution 18
(2003): 469–96; Neil Vidmar and Jeffrey Rice,
"Jury-Determined Settlements and Summary
Jury Trials: Observations About Alternative
Dispute Resolution in an Adversary Culture,"
Florida State University Law Review 19 (1991):
89–104.

25. Lisa B. Bingham and Debra J. Mesch,
"Decision-Making in Employment and Labor
Arbitration," *Industrial Relations* 39 (2000):
671–94; Robert J. MacCoun, "Comparing Legal
Factfinders: Real and Mock, Amateur and Professional," *Florida State University Law Review*
32, no. 2 (2005): 511–18.

26. For one mechanism for handling
arbitration costs, arguing that arbitration costs
are generally not a barrier to asserting a claim
in arbitration, see Christopher R. Drahozal,
"Arbitration Costs and Contingent Free
Contracts," *Vanderbilt Law Review* 59 (2006):
729–91.

27. Joseph S. Wholey, Harry P. Hatry, and
Kathryn E. Newcomer, *The Handbook of Prac-
tical Program Evaluation* (San Francisco, CA:
Jossey-Bass, 2004), 33.

28. Ibid., 34.

29. Donna Shestowsky and Jeanne M. Brett,
"Disputants' Perceptions of Dispute Resolution
Procedures: An Ex Ante and Ex Post Longitu-

dinal Empirical Study," *Connecticut Law Review* 41 (2008): 63–107.

30. For more discussion of how courts have evaluated their ADR programs, see Chapter 7; for detailed findings from this research program, see Donna Shestowsky, "The Psychology of Procedural Preference: How Litigants Evaluate Legal Procedures Ex Ante," *Iowa Law Review* 99 (2014): 637–710; Donna Shestowsky, "How Litigants Evaluate the Characteristics of Legal Procedures: A Multi-court Empirical Study," *University of California Davis Law Review* 49 (2016): 793-841; and Donna Shestowsky, "When Ignorance Is Not Bliss: An Empirical Study of Litigants' Awareness of Court-Sponsored Alternative Dispute Resolution Programs," *Harvard Negotiation Law Review* 22 (2017): 189–239.

31. Elinor Ostrom, "Collective Action and the Evolution of Social Norms," *Journal of Economic Perspectives* 14, no. 3 (2000): 137–58.

32. American Bar Association Section of Dispute Resolution, "Report of the Task Force on Research on Mediator Techniques"; Nancy A. Welsh, "Magistrate Judges, Settlements, and Procedural Justice," *Nevada Law Journal* 16 (2016): 983–1060; Nancy A. Welsh and Bobbi McAdoo, "Look Before You Leap and Keep on Looking: Lessons from the Institutionalization of Court-Connected Mediation," *Nevada Law Journal* 5 (2004–2005): 399–432.

33. Carrie J. Menkel-Meadow, "Dispute Resolution," in *Oxford Handbook of Empirical Legal Research*, ed. Peter Cane and Herbert Kritzer (Oxford: Oxford University Press, 2010), 596–624; Carrie J. Menkel-Meadow et al., *Dispute Resolution: Beyond the Adversarial Model* (New York: Wolters Kluwer, 2019), 536; Felix Steffek et al., eds., *Regulating Dispute Resolution: ADR and Access to Justice at the Crossroads* (Oxford: Hart, 2013).

34. Jeanne M. Brett et al., "Sticks and Stones: Language, Face, and Online Dispute Resolution," *Academy of Management Journal* 50, no. 1 (2007): 85–99. This groundbreaking study of eBay's DSD uses qualitative data (text from online claims resolution communications) and quantitative analysis using an event history model.

35. Tests for differences are analysis of variance (ANOVA), *T*-tests, chi squares, linear multiple regression, logistic regression (logits), and probits, among others. For example, you can use ANOVA to test for significant differences between the means of two random samples.

36. See Chester L. Olson, *Statistics: Making Sense of Data* (Boston, MA: Allyn and Bacon, 1987).

37. In control theory, giving disputants control over the outcome in mediation allows them to shape the outcome directly; control over the process in arbitration allows them to present evidence and argument to shape the outcome indirectly. John W. Thibaut and Laurens Walker, *Procedural Justice* (Mahwah, NJ: Lawrence Erlbaum, 1975).

38. In group value theory, people prefer neutrality and respectful, dignified treatment because it signals their value and standing within a social group. Tom R. Tyler, "The Psychology of Procedural Justice: A Test of the Group Value Model," *Journal of Personality and Social Psychology* 57 (1989): 830–38; Tom R. Tyler and E. Allan Lind, "A Relational Model of Authority in Groups," *Advances in Experimental Social Psychology* 25 (1992): 115–91.

39. In fairness heuristic theory, when people perceive a process or outcome as fair, they use it as a shortcut (heuristic) to decide whether to trust an authority. Kees van den Bos, "Uncertainty Management: The Influence of Uncertainty Salience on Reactions to Perceived Procedural Fairness," *Journal of Personality and Social Psychology* 80 (2001): 931–41; Kees van den Bos and Allan Lind, "Uncertainty Management by Means of Fairness Judgments," *Advances in Experimental Social Psychology*

34 (2002): 1–60. For a review of the literature, see Robert J. MacCoun, "Voice, Control, and Belonging: The Double-Edged Sword of Procedural Fairness," *Annual Review of Law and Society Science* 1 (2005): 171–201.

40. Roy J. Lewicki and Edward C. Tomlinson, "Trust, Trust Development, and Trust Repair," in *The Handbook of Conflict Resolution: Theory and Practice*, 3rd ed., ed. Peter T. Coleman, Morton Deutsch, and Eric C. Marcus (San Francisco, CA: Jossey-Bass, 2014), 104–36.

41. For example, administrative procedure identifies values related to the legitimacy of agency action; these include the transparency of the process, participation in the process, and a decision maker's accountability for its results. Richard B. Stewart examines how U.S. administrative law might provide a model for making global regulatory regimes more accountable through participation, transparency, and judicial review. See Richard B. Stewart, "U.S. Administrative Law: A Model for Global Administrative Law?," *Law and Contemporary Problems* 68, nos. 3–4 (2005): 63–108.

42. Rory Van Loo, "The Corporation as Courthouse," *Yale Journal on Regulation* 33 (2016): 547–602.

43. Robert J. MacCoun, "Unintended Consequences of Court-Annexed Arbitration: A Cautionary Tale from New Jersey," *Justice System Journal* 14 (1991): 229–43.

44. See the discussion of the Kaiser independent evaluation process in Chapter 14.

45. Mariana Hernandez Crespo, "Building the Latin America We Want: Supplementing Representative Democracies with Consensus-Building," *Cardozo Journal of Conflict Resolution* 10 (2009): 425–90.

46. Lisa B. Bingham and Cristina M. Novac, "Mediation's Impact on Formal Complaint Filing: Before and After the REDRESS™ Program at the United States Postal Service," *Review of Public Personnel Administration* 21, no. 4 (2001): 308–31.

47. Lisa B. Bingham et al., "Dispute Resolution and the Vanishing Trial: Comparing Federal Government Litigation and ADR Outcomes," *Ohio State Journal on Dispute Resolution* 24, no. 2 (2009): 225–62.

Chapter 6

1. This book touches only briefly on large-group processes such as dialogue and deliberation or public engagement, which also entail system design (Chapter 17). For professionals who study or practice intervention in community disputes involving large-scale protest or racial or ethnic conflict, commentators recommend ethical consideration of how the process promotes "core values of freedom, justice, and proportional empowerment." James Laue and Gerald Cormick, "The Ethics of Intervention in Community Disputes," in *The Ethics of Social Intervention*, ed. Gordon Bermant, Herbert C. Kelman, and Donald P. Warwick (New York: Halstead Press, 1978), 217. The authors define justice as "the ultimate social good" and note that a "just social system is one in which power

(control over decisions) is diffused, decision-making is participatory, accountability for decisions is visible, and resources are adequate and equally distributed" (219). See also Preston M. Williams, "Comments on 'The Ethics of Intervention in Community Disputes,'" in Bermant, Kelman, and Warwick, *The Ethics of Social Intervention*, 233–42.

2. Carrie Menkel-Meadow, "Are There Systemic Ethics Issues in Dispute System Design? And What We Should [Not] Do About It: Lessons from International and Domestic Fronts," *Harvard Negotiation Law Review* 14 (2009): 195, 205.

3. International Institute for Conflict Prevention and Resolution, "Principles for ADR Provider Organizations: CPR-Georgetown

Commission on Ethics and Standards of Practice in ADR," May 1, 2002, https://www.cpradr .org/resource-center/protocols-guidelines/ ethics-codes/principles-for-adr-provider -organizations. This website defines a provider organization as "any entity or individual which holds itself out as managing or administering dispute resolution or conflict management services." An excellent taxonomy of ADR provider organizations is contained as Appendix A to these principles, addressing such topics as types of organizational structure, relationship to neutrals, quality control, transparency, nature of cases, and nature of processes offered. In the last category, "system design" is the first process listed, along with training, facilitation, mediation, arbitration, and other processes and related services.

4. See, for example, American Arbitration Association, "About the AAA and ICDR," https://www.adr.org/about (accessed May 23, 2019); and Judicial Arbitration and Mediation Services, "About Us: JAMS Mediation, Arbitration and ADR Services," https://www.jamsadr .com/about (accessed May 23, 2019).

5. CPR is now the International Institute for Conflict Prevention and Resolution; see its website at https://www.cpradr.org.

6. See International Institute for Conflict Prevention and Resolution, "Principles for ADR Provider Organizations." Although the CPR-Georgetown principles note their applicability to "internal cases," their focus is on organizations, public and private, that serve as "middlemen" in provision of ADR services, as evidenced by the title.

7. Society of Professionals in Dispute Resolution, "Designing Integrated Conflict Management Systems: Guidelines for Practitioners and Decision Makers in Organizations," January 1, 2001, http://digitalcommons.ilr.cor nell.edu/icrpubs/2. Though focused on internal disputes, the guidelines state that its principles "can also be used to manage external con-

flict with customers, clients, and the public" (6).

8. The term "fourth party" was introduced by Ethan Katsh and Janet Rifkin in *Online Dispute Resolution: Resolving Conflicts in Cyberspace* (San Francisco, CA: Jossey-Bass, 2001), 93.

9. Susan Nauss Exon, "Ethics and Online Dispute Resolution: From Evolution to Revolution," *Ohio State Journal on Dispute Resolution* 32, no. 4 (2017): 609, 623.

10. Ibid., 659–64. See also ICANN, "Online Dispute Resolution: Standards of Practice," July 2009, https://www.icann.org/ombudsman/ odr-standards-of-practice-en.pdf; and the discussion of EU Regulation on Online Dispute Resolution for Consumer Disputes, "Directive 2013/11/EU, of the European Parliament and of the Council of 21 May 2013 on Alternative Dispute Resolution for Consumer Disputes and Amending Regulation," in Exon, "Ethics and Online Dispute Resolution."

11. Standard I of the "Model Standards of Conduct for Mediators" states that mediations shall be conducted on the basis of "the principle of party self-determination." American Bar Association, American Arbitration Association, and Association for Conflict Resolution, "Model Standards of Conduct for Mediators," September 2005, Standard I.A, https://www.americanbar.org/content/dam/ aba/migrated/2011_build/dispute_resolution/ model_standards_conduct_april2007.pdf.

12. Ibid.

13. Robert A. Baruch Bush and Joseph P. Folger, *The Promise of Mediation: Responding to Conflict Through Empowerment and Recognition* (San Francisco, CA: Jossey-Bass, 1994).

14. See, for example, Robert A. Baruch Bush, "A Study of Ethical Dilemmas and Policy Implications," *Journal of Dispute Resolution* 1994, no. 1 (1994): 1–56; and Nancy A. Welsh, "The Thinning Vision of Self-Determination

in Court-Connected Mediation: The Inevitable Price of Institutionalization?" *Harvard Negotiation Law Review* 6, no. 1 (2001): 1–96.

15. American Bar Association, American Arbitration Association, and Association for Conflict Resolution, "Model Standards of Conduct for Mediators."

16. Exon, "Ethics and Online Dispute Resolution," 649.

17. Society of Professionals in Dispute Resolution, "Designing Integrated Conflict Management Systems," 16–17.

18. International Ombudsman Association, "IOA Best Practices: A Supplement to IOA's Standards of Practice," October 13, 2009, https://www.ombudsassociation.org/assets/docs/IOA_Best_Practices_Version3_101309_0.pdf.

19. American Bar Association, American Arbitration Association, and Association for Conflict Resolution, "Model Standards of Conduct for Mediators."

20. Phyllis Bernard and Bryant Garth, eds., *Dispute Resolution Ethics: A Comprehensive Guide* (Washington, DC: American Bar Association, 2002), 267. These standards were developed by a broad-based group of representatives from the ABA Section of Family Law, the Association of Family and Conciliation Courts, the Academy of Family Mediators, and others (271–73).

21. Society of Professionals in Dispute Resolution, "Designing Integrated Conflict Management Systems," 17.

22. Menkel-Meadow, "Are There Systemic Ethics Issues in Dispute System Design?," 230.

23. As discussed in Chapter 3, there are also nonbinding arbitration variants.

24. For the argument that all standard contract defenses should apply in disputes over voluntary consent to adhesive and forced arbitration clauses, focusing on duress, see Stephen J. Ware, "Employment Arbitration and Voluntary Consent," *Hofstra Law Review* 25, no. 1

(1996): 83. For the suggestion that, in addition to duress and unconscionability, a public policy defense can be used in situations in which "Congress or a state legislature has created statutory rights benefiting one party . . . [that] arguably limit the ability to arbitrate disputes relating to those rights," see Sharona Hoffman, "Mandatory Arbitration: Alternative Dispute Resolution or Coercive Dispute Suppression?," *Berkeley Journal of Employment and Labor Law* 17 (1996): 149.

25. For the argument that a predispute arbitration agreement is a contract, see Ware, "Employment Arbitration and Voluntary Consent," 106; and Samuel Estreicher, "Predispute Agreements to Arbitrate Statutory Employment Claims," *New York University Law Review* 72 (December 1997): 1344.

26. Internal mediation systems are less controversial than binding arbitration systems, because the court option is still available, although these systems can also raise ethical issues.

27. *Hooters of Am., Inc. v. Phillips*, 173 F.3d 933, 941 (4th Cir. 1999), held that the employment arbitration agreement was voidable by the employee if the purported arbitrators are other Hooters managers. *Green Tree Finance Corp.-Ala. v. Randolph*, 531 U.S. 79, 91–92 (2000), provides that a party subject to mandatory arbitration may be able to avoid the process upon a showing that arbitration would be prohibitively expensive.

28. Richard A. Bales, "The Employment Due Process Protocol at Ten: Twenty Unresolved Issues, and a Focus on Conflicts of Interest," *Ohio State Journal on Dispute Resolution* 21 no. 1 (2005): 165. The Due Process Protocol for Mediation and Arbitration of Statutory Disputes Arising out of the Employment Relationship is posted on the website of the convening organization for the group that developed it, the American Arbitration Asso-

ciation. See American Arbitration Association, "Employment Due Process Protocol," May 9, 1995, https://www.adr.org/sites/default/files/document_repository/Employment%20Due%20Process%20Protocol_0.pdf. For a detailed analysis, see John T. Dunlop and Arnold M. Zack, *Mediation and Arbitration of Employment Disputes* (San Francisco, CA: Jossey-Bass, 1997).

29. Engalla v. Permanente Medical Group, Inc., 64 Cal. Rptr. 2d 843 (Cal. 1997).

30. For a description of the program as first implemented, see Kaiser Permanente Office of the Independent Administrator, "First Annual Report of the Office of the Independent Administrator of the Kaiser Foundation Health Plan, Inc. Mandatory Arbitration System for Disputes with Health Plan Members, March 29, 1999–March 28, 2000," http://www.oia-kaiserarb.com/pdfs/annrptyr1.pdf (accessed November 28, 2019). The program's current rules reflect the evolution of the program as well as intervening changes to arbitration law and regulation. Kaiser Permanente Office of the Independent Administrator, "Rules for Kaiser Permanente Member Arbitrations," January 1, 2019, http://oia-kaiserarb.com/pdfs/Rules.pdf. The Kaiser case is discussed in more detail in Chapter 4 and Chapter 14.

31. Tracy Lien, "Uber Stops Requiring Sexual Misconduct Victims to Quietly Use Arbitration Instead of Suing," *Los Angeles Times*, May 15, 2018, http://www.latimes.com/business/technology/la-fi-tn-uber-misconduct-policy-20180515-story.html. For how Uber previously enforced coercive and forced arbitration, see Neil Eddington, "Uber Hitches a Ride with Arbitration: How Pro-arbitration Attitudes and Uber Will Prevail in California and the Ninth Circuit," *Pepperdine Dispute Resolution Law Journal* 17, no. 2 (2017): 203–32.

32. International Institute for Conflict Prevention and Resolution, "Principles for ADR Provider Organizations."

33. Standard III of the "Model Standards of Practice for Family and Divorce Mediation" provides that a mediator may invite additional persons into the confidential mediation if the mediator feels such person is necessary to prevent violence. See Bernard and Garth, *Dispute Resolution Ethics*.

34. "ADR Local Rules" for the U.S. District Court for the Northern District of California lists examples, providing statutory and case law citations from other jurisdictions, including "threats of death or substantial bodily injury (see Or. Rev. Stat. § 36.220(6)); use of mediation to commit a felony (see Colo. Rev. Stat. § 13-22-307); right to effective cross examination in a quasi-criminal proceeding (see *Rinaker v. Superior Court*, 62 Cal. App. 4th 155 (3d Dist. 1998); lawyer duty to report misconduct (see *In re Waller*, 573 A.2d 780 (D.C. App. 1990); need to prevent manifest injustice (see Ohio Rev. Code, § 2317.023(c)(4); see also Uniform Mediation Act § 6 (2001). . . . See amended opinion in *Olam v. Congress Mortgage Co.*, 68 F.Supp. 2d 1110 (N.D. Cal. 1999)." U.S. District Court–Northern District of California, "ADR Local Rules," May 1, 2018, Rule 6-12, http://www.cand.uscourts.gov/localrules/ADR. For an overview and analysis of case law on these issues, see James R. Coben and Peter N. Thompson, "Disputing Irony: A Systematic Look at Litigation About Mediation," *Harvard Negotiation Law Review* 11 (2006): 43.

35. The Northern District of California's ADR Local Rule 2-6 notes that Congress has mandated that the court's ADR programs be evaluated and directs "neutrals, counsel and clients" to "promptly respond to any inquiries or questionnaires from persons authorized by the Court to evaluate the programs." It promises that "sources of data" will not be identified to judges or in any report. See U.S. District Court–Northern District of California, "ADR Local Rules," Rule 2-6.

36. "Model Standards of Conduct for Mediators" states that mediators who are involved in teaching, research, or evaluation "should protect the anonymity of the parties and abide by their reasonable expectations regarding confidentiality." See American Bar Association, American Arbitration Association, and Association for Conflict Resolution, "Model Standards of Conduct for Mediators," Standard V.A.3.

37. International Ombudsman Association, "IOA Code of Ethics," January 2007, https://www.ombudsassociation.org/assets/IOA%20Code%20of%20Ethics.pdf.

38. For a description of situations in which ombuds employed by corporations requested specific arbitrators for certain cases and decided to represent employees themselves in company arbitrations, see Lisa B. Bingham, "Emerging Due Process Concerns in Employment Arbitration: A Look at Actual Cases," *Labor Law Journal* 47, no. 2 (1996): 108–26.

39. For a discussion of the history of case law on the ombuds privilege, as well as possible support through the Uniform Mediation Act, the Administrative Dispute Resolution Act, and other sources, see Charles L. Howard, *The Organizational Ombudsman: Origins, Roles, and Operations—a Legal Guide* (Chicago: American Bar Association, 2010), 220–77. See also Scott C. Van Soye, "Illusory Ethics: Legal Barriers to an Ombudsman's Compliance with Accepted Ethical Standards," *Pepperdine Dispute Resolution Law Journal* 8 (2007): 117–46.

40. For a broader discussion of ethics in ODR, see Jo DeMars et al., "Virtual Virtues: Ethical Considerations for an Online Dispute Resolution (ODR) Practice," *Dispute Resolution Magazine*, Fall 2010, pp. 6–10; and Exon, "Ethics and Online Dispute Resolution."

41. International Institute for Conflict Prevention and Resolution, "Principles for ADR Provider Organizations."

42. It is very rare for the budget not to be an issue, but in creating the September 11th Victim Compensation Fund, Congress authorized a compensation fund for victims without setting a limit on the ultimate payout. This rare, and perhaps unique, example is discussed in Chapter 8.

43. The employment protocol provides the following: "6. Compensation of the Mediator and Arbitrator. Impartiality is best assured by the parties sharing the fees and expenses of the mediator and arbitrator. In cases where the economic condition of a party does not permit equal sharing, the parties should make mutually acceptable arrangements to achieve that goal if at all possible. In the absence of such agreement, the arbitrator should determine allocation of fees. The designating agency, by negotiating the parties share of costs and collecting such fees, might be able to reduce the bias potential of disparate contributions by forwarding payment to the mediator and/or arbitrator without disclosing the parties' share therein." American Arbitration Association, "Employment Due Process Protocol," 4.

44. American Bar Association, American Arbitration Association, and Association for Conflict Resolution, "Model Standards of Conduct for Mediators," Standard VIII.B.2.

45. American Bar Association, "Reporter's Notes," September 9, 2005, pp. 20–21, https://www.americanbar.org/content/dam/aba/migrated/2011_build/dispute_resolution/mscm_reporternotes.pdf.

46. "The amount or nature of a mediator's fee must not be made contingent on the outcome of the mediation." Judicial Council of California, "California Rules of Court," Rule 3.859(c), https://www.courts.ca.gov/cms/rules/index.cfm?title=three&linkid=rule3_859 (accessed October 3, 2019).

47. American Bar Association, "The Code of Ethics for Arbitrators in Commercial Disputes," February 9, 2004, p. 10, http://www.americanbar.org/content/dam/aba/migrated/dispute/commercial_disputes.pdf.

48. For the rising use of arbitration clauses in general consumer transactions and the finding that 30 percent of businesses surveyed were using arbitration clauses, see Linda J. Demain and Deborah R. Hensler, "'Volunteering' to Arbitrate Through Predispute Arbitration Clauses: The Average Consumer's Experience," *Law and Contemporary Problems* 67 (Winter 2004): 55, 64; and Cliff Palefsky, "Mandatory Binding Arbitration: Is It Fair and Voluntary?," September 15, 2009, https://www.ca-employment-lawyers .com/Articles/MandatoryArbitrationTaskForce .NELA.Palefksy.pdf. Since 2004, the use of such clauses in consumer transactions has increased. See also Chapter 12. For testimony that the American Arbitration Association marketed its arbitration services to employers by referring to new civil rights antidiscrimination statutes and stated "that [it] could limit discovery, eliminate punitive damages and keep all proceedings off limits to the public and the press," see Palefsky, "Mandatory Binding Arbitration," 3.

49. See, generally, Chapter 12. For the finding that employers that arbitrate more than once in the case sample have statistically significantly higher win rates in employment arbitration, see Lisa B. Bingham, "Employment Arbitration: The Repeat Player Effect," *Employee Rights and Employment Policy Journal* 1 (1997): 189. See also David Horton and Andrea Cann Chandrasekher, "After the Revolution: An Empirical Study of Consumer Arbitration," *Georgetown Law Journal* 104 (2015): 57–124; and David Horton and Andrea Cann Chandrasekher, "Employment Arbitration after the Revolution," *DePaul Law Review* 65 (2016): 457–96.

50. International Institute for Conflict Prevention and Resolution, "Principles for ADR Provider Organizations." In 2002, California enacted significant disclosure requirements for consumer and employment disputes submitted to arbitration under the supervision of a private arbitration company. The statute, subsequently revised, requires private arbitration companies,

with limited exceptions, to make available online at least quarterly substantial data on consumer cases they have administered. The required information includes whether arbitration was demanded pursuant to a predispute arbitration clause and, if so, whether that clause designated the administering private arbitration company. It also requires disclosure of the type of dispute, names of the nonconsumer parties (if corporations or other business entities), the prevailing party, case disposition, arbitrator fees and how they were allocated, and the number of times the nonconsumer party has been a party in arbitrations or mediations administered by the reporting private provider. California Code of Civil Procedure § 1281.96 (2014).

51. "Firm Agrees to End Role in Arbitrating Card Debt," *New York Times*, July 20, 2009, p. B8.

52. Trans Atlantic Consumer Dialogue, "Alternative Dispute Resolution in the Context of Electronic Commerce," February 2000, https:// tacd.org/wp-content/uploads/2013/09/TACD -ECOM-12-00-Alternative-Dispute-Resolution -in-the-Context-of-Electronic-Commerce.pdf.

53. The value of an ADR option is often contrasted with the other available process options, particularly the court system. The cost of litigation continues to increase, and as the availability of legal aid declines, the court option may also be out of reach for many claimants in the United States.

54. An exception is the use of non-neutral arbitrators selected by one party on some three-person arbitration panels. This practice has been common in the United States but not internationally. Changes in the 2004 Code of Ethics for Arbitrators in Commercial Disputes create a presumption in favor of neutrality for all arbitrators and provide a specialized subset of rules for cases in which parties choose to retain the older model. See American Bar Association, "The Code of Ethics for Arbitrators

in Commercial Disputes," Canons IX and X; and Bruce Meyerson and John M. Townsend, "Revised Code of Ethics for Commercial Arbitrators Explained," *Dispute Resolution Journal* 59, no. 1 (2004): 10–17. The Code of Professional Responsibility for Arbitrators of Labor-Management Disputes states that the code "does not apply to partisan representatives on tripartite boards." National Academy of Arbitrators, American Arbitration Association, and Federal Mediation and Conciliation Service, "Code of Professional Responsibility for Arbitrators of Labor-Management Disputes," September 2007, p. 4, https://www.adr.org/sites/default/files/document_repository/Code%20of%20Professional%20Responsibility%20for%20Arbitrators%20of%20Labor-Management%20Disputes_0.pdf.

55. American Bar Association, American Arbitration Association, and Association for Conflict Resolution, "Model Standards of Conduct for Mediators," Standard II.A.

56. American Bar Association, "The Code of Ethics for Arbitrators in Commercial Disputes," 6.

57. Ibid., 3. Parties in some cases may knowingly choose a mediator with some party affiliation. National Conference of Commissioners on Uniform State Laws, "Uniform Mediation Act," August 2001, section 9(a), (g), http://www.mediate.com/articles/umafinalstyled.cfm.

58. American Bar Association, "The Code of Ethics for Arbitrators in Commercial Disputes," 5.

59. See Bingham, "Emerging Due Process Concerns in Employment Arbitration," 116–17. See also Van Soye, "Illusory Ethics."

60. International Ombudsman Association, "IOA Code of Ethics."

61. International Ombudsman Association, "IOA Best Practices," 2.

62. Cathy A. Costantino, "Second Generation Organizational Conflict Management Systems Design: A Practitioner's Perspective on Emerging Issues," *Harvard Negotiation Law Review* 14 (Winter 2009): 81, 90–92.

63. On universality versus particularity, see Menkel-Meadow, "Are There Systemic Ethics Issues in Dispute System Design?," 201–202, 212.

64. Society of Professionals in Dispute Resolution, "Designing Integrated Conflict Management Systems," 17.

65. See Standard II.A.4 of the "Model Standards of Practice for Family and Divorce Mediation," in Bernard and Garth, *Dispute Resolution Ethics*.

66. Standard VIII.B in ibid. It adds that such mediators should "[advise] the participants, in appropriate cases, that they can seek the advice of religious figures, elders or other significant persons in their community whose opinions they value." Standard III.A.5 in ibid.

67. Jacqueline Nolan-Haley, Ellen E. Deason, and Mariana Hernandez-Crespo Gonstead, *Global Issues in Mediation* (St. Paul, MN: West Academic, 2019), 157–180.

68. "European Code of Conduct for Mediators," http://ec.europa.eu/civiljustice/adr/adr_ec_code_conduct_en.pdf (accessed May 23, 2019).

69. Lukasz Rozdeiczer and Alejandro Alvarez de la Campa, *Alternative Dispute Resolution Manual: Implementing Commercial Mediation* (Washington, DC: World Bank, 2006), http://documents.worldbank.org/curated/en/922161468339057329/pdf/384810ADR1Manu1l1Mediation01PUBLIC1.pdf.

70. International Mediation Institute, "Criteria for Approving Programs to Qualify Mediators for IMI Inter-cultural Certification," https://www.imimediation.org/wp-content/uploads/2018/04/imi-intercultural-criteria-and-cfa-final-draft-modified-.pdf (accessed May 23, 2019).

71. Rozdeiczer and Alvarez de la Campa, *Alternative Dispute Resolution Manual*, 7–8.

72. Menkel-Meadow, "Are There Systemic Ethics Issues in Dispute System Design?," 211–12; Costantino, "Second Generation Organizational Conflict Management Systems Design," 82–86, 98.

73. See Cathy A. Costantino and Christina Sickles Merchant, *Designing Conflict Management Systems: A Guide to Creating Productive and Healthy Organizations* (San Francisco, CA: Jossey-Bass, 1996), chap. 5.

74. See, generally, Carrie Menkel-Meadow, "Ethics in ADR: The Many 'C's' of Professional Responsibility and Dispute Resolution," *Fordham Urban Law Journal* 28 (2001): 979–90. In response to the recommendations of the ABA Ethics 2000 Commission, the ABA in 2002 added a new provision: Model Rule 2.4 Lawyer Serving as Third Party Neutral. At the same time, the ABA expanded Model Rule 1.12, previously addressing conflicts of interest for former judges, to also cover arbitrators, mediators, and other third-party neutrals. American Bar Association, *Model Rules of Professional Conduct* (Chicago: American Bar Association, 2002), Rules 1.12, 2.4.

75. Note that under the ABA model rules, lawyers, in their role as counselors and advisors, may refer not only to the law but also to "moral, economic, social and political factors." See American Bar Association, *Model Rules of Professional Conduct*, Rule 2.1.

76. Menkel-Meadow, "Are There Systemic Ethics Issues in Dispute System Design?," 204–6, 229–30.

77. For a discussion of bottom-up and top-down process choices, see, for example, Stephanie E. Smith, "Comment: Trends and Challenges in Bringing Together ADR and Rule of Law," *Journal of Dispute Resolution* 2011, no. 1 (2011): 189, 190–91; Andrea Kupfer Schneider, "The Intersection of Dispute Systems Design and Transitional Justice," *Harvard Negotiation Law Review* 14 (Winter 2009): 289, 297–302; and Menkel-Meadow, "Are There Systemic Ethics Issues in Dispute System Design?," 209, 229–30.

78. Howard Gadlin, "Bargaining in the Shadow of Management: Integrated Conflict Management Systems," in *The Handbook of Dispute Resolution*, ed. Michael L. Moffitt and Robert C. Bordone (San Francisco, CA: Jossey-Bass, 2005), 371, 380–83.

79. Menkel-Meadow, "Are There Systemic Ethics Issues in Dispute System Design?," 204; Costantino, "Second Generation Organizational Conflict Management Systems Design," 98.

80. Menkel-Meadow, "Are There Systemic Ethics Issues in Dispute System Design?," 221, 229. See, generally, Mary B. Anderson, *Do No Harm: How Aid Can Support Peace—or War* (Boulder, CO: Lynne Rienner, 1999).

Chapter 7

1. For a more complete discussion of some of these perspectives, see Robert A. Baruch Bush, "Mediation and Adjudication, Dispute Resolution and Ideology: An Imaginary Conversation," *Journal of Contemporary Legal Issues* 3, no. 1 (1989): 1–36.

2. For further discussion of formal and informal justice, see Chapter 1; and Carrie Menkel-Meadow, "Regulation of Dispute Resolution in the United States of America: From the Formal to the Informal to the 'Semi-formal,'" in *Regulating Dispute Resolution: ADR and Access to Justice at the Crossroads*, ed. Felix Steffek and Hannes Unberath (Oxford: Hart, 2013), 419–54. For a discussion of informal justice values as including party empowerment and participation, self-determination, consent, tailored solutions, nonmonetized outcomes and solutions, future-oriented problem-solving (not just past-oriented), confidentiality, reduction of elite and professional decision makers' involvement, reorientation of the parties to each

other, efficiency, and greater legitimacy and
compliance, see Menkel-Meadow, "Regulation
of Dispute Resolution in the United States of
America," 430–34.

3. For a discussion of the evolution of
Anglo-American dispute resolution from
violence and self-help to trial by ordeal and by
combat to our current secular trials with and
without juries, see Carrie Menkel-Meadow, "Is
the Adversary System Really Dead? Dilemmas
of Legal Ethics as Legal Institutions and Roles
Evolve," in *Current Legal Problems*, vol. 57, ed.
Jane Holder, Colm O'Cinneide, and Michael
Freeman (Oxford: Oxford University Press,
2004), 85–99.

4. Lawrence M. Friedman, *American Law
in the 20th Century* (New Haven, CT: Yale
University Press, 2002), 251. Friedman also describes the federal procedural rules in that era
as "a complex and ramshackle mess" (252).

5. Notice pleading enabled plaintiffs who
lacked sophisticated counsel to have their
claims heard. But it is not only the creation of
procedural rules that affects claimants' access
to the courts but also the courts' interpretation
of those rules. Nancy Welsh analyzed the likely
adverse impact of the U.S. Supreme Court's
opinions in *Ashcroft v. Iqbal* and *Bell Atlantic
Corp. v Twombly*. She proposed, as a system
design response, reviving the summary jury
trial process to address certain civil rights
claims. Nancy A. Welsh, "I Could Have Been a
Contender: Summary Jury Trial as a Means to
Overcome Iqbal's Negative Effects upon Pre-
litigation Communication, Negotiation and
Early, Consensual Dispute Resolution," *Penn
State Law Review* 114 (2010): 1149–89.

6. For a description of the drafters' and
the courts' hopes that the 1938 rule revisions
would promote just outcomes at trial and
by settlement by decreasing gamesmanship,
adversariness, cost, and delay, see, for example,
Wayne D. Brazil, "The Adversary Character

of Civil Discovery: A Critique and Proposals
for Change," *Vanderbilt Law Review* 31 (1978):
1298–303.

7. Friedman, *American Law*, 254–55.

8. Brazil, "The Adversary Character." Brazil
describes how "adversary pressures and competitive economic impulses inevitably work to
impair significantly, if not to frustrate com-
pletely, the attainment of the discovery system's
primary objectives" (1303).

9. Frank E. A. Sander, "Varieties of Dispute
Processing," in *The Pound Conference: Perspectives on Justice in the Future*, ed. A. Leo Levin
and Russell R. Wheeler (St. Paul, MN: West,
1979), 65–87.

10. Donna Stienstra, "ADR in the Federal
District Courts: An Initial Report," Federal Judicial Center, November 16, 2011, p. 5, https://www
.fjc.gov/sites/default/files/2012/ADR2011.pdf.

11. National Center for State Courts, "Comparing State Courts," http://www.ncsc.org/
information-and-resources/comparing-state
-courts.aspx (accessed May 30, 2019).

12. James Michel, "Alternative Dispute
Resolution and the Rule of Law in International
Development Cooperation," *Journal of Dispute
Resolution* 2011, no. 1 (2011): 36–41.

13. For a discussion of restorative and
retributive justice, see Chapter 1.

14. For a discussion of the evolution of
problem-solving courts, see Greg Berman
and John Feinblatt, *Good Courts—the Case for
Problem-Solving Justice* (New York: New Press,
2005), 38–58.

15. Michael C. Dorf and Charles F. Sabel,
"Drug Treatment Courts and Emergent Experimentalist Government," *Vanderbilt Law Review*
53 (2000): 843–55; Berman and Feinblatt, *Good
Courts*, 9.

16. As of June 2015, there were over 4,400
problem-solving courts in the United States
(over 3,000 drug courts and over 1,300 other
specialized courts). See National Institute of

Justice, "Drug Courts," August 23, 2018, https://www.nij.gov/topics/courts/drug-courts/pages/welcome.aspx; and National Institute of Justice, "Specialized Courts," May 30, 2018, https://www.nij.gov/topics/courts/pages/specialized-courts.aspx.

17. An earlier version of this case study appeared in Stephanie Smith and Janet Martinez, "Analytic Framework for Dispute Systems Design," *Harvard Negotiation Law Review* 14 (Winter 2009): 123–69.

18. Civil Justice Reform Act, Pub. L. No. 101-650, § 104, 104 Stat 5089, 5097 (1990) (before 1991 amendment).

19. See Chapter 3 and U.S. District Court–Northern District of California, "Alternative Dispute Resolution," https://www.cand.uscourts.gov/adr (accessed February 23, 2019).

20. Joshua D. Rosenberg and H. Jay Folberg, "Alternative Dispute Resolution: An Empirical Analysis," *Stanford Law Review* 46 (1994): 1487–551.

21. For an in-depth discussion of early neutral evaluation, including ethical issues, see Wayne D. Brazil, *Early Neutral Evaluation* (Chicago: American Bar Association, 2012).

22. Brazil cited studies showing that "between twenty percent and thirty-five percent of civil cases leave the federal system without any action by or direct contact with a judge" and nearly three-quarters leave "before a judge holds a pretrial conference." Wayne D. Brazil, "Should Court-Sponsored ADR Survive?," *Ohio State Journal on Dispute Resolution* (2006): 244–45.

23. Ibid.

24. Civil Justice Reform Act, § 478.

25. As a demonstration district under the Civil Justice Reform Act, the Northern District of California court was able to obtain additional resources to hire several staff.

26. The pilot format featured five volunteer judges and most, but not all, civil case categories. For a discussion of the benefits of starting with a pilot program, see Cathy A. Costantino and Christina Sickles Merchant, *Designing Conflict Management Systems: A Guide to Creating Productive and Healthy Organizations* (San Francisco, CA: Jossey-Bass, 1996), 152–67.

27. As an alternative to requesting a court-based ADR option, parties were free to retain a private ADR provider of their choosing.

28. Attorneys were required to participate; clients were encouraged to do so (though they rarely did).

29. A purely voluntary system was avoided because of the perceived likelihood of low use as a result of advice from lawyers, then largely untrained and unaccustomed to these procedures, who might be concerned about possible loss of income if cases resolved earlier by use of ADR.

30. For a more detailed discussion of five different staffing models and their strengths and weaknesses, see Wayne D. Brazil, "Comparing Structures for the Delivery of ADR Services by Courts: Critical Values and Concerns," *Ohio State Journal on Dispute Resolution* 14 (1999): 715–33. Note that some federal district courts provide no ADR options beyond use of judges, particularly magistrate judges, for court-sponsored settlement assistance.

31. With Civil Justice Reform Act funds, the court hired three new full-time staff: two attorneys and an administrative assistant. Additional critical judicial and court staff supported the ADR program. Staff in the clerk's office helped administer arbitration and ENE.

32. The mediator or evaluator volunteers up to two hours of preparation time and four hours of services. After that time, the neutral may continue to volunteer or charge a market rate or other rate agreed to by the parties if they choose to continue the process. See U.S. District Court–Northern District of California, "ADR Local Rules," ADR L.R. 5-3(b) and 6-3(c), May 1, 2018, https://www.cand.uscourts.gov/localrules/ADR.

33. Initially only attorneys could serve as ADR neutrals in the court's programs, though later other trained professionals served as mediators. See U.S. District Court–Northern District of California, "ADR Local Rules," 2-5(b)(3).

34. For a more in-depth discussion on the "competition" between court ADR and private sector ADR providers, see Brazil, "Should Court-Sponsored ADR Survive?," 271–77.

35. See Donna Stienstra, Molly Johnson, and Patricia Lombard, "Report to the Judicial Conference Committee on Court Administration and Case Management: A Study of the Five Demonstration Programs Established Under the Civil Justice Report Act of 1990," January 24, 1997, p. 192, https://www.fjc.gov/sites/default/files/2012/0024.pdf.

36. Brazil, "Comparing Structures for the Delivery of ADR Services by Courts," 721n6.

37. Superior Court of California, "Multi-option ADR Project: Evaluation Report, July 2007–July 2008," January 2009, p. 38, https://www.sanmateocourt.org/documents/adr/2007_2008_evaluation_report.pdf.

38. Sheila Purcell, personal communication, March 3, 2018.

39. Sheila Purcell, "Growing Mediation in Our Courts: Why and How One Court Made the Journey," California Courts Review 12 (Spring 2007): 12–19.

40. Purcell, personal communication.

41. Sheila Purcell and Monica Rands-Preuss, personal communications, October 14, 2011, and January 23, 2013.

42. See, for example, Nancy Ver Steegh, Gabrielle Davis, and Loretta Frederick, "Look Before You Leap: Court System Triage of Family Law Cases Involving Intimate Partner Violence," Marquette Law Review 95 (2012): 955–68.

43. Superior Court of California, "The Multi-option ADR Project," 39; Purcell and Rands-Preuss, personal communications.

44. Superior Court of California, "The Multi-option ADR Project," 42–48.

45. Berman and Feinblatt, Good Courts, 76–78.

46. See the Center for Court Innovation's website, at https://www.courtinnovation.org.

47. Greg Berman and John Feinblatt, "Problem-Solving Courts: A Brief Primer," Law and Policy 23, no. 2 (2001): 127. For history and evaluation of the Midtown Community Court, see Michele Sviridoff et al., Dispensing Justice Locally: The Implementation and Effects of the Midtown Community Court (Amsterdam: Harwood Academic, 2000).

48. Greg Berman and Aubrey Fox, "Justice in Red Hook," Justice System Journal 26 (2005): 79–89.

49. Ibid., 80.

50. Ibid., 81–82.

51. Ibid., 79.

52. Ibid.

53. The facility includes the Housing Resource Center, which offers mediation services for neighbor and family disputes not involving domestic violence. Cynthia G. Lee et al., A Community Court Grows in Brooklyn—a Final Report: A Comprehensive Evaluation of the Red Hook Community Justice Center (Williamsburg, VA: National Center for State Courts, 2013), 42.

54. Berman and Fox, "Justice in Red Hook," 82–84.

55. Lee et al., A Community Court Grows in Brooklyn, 153–55, 174–77.

56. Ibid., 167, 178.

57. See, generally, Jean R. Sternlight, "Is Alternative Dispute Resolution Consistent with the Rule of Law? Lessons from Abroad," DePaul Law Review 56 (2007): 569–84. Sternlight discusses the history of ADR as part of international aid and analyzes the arguments for and against ADR's compatibility with rule of law. See also Michel, "Alternative Dispute Resolution and the Rule of Law." Michel discusses development funders' support for ADR as part of rule of law and governance reform efforts, particularly in Latin America.

58. Mariana Hernandez Crespo critiques the top-down rule of law models used in Latin America and highlights the disconnect between the masses and the government, including courts. She proposes using DSD principles to create an integrated model, adapting and connecting the existing Casas de Justicia (based on the multidoor courthouse model) with the formal courts to advance participatory governance, citizen inclusion and empowerment, and rule of law. Mariana Hernandez Crespo, "From Noise to Music: The Potential of the Multi-door Courthouse (Casas de Justicia) Model to Advance Systemic Inclusion and Participation as a Foundation for Sustainable Rule of Law in Latin America," *Journal of Dispute Resolution* 2012, no. 2 (2012): 335–402.

59. See also Cynthia Alkon, "The Flawed U.S. Approach to Rule of Law Development," *Penn State Law Review* 117 (2013): 797–814. Alkon critiques the inclusion of rule of law as a standard part of development assistance and calls for thorough understanding of the political, social, economic, and security context before designing any rule of law program.

60. The Netherlands has been an exception. Nadja Alexander, ed., *Global Trends in Mediation*, 2nd ed. (Alphen aan den Rijn, Netherlands: Kluwer Law International, 2006), 7.

61. Ibid., 20–21.

62. Ibid., 20–24.

63. Ibid., 33. Alexander cites the Netherlands and Austria as examples. This difference in leadership has contributed to training models in civil law different from common law countries.

64. "Directive 2008/52/EC of the European Parliament and of the Council of 21 May 2008 on Certain Aspects of Mediation in Civil and Commercial Matters," *Official Journal of the European Union*, May 24, 2008, pp. L 136/3–L 136/8. For an overview of historical developments in Europe leading up to this directive,

see Jacqueline Nolan-Haley, "Evolving Paths to Justice: Assessing the EU Directive on Mediation," in *Proceedings of the Sixth Annual Conference on International Arbitration and Mediation* (Leiden, Netherlands: Brill-Nijhoff, 2012), 2–5.

65. "Directive 2008/52/EC of the European Parliament," L 136/6.

66. Ibid., L 136/4.

67. Those thirteen are Bulgaria, Croatia, Cyprus, Czech Republic, Estonia, Finland, Greece, Latvia, Lithuania, Luxembourg, Malta, Portugal, and Sweden. See Giuseppe De Palo et al., "'Rebooting' the Mediation Directive: Assessing the Limited Impact of Its Implementation and Proposing Measures to Increase the Number of Mediations in the EU," January 15, 2014, p. 6, http://www.europarl.europa.eu/thinktank/en/document.html?reference=IPOL-JURI_ET(2014)493042.

68. Loukas A. Mistelis, "ADR in England and Wales: A Successful Case of Public Private Partnership," in Alexander, *Global Trends in Mediation*, 151–52.

69. Ibid., 143–48.

70. Lord Woolf, *Access to Justice: Interim Report to the Lord Chancellor on the Civil Justice System in England and Wales* (London: Her Majesty's Stationery Office, 1995); Lord Woolf, *Access to Justice: Final Report to the Lord Chancellor on the Civil Justice System in England and Wales* (London: Her Majesty's Stationery Office, 1996); Supreme Court of England and Wales County Courts, "The Civil Procedure Rules, 1998," March 12, 2014, http://www.wipo.int/edocs/lexdocs/laws/en/gb/gb317en.pdf.

71. Mistelis, "ADR in England and Wales," 148.

72. Ibid., 149; see also the Civil Procedure Act 1997, at https://www.legislation.gov.uk/ukpga/1997/12/contents.

73. De Palo et al., "'Rebooting' the Mediation Directive," 67–68.

74. Hazel Genn, Shiva Riahi, and Katherine Pleming, "Regulation of Dispute Resolution in England and Wales: A Sceptical Analysis of Government and Judicial Promotion of Private Mediation," in *Regulating Dispute Resolution: ADR and Access to Justice at the Crossroads*, ed. Felix Steffek and Hannes Unberath (Oxford: Hart, 2013), 135, 153–54; Mistelis, "ADR in England and Wales," 165–71.

75. De Palo et al., "'Rebooting' the Mediation Directive," 65, 69–70. De Palo and colleagues note the role of the Civil Mediation Council, a membership organization for private mediation providers, in accreditation.

76. Ibid., 71.

77. Ibid., 39. Although, here, De Palo and colleagues note that mediation was used in certain sectors, such as labor, business-to-business disputes, and some other commercial disputes.

78. In 2000–2003, the average civil case was completed at the trial level in 3.5 years. A case involving appeals could expect to receive a final judgment in 10 years. Giuseppe De Palo and Luigi Cominelli, "Mediation in Italy: Waiting for the Big Bang," in Alexander, *Global Trends in Mediation*, 260–61.

79. Ibid., 262–63.

80. De Palo et al., "'Rebooting' the Mediation Directive," 39–40; Owen Bowcott, "Compulsory Mediation Angers Lawyers Working in Italy's Unwieldy Legal System," *The Guardian*, May 23, 2011, https://www.theguardian.com/law/butterworth-and-bowcott-on-law/2011/may/23/italian-lawyers-strike-mandatory-mediation.

81. De Palo et al., "'Rebooting' the Mediation Directive," 40.

82. Ibid., 42; Giuseppe De Palo and Leonardo D'Urso, "Achieving a Balanced Relationship Between Mediation and Judicial Proceedings," in *The Implementation of the Mediation Directive Workshop 29 November 2016:*

Compilation of In-Depth Analyses (Brussels: European Parliament, 2016), 13, https://docplayer.net/69471160-The-implementation-of-the-mediation-directive-workshop-29-november-2016.html.

83. De Palo et al., "'Rebooting' the Mediation Directive," 42.

84. De Palo and D'Urso, "Achieving a Balanced Relationship Between Mediation and Judicial Proceedings," 7.

85. European Commission, "Report from the Commission to the European Parliament, the Council and the European Economic and Social Committee on the Application of Directive 2008/52/EC of the European Parliament and of the Council on Certain Aspects of Mediation in Civil and Commercial Matters," August 26, 2016, https://eur-lex.europa.eu/legal-content/EN/TXT/?uri=COM%3A2016%3A542%3AFIN.

86. Giuseppe De Palo, "A Ten-Year-Long 'EU Mediation Paradox': When an EU Directive Needs to Be More . . . Directive," November 2018, pp. 1, 5–6, 8–9, http://www.europarl.europa.eu/RegData/etudes/BRIE/2018/608847/IPOL_BRI(2018)608847_EN.pdf.

87. This discussion of Bhutan draws on the experiences of two of the authors as we consulted with its courts in 2009 and 2010.

88. Pema Needup, "Traditional Dispute Resolution System in Bhutan," November 10, 2011, p. 2 (unpublished paper in authors' possession); Pema Needup, "Training and Consultation on ADR for Local Leaders: Taking Justice Closer to the People," 2012 (unpublished paper in authors' possession).

89. David Martinez, "Mediation Design in Bhutan," 2012, pp. 2–3, 6 (unpublished fieldwork research notes in authors' possession).

90. Needup, "Training and Consultation on ADR for Local Leaders."

91. Many commentators have expressed concerns that courts that prioritize the goal

of efficiency, in order to reduce caseloads, are inappropriately pressuring parties to settle and thereby undercutting the right to trial. This risk increases when a court mediator uses a coercive, evaluative mediation model. See, for example, Nancy A. Welsh, "The Thinning Vision of Self-Determination in Court-Connected Mediation: The Inevitable Price of Institutionalization?," *Harvard Negotiation Law Review* 6, no. 1 (2001): 1; and Brazil, "Should Court-Sponsored ADR Survive?," 266. For academic perspectives critiquing the propriety of ADR in the courts, see, e.g., Owen M. Fiss, "Against Settlement," *Yale Law Journal* 93, no. 6 (1984): 1073–92; Judith Resnik, "Managerial Judges," *Harvard Law Review* 96, no. 2 (1982): 374–448; Deborah R. Hensler, "Suppose It's Not True: Challenging Mediation Ideology," *Journal of Dispute Resolution* 2002, no. 1 (2002): 81–99; and Judith Resnik, "The Contingency of Openness in Courts: Changing the Experiences and Logics of the Public's Role in Court-Based ADR," *Nevada Law Journal* 15, no. 3 (2015): 1631–88.

92. Self-represented parties are also referred to as pro se or pro per litigants.

93. Magistrate judges continued to be available to hold settlement conferences in cases with self-represented parties, in appropriate cases.

94. Stienstra, "ADR in the Federal District Courts," 7–9. The Northern District of California court recommends that self-represented parties participate in settlement conferences with magistrate judges but does not bar them from participation in mediation or ENE in appropriate circumstances. U.S. District Court–Northern District of California, "Alternative Dispute Resolution Procedures Handbook," May 2018, p. 14, https://www.cand.uscourts .gov/adr/adr-handbook.

95. See Victoria Malkin, "Problem-Solving in Community Courts: Who Decides the

Problem?," in *Problem-Solving Courts: Justice for the Twenty-First Century*, ed. Paul Higgins and Mitchell B. Mackinem (Santa Barbara, CA: ABC-CLIO, 2009), 139–59.

96. For a discussion of therapeutic jurisprudence, its history, and its focus on the mental health impacts of legal actions, see Bruce J. Winick, "Therapeutic Jurisprudence and Problem Solving Courts," *Fordham Urban Law Journal* 30, no. 3 (2003): 1055–90. For more discussion of the varieties of justice, see Chapter 1.

97. For more information on problem-solving courts, see the website of the National Center for State Courts, at https://www.ncsc .org/Topics/Alternative-Dockets/Problem -Solving-Courts/Home.aspx and https://www .ncsc.org/Topics/Special-Jurisdiction.aspx; Tribal Law and Policy Institute, "Tribal Healing to Wellness Courts: The Key Components," April 2003, https://www.ncjrs.gov/pdffiles1/ bja/188154.pdf; Suzanne M. Strong, Ramona R. Rantala, and Tracey Kyckelhahn, "Census of Problem-Solving Courts, 2012," *Bureau of Justice Statistics Bulletin*, September 2016, https://www.bjs.gov/content/pub/pdf/cpsc12 .pdf; and Amy J. Cohen, "Trauma and the Welfare State: A Genealogy of Prostitution Courts in New York City," *Texas Law Review* 95, no. 5 (2017): 915–92. For a description of problem-solving court programs of the Center for Court Innovation, see its website, at https:// www.courtinnovation.org/programs. For information on opioid intervention courts, see Center for Court Innovation, "The 10 Essential Elements of Opioid Intervention Courts," 2019, https://www.courtinnovation.org/sites/ default/files/media/documents/2019-07/report _the10essentialelements_07092019.pdf.

98. Craig A. Marvinney, "Mediation in the United States Circuit Courts of Appeals: A Survey," *FDCC Quarterly* 64, no. 1 (Fall 2014): 53, 58.

99. Private sector innovation in ODR is discussed in Chapter 14.

100. Ethan Katsh and Orna Rabinovich-Einy, *Digital Justice: Technology and the Internet of Disputes* (New York: Oxford University Press, 2017), 160.

101. Ibid., 160–61.

102. Ibid., 159–62; Colin Rule and Mark Wilson, "Online Resolution and Citizen Empowerment: Property Tax Appeals in North America," in *Revolutionizing the Interaction Between State and Citizens Through Digital Communications*, ed. Sam B. Edwards III and Diogo Santos (Hershey, PA: Information Science Reference, 2015), 185–205.

103. In re NLO, Inc., 5 F.3d 154, 157–58 (6th Cir. 1993); Strandell v. Jackson County, 838 F.2d 884 (7th Cir. 1987). But see also In re Atlantic Pipe Corp., 304 F.3d 135 (1st Cir. 2002).

104. In re Atlantic Pipe Corp., 304 F.3d 135 (1st Cir. 2002).

105. Alternative Dispute Resolution Act of 1998, 28 U.S.C. § 651 (October 30, 1998).

106. See, for example, Foxgate Homeowners' Association v. Bramalea, 25 P.3d 1117 (Cal. 2001).

107. See Rinaker v. Superior Court, 62 Cal. App. 4th 155 (3d Dist. 1998). This case ruled mediation confidentiality is overridden when obtaining key evidence in a juvenile delinquency case.

108. For the roster of jurisdictions that have adopted the Uniform Mediation Act, see Uniform Law Commission, "2001 Mediation Act," https://www.uniformlaws.org/committees/community-home?CommunityKey=45565a5f-0c57-4bba-bbab-fc7de9a59110 (accessed May 30, 2019).

109. National Conference of Commissioners on Uniform State Laws, "Uniform Mediation Act," December 10, 2003, https://www.uniformlaws.org/HigherLogic/System/DownloadDocumentFile.ashx?DocumentFileKey=9b244b42-269c-769e-9f89-590ce048d0dd&forceDialog=0.

110. See, for example, "Model Standards of Practice for Family and Divorce Mediation, Standard IX," reprinted in Phyllis Bernard and Bryant Garth, eds., *Dispute Resolution Ethics: A Comprehensive Guide* (Washington, DC: American Bar Association, 2002), 269, appendix B. See also National Conference of Commissioners on Uniform State Laws, "Uniform Mediation Act" (2003), sec. 6.

111. See, for example, U.S. District Court–Northern District of California, "ADR Local Rules," 6-12(b)(4). For an overview of litigation about mediation, see James R. Coben and Peter N. Thompson, "Disputing Irony: A Systematic Look at Litigation About Mediation," *Harvard Negotiation Law Review* 11 (2006): 70; and Nancy A. Welsh, "The Current Transitional State of Court-Connected ADR," *Marquette Law Review* 95 (2012): 875–76. Welsh cites cases in which attorneys have attempted to use mediation confidentiality and privilege to shield themselves from claims of malpractice. In the case of *Cassel v. Superior Court*, 51 Cal. 4th 113 (2011), the court preserved confidentiality, thereby shielding an attorney from a claim of malpractice during a mediation and leading to an effort to change California law. See California Law Revision Commission, "Relationship Between Mediation Confidentiality and Attorney Malpractice and Other Misconduct," December 2017, http://www.clrc.ca.gov/pub/Printed-Reports/RECpp-K402.pdf.

112. For more in-depth discussion of concerns regarding the changed role of judges in problem-solving courts, see Berman and Feinblatt, *Good Courts*, chap. 4; and Malkin, "Problem-Solving in Community Courts."

113. Robin Steinberg and Skylar Albertson, "Broken Windows Policing and Community Courts: An Unholy Alliance," *Cardozo Law*

Review 37 (2016): 995–1024; Berman and Feinblatt, *Good Courts*, 109–12.

114. Berman and Feinblatt, *Good Courts*, 49; Lee et al., *A Community Court Grows in Brooklyn*, 2, 5–6.

115. Steinberg and Albertson, "Broken Windows Policing and Community Courts," 997–98. As an alternative to community courts, Steinberg and Albertson advocate for "holistic defense," in which the defense counsel, not the court, are the catalysts and conduits advising and connecting their clients to social services, education, or other needed community connection and assistance.

116. For other examples of the impacts of budget cuts on court ADR programs in this period, see Donna Shestowsky, "The Psychology of Procedural Preference: How Litigants Evaluate Legal Procedures Ex Ante," *Iowa Law Review* 99 (2014): 640.

117. Monica Rands-Preuss, personal communication, February 9, 2015.

118. See U.S. District Court–Northern District of California, "ADR Program Report: Fiscal Year 2018," 1, https://www.cand.uscourts.gov/adr/annualreports (accessed May 30, 2019).

119. In the design phase alone, the Red Hook initiative received funds from the U.S. Department of Justice, the New York City Housing Authority, and private nonprofit funders such as the Schubert Foundation and the Scherman Foundation. Lee et al., *A Community Court Grows in Brooklyn*, 26.

120. For a good overview of court ADR program evaluations, see Deborah Thompson Eisenberg, "What We Know and Need to Know About Court-Annexed Dispute Resolution," *South Carolina Law Review* 67 (2016): 245–65. Also see Chapter 5; Roselle L. Wissler, "The Effectiveness of Court-Connected Dispute Resolution in Civil Cases," *Conflict Resolution Quarterly* 22, nos. 1–2 (2004): 55–72; Heather

Anderson and Ron Pi, *Evaluation of the Early Mediation Pilot Programs* (San Francisco, CA: Judicial Council of California, 2004), 61–64; and James S. Kakalik et al., *Just, Speedy, and Inexpensive? An Evaluation of Judicial Case Management Under the Civil Justice Reform Act* (Santa Monica, CA: RAND, 1997). Good sources for evaluations of court programs in the United States include the National Center for State Courts (https://www.ncsc.org), the Federal Judicial Center (https://www.fjc.gov), and the Resolution Systems Institute (https://www.aboutrsi.org). For evaluations of court mediation programs in ten countries, including survey research on mandatory versus voluntary programs, see Shahla F. Ali, *Court Mediation Reform: Efficiency, Confidence and Perceptions of Justice* (Cheltenham, UK: Edward Elgar, 2018).

121. See, e.g., John Lande, "Commentary: Focusing on Program Design Issues in Future Research on Court-Connected Mediation," *Conflict Resolution Quarterly* 22, nos. 1–2 (2004): 89–100; Bobbi McAdoo, Nancy A. Welsh, and Roselle L. Wissler, "Institutionalization: What Do Empirical Studies Tell Us About Court Mediation?," *Dispute Resolution Magazine* 9 (Winter 2003): 8–10; Bobbi McAdoo and Nancy A. Welsh, "Look Before You Leap and Keep on Looking: Lessons from the Institutionalization of Court-Connected Mediation," *Nevada Law Journal* 5 (2004–2005): 399–421.

122. For instance, an earlier ENE or mediation may have been crucial to a settlement that occurs months later.

123. These comparison courts were different from the demonstration districts, such as the Northern District of California court, which, as noted above, were evaluated by the Federal Judicial Center.

124. James S. Kakalik et al., *An Evaluation of Mediation and Early Neutral Evaluation*

Under the Civil Justice Reform Act (Santa Monica, CA: RAND, 1995).

125. Menkel-Meadow, "Regulation of Dispute Resolution in the United States of America," 437.

126. Ibid.

127. Lorig Charkoudian, "What Works in District Court Day of Trial Mediation: Effectiveness of Various Mediation Strategies on Short- and Long-Term Outcomes," January 2016, pp. 6–7, http://mdmediation.org/sites/default/files/What%20Works%20in%20District%20Court%20DOT%20Mediation.pdf. The style categorizations were based on clusters of the twenty-five coded mediator behaviors. Ibid., 13–19. See also Lorig Charkoudian, "What Works in Child Access Mediation: Effectiveness of Various Mediation Strategies on Short- and Long-Term Outcomes," January 2016, pp. iii–vii, http://mdmediation.org/sites/default/files/What%20Works%20in%20Child%20Access%20Mediation%20FINAL%20REV.pdf.

128. Charkoudian, "What Works in District Court Day of Trial Mediation," 7. Cases in which the mediator used more of the elicitive strategy were also less likely to be back in court within twelve months.

129. Ibid., 6.

130. Shestowsky's first report from this multijurisdictional study found that at the beginning of the litigation the parties preferred mediation over nonbinding arbitration and bench trials over jury trials. Shestowsky, "The Psychology of Procedural Preference," 637–54. See also Donna Shestowsky, "Inside the Mind of the Client: An Analysis of Litigants' Decision Criteria for Choosing Procedures," *Conflict Resolution Quarterly* 36, no. 1 (2018): 69–87. For an overview and critique of previous procedural justice studies, see Donna Shestowsky, "Disputants' Preferences for Court-Connected Dispute Resolution Procedures: Why We Should Care and Why We Know So Little," *Ohio State Journal on Dispute Resolution* 23 (2008): 598–622.

131. Lee et al., *A Community Court Grows in Brooklyn*, 139–41. Recidivism was defined as rearrest, not reconviction (122–23).

132. Ibid., 177–78, 182–83.

133. See Chapter 5 and American Bar Association Section of Dispute Resolution Task Force on Research and Statistics, "Top Ten Pieces of Information Courts Should Collect on ADR," June 9, 2006, https://www.americanbar.org/content/dam/aba/events/dispute_resolution/cle_and_mtg_planning_board/teleconferences/2012-2013/May_2013/topten.authcheckdam.pdf.

Chapter 8

1. For more information, see National Center for Victims of Crime, "National Compassion Fund," http://www.victimsofcrime.org/our-programs/national-compassion-fund (accessed June 3, 2019).

2. Francis E. McGovern, "The What and Why of Claims Resolution Facilities," *Stanford Law Review* 57 (2005): 1361. Such facilities are also known by other terms, including claims fund, claims resolution program, claims facility, and claims program equivalent.

3. Marshall Shapo, *Principles of Tort Law*, 3rd ed. (St. Paul, MN: West Academic, 2010). A more advanced definition of tort is "an event, arising out of the action or omission of another party, which causes injury to the human body or personality, to property or to economic interests, in circumstances where the law deems it just to require compensation from the person who has acted or failed to act." See Marshall S. Shapo and American Bar Association Special Committee on the Tort Liability System, *Towards a Jurisprudence of Injury: The Continuing Creation of a System of Substantive Justice in American Tort Law* (Chicago: American Bar Association, 1984), 1–3.

4. Nora Freeman Engstrom, "Exit, Adversarialism, and the Stubborn Persistence of Tort," *Journal of Tort Law* 6 (2015): 75–115; Stephen D. Sugarman, *Doing Away with Personal Injury Law: New Compensation Mechanisms for Victims, Consumers, and Business* (Westport, CT: Quorum Books, 1989), 38, 40. For an explanation of the unpredictability of the decisions and the costliness of the legal proceedings by the American "lawyer-driven, jury-centered methods of adjudication," see Robert A. Kagan, *Adversarial Legalism: The American Way of Law* (Cambridge, MA: Harvard University Press, 2003), 127.

5. Deborah R. Hensler and Mark A. Peterson, "Understanding Mass Personal Injury Litigation: A Socio-legal Analysis," *Brooklyn Law Review* 59, no. 3 (1995): 961.

6. Ibid., 965–66.

7. Ibid., 1031–33. For a discussion of tactics used by the courts in the East Texas asbestos cases and the Dalkon Shield bankruptcy, see Francis M. McGovern, "Resolving Mature Mass Tort Litigation," *Boston University Law Review* 69 (1989): 659–94.

8. Under Rule 23 of the Federal Rules of Civil Procedure, a "class action may be maintained" if two conditions are met: "the suit must satisfy the criteria set forth in subdivision (a)" (i.e., numerosity, commonality, typicality, and adequacy of representation) and the suit fits into one of the three categories described in subdivision (b). The third category, Rule 23(b) (3), permits a class action if "the court finds that the questions of law or fact common to class members predominate over any questions affecting only individual members" and "that a class action is superior to other available methods for fairly and efficiently adjudicating the controversy." See Cornell Law School Legal Information Institute, "Rule 23. Class Actions," https://www.law.cornell.edu/rules/frcp/rule _23 (accessed June 3, 2019). For a call to adopt the class action tool in mass torts cases, see

also Sergio J. Campos, "Mass Torts and Due Process," *Vanderbilt Law Review* 65, no. 4 (2012): 1059, 1065; and Shady Grove Orthopedic Assocs., P.A. v. Allstate Ins. Co., 130 S. Ct. 1431, 1437 (2010).

9. Campos, "Mass Torts and Due Process," 1065–66. One of the explanations for such judicial reluctance was explained by the Advisory Committee's Note regarding Rule 23, stating that "mass accident" cases are usually not appropriate for a class action. See Kenneth Feinberg, "Dalkon Shield Claimants Trust," in "Claims Resolution Facilities and the Mass Settlement of Mass Torts," ed. Francis E. McGovern, special issue, *Law and Contemporary Problems* 53, no 4 (Autumn 1990): 86.

10. Peter H. Schuck, *Agent Orange on Trial: Mass Toxic Disasters in the Courts* (Cambridge, MA: Belknap Press, 1986), 263; Deborah Hensler, "Resolving Mass Toxic Torts: Myths and Realities," *University of Illinois Law Review* 89, no. 91 (1989): 89–104.

11. Schuck, *Agent Orange on Trial*, 264.

12. Another solution attempting to address mass tort claims is the no-fault approach, intended to replace litigation with insurance funded either by private insurers or public agencies. Designers of claims facilities should be familiar with this alternative but be aware that it has generally failed in the United States. The original no-fault mechanisms were the workers' compensation laws of the 1970s, later expanded to other areas such as automobile insurance and coal miners. The National Childhood Vaccine Injury Act of 1986, enacted as a response to pharmaceutical fear of litigation crisis, attempts to protect firms from liability. Congress thus established the tax-funded Vaccine Injury Compensation Program. For more on the VICP, see Nora Freeman Engstrom, "A Dose of Reality for Specialized Courts: Lessons from the VICP," *University of Pennsylvania Law Review* 163 (2015): 1631–717. More broadly, see Mark A. Peterson, "Giving Away Money:

Comparative Comments on Claims Resolution Facilities," *Law and Contemporary Problems* 53, no. 4 (1990): 113, 116.

13. The EPA named asbestos a hazardous air pollutant in the Clean Air Act of 1970, Section 112, 42 U.S.C. § 7412.

14. Stephen J. Carroll et al., *Asbestos Litigation Costs and Compensation: An Interim Report* (Santa Monica, CA: RAND, 2002), https://www.rand.org/content/dam/rand/pubs/documented_briefings/2005/DB397.pdf; Paul D. Carrington, "Asbestos Lessons: The Unattended Consequences of Asbestos Litigation," *Review of Litigation* 26, no. 3 (2007): 583–612.

15. Borel v. Fibreboard Paper Prods. Corp., 493 F.2d 1076 (5th Cir. 1973).

16. By the mid-1980s asbestos cases constituted a meaningful fraction of the civil case docket in the ten federal and state courts in which they were concentrated. See Deborah Hensler, "As Time Goes By: Asbestos Litigation After Amchem and Ortiz," *Texas Law Review* 80 (2002): 1900.

17. For the role of indeterminate defendants in certain tort claim actions, see the panel discussion among Henry Nickel, William Anderson, Kenneth Feinberg, and Nicholas Yost, panel discussion, *Environmental Law Reporter* 16, no. 8 (1986):10216–19.

18. Hensler and Peterson, "Understanding Mass Personal Injury Litigation," 1004–5.

19. Carrington, "Asbestos Lessons," 593–94.

20. Carroll et al., *Asbestos Litigation Costs and Compensation*, 25–26.

21. Hensler and Peterson, "Understanding Mass Personal Injury Litigation," 1004–5. For more on these funds, see Lloyd Dixon, Geoffrey McGovern, and Amy Coombe, *Asbestos Bankruptcy Trusts: An Overview of Trust Structure and Activity with Detailed Reports on the Largest Trusts* (Santa Monica, CA: RAND, 2010), http://www.rand.org/content/dam/rand/pubs/technical_reports/2010/RAND_TR872.pdf.

22. Hensler and Peterson, "Understanding Mass Personal Injury Litigation," 1005–6.

23. Ortiz v. Fibreboard Corp., 527 U.S. 815 (1999); Amchem Prods., Inc. v. Windsor, 521 U.S. 591 (1997). See also Francis E. McGovern, ed., "Claims Resolution Facilities and the Mass Settlement of Mass Torts," special issue, *Law and Contemporary Problems* 53, no. 4 (1990): 79–112; and Elizabeth J. Cabraser, "Life After Amchem: The Class Struggle Continues," *Loyola Law Review* 31 (1998): 373–394.

24. Carroll et al., *Asbestos Litigation Costs and Compensation*.

25. Deborah R. Hensler et al., *Asbestos in the Courts: The Challenge of Mass Toxic Torts* (Santa Monica, CA: RAND, 1985); Deborah R. Hensler, "Justice for the Masses? Aggregate Litigation and Its Alternatives," *Daedalus* 143 (Summer 2014): 73. For a comparison of management of mass toxic torts through a hybrid tort or no-fault system, see Robert L. Rabin, "Some Thoughts on the Efficacy of a Mass Administrative Compensation Scheme," *Maryland Law Review* 52, no. 4 (1993): 964–78. Rabin highlights the challenge of establishing claim boundaries and limits and forming special early-warning judicial panels to switch from the court to administrative process to achieve greater fairness and efficiency.

26. Georgene M. Vairo, "The Dalkon Shield Claimants Trust: Paradigm Lost (or Found)?," *Fordham Law Review* 61, no. 3 (1992): 625–26; Feinberg, "Dalkon Shield Claimants Trust," 100–101.

27. Vairo, "Dalkon Shield Claimants Trust," 628–29.

28. Feinberg, "Dalkon Shield Claimants Trust," 104–5.

29. For an extensive review of the asbestos and Dalkon Shield facilities, see McGovern, "Claims Resolution Facilities and the Mass Settlement of Mass Torts." For the Dalkon Shield claims facility, see Feinberg, "Dalkon Shield Claimants Trust," 79.

30. Feinberg, "Dalkon Shield Claimants Trust," 111.

31. Engstrom, "A Dose of Reality for Specialized Courts," 1635.

32. U.S. District Court–Northern District of Ohio, "In re National Prescription Opiate Litigation: Transcript of Proceedings," January 9, 2019, p. 9, http://psych-history.weill.cornell.edu/pdf/Polster%20Transcript.pdf.

33. Nora Freeman Engstrom and Michelle M. Mello, "Suing the Opioid Companies," *Stanford Law School* (blog), August 30, 2018, https://law.stanford.edu/2018/08/30/q-and-a-with-mello-and-engstrom; Jan Hoffman, "Looking for Someone to Clean Opioid Mess," *New York Times*, February 1, 2019, p. A21.

34. "Large Morass: Dalkon Shield Trust, Hailed as Innovative, Stirs a Lot of Discord," *Wall Street Journal*, June 3, 1991, p. 1.

35. Carrie Menkel-Meadow, "Taking the Mass out of Mass Torts: Reflections of a Dalkon Shield Arbitrator on Alternative Dispute Resolution, Judging, Neutrality, Gender, and Process," *Loyola Los Angeles Law Review* 31 (1997–1998): 531–50.

36. Vairo, "Dalkon Shield Claimants Trust," 640–41.

37. The *Exxon Valdez*, a U.S. oil tanker, ran aground in Alaska's Prince William Sound, spilling up to 750,000 barrels of crude oil; the resulting litigation still continued nearly thirty years later.

38. Kimberley A. Strassel, "Mr. Fairness," *Wall Street Journal*, August 7, 2011, p. A11 (ellipsis in original). As of April 2011, $3.8 billion had been distributed ($2.6 billion in emergency payments) to half a million claimants. John Schwartz, "Man with $20 Billion to Disburse Finds No Shortage of Claims or Critics," *New York Times*, April 19, 2011, p. A1. Decisions by the administrator can be appealed to the courts or the U.S. Coast Guard. For a summary of the U.S. General Accountability Office report on $2 billion in cleanup and $1.8 billion for habitat restoration and personal damages, see "Exxon Valdez Oil Spill—Lessons Learned 30 Years After the Event," *HazMat* (blog), February 6, 2019, http://hazmatmag.com/2019/02/exxon-valdez-oil-spill-lessons-learned-30-years-after-the-event.

39. Myriam Gilles, "Public-Private Approaches to Mass Tort Victim Compensation: Some Thoughts on the Gulf Coast Claims Facility," *DePaul Law Review* 61, no. 2 (2012): 433–34.

40. Colin McDonell, "The Gulf Coast Claims Facility and the Deepwater Horizon Litigation: Judicial Regulation of Private Compensation Schemes," *Stanford Law Review* 64 (2012): 765.

41. Ibid., 770–71.

42. Joe Nocera, "BP Makes Amends," *New York Times*, January 10, 2012, p. A21.

43. Linda S. Mullenix, "Prometheus Unbound: The Gulf Coast Claims Facility as a Means for Resolving Mass Tort Claims—a Fund Too Far," *Louisiana Law Review* 71, no. 3 (2011): 819–916; Nicholas Guidi, "Oil, Fire, Smoke and Mirrors: The Gulf Coast Claims Facility and Its Dangerous Precedent," *William and Mary Environmental Law and Policy Review* 39, no. 3 (2015): 739–64.

44. McDonell, "The Gulf Coast Claims Facility and the Deepwater Horizon Litigation," 772–73.

45. In re Oil Spill by the Oil Rig "Deepwater Horizon" in the Gulf of Mexico on April 20, 2010, MDL No. 2179, 2011 WL 323866, at *8 (E.D. La. February 2, 2011).

46. BDO Consulting, "Independent Evaluation of the Gulf Coast Claims Facility: Report of Findings and Observations to the U.S. Department of Justice," June 5, 2012, https://www.justice.gov/iso/opa/resources/66520126611210351178.pdf.

47. "Deepwater Horizon Court-Supervised Settlement Program," December 22, 2012, http://www.deepwaterhorizonsettlements.com.

48. U.S. District Court Judge Carl J. Barbier ruled that "BP was indeed the primary culprit and that it had acted with 'conscious disregard of known risks,' its 'conduct was reckless' . . . and opened the possibility of $18 billion in new civil penalties" beyond the $28 billion that BP has already paid in claim payments and cleanup costs. The ruling addresses the first of three phases of litigation, dealing with liability for the blowout. Judge Barbier has yet to rule on how much oil was spilled; the third phase will determine penalties under the Clean Water Act. Campbell Robertson and Clifford Krauss, "BP May Be Fined up to $18 Billion for Spill in Gulf," *New York Times*, September 5, 2014, p. A1.

49. Deepwater Horizon Claims Center, "Public Statistics for the Deepwater Horizon Economic and Property Damages Settlement," http://www.deepwaterhorizoneconomic settlement.com/docs/statistics.pdf (accessed August 25, 2019).

50. Lawrence Susskind, "Make Compensatory Payments in the Gulf Coast NOW!," *Consensus Building Approach* (blog), June 2, 2010, http://theconsensusbuildingapproach.blogspot .com/search?q=gulf+coast+now.

51. The final claim filing deadline was June 8, 2015. For status of the MDL 2179 court proceedings, see Claims Administration Website, "Deepwater Horizon Claims Center," http://deepwaterhorizoneconomicsettlement .com (accessed July 1, 2019).

52. Jack B. Weinstein, *Individual Justice in Mass Tort Litigation* (Evanston, IL: Northwestern University Press, 1995), 1–8, 166–67. Geoffrey C. Hazard Jr. observed the adaptations to both procedural mechanisms and standardized provisions for eligibility and formulas for recovery from settlement funds and the applicable professional ethical norms. Geoffrey C. Hazard Jr., "Reflections on Judge Weinstein's Ethical Dilemmas in Mass Tort Litigation,"

Northwestern University Law Review 88 (1994): 576–78.

53. Carrie Menkel-Meadow, "Ethics and the Settlement of Mass Torts: When the Rules Meet the Road," *Cornell Law Review* 80 (1995): 1213–21.

54. Lynn P. Cohn, "A Model for the Use of ADR to Efficiently Distribute a Significant Settlement Fund in Mass Claims Litigation Without Sacrificing an Individualized Assessment of Claims," *Cardozo Journal of Conflict Resolution* 18, no. 3 (2017): 699–715.

55. Lindy Rouillard-Labbe, "Justice Among the Ashes: How Government Compensation Facilities Can Bring Justice to Disaster Victims," *Fordham International Law Journal* 38, no. 1 (2015): 245–297.

56. Insured losses were $40.6 billion. Damage to infrastructure (including roads and bridges) was $5.5 billion; 300,000 vehicles were destroyed, 2,400 ships and vessels wrecked, and 450,000 people displaced; and 800,000 Louisiana citizens requested assistance from federal and state relief programs and agencies. The Small Business Administration reported requests for $229 million in home and small business loans. FEMA, "Hurricane Katrina in the Gulf Coast: Mitigation Assessment Team Report, Building Performance Observations, Recommendations, and Technical Guidance," July 2006, chap. 1, https://www.fema.gov/media-library/assets/ documents/4069.

57. For firsthand accounts of conditions in the Superdome during and after Hurricane Katrina, see Ira Glass, "After the Flood," *This American Life*, September 9, 2005, http://www .thisamericanlife.org/radio-archives/episode/ 296/transcript.

58. Upon request by the governor of the affected state, the president is authorized to declare a disaster, thus enabling the affected area to access federal resources. Robert T. Stafford

Disaster Relief and Emergency Assistance Act, 42 U.S.C. §§ 5121–5207, § 401.

59. 42 U.S.C. § 5121 et seq. § 406, the Public Assistance Program, provides for the cost of repairing, restoring, reconstructing, or replacing public facilities.

60. While an insurance model might make more sense than relying on taxpayers for natural disaster relief, from both an efficiency and a preventive perspective, it has been difficult to identify effective structures and incentives. The National Flood Insurance Program, enacted in 1968 to limit disaster losses, was insufficient to handle the string of floods in the 1990s through Hurricane Sandy in 2012. The program is now more than $25 billion in debt. The National Flood Insurance Reform Act of 2012, with strong bilateral support, phased out some subsidies and increased premiums significantly. Congress has since been pressured to repeal the plan because constituents are unwilling to pay the insurance premiums.

61. Howard Kunreuther and Mark Pauly, "Rules Rather than Discretion: Lessons from Hurricane Katrina," *Journal of Risk and Uncertainty* 33, no. 1 (2006): 102. In November 2009, Judge Stanwood R. Duval found the Army Corps of Engineers liable for poor maintenance; in September 2012, the Court of Appeals for the Fifth Circuit ruled the government immune from lawsuits for decisions made by the corps that might have left the Mississippi River Gulf outlet vulnerable. See Nicholas Pinter, "The New Flood Insurance Disaster," *New York Times*, August 29, 2013, p. A21.

62. With limited court resources, the plaintiffs, defendants, cross-defendants, and the court designed a mediation system that resulted in settlement of 98 percent of cases for $800 million. The Fourth District California Court of Appeal Justice John Trotter oversaw the process. See John Pardun, "How ADR Can Be Used to Resolve Mass Disaster and Insurance Claims," *International In-House Counsel Journal* 6, no. 23 (2013): 1. This incident triggered controversy over the extent to which a utility such as Pacific Gas and Electric can be held liable for sparking wildfires and whether the utility's customers should pay; legislators pursue how to balance the risk of harm and the security of the electric grid. Ivan Penn, "When Utilities Spark Wildfires," *New York Times*, June 15, 2018, p. B1; David Baker, "PG&E Chief: Liability Proposal Is Not Enough," *San Francisco Chronicle*, July 27, 2018, p. C1.

63. See Rouillard-Labbe, "Justice Among the Ashes," 245.

64. Ibid., 262, 285. See also Gillian K. Hadfield, "Framing the Choice Between Cash and the Courthouse: Experiences with the 9/11 Victim Compensation Fund," *Law and Society Review* 42, no. 3 (2008): 660–73.

65. Janet Cooper Alexander, "Procedural Design and Terror Victim Compensation," *DePaul Law Review* 53, no. 2 (2003–2004): 627; Lisa Belkin, "Just Money," *New York Times*, December 8, 2002, p. 92. For the compensation fund statute, see Pub. L. No. 107-42, September 11th Victim Compensation Fund of 2001, 115 Stat. 230 (2001) (codified at 49 U.S.C.A. § 40101).

66. Kenneth R. Feinberg, *What Is Life Worth? The Unprecedented Effort to Compensate the Victims of 9/11* (New York: BBS, 2005).

67. Aviation and Transportation Security Act, § 405(b)(1)(B)(i)–(ii).

68. George L. Priest, "The Problematic Structure of the September 11th Victim Compensation Fund," *DePaul Law Review* 53 (2003): 530–31.

69. Alexander, "Procedural Design and Terror Victim Compensation."

70. Ibid., 634–35.

71. Priest, "The Problematic Structure of the September 11th Victim Compensation Fund," 542–44.

72. Gillian K. Hadfield, "Framing the Choice Between Cash and the Courthouse."

73. Feinberg, *What Is Life Worth?*

74. Robert L. Rabin, "Review of *What Is Life Worth? The Unprecedented Effort to Compensate the Victims of 9/11*, by Kenneth R. Feinberg," *Columbia Law Review* 106, no. 2 (2006): 479–82. For the history of federal disaster relief programs, see Michele Landis Dauber, "The War of 1812, September 11th, and the Politics of Compensation," *DePaul Law Review* 53, no. 2 (2003): 289. For administrative programs that compensate victims of terrorist attacks, see Robert L. Rabin, "The September 11th Victim Compensation Fund: A Circumscribed Response or an Auspicious Model?," *DePaul Law Review* 53, no. 2 (2003): 769.

75. Public Law 116-34 permanently reauthorizes the 9/11 Victim Compensation Fund. For the text of the act, see https://www.congress .gov/bill/116th-congress/house-bill/1327.

76. Special thanks go to Noah Susskind for his research compilation of the One Fund Boston.

77. Scott Neuman, "Social Media Helped Find Loved Ones After Marathon Bombing," *National Public Radio*, April 16, 2013, https:// www.npr.org/sections/thetwo-way/2013/04/ 16/177443006/social-media-helped-find-loved -ones-after-marathon-bombing; "Lessons Learned from the Media's Coverage of Boston Bombing," *National Public Radio*, April 20, 2013, http://www.npr.org/2013/0420/178090655/ lessons-learned-from-the-medias-coverage-of -boston-bombing.

78. Ed Pilkington, "Kenneth Feinberg Prepares to Put a Price on Trauma of Boston Bombings," *The Guardian*, April 26, 2013, https://www.theguardian.com/world/2013/apr/ 26/kenneth-feinberg-boston-bombings-trauma -compensation.

79. "Managing the $30 million 'One Fund' to Aid Boston Victims," *National Public Radio*,

May 16 2013, http://www.npr.org/templates/ story/story.php?storyId=184524656.

80. Richard Weir, "One Fund's Second Act 'Uncharted Territory,'" *Boston Herald*, September 12, 2013, http://bostonherald.com/news _opinion/local_coverage/2013/09/one_fund_s _second_act_uncharted_territory.

81. City of Boston, "One Fund Boston Administrator Ken Feinberg Distributes Nearly $61 Million Among 232 Eligible Claimants," July 1, 2013, http://www.cityofboston.gov/news/ default.aspx?id=6211.

82. Neuman, "Social Media Helped Find Loved Ones After Marathon Bombing."

83. Martha Bebinger, "No Clear Targets for Civil Suits in Marathon Bombings," *WBUR*, May 10, 2013, http://www.wbur.org/2013/05/10/ marathon-victims-lawsuits.

84. Eric Moskowitz, "Marathon Victim Payout Method Faulted," *Boston Globe*, July 4, 2013, http://www.bostonglobe.com/metro/ 2013/07/03/methodology-marathon-victim -payout-faulted-lawyer-group/sqxc7kjTz2OF pdxOTLT5VP/story.html.

85. National Insurance Institute of Israel, "Hostile Action Casualties," https://www.btl .gov.il/English%20Homepage/Benefits/Benefits %20for%20Victims%20of%20Hostilities/Pages/ default.aspx (accessed June 3, 2019). For the Compensation for Victims of Hostile Acts Law in Hebrew, see https://www.btl.gov.il/ SiteCollectionDocuments/btl/Publications/ SocialSecurity/67/article5.pdf. See also Guy Mundlak, "Fifty Years of the National Insurance Law: The Celebrations Will Take Place in the Courtroom," *Social Security* 67 (2004): 83–108 (in Hebrew).

86. Francis McGovern, "Second Generation Dispute System Design Issues in Managing Settlements," *Harvard Negotiation Law Review* 14 (2009): n.p.

87. Carrie Menkel-Meadow, "Taking the Mass out of Mass Torts," 528.

88. Compare Mullenix, "Prometheus Unbound."

89. Ibid.

90. See McGovern, "The What and Why of Claims Resolution Facilities"; and Peter H. Schuck, "Mass Torts: An Institutional Evolutionist Perspective," *Cornell Law Review* 80, no. 4 (1995): 941–89.

91. Francis E. McGovern, "The Second Generation of Dispute System Design: Reoccurring Problems and Potential Solutions," *Ohio State Journal on Dispute Resolution* 24 (2008): 68.

92. Kenneth Feinberg, "The Building Blocks for Successful Victim Compensation Programs," *Ohio State Journal on Dispute Resolution* 20 (2005): 273–78. For a discussion of the array of factors considered in compensated and pro bono cases, designing the distribution process and protocol, and unexpected obstacles, see Roger Parloff, "Steering Billions to Victims," *New York Times*, June 24, 2017, p. B1.

93. Nicole Raz, "Las Vegas Victims' Fund to Distribute $31.4M to Victims in March," *Las Vegas Review-Journal*, March 2, 2018, https://www.reviewjournal.com/crime/shootings/las-vegas-victims-fund-to-distribute-31-4m-to-victims-in-march.

94. Robert J. MacCoun, "Voice, Control, and Belonging: The Double-Edged Sword of Procedural Fairness," *Annual Review of Law and Social Science* 1 (2005): 171–201. MacCoun reviews the procedural-justice literature and renames it "procedural fairness," which is a function of claimants' standing to have a voice, trust in process (if treated with respect by a decision maker), and a neutral, legitimate decision maker.

95. McGovern, "The What and Why of Claims Resolution Facilities."

Chapter 9

1. *Merriam-Webster Dictionary*, s.v. "community," https://www.merriam-webster.com/dictionary/community (accessed June 3, 2019).

2. Elinor Ostrom, *Understanding Institutional Diversity* (Princeton, NJ: Princeton University Press, 2005).

3. Jerome T. Barrett, with Joseph P. Barrett, *A History of Alternative Dispute Resolution: The Story of a Political, Cultural, and Social Movement* (San Francisco, CA: Jossey-Bass, 2004).

4. Ibid., 2–6.

5. Timothy Hedeen and Patrick G. Coy, "Community Mediation and the Court System: The Ties That Bind," *Mediation Quarterly* 17, no. 4 (2000): 351–67.

6. Timothy Hedeen, "The Evolution and Evaluation of Community Mediation: Limited Research Suggests Unlimited Progress," *Conflict Resolution Quarterly* 22, nos. 1–2 (2004): 102.

7. Raymond Shonholtz, "Justice from Another Perspective: The Ideology and Developmental History of the Community Boards Program," in *The Possibility of Popular Justice*, ed. Sally Engle Merry and Neal Milner (Ann Arbor: University of Michigan Press, 1993), 201–38.

8. See the organization's website, at https://communityboards.org.

9. See, for example, the websites of the Center for Community Justice, at https://centerforcommunityjustice.org, and the National Association for Community Mediation, at https://www.nafcm.org.

10. National Association for Community Mediation, "Purpose," https://www.nafcm.org/page/Purpose? (accessed June 3, 2019).

11. Beth Gazley, Won Kyung Chang, and Lisa Blomgren Bingham, "Collaboration and Citizen Participation in Community Mediation Centers," *Review of Policy Research* 23, no. 4 (2006): 843–63. Percentages are reported only for members of the National Association of Community

Mediation who participated in a 2005 survey by the Indiana Conflict Resolution Institute.

12. Shonholtz, "Justice from Another Perspective."

13. John Braithwaite, *Restorative Justice and Responsive Regulation* (New York: Oxford University Press, 2002).

14. Mark S. Umbreit, Robert B. Coates, and Betty Vos, "Victim-Offender Mediation: Three Decades of Practice and Research," *Conflict Resolution Quarterly* 22, nos. 1–2 (2004): 279–303; Mark S. Umbreit, *The Handbook of Victim-Offender Mediation: An Essential Guide to Practice and Research* (San Francisco, CA: Jossey-Bass, 2000). See also the Center for Community Justice website, at https://centerforcommunityjustice.org.

15. Lisa Blomgren Bingham, "Collaborative Governance: Emerging Practices and the Incomplete Legal Framework for Citizen and Stakeholder Voice," *Journal of Dispute Resolution* 2009, no. 2 (2010): 269–326. See also John Gastil and Peter Levine, eds., *The Deliberative Democracy Handbook: Strategies for Effective Civic Engagement in the Twenty-First Century* (San Francisco, CA: Jossey-Bass, 2005).

16. Gazley, Chang, and Bingham, "Collaboration and Citizen Participation in Community Mediation Centers."

17. See the Participatory Budgeting Project website, at https://www.participatorybudgeting.org.

18. See, for example, Bruce P. Archibald, "Let My People Go: Human Capital, Investment and Community Capacity Building via Meta/Regulation in a Deliberative Democracy—a Modest Contribution to Criminal Law and Restorative Justice," *Cardozo Journal of International and Comparative Law* 16, no. 1 (2008): 1–85.

19. For a discussion of discursive democracy as a system, see Russell A. Miller, "Theoretical Approaches to International Indigenous Rights: Collective Discursive Democracy as the Indigenous Right to Self-Determination," *American Indian Law Review* 31 (2007): 341–73, esp. 342.

20. Hedeen, "The Evolution and Evaluation of Community Mediation."

21. Hedeen and Coy, "Community Mediation and the Court System."

22. Beth Gazley, Won Kyung Chang, and Lisa Blomgren Bingham, "External Linkages, Board Diversity, and Organizational Effectiveness in Community Mediation Centers," *Public Administration Review* 70, no. 4 (2010): 610–20.

23. William C. Bradford, "Reclaiming Indigenous Legal Autonomy on the Path to Peaceful Coexistence: The Theory, Practice and Limitations of Tribal Peacemaking in Indian Dispute Resolution," *North Dakota Law Review* 76 (2000): 551–604.

24. James A. Wall Jr., John B. Stark, and Rhetta L. Standifer, "Mediation: A Current Review and Theory Development," *Journal of Conflict Resolution* 45, no. 3 (2001): 370–91.

25. Alison Brysk, *From Tribal Village to Global Village: Indian Rights and International Relations in Latin America* (Stanford, CA: Stanford University Press, 2000).

26. Carlo Osi, "Understanding Indigenous Dispute Resolution Processes and Western Alternative Dispute Resolution: Cultivating Culturally Appropriate Methods in Lieu of Litigation," *Cardozo Journal of Conflict Resolution* 10 (2008): 163–231.

27. Bradford, "Reclaiming Indigenous Legal Autonomy on the Path to Peaceful Coexistence," 578.

28. Joseph Stahlman, interview by the authors, September 18, 2014, Bloomington, Indiana. An example of an Iroquois Peacemaker court is the Seneca court in New York. See Seneca Nation of Indians, "Peacemaker's Court," https://sni.org/government/peacemakers-court (accessed June 3, 2019).

29. Clark Freshman, "The Promise and Perils of 'Our' Justice: Psychological, Critical and Economic Perspectives on Communities and Prejudices in Mediation," *Cardozo Journal of Conflict Resolution* 6 (2004): 1–18.

30. James A. Wall Jr. and Ronda Roberts Callister, "Malaysian Community Mediation," *Journal of Conflict Resolution* 43 (1999): 343–65; James A. Wall Jr. et al., "Mediation in the USA, China, Japan and Korea," *Security Dialogue* 29 (1998): 235–48; Dong-Won Sohn and James A. Wall Jr., "Community Mediation in South Korea: A City-Village Comparison," *Journal of Conflict Resolution* 37 (1993): 536–43; James A. Wall, "Community Mediation in China and Korea: Some Similarities and Differences," *Harvard Negotiation Journal* 9 (1993): 141–53; Nam Kim et al., "Community and Industrial Mediation in South Korea," *Journal of Conflict Resolution* 37 (1993): 361–82.

31. William C. Warters, *Mediation in the Campus Community: Designing and Managing Effective Programs* (San Francisco, CA: Jossey-Bass, 2000).

32. Hedeen, "The Evolution and Evaluation of Community Mediation," 105. See also Gazley, Chang, and Bingham, "Collaboration and Citizen Participation in Community Mediation Centers."

33. Won Kyung Chang, "The Practice of Restorative Justice: An Ethnographic Exploration of One Community's Attempt to Implement a Community-Based System" (PhD diss., Indiana University, Bloomington, 2010).

34. Antoinette Sedillo Lopez, "Evolving Indigenous Law: Navajo Marriage—Cultural Traditions and Modern Challenges," *Arizona Journal of International and Comparative Law* 17 (2000): 283–307.

35. Tavis Smiley, ed., *The Covenant with Black America: Ten Years Later* (Carlsbad, CA: SmileyBooks, 2016).

36. See the home page of the Victim Offender Mediation Association, at http://www.voma.org.

37. Umbreit, Coates, and Vos, "Victim-Offender Mediation." For a description of other models of restorative justice, including family group conferences and peacemaking circles, see Howard Zehr, "Commentary: Restorative Justice: Beyond Victim-Offender Mediation," *Conflict Resolution Quarterly* 22 (2004): 305.

38. Christine B. Harrington, *Shadow Justice: The Ideology and Institutionalization of Alternatives to Court* (Westport, CT: Greenwood Press, 1985).

39. One example is a minigrant program for community mediation sponsored by JAMS in collaboration with the National Association for Community Mediation. See Judicial Arbitration and Mediation Services, "JAMS Foundation/NAFCM Mini-grant Program," https://www.jamsadr.com/nafcm (accessed June 3, 2019).

40. Daniel McGillis, *Community Mediation Programs: Developments and Challenges* (Washington, DC: National Institute of Justice, 1997).

41. Patrick G. Coy and Timothy Hedeen, "A Stage Model of Social Movement Co-optation: Community Mediation in the United States," *Sociological Quarterly* 46, no. 3 (2005): 405–35.

42. Gazley, Chang, and Bingham, "Collaboration and Citizen Participation in Community Mediation Centers."

43. Ibid.

44. Ibid.

45. See Sally Engle Merry and Neal Milner, eds., *The Possibility of Popular Justice* (Ann Arbor: University of Michigan Press, 1993), 201–38.

46. Hedeen, "The Evolution and Evaluation of Community Mediation."

47. Ibid., 121.

48. Ibid., 122.

49. Umbreit, Coates, and Vos, "Victim-Offender Mediation."

50. See Craig A. McEwen and Richard J. Maiman, "Small Claims Mediation in Maine: An Empirical Assessment," *Maine Law Review* 33 (1981): 237–68.

51. Craig A. McEwen and Richard J. Maiman, "Mediation in Small Claims Court: Achieving Compliance Through Consent," *Law and Society Review* 18, no. 1 (1984): 11–50.

52. Hedeen, "The Evolution and Evaluation of Community Mediation," 123–24.

53. Gazley, Chang, and Bingham, "External Linkages, Board Diversity, and Organizational Effectiveness in Community Mediation Centers."

54. Lisa Bernstein, "Opting Out of the Legal System: Extralegal Contractual Relations in the Diamond Industry," *Journal of Legal Studies* 21, no. 1 (1992): 115–57; Lisa Bernstein, "Private Commercial Law in the Cotton Industry: Creating Cooperation Through Rules, Norms, and Institutions," *Michigan Law Review* 99 (2001): 1724–90.

55. For information about the arbitration system, see Diamond Dealers Club New York, "Non-members and Arbitration," https://www.nyddc.com/arbitration.html (accessed June 3, 2019).

56. Bernstein, "Opting Out of the Legal System," 115. Beyond this observation, Bernstein does not report on the nature of discussions leading to the DDC's arbitration system. The DDC does not have a website or public means of verifying the status of its current dispute resolution system. Presumably, it has not changed.

57. Ibid., 124.

58. Ibid., 126. Members may now insert DDC arbitration clauses in documents for transactions with nonmembers.

59. Ibid., 125–26.

60. Ibid., 126.

61. Ibid., 127.

62. Bernstein, "Private Commercial Law in the Cotton Industry," 1726–27.

63. Ibid., 1728.

64. Ibid., 1744n90.

65. Ibid., 1728.

66. Ibid., 1744n90.

67. Ibid., 1731–39.

68. Ibid., 1725.

69. Nancy H. Rogers, "When Conflicts Polarize Communities: Designing Localized Offices That Intervene Collaboratively," *Ohio State Journal on Dispute Resolution* 30, no. 2 (2015): 173–231.

70. U.S. Department of Justice Community Relations Service, "What We Do," February 14, 2017, https://www.justice.gov/crs/what-we-do.

71. Neil A. Levine, "Hands Up, Don't Shoot: A Case for the Community Relations Service," Levine Strategies, August 25, 2104, https://www.levinestrategies.com/all-posts/2014/8/25/hands-up-dont-shoot-a-case-for-the-community-relations-service.

72. Community Justice and Mediation Center, "Downtown Safety, Civility, and Justice Project: Report Summary; What the Community Said," January 30, 2017, https://bloomington.in.gov/sites/default/files/2017-06/CJAM%20Downtown%20Safety%2C%20Civility%20and%20Justice_What%20the%20Community%20Said_Report%20Summary%20%281%29.pdf.

73. In a storyboarding process, members anonymously write on individual sheets of paper their observations and experiences, in this case, related to downtown safety, civility, and justice, including issues of aggressive panhandling, people experiencing homelessness, and substance and alcohol abuse and addiction. They then taped their comments to the walls and rearranged them to form themes.

74. For using similar examples to teach DSD, see Andrea Kupfer Schneider, "How Does DSD Help Us Teach About Community Con-

flict (and How Can Community Conflict Help Illustrate DSD)?," *University of St. Thomas Law Journal* 13, no. 2 (2017): 370–80.

75. Gazley, Chang, and Bingham, "Collaboration and Citizen Participation in Community Mediation Centers," 853.

76. Maisha T. Winn, *Justice on Both Sides: Transforming Education Through Restorative Justice* (Cambridge, MA: Harvard Education Press, 2018).

77. Thomas A. Mayes, "A Brief Model for Explaining Dispute Resolution Options in Special Education," *Ohio State Journal on Dispute Resolution* 34, no. 1 (2019): 153–70.

78. Nancy A. Welsh, "Stepping Back Through the Looking Glass: Real Conversations with Real Disputants About Institutionalized Mediation and Its Value," *Ohio State Journal on Dispute Resolution* 19, no. 2 (2004): 573–678.

79. Grace E. D'Alo, "Accountability in Special Education Mediation: Many a Slip Twixt Vision and Practice," *Harvard Negotiation Law Review* 8 (2003): 201–70.

80. Ostrom, *Understanding Institutional Diversity.*

81. For extensive resources on mediation in special education, see the website of the Center for Appropriate Dispute Resolution in Special Education, at https://www.cadreworks.org/resources/main-library.

82. Amy J. Cohen, "Dispute Systems Design, Neoliberalism, and the Problem of Scale," *Harvard Negotiation Law Review* 14, no. 1 (2009): 53.

83. Terry Amsler, "Community Dispute Resolution: Assessing Its Importance and Addressing Its Challenges," *Dispute Resolution Magazine* 19, no. 2 (2013): 4–6.

Chapter 10

1. Ellen Dannin, *Taking Back the Workers' Law* (Ithaca, NY: ILR Press, 2006), 21–29.

2. Jerome T. Barrett, with Joseph P. Barrett, *A History of Alternative Dispute Resolution: The Story of a Political, Cultural, and Social Movement* (San Francisco, CA: Jossey-Bass, 2004), 84–118.

3. Ibid., 118–23.

4. National Labor Relations Act of 1935, 29 U.S. Code §§ 151–169 (1935).

5. There is a DSD for unfair labor practice charges that allows administrative law judges to serve as settlement judges, acting much like mediators, who help the parties reach negotiated settlements; the program is well received by disputants. For the finding of substantial participant satisfaction, see Lamont Stallworth, Arup Varma, and John T. Delaney, "The NLRB's Unfair Labor Practice Settlement Program: An Empirical Analysis of Participant Satisfaction," *Dispute Resolution Journal* 59, no. 4 (2004–2005): 16–29.

6. For the leading and comprehensive treatise on federal labor law in the private sector, see John E. Higgins Jr., ed., *The Developing Labor Law: The Board, the Courts, and the National Labor Relations Act*, 6th ed. (Washington, DC: Bloomberg BNA, 2012).

7. Barrett and Barrett, *A History of Alternative Dispute Resolution*, 121–24.

8. Labor-Management Relations Act of 1947, 29 U.S. Code §§ 141–197 (1947); Barrett and Barrett, *A History of Alternative Dispute Resolution*, 125–39.

9. Kenneth May, Patrick M. Sanders, and Michelle T. Sullivan, eds., *Elkouri and Elkouri: How Arbitration Works*, 7th ed. (Washington, DC: Bloomberg BNA, 2012).

10. See W. Daniel Boone, "Steelworkers Trilogy: Collective Bargaining as the Foundation for Industrial Democracy and Arbitration as an Integral Part of Workplace Self-Government," in *National Academy of*

Arbitrators Annual Proceedings 2010 (Edison, NJ: BNA Books, 2010), 100–142.

11. "The function of the court is very limited when the parties have agreed to submit all questions of contract interpretation to the arbitrator." United Steelworkers of Am. v. Am. Mfg. Co., 363 U.S. 564 (1960), 567–68, 80 S. Ct. 1343 (1960), 1346, 4 L. Ed. 2d 1403 (1960).

12. *United Steelworkers*, 363 U.S. 564 (1960).

13. Ibid., 568.

14. United Steelworkers v. Warrior and Gulf Navigation Co., 363 U.S. 574 (1960).

15. Ibid., 582–83.

16. United Steelworkers of Am. v. Enter. Wheel and Car Corp., 363 U.S. 593 (1960), 80 S. Ct. 1358 (1960), 4 L. Ed. 2d 1424 (1960).

17. *United Steelworkers.*, 363 U.S. 593 (1960), 597.

18. Dannin, *Taking Back the Workers' Law.*

19. For a cutting-edge analysis of the effect unionization has on management ADR choices for nonunion employees in the public and private sectors, see Ariel C. Avgar et al., "Unions and ADR: The Relationship Between Labor Unions and Workplace Dispute Resolution in U.S. Corporations," *Ohio State Journal on Dispute Resolution* 28 (2013): 63–106. Avgar and colleagues discuss strategic choices on whether companies seek to substitute ADR for unionization or view ADR as complementing collective bargaining.

20. Ibid., 100.

21. Ibid., 66.

22. David B. Lipsky, Ronald L. Seeber, and Richard D. Fincher, *Emerging Systems for Managing Workplace Conflict: Lessons from American Corporations for Managers and Dispute Resolution Professionals* (San Francisco, CA: Jossey-Bass, 2003).

23. For an empirical examination of workplace representation in twenty-seven European Union countries, see John Forth, Alex Bryson, and Anitha George, "Explaining Cross-National Variation in Workplace Employee Representation," *European Journal of Industrial Relations* 23, no. 4 (2017): 415–33.

24. Higgins, *The Developing Labor Law.*

25. Karen L. Ertel, *Grievance Guide*, 13th ed. (Edison, NJ: Bloomberg BNA, 2012).

26. For example, "a grievance is defined as a dispute, difference, disagreement or complaint between the parties related to wages, hours, and conditions of employment. A grievance shall include, but is not limited to, the complaint of an employee or of the Union which involves the interpretation, application of, or compliance with the provisions of this Agreement or any local Memorandum of Understanding not in conflict with this Agreement." American Postal Workers Union, "Collective Bargaining Agreement Between the American Postal Workers Union, AFL-CIO and the U.S. Postal Service, November 21, 2006–November 20, 2010," 2006, article 15, section 1, https://apwu.org/contracts/2006-2010-collective-bargaining-agreement-nov-21-2006.

27. Michael J. Duane, *The Grievance Process in Labor-Management Cooperation* (Westport, CT: Quorum Books, 1993).

28. May, Sanders, and Sullivan, *Elkouri and Elkouri.*

29. Theodore J. St. Antoine, ed., *The Common Law of the Workplace: The Views of Arbitrators*, 2nd ed. (Washington, DC: BNA, 2005).

30. Marvin F. Hill Jr. and Anthony V. Sinicropi, *Remedies in Arbitration*, 2nd ed. (Washington, DC: Bloomberg BNA, 1991), 329–476.

31. Ibid., 137–281; Marvin F. Hill Jr. and James A. Wright, *Employee Lifestyle and Off-Duty Conduct Regulation* (Washington, DC: Bloomberg BNA, 1993), 167–254.

32. Federal Arbitration Act, 9 U.S.C. § 1 et seq. (2012).

33. National Conference of Commissioners on Uniform State Laws, "Uniform Arbitration Act," December 13, 2000, https://www.uniformlaws.org/HigherLogic/

System/DownloadDocumentFile.ashx
?DocumentFileKey=cf35cea8-4434-0d6b-408d
-756f961489af&forceDialog=0.

34. Ray J. Schoonhoven, ed., *Fairweather's Practice and Procedure in Labor Arbitration*, 3rd ed. (Washington, DC: Bloomberg BNA, 1991).

35. John T. Dunlop and Arnold M. Zack, *Mediation and Arbitration of Employment Disputes* (San Francisco, CA: Jossey-Bass, 1997).

36. See the National Academy of Arbitrators website, at http://www.naarb.org. For one example of its policy making, see National Academy of Arbitrators, "National Academy of Arbitrators Policy Statement on Employment Arbitration," May 20, 2009, https://naarb.org/employment-arbitration-policy-and-guidelines.

37. Lisa Blomgren Bingham et al., "Mediation in Employment and Creeping Legalism: Implications for Dispute Systems Design," *Journal of Dispute Resolution* 2010, no. 2 (2010): 129–50.

38. For the classic early evaluation of grievance mediation, see Jeanne M. Brett and Stephen B. Goldberg, "Grievance Mediation in the Coal Industry: A Field Experiment," *ILR Review* 37 (1983): 49–69.

39. A review of this literature is outside the scope of this book. See, generally, David Lewin and Richard B. Peterson, *The Modern Grievance Procedure in the United States* (Westport, CT: Greenwood Press, 1988); and Blair H. Sheppard, Roy J. Lewicki, and John W. Minton, *Organizational Justice* (Lexington, MA: Lexington Press, 1992). For a comparison of the research related to design issues presented in union and nonunion dispute resolution procedures, see Lisa Blomgren Bingham and Denise R. Chachere, "Dispute Resolution in Employment: The Need for Research," in *Employment Dispute Resolution and Worker Rights in the Changing Workplace*, ed. Adrienne E. Eaton and Jeffrey H. Keefe (Champaign, IL: Industrial Relations Research Association, 1999), 95–135.

40. Albert O. Hirschman, *Exit, Voice, and Loyalty* (Cambridge, MA: Harvard University Press, 1970).

41. Elinor Ostrom, *Understanding Institutional Diversity* (Princeton, NJ: Princeton University Press, 2005), 138.

42. William B. Gould IV, "Using an Independent Monitor to Resolve Union-Organizing Disputes Outside the NLRB: The FirstGroup Experience," *Dispute Resolution Journal* 66 (May–July 2011): 46–58.

43. Ibid., 52.

44. Ibid., 57.

45. William L. Ury, Jeanne M. Brett, and Stephen B. Goldberg, *Getting Disputes Resolved: Designing Systems to Cut the Costs of Conflict* (San Francisco, CA: Jossey-Bass, 1988).

46. Jeanne M. Brett and Stephen P. Goldberg, "Wildcat Strikes in Bituminous Coal Mining," *ILR Review* 32 (1979): 465–83.

47. Ury, Brett, and Goldberg, *Getting Disputes Resolved*, 51–52.

48. Ibid.

49. Stephen B. Goldberg, "How Interest-Based, Grievance Mediation Performs over the Long Term," *Dispute Resolution Journal* 59 (November 2004–January 2005): 8–15.

50. Ibid., 11–13.

51. Debra L. Shapiro and Jeanne M. Brett, "Comparing Three Processes Underlying Judgments of Procedural Justice: A Field Study of Mediation and Arbitration," *Journal of Personality and Social Psychology* 65, no. 6 (1993): 1167–77.

52. See generally Frits M. van der Meer, Jos C. N. Raadschelders, and Theo A. J. Toonen, eds., *Comparative Civil Service Systems in the 21st Century*, 2nd ed. (New York: Palgrave Macmillan, 2015).

53. Barrett and Barrett, *A History of Alternative Dispute Resolution*, 141–48; Dale Belman, Morley Gunderson, and Douglas Hyatt, eds., *Public Sector Employment in a Time of Transition* (Champaign, IL: Industrial Relations Research Association, 1996), 1.

54. Conn. Gen. Stat. § 31-91 et seq. (2013). Section 31-91 illustrates a form of third-party DSD, because the legislature provides, in part, for the membership of board and appointments and officers.

55. Lisa Blomgren Bingham and Rosemary O'Leary, eds., *Big Ideas in Collaborative Public Management* (Armonk, NY: M. E. Sharpe, 2008); Rosemary O'Leary and Lisa Blomgren Bingham, eds., *The Collaborative Public Manager* (Washington, DC: Georgetown University Press, 2009).

56. James L. Perry, "Measuring Public Service Motivation: An Assessment of Construct Reliability and Validity," *Journal of Public Administration Research and Theory* 6 (1996): 5–22.

57. Martin H. Malin, "Public Employees' Right to Strike: Law and Experience," *University of Michigan Journal of Law Reform* 26 (1993): 313–402.

58. For the argument that interest arbitration should be viewed as an extension of collective bargaining and not as an adjudicative procedure, see Martin H. Malin, "Two Models of Interest Arbitration," *Ohio State Journal on Dispute Resolution* 28 (2013): 144–69.

59. Amy Howe, "Opinion Analysis: Court Strikes Down Public-Sector Union Fees," *SCOTUSblog*, June 27, 2108, http://www.scotus blog.com/2018/06/opinion-analysis-court -strikes-down-public-sector-union-fees.

60. American Postal Workers Union, "Collective Bargaining Agreement," article 15, section 3.

61. Thomas Kochan et al., "The Long-Haul Effects of Interest Arbitration: The Case of New York State's Taylor Law," *ILR Review* 63 (2010): 570–72. See also New York State Governor's Office of Employee Relations, "New York State Public Employees' Fair Employment Act—the Taylor Law," https://goer.ny.gov/new-york-state -public-employees-fair-employment-act-taylor

-law (accessed October 12, 2019). For a comparison of eight states' public sector bargaining laws, see Joyce M. Najita and James L. Stern, *Collective Bargaining in the Public Sector: The Experience of Eight States* (New York: Routledge, 2001).

62. Ibid., 573.

63. Debra J. Mesch, "Grievance Arbitration in the Public Sector: A Conceptual Framework and Empirical Analysis of Public and Private Sector Arbitration Cases," *Review of Public Personnel Administration* 15 (1995): 22–36.

64. For more information about how this system functions, see the law firm Shipman and Goodwin's blog, *School Law*, at http://www .shipmangoodwin.com/schoollaw.

65. Conn. Gen. Stat. § 10-153f(a) (2013) of the statute constructs the arbitral body.

66. Conn. Gen. Stat. § 10-153f(c)(4) (2013).

67. Conn. Gen. Stat. § 10-153f(c)(8) (2013).

68. Federal Arbitration Act, 9 U.S.C. § 10 (2012).

69. Martin H. Malin, "The Legislative Upheaval in Public-Sector Labor Law: A Search for Common Elements," *ABA Journal of Labor and Employment Law* 27 (2012): 149–64; Martin H. Malin, "The Paradox of Public Sector Labor Law," *Indiana Law Journal* 84 (2009): 1369–99.

70. Labor-Management Relations Act, 29 U.S.C.A. §§ 141–197 (1947), as amended by the Labor Management Cooperation Act of 1978, 29 U.S.C. § 203(e) (1978).

71. Federal Mediation and Conciliation Service, "Planning for Progress: Labor-Management Committees," June 2015, https://www .fmcs.gov/wp-content/uploads/2015/06/FMCS _LMC_Planning_for_Progess.pdf.

72. Ibid., 11.

73. Ibid., 5.

74. Federal Mediation and Conciliation Service, "Labor-Management Cooperation Grant Application Materials," https://www .fmcs.gov/resources/forms-applications/

labor-management-grants-program/labor
-management-cooperation-grant-program
(accessed June 4, 2019).

75. This narrative is based on interviews
and a focus group conducted by Lisa Blomgren
Amsler (formerly Bingham) on May 20, 2008,
in Crane, Indiana.

76. Organization for Economic Cooperation and Development, "OECD Employment
Outlook, 2017," June 13, 2017, http://dx.doi.org/
10.1787/empl_outlook-2017-en.

77. Bureau of Labor Statistics, "Union
Members Summary," January 18, 2019, https://
www.bls.gov/news.release/union2.nr0.htm.

78. David Weil, *The Fissured Workplace:
Why Work Became So Bad for So Many and
What Can Be Done to Improve It* (Cambridge,
MA: Harvard University Press, 2014).

79. Darrell M. West, *Billionaires: Reflections
on the Upper Crust* (Washington, DC: Brookings Institution Press, 2014).

80. Christian E. Weller, ed., *Inequality,
Uncertainty, and Opportunity: The Varied and
Growing Role of Finance in Labor Relations*
(Champaign, IL: Labor and Employment Rela-
tions Association, 2015).

81. Edward J. Carberry, ed., *Employee Ownership and Shared Capitalism: New Directions in
Research* (Champaign, IL: Labor and Employment Relations Association, 2011).

82. Henry Hansmann, *The Ownership of
Enterprise* (Cambridge, MA: Belknap Press,
2000).

83. Thomas A. Kochan and David B. Lipsky,
eds., *Negotiations and Change: From the Workplace to Society* (Ithaca, NY: Cornell University
Press, 2003).

84. See generally, Janice Fine et al., eds., *No
One Size Fits All: Worker Organization, Policy,
and Movement in a New Economic Age* (Champaign, IL: Labor and Employment Relations
Association, 2018).

Chapter 11

1. William L. Ury, Jeanne M. Brett, and
Stephen B. Goldberg, *Getting Disputes Resolved:
Designing Systems to Cut the Costs of Conflict*
(San Francisco, CA: Jossey-Bass, 1988).

2. David W. Ewing, *Justice on the Job: Re-
solving Grievances in the Non-union Workplace*
(Cambridge, MA: Harvard Business School
Press, 1989); Douglas C. McCabe, *Corporate
Nonunion Complaint Procedures and Systems:
A Strategic Human Resources Management
Analysis* (New York: Praeger, 1988); M. Afzalur
Rahim, *Managing Conflict in Organizations*,
4th ed. (London: Routledge, Taylor and
Francis, 2017).

3. Bureau of Labor Statistics, "Union Members Summary," January 18, 2019, https://www
.bls.gov/news.release/union2.nr0.htm.

4. Ibid. For a report that shows decline in
union membership among virtually all OECD
countries, see Organization for Economic

Cooperation and Development, "OECD
Employment Outlook, 2017," June 13, 2017,
p. 136, http://dx.doi.org/10.1787/empl_outlook
-2017-en.

5. Mingwei Liu, "Conflict Resolution in
China," in *The Oxford Handbook of Conflict
Management in Organizations*, ed. William
K. Roche, Paul Teague, and Alexander J. S.
Colvin (Oxford: Oxford University Press, 2014),
494–517.

6. For a discussion of how organizations
misclassify employees as interns, temporary
employees, and independent contractors, see
generally David Weil, *The Fissured Workplace:
Why Work Became So Bad for So Many and
What Can Be Done to Improve It* (Cambridge,
MA: Harvard University Press, 2014).

7. For example, employers may seek to minimize liability for workplace violence. See Mark
Braverman, *Preventing Workplace Violence: A*

Guide for Employers and Practitioners (Thousand Oaks, CA: Sage, 1999); Mark A. Lies II, ed., *Preventing and Managing Workplace Violence: Legal and Strategic Guidelines* (Chicago: American Bar Association, 2008).

8. Jason A. Colquitt et al., "Justice at the Millennium: A Meta-analytic Review of 25 Years of Organizational Justice Research," *Journal of Applied Psychology* 86, no. 3 (2001): 425–45; Jerald Greenberg, "Everybody Talks About Organizational Justice, but Nobody Does Anything About It," *Industrial and Organizational Psychology* 2 (2009): 181–95; Blair H. Sheppard, Roy J. Lewicki, and John W. Minton, *Organizational Justice: The Search for Fairness in the Workplace* (New York: Lexington Books, 1992).

9. Sheppard, Lewicki, and Minton, *Organizational Justice*.

10. Albert O. Hirschman, *Exit, Voice, and Loyalty: Responses to Decline in Firms, Organizations, and States* (Cambridge, MA: Harvard University Press, 1970).

11. Roche, Teague, and Colvin, *Oxford Handbook of Conflict Management in Negotiations*, 13.

12. Ibid., 24.

13. Dean Tjosvold, "The Conflict-Positive Organization: It Depends upon Us," *Journal of Organizational Behavior* 29, no. 1 (2008): 19–28.

14. Carsten K. W. De Dreu, "The Virtue and Vice of Workplace Conflict: Food for (Pessimistic) Thought," *Journal of Organizational Behavior* 29 (2008): 5–18.

15. See, for example, Paul S. Hempel, Zhi-Xue Zhang, and Dean Tjosvold, "Conflict Management Between and Within Teams for Trusting Relationships and Performance in China," *Journal of Organizational Behavior* 30 (2009): 41–65.

16. Douglas M. Mahony and Brian S. Klass, "HRM and Conflict Management," in Roche, Teague, and Colvin, *Oxford Handbook of Conflict Management in Organizations*, 79–104.

17. Ibid., 87.

18. Lisa B. Bingham, "Self-Determination in Dispute System Design and Employment Arbitration," *University of Miami Law Review* 56, no. 4 (2002): 873–908; Lisa B. Bingham, "Control over Dispute System Design and Mandatory Commercial Arbitration," *Law and Contemporary Problems* 67, nos. 1–2 (2004): 221–51.

19. Corinne Bendersky, "Culture: This Missing Link in Dispute Systems Design," *Negotiation Journal* 14, no. 4 (1998): 307–11.

20. Lauren B. Edelman, *Working Law: Courts, Corporations, and Symbolic Civil Rights* (Chicago: University of Chicago Press, 2016).

21. Lauren B. Edelman and Shauhin A. Talesh, "To Comply or Not to Comply—That Isn't the Question: How Organizations Construct the Meaning of Compliance," in *Explaining Compliance: Business Responses to Regulation*, ed. Christine Parker and Vibeke Lehmann Nielsen (Northampton, MA: Edward Elgar, 2011), 103–22.

22. Tina Nabatchi, "The Institutionalization of Alternative Dispute Resolution in the Federal Government," *Public Administration Review* 67, no. 4 (2007): 646–61.

23. Lisa Blomgren Bingham and David H. Good, "A Better Solution to Moral Hazard in Employment Arbitration: It Is Time to Ban Pre-dispute Arbitration Clauses," *Minnesota Law Review Headnotes* 93, no. 1 (2009): 1–14.

24. Edward E. Lawler III, *High-Involvement Management* (San Francisco, CA: Jossey-Bass, 1986).

25. Karl A. Slaikeu and Ralph H. Hasson, *Controlling the Costs of Conflict: How to Design a System for Your Organization* (San Francisco, CA: Jossey-Bass, 1998).

26. Elayne E. Greenberg, "Fitting the Forum to the Pernicious Fuss: A Dispute System Design to Address Implicit Bias and 'Isms in the Workplace," *Cardozo Journal of Conflict Resolution* 75 (2015): 75–113.

27. Ibid., 102–5.

28. But see Jones v. Halliburton Co., 583 F.3d 228 (5th Cir. 2009). The court refused to compel arbitration for claims for assault and battery; intentional infliction of emotional distress; negligent hiring, retention, and supervision of employees involved in a sexual assault; and false imprisonment by coworkers when the employee worked in Iraq, because the claims were not related to her employment contract.

29. Bingham, "Self-Determination in Dispute System Design and Employment Arbitration."

30. David Lipsky, Ronald Seeber, and Richard Fincher, *Emerging Systems for Managing Workplace Conflict: Lessons from American Corporations for Managers and Dispute Resolution Professionals* (San Francisco, CA: Jossey-Bass, 2003).

31. 14 Penn Plaza LLC v. Pyett, 556 U.S. 247 (2009).

32. Corinne Bendersky, "Organizational Dispute Resolution Systems: A Complementarities Model," *Academy of Management Review* 28, no. 4 (2003): 643–56.

33. Charles L. Howard, *The Organizational Ombudsman: Origins, Roles, and Operations—a Legal Guide* (Washington, DC: American Bar Association, 2010).

34. Mary Rowe, "Dispute Resolution in the Non-union Environment," in *Workplace Dispute Resolution: Direction for the 21st Century*, ed. Sandra E. Gleason (East Lansing: Michigan State University Press, 1997), 79–106.

35. Ury, Brett, and Goldberg, *Getting Disputes Resolved*, 11–12.

36. Arnold M. Zack and Michael T. Duffy, "ADR and Employment Discrimination: A Massachusetts Agency Leads the Way," *Dispute Resolution Journal* 29 (1996): 28–53.

37. Ibid., 30–31.

38. Thomas Kochan, Brenda Lautsch, and Corinne Bendersky, "An Evaluation of the Massachusetts Commission Against Alternative Dispute Resolution Program," *Harvard Negotiation Law Review* 5 (2000): 233–74.

39. Ibid., 238.

40. Ibid., 273.

41. Ibid., 256.

42. Ibid., 274.

43. Colquitt et al., "Justice at the Millennium."

44. Tina Nabatchi, David H. Good, and Lisa Blomgren Bingham, "Organizational Justice and Workplace Mediation: A Six-Factor Model," *International Journal of Conflict Management* 18, no. 2 (2007): 148–74.

45. 42 U.S.C. § 2000e-3 et seq.

46. 42 U.S.C. § 12101 et seq.

47. 29 U.S.C. § 621 et seq.

48. Alexander v. Gardner-Denver, 415 U.S. 36 (1974). The case reasons that Congress provided for cooperation and voluntary compliance as the preferred means to resolve equal employment opportunity complaints.

49. U.S. General Accounting Office, "Equal Employment Opportunity: Rising Trends in EEO Complaint Caseloads in the Federal Sector," July 24, 1998, https://www.gao.gov/archive/1998/gg98157b.pdf; U.S. General Accounting Office, "Equal Employment Opportunity: Complaint Caseloads Rising, with Effects of New Regulations on Future Trends Unclear," August 16, 1999, https://www.gao.gov/assets/230/227882.pdf.

50. Lisa Blomgren Bingham and Lisa Marie Napoli, "Employment Dispute Resolution and Workplace Culture: The REDRESS™ Program at the United States Postal Service," in *The Federal Alternative Dispute Deskbook*, ed. Marshall J. Breger and Gerald M. Schatz (Washington, DC: American Bar Association), 507–26.

51. Lisa Blomgren Bingham, Kiwhan Kim, and Susan Summer Raines, "Exploring the Role of Representation in Employment Mediation at the USPS," *Ohio State Journal on Dispute Resolution* 17 (2002): 341–77.

52. Jonathan F. Anderson and Lisa Blomgren Bingham, "Upstream Effects from Mediation of Workplace Disputes: Some

Preliminary Evidence from the USPS," *Labor Law Journal* 48 (1997): 601–15, esp. 606–7.

53. Lisa B. Bingham, "Mediating Employment Disputes: Perceptions of REDRESS at the United States Postal Service," *Review of Public Personnel Administration* 17, no. 2 (1997): 20–30.

54. Lisa B. Bingham et al., "Mediating Employment Disputes at the United States Postal Service: A Comparison of In-House and Outside Neutral Mediators," *Review of Public Personnel Administration* 20, no. 1 (2000): 5–19. The inside neutral mean process index was 30.51, and outside was 31.78 (marginally significant at the .07 level); inside mediator index was 22.98, and outside was 24.23 (significant at the .01 level); and inside mediator outcome index was 18.39, and outside was 19.98 (significant at the .05 level). Also, outside mediators resolved more cases fully or partially (75 percent) than insiders (56 percent).

55. Robert A. Baruch Bush and Joseph P. Folger, *The Promise of Mediation: Responding to Conflict Through Empowerment and Recognition* (Hoboken, NJ: Wiley, 1994).

56. Edith Primm, "The Neighbor Justice Center Movement," *Kentucky Law Journal* 81 (1993): 1067–83.

57. Nabatchi, Bingham, and Good, "Organizational Justice and Workplace Mediation."

58. Lisa Blomgren Bingham et al., "Dispute System Design and Justice in Employment Dispute Resolution: Mediation at the Workplace," *Harvard Negotiation Law Review* 14 (2009): 1–50; Yuseok Moon and Lisa Blomgren Bingham, "Transformative Mediation at Work: Employee and Supervisor Perceptions on USPS REDRESS Program," *International Review of Public Administration* 11 (2007): 43–55.

59. The mean employee process index was 31.49 and supervisor process index was 31.79 out of a maximum of 35. Moon and Bingham, "Transformative Mediation at Work."

60. Lisa B. Bingham and Cristina M. Novac, "Mediation's Impact on Formal Complaint Filing: Before and After the REDRESS™ Program at the United States Postal Service," *Review of Public Personnel Administration* 21, no. 4 (2001): 308–31.

61. Nabatchi, Good, and Bingham, "Organizational Justice and Workplace Mediation."

62. Howard Gadlin, "Careful Maneuvers: Mediating Sexual Harassment," *Negotiation Journal* 7, no. 2 (1991): 139–53; Lee P. Robbins and William B. Deane, "The Corporate Ombuds: A New Approach to Conflict Management," *Negotiation Journal* 2, no. 2 (1986): 195–205.

63. Deborah M. Kolb, "Corporate Ombudsman and Organization Conflict Resolution," *Journal of Conflict Resolution* 31, no. 4 (1987): 673–91.

64. For a study based on qualitative interviews of key agency stakeholders, see Leah Meltzer, "The Federal Workplace Ombuds," *Ohio State Journal on Dispute Resolution* 13, no. 2 (1998): 549–609.

65. Howard, *The Organizational Ombudsman.*

66. International Ombudsman Association, "IOA Standards of Practice," October 2009, https://www.ombudsassociation.org/assets/docs/IOA_Standards_of_Practice_Oct09.pdf.

67. Compliance Advisor Ombudsman, "How We Work: Ombudsman," http://www.cao-ombudsman.org/howwework/ombudsman (accessed June 13, 2019).

68. Lisa B. Bingham, "Emerging Due Process Concerns in Employment Arbitration," *Labor Law Journal* 47, no. 2 (1996): 108–26.

69. Mary Rowe, "Dispute Resolution in the Non-union Environment: An Evolution Toward Integrated Systems for Conflict Management?," in *Workplace Dispute Resolution: Directions for the 21st Century*, ed. Sandra E. Gleason (East Lansing: Michigan State University Press, 1997), 79–106.

70. Society of Professionals in Dispute Resolution, "Guidelines for the Design of Integrated Conflict Management Systems Within

Organizations: Executive Summary," https://www.mediate.com/articles/spidrtrack1.cfm (accessed June 13, 2019).

71. Ibid.

72. Raytheon Corporation explored the transformative model in employment. It ultimately changed its ADR program from adhe-

Chapter 12

1. Hooters of Am., Inc. v. Phillips, 173 F.3d 933 (4th Cir. 1999). The decision declined to compel the employee to arbitrate a Title VII claim of egregiously one-sided and unfair arbitration rules. See also Murray v. United Food and Commercial Workers Int'l Union, 289 F.3d 297, 302–4 (4th Cir. 2002) ("And, as in *Hooters*, the one-sided nature of the arbitration agreement [includes] the employer providing itself with the exclusive right to select the list of potential arbitrators from which the ultimate decisionmaker will be selected").

2. See Sandra F. Gavin, "Unconscionability Found: A Look at Pre-dispute Mandatory Arbitration Agreements 10 Years After *Doctor's Associates, Inc. v. Casarotto*," *Cleveland State Law Review* 54 (2006): 249–72, esp. 263–68.

3. European Parliament Directorate-General for Internal Policies, "Legal Instruments and Practice of Arbitration in the EU," November 2014, http://www.europarl.europa.eu/RegData/etudes/STUD/2015/509988/IPOL_STU(2015)509988_EN.pdf. The policy notes that mandatory predispute arbitration clauses are often found invalid in European jurisdictions.

4. Paul B. Marrow, "Determining If Mandatory Arbitration Is Fair: Asymmetrically Held Information and the Role of Mandatory Arbitration in Modulating Uninsurable Contract Risks," *New York Law School Law Review* 54, no. 1 (2009): 187–239. Marrow argues that mandatory arbitration valuably "transfers some of the risk created by asymmetrically held information back to the party creating that risk" (189). But see Lisa B. Bingham, "Control over Dispute-System Design and Mandatory

sive, or forced, arbitration to mediation. Charles D. Coleman, "Is Mandatory Employment Arbitration Living Up to Its Expectations? A View from the Employer's Perspective," *ABA Journal of Labor and Employment Law* 25, no. 2 (2010): 227–40.

Commercial Arbitration," *Law and Contemporary Problems* 67, nos. 1–2 (2004): 223–24. Bingham argues that repeat players that control the design of arbitration systems manage risk by shifting transaction costs to the one-shot player to reduce the settlement value of a case and discourage litigation.

5. Lisa B. Bingham, "Employment Arbitration: The Repeat Player Effect," *Employee Rights and Employment Policy Journal* 1, no. 1 (1997): 189–220; Marc Galanter, "Why the 'Haves' Come Out Ahead: Speculation on the Limits of Legal Change," *Law and Society Review* 9, no. 1 (1974): 95–160; Carrie Menkel-Meadow, "Do the 'Haves' Come Out Ahead in Alternative Justice Systems? Repeat Players in ADR," *Ohio State Journal on Dispute Resolution* 15 (1999): 19–61.

6. For a review of the literature, see Thomas J. Stipanowich, "The Arbitration Fairness Index: Using a Public Rating System to Skirt the Legal Logjam and Promote Fairer and More Effective Arbitration of Employment and Consumer Disputes," *Kansas Law Review* 60 (2012): 985–1069; and Thomas J. Stipanowich, "The Third Arbitration Trilogy: *Stolt-Nielsen, Rent-A-Center, Concepcion* and the Future of American Arbitration," *American Review of International Arbitration* 22 (2011): 323–434.

7. Jill Gross, "Justice Scalia's Hat Trick and the Supreme Court's Flawed Understanding of Twenty-First Century Arbitration," *Brooklyn Law Review* 81, no. 1 (2015): 111–48.

8. Lisa B. Bingham, "Employment Dispute Resolution: The Case for Mediation," *Conflict Resolution Quarterly* 22 (2004): 145–74; H. John Bernardin, Brenda E. Richey, and Stephanie L.

Castro, "Mandatory and Binding Arbitration: Effects on Employee Attitudes and Recruiting Results," *Human Resource Management* 50, no. 2 (2011): 175–200.

9. Yadong Luo, John Hongxin Zhao, and Jianjun Du, "The Internationalization Speed of E-commerce Companies: An Empirical Analysis," *International Marketing Review* 22, no. 6 (2005): 693–709; Cliff Wymbs, "How E-commerce Is Transforming and Internationalizing Service Industries," *Journal of Services Marketing* 14, no. 6 (2000): 463–77.

10. Pablo Cortés, *Online Dispute Resolution for Consumers in the European Union* (New York: Taylor and Francis, 2011); Catherine A. Rogers, "Transparency in International Commercial Arbitration," *Kansas Law Review* 54 (2006): 1301–38; Donna M. Bates, "A Consumer's Dream or Pandora's Box: Is Arbitration a Viable Option for Cross-Border Consumer Disputes?," *Fordham International Law Journal* 27 (2003): 823–98. More broadly, see also Stephen E. Gent, "The Politics of International Arbitration and Adjudication," *Penn State Journal of Law and International Affairs* 2, no. 1 (2013): 66–77; and Stephen E. Gent and Megan Shannon, "The Effectiveness of International Arbitration and Adjudication: Getting into a Bind," *Journal of Politics* 72, no. 2 (2010): 366–80.

11. See Directive 2013/11/EU of the European Parliament and of the Council, May 21, 2013, at https://eur-lex.europa.eu/LexUriServ/LexUriServ.do?uri=OJ:L:2013:165:0063:0079:EN:PDF. See also Chris Gill, Jane Williams, Carol Brennan, and Carolyn Hirst, "Designing Consumer Redress: A Dispute System Design (DSD) Model for Consumer-to-Business Disputes," *Legal Studies* 36, no. 3 (2016): 438–63.

12. Carrie Menkel-Meadow, "Mothers and Fathers of Invention: The Intellectual Founders of ADR," *Ohio State Journal on Dispute Resolution* 16 (2000): 1–37.

13. Elinor Ostrom, *Understanding Institutional Diversity* (Princeton, NJ: Princeton University Press, 2005).

14. Lisa Blomgren Amsler, "The Evolution of Social Norms in Conflict Resolution," *Journal of Natural Resources Policy Research* 6, no. 4 (2014): 285–90.

15. National Labor Relations Act, 29 U.S.C. §§ 151–169 (1935).

16. See W. Daniel Boone, "Steelworkers Trilogy: Collective Bargaining as the Foundation for Industrial Democracy and Arbitration as an Integral Part of Workplace Self-Government," in *National Academy of Arbitrators Annual Proceedings 2010* (Edison, NJ: BNA Books, 2010), 100–142.

17. United Steelworkers of Am. v. Am. Mfg. Co., 363 U.S. 564 (1960).

18. United Steelworkers v. Warrior and Gulf Navigation Co., 363 U.S. 574 (1960).

19. United Steelworkers of Am. v. Enter. Wheel and Car Corp., 363 U.S. 593 (1960), 80 S. Ct. 1358 (1960), 4 L. Ed. 2d 1424 (1960).

20. Henry Drummonds, "A Closer Look at the US Supreme Court's Public Policy Trilogy: A BROADER View of the Public Policy Exception to Labor Arbitration Award Enforcement," *Labor Law Journal* 65, no. 3 (2014): 136–70. Drummonds argues that many arbitrators and labor lawyers give the public policy exception "too cribbed an interpretation" under the principles announced by the Supreme Court (137).

21. Alexander v. Gardner-Denver, 415 U.S. 36 (1974). As noted in Chapter 11, the Supreme Court may reconsider this holding in the near future.

22. See David Horton, "Arbitration as Delegation," *New York University Law Review* 86 (2011): 437–99, esp. 444–45n34. Horton observes that "in 1925, business groups and the American Bar Association persuaded Congress to pass the [Federal Arbitration Act] to eliminate judicial hostility to arbitration" (445).

23. Federal Arbitration Act, 9 U.S.C. § 1 et seq. (2012).

24. Federal Arbitration Act, 6 Pub. L. No. 68-401, 43 Stat. 883 (1925). See, generally, Ian R. Macneil, *American Arbitration Law* (Oxford: Oxford University Press, 1992), 83–101.

25. See, generally, Imre Stephen Szalai, "Exploring the Federal Arbitration Act Through the Lens of History," *Journal of Dispute Resolution* 2016, no. 1 (2016): 115–39, esp. 116–22; and Macneil, *American Arbitration Law*, 102–21.

26. See, generally, Gross, "Justice Scalia's Hat Trick."

27. Federal Arbitration Act, 9 U.S.C. § 1 (2012).

28. Federal Arbitration Act, 9 U.S.C. § 2 (2012). The act says, "A written provision in any maritime transaction or a contract evidencing a transaction involving commerce to settle by arbitration a controversy thereafter arising out of such contract or transaction, or the refusal to perform the whole or any part thereof, or an agreement in writing to submit to arbitration an existing controversy arising out of such a contract, transaction, or refusal, shall be valid, irrevocable, and enforceable, save upon such grounds as exist at law or in equity for the revocation of any contract."

29. Federal Arbitration Act, 9 U.S.C. § 10, authorizes awards to be vacated only as follows: "(a) In any of the following cases the United States court in and for the district wherein the award was made may make an order vacating the award upon the application of any party to the arbitration—(1) where the award was procured by corruption, fraud, or undue means; (2) where there was evident partiality or corruption in the arbitrators, or either of them; (3) where the arbitrators were guilty of miscon- duct in refusing to postpone the hearing, upon sufficient cause shown, or in refusing to hear evidence pertinent and material to the contro-

versy; or of any other misbehavior by which the rights of any party have been prejudiced; or (4) where the arbitrators exceeded their powers, or so imperfectly executed them that a mutual, final, and definite award upon the subject mat- ter submitted was not made."

30. Sarah Rudolph Cole, "Revising the FAA to Permit Expanded Judicial Review of Arbitration Awards," *Nevada Law Journal* 8 (2007): 214–33.

31. Administrative Procedure Act, 5 U.S.C. § 706.

32. Lisa Bernstein, "Opting out of the Legal System: Extralegal Contractual Relations in the Diamond Industry," *Journal of Legal Studies* 21, no. 1 (1992): 115–57; Ersoy Zirhlioglu, "The Diamond Industry and the Industry's Dispute Resolution Mechanisms," *Arizona Journal of International and Comparative Law* 30, no. 3 (2013): 477–506.

33. Lisa Bernstein, "Private Commercial Law in the Cotton Industry: Creating Cooper- ation Through Rules, Norms, and Institutions," *Michigan Law Review* 99 (2001): 1724–90; Jean-Baptiste Zoma, "Communication sur les interprofessions au Burkina Faso" [Commu- nication on interprofessions in Burkina Faso], October 2006, http://www.inter-reseaux.org/ IMG/pdf/Burkina_Etatdeslieux_Interpro_PAF .pdf. Zoma argues that interprofessional agri- cultural associations, such as those for cotton, should be recognized as arbitrators of disputes within the production chain.

34. See, for example, Bernstein, "Private Commercial Law in the Cotton Industry," 1726–28.

35. Gilmer v. Interstate/Johnson Lane Corp., 500 U.S. 20 (1991).

36. Ibid., 40.

37. For a historical analysis that dem- onstrates an intent to keep them separate, consider Imre Szalai, *Outsourcing Justice: The Rise of Modern Arbitration Laws in America*

(Durham, NC: Carolina Academic Press, 2016), 191–92. Szalai examines how the FAA was never intended to apply to employment disputes.

38. Mark D. Gough, "Employment Lawyers and Mandatory Arbitration: Facilitating or Forestalling Access to Justice?," in *Managing and Resolving Workplace Conflict*, ed. David B. Lipsky, Ariel C. Avgar, and J. Ryan Lamare (Bingley, UK: Emerald, 2016), 105–34; Kathryn A. Sabbeth and David C. Vladeck, "Contracting (out) Rights," *Fordham Urban Law Journal* 36, no. 4 (2009): 803–38.

39. Richard C. Reuben, "Process Purity and Innovation: Response to Professors Stempel, Cole, and Drahozal," *Nevada Law Journal* 8, no. 1 (2007): 271–313, esp. 278–79.

40. Marc Galanter, "The Quality of Settlements," *Journal of Dispute Resolution* 1988 (1988): 55–84. The discussion that follows of Galanter's work is drawn from Bingham, "Control over Dispute-System Design and Mandatory Commercial Arbitration."

41. It is also sometimes called the "bottom line." David A. Lax and James K. Sebenius, *The Manager as Negotiator: Bargaining for Cooperation and Competitive Gain* (New York: Free Press, 1986), 51.

42. The settlement range is also sometimes referred to as the bargaining zone or set. It is defined as the difference between the parties' reservation prices. Ibid., 119–21. If, for example, the seller has a reservation price of ten dollars (the least she will accept) and the buyer has a reservation price of twelve dollars (the most he will pay), there is a settlement range of between ten dollars and twelve dollars. If the seller instead has a reservation price of twelve dollars and the buyer ten dollars, there is no settlement range or bargaining zone at all. Roy J. Lewicki, David M. Saunders, and Bruce Barry call this a negative bargaining zone. Roy J. Lewicki, David M. Saunders, and Bruce Barry, *Negotiation* (New York: McGraw-Hill, 2015).

43. Galanter, "The Quality of Settlements," 69–71n10. If A expects to recover $100 and B to pay $100 in damages, both expect to pay $20 in transaction costs such as attorneys' fees, and A expects to lose $5 while B gains $5 in interest on the use of the money during the delay, these transaction costs produce a settlement range of between $75, as the lowest A will accept, and $115, as the most B will pay. If A and B have different estimates of what will happen in court, the transaction costs make the difference. If A thinks she will recover $110, B expects to pay only $90, and there are no transaction costs, there is no settlement range. If you factor in the $20 in attorneys' fees or costs and $5 for the time-value of money, you now have a settlement range between $85, as the least A will accept, and $105, as the most B will pay.

44. For a detailed discussion of the settlement range, or "bargaining set," see Lax and Sebenius, *The Manager as Negotiator*, 46–62.

45. This alternative is what each party can do unilaterally, without the agreement of the other, to meet its own needs or interests. See Roger Fisher, William L. Ury, and Bruce Patton, *Getting to Yes: Negotiating Agreement Without Giving In*, 3rd ed. (New York: Penguin, 2011), 97–106. See also Lax and Sebenius, *The Manager as Negotiator*, 46–62.

46. Most cases result in "litigotiation," or settlement in the shadow of litigation, with full adjudication occurring with relative infrequency. For a review of the decline in contract litigation and a survey of available empirical findings on its extent and causes, including referral to ADR, see Marc Galanter, "Contract in Court; Or, Almost Everything You May or May Not Want to Know About Contract Litigation," *Wisconsin Law Review* 2001 (2001): 577–620, esp. 596.

47. See, for example, Lax and Sebenius, *The Manager as Negotiator*, 55–69.

48. Ibid., 55.

49. For an example, consider David Horton and Andrea Cann Chandrasekher, "After the Revolution: An Empirical Study of Consumer Arbitration," *Georgetown Law Review* 104 (2015): 57–124.

50. Lisa B. Bingham, "McGeorge Symposium on Arbitration: On Repeat Players, Adhesive Contracts, and the Use of Statistics in Judicial Review of Arbitration Awards," *McGeorge Law Review* 29, no. 2 (1998): 223–59; Bingham, "Employment Arbitration"; Lisa B. Bingham, "Self-Determination in Dispute System Design and Employment Arbitration," *University of Miami Law Review* 56, no. 4 (2002): 873–908; Alexander J. S. Colvin, "An Empirical Study of Employment Arbitration: Case Outcomes and Processes," *Journal of Empirical Legal Studies* 8, no. 1 (2011): 1–23; David Horton and Andrea Cann Chandrasekher, "Employment Arbitration After the Revolution," *Georgetown Law Journal* 104 (2015): 57–124; J. Ryan Lamare and David B. Lipsky, "Employment Arbitration in the Securities Industry: Lessons Drawn from Recent Empirical Research," *Berkeley Journal of Employment and Labor Law* 35 (2014): 113–33.

51. The Due Process Protocol for Mediation and Arbitration of Statutory Disputes Arising out of the Employment Relationship is posted on the website of the convening organization for the group that developed it, the American Arbitration Association. See American Arbitration Association, "Employment Due Process Protocol," May 9, 1995, https://www.adr .org/sites/default/files/document_repository/ Employment%20Due%20Process%20Protocol _0.pdf. A decade later, Richard A. Bales identified six areas in which the employment protocol either provided no or insufficient guidance or has been left behind by case law: contract formation issues, barriers to access, process issues, remedies issues, FAA issues, and conflicts of interest. Richard A. Bales, "The Employment Due Process Protocol at Ten: Twenty

Unresolved Issues, and a Focus on Conflicts of Interest," *Ohio State Journal on Dispute Resolution* 21, no. 1 (2005): 185.

52. For the Consumer Due Process Protocol, see American Arbitration Association, "Consumer Due Process Protocol: Statement of Principles," 1998, https://www.adr.org/sites/ default/files/document_repository/Consumer %20Due%20Process%20Protocol%20(1).pdf.

53. Lisa B. Bingham and Shimon Sarraf, "Employment Arbitration Before and After the Due Process Protocol for Mediation and Arbitration of Statutory Disputes Arising out of Employment: Preliminary Evidence that Self-Regulation Makes a Difference," in *Alternative Dispute Resolution in the Employment Arena: Proceedings of New York University 53rd Annual Conference on Labor* (New York: Kluwer Law International, 2004), 303–29. Bingham and Sarraf find that employee outcomes improved after the American Arbitration Association implemented the employee protocol in its employment arbitration cases.

54. Goldberg v. Kelly, 397 U.S. 254 (1970); Mathews v. Eldridge, 424 U.S. 319 (1976).

55. Carrie J. Menkel-Meadow et al., *Dispute Resolution: Beyond the Adversarial Model*, 2nd ed. (Danvers, MA: Wolters Kluwer, 2010), 413–81.

56. In a systematic comparison of arbitration and litigation that accounts for several key factors that differentiate the types of cases brought in each of the two forums, "settlement amounts are lower in mandatory arbitration cases than in litigation." Alexander J. S. Colvin and Mark D. Gough, "Comparing Mandatory Arbitration and Litigation: Access, Process, and Outcomes," April 2, 2014, http:// digitalcommons.ilr.cornell.edu/reports/60.

57. Sajida A. Mahdi, "Gateway to Arbitration: Issues of Contract Formation Under the U.C.C. and the Enforceability of Arbitration Clauses Included in Standard Form Contracts

Shipped with Goods," *Northwestern University Law Review* 96 (2001): 403–46 esp. 430–35.

58. For a view into the wider commercial context of "customized procedure," see W. Mark C. Weidenmaier, "Customized Procedure in Theory and Reality," *Washington and Lee Law Review* 72, no. 4 (2015): 1865–946. For a more in-depth discussion, see Menkel-Meadow et al., *Dispute Resolution*.

59. Erin A. O'Hara O'Connor, Kenneth J. Martin, and Randall S. Thomas, "Customizing Employment Arbitration," *Iowa Law Review* 98, no. 1 (2012): 133–82.

60. Prima Paint Corp. v. Flood and Conklin Mfg. Co., 388 U.S. 395 (1967).

61. Ibid., 400–401.

62. Ibid., 406.

63. Buckeye Check Cashing, Inc. v. Cardegna, 546 U.S. 440 (2006).

64. Ibid., 447–48.

65. Ibid., 449.

66. 26 A.L.R.3d 604 (1993) ("[Is] the court or the arbitrator . . . the proper forum to decide whether a party seeking arbitration, or opposing another's right to arbitration, has waived the right to arbitration or any other substantive right[?]").

67. New Prime Inc. v. Oliveira, No. 17-340, 586 U.S. ___ (U.S. Jan. 15, 2019). In an 8–0 decision, the court held that FAA excludes disputes concerning contracts of employment involving transportation workers engaged in foreign or interstate commerce.

68. Granite Rock Co. v. Teamsters, 561 U.S. 287 (2010).

69. Ibid., 299–300.

70. For an example, see Lara K. Richards and Jason W. Burge, "Analyzing the Applicability of Statutes of Limitations in Arbitration," *Gonzaga Law Review* 49, no. 2 (2013): 213–48. In *Henry Schein Inc. v. Archer and White Sales Inc.*, No. 17-1272 (U.S. Jan. 8, 2019), the Supreme Court held (9–0) that the arbitrator had the power to determine whether a dispute over arbitration clause language that excluded claims for injunctive relief was arbitrable, rejecting an exception for "wholly groundless" claims.

71. For a discussion of *Howsam v. Dean Witter Reynolds, Inc.*, 537 U.S. 79 (2002), see Menkel-Meadow et al., *Dispute Resolution*, 455.

72. Rent-a-Center, West, Inc. v. Jackson, 561 U.S. 63 (2010), WL 2471058 (2010). See, generally, Charles L. Knapp, "Blowing the Whistle on Mandatory Arbitration: Unconscionability as a Signaling Device," *San Diego Law Review* 46 (2009): 609–28. Knapp studies the increase in use and success of unconscionability arguments from 1990 through 2008.

73. For a compelling narrative that answers this question in the negative by suggesting arbitration is undermining public law, see J. Maria Glover, "Disappearing Claims and the Erosion of Substantive Law," *Yale Law Journal* 124 (2015): 3052–93.

74. See Timothy E. Travers, annotation, "Arbiter's Power to Award Punitive Damages," 83 A.L.R.3d 1037 (1978).

75. PacifiCare Health Systems, Inc. v. Book, 538 U.S. 401 (2003).

76. Ibid., 403–7.

77. AT&T Mobility v. Concepcion, 131 S. Ct. 1740 (2011). In 2019, the Supreme Court held that under the FAA, an ambiguous agreement to arbitrate does not provide the basis to conclude that the parties agreed to submit to class arbitration. Lamps Plus, Inc. et al. v. Varela, 587 U.S. ___ (2019).

78. AT&T Mobility v. Concepcion, 341–43.

79. American Express Co. et al. v. Italian Colors Restaurant et al., 570 U.S. 228 (2013).

80. Epic Systems Corp. v. Lewis, 584 U.S., 138 S. Ct. 1612 (2018), Slip. Op. 16-285.

81. Imre S. Szalai, "A Constitutional Right to Discovery? Creating and Reinforcing Due Process Norms Through the Procedural Laboratory of Arbitration," *Pepperdine Dispute Resolution Law Journal* 15 (2015): 337–75, esp. 339–55.

82. Hall Street Associates L.L.C. v. Mattel, Inc., 552 U.S. 576 (2008).

83. Ibid., 579.

84. Ibid., 590.

85. But see Helen LaVan, Michael J. Jedel, and Robert Perkovich, "Vacating of Arbitration Awards as Diminishment of Conflict Resolution," *Negotiation and Conflict Management Research* 5 (2012): 29–48.

86. S. I. Strong, "Limits of Procedural Choice of Law," *Brooklyn Journal of International Law* 39, no. 3 (2014): 1027–122.

87. Bruce Wardhaugh, "Unveiling Fairness for the Consumer: The Law, Economics and Justice of Expanded Arbitration," *Loyola Consumer Law Review* 26 (2014): 42–69.

88. Green Tree Financial Corp.-Ala. v. Randolph, 531 U.S. 79 (2000).

89. Christopher R. Drahozal, "Arbitration Costs and Forum Accessibility: Empirical Evidence," *University of Michigan Journal of Law Reform* 41, no. 4 (2008): 813–41. Drahozal finds that upfront arbitration costs are higher than court, that arbitration may be more accessible for low-cost claims but less so for larger claims, and that even for low-cost claims, cost may depend on the accessibility of class actions. Drahozal reached these conclusions before the *Concepcion* ruling.

90. Thomas J. Stipanowich, "Arbitration: The 'New Litigation,'" *University of Illinois Law Review* 2010, no. 1 (2010): 1–60.

91. David Lipsky, Ronald L. Seeber, and Richard D. Fincher, *Emerging Systems for Managing Workplace Conflict: Lessons from American Corporations for Managers and Dispute Resolution Professionals* (San Francisco, CA: Jossey-Bass, 2003).

92. Bernardin, Richey, and Castro, "Mandatory and Binding Arbitration."

93. Galanter, "Why the 'Haves' Come Out."

94. Cedric Dawkins, "Agonistic Pluralism and Stakeholder Engagement," *Business Ethics Quarterly* 25 (2015): 1–28.

95. Bernardin, Richey, and Castro, "Mandatory and Binding Arbitration." An empirical study found that the more the public learns about adhesive arbitration, the less fair it believes it to be. Victor D. Quintanilla and Alexander B. Avtgis, "The Public Believes Predispute Binding Arbitration Clauses Are Unjust: Ethical Implications for Dispute-System Design in the Time of Vanishing Trials," *Fordham Law Review* 85 (2017): 2119–49. Contrast this with Kaiser Permanente, described in Chapters 4 and 14, which after its initial one-party design, brought in multiple parties and stakeholder input to redesign the system.

96. Christopher R. Drahozal and Erin A. O'Hara O'Connor, "Unbundling Procedure: Carve-Outs from Arbitration Clauses," *Florida Law Review* 66, no. 5 (2013): 1945–2006.

97. The implications for this debate are far-flung and fundamental, touching on several of America's bedrock principles, such as federalism. See David S. Schwartz, "State Judges as Guardians of Federalism: Resisting the Federal Arbitration Act's Encroachment on State Law," *Washington University Journal of Law and Policy* 16 (2004): 129–62.

98. Nancy A. Welsh, "Class Action–Barring Mandatory Pre-dispute Consumer Arbitration Clauses: An Example," *University of St. Thomas Law Journal* 13, no. 2 (2017): 381–433.

99. Matthew R. Salzwedel and Devona Wells, "National Arbitration Forum Settlement with Minnesota Attorney General," *State AG Tracker* 1, no. 4 (2009), https://fedsoc-cms -public.s3.amazonaws.com/update/pdf/ RNhzz01Xy8MkGjKXRSlexfbd58K2EO0e9Lk Jtwq5.pdf.

100. Lisa Blomgren Bingham and David H. Good, "A Better Solution to Moral Hazard in Employment Arbitration: It Is Time to Ban Pre-dispute Arbitration Clauses," *Minnesota Law Review Headnotes* 93, no. 1 (2009): 1–14. Congressional considerations are arguably reasonable: the premise that predispute adhesive

arbitration in the employment context expands employee access to justice is highly disputed. See Gough, "Employment Lawyers and Mandatory Arbitration."

101. For a more detailed analysis of its genesis, see Todd Zywicki, "The Consumer Financial Protection Bureau: Savior or Menace?," *George Washington Law Review* 81 (2013): 856–921.

102. Ibid., 907, citing Dodd-Frank Wall Street Reform and Consumer Protection Act, Pub. L. No. 111-203, § 1414(a), § 129C(e)(1), 124 Stat. 1376, 2151 (2010) (codified at 15 U.S.C. § 1639c(e)(1) (Supp. IV 2011)).

103. Bureau of Consumer Financial Protection, "12 CFR Part 1026, Loan Originator Compensation Requirements Under the Truth in Lending Act (Regulation Z): Final Rule," 78 Fed. Reg. 11280 (February 15, 2013). The relevant mortgage language appears in § 1026.36(h).

104. Zywicki, "Consumer Financial Protection Bureau," 907–8.

105. The Consumer Financial Protection Bureau Credit Card Database is available at http://www.consumerfinance.gov/credit-cards/agreements.

106. Consumer Financial Protection Bureau, "Arbitration Study Preliminary Results," December 12, 2013, http://files.consumerfinance.gov/f/201312_cfpb_arbitration-study-preliminary-results.pdf. On pages 19–22, the report shows that banks and credit card issuers use arbitration clauses more often if they are larger institutions and that the majority of outstanding loans thus have such clauses, even though they represent only 17 percent of the contracts.

107. Kenneth Richards, David Bach, and Robert K. Fleming, "Golden Agri Resources and Sustainability," *Yale University Teaching Case Study*, 2013, https://som.yale.edu/case/2013/golden-agri-resources-and-sustainability.

108. Stipanowich, "The Arbitration Fairness Index."

109. Ibid., 1030.

110. Nancy A. Welsh, "Mandatory Predispute Arbitration, Structural Bias, and Incentivizing Procedural Safeguards," *Southwestern University Law Review* 42 (2012): 187–228, esp. 187–213.

111. Metropolitan Life Ins. Co. v. Glenn, 554 U.S. 105 (2008).

112. Welsh, "Mandatory Predispute Arbitration," 220. She also observes, "*Glenn* now entitles claimants to request discovery regarding the details of insurers' and employers' claims handling" (220).

113. "The potential transparency and accountability offered by discovery into administrators' claims processing, would at least create the potential to enhance the reality of, and a skeptical public's perception of, the thoroughness and accuracy of decision-making in mandatory predispute arbitration." Ibid., 222.

114. Nancy A. Welsh, "I Could Have Been a Contender: Summary Jury Trial as a Means to Overcome Iqbal's Negative Effects upon Pre-litigation Communication, Negotiation and Early, Consensual Dispute Resolution," *Penn State Law Review* 114 (2010): 1149–89, esp. 1172–88.

115. For reviews of research, see Colvin, "An Empirical Study of Employment Arbitration"; and Lamare and Lipsky, "Employment Arbitration in the Securities Industry."

116. Lisa Blomgren Amsler, "Combating Structural Bias in Dispute System Designs That Use Arbitration: Transparency, the Universal Sanitizer," *Yearbook on Arbitration and Mediation* 6 (2014): 32–55.

117. Alexander J. S. Colvin, "The Metastasization of Mandatory Arbitration," *Chicago-Kent Law Review* 94 (2019): 3–24; Cynthia Estlund, "The Black Hole of Mandatory Arbitration," *North Carolina Law Review* 96 (2018): 679–710.

118. Judith Resnik, "Diffusing Disputes: The Public in the Private of Arbitration, the Private in Courts, and the Erasure of Rights," *Yale Law Journal* 124 (2015): 2804–939.

119. Colin Rule, Vikki Rogers, and Louis F. Del Duca, "Designing a Global Consumer Online Dispute Resolution (ODR) System for Cross-Border Small Value–High Volume Claims—OAS Developments," *Uniform Commercial Code Law Journal* 42, no. 3 (2010): 221–64.

120. Jean R. Sternlight, "Mandatory Arbitration Stymies Progress Towards Justice in Employment Law: Where to, #MeToo?," *Harvard Civil Rights–Civil Liberties Law Review* 54 (2019): 1–51.

Chapter 13

1. Christopher W. Moore, *The Mediation Process: Practical Strategies for Resolving Conflict*, 4th ed. (San Francisco, CA: Jossey-Bass, 2014): 3–18, 60.

2. Y. P. Kamminga, "Towards Effective Governance Structures for Contractual Relations: Recommendations from Social Psychology, Economics, and Law for Improving Project Performance in Infrastructure Projects" (PhD diss., Tilburg University, Netherlands, 2008). See also Michael Latham, *Constructing the Team: Joint Review of Procurement and Contractual Arrangements in the United Kingdom Construction Industry* (London: HMSO, July 1994); and John Egan, *Rethinking Construction: The Report of the Construction Task Force* (London: HMSO, November 1998). We acknowledge and thank Peter Kamminga for his research in the field of construction dispute resolution.

3. In the United States, ADR was introduced as an alternative to construction litigation and took the form of partnering agreements and dispute boards. See David C. Weston and G. Edward Gibson Jr., "Partnering-Project Performance in U.S. Army Corps of Engineers," *Journal of Management Engineering* 9, no. 4 (1993): 410–25; Contract Disputes Act of 1978, 92 Stat. 2383 (1978); Administrative Dispute Resolution Act of 1990, 104 Stat. 2736 (1990); and Administrative Dispute Resolution Act of 1996, Pub. L. No. 104-320.

4. See American Arbitration Association, "The Construction Industry's Guide to Dispute Avoidance and Resolution," October 1, 2009, pp. 3–6, https://www.adr.org/sites/default/files/document_repository/The%20Construction%20Industry's%20Guide%20to%20Dispute%20Avoidance%20and%20Resolution.pdf.

5. James P. Groton, Robert A. Rubin, and Bettina Quintas, "Comparing Dispute Review Boards and Adjudication," in *American Arbitration Association Handbook on Construction Arbitration and ADR*, 3rd ed. (Huntington, NY: JurisNet, 2016), 501–6; Shamil Naoum, "An Overview into the Concept of Partnering," *International Journal of Project Management* 21, no. 1 (2003): 71–76; Kamminga, "Towards Effective Governance Structures for Contractual Relations," 97–98.

6. See American Arbitration Association, "Construction Industry Arbitration Rules and Mediation Procedures," July 1, 2015, https://www.adr.org/sites/default/files/Construction_Arbitration_Rules_7May2018.pdf.

7. We acknowledge and thank Noah Susskind for his extensive research on the design and experience of dispute resolution for the Big Dig.

8. Kurt L. Dettman, Martin J. Harty, and Joel Lewin, "Resolving Megaproject Claims: Lessons from Boston's 'Big Dig,'" *Construction Lawyer* 30, no. 2 (2010): 1–13.

9. Kathleen M. J. Harmon, "Case Study as to the Effectiveness of Dispute Review Boards on the Central Artery/Tunnel Project," *Journal of Legal Affairs and Dispute Resolution in Engineering and Construction* 1, no. 1 (2009): 18–31.

10. Kamminga, "Towards Effective Governance Structures for Contractual Relations," 43–81; Barbara Epstein Stedman, "A Multi-option System Helps Get to the Bottom of 'Big Dig' Conflicts," *Negotiation Journal* 15, no. 1 (1999): 5–10.

11. Janet Shprintz, "John Schulman: Hollywood Law Impact Report," *Variety*, March 28, 2007, https://variety.com/2007/biz/markets-festivals/john-schulman-1117961951.

12. For more about CPR (formerly the Center for Public Resources), see its website, at http://www.cpradr.org.

13. P. D. Villarreal, "Unnecessary Litigation: A System Flaw—GE Launches Zero Defect Campaign," *Metropolitan Corporate Counsel Annual Index* 7, no. 8 (1999): 1–36.

14. See Center for Public Resources, *Corporate Early Case Assessment Toolkit* (New York: International Institute for Conflict Prevention and Resolution, 2009); and Frank Aquila and Kathy Bryan, "Avoiding the 'Boomerang': Resolving Disputes Before They Ruin the Deal," *M&A Journal* 10, no. 5 (2010): 17–20.

15. An integrated conflict management system is "a systematic approach to preventing, managing, and resolving conflict that focuses on the causes of conflict within the organization." Society of Professionals in Dispute Resolution, "Guidelines for the Design of Integrated Conflict Management Systems Within Organizations: Executive Summary," https://www.mediate.com/articles/spidrtrack1.cfm (accessed June 13, 2019).

16. Michael A. Wheeler and Gillian Morris, "GE's Early Dispute Resolution Initiative (A)," Harvard Business School case HBS 9801395-E, June 19, 2001, p. 9.

17. P. D. Villarreal (senior vice president of global litigation of GlaxoSmithKline), presentation at Stanford Law School, November 28, 2017, copy in the authors' possession.

18. See Thomas L. Sager and Richard L. Horwitz, "Early Case Assessment: DuPont's Experience," in *Successful Partnering Between Inside and Outside Counsel*, ed. Robert L. Haig (Wilmington, DE: Potter, Anderson, Corroon, 2012), 4:19.

19. The Early Case Assessment Toolkit can be downloaded at https://www.cpradr.org/resource-center/toolkits/early-case-assessment-guidelines.

20. Scott Partridge, "The Monsanto Case Study: A Practical Roadmap to Relationship-Based Conflict Resolution," presentation to the International Institute for Conflict Prevention and Resolution, February 15, 2016, New York, NY, https://slideplayer.com/slide/11714593; Scott Partridge, Jeremy Lack, and Debra Gerardi, "Session 2: Navigating, Building, and Strengthening Relationships," *Pepperdine Dispute Resolution Law Journal* 16, no. 2 (2016): 163–92.

21. International Institute for Conflict Prevention and Resolution, "21st Century Pledge," https://www.cpradr.org/resource-center/adr-pledges/21st-century-pledge (accessed June 14, 2019).

22. Rebecca Lowe, "Back to Basics," International Bar Association, January 23, 2014, https://www.ibanet.org/Article/Detail.aspx?ArticleUid=2ce3cb9b-55a1-48e0-b6a7-2db47771aa85.

23. For an example of the literature targeting counsel who draft and implement dispute resolution provisions, see Michael McIlwrath and John Savage, *International Arbitration and Mediation: A Practical Guide* (Dordrecht, Netherlands: Kluwer Law International, 2010).

24. Federal Acquisition Regulation implements this provision in section 33.214; recent amendments to the regulation encourage federal agencies to "use ADR procedures to the maximum extent practicable." See Interagency Alternative Dispute Resolution Working Group, "FAR Provisions Pertinent to ADR," in "Electronic Guide to Federal Procurement ADR," §§ 33.214, 33.204, https://www.adr.gov/adrguide (accessed June 14, 2019).

25. The Interagency Alternative Dispute Resolution Working Group's contracts and procurement section, chaired by Air Force Brig. Gen. Frank Anderson, developed the "Electronic Guide to Federal Procurement ADR" specifically for the use of federal procurement professionals. This guide is published at https://www.adr.gov/adrguide. See also American Bar Association, *Alternative Dispute Resolution: A Practical Guide for Resolving Government Contract Controversies*, 2nd ed. (Chicago: American Bar Association, 2005).

26. Department of the Navy, "Introduction to the DON ADR Program," May 2003, http://www.secnav.navy.mil/ADR/Documents/IntroDONADRProgram.pdf.

27. Ibid.

28. Department of the Navy, https://www.secnav.navy.mil/ADR/Pages/etraining.aspx; Shannon Barnard, "Understanding the Importance of Alternative Dispute Resolution in the United States Military: An Analysis of ADR in the Navy," December 2010, unpublished research paper in Shannon Barnard's possession. The Department of the Navy has expanded its outreach with its "Online Introduction to Alternative Dispute Resolution," available at https://www.secnav.navy.mil/ADR/Pages/etraining.aspx (accessed November 5, 2019).

29. Robert E. Scott and George G. Triantis, "Anticipating Litigation in Contract Design," *Yale Law Journal* 115 (2006): 814–79.

30. For example, see Helena Tavares Erickson, *Drafting Dispute Resolution Clauses, 2008 Supplement* (New York: International Institute for Conflict Prevention and Resolution, 2008).

31. John Lande, Kurt L. Dettman, and Catherine E. Shanks, "User Guide: Planned Early Dispute Resolution," 2016, http://www.americanbar.org/content/dam/aba/events/dispute_resolution/committees/PEDR/abadr_pedr_guide.authcheckdam.pdf; John Lande and Peter Benner, "Why and How Businesses Use Planned Early Dispute Resolution,"

University of St. Thomas Law Journal 13 (2017): 248–96.

32. Thomas J. Stipanowich and J. Ryan Lamare, "Living with ADR: Evolving Perceptions and Use of Mediation, Arbitration, and Conflict Management in Fortune 1000 Corporations," *Harvard Negotiation Law Review* 19, no. 1 (2014): 1–68.

33. Ibid., 6.

34. Ibid., 6, 34, 44.

35. For a historical example, see Amalia D. Kessler, *A Revolution in Commerce: The Parisian Merchant Court and the Rise of Commercial Society in Eighteenth-Century France* (New Haven, CT: Yale University Press, 2007).

36. Kathleen M. Scanlon and International Institute for Conflict Prevention and Resolution, *Drafting Dispute Resolution Clauses: Better Solutions for Business*, ed. Helena Tavares Erickson (New York: International Institute for Conflict Prevention and Resolution, 2006); Erickson, *Drafting Dispute Resolution Clauses, 2008 Supplement.*

37. Catherine Cronin-Harris and International Institute for Conflict Prevention and Resolution, *Building ADR into the Corporate Law Department: ADR Systems Design* (New York: International Institute for Conflict Prevention and Resolution, 1997). For complex litigation, CPR has developed a guide to selecting administered processes, whether under the auspices of the court or an independent ADR entity, or self-administered by a neutral with the parties. International Institute for Conflict Prevention and Resolution, "A Guide to Self-Administered ADR and CPR's Dispute Resolution Services," https://www.yumpu.com/en/document/read/29802392/cprs-guide-to-self-administered-adr-cpr-institute-for-dispute- (accessed June 14, 2019). For cross-border disputes, see International Institute for Conflict Prevention and Resolution, "The CPR Corporate Counsel Manual for Cross-Border Dispute Resolution," https://www.cpradr.org/news-publications/store/

corporate-counsel-manual-for-cross-border
-dispute-resolution (accessed June 14, 2019).

38. At the original Roscoe Pound Confer-
ence on the Causes of Popular Dissatisfaction
with the Administration of Justice, held in 1976,
Frank Sander introduced ideas that led to the
concept of the multidoor courthouse. A. Leo
Levin and Russell R. Wheeler, eds., *The Pound
Conference: Perspectives on Justice in the Future*
(St. Paul, MN: West, 1979).

39. The four core questions were posed at
all forty events in the series; these responses
were from San Francisco. As a center of ADR
practice development, the San Francisco
community has taken mediation for granted
as a staple of our legal system and our legal
culture, and innovation may be harder to
achieve. Deborah Masucci, "2016–2017 Global
Pound Conference," *Dispute Resolution Section
Magazine* 73 (Spring 2018): 6–8. See also "Jed
D. Melnick Symposium: The Pound Conferences; Where Do We Come From? What Are
We? Where Are We Going?," *Cardozo Journal
of Conflict Resolution* 18, no. 3 (2017): 513–698.

40. Deborah Masucci and Shravanthi
Suresh, "Transforming Business Through Pro-
active Dispute Management," *Cardozo Journal of
Conflict Resolution* 18, no. 3 (2017): 659–76.

41. For a preliminary evaluation of mediation's use and effect, see European Parliament

Directorate-General for Internal Policies, *The
Implementation of the Mediation Directive
Workshop, 29 November 2016: Compilation of
In-Depth Analyses* (Brussels: European Parliament, 2016), http://www.europarl.europa.eu/
RegData/etudes/IDAN/2016/571395/IPOL_IDA
%282016%29571395_EN.pdf. See also Directive
2008/52/EC of the European Parliament and
of the Council, May 21, 2008, at https://eur-lex
.europa.eu/LexUriServ/LexUriServ.do?uri=OJ:
L:2008:136:0003:0008:En:PDF; and United Nations, "Annex I: United Nations Convention on
International Settlement Agreements Resulting
from Mediation," http://www.uncitral.org/
pdf/english/commissionsessions/51st-session/
Annex_I.pdf (accessed June 14, 2019).

42. Blockchain is the digital structure
used by cryptocurrencies; agreements consist
of computer code built on nodes distributed
in a decentralized ledger. Traditional civil or
common law may not fit smart contracts. See
David Zaslowsky, "What to Expect When
Litigating Smart Contract Disputes," *Law360*,
April 4, 2018, https://www.law360.com/articles/
1028009/what-to-expect-when-litigating-smart
-contract-disputes.

43. Amy J. Schmitz and Colin Rule, "Online
Dispute Resolution for Smart Contracts,"
Journal of Dispute Resolution 2019, no. 2 (2019):
103–25.

Chapter 14

1. State consumer auto lemon laws provide
an interesting example on design and effect.
California and Vermont both claimed an informal, flexible adjudicatory environment with
due process protections, but they differed in
neutral training, claimants' voice, fact-finding,
and procedural rules. Shauhin A. Talesh, "How
Dispute Resolution System Design Matters: An
Organizational Analysis of Dispute Resolution
Structures and Consumer Lemon Laws," *Law
and Society Review* 46, no. 3 (2012): 463–96.

2. Engalla v. Permanente Medical Group,
Inc., 64 Cal. Rptr. 2d 843, 856 (1997).

3. Blue Ribbon Advisory Panel on Kaiser
Permanente Arbitration, "The Kaiser Permanente Arbitration System: A Review and Recommendations for Improvement," January 5,
1998, http://www.oia-kaiserarb.com/pdfs/BRP
-Report.pdf.

4. The National Academy of Science's Committee on Science, Technology, and Law published an article recognizing the information

available from the Office of the Independent Administrator. See Alan B. Morrison, "Can Mandatory Arbitration of Medical Malpractice Claims Be Fair? The Kaiser Permanente System," *Dispute Resolution Journal* 70, no. 3 (2015): 35–79.

5. Kaiser Permanente Office of the Independent Administrator, "Report Summary," http://www.oia-kaiserarb.com/pdfs/Summary .pdf (accessed October 14, 2019).

6. Kaiser Arbitration Oversight Board, "Board Comments on the Annual Report for 2018," http://www.oia-kaiserarb.com/pdfs/AOB -Comments.pdf (accessed June 14, 2019).

7. See Kaiser Arbitration Oversight Board, "Status of Blue Ribbon Panel Recommendations," December 31, 2018, p. 8, http://www.oia -kaiserarb.com/pdfs/BRP-Status-Report.pdf; and Mark Montijo et al., "Bridging Physician-Patient Perspectives Following an Adverse Medical Outcome," *Permanente Journal* 15, no. 4 (2011): 85–88.

8. Tracey Walker, "Advocacy with Compassion: Dorothy Tarrant's Role as Healthcare Ombudsman/Mediator Places Her at the Nexus of Patient-Provider Interaction," *Managed Health Care Executive*, June 1, 2006, pp. 34–36. See also Montijo et al., "Bridging Physician-Patient Perspectives Following an Adverse Medical Outcome," 6n5; and Paul Charlton, "Indicators of Success: An Exploration of Successful Conflict Management in U.S. Hospital Settings," master's thesis, Georgetown University, June 15, 2010.

9. Carole S. Houk and Lauren M. Edelstein, "Beyond Apology to Early Non-judicial Resolution: The MedicOm Program as a Patient Safety–Focused Alternative to Malpractice Litigation," *Hamline Journal of Public Law and Policy* 29 (Spring 2008): 415.

10. Chris Stern Hyman et al., "Interest-Based Mediation of Medical Malpractice Lawsuits: A Route to Improved Patient Safety,"

Journal of Health Politics, Policy, and Law 35, no. 5 (2010): 797–828.

11. Houk and Edelstein, "Beyond Apology to Early Non-judicial Resolution," 411–19.

12. Ibid., 413. See also Joint Commission on Accreditation of Healthcare Organizations, "Health Care at the Crossroads: Strategies for Improving the Medical Liability System and Preventing Patient Injury," 2005, https://www .jointcommission.org/assets/1/18/Medical _Liability.pdf.

13. For findings that success of such programs depends on having a strong institutional champion, investing in building and marketing the program to clinicians, and recognizing that they take time, see Michelle M. Mello et al., "Communication-and-Resolution Programs: The Challenges and Lessons Learned from Six Early Adopters," *Health Affairs* 33, no. 1 (2014): 20–29.

14. Viggo Boserup et al., *What Is . . . ADR in Health Care Disputes?* (New York: American Bar Association, 2015), 50. Also see Carol B. Liebman, "Medical Malpractice Mediation: Benefits Gained, Opportunities Lost," *Law and Contemporary Problems* 74, no. 3 (2011): 135–49; and Chris Stern Hyman, "Mediation and Medical Malpractice: Why Plaintiffs, Hospitals and Physicians Should Be at the Table," *Dispute Resolution Journal* 66, no. 3 (2011): 32–37.

15. Jennifer Moore, Marie Bismark, and Michelle M. Mello, "Patients' Experiences with Communication-and-Resolution Programs After Medical Injury," *JAMA Internal Medicine* 177, no. 11 (2017): 1600.

16. Morrison, "Can Mandatory Arbitration of Medical Malpractice Claims Be Fair?" 59.

17. For background on costs from the current liability system, see David M. Studdert et al., "Claims, Errors, and Compensation Payments in Medical Malpractice Litigation," *New England Journal of Medicine* 354, no. 19 (2006): 2014–33.

18. Randall C. Jenkins et al., "Mandatory Pre-suit Mediation for Medical Malpractice: Eight-Year Results and Future Innovations," *Conflict Resolution Quarterly* 35, no. 1 (2017): 73–88. See also Susan J. Szmania, Addie M. Johnson, and Margaret Mulligan, "Alternative Dispute Resolution in Medical Malpractice: A Survey of Emerging Trends and Practices," *Conflict Resolution Quarterly* 26, no. 1 (2008): 71–96; Carol B. Liebman and Chris Stern Hyman, "Medical Error Disclosure, Mediation Skills, and Malpractice Litigation: A Demonstration Project in Pennsylvania," 2005, http://www.pewtrusts.org/-/media/legacy/uploadedfiles/wwwpewtrustsorg/reports/medical_liability/liebmanreportpdf.pdf; and Orna Rabinovich-Einy, "Escaping the Shadow of Malpractice Law," *Law and Contemporary Problems* 74 (Summer 2011): 241–78.

19. See the excellent overview of the market conditions, legal options, and incentives for borrowers, lenders, and loan providers in Lydia Nussbaum, "ADR's Place in Foreclosure: Remedying the Flaws of a Securitized Housing Market," *Cardozo Law Review* 34 (2013): 1889–953.

20. See Federal Reserve Bank of San Francisco, "Arizona: Housing and Labor Market Trends," January 2013, http://www.frbsf.org/community-development/files/Arizona-0113.pdf.

21. Art Hinshaw and Timothy Burr, "Foreclosure Mediation in Arizona," *Arizona State Law Journal* 45 (2013): 749–59.

22. Sharon Press, "Mortgage Foreclosure Mediation in Florida: Implementation Challenges for an Institutionalized Program," *Nevada Law Journal* 11, no. 2 (2011): 306–67.

23. Administrative Order AOSC09-54 recognized that "the best method to open communication and facilitate problem-solving between the parties to foreclosure cases while conserving limited judicial resources . . . was that the court adopt a uniform, statewide managed mediation program implemented through a model administrative order to be issued by each circuit chief judge." In re Final Report and Recommendation on Residential Mortgage Foreclosure Cases, no. AOSC09-54 (Fla., December 28, 2009), http://www.floridasupremecourt.org/clerk/adminorders/2009/AOSC09-54.pdf.

24. Kathleen Haughney, "Florida Justice Shuts Down Foreclosure Mediation," *Orlando Sentinel*, December 20, 2011, p. A10.

25. Jennifer Shack and Hanna Kaufman, "Promoting Access to Justice: Applying Lessons Learned from Foreclosure Mediation," *Dispute Resolution Magazine* 71 (Spring 2016): 16–20.

26. State of Nevada Foreclosure Mediation Program, "Foreclosure Mediation Factsheet," https://www.scribd.com/document/46273434/Nevada-Foreclosure-Mediation-Program-Factsheet (accessed July 2, 2019).

27. The advisory committee had fourteen members as of May 2013, including homeowner, lender, realtor, mediator, title company, lender counsel representatives, and homeowner counsel representatives.

28. The Milwaukee Foreclosure Initiative is reviewed in detail in Andrea Kupfer Schneider and Natalie C. Fleury, "There's No Place Like Home: Applying Dispute Systems Design Theory to Create a Foreclosure Mediation System," *Nevada Law Journal* 11 (2011): 368–96.

29. Ibid., 371.

30. Ibid., 381.

31. Nussbaum, "ADR's Place in Foreclosure."

32. Nussbaum, "ADR's Place in Foreclosure," 1952; see also 1889, 1893, 1915. For a discussion of transparency and confidentiality, see Nancy A. Welsh, "Dispute Resolution Neutrals' Ethical Obligation to Support Measured Transparency," *Oklahoma Law Review* 71, no. 3 (2019): 823–84.

33. See, for example, its tool for finding a housing counselor or housing intermediary, at http://www.consumerfinance.gov/find-a-housing-counselor, and "Get Answers to Your Mortgage Questions" page, at http://www.consumerfinance.gov/mortgage/#homeowners. See also Ann Carrns, "With the New Year, New Consumer Protections on Mortgages," *New York Times*, January 4, 2014, p. B4. The Consumer Finance Protection Bureau has established an ombuds office to assist in the handling of consumer complaints. See Consumer Financial Protection Bureau, "CFPB Ombudsman," http://www.consumerfinance.gov/ombudsman (accessed June 14, 2019). The bureau has a site for filing a complaint or just "tell[ing] your story" relative to the provision of any financial product or service. See Consumer Financial Protection Bureau, "Having a Problem with a Financial Product or Service?," http://www.consumerfinance.gov/complaint (accessed June 14, 2019).

34. Judith Scott-Clayton, "The Looming Student Loan Default Crisis Is Worse than We Thought," Brookings, January 11, 2018, https://www.brookings.edu/research/the-looming-student-loan-default-crisis-is-worse-than-we-thought.

35. eBay, "Fast Facts," https://investors.ebayinc.com/fast-facts/default.aspx (accessed October 14, 2019); Colin Rule, "Making Peace on eBay: Resolving Disputes in the World's Largest Marketplace," speech to the Association for Conflict Resolution, Harvard Law School, Cambridge, MA, October 19, 2008.

36. A major study describes the importance of word usage in online dispute resolution of seller-buyer disputes on eBay. Words that give face—respect for the counterpart—enhance the probability of settlement, whereas words that attack face (negative emotions, commands) reduce the likelihood of settlement. Jeanne M. Brett et al., "Sticks and Stones:

Language, Face, and Online Dispute Resolution," *Academy of Management Journal* 50, no. 1 (2007): 85–99.

37. eBay is an interesting example of corporation as (private) courthouse, described by Rory Van Loo, who explores the corporation through three roles: customer service provider, third-party dispute resolver (between the customer and a third party), and reputation sanction imposer—all with varying levels of transparency. Rory Van Loo, "The Corporation as Courthouse," *Yale Journal on Regulation* 33 (2016): 547–602.

38. See American Bar Association, "Recommended Best Practices for Online Dispute Resolution Service Providers," http://www.abanet.org/dispute/documents/BestPracticesFinal102802.pdf (accessed June 14, 2019). See, generally, Mohamed S. Abdel Wahab, Ethan Katsh, and Daniel Rainey, eds., *Online Dispute Resolution: Theory and Practice: A Treatise on Technology and Dispute Resolution* (The Hague: Eleven International, 2012). For a discussion of international systems of ODR, see Chapter 16. Chris Gill and colleagues have designed a DSD model specifically for consumer-to-business disputes, urging deliberate dispute system design for consumer redress, in what they term consumer dispute resolution, or CDR. Chris Gill et al., "Designing Consumer Redress: A Dispute System Design (DSD) Model for Consumer-to-Business Disputes," *Legal Studies* 36, no. 3 (2016): 450.

39. Amy J. Schmitz and Colin Rule, *The New Handshake: Online Dispute Resolution and the Future of Consumer Protection* (Chicago: ABA Press, 2017).

40. Directive 2013/22, 2013 O.J. (L 165) 63(EC); Regulation 524/2013, 2013 O.J. (L 165) 1. The European Union's ODR portal is available at http://ec.europa.eu/odr.

41. Pablo Cortés, "The Brave New World of Consumer Redress in the European Union and

the United Kingdom," *Dispute Resolution Magazine* 71 (Spring 2016): 41–45. For a more detailed overview of the EU experience, see Pablo Cortés, ed., *The New Regulatory Framework for Consumer Dispute Resolution* (New York: Oxford University Press, 2017).

42. United Nations Commission on International Trade Law, "UNCITRAL Technical Notes on Online Dispute Resolution," April 2017, http://www.uncitral.org/pdf/english/texts/odr/V1700382_English_Technical_Notes_on_ODR.pdf.

43. See Ethan Katsh and Orna Rabinovich-Einy, *Digital Justice: Technology and the Internet of Disputes* (London: Oxford University Press, 2017), 158–65. The Rechtwijzer is a platform operated with the court that was established by the Hague Institute of International Law with the Netherlands Ministry of Justice for family law mediation; after several months' operation, it is currently under platform redesign. The British Columbia Administrative Law Tribunal was established to handle civil claims and condominium disputes. See the website of its Civil Resolution Tribunal, at https://www.civilresolutionbc.ca. The Hangzhou Internet Court was opened in August 2017 to handle a range of commercial disputes. See Dani Deahl, "China Launches Cyber-Court to Handle Internet-Related Disputes," *The Verge*, August 18, 2017, https://www.theverge.com/tech/2017/8/18/16167836/china-cyber-court-hangzhou-internet-disputes. Her Majesty's Online Court is ex-

pected to open in the United Kingdom in 2020 to handle civil claims up to 25,000 pounds. See Online Dispute Resolution Advisory Group, "Online Dispute Resolution for Low Value Civil Claims," February 2015, https://www.judiciary.uk/wp-content/uploads/2015/02/Online-Dispute-Resolution-Final-Web-Version1.pdf.

44. Orna Rabinovich-Einy and Ethan Katsh, "A New Relationship Between Public and Private Dispute Resolution: Lessons from Online Dispute Resolution," *Ohio State Journal on Dispute Resolution* 32 (2017): 695–723.

45. See Leah Wing, "Cyberbullying Hackathon Challenge Report," presentation at 2014 ODR Forum, San Francisco/Palo Alto, CA, June 21–22, 2014. See also J. Nathan Matias et al., "Reporting, Reviewing, and Responding to Harassment on Twitter," May 13, 2015, https://arxiv.org/ftp/arxiv/papers/1505/1505.03359.pdf.

46. For a parallel effort from the perspective of ethical behavior of virtual mediators, see Susan Nauss Exon, "Ethics and Online Dispute Resolution: From Evolution to Revolution," *Ohio State Journal on Dispute Resolution* 32, no. 4 (2017): 609–64.

47. See Chapter 12 for a review of the U.S. Supreme Court case history on mandatory arbitration.

48. Consumer Financial Protection Bureau, "Arbitration Agreements," 2017, http://files.consumerfinance.gov/f/documents/201707_cfpb_Arbitration-Agreements-Rule.pdf.

Chapter 15

1. International Criminal Court, "Rome Statute of the International Criminal Court," 2011, http://www.icc-cpi.int/nr/rdonlyres/ea9aeff7-5752-4f84-be94-0a655eb30e16/0/rome_statute_english.pdf. Jurisdiction encompasses the crime of genocide, crimes against humanity, war crimes, and the crime of aggression. Ibid., article V.

2. The term "impunity gap" was coined by the International Center for Transitional

Justice. See International Center for Transitional Justice, "Criminal Justice," https://www.ictj.org/our-work/transitional-justice-issues/criminal-justice (accessed June 21, 2019).

3. Estimated deaths from the genocide range from 500,000 to almost 1 million. Maya Goldstein Bolocan, "Rwandan Gacaca: An Experiment in Transitional Justice," *Journal of Dispute Resolution*, no. 2 (2004): 368n80.

Bolocan estimates 800,000 and cites government reports of 937,000. See also Alison Des Forges and Timothy Longman, "Legal Responses to Genocide in Rwanda," in *My Neighbor, My Enemy: Justice and Community in the Aftermath of Mass Atrocity*, ed. Eric Stover and Harvey M. Weinstein (Cambridge: Cambridge University Press, 2004). Des Forges and Longman estimate "at least 500,000" deaths (50).

4. Participation in the genocide was widespread, at all levels of the community, though estimates of the number of participants range widely. See, for example, Des Forges and Longman, "Legal Responses to Genocide in Rwanda," 51. Des Forges and Longman cite "tens of thousands." See also Erin Daly, "Between Punitive and Reconstructive Justice: The Gacaca Courts in Rwanda," *NYU Journal of International Law and Politics* 34 (2004): 364. Daly cites 650,000.

5. For a history of the development of the *gacaca* courts and the other Rwandan transitional justice processes, see Bolocan, "Rwandan Gacaca."

6. This history draws on Spencer Zifcak, "Restorative Justice in East Timor: An Evaluation of the Community Reconciliation Process of the CAVR," http://pdf.usaid.gov/pdf_docs/Pnado632.pdf (accessed June 21, 2019); and Edith Bowles and Tanja Chopra, "East Timor: Statebuilding Revisited," in *Building States to Build Peace*, ed. Charles T. Call (Boulder, CO: Lynne Rienner, 2008), 271–302.

7. In international humanitarian law, "combatant" commonly refers only to state-sponsored armed fighters in international conflicts. In this chapter, "combatant" includes all armed fighters.

8. Office of the United Nations High Commissioner for Human Rights, *Rule-of-Law Tools for Post-conflict States: Amnesties* (New York: United Nations, 2009), 27, http://www.ohchr .org/Documents/Publications/Amnesties_en .pdf.

9. For a discussion of the evolution of this jurisprudence and some critique, see Lisa J. La Plante, "Outlawing Amnesty: The Return of Criminal Justice in Transitional Justice Schemes," *Virginia Journal of International Law* 49, no. 15 (2009): 22–47; Christina Binder, "The Prohibition of Amnesties by the Inter-American Court of Human Rights," *German Law Journal* 12, no. 5 (2011): 1203–30; and Wayne Sandholtz and Mariana Rangel Padilla, "Law and Politics in the Inter-American System: The Amnesty Cases," *Journal of Law and Courts* 8, no. 1 (forthcoming).

10. Naomi Roht-Arriaza, "After Amnesties Are Gone: Latin American National Courts and the New Contours of the Fight Against Impunity," *Human Rights Quarterly* 37 (2015): 341–82.

11. In re Pinochet (House of Lords, January 15, 1999), https://www.publications.parliament .uk/pa/ld199899/ldjudgmt/jd990115/pin001 .htm.

12. The U.S. Supreme Court rejected the concept of universal jurisdiction in the case of *Kiobel v. Royal Dutch Petroleum Co.*, 569 U.S. 108 (2013). See Julian G. Ku, "Kiobel and the Surprising Death of Universal Jurisdiction Under the Alien Tort Statute," *American Journal of International Law* 107 (2013): 835–41. Ku states, "All nine justices rejected decades of lower-court precedent and widespread scholarly opinion when they held that the [Alien Tort Statute] excluded cases involving purely extraterritorial conduct, even if the alleged conduct constituted acts that are universally proscribed under international law" (835). See also Jesner et al. v. Arab Bank, PLC, 584 U.S. ___, 138 S. Ct. 1386 (2018).

13. United Nations, "Guidance Note of the Secretary-General: United Nations Approach to Transitional Justice," March 2010, p. 8, https:// www.un.org/ruleoflaw/files/TJ_Guidance_Note _March_2010FINAL.pdf.

14. Paul Seils, "The Place of Reconciliation in Transitional Justice: Conceptions and Misconceptions," *ICTJ Briefing*, June 2017, p. 1, https://www.ictj.org/sites/default/files/ICTJ -Briefing-Paper-Reconciliation-TJ-2017.pdf.

15. Priscilla B. Hayner, *Unspeakable Truths: Transitional Justice and the Challenge of Truth Commissions* (New York: Routledge, 2011), 28.

16. Ibid.

17. "Greensboro Truth and Reconciliation Report: Executive Summary," May 25, 2006, http://www.greensborotrc.org/exec_summary .pdf; International Center for Transitional Justice, "U.S.A: Greensboro, NC," https://www .ictj.org/our-work/regions-and-countries/usa -greensboro-nc (accessed June 21, 2019).

18. Hayner, *Unspeakable Truths*, 47.

19. Ibid., 60–61.

20. Factory at Chorzów, Germany v. Poland, series A, no. 17 (PCIJ 1928), 47.

21. United Nations General Assembly, "The Basic Principles and Guidelines on the Right to a Remedy and Reparation for Victims of Gross Violations of International Human Rights Law and Serious Violations of International Humanitarian Law," December 16, 2005, articles 22, 23, http://www.un.org/ga/search/view_doc .asp?symbol=A/RES/60/147; Martha Minow, *Between Vengeance and Forgiveness: Facing History After Genocide and Mass Violence* (Boston, MA: Beacon Press, 1998), 91–117; Hayner, *Unspeakable Truths*, 163–81. Hayner includes critiques of reparations programs from a gender perspective and for failure to address "structural violence" (165).

22. Hayner, *Unspeakable Truths*, 176–77.

23. Ibid., 167.

24. Ibid., 60–62, 168.

25. Extraordinary Chambers in the Courts of Cambodia, "ECCC at a Glance," April 2014, https://www.eccc.gov.kh/sites/default/files/ ECCC%20at%20a%20Glance%20-%20EN%20 -%20April%202014_FINAL.pdf.

26. Christoph Sperfeldt, "Collective Reparations at the Extraordinary Chambers in the Courts of Cambodia," *International Criminal Law Review* 12 (2012): 457–72, esp. 461.

27. Ibid., 477–78.

28. The reparations included thirteen projects "concerning remembrance of the victims and memorialisation of the suffering endured, therapy and psychological assistance to the victims, and documentation and education." Extraordinary Chambers in the Courts of Cambodia, "Trial Chamber Summary of Judgment: Case 002/02," November 16, 2018, p. 31, https://www.eccc.gov.kh/sites/default/ files/documents/courtdoc/%5Bdate-in-tz%5D/ 20181217%20Summary%20of%20Judgement %20Case%20002-02%20ENG_FINAL%20FOR %20PUBLICATION.pdf.

29. For a discussion of these terms and "lustration," "screening," and "administrative justice," see Roger Duthie, "Introduction," in *Justice as Prevention: Vetting Public Employees in Transitional Societies*, ed. Alexander Mayer-Rieckh and Pablo de Greiff (New York: Social Science Research Council, 2007), 17–38.

30. Ana Cutter Patel, Pablo de Greiff, and Lars Waldorf, eds., *Disarming the Past: Transitional Justice and Ex-Combatants* (New York: Social Science Research Council, 2009). Patel, de Greiff, and Waldorf note that "approximately thirty-four DDR programs were created between 1994 and 2005" (18).

31. Civil society actors are, for example, nongovernmental organizations, religious leaders, community leaders, media, medical and legal communities, human rights activists, sociologists, psychologists, and historians.

32. Alex Boraine, "Truth and Reconciliation in South Africa: The Third Way," in *Truth v. Justice: The Morality of Truth Commissions*, ed. Robert I. Rotberg and Dennis Thompson (Princeton, NJ: Princeton University Press, 2000), 141.

33. Ibid.

34. As discussed in Chapter 1, there are many types of justice. Lisa Blomgren Bingham, "Designing Justice: Legal Institutions and Other Systems for Managing Conflict," *Ohio State Journal on Dispute Resolution* 24, no. 1 (2008): 1–52. Ruti Teitel analyzes the transitional justice field under five major justice headings: criminal, historical, reparatory, administrative, and constitutional. Ruti Teitel, *Transitional Justice* (New York: Oxford University Press, 2000).

35. For a critical perspective on the history of the rule of law and legal pluralism from the colonial period to the present, see Laura Grenfell, *Promoting the Rule of Law in Post-conflict States* (Cambridge: Cambridge University Press, 2013), 14–58.

36. Ibid., 58.

37. Boraine, "Truth and Reconciliation in South Africa," 153.

38. See, for example, Human Rights Watch, *Selling Justice Short: Why Accountability Matters for Peace* (New York: Human Rights Watch, 2009).

39. See Andrea Kupfer Schneider, "The Intersection of Dispute Systems Design and Transitional Justice," *Harvard Negotiation Law Review* 14 (2009): 291–97.

40. Ibid., 293.

41. Ibid., 294–95.

42. Mark Freeman, *Necessary Evils: Amnesties and the Search for Justice* (Cambridge: Cambridge University Press, 2009), 109.

43. This debate was reflected in a dialogue, in a series of articles, between Diane Orentlicher and Carlos Nino. Diane F. Orentlicher, "Settling Accounts: The Duty to Punish Human Rights Violations of a Prior Regime," *Yale Law Journal* 100 (1991): 2537–615; Carlos Nino, "The Duty to Punish Past Abuses of Human Rights in Context: The Case of Argentina," *Yale Law Journal* 100 (1991): 2619–40; and Diane F. Orentlicher, "A Reply to Professor Nino," *Yale Law Journal* 100 (1991): 2641–43.

44. See, for example, Diane F. Orentlicher, "'Settling Accounts' Revisited: Reconciling Global Norms with Local Agency," *International Journal of Transitional Justice* 1 (2007): 10, 16.

45. Center for Strategic and International Studies and Association of the United States Army, "Post-conflict Reconstruction: Task Framework," May 2002, http://csis.org/files/media/csis/pubs/framework.pdf. This framework was subsequently adapted by the U.S. State Department. See U.S. Department of State, "Post Conflict Reconstruction Essentials Tasks Matrix," April 1, 2005, http://2001-2009.state.gov/s/crs/rls/52959.htm.

46. Center for Strategic and International Studies and Association of the United States Army, "Post-conflict Reconstruction," 2.

47. Boraine, "Truth and Reconciliation in South Africa," 144–45. Parliament passed the Promotion of National Unity and Reconciliation Act in May 1995 after broad stakeholder input including "two international conferences to explore the transitional justice policies instituted in other countries" and "hundreds of hours of hearings." Hayner, *Unspeakable Truths*, 27.

48. Orentlicher, "'Settling Accounts' Revisited," 17.

49. William A. Schabas, "The Sierra Leone Truth and Reconciliation Commission," in *Transitional Justice in the Twenty-First Century: Beyond Truth Versus Justice*, ed. Naomi Roht-Arriaza and Javier Mariezcurrena (Cambridge: Cambridge University Press, 2006), 31–32.

50. Women are also participants in war but in an array of roles. They are combatants and spies but also porters, cooks, and sex slaves. Some women have been kidnapped and forced into participation; others participate voluntarily. See Luisa Maria Dietrich Ortega, "Transitional Justice and Female Ex-Combatants: Lessons Learned from International Experience,"

in Patel, De Greiff, and Waldorf, *Disarming the Past*, 158–88.

51. Françoise Nduwimana, "United Nations Security Council Resolution 1325 (2000) on Women, Peace and Security: Understanding the Implications, Fulfilling the Obligations," pp. 161–63, http://www.un.org/womenwatch/osagi/cdrom/documents/Background_Paper_Africa.pdf (accessed June 21, 2019). Subsequent Security Council resolutions have expanded on this resolution. See United Nations Security Council, "Resolution 1820," June 19, 2008, https://www.un.org/ruleoflaw/files/women_peace_security_resolution1820.pdf. This resolution states that sexual violence can constitute a war crime and "*stresses the need for* the exclusion of sexual violence crimes from amnesty provisions" (3; emphasis in original).

52. United Nations General Assembly, "Transforming Our World: The 2030 Agenda for Sustainable Development," September 25, 2015, http://www.un.org/en/development/desa/population/migration/generalassembly/docs/globalcompact/A_RES_70_1_E.pdf. See especially goals 5 and 16.

53. See, for example, Thomas Carothers, *Critical Mission: Essays on Democracy Promotion* (Washington, DC: Carnegie Endowment for International Peace, 2004), 24–25, 129.

54. Ruti G. Teitel, *Globalizing Transitional Justice: Contemporary Essays* (New York: Oxford University Press, 2014), xvii.

55. See, for example, Rachel Kleinfeld, *Advancing the Rule of Law Abroad: Next Generation Reform* (Washington, DC: Carnegie Endowment for International Peace, 2012); and Stephanie E. Smith, "Comment: Trends and Challenges in Bringing Together ADR and Rule of Law," *Journal of Dispute Resolution* 2011, no. 1 (2011): 189–91.

56. James Michel, "Alternative Dispute Resolution and the Rule of Law in International Development Cooperation," *Journal of Dispute Resolution* 2011, no. 1 (2011): 21, 42. See also Organization for Economic Cooperation and Development, "The Paris Declaration on Aid Effectiveness and the Accra Agenda for Action," http://www.oecd.org/dac/effectiveness/34428351.pdf (accessed June 21, 2019). This declaration strongly emphasizes the importance of harmonizing efforts with partner countries and their needs and capabilities. For recommendations on how to engage effectively with customary justice systems to advance the rule of law, see Deborah Isser, ed., *Customary Justice and the Rule of Law in War-Torn Societies* (Washington, DC: United States Institute of Peace Press, 2011), 341–67.

57. Boraine, "Truth and Reconciliation in South Africa," 143.

58. Neil Kritz, "Policy Implications of Empirical Research on Transitional Justice," in *Assessing the Impact of Transitional Justice: Challenges for Empirical Research*, ed. Hugo van der Merwe, Victoria Baxter, and Audrey R. Chapman (Washington, DC: United States Institute of Peace Press, 2009), 14.

59. Hayner, *Unspeakable Truths*. Hayner notes that "by the end of 2009, 779 former officials had been charged with human rights crimes, and over 200 had been tried and convicted, with 59 serving sentences in jail" (49). The U.S. Department of State reported that "as of November 2015, according to the [Chilean] Ministry of the Interior, a total of 1,373 former military and law enforcement officials had been charged or convicted of complicity in murder or disappearance during the Pinochet government years (1973–90). In its 2016 annual Human Rights Report, the University of Diego Portales reported that 177 of these were in prison as of December 2015." U.S. Department of State, "Chile 2017 Human Rights Report," p. 1, https://cl.usembassy.gov/wp-content/uploads/sites/104/Chile-Human

-Rights-Report-2017.pdf (accessed October 14, 2019).

60. Zifcak, "Restorative Justice in East Timor," 3-4.

61. See, for example, David Cohen, "Justice on the Cheap Revisited: The Failure of the Serious Crimes Trials in East Timor," *Asia-Pacific Issues* 80 (2006): 1-12; and Megan Hirst, *Too Much Friendship, Too Little Truth: Monitoring Report on the Commission of Truth and Friendship in Indonesia and Timor-Leste* (New York: International Center for Transitional Justice, 2008), 7.

62. Zifcak, "Restorative Justice in East Timor," 4.

63. Bolocan, "Rwandan Gacaca," 369-71.

64. United Nations, "Guidance Note of the Secretary-General," 8.

65. For a discussion of how truth commissions in different countries have answered these questions, see Hayner, *Unspeakable Truths*, 121-44.

66. Some have questioned whether the *gacaca* court process was a true hybrid of traditional and modern processes. Lars Waldorf has described the *gacaca* courts, as they evolved, as so heavily formalized, imposed top-down by the government, that this "gacaca bore no resemblance to customary dispute resolution other than the name." Lars Waldorf, "'Like Jews Waiting for Jesus': Posthumous Justice in Post-genocide Rwanda," *Localizing Transitional Justice: Interventions and Priorities After Mass Violence*, ed. Rosalind Shaw and Lars Waldorf (Stanford, CA: Stanford University Press, 2010), 188.

67. Bolocan, "Rwandan Gacaca," 380.

68. Waldorf, "Like Jews Waiting for Jesus," 185; Bolocan, "Rwandan Gacaca," 372.

69. Grenfell, *Promoting the Rule of Law in Post-conflict States*, 43. Grenfell discusses the lawsuit brought by Amnesty International challenging the *gacaca* courts for failing to provide due process, including impartiality, full appeal rights, and judicial competence (41-42). For an illuminating description and analysis of the postwar Rwandan context for DSD—in particular, the situation for women and children suffering from HIV/AIDS—see Phyllis E. Bernard, "Begging for Justice? Or, Adaptive Jurisprudence? Initial Reflections on Mandatory ADR to Enforce Women's Rights in Rwanda," *Cardozo Journal of Conflict Resolution* 7, no. 2 (2006): 325-52.

70. Hirst, *Too Much Friendship, Too Little Truth*, 8.

71. Zifcak, "Restorative Justice in East Timor"; Shaw and Waldorf, *Localizing Transitional Justice*, 17.

72. *The Report of the Iraq Inquiry: Report of a Committee of Privy Counsellors* (London: Her Majesty's Stationery Office, 2016), 58-61, http://webarchive.nationalarchives.gov.uk/ 20171123122743/http://www.iraqinquiry.org.uk/ the-report.

73. See, generally, Elizabeth A. Cole and Judy Barsalou, *Unite or Divide? The Challenges of Teaching History in Societies Emerging from Violent Conflict* (Washington, DC: United States Institute of Peace Press, 2006), 163. For an example of an evaluation of postconflict educational reforms, see Sarah Warshauer Freedman et al., "Confronting the Past in Rwandan Schools," in Stover and Weinstein, *My Neighbor, My Enemy*, 248-65.

74. Hayner, *Unspeakable Truths*, 165.

75. Ibid., 173-74. Hayner cites the case of Peru, where government reparations made to whole villages were criticized by victims and community members.

76. International Criminal Court, "Rome Statute," art. 75.

77. Sperfeldt, "Collective Reparations at the Extraordinary Chambers in the Courts of Cambodia," 459. See also Christine Van den Wyngaert, "Victims Before International

Criminal Courts: Some Views and Concerns of an ICC Trial Judge," *Case Western Reserve Journal of International Law* 44 (2011): 475–96.

78. David L. Attanasio, "Extraordinary Reparations, Legitimacy, and the Inter-American Court," *University of Pennsylvania Journal of International Law* 37, no. 3 (2016), 813–70, esp. 828, 829.

79. Ibid., 820. Attanasio refers to the case of *Rio Negro Massacres v. Guatemala*.

80. Donor countries fund transitional justice mechanisms in other nations through direct bilateral aid or through assessed or voluntary contributions to the UN. See, for example, United Nations, "Special Court for Sierra Leone Faces Funding Crisis, as Charles Taylor Trial Gets Under Way, Security Council Told Today in Briefing by Court's Senior Officials," June 8, 2007, https://www.un.org/press/en/2007/sc9037.doc.htm. This press release notes voluntary contributions through the UN for the Special Court for Sierra Leone. Des Forges and Longman discuss the controversy over the levels of USAID support for different transitional justice mechanisms in Rwanda. Des Forges and Longman, "Legal Responses to Genocide in Rwanda," 59.

81. See Shepard Forman and Stewart Patrick, eds., *Good Intentions: Pledges of Aid for Post-conflict Recovery* (Boulder, CO: Lynne Rienner, 2000).

82. Alistair Leithead, "Rwanda Genocide: International Criminal Tribunal Closes," *BBC News*, December 14, 2015, https://www.bbc.com/news/world-africa-35070220.

83. Jessica Hatcher-Moore, "Is the World's Highest Court Fit for Purpose?" *The Guardian*, April 5, 2017, https://www.theguardian.com/global-development-professionals-network/2017/apr/05/international-criminal-court-fit-purpose. For information on International Criminal Court convictions, acquittals, and the status of open cases, see its website, at https://www.icc-cpi.int/Pages/cases.aspx.

84. Deborah H. Isser, Stephen C. Lubkemann, and Saah N'Tow, *Looking for Justice: Liberian Experiences with and Perceptions of Local Justice Options* (Washington, DC: United States Institute of Peace Press, 2009), 6.

85. Colleen Duggan, "Editorial Note," *International Journal on Transitional Justice* 4 (2010): 320.

86. Isser et al., *Looking for Justice*.

87. Ibid., 3–4.

88. Duggan, "Editorial Note," 322–25.

89. See, for example, Bolocan, "Rwandan Gacaca," 366.

90. James L. Gibson, *Overcoming Apartheid* (New York: Russell Sage Foundation, 2004), 3–4.

91. James L. Gibson, "Truth, Reconciliation, and the Creation of a Human Rights Culture in South Africa," *Law and Society Review* 38 (2004): 21, 34–35. See also Oskar N. T. Thoms, James Ron, and Roland Paris, "State-Level Effects of Transitional Justice: What Do We Know?," *International Journal of Transitional Justice* 4 (2010): 329–54; see esp. 329–30 for an overview of research on state-level effects of transitional justice and the uncertainties in social science outcomes in this area, including Gibson's work.

92. Boraine, "Truth and Reconciliation in South Africa," 142–43.

93. Civil Liberties Act of 1988 (Pub. L. No. 100-383, Title I, August 10, 1988, 102 Stat. 904, 50a U.S.C. § 1989b et seq.).

94. New memorials are being created in the United States. In 2018, the National Memorial for Peace and Justice opened in Montgomery, Alabama. This memorial is "dedicated to the legacy of enslaved black people, people terrorized by lynching, African Americans humiliated by racial segregation and Jim Crow, and people of color burdened with contemporary presumptions of guilt and police violence." Equal Justice Initiative, "The National Memorial for Peace and Justice," https://eji.org/

national-lynching-memorial (accessed June 21, 2019).

Chapter 16

1. For an excellent overview, see Louise Reilly, "An Introduction to the Court of Arbitration for Sport (CAS) and the Role of National Courts in International Sports Disputes," *Journal of Dispute Resolution* 63, no. 1 (2012): 63–81.

2. See Court of Arbitration for Sport, "Frequently Asked Questions," https://www.tas -cas.org/en/general-information/frequently -asked-questions.html (accessed June 22, 2019).

3. See Guillermo Cañas v. ATP Tour, CAS 2005/A/951 (Ct. Arb. Sport, March 22, 2007); and Cañas v. ATP Tour, 4P.172/2006 (Swiss Federal Tribunal, March 22, 2007). The Swiss Federal Tribunal judgment is also noteworthy because it was the first time the Swiss Federal Tribunal annulled a CAS award.

4. Jacques Rogge, "IOC President Addresses Sports Ministers at First World Olympic Sport Convention," October 23, 2010, https://www.olympic.org/news/ioc-president -addresses-sports-ministers-at-first-world -olympic-sport-convention.

5. The World Anti-Doping Agency and World Anti-Doping Code have advanced harmonization of antidoping policies in all sports worldwide.

6. See Court of Arbitration for Sport, "Statistics," 2016, https://www.tas-cas.org/ fileadmin/user_upload/CAS_statistics_2016_ .pdf.

7. The New York Convention on the Recognition and Enforcement of Foreign Arbitral Awards provides that any arbitral award may be enforced in the courts of a party who is a signatory country. The text of the convention is available at http://www.newyorkconvention.org.

8. See the papers presented at the International Parental Child Abduction and Mediation in a Globalized World symposium at Stanford University, Stanford, CA, April 10, 2018, which are available in *World Arbitration and Mediation Review* 12, no. 1 (2018).

9. See International Centre for Settlement of Investment Disputes, "About ICSID," https:// icsid.worldbank.org/en/Pages/about/default .aspx (accessed November 5, 2019).

10. See Jonathan D. Greenberg and Evan Darwin Winet, "International Investment Law and Dispute Resolution," in *Handbook on the Geopolitics of Business*, ed. Joseph Mark S. Munoz (Northampton, MA: Edward Elgar, 2013); Antonio R. Parra, *The History of ICSID* (Oxford: Oxford University Press, 2017); and Ucheora Onwuamaegbu, "Limiting the Participation of Developed States: Impacts on Investor-State Arbitration," Investor-State Arbitration Series paper no. 11, September 2016, https://www.cigionline.org/sites/default/files/ isa_paper_no.11_web.pdf.

11. See United Nations Commission on Trade and Development, "Most Recent IIAs," http://investmentpolicyhub.unctad.org/IIA (accessed June 22, 2019).

12. Jeswald Salacuse, "The Emerging Global Regime for Investment," *Harvard International Law Journal* 51 (2010): 427–73. Building on regime theory, Salacuse posits five possible motivating interests: encouraging foreign investment, encouraging domestic investment, building relationships, liberalizing economic transactions, and improving governance. Also see Tom Ginsburg, "International Substitutes for Domestic Institutions: Bilateral Investment Treaties and Governance," *International Review of Law and Economics* 25, no. 1 (2005): 107–23; and Susan D. Franck, "Foreign Direct Investment, Investment Treaty Arbitration, and the Rule of Law," *Pacific McGeorge Global*

95. Ta-Nehisi Coates, "The Case for Reparations," *Atlantic Monthly*, June 2014, pp. 54–71.

Business and Development Review 19 (2007): 337–73.

13. United Nations, "UN Charter," October 24, 1945, https://www.un.org/en/sections/un -charter/un-charter-full-text.

14. Of the cases filed with International Convention on the Settlement of Investment Disputes, about 30 percent are settled. Jack Coe Jr., "Toward a Complementary Use of Concilia- tion in Investor-State Disputes—a Preliminary Sketch," *UC Davis Journal of International Law and Policy* 12, no. 7 (2005): 7–46. Of the cases submitted to arbitration before the International Chamber of Commerce in Paris, two-thirds are settled. Eric Schwartz, "Inter- national Conciliation and the ICC," *ICSID Review—Foreign Investment Law Journal* 10, no. 1 (1995): 99.

15. See International Court of Justice, "Stat- ute of the International Court of Justice," article 59, https://www.icj-cij.org/en/statute (accessed November 5, 2019).

16. Greenberg and Winet, "International Investment Law and Dispute Resolution," 244. United Nations Commission on Trade and Development, *Investor-State Disputes: Preven- tion and Alternatives to Arbitration* (New York: United Nations, 2010), 14, http://unctad.org/en/ docs/diaeia200911_en.pdf.

17. Laurence Helfer and Anne-Marie Slaughter, "Toward a Theory of Effective Supra- national Adjudication," *Yale Law Journal* 107 (1997): 273–391.

18. Joseph E. Stiglitz, "Regulating Multi- national Corporations: Towards Principles of Cross-Border Legal Frameworks in a Global- ized World Balancing Rights with Responsibil- ities," *American University International Law Review* 23 (2008): 451–558; Susan D. Franck, "The ICSID Effect? Consideration of Potential Variations in Arbitration Awards," *Virginia Journal of International Law* 51, no. 4 (2011): 825–1014.

19. A further complication is raised by the status of the parties. "State to state" investment traditionally meant a developed country inves- tor and a developing country host. Since the North American Free Trade Agreement came into effect, in 1994, there has been an increase in investments among developed and devel- oping states and a call for rebalancing the rela- tionship with enhanced procedural protections. See Onwuamaegbu, "Limiting the Participation of Developed States"; and Parra, *The History of ICSID*, 289–93.

20. Mariana Hernandez Crespo, "From Paper to People: Building Conflict Resolution Capacity and Frameworks for Sustainable Im- plementation of IIAs to Increase Investor-State Satisfaction," in *Investor-State Disputes: Preven- tion and Alternatives to Arbitration II*, ed. Susan D. Franck and Anna Joubin-Bret (New York: United Nations, 2011), 55–62, http://unctad .org/en/docs/webdiaeia20108_en.pdf; Mariana Hernandez Crespo, "From Problem to Poten- tial: The Need to Go Beyond Investor-State Disputes and Integrate Civil Society, Investors and State at the Local Level," in *Poverty and the International Economic Legal System*, ed. Krista Nadakavukaren Schefer (Cambridge: Cam- bridge University Press, 2013), 225–40.

21. George Kahale III, "Is Investor-State Arbitration Broken?," *Transnational Dispute Management*, October 2012, http://www.curtis .com/siteFiles/News/Is%20Investor-State %20Arbitration%20Broken.pdf.

22. European Parliament, "Multilateral Investment Court (MIC)," October 20, 2019, http://www.europarl.europa.eu/legislative -train/theme-a-balanced-and-progressive -trade-policy-to-harness-globalisation/file -multilateral-investment-court-(mic). The Eu- ropean Union is demanding that an investment court system (including appellate mechanism) replace investment treaty arbitration in its future trade and investment agreements. Such

an investment court system would include a cooling-off period, use of conciliation and mediation as more flexible resolution options, and greater transparency pursuant to the Mauritius Convention. The adoption of these features in various regional agreements (e.g., the Comprehensive and Economic Trade Agreement, the European Union–Viet Nam Investment Protection Agreement, and the revised NAFTA) results in regional fragmentation of resolution provisions. Paul Barker, "Investor-State Dispute Settlement Under Investment Treaties and Free Trade Agreements: Ad Hoc Arbitration or Investment Court System?" *International Law Bulletin*, no. 1 (February 2017), http://doughty-street-chambers.newsweaver.com/International/19q5vjt0076?a=1&p=1456996&t=174031; Shilpa Singh, "Analyzing Features of Investment Court System Under CETA and EUVIPA: Discussing Improvement in the System and Clarity to Clauses," *Kluwer Arbitration Blog*, February 8, 2019, http://arbitrationblog.kluwerarbitration.com/2019/02/08/analyzing-features-of-investment-court-system-under-ceta-and-euvipa-discussing-improvement-in-the-system-and-clarity-to-clauses.

23. Parra, *The History of ICSID*, 289. See also Stephen M. Schwebel, "Is Mediation of Foreign Investment Disputes Plausible?," *ICSID Review—Foreign Investment Law Journal* 22, no. 2 (2007): 237–41.

24. Greenberg and Winet, "International Investment Law and Dispute Resolution," 249.

25. See World Trade Organization, "A Unique Contribution," https://www.wto.org/english/thewto_e/whatis_e/tif_e/disp1_e.htm (accessed November 5, 2019).

26. Decision-making by consensus means "the body concerned shall be deemed to have decided by consensus on a matter submitted for its consideration, if no Member, present at the meeting when the decision is taken, formally objects to the proposed decision." See World

Trade Organization, "WTO Analytical Index: WTO Agreement, Article IX," February 2018, https://www.wto.org/english/res_e/publications_e/ai17_e/wto_agree_art9_oth.pdf.

27. The Doha Round was launched in Doha, Qatar, in November 2001. The Doha Development Agenda started with a focus on agriculture, services, intellectual property, and implementation of the previously adopted WTO agreements and now spans twenty issues. See World Trade Organization, "The Doha Round Texts—Introduction," https://www.wto.org/english/tratop_e/dda_e/texts_intro_e.htm (accessed November 5, 2019).

28. I. William Zartman, "The Elephant and the Holograph: Toward a Theoretical Synthesis and a Paradigm," in *International Multilateral Negotiation: Approaches to the Management of Complexity*, ed. I. William Zartman (San Francisco, CA: Jossey-Bass, 1994), 215.

29. In a review by Janet Martinez of WTO disputes from 1995 to 2003, over half the 304 cases involved the four largest trading countries as complainant or respondent. In nearly half the cases, the largest industrialized countries were both complainant and respondent. The balance of cases was equally distributed among industrialized versus developing, developing versus industrialized, and developing versus developing countries.

30. See World Trade Organization, "A Unique Contribution."

31. See World Trade Organization, "Negotiations to Improve Dispute Settlement Procedures," https://www.wto.org/english/tratop_e/dispu_e/dispu_negs_e.htm (accessed November 5, 2019).

32. Vikki Rogers, "Managing Disputes in the Online Global Marketplace," *Dispute Resolution Magazine* 19, no. 3 (2013): 20–24; Colin Rule, Vikki Rogers, and Louis Del Duca, "Designing a Global Consumer Online Dispute Resolution (ODR) System for Cross-Border

Small Value–High Volume Claims—OAS Developments," *Uniform Commercial Code Law Journal* 42, no. 3 (2010): 221–64.

33. See Organization for Economic Co-operation and Development, "Conference on Empowering E-Consumers: Strengthening Consumer Protection in the Internet Economy; Background Report," December 2009, http://www.oecd.org/ict/econsumerconference/44047583.pdf.

34. Guillermo Palao Moreno, "Cross-Border Consumer Redress After the ADR Directive and the ODR Regulation," in *The New Regulatory Framework for Consumer Dispute Resolution*, ed. Pablo Cortés (New York: Oxford University Press, 2016), 393–406; Pablo Cortés, "The New Landscape of Consumer Redress: The European Directive on Consumer Alternative Dispute Resolution and the Regulation on Online Dispute Resolution," in Cortés, *The New Regulatory Framework for Consumer Dispute Resolution*, 17–40; Pablo Cortés, "The Consumer Arbitration Conundrum: A Matter of Statutory Interpretation or Time for Reform?" in Cortés, *The New Regulatory Framework for Consumer Dispute Resolution*, 65–78.

35. In 2010, the Pace Law School Institute of International Commercial Law, the UNCITRAL Secretariat, and Penn State Dickinson School of Law organized a colloquium of leading experts in the ODR field. For podcasts of presentations, see Pace University Elisabeth Haub School of Law, "Speaker Presentations," http://law.pace.edu/speaker-presentations (accessed June 22, 2019).

36. As noted on the UNCITRAL website, "The Commission is composed of sixty member States elected by the General Assembly. Membership is structured so as to be representative of the world's various geographic regions and its principal economic and legal systems." See United Nations Commission on International Trade Law, "Origin, Mandate and Composition of UNCITRAL," http://www.uncitral.org/uncitral/en/about/origin.html (accessed June 23, 2019).

37. United Nations General Assembly, "Report of Working Group III (Online Dispute Resolution) on the Work of Its Thirty-Second Session (Vienna, 30 November–4 December 2015)," December 16, 2015, https://documents-dds-ny.un.org/doc/UNDOC/GEN/V15/089/16/PDF/V1508916.pdf?OpenElement. Reports of Working Group III and the draft procedural rules are available on the UNCITRAL website, at http://www.uncitral.org/uncitral/commission/working_groups/3Online_Dispute_Resolution.html.

38. Julia Salasky, "ODR Rulebook," presentation at 13th Annual Online Dispute Resolution Forum, June 26–28, 2014, Stanford Law School, Stanford, CA.

39. Rogers, "Managing Disputes in the Online Global Marketplace," 23.

40. United Nations Commission on International Trade Law, "UNCITRAL Technical Notes on Online Dispute Resolution," April 2017, http://www.uncitral.org/pdf/english/texts/odr/V1700382_English_Technical_Notes_on_ODR.pdf. The technical notes were adopted by the General Assembly on December 16, 2016.

41. Ibid.

42. United Nations Commission on International Trade Law, "United Nations Convention on International Settlement Agreements Resulting from Mediation," https://www.uncitral.org/pdf/english/commissionsessions/51st-session/Annex_I.pdf (accessed November 5, 2019). For a review of the design process, see S. I. Strong, "The Role of Empirical Research and Dispute System Design in Proposing and Developing International Treaties: A Case Study of the Singapore Convention on Mediation," *Cardozo Journal of Conflict Resolution* 20 (forthcoming).

43. United Nations General Assembly, "Report of Working Group II (Dispute

Settlement) on the Work of Its Sixty-Seventh
Session (Vienna, 2–6 October 2017)," October
11, 2017, https://documents-dds-ny.un.org/doc/
UNDOC/GEN/V17/072/79/PDF/V1707279
.pdf?. While the Singapore Convention represents a significant recognition of mediation
of international disputes, for it to enter into
force will require great effort and perseverance
to persuade states to join the convention and
the private sector and nongovernmental organizations to support it.

44. See International Council for Online
Dispute Resolution, "ICODR Standards,"
https://icodr.org/standards (accessed November 5, 2019).

45. United Nations, "UN Charter," October 24, 1945, Article 33, https://www.un.org/
en/sections/un-charter/un-charter-full-text.
See also Abram Chayes and Antonia Handler
Chayes, *The New Sovereignty: Compliance with
International Regulatory Agreements* (Cambridge, MA: Harvard University Press, 1997),
201.

46. The United Nations Convention on
Law of the Sea, which encompasses a web of
technical, commercial and security issues, has
the most simple and sophisticated dispute handling system: whatever forum or procedure the
parties agree to. International environmental
treaties like the UN Framework Convention on
Climate Change provide a consultative process

for questions of implementation and compulsory conciliation for dispute settlement. Chayes
and Chayes, *The New Sovereignty*, 217–23.

47. Deborah R. Hensler, "The Private in
Public, the Public in Private: The Blurring
Boundary Between Public and Private Dispute
Resolution," in *Formalisation and Flexibilisa-
tion in Dispute Resolution*, ed. Joachim Zekoll,
Moritz Balz, and Iwo Amelung (Leiden, Neth-
erlands: Brill/Nijhoff, 2014): 47.

48. At its forty-sixth session in 2013
UNCITRAL adopted Rules on Transparency
in Treaty-Based Investor-State Arbitration. To
ensure a widespread application of the Rules
on Transparency, the Working Group II of the
commission drafted the convention, which
was adopted by the UN General Assembly
on December 10, 2014. The convention was
opened for signature in Port Louis, Mauritius,
on March 17, 2015. United Nations Commission
on International Trade Law, "United Nations
Convention on Transparency in Treaty-Based
Investor-State Arbitrator," December 10,
2014, http://www.uncitral.org/uncitral/en/
uncitral_texts/arbitration/2014Transparency
_Convention.html. For a perspective on the
neutral's responsibility regarding transparency,
see Nancy A. Welsh, "Dispute Resolution Neutrals' Ethical Obligation to Support Measured
Transparency," *Oklahoma Law Review* 71, no. 3
(2019): 823–84.

Chapter 17

1. See South Africa's Promotion of National
Unity and Reconciliation Act 34 of 1995, available at http://www.justice.gov.za/legislation/
acts/1995-034.pdf.

2. Ibid.; James L. Gibson, "Truth, Recon-
ciliation, and the Creation of a Human Rights
Culture in South Africa," *Law and Society
Review* 38, no. 1 (2004): 5–40.

3. See, for example, the Truth and Reconciliation Commission's Register of Reconciliation,
at http://www.justice.gov.za/trc/ror/index.htm.

Transcripts of amnesty hearings and decisions
on amnesty are available on the Truth and Reconciliation Commission's "Amnesty Hearings
and Decisions" web page, at http://www.justice
.gov.za/trc/amntrans/index.htm.

4. See, generally, James L. Gibson, "The
Truth About Truth and Reconciliation in
South Africa," *International Political Science
Review* 26 (2005): 341–61. Gibson reports
the results of a large-scale empirical study
finding that the commission was viewed as

largely successful. See also James L. Gibson and Amanda Gouws, *Overcoming Intolerance in South Africa: Experiments in Democratic Persuasion* (Cambridge: Cambridge University Press, 2003).

5. Elinor Ostrom, *Understanding Institutional Diversity* (Princeton, NJ: Princeton University Press, 2005), 11–15.

6. Ibid., 16–22. Ostrom uses rules in the sense of regulations defined by an authority, distinguished from norms and strategies (16–17). See also Neil MacCormick, *Institutions of Law: An Essay in Legal Theory* (Oxford: Oxford University Press, 2008).

7. See, generally, Richard C. Feiock and John T. Scholz, eds., *Self-Organizing Federalism: Collaborative Mechanisms to Mitigate Institutional Collective Action Dilemmas* (Cambridge: Cambridge University Press, 2009).

8. See, generally, Susan L. Podziba, *Civic Fusion: Mediating Polarized Public Disputes* (Washington, DC: American Bar Association, 2012); see also Chapter 18's discussion of consensus building and conflict resolution in environmental disputes.

9. See, generally, Konrad Zweigert and Hein Kötz, *An Introduction to Comparative Law*, trans. Tony Weir, 3rd ed. (Oxford: Oxford University Press, 1998).

10. For reviews and a discussion of current theories and literature on governance, see Scott Burris, Michael Kempa, and Clifford Shearing, "Changes in Governance: A Cross-Disciplinary Review of Current Scholarship," *Akron Law Review* 41 (2008): 1–66.

11. Ibid., 3.

12. Mark Bevir, "Governance as Theory, Practice, and Dilemma," in *The Sage Handbook of Governance*, ed. Mark Bevir (London: Sage, 2011), 1. DSD applies to nested agency governance structures that use voice processes along the policy continuum, such as the mediation program using administrative law judges in the Occupational Safety and Health Review Commission, which hears appeals from the Occupational Safety and Health Administration. See Lisa Blomgren Bingham et al., "Dispute Resolution in the Administrative Process: Evaluation of the Occupational Safety and Health Review Commission Settlement Part Program," 2013, https://www.oshrc.gov/assets/1/6/IU_Final_Report.pdf.

13. See, generally, Jonathan G. S. Koppell, *The Politics of Quasi-government: Hybrid Organizations and the Dynamics of Bureaucratic Control* (Cambridge: Cambridge University Press, 2003).

14. Ibid., 2.

15. See the papers from the "Transatlantic Conference on New Governance and the Transformation of Law" symposium at the University of Wisconsin Law School, Madison, WI, November 20–21, 2009, which are available in *Wisconsin Law Review* 10, no. 2 (2010).

16. See, generally, Glenn Morgan et al., eds., *The Oxford Handbook of Comparative Institutional Analysis* (Oxford: Oxford University Press, 2011).

17. See, generally, Lester Salamon, ed., *The Tools of Government: A Guide to the New Governance* (New York: Oxford University Press, 2002).

18. See, generally, Eugene Bardach, "Policy Dynamics," in *The Oxford Handbook of Public Policy*, ed. Michael Moran, Martin Rein, and Robert E. Goodin (Oxford: Oxford University Press, 2008), 336–66. Bardach examines system dynamics in governance, a relatively new perspective and field. For a comprehensive examination of both the theory and the practice of governance, see Bevir, *The Sage Handbook of Governance*.

19. Robert Agranoff and Michael McGuire, *Collaborative Public Management: New Strategies for Local Governments* (Washington, DC: Georgetown University Press, 2003), 24.

20. See, generally, Steve Cropper et al., eds., *The Oxford Handbook of Inter-organizational Relations* (Oxford: Oxford University Press, 2008).

21. See, generally, Kaifeng Yang and Erik Bergrud, eds., *Civic Engagement in a Network Society* (Charlotte, NC: Information Age, 2008).

22. Bardach, "Policy Dynamics."

23. See, generally, Robert Agranoff, *Collaborating to Manage: A Primer for the Public Sector* (Washington, DC: Georgetown University Press, 2009).

24. See, generally, Nancy C. Roberts, ed., *The Age of Direct Citizen Participation* (Armonk, NY: M. E. Sharpe, 2008).

25. See, generally, Archon Fung and Erik Olin Wright, eds., *Deepening Democracy: Institutional Innovations in Empowered Participatory Governance* (London: Verso, 2003); and Jane J. Mansbridge, *Beyond Adversary Democracy* (Chicago: University of Chicago Press, 1983).

26. For case studies and essays on deliberative democracy, see John Gastil and Peter Levine, eds., *The Deliberative Democracy Handbook: Strategies for Effective Civic Engagement in the Twenty-First Century* (San Francisco, CA: Jossey-Bass, 2005); and Tina Nabatchi et al., *Democracy in Motion: Evaluating the Practice and Impact of Deliberative Civic Engagement* (New York: Oxford University Press, 2012).

27. For an extensive compendium of processes, see National Coalition for Dialogue and Deliberation, "Dialogue and Deliberation Methods," September 12, 2010, http://ncdd.org/rc/item/4856.

28. Jody Freeman, "The Private Role in Public Governance," *New York University Law Review* 75 (2000): 543–675. Freeman argues that institutional design should move away from the traditional legislative, executive, and judicial branches to an examination of alternative private institutions and stakeholders and the role they can play in governance.

29. See, generally, Robert Agranoff, *Managing Within Networks: Adding Value to Public Organizations* (Washington, DC: Georgetown University Press, 2007); Agranoff and McGuire, *Collaborative Public Management*; Eugene Bardach, *Getting Agencies to Work Together: The Practice and Theory of Managerial Craftsmanship* (Washington, DC: Brookings Institute, 1998); Lisa Blomgren Bingham and Rosemary O'Leary, eds., *Big Ideas in Collaborative Public Management* (Armonk, NY: M. E. Sharpe, 2008); and Rosemary O'Leary and Lisa Blomgren Bingham, eds., *The Collaborative Public Manager* (Washington, DC: Georgetown University Press, 2009).

30. See, generally, Jerome T. Barrett with Joseph Barrett, *A History of Alternative Dispute Resolution: The Story of a Political, Social, and Cultural Movement* (San Francisco, CA: Jossey-Bass, 2004). See also the website of the federal Interagency Alternative Dispute Resolution Working Group, at https://www.adr.gov.

31. Carrie Menkel-Meadow, "The Lawyer's Role(s) in Deliberative Democracy," *Nevada Law Journal* 5 (2004–2005): 347–69.

32. See, for example, Barack Obama, "Transparency and Open Government: Memorandum for the Heads of Executive Departments and Agencies," *Federal Register* 74 (2009): 4685–86.

33. Ibid.

34. Jane Mansbridge et al., "Norms of Deliberation: An Inductive Study," *Journal of Public Deliberation* 2, no. 1 (2006): 1–47, esp. 2–3.

35. Ibid., 5–6.

36. Tina Nabatchi and Lisa Blomgren Amsler, "Direct Public Engagement in Local Government," suppl., *American Review of Public Administration* 44, no. S4 (2014): 63S–88S.

37. Lawrence E. Susskind, "Can Public Policy Dispute Resolution Meet the Challenges Set by Deliberative Democracy?," *Dispute Resolution Magazine* 12 (2006): 5–6, reprinted in Lawrence E. Susskind and Larry Crump, eds., *Multiparty Negotiation*, vol. 2, *Theory and Practice of Public Dispute Resolution*, (Los Angeles: Sage, 2008), 1–4.

38. John Gastil, *By Popular Demand: Revitalizing Representative Democracy Through Deliberative Elections* (Berkeley: University of California Press, 2000), 22.

39. Mansbridge et al., "Norms of Deliberation," 1–2.

40. See, e.g., Stephen Coleman and Peter M. Shane, *Connecting Democracy: Online Consultation and the Flow of Political Communication* (Cambridge, MA: MIT Press, 2012); Fung, and Wright, *Deepening Democracy*; Mansbridge, *Beyond Adversary Democracy*; Beth Simone Noveck, *Smart Citizens, Smarter State: The Technologies of Expertise and the Future of Governing* (Cambridge, MA: Harvard University Press, 2015); Yang and Bergrud, *Civic Engagement in a Network Society*; and Daniel Yankelovich, *The Magic of Dialogue: Transforming Conflict into Cooperation* (New York: Simon and Schuster, 1999). For a review of this literature respecting local government and community level engagement, see Nabatchi and Amsler, "Direct Public Engagement in Local Government."

41. For a review of literature on dialogue and deliberation, see Laura W. Black, Nancy L. Thomas, and Timothy J. Shaffer, eds., "State of the Field," special issue, *Journal of Public Deliberation* 10, no. 1 (2014), http://www.publicdeliberation.net/jpd/vol10/iss1.

42. Many design choices have been identified in Lisa Blomgren Bingham, Tina Nabatchi, and Rosemary O'Leary, "The New Governance: Practices and Processes for Stakeholder and Citizen Participation in the Work of Government," *Public Administration Review* 65, no. 5 (2005): 547–58; Archon Fung, "Recipes for Public Spheres: Eight Institutional Design Choices and Their Consequences," *Journal of Political Philosophy* 11 (2003): 338–67; Archon Fung, "Varieties of Participation in Complex Governance," *Public Administration Review* 66 (2006): 66–75; and Tina Nabatchi, "An Introduction to Deliberative Civic Engagement," in Nabatchi et al., *Democracy in Motion*, 3–17.

43. See the websites of the National Issues Forums, at https://www.nifi.org, and the Kettering Foundation National Issues Forums, at https://www.kettering.org/tags/national-issues-forums. For another model using community-wide dialogue, see Everyday Democracy, "About Everyday Democracy," https://www.everyday-democracy.org/about (accessed March 3, 2019).

44. See, for example, Center for Deliberative Democracy, "Summary Results from the National Deliberative Poll in Mongolia on Constitutional Reform," August 29, 2017, http://cdd.stanford.edu/polls/docs/summary.

45. Carolyn J. Lukensmeyer, Joe Goldman, and Steven Brigham, "A Town Meeting for the 21st Century," in Gastil and Levine, *Deliberative Democracy Handbook*, 157; Carolyn Lukensmeyer and Steven Brigham, "Taking Democracy to Scale: Large Scale Interventions—for Citizens," *Journal of Applied Behavioral Science* 41 (2005): 47–58, esp. 47, 48, 53–56. For case studies and essays on deliberative democracy, see Fung and Wright, *Deepening Democracy*.

46. Christopher Ansell and Allison Gash, "Collaborative Governance in Theory and Practice," *Journal of Public Administration Research and Theory* 18, no. 4 (2008): 543–71; Kirk Emerson and Tina Nabatchi, *Collaborative Governance Regimes* (Washington, DC: Georgetown University Press, 2015).

47. Lisa Blomgren Amsler, "Collaborative Governance: Integrating Management, Politics, and Law," *Public Administration Review* 76, no. 5 (2016): 700–711.

48. John M. Bryson, Barbara C. Crosby, and Melissa Middleton Stone, "Designing and Implementing Cross-Sector Collaborations: Needed and Challenging," *Public Administration Review* 75, no. 5 (2015): 647–63; John M. Bryson et al., "Designing Public Participation Processes," *Public Administration Review* 73, no. 1 (2012): 23–34; Tina Nabatchi, "Putting the 'Public' Back in Public Values Research: Designing Participation to Identify and Respond to Values," *Public Administration Review* 72, no. 5 (2012): 699–708.

49. Koppell, *The Politics of Quasi-government.*

50. Udall Foundation, "U.S. Institute for Environmental Conflict Resolution," http://www.udall.gov/OurPrograms/Institute/Institute.aspx (accessed June 30, 2019).

51. John Kiefer and Robert Montjoy, "Incrementalism Before the Storm: Network Performance for the Evacuation of New Orleans," *Public Administration Review* 66 (2006): 122–30.

52. Susskind and Crump, *Multiparty Negotiation*; Rosemary O'Leary and Lisa Bingham, eds., *The Promise and Performance of Environmental Conflict Resolution* (Washington, DC: Resources for the Future Press, 2003); Lawrence Susskind, Sarah McKearnan, and Jennifer Thomas-Larmer, eds., *The Consensus Building Handbook: A Comprehensive Guide to Reaching Agreement* (Thousand Oaks, CA: Sage, 1999).

53. Richard Feiock, Hyung Jun Park, and In Won Lee, "Administrators' and Elected Officials' Collaboration Networks: Selecting Partners to Reduce Risk in Economic Development," *Public Administration Review* 72, no. S1 (2012): S58–S68.

54. Terry Cooper, Thomas Bryer, and Jack Meek, "Citizen-Centered Collaborative Public Management," *Public Administration Review* 66 (2006): 76–88.

55. William Leach and Paul Sabatier, "Facilitators, Coordinators, and Outcomes," in O'Leary and Bingham, *Promise and Performance of Environmental Conflict Resolution,* 148–71.

56. Stephanie E. Smith and Janet K. Martinez, "Analytic Framework for Dispute Systems Design," *Harvard Negotiation Law Review* 14 (2009): 123–69. This article introduced the original version of the DSD Analytic Framework. As our thinking progressed, we added culture and context and reordered the categories.

57. Daniel B. Rodriguez, Mathew D. McCubbins, and Barry R. Weingast, "The Rule of Law Unplugged," *Emory Law Journal* 59 (2010): 1455–94.

58. Thomas Carothers, *Promoting the Rule of Law Abroad: In Search of Knowledge* (Washington, DC: Carnegie Endowment for International Peace, 2006); Terence C. Halliday, "The Fight for Basic Legal Freedoms: Mobilization by the Legal Complex," in *Global Perspectives on the Rule of Law*, ed. James J. Heckman, Robert L. Nelson, and Lee Cabatingan (London: Routledge, Taylor and Francis, 2010), 210.

59. Kenneth W. Dam, *The Law-Growth Nexus: The Rule of Law and Economic Development* (Washington, DC: Brookings Institute, 2006), 15.

60. Margaret Levi and Brad Epperly, "Principled Principals in the Founding Moments of the Rule of Law," in Heckman, Nelson, and Cabatingan, *Global Perspectives on the Rule of Law*, 192.

61. James J. Heckman, "The Viability of the Welfare State," in Heckman, Nelson, and Cabatingan, *Global Perspectives on the Rule of Law*, 94.

62. Tom R. Tyler, *Why People Obey the Law* (Princeton, NJ: Princeton University Press, 2006).

63. William D. Leach, "Collaborative Public Management and Democracy: Evidence from Western Watershed Principles," *Public Administration Review* 68 (2006): 100–110.

64. James Laue and Gerald Cormick, "The Ethics of Intervention in Community Disputes," in *The Ethics of Social Intervention*, ed. Gordon Bermant, Herbert C. Kelman, and Donald P. Warwick (New York: Halstead Press, 1978), 217. For a proposed ethics for public deliberation, see Archon Fung, "Deliberation Before the Revolution: Toward an Ethics of Deliberative Democracy in an Unjust World," *Political Theory* 33, no. 2 (2005): 397–419.

65. See, for example, E-government Act, 44 U.S.C. §§ 3601–3606 (2002).

66. Chris Carlson, "Convening," in Susskind, McKearnan, and Thomas-Larmer, *Consensus Building Handbook*, 169–97.

67. David Laws, "Representation of Stake-holding Interests," in Susskind, McKearnan, and Thomas-Larmer, *Consensus Building Handbook*, 241–85.

68. See Ran Hirschl, "The 'Design Sciences' and Constitutional 'Success,'" *Texas Law Review* 87 (2009): 1339–74.

69. For case studies about language accessibility in public engagement, see the website of the Institute for Local Government, at https://www.ca-ilg.org.

70. Beth Glick and Laina Reynolds Levy, "The Institution as Innovator: Laying the Foundation for Peaceful Change," in *Building Peace: Practical Reflections from the Field*, ed. Craig Zelizer and Robert A. Rubinstein (Sterling, VA: Kumarian Press, 2009), 39–53.

71. Ibid., 41.

72. Ibid., 45.

73. Lisa Blomgren Bingham, "The Next Generation of Administrative Law: Building the Legal Infrastructure for Collaborative Governance," *Wisconsin Law Review* 10, no. 2 (2010): 297–356.

74. Susskind and Crump, *Multiparty Negotiation.*

75. John R. Ehrmann and Barbara L. Stinson, "Joint Fact-Finding and the Use of Technical Experts," in Susskind, McKearnan, and Thomas-Larmer, *Consensus Building Handbook*, 375–400.

76. Michael L. Poirier Elliott, "The Role of Facilitators, Mediators, and Other Consensus Building Practitioners," in Susskind, McKearnan, and Thomas-Larmer, *Consensus Building Handbook*, 199–239.

77. Lawrence Susskind and Jeffrey L. Cruikshank, *Breaking Robert's Rules: The New Way to Run Your Meeting, Build Consensus, and Get Results* (New York: Oxford University Press, 2006), 18–39. See also Susskind, McKearnan, and Thomas-Larmer, *Consensus Building Handbook.*

78. Susskind, McKearnan, and Thomas-Larmer, *Consensus Building Handbook*, 102.

79. Gerald W. Cormick, "Strategic Issues in Structuring Multi-party Public Policy Negotiations," *Negotiation Journal* 5, no. 2 (1989): 125–32.

80. Lawrence E. Susskind and Jeffrey L. Cruikshank, "What Is Consensus?," in Susskind and Cruikshank, *Breaking Robert's Rules*, 18–40.

81. Chester A. Crocker, Fen Osler Hampson, and Pamela Aall, eds., *Herding Cats: Multiparty Mediation in a Complex World* (Washington, DC: United States Institute of Peace Press, 2003).

82. For a discussion of a meta-analysis of many case studies of online or online combined with in-person dialogue, see Joachim Astrom and Ake Gronlund, "Online Consultations in Local Government: What Works, When, and Why?," in *Connecting Democracy: Online Consultation and the Flow of Political Com-*

munication, ed. Stephen Coleman and Peter M. Shane (Cambridge, MA: MIT Press, 2012), 75–96.

83. Lisa Blomgren Amsler and Susanna Foxworthy, "Collaborative Governance and Collaborating Online: The Open Government Initiative in the United States," in *Trends in the Modern State*, ed. Eberhard E. Bohne, John D. Graham, and Jos Raadschelders (New York: Palgrave Macmillan, 2014), 189–202.

84. Burris, Kempa, and Shearing observe, "'Governance' is not synonymous with 'good governance.' . . . Any given contemporary governance system may be inefficient, corrupt, or unresponsive to the needs of the governed. Governance can be 'good' in at least two senses: it can deliver good results . . . and it can work through processes and institutions that meet broadly accepted standards of justice and due process. Ideally governance is good in both of these ways, and many people believe that governance that fails the second criterion will normally have difficulty delivering on the first." This definition also recognizes the distinction between means and ends in discussions of the rule of law. Burris, Kempa, and Shearing, "Changes in Governance," 3.

85. World Bank, "Worldwide Governance Indicators," http://info.worldbank.org/governance/wgi/#home (accessed June 30, 2019).

86. See, generally, Adrian Karatnycky and Peter Ackerman, "How Freedom Is Won: From Civic Resistance to Durable Democracy," 2005, https://freedomhouse.org/sites/default/files/How%20Freedom%20is%20Won.pdf.

87. Judith E. Innes, "Evaluating Consensus Building," in Susskind, McKearnan, and Thomas-Larmer, *Consensus Building Handbook*, 632–77.

88. Maarten A. Hajer and Hendrik Wagenaar, eds., *Deliberative Policy Analysis:*

Understanding Governance in a Network Society (Cambridge: Cambridge University Press, 2003).

89. See Howard Kunreuther, Lawrence Susskind, and Thomas D. Aarts, "The Facility Siting Credo: Guidelines for an Effective Facility Siting Process," 1991, http://web.mit.edu/publicdisputes/practice/credo.pdf.

90. See Jonathan Raab, *Using Consensus Building to Improve Utility Regulation* (Washington, DC: American Council for an Energy Efficient Economy, 1994).

91. Jonathan Raab and Lawrence Susskind, "New Approaches to Consensus Building and Speeding Up Large-Scale Energy Infrastructure Projects," paper presented at Expansion of the German Transmission Grid, Gottingen University, Gottingen, Germany, June 23, 2009.

92. Cary Coglianese, "Assessing Consensus: The Promise and Performance of Negotiated Rulemaking," *Duke Law Journal* 46 (1997): 1255–349; Philip J. Harter, "Assessing the Assessors: The Actual Performance of Negotiated Rulemaking," *New York University Environmental Law Journal* 9, no. 1 (2000–2001): 32–59; Cary Coglianese, "Assessing the Advocacy of Negotiated Rulemaking: A Response to Philip Harter," *New York University Environmental Law Journal* 9, no. 2 (2001): 386–447.

93. In the United States, the Participatory Budgeting Project (https://www.participatorybudgeting.org) has ongoing projects in Chicago and Vallejo, California. Coexecutive Director Josh Lerner advocates game structures in deliberative democracy. See, generally, Josh Lerner, *Making Democracy Fun: How Game Design Can Empower Citizens and Transform Politics* (Cambridge, MA: MIT Press, 2014).

94. Gianpaolo Baiocchi, "Participation, Activism, and Politics: the Porto Alegre Experiment," in *Deepening Democracy: Institutional Innovations in Empowered Participatory*

Governance, ed. Archon Fung and Erik Olin Wright (London: Verso Press, 2003), 45–76.

95. Ibid.

96. Stephan Haggard, Andrew MacIntyre, and Lydia Tiede, "The Rule of Law and Economic Development," *Annual Review Political Science* 11 (2008): 205–34.

97. Jeffrey K. Staton, "A Comment on the Rule of Law Unplugged," *Emory Law Journal* 59 (2010): 1495–514, esp. 1512–13.

Chapter 18

1. See, generally, John T. Scholz and Bruce Stiftel, eds., *Adaptive Governance and Water Conflict: New Institutions for Collaborative Planning* (Washington, DC: Resources for the Future Press, 2005).

2. Horst W. J. Rittel and Melvin M. Webber, "Dilemmas in a General Theory of Planning," *Policy Sciences* 4, no. 2 (1973): 155; P. J. Balint et al., *Wicked Environmental Problems: Managing Uncertainty and Conflict* (Washington, DC: Island Press, 2011).

3. See, generally, Alissa J. Stern and Tim Hicks, *The Process of Business/Environmental Collaborations: Partnering for Sustainability* (Westport, CT: Quorum Books, 2000).

4. See Udall Foundation, "U.S. Institute for Environmental Conflict Resolution," https://www.udall.gov/OurPrograms/Institute/Institute.aspx (accessed June 30, 2019).

5. See, generally, J. Walton Blackburn and Willa Marie Bruce, eds., *Mediating Environmental Conflicts: Theory and Practice* (Westport, CT: Quorum Books, 1995); and Lon L. Fuller and Kenneth I. Winston, "The Forms and Limits of Adjudication," *Harvard Law Review* 92, no. 2 (1978): 353–409.

6. For the foundational theory of ECR and numerous case applications, see Lawrence E. Susskind, Sarah McKearnan, and Jennifer Thomas-Larmer, eds., *The Consensus Building Handbook: A Comprehensive Guide to Reaching Agreement* (Thousand Oaks, CA: Sage, 1999).

7. Gail Bingham, *Resolving Environmental Disputes: A Decade of Experience* (Washington, DC: Conservation Foundation, 1986); Rosemary O'Leary et al., *Managing for the Environment: Understanding the Legal, Organizational, and Policy Challenges* (San Francisco, CA: Jossey-Bass, 1999), 202–3.

8. O'Leary et al., *Managing for the Environment*, 196–97.

9. See Janet Martinez, Esther Conrad, and Tara Moran, "Upstream, Midstream, and Downstream: Dispute System Design for Sustainable Groundwater Management," *University of St. Thomas Law Journal* 13, no. 2 (2017): 297–314.

10. Scott Mernitz, *Mediation of Environmental Disputes: A Sourcebook* (New York: Praeger, 1980).

11. Edwardo Lao Rhodes, *Environmental Justice in America: A New Paradigm* (Bloomington: Indiana University Press, 2003).

12. David M. Konisky, "Environmental Justice," in *Environmental Governance Reconsidered: Challenges, Choices and Opportunities*, 2nd ed., ed. Robert F. Durant, Daniel J. Fiorino, and Rosemary O'Leary (Cambridge, MA: MIT Press, 2017), 205.

13. For a study of indigenous communities protecting traditional lands and waters, see Sibyl Diver, "Native Water Protection Flows Through Self-Determination: Understanding Tribal Water Quality Standards and 'Treatment as a State,'" *Journal of Contemporary Water Research and Education*, no. 163 (2018): 6–30.

14. Regina S. Axelrod and Stacy D. VanDeveer, "Global Environmental Governance," in Durant, Fiorino, and O'Leary, *Environmental Governance Reconsidered*, 43–74.

15. Yoshifumi Tanaka, *The International Law of the Sea*, 2nd ed. (Cambridge: Cambridge University Press, 2015).

16. In the international context intragovernmental agencies disagree (e.g., ministers holding economic versus environmental portfolios struggle over issues like greenhouse gas emissions, farm subsidies, and genetically modified food regulation) and developed and developing nations dispute state sovereignty and biodiversity preservation and risk management versus the precautionary principle. See, generally, Kathryn M. Mutz et al., *Justice and Natural Resources: Concepts, Strategies, and Applications* (Washington, DC: Island Press, 2002).

17. Udall Foundation, "U.S. Institute for Environmental Conflict Resolution: Find a Mediator or Facilitator," https://www.udall.gov/OurPrograms/Institute/FindMediatorFacilitator.aspx (accessed June 30, 2019).

18. John T. Dunlop, "The Limits of Legal Compulsion," *Labor Law Journal* 27, no. 2 (1976): 70. More broadly, for a discussion between cases that pose polycentric problems, or problems that are "many centered" and that the courts are not well suited to resolve well, see Fuller and Winston, "The Forms and Limits of Adjudication."

19. Lawrence S. Bacow and Michael Wheeler, *Environmental Dispute Resolution* (New York: Plenum Press, 1984).

20. O'Leary et al., *Managing for the Environment*, 194–95.

21. Susan L. Carpenter and W. J. D. Kennedy, *Managing Public Disputes* (San Francisco, CA: Jossey-Bass, 1988), 29.

22. 5. U.S.C. § 562(2).

23. For conflict resolution information, see the website of Beyond Intractability, at http://www.crinfo.org.

24. For more information on consensus building, see Barbara Gray, *Collaborating: Finding Common Ground for Multiparty Problems* (San Francisco, CA: Jossey-Bass, 1989); Lawrence Susskind and Jeffrey Cruikshank, *Breaking the Impasse: Consensual Approaches to Resolving Public Disputes* (New York: Basic Books, 1987); Judith E. Innes, "Evaluating Consensus Building," in Susskind, McKearnan, and Thomas-Larmer, *The Consensus Building Handbook*, 631–75; and Cary Coglianese, "Is Consensus an Appropriate Basis for Regulatory Policy?," in *Environmental Contracts: Comparative Approaches to Regulatory Innovation in the United States and Europe*, ed. Eric Orts and Kurt Deketelaere (New York: Kluwer Academic, 2001), 93–113. See also the website of Kitchen Table Democracy (formerly the Policy Consensus Initiative), at http://www.policyconsensus.org.

25. Collaborative adaptive management is a form of structured decision-making that is similar to ECR; it focuses on the importance of setting clear goals and concrete and measurable objectives while facilitating participation and joint fact-finding to share learning and manage scientific uncertainty over time. However, the extensive time and resources involved suggest caution in weighing the plausible and valuable benefits against the costs. See Lawrence Susskind, Alejandro E. Camacho, and Todd Schenk, "A Critical Assessment of Collaborative Adaptive Management in Practice," *Journal of Applied Ecology* 49, no. 1 (2011): 47–51; and Holly Doremus, "Adaptive Management as an Information Problem," *North Carolina Law Review* 89 (2010): 1455–98.

26. Roger Fisher, William L. Ury, and Bruce Patton, *Getting to Yes: Negotiating Agreement Without Giving In*, 3rd ed. (New York: Penguin Books, 2011); Ellen A. Waldman, "Identifying the Role of Social Norms in Mediation: A Multiple Model Approach," *Hastings Law Journal* 48, no. 4 (1998): 703–69; Ellen A. Waldman, "The Evaluative-Facilitative Debate in Mediation: Applying the Lens of Therapeutic Jurisprudence," *Marquette Law Review* 82, no. 1 (1998): 155–70.

27. Adrienne E. Eaton and Jeffrey H. Keefe, *Employment Dispute Resolution and Worker Rights in the Changing Workplace*

(Champaign, IL: Industrial Relations Research Association, 1999), 95–135.

28. Waldman, "The Evaluative-Facilitative Debate in Mediation."

29. Steven E. Daniels and Gregg B. Walker, *Working Through Environmental Conflict: The Collaborative Learning Approach* (Westport, CT: Praeger, 2001), 97–100.

30. William D. Leach, "Watershed Partnerships in California and Washington: Final Report for the Watershed Partnerships Project," *SSRN*, February 2002, https://papers.ssrn.com/sol3/papers.cfm?abstract_id=2268676.

31. See the website of the William and Flora Hewlett Foundation, at https://hewlett.org.

32. Zachary D. Clopton, "Redundant Public-Private Enforcement," *Vanderbilt Law Review* 69, no. 2 (2016): 285–332.

33. Elinor Ostrom, *Understanding Institutional Diversity* (Princeton, NJ: Princeton University Press, 2005).

34. O'Leary et al., *Managing for the Environment*, 193.

35. Rosemary O'Leary and Lisa B. Bingham, eds., *The Promise and Performance of Environmental Conflict Resolution* (Washington, DC: Resources for the Future Press, 2003).

36. Kirk Emerson et al., "Environmental Conflict Resolution: Evaluating Performance Outcomes and Contributing Factors," *Conflict Resolution Quarterly* 27, no. 1 (2009): 27–64.

37. Kirk Emerson and Tina Nabatchi, *Collaborative Governance Regimes* (Washington, DC: Georgetown University Press, 2015). For a different model of collaborative governance processes and a review of environmental conflict resolution case studies, see Christopher Ansell and Allison Gash, "Collaborative Governance in Theory and Practice," *Journal of Public Administration Research and Theory* 18, no. 4 (2008) 543–71.

38. Kirk Emerson and Tina Nabatchi, "Evaluating the Productivity of Collaborative

Governance Regimes: A Performance Matrix," *Public Performance and Management Review* 38, no. 4 (2015): 717–47.

39. Adapted by Rosemary O'Leary, Tina Nabatchi, and Lisa Blomgren Bingham, "Assessing and Improving Conflict Resolution in Multiparty Environmental Negotiations," *International Journal of Organizational Theory and Behavior* 8, no. 2 (2005): 191, from Lawrence Susskind et al., *Using Assisted Negotiation to Settle Land Use Disputes: A Guidebook for Public Officials* (Cambridge, MA: Lincoln Institute of Land Policy, 1999).

40. Bingham, *Resolving Environmental Disputes.*

41. Blackburn and Bruce, *Mediating Environmental Conflicts.*

42. See perspectives raised by Lawrence Susskind, "Environmental Mediation and the Accountability Problem," *Vermont Law Review* 6, no. 1 (1981): 4–8; and Joseph B. Stulberg, "The Theory and Practice of Mediation: A Reply to Professor Susskind," *Vermont Law Review* 6, no. 1 (1981): 110–14.

43. This narrative is paraphrased from Sarah McKearnan and Patrick Field, "The Northern Oxford County Coalition," in Susskind, McKearnan, and Thomas-Larmer, *The Consensus Building Handbook*, 711–41.

44. Ibid., 716.

45. Ibid., 719.

46. Ibid., 723.

47. Ibid., 735.

48. Ibid., 738.

49. Ibid.

50. Chris F. Sabel, "Commentary," in Susskind, McKearnan, and Thomas-Larmer, *The Consensus Building Handbook*, 720.

51. Michael Osmond et al., "Lessons for Marine Conservation Planning: A Comparison of Three Marine Protected Area Planning Processes," *Ocean and Coastal Management* 53 (2010): 46.

52. Amanda E. Cravens, "Negotiation and Decision-Making with Collaborative Software: How MarineMap 'Changed the Game' in California's Marine Life Protected Act Initiative," *Environmental Management* 57, no. 2 (2016): 474–97.

53. California Fish and Game Code § 5341 et seq.

54. Jonathan Raab, "Report on Lessons Learned from the Marine Life Protection Act Initiative: North Central Coast Study Region," October 31, 2008, p. vi (in the authors' possession). See also Jonathan Raab, "California Marine Life Protection Act: Evaluation of the Central Coast Regional Stakeholder Group Process," August 14, 2006, https://www.dfg.ca.gov/marine/pdfs/agenda_090606e.pdf.

55. MarineMap was created to help stakeholders analyze, design, and evaluate the consequence of proposed protected areas on marine life and habitats. See Marine Science Institute, "MarineMap," http://msi.ucsb.edu/marinemap (accessed June 30, 2019). See also Cravens, "Negotiation and Decision-Making with Collaborative Software." For use of models more broadly, see Stacy Langsdale et al., "Collaborative Modeling for Decision Support in Water Resources: Principles and Best Practices," *Journal of the American Water Resources Association* 49, no. 3 (2013): 629–38.

Conclusion

1. For a brief history, see Larry Kramer, "Beyond Neoliberalism: Rethinking Political Economy," April 26, 2018, https://hewlett.org/wp-content/uploads/2018/04/Beyond-Neoliberalism-Public-Board-Memo.pdf. The Hewlett Foundation funded the field of conflict resolution for twenty years (1984–2004), creating ADR Theory Centers, with one at Northwestern University, where Jeanne Brett and Stephen Goldberg were faculty. Brett and Goldberg were coauthors of the original book on DSD with William Ury, who was at the Harvard Program on Negotiation, also a Hewlett Theory Center. William L. Ury, Jeanne M. Brett, and Stephen B. Goldberg, *Getting Disputes Resolved: Designing Systems to Cut the Costs of Conflict* (San Francisco, CA: Jossey-Bass, 1988).

2. Frances Moore Lappé and Adam Eichen, *Daring Democracy: Igniting Power, Meaning, and Connection for the America We Want* (Boston, MA: Beacon Press, 2017), chap 1. Lappé also authored *Diet for a Small Planet* (New York: Ballantine Books, 1971).

3. Amartya Sen, *The Idea of Justice* (Cambridge, MA: Belknap Press, 2009), 18.

4. Michael J. Sandel, *Justice: What's the Right Thing to Do* (New York: Farrar, Straus and Giroux, 2009), 260. Sandel concludes, "A just society can't be achieved simply by maximizing utility or by securing freedom of choice. To achieve a just society, we have to reason together about the meaning of the good life, and to create a public culture hospitable to the disagreements that will inevitably arise" (261).

5. Ury, Brett, and Goldberg, *Getting Disputes Resolved*.

BIBLIOGRAPHY

Ackerman, Bruce, and James S. Fishkin. *Deliberation Day.* New Haven, CT: Yale University Press, 2004.

Adjudication Society. "About Us." http://www.adjudication.org/about (accessed May 20, 2019).

Adler, Peter S., Robert C. Barrett, Martha C. Bean, Juliana E. Birkhoff, Connie P. Ozawa, and Emily B. Rudin. *Managing Scientific and Technical Information in Environmental Cases: Principles and Practices for Mediators and Facilitators.* Tucson, AZ: U.S. Institute for Environmental Conflict Resolution, 1999.

"*Against Settlement*: Twenty-Five Years Later." Special issue, *Fordham Law Review* 78, no. 3 (2009).

Agranoff, Robert. *Collaborating to Manage: A Primer for the Public Sector.* Washington, DC: Georgetown University Press, 2009.

———. *Managing Within Networks: Adding Value to Public Organizations.* Washington, DC: Georgetown University Press, 2007.

Agranoff, Robert, and Michael McGuire. *Collaborative Public Management: New Strategies for Local Governments.* Washington, DC: Georgetown University Press, 2003.

Alexander, Janet Cooper. "Procedural Design and Terror Victim Compensation." *DePaul Law Review* 53, no. 2 (2003–2004): 627–718.

Alexander, Nadja, ed. *Global Trends in Mediation.* 2nd ed. Alphen aan den Rijn, Netherlands: Kluwer Law International, 2006.

———, ed. *International Comparative Mediation: Legal Perspectives.* The Hague, Netherlands: Kluwer International, 2009.

Alexander v. Gardner-Denver. 415 U.S. 36 (1974).

Ali, Shahla F. *Court Mediation Reform: Efficiency, Confidence and Perceptions of Justice.* Cheltenham, UK: Edward Elgar, 2018.

Alkon, Cynthia. "The Flawed U.S. Approach to Rule of Law Development." *Penn State Law Review* 117 (2013): 797–814.

———. "The Increased Use of 'Reconciliation' in Criminal Cases in Central Asia: A Sign of Restorative Justice, Reform, or Cause for Concern?" *Pepperdine Dispute Resolution Law Journal* 8 (2007): 41–116.

Alternative Dispute Resolution: A Resource Guide. Washington, DC: U.S. Office of Personnel Management. http://www.au.af.mil/au/awc/awcgate/dispute_resolution/opm_adrguide.pdf (accessed May 20, 2019).

Amchem Prods., Inc. v. Windsor. 521 U.S. 591 (1997).

American Arbitration Association. "About the AAA and ICDR." https://www.adr.org/about (accessed May 23, 2019).

———. "Construction Industry Arbitration Rules and Mediation Procedures." July 1, 2015. https://www.adr.org/sites/default/files/Construction_Arbitration_Rules_7May2018.pdf.

———. "The Construction Industry's Guide to Dispute Avoidance and Resolution." October 1, 2009. https://www.adr.org/sites/default/files/document_repository/The%20Construction%20Industry's%20Guide%20to%20Dispute%20Avoidance%20and%20Resolution.pdf.

———. "Employment Due Process Protocol." May 9, 1995. https://www.adr.org/sites/default/files/document_repository/Employment%20Due%20Process%20Protocol_0.pdf.

American Bar Association. *Alternative Dispute Resolution: A Practical Guide for Resolving Government Contract Controversies*. 2nd ed. Chicago: American Bar Association, 2005.

———. "The Code of Ethics for Arbitrators in Commercial Disputes." February 9, 2004. http://www.americanbar.org/content/dam/aba/migrated/dispute/commercial_disputes.pdf.

———. *Model Rules of Professional Conduct*. Chicago: American Bar Association, 2002.

———. "Recommended Best Practices for On-line Dispute Resolution Service Providers." http://www.abanet.org/dispute/documents/BestPracticesFinal102802.pdf (accessed June 14, 2019).

———. "Reporter's Notes." September 9, 2005. https://www.americanbar.org/content/dam/aba/migrated/2011_build/dispute_resolution/mscm_reporternotes.pdf.

American Bar Association, American Arbitration Association, and Association for Conflict Resolution. "Model Standards of Conduct for Mediators." September 2005. https://www.americanbar.org/content/dam/aba/migrated/2011_build/dispute_resolution/model_standards_conduct_april2007.authcheckdam.pdf.

American Bar Association Section of Dispute Resolution. "Report of the Task Force on Research on Mediator Techniques." June 12, 2017. https://www.americanbar.org/content/dam/aba/administrative/dispute_resolution/med_techniques_tf_report.pdf.

American Bar Association Section of Dispute Resolution Task Force on Research and Statistics. "Top Ten Pieces of Information Courts Should Collect on ADR." June 9, 2006. https://www.americanbar.org/content/dam/aba/events/dispute_resolution/cle_and_mtg_planning_board/teleconferences/2012-2013/May_2013/topten.authcheckdam.pdf.

American Express Co. et al. v. Italian Colors Restaurant et al. 570 U.S. 228 (2013).

American Family Mutual Ins. Co. v. Farmers Insurance Exchange. 26 A.L.R.3d 604 (1993).

American Postal Workers Union. "Collective Bargaining Agreement Between the American Postal Workers Union, AFL-CIO and the U.S. Postal Service, November 21, 2006–November 20, 2010." 2006. https://apwu.org/contracts/2006-2010-collective-bargaining-agreement-nov-21-2006.

Amsler, Lisa Blomgren. "Collaborative Governance: Integrating Management, Politics, and Law." *Public Administration Review* 76, no. 5 (2016): 700–11.

———. "Combating Structural Bias in Dispute System Designs That Use Arbitration: Transparency, the Universal Sanitizer." *Yearbook on Arbitration and Mediation* 6 (2014): 32–55.

———. "Dispute System Design and the Global Pound Conference." *Cardozo*

Journal of Conflict Resolution 18 (2017): 621–35.

———. "The Evolution of Social Norms in Conflict Resolution." *Journal of Natural Resources Policy Research* 6, no. 4 (2014): 285–90.

Amsler, Lisa Blomgren, and Susanna Foxworthy. "Collaborative Governance and Collaborating Online: The Open Government Initiative in the United States." In *Trends in the Modern State*, edited by Eberhard E. Bohne, John D. Graham, and Jos Raadschelders, 189–202. New York: Palgrave Macmillan, 2014.

Amsler, Lisa Blomgren, and Jessica Sherrod. "Accountability Forums and Dispute System Design." *Public Performance Management Review* 40, no. 3 (2017): 529–50.

Amsler, Terry. "Community Dispute Resolution: Assessing Its Importance and Addressing Its Challenges." *Dispute Resolution Magazine* 19, no 2 (2013): 4–6.

Anderson, Heather, and Ron Pi. *Evaluation of the Early Mediation Pilot Programs.* San Francisco, CA: Judicial Council of California, 2004.

Anderson, Jonathan F., and Lisa Blomgren Bingham. "Upstream Effects from Mediation of Workplace Disputes: Some Preliminary Evidence from the USPS." *Labor Law Journal* 48 (1997): 601–15.

Anderson, Mary B. *Do No Harm: How Aid Can Support Peace—or War.* Boulder, CO: Lynne Rienner, 1999.

Ansell, Christopher, and Allison Gash. "Collaborative Governance in Theory and Practice." *Journal of Public Administration Research and Theory* 18, no. 4 (2008): 543–71.

Apple, James G., and Robert P. Deyling. *A Primer on the Civil-Law System.* Washington, DC: Federal Judicial Center, 1995.

Aquila, Frank, and Kathy Bryan. "Avoiding the 'Boomerang': Resolving Disputes Before They Ruin the Deal." *M&A Journal* 10, no. 5 (2010): 17–20.

Archibald, Bruce P. "Let My People Go: Human Capital, Investment and Community Capacity Building via Meta/Regulation in a Deliberative Democracy—a Modest Contribution to Criminal Law and Restorative Justice." *Cardozo Journal of International and Comparative Law* 16, no. 1 (2008): 1–85.

Arrow, Kenneth J., Robert H. Mnookin, Lee Ross, Amos Tversky, and Robert B. Wilson. *Barriers to Conflict Resolution.* New York: W. W. Norton, 1995.

Association for Conflict Resolution. "Report on Competencies in Conflict Management Systems Design." 2000. https://cdn.ymaws.com/acrnet.org/resource/resmgr/docs/SPIDR_Report_on_Competencies.pdf.

Astrom, Joachim, and Ake Gronlund. "Online Consultations in Local Government: What Works, When, and Why?" In *Connecting Democracy: Online Consultation and the Flow of Political Communication*, edited by Stephen Coleman and Peter M. Shane, 75–96. Cambridge, MA: MIT Press, 2012.

Attanasio, David L. "Extraordinary Reparations, Legitimacy, and the Inter-American Court." *University of Pennsylvania Journal of International Law* 37, no. 3 (2016): 813–71.

AT&T Mobility v. Concepcion. 131 S. Ct. 1740 (2011).

Austin, William G., and Joyce M. Tobiasen. "Legal Justice and the Psychology of Conflict Resolution." In *The Sense of Injustice: Social Psychological Perspectives*, edited by Robert G. Folger, 227–74. Boston, MA: Springer, 1984.

Avgar, Ariel C., J. Ryan Lamare, David B. Lipsky, and Abhishek Gupta. "Unions and ADR: The Relationship Between Labor Unions and Workplace Dispute Resolution in U.S. Corporations." *Ohio State Journal on Dispute Resolution* 28 (2013): 63–106.

Avruch, Kevin. *Culture and Conflict Resolution.* Washington, DC: U.S. Institute of Peace, 1998.

Axelrod, Regina S., and Stacy D. VanDeveer. "Global Environmental Governance." In *Environmental Governance Reconsidered: Challenges, Choices and Opportunities*, 2nd ed., edited by Robert F. Durant, Daniel J. Fiorino, and Rosemary O'Leary, 43–74. Cambridge, MA: MIT Press, 2017.

Axelrod, Robert. *The Complexity of Cooperation: Agent-Based Models of Competition and Collaboration*. Princeton, NJ: Princeton University Press, 1998.

———. *The Evolution of Cooperation*. New York Basic Books, 1984.

Bacow, Lawrence, and Michael Wheeler. *Environmental Dispute Resolution*. New York: Plenum Press, 1984.

Baiocchi, Gianpaolo. "Participation, Activism, and Politics: the Porto Alegre Experiment." In *Deepening Democracy: Institutional Innovations in Empowered Participatory Governance*, edited by Archon Fung and Erik Olin Wright, 45–76. London: Verso Press, 2003.

Baker, David. "PG&E Chief: Liability Proposal Is Not Enough." *San Francisco Chronicle*, July 27, 2018, p. C1.

Baldwin, Elizabeth, Tingjia Chen, and Daniel Cole. "Institutional Analysis for New Public Governance Scholars." *Public Management Review* 21, no. 6 (2019): 890–917.

Bales, Richard A. "The Employment Due Process Protocol at Ten: Twenty Unresolved Issues, and a Focus on Conflicts of Interest." *Ohio State Journal on Dispute Resolution* 21, no. 1 (2005): 165–97.

Balint, Peter J., Lawrence C. Walters, Ronald Eugene Stewart, Anand Desai. *Wicked Environmental Problems: Managing Uncertainty and Conflict*. Washington, DC: Island Press, 2011.

Bardach, Eugene. *Getting Agencies to Work Together: The Practice and Theory of Managerial Craftsmanship*. Washington, DC: Brookings Institute, 1998.

———. "Policy Dynamics." In *The Oxford Handbook of Public Policy*, edited by Michael Moran, Martin Rein, and Robert E. Goodin, 336–66. Oxford: Oxford University Press, 2008.

Barker, Paul. "Investor-State Dispute Settlement Under Investment Treaties and Free Trade Agreements: Ad Hoc Arbitration or Investment Court System?" *International Law Bulletin*, no. 1 (February 2017). http://doughty-street-chambers.newsweaver.com/International/19q5vjto076?a=1&p=1456996&t=174031.

Barnard, Shannon. "Understanding the Importance of Alternative Dispute Resolution in the United States Military: An Analysis of ADR in the Navy." December 2010. Unpublished paper.

Barrett, Jerome, with Joseph Barrett. *A History of Alternative Dispute Resolution: The Story of a Political, Cultural and Social Movement*. San Francisco, CA: Jossey-Bass, 2004.

Bassiouni, M. Cherif, ed. *Post-conflict Justice*. Ardsley, NY: Transnational, 2002.

Bates, Donna M. "A Consumer's Dream or Pandora's Box: Is Arbitration a Viable Option for Cross-Border Consumer Disputes?" *Fordham International Law Journal* 27 (2003): 823–98.

Bayles, Michael D. *Procedural Justice: Allocating to Individuals*. Boston: Kluwer Academic, 1990.

Bazerman, Max H., and Margaret A. Neale. *Negotiating Rationally*. New York: Free Press, 1992.

BDO Consulting. "Independent Evaluation of the Gulf Coast Claims Facility: Report of Findings and Observations to the U.S. Department of Justice." June 5, 2012. https://www.justice.gov/iso/opa/resources/66520126611210351178.pdf.

Bebinger, Martha. "No Clear Targets for Civil Suits in Marathon Bombings." *WBUR*,

May 10, 2013. http://www.wbur.org/2013/05/10/marathon-victims-lawsuits.

Belkin, Lisa. "Just Money." *New York Times*, December 8, 2002, p. 92.

Belman, Dale, Morley Gunderson, and Douglas Hyatt, eds. *Public Sector Employment in a Time of Transition*. Champaign, IL: Industrial Relations Research Association, 1996.

Bendersky, Corinne. "Culture: The Missing Link in Dispute Systems Design." *Negotiation Journal* 14, no. 4 (1998): 307–11.

———. "Organizational Dispute Resolution Systems: A Complementarities Model." *Academy of Management Review* 28, no. 4 (2003): 643–56.

Berman, Greg, and John Feinblatt. *Good Courts—the Case for Problem-Solving Justice*. New York: New Press, 2005.

———. "Problem-Solving Courts: A Brief Primer." *Law and Policy* 23, no. 2 (2001): 125–40.

Berman, Greg, and Aubrey Fox. "Justice in Red Hook." *Justice System Journal* 26 (2005): 79–94.

Bernard, Phyllis E. "Begging for Justice? Or, Adaptive Jurisprudence? Initial Reflections on Mandatory ADR to Enforce Women's Rights in Rwanda." *Cardozo Journal of Conflict Resolution* 7, no. 2 (2006): 325–52.

Bernard, Phyllis, and Bryant Garth, eds. *Dispute Resolution Ethics: A Comprehensive Guide*. Washington, DC: American Bar Association, 2002.

Bernardin, H. John, Brenda E. Richey, and Stephanie L. Castro. "Mandatory and Binding Arbitration: Effects on Employee Attitudes and Recruiting Results." *Human Resource Management* 50, no. 2 (2011): 175–200.

Bernstein, Lisa. "Opting out of the Legal System: Extralegal Contractual Relations in the Diamond Industry." *Journal of Legal Studies* 21, no. 1 (1992): 115–57.

———. "Private Commercial Law in the Cotton Industry: Creating Cooperation Through Rules, Norms, and Institutions." *Michigan Law Review* 99 (2001): 1724–90.

Bevir, Mark. "Governance as Theory, Practice, and Dilemma." In *The Sage Handbook of Governance*, edited by Mark Bevir, 1–17. London: Sage, 2011.

Bevir, Mark, ed. *The Sage Handbook of Governance*. London: Sage, 2011.

Bies, Robert J. "The Predicament of Injustice: The Management of Moral Outrage." *Research in Organizational Behavior* 9 (1987): 289–319.

Bies, Robert J., and Joseph S. Moag. "Interactional Justice: Communication Criteria of Fairness." In *Research on Negotiation in Organizations*, edited by Roy J. Lewicki, Robert J. Bies, and Blair H. Sheppard, 43–55. Newton, MA: JAI Press, 1986.

Bies, Robert J., and Debra L. Shapiro. "Voice and Justification: Their Influence on Procedural Fairness Judgments." *Academy of Management Journal* 31 (1988): 676–85.

Bies, Robert J., Debra L. Shapiro, and L. L. Cummings. "Casual Accounts and Managing Organizational Conflict: Is It Enough to Say It's Not My Fault?" *Communication Research* 15, no. 4 (1988): 381–99.

Binder, Christina. "The Prohibition of Amnesties by the Inter-American Court of Human Rights." *German Law Journal* 12, no. 5 (2011): 1203–30.

Bingham, Gail. *Resolving Environmental Disputes: A Decade of Experience*. Washington, DC: Conservation Foundation, 1986.

Bingham, Lisa B. "Control over Dispute-System Design and Mandatory Commercial Arbitration." *Law and Contemporary Problems* 67, nos. 1–2 (2004): 221–51.

———. "Collaborative Governance: Emerging Practices and the Incomplete Legal Framework for Citizen and Stakeholder Voice."

Journal of Dispute Resolution 2009, no. 2 (2010): 269–326.

———. "Designing Justice: Legal Institutions and Other Systems for Managing Conflict." *Ohio State Journal on Dispute Resolution* 24, no. 1 (2008): 1–52.

———. "Emerging Due Process Concerns in Employment Arbitration: A Look at Actual Cases." *Labor Law Journal* 47, no. 2 (1996): 108–26.

———. "Employment Arbitration: The Repeat Player Effect." *Employee Rights and Employment Policy Journal* 1, no. 1 (1997): 189–221.

———. "Employment Dispute Resolution: The Case for Mediation." *Conflict Resolution Quarterly* 22 (2004): 145–74.

———. "McGeorge Symposium on Arbitration: On Repeat Players, Adhesive Contracts, and the Use of Statistics in Judicial Review of Arbitration Awards." *McGeorge Law Review* 29, no. 2 (1998): 223–60.

———. "Mediating Employment Disputes: Perceptions of REDRESS at the United States Postal Service." *Review of Public Personnel Administration* 17, no. 2 (1997): 20–30.

———. "Mediation at Work: Transforming Workplace Conflict at the United States Postal Service." October 2003. http://www .businessofgovernment.org/sites/default/ files/Mediation.pdf.

———. "The Next Generation of Administrative Law: Building the Legal Infrastructure for Collaborative Governance." *Wisconsin Law Review* 10, no. 2 (2010): 297–356.

———. "Reflections on Designing Governance to Produce the Rule of Law." *Journal of Dispute Resolution* 2011, no. 1 (2011): 67–89.

———. "Self-Determination in Dispute System Design and Employment Arbitration." *University of Miami Law Review* 56, no. 4 (2002): 873–908.

———. "When We Hold No Truths to Be Self-Evident: Truth, Belief, Trust, and the Decline in Trials." *Journal of Dispute Resolution* 2006 (2006): 131–63.

Bingham, Lisa Blomgren, and Denise R. Chachere. "Dispute Resolution in Employment: The Need for Research." In *Employment Dispute Resolution and Worker Rights in the Changing Workplace*, edited by Adrienne E. Eaton and Jeffrey H. Keefe, 95–135. Champaign, IL: Industrial Relations Research Association, 1999.

Bingham, Lisa Blomgren, Gregory Chesmore, Yuseok Moon, and Lisa Marie Napoli. "Mediating Employment Disputes at the United States Postal Service: A Comparison of In-House and Outside Neutral Mediators." *Review of Public Personnel Administration* 20, no. 1 (2000): 5–19.

Bingham, Lisa Blomgren, and David H. Good. "A Better Solution to Moral Hazard in Employment Arbitration: It Is Time to Ban Pre-dispute Arbitration Clauses." *Minnesota Law Review Headnotes* 93, no. 1 (2009): 1–14.

Bingham, Lisa Blomgren, Cynthia. J. Hallberlin, Denise A. Walker, and Won Tae Chung. "Dispute System Design and Justice in Employment Dispute Resolution: Mediation at the Workplace." *Harvard Negotiation Law Review* 14 (2009): 1–50.

Bingham, Lisa Blomgren, Kiwhan Kim, and Susan Summer Raines. "Exploring the Role of Representation in Employment Mediation at the USPS." *Ohio State Journal on Dispute Resolution* 17 (2002): 341–77.

Bingham, Lisa Blomgren, Deanna Malatesta, Susanna Foxworthy, and Timothy Reuter. "Dispute Resolution in the Administrative Process: Evaluation of the Occupational Safety and Health Review Commission Settlement Part Program." 2013. https:// www.oshrc.gov/assets/1/6/IU_Final _Report.pdf.

Bingham, Lisa B., and Debra J. Mesch. "Decision-Making in Employment and Labor

Arbitration." *Industrial Relations* 39 (2000): 671–94.

Bingham, Lisa Blomgren, Tina Nabatchi, and Rosemary O'Leary. "The New Governance: Practices and Processes for Stakeholder and Citizen Participation in the Work of Government." *Public Administration Review* 65, no. 5 (2005): 547–58.

Bingham, Lisa B., Tina Nabatchi, Jeffrey Senger, and M. Scott Jackman. "Dispute Resolution and the Vanishing Trial: Comparing Federal Government Litigation and ADR Outcomes." *Ohio State Journal on Dispute Resolution* 24, no. 2 (2009): 225–62.

Bingham, Lisa Blomgren, and Lisa Marie Napoli. "Employment Dispute Resolution and Workplace Culture: The REDRESS™ Program at the United States Postal Service." In *The Federal Alternative Dispute Deskbook*, edited by Marshall J. Breger and Gerald M. Schatz, 507–26. Washington, DC: American Bar Association.

Bingham, Lisa B., and Cristina M. Novac. "Mediation's Impact on Formal Complaint Filing: Before and After the REDRESS™ Program at the United States Postal Service." *Review of Public Personnel Administration* 21, no. 4 (2001): 308–31.

Bingham, Lisa Blomgren, and Rosemary O'Leary, eds. *Big Ideas in Collaborative Public Management*. Armonk, NY: M. E. Sharpe, 2008.

———. *A Manager's Guide to Resolving Conflict in Collaborative Networks*. Washington, DC: IBM Center for the Business of Government, 2007.

Bingham, Lisa Blomgren, Susan Summers Raines, Timothy K. Hedeen, and Lisa Marie Napoli. "Mediation in Employment and Creeping Legalism: Implications for Dispute Systems Design." *Journal of Dispute Resolution* 2010, no. 2 (2010): 129–50.

Bingham, Lisa Blomgren, and Charles R. Wise. "The Administrative Dispute Resolu-

tion Act of 1990: How Do We Evaluate Its Success?" *Journal of Public Administration, Research and Theory* 6 (1996): 383–414.

Birke, Richard, and Craig Fox. "Psychological Principles in Negotiating Civil Settlements." *Harvard Negotiation Law Review* 14 (1999): 1–28.

Black, Laura W., Nancy L. Thomas, and Timothy J. Shaffer, eds. "State of the Field." Special issue, *Journal of Public Deliberation* 10, no. 1 (2014). http://www.publicdeliberation.net/jpd/vol10/iss1.

Blackburn, J. Walton, and Willa Marie Bruce, eds. *Mediating Environmental Conflicts: Theory and Practice*. Westport, CT: Quorum Books, 1995.

Blue Ribbon Advisory Panel on Kaiser Permanente Arbitration. "The Kaiser Permanente Arbitration System: A Review and Recommendations for Improvement." January 5, 1998. http://www.oia-kaiserarb.com/pdfs/BRP-Report.pdf.

Bohne, Eberhard E., John D. Graham, and Jos Raadschelders. *Trends in the Modern State*. New York: Palgrave Macmillan, 2014.

Bolocan, Maya Goldstein. "Rwandan Gacaca: An Experiment in Transitional Justice." *Journal of Dispute Resolution* 2004, no. 2 (2004): 355–400.

Boone, W. Daniel. "Steelworkers Trilogy: Collective Bargaining as the Foundation for Industrial Democracy and Arbitration as an Integral Part of Workplace Self-Government." In *National Academy of Arbitrators Annual Proceedings 2010*, edited by National Academy of Arbitrators, 100–142. Edison, NJ: BNA Books, 2010.

Boraine, Alex. "Truth and Reconciliation in South Africa: The Third Way." In *Truth v. Justice: The Morality of Truth Commissions*, edited by Robert I. Rotberg and Dennis Thompson, 141–57. Princeton, NJ: Princeton University Press, 2000.

Bordone, Robert, and Michael Moffitt, eds. *The Conflict Resolution Handbook*. San Francisco, CA: Jossey-Bass, 2005.

Borel v. Fibreboard Paper Prods. Corp. 493 F.2d 1076 (5th Cir. 1973).

Boserup, Viggo, Brian Parmelee, Jerry Roscoe, Janice Symchych, Wayne Thorpe, and Cathy Yanni. *What Is . . . ADR in Health Care Disputes?* New York: American Bar Association, 2015.

Bovens, Mark. "Two Concepts of Accountability: Accountability as a Virtue and as a Mechanism." *West European Politics* 33, no. 5 (2010): 946–67.

Bovens, Mark, Robert E. Goodin, and Thomas Schillermans. *The Oxford Handbook of Public Accountability*. Oxford: Oxford University Press, 2014.

Bovens, Mark, and Thomas Schillermans. "Meaningful Accountability." In *The Oxford Handbook of Public Accountability*, edited by Mark Bovens, Robert E. Goodin, and Thomas Schillermans, 673–83 Oxford: Oxford University Press, 2014.

Bowcott, Owen. "Compulsory Mediation Angers Lawyers Working in Italy's Unwieldy Legal System." *The Guardian*, May 23, 2011. https://www.theguardian.com/law/butterworth-and-bowcott-on-law/2011/may/23/italian-lawyers-strike-mandatory-mediation.

Bowles, Edith, and Tanja Chopra. "East Timor: Statebuilding Revisited." In *Building States to Build Peace*, edited by Charles T. Call and Vanessa Wyeth, 271–302. Boulder, CO: Lynne Rienner, 2008.

Bradford, D. L., and W. W. Burke. *Organizational Development*. San Francisco, CA: Pfeiffer, 2005.

Bradford, William C. "Reclaiming Indigenous Legal Autonomy on the Path to Peaceful Coexistence: The Theory, Practice and Limitations of Tribal Peacemaking in Indian Dispute Resolution." *North Dakota Law Review* 76 (2000): 551–604.

Braithwaite, John. "Holism, Justice, and Atonement." *Utah Law Review* 2003 (2003): 389–412.

———. *Restorative Justice and Responsive Regulation*. New York: Oxford University Press, 2002.

Braverman, Mark. *Preventing Workplace Violence: A Guide for Employers and Practitioners*. Thousand Oaks, CA: Sage, 1999.

Brazil, Wayne D. "The Adversary Character of Civil Discovery: A Critique and Proposals for Change." *Vanderbilt Law Review* 31 (1978): 1295–361.

———. "Comparing Structures for the Delivery of ADR Services by Courts: Critical Values and Concerns." *Ohio State Journal on Dispute Resolution* 14 (1999): 715–811.

———. *Early Neutral Evaluation*. Chicago: American Bar Association, 2012.

———. "Should Court-Sponsored ADR Survive?" *Ohio State Journal on Dispute Resolution* 21 (2006): 244–51.

Breger, Marshall J., and Gerald M. Schatz, eds. *The Federal Alternative Dispute Deskbook*. Washington, DC: American Bar Association.

Brest, Paul, and Linda Hamilton Krieger. *Problem Solving, Decision Making, and Professional Judgment: A Guide for Lawyers and Policymakers*. New York: Oxford University Press, 2010.

Brett, Jeanne M. *Negotiating Globally: How to Negotiate Deals, Resolve Disputes, and Make Decisions Across Cultural Boundaries*. San Francisco, CA: Jossey-Bass, 2007.

Brett, Jeanne M., and Stephen B. Goldberg. "Grievance Mediation in the Coal Industry: A Field Experiment." *ILR Review* 37, no. 1 (1983): 49–69.

———. "Wildcat Strikes in Bituminous Coal Mining." *ILR Review* 32 (1979): 465–83.

Brett, Jeanne M., Mara Olekalns, Ray Friedman, Nathan Goates, Cameron Anderson, and Cara Cherry Lisco. "Sticks and Stones: Language, Face, and Online Dispute Resolution." *Academy of Management Journal* 50, no. 1 (2007): 85–99.

Briggs, Lord Justice. "Civil Courts Structure Review: Final Report." July 2016. https://www.judiciary.uk/wp-content/uploads/2016/07/civil-courts-structure-review-final-report-jul-16-final-1.pdf.

Brinkert, Ross, and Tricia S. Jones. *Conflict Coaching: Conflict Management Strategies and Skills for the Individual.* Los Angeles: Sage, 2008.

Brown, Tim. "Design Thinking." *Harvard Business Review* 86, no. 6 (2008): 84–92.

Brunet, Edward, Richard Speidel, Jean E. Sternlight, and Stephen H. Ware. *Arbitration Law in America: A Critical Assessment.* Cambridge: Cambridge University Press, 2006.

Brysk, Alison. *From Tribal Village to Global Village: Indian Rights and International Relations in Latin America.* Stanford, CA: Stanford University Press, 2000.

Bryson, John M., Barbara C. Crosby, and Melissa Middleton Stone. "Designing and Implementing Cross-Sector Collaborations: Needed and Challenging." *Public Administration Review* 75, no. 5 (2015): 647–63.

Bryson, John M., Kathryn S. Quick, Carissa Schively Slotterback, and Barbara C. Crosby. "Designing Public Participation Processes." *Public Administration Review* 73, no. 1 (2012): 23–34.

Buckeye Check Cashing, Inc. v. Cardegna. 546 U.S. 440 (2006).

Bureau of Consumer Financial Protection. "12 CFR Part 1026, Loan Originator Compensation Requirements Under the Truth in Lending Act (Regulation Z): Final Rule." 78 Fed. Reg. 11280 (February 15, 2013).

Bureau of Labor Statistics. "Union Members Summary." January 18, 2019. https://www.bls.gov/news.release/union2.nr0.htm.

Burris, Scott, Michael Kempa, and Clifford Shearing. "Changes in Governance: A Cross-Disciplinary Review of Current Scholarship." *Akron Law Review* 41 (2008): 1–66.

Bush, Robert A. Baruch. "Mediation and Adjudication, Dispute Resolution and Ideology: An Imaginary Conversation." *Journal of Contemporary Legal Issues* 3, no. 1 (1989): 1–36.

———. "A Study of Ethical Dilemmas and Policy Implications." *Journal of Dispute Resolution* 1994, no. 1 (1994): 1–56.

Bush, Robert A. Baruch, and Lisa Blomgren Bingham. "Knowledge Gaps: The Final Conference of the Hewlett ADR Theory Centers." *Conflict Resolution Quarterly* 23, no. 1 (2005): 99–122.

Bush, Robert A. Baruch, and Joseph P. Folger. *The Promise of Mediation: Responding to Conflict Through Empowerment and Recognition.* San Francisco, CA: Jossey-Bass, 1994.

———. *The Promise of Mediation: The Transformative Approach to Conflict.* 2nd ed. San Francisco, CA: Jossey-Bass, 2004.

Cabraser, Elizabeth J. "Life After Amchem: The Class Struggle Continues." *Loyola Los Angeles Law Review* 31 (1998): 373–94.

California Courts. "ADR Types and Benefits." https://www.courts.ca.gov/programs-adr.htm (accessed May 20, 2019).

California Law Revision Commission. "Relationship Between Mediation Confidentiality and Attorney Malpractice and Other Misconduct." December 2017. http://www.clrc.ca.gov/pub/Printed-Reports/RECpp-K402.pdf.

Call, Charles T., and Vanessa Wyeth, eds. *Building States to Build Peace.* Boulder, CO: Lynne Rienner, 2008.

Campos, Sergio J. "Mass Torts and Due Process." *Vanderbilt Law Review* 65, no. 4 (2012): 1059–124.

Cane, Peter, and Herbert Kritzer, eds. *Oxford Handbook of Empirical Legal Research*. Oxford: Oxford University Press, 2010.

Carberry, Edward J., ed. *Employee Ownership and Shared Capitalism: New Directions in Research*. Champaign, IL: Labor and Employment Relations Association, 2011.

Carbonneau, Thomas E. *Arbitration in a Nutshell*. 3rd ed. St. Paul, MN: Thomson West, 2011.

———. *The Law and Practice of Arbitration*. 2nd ed. Huntington, NY: Juris, 2012.

Carlson, Chris. "Convening." In *Consensus Building Handbook: A Comprehensive Guide to Reaching Agreement*, edited by Lawrence Susskind, Sarah McKearnan, and Jennifer Thomas-Larmer, 169–97. Thousand Oaks, CA: Sage, 1999.

Carothers, Thomas. *Critical Mission: Essays on Democracy Promotion*. Washington, DC: Carnegie Endowment for International Peace, 2004.

———. *Promoting the Rule of Law Abroad: In Search of Knowledge*. Washington, DC: Carnegie Endowment for International Peace, 2006.

Carpenter, Susan L., and W. J. D. Kennedy. *Managing Public Disputes*. San Francisco, CA: Jossey-Bass, 1988.

Carrington, Paul D. "Asbestos Lessons: The Unattended Consequences of Asbestos Litigation." *Review of Litigation* 26, no. 3 (2007): 583–612.

Carrns, Ann. "With the New Year, New Consumer Protections on Mortgages." *New York Times*, January 4, 2014, p. B4.

Carroll, John S., ed. *Applied Social Psychology and Organizational Settings*. Hillsdale, NJ: Lawrence Erlbaum, 1990.

Carroll, Stephen J., Deborah Hensler, Allan Abrahamse, Jennifer Gross, Michelle White, Scott Ashwood, and Elizabeth Sloss. *Asbestos Litigation Costs and Compensation: An Interim Report*. Santa Monica, CA: RAND, 2002. https://www.rand.org/content/dam/rand/pubs/documented _briefings/2005/DB397.pdf.

Carroll, Stephan J., Deborah Hensler, Jennifer Gross, Elizabeth Sloss, Matthias Schonlau, Allan Abrahamse, and J. Scott Ashwood. *Asbestos Litigation*. Santa Monica, CA: RAND, 2005.

Carson, Lyn, and Janette Hartz-Karp. "Adapting and Combining Deliberative Designs: Juries, Polls and Forums." In *The Deliberative Democracy Handbook: Strategies for Effective Civic Engagement in the Twenty-First Century*, edited by John Gastil and Peter Levine, 120–38. San Francisco, CA: Jossey-Bass, 2005.

Cassel v. Superior Court. 51 Cal. 4th 113 (2011).

"Cathy A. Costantino." Georgetown Law. https://www.law.georgetown.edu/faculty/cathy-a-costantino (accessed May 20, 2019).

Center for Court Innovation. "The 10 Essential Elements of Opioid Intervention Courts." 2019. https://www.courtinnovation.org/sites/default/files/media/documents/2019-07/report_the10essentialelements _07092019.pdf.

Center for Deliberative Democracy. "Summary Results from the National Deliberative Poll in Mongolia on Constitutional Reform." August 29, 2017. http://cdd.stanford .edu/polls/docs/summary.

Center for Public Resources. *Corporate Early Case Assessment Toolkit*. New York: International Institute for Conflict Prevention and Resolution, 2009.

Center for Strategic and International Studies and Association of the United States Army. "Post-conflict Reconstruction: Task Framework." May 2002. http://csis.org/files/media/csis/pubs/framework.pdf.

Cernansky, Rachel. "It Takes Consultation to Help a Village." *New York Times*, July 17, 2018. https://www.nytimes.com/2018/07/17/opinion/development-aid-liberia.html.

Chang, Won Kyung. "The Practice of Restorative Justice: An Ethnographic Exploration of One Community's Attempt to Implement a Community-Based System." PhD diss., Indiana University, Bloomington, 2010.

Charkoudian, Lorig. "What Works in Child Access Mediation: Effectiveness of Various Mediation Strategies on Short- and Long-Term Outcomes." January 2016. http://mdmediation.org/sites/default/files/What%20Works%20in%20Child%20Access%20Mediation%20FINAL%20REV.pdf.

———. "What Works in District Court Day of Trial Mediation: Effectiveness of Various Mediation Strategies on Short-Term and Long-Term Outcomes." January 2016. http://mdmediation.org/sites/default/files/What%20Works%20in%20District%20Court%20DOT%20Mediation.pdf.

Charlton, Paul. "Indicators of Success: An Exploration of Successful Conflict Management in U.S. Hospital Settings." Master's thesis, Georgetown University, June 15, 2010.

Chayes, Abram, and Antonia Handler Chayes. *The New Sovereignty: Compliance with International Regulatory Agreements.* Cambridge, MA: Harvard University Press, 1997.

Chetwynd, Josh. "Play Ball? An Analysis of Final Offer Arbitration, Its Use in Major League Baseball and Its Potential Applicability to European Football Wage and Transfer Disputes." *Marquette Sports Law Review* 20 (2009): 109–46.

City of Boston. "One Fund Boston Administrator Ken Feinberg Distributes Nearly $61 Million Among 232 Eligible Claimants." July 1, 2013. http://www.cityofboston.gov/news/default.aspx?id=6211.

Civil Resolution Tribunal. "Welcome to the Civil Resolution Tribunal." https://civilresolutionbc.ca (accessed May 20, 2019).

Claims Administration Website. "Deepwater Horizon Claims Center." http://deepwaterhorizoneconomicsettlement.com (accessed July 1, 2019).

Clopton, Zachary D. "Redundant Public-Private Enforcement." *Vanderbilt Law Review* 69, no. 2 (2016): 285–332.

Coates, Ta-Nehisi. "The Case for Reparations." *Atlantic Monthly*, June 2014, pp. 54–71.

Coben, James R., and Peter N. Thompson. "Disputing Irony: A Systematic Look at Litigation About Mediation." *Harvard Negotiation Law Review* 11 (2006): 43–146.

Coe, Jack, Jr. "Toward a Complementary Use of Conciliation in Investor-State Disputes—a Preliminary Sketch." *UC Davis Journal of International Law and Policy* 12, no. 7 (2005): 7–46.

Coglianese, Cary. "Assessing the Advocacy of Negotiated Rulemaking: A Response to Philip Harter." *New York University Environmental Law Journal* 9, no. 2 (2001): 386–447.

———. "Assessing Consensus: The Promise and Performance of Negotiated Rulemaking." *Duke Law Journal* 46 (1997): 1255–349.

———. "Is Consensus an Appropriate Bases for Regulatory Policy?" In *Environmental Contracts: Comparative Approaches to Regulatory Innovation in the United States,* edited by Eric Orts and Kurt Deketelaere, 93–113. New York: Kluwer Academic, 2001.

Cohen, Amy J. "Dispute Systems Design, Neoliberalism, and the Problem of Scale." *Harvard Negotiation Law Review* 14, no. 1 (2009): 51–80.

———. "Trauma and the Welfare State: A Genealogy of Prostitution Courts in New

York City." *Texas Law Review* 95, no. 5 (2017): 915–92.

Cohen, David. "Justice on the Cheap Revisited: The Failure of the Serious Crimes Trials in East Timor." *Asia-Pacific Issues* 80 (2006): 1–12.

Cohn, Lynn P. "A Model for the Use of ADR to Efficiently Distribute a Significant Settlement Fund in Mass Claims Litigation Without Sacrificing an Individualized Assessment of Claims." *Cardozo Journal of Conflict Resolution* 18, no. 3 (2017): 699–715.

Cole, Daniel H. "Laws, Norms, and the Institutional Analysis and Development Framework." *Journal of Institutional Economics* 13, no. 4 (2017): 829–47.

Cole, Elizabeth A., and Judy Barsalou. *Unite or Divide? The Challenges of Teaching History in Societies Emerging from Violent Conflict.* Washington, DC: United States Institute of Peace Press, 2006.

Cole, Sarah Rudolph. "Revising the FAA to Permit Expanded Judicial Review of Arbitration Awards." *Nevada Law Journal* 8 (2007): 214–33.

Cole, Sarah R., Craig A. McEwen, Nancy H. Rogers, James R. Coben, and Peter N. Thompson. *Mediation: Law, Policy and Practice.* 3 vols. Eagan, MN: West, 2012.

Coleman, Charles D. "Is Mandatory Employment Arbitration Living Up to Its Expectations? A View from the Employer's Perspective." *ABA Journal of Labor and Employment Law* 25, no. 2 (2010): 227–40.

Coleman, Stephen, and Peter M. Shane. *Connecting Democracy: Online Consultation and the Flow of Political Communication.* Cambridge, MA: MIT Press, 2012.

Colquitt, Jason A. "On the Dimensionality of Organizational Justice: A Construct Validation of a Measure." *Journal of Applied Psychology* 86 (2001): 386–400.

Colquitt, Jason A., Donald E. Conlan, Michael J. Wesson, Christopher O. H. L. Por-

ter, and K. Yee Ng. "Justice at the Millennium: A Meta-analytic Review of 25 Years of Organizational Justice Research." *Journal of Applied Psychology* 86, no. 3 (2001): 425–45.

Colvin, Alexander J. S. "An Empirical Study of Employment Arbitration: Case Outcomes and Processes." *Journal of Empirical Legal Studies* 8, no. 1 (2011): 1–23.

———. "The Metastasization of Mandatory Arbitration." *Chicago-Kent Law Review* 94 (2019): 3–24.

Colvin, Alexander J. S., and Mark D. Gough. "Comparing Mandatory Arbitration and Litigation: Access, Process, and Outcomes." April 2, 2014. http://digitalcommons.ilr .cornell.edu/reports/60.

Community Justice and Mediation Center. "Downtown Safety, Civility, and Justice Project: Report Summary; What the Community Said." January 30, 2017. https:// bloomington.in.gov/sites/default/files/ 2017-06/CJAM%20Downtown%20Safety %2C%20Civility%20and%20Justice_What %20the%20Community%20Said_Report %20Summary%20%281%29.pdf.

Compliance Advisor Ombudsman. "How We Work: Ombudsman." http://www .cao-ombudsman.org/howwework/ ombudsman (accessed June 13, 2019).

Conbere, John. "Theory Building for Conflict Management System Design." *Conflict Resolution Quarterly* 19 (2001): 213–36.

Consumer Financial Protection Bureau. "Arbitration Agreements." 2017. http://files .consumerfinance.gov/f/documents/201707 _cfpb_Arbitration-Agreements-Rule.pdf.

———. "Arbitration Study Preliminary Results." December 12, 2013. http://files .consumerfinance.gov/f/201312_cfpb _arbitration-study-preliminary-results.pdf.

———. "CFPB Ombudsman." http://www .consumerfinance.gov/ombudsman (accessed June 14, 2019).

———. "Finding a Housing Counselor." http://www.consumerfinance.gov/find-a-housing-counselor (accessed July 2, 2019).

———. "Get Answers to Your Mortgage Questions." http://www.consumerfinance.gov/mortgage/#homeowners (accessed July 2, 2019).

———. "Having a Problem with a Financial Product or Service?" http://www.consumerfinance.gov/complaint (accessed June 14, 2019).

Cooper, Terry, Thomas Bryer, and Jack Meek. "Citizen-Centered Collaborative Public Management." *Public Administration Review* 66 (2006): 76–88.

Cormick, Gerald W. "Strategic Issues in Structuring Multi-party Public Policy Negotiations." *Negotiation Journal* 5, no. 2 (1989): 125–32.

Cornell Law School Legal Information Institute. "Rule 23. Class Actions." https://www.law.cornell.edu/rules/frcp/rule_23 (accessed June 3, 2019).

Cortés, Pablo. "The Brave New World of Consumer Redress in the European Union and the United Kingdom." *Dispute Resolution Magazine* 71 (Spring 2016): 41–45.

———. "The Consumer Arbitration Conundrum: A Matter of Statutory Interpretation or Time for Reform?" In *The New Regulatory Framework for Consumer Dispute Resolution*, edited by Pablo Cortés, 65–78. New York: Oxford University Press, 2016.

———. "The New Landscape of Consumer Redress: The European Directive on Consumer Alternative Dispute Resolution and the Regulation on Online Dispute Resolution." In *The New Regulatory Framework for Consumer Dispute Resolution*, edited by Pablo Cortés, 17–40. New York: Oxford University Press, 2016.

———, ed. *The New Regulatory Framework for Consumer Dispute Resolution*. New York: Oxford University Press, 2016.

———. *Online Dispute Resolution for Consumers in the European Union*. New York: Taylor and Francis, 2011.

Coser, Lewis. *The Functions of Social Conflict*. New York: Free Press, 1956.

Costantino, Cathy. "Second Generation Organizational Conflict Management Systems Design: A Practitioner's Perspective on Emerging Issues." *Harvard Negotiation Law Review* 14 (2009): 81–100.

Costantino, Cathy, and Christina Sickles Merchant. *Designing Conflict Management Systems: A Guide to Creating Productive and Healthy Organizations*. San Francisco, CA: Jossey-Bass, 1996.

Court of Arbitration for Sport. "Frequently Asked Questions." https://www.tas-cas.org/en/general-information/frequently-asked-questions.html (accessed June 22, 2019).

———. "Statistics." 2016. https://www.tas-cas.org/fileadmin/user_upload/CAS_statistics_2016_.pdf.

Coy, Patrick G., and Timothy Hedeen. "A Stage Model of Social Movement Co-optation: Community Mediation in the United States." *Sociological Quarterly* 46, no. 3 (2005): 405–35.

Cravens, Amanda E. "Negotiation and Decision Making with Collaborative Software: How MarineMap 'Changed the Game' in California's Marine Life Protection Act Initiative." *Environmental Management* 57, no. 2 (2016): 474–97.

Crespo, Mariana Hernandez. "Building the Latin America We Want: Supplementing Representative Democracies with Consensus-Building." *Cardozo Journal of Conflict Resolution* 10 (2009): 425–90.

———. "From Noise to Music: The Potential of the Multi-door Courthouse (Casas de Justicia) Model to Advance Systemic Inclusion and Participation as a Foundation for Sustainable Rule of Law in Latin America."

Journal of Dispute Resolution 2012, no. 2 (2012): 335–423.

———. "From Paper to People: Building Conflict Resolution Capacity and Frameworks for Sustainable Implementation of IIAs to Increase Investor-State Satisfaction." In *Investor-State Disputes: Prevention and Alternatives to Arbitration II*, edited by Susan D. Franck and Anna Joubin-Bret, 55–62. New York: United Nations, 2011. http://unctad.org/en/docs/webdiaeia20108_en.pdf.

———. "From Problem to Potential: The Need to Go Beyond Investor-State Disputes and Integrate Civil Society, Investors and State at the Local Level." In *Poverty and the International Economic Legal System*, edited by Krista Nadakavukaren Schefer, 225–40. Cambridge: Cambridge University Press, 2013.

Crocker, Chester A., Fen Osler Hampson, and Pamela Aall, eds. *Herding Cats: Multiparty Mediation in a Complex World*. Washington, DC: United States Institute of Peace Press, 2003.

Cronin-Harris, Catherine, and International Institute for Conflict Prevention and Resolution. *Building ADR into the Corporate Law Department: ADR Systems Design*. New York: International Institute for Conflict Prevention and Resolution, 1997.

Cropanzano, Russell. *Justice in the Workplace: Approaching Fairness in Human Resource Management*. Hillsdale, NJ: Lawrence Erlbaum, 1993.

Cropper, Steve, Mark Ebers, Chris Huxham, and Peter Smith Ring, eds. *The Oxford Handbook of Inter-organizational Relations*. Oxford: Oxford University Press, 2008.

Cruikshank, Jeffrey, and Lawrence Susskind. *Breaking the Impasse: Consensual Approaches to Resolving Public Disputes*. New York: Basic Books, 1987.

D'Alo, Grace E. "Accountability in Special Education Mediation: Many a Slip Twixt

Vision and Practice." *Harvard Negotiation Law Review* 8 (2003): 201–70.

Daly, Erin. "Between Punitive and Reconstructive Justice: The Gacaca Courts in Rwanda." *NYU Journal of International Law and Politics* 34 (2004): 355–96.

Dam, Kenneth W. *The Law-Growth Nexus: The Rule of Law and Economic Development*. Washington, DC: Brookings Institute, 2006.

Daniels, Steven E., and Gregg B. Walker. *Working Through Environmental Conflict: The Collaborative Learning Approach*. Westport, CT: Praeger, 2001.

Dannin, Ellen. *Taking Back the Workers' Law*. Ithaca, NY: ILR Press, 2006.

Dauber, Michele Landis. "The War of 1812, September 11th, and the Politics of Compensation." *DePaul Law Review* 53, no. 2 (2003): 289–354.

Dawkins, Cedric. "Agonistic Pluralism and Stakeholder Engagement." *Business Ethics Quarterly* 25 (2015): 1–28.

Deahl, Dani. "China Launches Cyber-Court to Handle Internet-Related Disputes." *The Verge*, August 18, 2017. https://www.theverge.com/tech/2017/8/18/16167836/china-cyber-court-hangzhou-internet-disputes.

De Dreu, Carsten K. W. "The Virtue and Vice of Workplace Conflict: Food for (Pessimistic) Thought." *Journal of Organizational Behavior* 29 (2008): 5–18.

Deepwater Horizon Claims Center. "Public Statistics for the Deepwater Horizon Economic and Property Damages Settlement." http://www.deepwaterhorizoneconomicsettlement.com/docs/statistics.pdf (accessed July 20, 2018).

"Deepwater Horizon Court-Supervised Settlement Program." December 22, 2012. http://www.deepwaterhorizonsettlements.com.

Demain, Linda J., and Deborah R. Hensler. "'Volunteering' to Arbitrate Through

Predispute Arbitration Clauses: The Average Consumer's Experience." *Law and Contemporary Problems* 67 (Winter 2004): 55–74.

DeMars, Jo, Susan Nauss Exon, Kimberlee K. Kovach, and Colin Rule. "Virtual Virtues: Ethical Considerations for Online Dispute Resolution Practice." *Dispute Resolution Magazine*, Fall 2010, pp. 6–10.

Denenberg, Richard, and Mark Braverman. *The Violence-Prone Workplace: A New Approach to Dealing with Hostile, Threatening, and Uncivil Behavior.* Ithaca, NY: Cornell University Press, 1999.

De Palo, Guiseppe. "A Ten-Year-Long 'EU Mediation Paradox': When an EU Directive Needs to Be More . . . Directive." November 2018. http://www.europarl.europa.eu/RegData/etudes/BRIE/2018/608847/IPOL_BRI(2018)608847_EN.pdf.

De Palo, Giuseppe, and Luigi Cominelli. "Mediation in Italy: Waiting for the Big Bang." In *Global Trends in Mediation*, edited by Nadja Alexander, 259–77. Alphen aan den Rijn, Netherlands: Kluwer Law International, 2006.

De Palo, Giuseppe, and Leonardo D'Urso. "Achieving a Balanced Relationship Between Mediation and Judicial Proceedings." In *The Implementation of the Mediation Directive Workshop 29 November 2016: Compilation of In-Depth Analyses*, 4–30. Brussels: European Parliament, 2016. https://docplayer.net/69471160-The-implementation-of-the-mediation-directive-workshop-29-november-2016.html.

De Palo, Giuseppe, Leonardo D'Urso, Mary Trevor, Bryan Branon, Romina Canessa, Beverly Cawyer, and L. Reagan Florence. "'Rebooting' the Mediation Directive: Assessing the Limited Impact of Its Implementation and Proposing Measures to Increase the Number of Mediations in the EU." January 15, 2014. http://www.europarl.europa.eu/thinktank/en/document.html?reference=IPOL-JURI_ET(2014)493042.

Department of the Navy. "Introduction to the DON ADR Program." May 2003. http://www.secnav.navy.mil/ADR/Documents/IntroDONADRProgram.pdf.

———. "Online Introduction to Alternative Dispute Resolution." https://www.secnav.navy.mil/ADR/Pages/etraining.aspx (accessed November 5, 2019).

Des Forges, Alison, and Timothy Longman. "Legal Responses to Genocide in Rwanda." In *My Neighbor, My Enemy: Justice and Community in the Aftermath of Mass Atrocity*, edited by Eric Stover and Harvey M. Weinstein, 49–68. Cambridge: Cambridge University Press, 2004.

DeSimone, Samuel G. "Summary Jury Trial—Untapped Tool for Effective State Courts." https://njcourts.gov/courts/civil/cdrappendices.html (accessed May 20, 2019).

Dettman, Kurt L., Martin J. Harty, and Joel Lewin. "Resolving Megaproject Claims: Lessons from Boston's 'Big Dig.'" *Construction Lawyer* 30, no. 2 (2010): 1–13.

Deutsch, Morton. *The Resolution of Conflict: Constructive and Destructive Processes.* New Haven, CT: Yale University Press, 1973.

Deutsch, Morton, and Peter T. Coleman. *The Handbook of Conflict Resolution.* San Francisco, CA: Jossey-Bass, 2000.

Diamond Dealers Club New York. "Non-members and Arbitration." https://www.nyddc.com/arbitration.html (accessed June 3, 2019).

"Directive 2008/52/EC of the European Parliament and of the Council of 21 May 2008 on Certain Aspects of Mediation in Civil and Commercial Matters." *Official Journal of the European Union*, May 24, 2008, pp. L 136/3–L 136/8.

Diver, Sibyl. "Native Water Protection Flows Through Self-Determination: Understanding Tribal Water Quality Standards and 'Treatment as a State.'" *Journal of Contemporary Water Research and Education*, no. 163 (2018): 6–30.

Dixon, Lloyd, Geoffrey McGovern, and Amy Coombe. *Asbestos Bankruptcy Trusts: An Overview of Trust Structure and Activity with Detailed Reports on the Largest Trusts*. Santa Monica, CA: RAND, 2010. http://www.rand.org/content/dam/rand/pubs/technical_reports/2010/RAND _TR872.pdf.

Doremus, Holly. "Adaptive Management as an Information Problem." *North Carolina Law Review* 89 (2010): 1455–98.

Dorf, Michael C., and Charles F. Sabel. "Drug Treatment Courts and Emergent Experimentalist Government." *Vanderbilt Law Review* 53 (2000): 831–83.

Drahozal, Christopher R. "Arbitration Costs and Contingent Free Contracts." *Vanderbilt Law Review* 59 (2006): 729–91.

———. "Arbitration Costs and Forum Accessibility: Empirical Evidence." *University of Michigan Journal of Law Reform* 41, no. 4 (2008): 813–41.

Drahozal, Christopher R., and Erin A. O'Hara O'Connor. "Unbundling Procedure: Carve-Outs from Arbitration Clauses." *Florida Law Review* 66, no. 5 (2013): 1945–2006.

Duggan, Colleen. "Editorial Note." *International Journal on Transitional Justice* 4 (2010): 315–28.

Drummonds, Henry. "A Closer Look at the US Supreme Court's Public Policy Trilogy: A BROADER View of the Public Policy Exception to Labor Arbitration Award Enforcement." *Labor Law Journal* 65, no. 3 (2014): 136–70.

Duane, Michael J. *The Grievance Process in Labor-Management Cooperation*. Westport, CT: Quorum Books, 1993.

Dubnick, Melvin J., and H. George Frederickson. "Accountable Agents: Federal Performance Measurement and Third-Party Government." *Journal of Public Administration Research and Theory* 20, suppl. 1 (2010): 143–59.

———, eds. *Accountable Governance: Problems and Promises*. Armonk, NY: M. E. Sharpe, 2011.

Dubnick, Melvin J., and Kaifeng Yang. "The Pursuit of Accountability: Promise, Problems, and Prospects." In *The State of Public Administration: Issues, Challenges, and Opportunities*, edited by Donald C. Menzel and Harvey L. White, 171–86. Armonk, NY: M. E. Sharpe, 2011.

Dunlop, John T. "The Limits of Legal Compulsion." *Labor Law Journal* 27, no. 2 (1976): 67–74.

Dunlop, John T., and Arnold M. Zack. *Mediation and Arbitration of Employment Disputes*. San Francisco, CA: Jossey-Bass, 1997.

Durant, Robert F., Daniel J. Fiorino, and Rosemary O'Leary, eds. *Environmental Governance Reconsidered: Challenges, Choices and Opportunities*. 2nd ed. Cambridge, MA: MIT Press, 2017.

Duthie, Roger. Introduction to *Justice as Prevention: Vetting Public Employees in Transitional Societies*, edited by Alexander Mayer-Rieckh and Pablo de Greiff, 17–38. New York: Social Science Research Council, 2007.

Eaton, Adrienne E., and Jeffrey H. Keefe. *Employment Dispute Resolution and Worker Rights in the Changing Workplace*. Champaign, IL: Industrial Relations Research Association, 1999.

eBay. "Fast Facts." https://investors.ebayinc .com/fast-facts/default.aspx (accessed October 14, 2019).

Ebner, Noam, James Coben, and Christopher Honeyman, eds. *Assessing Our Students,*

Assessing Ourselves. St. Paul, MN: DRI Press, 2012.

Eddington, Neil. "Uber Hitches a Ride with Arbitration: How Pro-arbitration Attitudes and Uber Will Prevail in California and the Ninth Circuit." *Pepperdine Dispute Resolution Law Journal* 17, no. 2 (2017): 203–32.

Edelman, Lauren B. *Working Law: Courts, Corporations, and Symbolic Civil Rights*. Chicago: University of Chicago Press, 2016.

Edelman, Lauren B., and Shauhin A. Talesh. "To Comply or Not to Comply—That Isn't the Question: How Organizations Construct the Meaning of Compliance." In *Explaining Compliance: Business Responses to Regulation*, edited by Christine Parker and Vibeke Lehmann Nielsen, 103–22. Northampton, MA: Edward Elgar, 2011.

Edwards, Sam B., III, and Diogo Santos. *Revolutionizing the Interaction Between State and Citizens Through Digital Communications*. Hershey, PA: Information Science Reference, 2015.

Egan, John. *Rethinking Construction: The Report of the Construction Task Force*. London: HMSO, 1998.

Ehrmann, John R., and Barbara L. Stinson. "Joint Fact-Finding and the Use of Technical Experts." In *Consensus Building Handbook: A Comprehensive Guide to Reaching Agreement*, edited by Lawrence Susskind, Sarah McKearnan, and Jennifer Thomas-Larmer, 375–400. Thousand Oaks, CA: Sage, 1999.

Eisenberg, Deborah Thompson. "What We Know and Need to Know About Court-Annexed Dispute Resolution." *South Carolina Law Review* 67 (2016): 245–65.

Elkouri, Frank, and Edna Elkouri. *How Arbitration Works*. Washington, DC: Bureau of National Affairs, 2003.

Elliott, Michael L. Poirier. "The Role of Facilitators, Mediators, and Other Consensus Building Practitioners." In *Consensus Building Handbook: A Comprehensive Guide to Reaching Agreement*, edited by Lawrence Susskind, Sarah McKearnan, and Jennifer Thomas-Larmer, 199–239. Thousand Oaks, CA: Sage, 1999.

Emerson, Kirk, and Tina Nabatchi. *Collaborative Governance Regimes*. Washington, DC: Georgetown University Press, 2015.

———. "Evaluating the Productivity of Collaborative Governance Regimes: A Performance Matrix." *Public Performance and Management Review* 38, no. 4 (2015): 717–47.

Emerson, Kirk, Patricia J. Orr, Dale L. Keyes, and Katherine M. Mcknight. "Environmental Conflict Resolution: Evaluating Performance Outcomes and Contributing Factors." *Conflict Resolution Quarterly* 27, no. 1 (2009): 27–64.

Engalla v. Permanente Medical Group, Inc. 64 Cal. Rptr. 2d 843 (Cal. 1997).

Engstrom, Nora Freeman. "A Dose of Reality for Specialized Courts: Lessons from the VICP." *University of Pennsylvania Law Review* 163 (2015): 1631–717.

———. "Exit, Adversarialism, and the Stubborn Persistence of Tort." *Journal of Tort Law* 6 (2015): 75–115.

Engstrom, Nora Freeman, and Michelle M. Mello. "Suing the Opioid Companies." *Stanford Law School* (blog), August 30, 2018. https://law.stanford.edu/2018/08/30/q -and-a-with-mello-and-engstrom.

Epic Systems Corp. v. Lewis. 584 U.S. ___, 138 S. Ct. 1612 (2018), Slip. Op. 16-285.

Epstein, Deborah. "Procedural Justice: Tempering the State's Response to Domestic Violence." *William and Mary Law Review* 43 (2002): 1843–905.

Equal Justice Initiative. "National Memorial for Peace and Justice." https://eji.org/ national-lynching-memorial (accessed June 21, 2019).

Erickson, Helena Tavares. *Drafting Dispute Resolution Clauses, 2008 Supplement.* New York: International Institute for Conflict Prevention and Resolution, 2008.

——, ed. *Drafting Dispute Resolution Clauses: Better Solutions for Business.* New York: International Institute for Conflict Prevention and Resolution, 2006.

Ertel, Karen L. *Grievance Guide.* 13th ed. Edison, NJ: Bloomberg BNA, 2012.

Estlund, Cynthia. "The Black Hole of Mandatory Arbitration." *North Carolina Law Review* 96 (2018): 679–709.

Estreicher, Samuel. "Predispute Agreements to Arbitrate Statutory Employment Claims." *New York University Law Review* 72 (December 1997): 1344–75.

Eur-Lex. "Mediation in Civil and Commercial Matters." August 17, 2015. http://europa.eu/legislation_summaries/justice_freedom_security/judicial_cooperation_in_civil_matters/l33251_en.htm.

"European Code of Conduct for Mediators." http://ec.europa.eu/civiljustice/adr/adr_ec_code_conduct_en.pdf (accessed May 23, 2019).

European Commission. "Report from the Commission to the European Parliament, the Council and the European Economic and Social Committee on the Application of Directive 2008/52/EC of the European Parliament and of the Council on Certain Aspects of Mediation in Civil and Commercial Matters." August 26, 2016. https://eur-lex.europa.eu/legal-content/EN/TXT/?uri=COM%3A2016%3A542%3AFIN.

European Parliament. "Multilateral Investment Court (MIC)." October 20, 2019. http://www.europarl.europa.eu/legislative-train/theme-a-balanced-and-progressive-trade-policy-to-harness-globalisation/file-multilateral-investment-court-(mic).

European Parliament Directorate-General for Internal Policies. *The Implementation of the Mediation Directive Workshop, 29 November 2016: Compilation of In-Depth Analyses.* Brussels: European Parliament, 2016. http://www.europarl.europa.eu/RegData/etudes/IDAN/2016/571395/IPOL_IDA%282016%29571395_EN.pdf.

——. "Legal Instruments and Practice of Arbitration in the EU." November 2014. http://www.europarl.europa.eu/RegData/etudes/STUD/2015/509988/IPOL_STU(2015)509988_EN.pdf.

Ewing, David W. *Justice on the Job: Resolving Grievances in the Non-union Workplace.* Cambridge, MA: Harvard Business School Press, 1989.

Exon, Susan Nauss. "Ethics and Online Dispute Resolution: From Evolution to Revolution." *Ohio State Journal on Dispute Resolution* 32, no. 4 (2017): 609–49.

Extraordinary Chambers in the Courts of Cambodia. "ECCC at a Glance." April 2014. https://www.eccc.gov.kh/sites/default/files/ECCC%20at%20a%20Glance%20-%20EN%20-%20April%202014_FINAL.pdf.

——. "Trial Chamber Summary of Judgment: Case 002/02." November 16, 2018. https://www.eccc.gov.kh/sites/default/files/documents/courtdoc/%5Bdate-in-tz%5D/20181217%20Summary%20of%20Judgement%20Case%20002-02%20ENG_FINAL%20FOR%20PUBLICATION.pdf.

"Exxon Valdez Oil Spill—Lessons Learned 30 Years After the Event." *HazMat* (blog), February 6, 2019. http://hazmatmag.com/2019/02/exxon-valdez-oil-spill-lessons-learned-30-years-after-the-event.

Factory at Chorzów, Germany v. Poland. Series A, no. 17 (PCIJ 1928).

FEMA (Federal Emergency Management Agency). "Hurricane Katrina in the Gulf Coast: Mitigation Assessment Team Report, Building Performance Observations, Recommendations, and Technical Guidance." July 2006. https://www.fema.gov/media-library/assets/documents/4069.

Federal Mediation and Conciliation Service. "Labor-Management Cooperation Grant Application Materials." https://www.fmcs.gov/resources/forms-applications/labor-management-grants-program/labor-management-cooperation-grant-program (accessed June 4, 2019).

———. "Planning for Progress: Labor-Management Committees." June 2015. https://www.fmcs.gov/wp-content/uploads/2015/06/FMCS_LMC_Planning_for_Progess.pdf.

———. "Shared Neutrals Programs." https://www.fmcs.gov/sharedneutrals (accessed May 20, 2019).

Federal Reserve Bank of San Francisco. "Arizona: Housing and Labor Market Trends." January 2013. http://www.frbsf.org/community-development/files/Arizona-0113.pdf.

Feinberg, Kenneth. "The Building Blocks for Successful Victim Compensation Programs." *Ohio State Journal on Dispute Resolution* 20 (2005): 273–78.

———. "Dalkon Shield Claimants Trust." In "Claims Resolution Facilities and the Mass Settlement of Mass Torts," edited by Francis E. McGovern. Special issue, *Law and Contemporary Problems* 53, no 4 (1990): 79–112.

———. *What Is Life Worth? The Unprecedented Effort to Compensate the Victims of 9/11.* New York: BBS, 2005.

Feiock, Richard C., Hyung Jun Park, and In Won Lee. "Administrators' and Elected Officials' Collaboration Networks: Selecting Partners to Reduce Risk in Economic Development." *Public Administration Review* 72, no. S1 (2012): S58–S68.

Feiock, Richard C., and John T. Scholz, eds. *Self-Organizing Federalism: Collaborative Mechanisms to Mitigate Institutional Collective Action Dilemmas.* Cambridge: Cambridge University Press, 2009.

Felstiner, William, Richard Abel, and Austin Sarat. "The Emergence and Transformation of Disputes: Naming, Blaming, Claiming." *Law and Society Review* 15, nos. 3–4 (1980–1981): 631–54.

Fine, Janice, Linda Burnham, Kati Griffith, Minsun Ji, Vicor Narro, and Steven Pitts, eds. *No One Size Fits All: Worker Organization, Policy, and Movement in a New Economic Age.* Champaign, IL: Labor and Employment Relations Association, 2018.

"Firm Agrees to End Role in Arbitrating Consumer Debt." *New York Times*, July 20, 2009, p. B8.

Fisher, Roger, and William Ury. *Getting to Yes.* New York: Penguin, 1981.

Fisher, Roger, William Ury, and Bruce Patton. *Getting to Yes: Negotiating Agreement Without Giving In.* 3rd ed. New York: Penguin, 2011.

Fishkin, James S. *When the People Speak: Deliberative Democracy and Public Consultation.* Oxford: Oxford University Press, 2010.

Fiss, Owen M. "Against Settlement." *Yale Law Journal* 93, no. 6 (1984): 1073–92.

Folberg, Jay, Dwight Golann, Thomas Stipanowich, and Lisa Kloppenberg. *Resolving Disputes: Theory, Practice, and Law.* 3rd ed. New York: Wolters Kluwer, 2016.

Folger, Robert G., ed. *The Sense of Injustice: Social Psychological Perspectives.* Boston, MA: Springer, 1984.

Folger, Robert G., and Russell Cropanzano. *Organizational Justice and Human Resource Management.* Thousand Oaks, CA: Sage, 1998.

Folger, Robert, David Rosenfield, and Thomas Robinson. "Relative Deprivation and Procedural Justification." *Journal of Personality and Social Psychology* 45 (1983): 268–73.

Forester, John. *Dealing with Differences: Dramas of Mediating Public Disputes.* New York: Oxford University Press, 2009.

———. *The Deliberative Practitioner: Encouraging Participatory Planning Processes.* Cambridge, MA: MIT Press, 1999.

Forman, Shepard, and Stewart Patrick, eds. *Good Intentions: Pledges of Aid for Post-conflict Recovery.* Boulder, CO: Lynne Rienner, 2000.

Forth, John, Alex Bryson, and Anitha George. "Explaining Cross-National Variation in Workplace Employee Representation." *European Journal of Industrial Relations* 23, no. 4 (2017): 415–33.

14 Penn Plaza LLC v. Pyett. 556 U.S. 247 (2009).

Foxgate Homeowners' Association v. Bramalea. 25 P.3d 1117 (Cal. 2001).

Franck, Susan D. "Foreign Direct Investment, Investment Treaty Arbitration, and the Rule of Law." *Pacific McGeorge Global Business and Development Review* 19 (2007): 337–74.

———. "The ICSID Effect? Consideration of Potential Variations in Arbitration Awards." *Virginia Journal of International Law* 51, no. 4 (2011): 825–1014.

Freedman, Sarah Warshauer, Deo Kambanda, Beth Lewis Samuelson, Innocent Mugisha, Immaculee Mukashema, Evode Mukama, Jean Mutabaruka, Harvey M. Weinstein, and Timothy Longman. "Confronting the Past in Rwandan Schools." In *My Neighbor, My Enemy: Justice and Community in the Aftermath of Mass Atrocity,* edited by Eric Stover and Harvey M. Weinstein, 248–65. Cambridge: Cambridge University Press, 2004.

Freeman, Jody. "The Private Role in Public Governance." *New York University Law Review* 75 (2000): 543–68.

Freeman, Mark. *Necessary Evils: Amnesties and the Search for Justice.* Cambridge: Cambridge University Press, 2009.

Freshman, Clark. "The Promise and Perils of 'Our' Justice: Psychological, Critical and Economic Perspectives on Communities and Prejudices in Mediation." *Cardozo Journal of Conflict Resolution* 6 (2004): 1–18.

Friedman, Lawrence M. *American Law in the 20th Century.* New Haven, CT: Yale University Press, 2002.

Fukiyama, Francis. *Political Order and Political Decay.* London: Farrar, Straus and Giroux, 2014.

Fuller, Lon L. "The Lawyer as an Architect of Social Structures." In *The Principles of Social Order: Selected Essays of Lon L. Fuller,* edited by Kenneth I. Winston, 264–70. Durham, NC: Duke University Press, 1981.

———. *The Morality of Law.* New Haven, CT: Yale University Press, 1964.

Fuller, Lon, and Kenneth I. Winston. "The Forms and Limits of Adjudication." *Harvard Law Review* 92, no. 2 (1978): 353–409.

Fung, Archon. "Deliberation Before the Revolution: Toward an Ethics of Deliberative Democracy in an Unjust World." *Political Theory* 33, no. 2 (2005): 397–419.

———. "Recipes for Public Spheres: Eight Institutional Design Choices and Their Consequences." *Journal of Political Philosophy* 11 (2003): 338–67.

———. "Varieties of Participation in Complex Governance." *Public Administration Review* 66 (2006): 66–75.

Fung, Archon, and Erik Olin Wright, eds. *Deepening Democracy: Institutional Innovations in Empowered Participatory Governance.* London: Verso, 2003.

Gadlin, Howard. "Bargaining in the Shadow of Management: Integrated Conflict Management Systems." In *The Handbook of Dispute Resolution,* edited by Michael L. Moffitt and Robert C. Bordone, 377–99. San Francisco, CA: Jossey-Bass, 2005.

———. "Careful Maneuvers: Mediating Sexual Harassment." *Negotiation Journal* 7, no. 2 (1991): 139–53.

Gaffney, John P. "Due Process in the World Trade Organization: The Need for Procedural Justice in the Dispute Settlement System." *American University International Law Review* 14 (1999): 1173–221.

Galanter, Marc. "Contract in Court; Or, Almost Everything You May or May Not Want to Know About Contract Litigation." *Wisconsin Law Review* 2001 (2001): 577–628.

———. "The Quality of Settlements." *Journal of Dispute Resolution* 1988 (1988): 55–84.

———. "The Vanishing Trial: An Examination of Trials and Related Matters in Federal and State Courts." *Journal of Empirical Legal Studies* 1, no. 3 (2004): 459–570.

———. "Why the 'Haves' Come Out Ahead: Speculations on the Limits of Legal Change." *Law and Society Review* 9, no. 1 (1974): 95–160.

Galanter, Marc, and Mia Cahill. "Symposium on Civil Justice Reform: 'Most Cases Settle'; Judicial Promotion and Regulation of Settlements." *Stanford Law Review* 46 (1994): 1339–91.

Gastil, John. *By Popular Demand: Revitalizing Representative Democracy Through Deliberative Elections.* Berkeley: University of California Press, 2000.

Gastil, John, and Peter Levine, eds. *The Deliberative Democracy Handbook: Strategies for Effective Civic Engagement in the Twenty-First Century.* San Francisco, CA: Jossey-Bass, 2005.

Gavin, Sandra F. "Unconscionability Found: A Look at Pre-dispute Mandatory Arbitration Agreements 10 Years After *Doctor's Associates, Inc. v. Casarotto.*" *Cleveland State Law Review* 54 (2006): 249–72.

Gazley, Beth, Won Kyung Chang, and Lisa Blomgren Bingham. "Collaboration and Citizen Participation in Community Mediation Centers." *Review of Policy Research* 23, no. 4 (2006): 843–63.

———. "External Linkages, Board Diversity, and Organizational Effectiveness in Community Mediation Centers." *Public Administration Review* 70, no. 4 (2010): 610–20.

Genn, Hazel, Shiva Riahi, and Katherine Pleming. "Regulation of Dispute Resolution in England and Wales: A Sceptical Analysis of Government and Judicial Promotion of Private Mediation." In *Regulating Dispute Resolution: ADR and Access to Justice at the Crossroads,* edited by Felix Steffek and Hannes Unberath, 135–74. Oxford, UK: Hart, 2013.

Gent, Stephen E. "The Politics of International Arbitration and Adjudication." *Penn State Journal of Law and International Affairs* 2, no. 1 (2013): 66–77.

Gent, Stephen E., and Megan Shannon. "The Effectiveness of International Arbitration and Adjudication: Getting into a Bind." *Journal of Politics* 72, no. 2 (2010): 366–80.

Gibson, James L. *Overcoming Apartheid.* New York: Russell Sage Foundation, 2004.

———. "The Truth About Truth and Reconciliation in South Africa." *International Political Science Review* 26 (2005): 341–61.

———. "Truth, Reconciliation, and the Creation of a Human Rights Culture in South Africa." *Law and Society Review* 38, no. 1 (2004): 5–40.

Gibson, James L., and Amanda Gouws. *Overcoming Intolerance in South Africa: Experiments in Democratic Persuasion.* Cambridge: Cambridge University Press, 2003.

Gill, Chris, Jane Williams, Carol Brennan, and Carolyn Hirst. "Designing Consumer Redress: A Dispute System Design (DSD) Model for Consumer-to-Business Disputes." *Legal Studies* 36, no. 3 (2016): 438–63.

Gilles, Myriam. "Public-Private Approaches to Mass Tort Victim Compensation: Some Thoughts on the Gulf Coast Claims Facility." *DePaul Law Review* 61, no. 2 (2012): 419–66.

Gilmer v. Interstate/Johnson Lane Corp. 500 U.S. 20 (1991).

Ginsburg. Tom. "International Substitutes for Domestic Institutions: Bilateral Investment Treaties and Governance." *International Review of Law and Economics* 25, no. 1 (2005): 107–23.

Glass, Ira. "After the Flood." *This American Life*, September 9, 2005. http://www .thisamericanlife.org/radio-archives/ episode/296/transcript.

Gleason, Sandra E., ed. *Workplace Dispute Resolution: Direction for the 21st Century*. East Lansing: Michigan State University Press, 1997.

Glick, Beth, and Laina Reynolds Levy. "The Institution as Innovator: Laying the Foundation for Peaceful Change." In *Building Peace: Practical Reflections from the Field*, edited by Craig Zelizer and Robert A. Rubinstein, 39–53. Sterling, VA: Kumarian Press.

Glover, J. Maria. "Disappearing Claims and the Erosion of Substantive Law." *Yale Law Journal* 124 (2015): 3052–92.

Goldberg, Stephen B. "How Interest-Based, Grievance Mediation Performs over the Long Term." *Dispute Resolution Journal* 59 (November 2004–January 2005): 8–15.

Goldberg, Stephen B., Frank E. A. Sander, Nancy H. Rogers, and Sarah Rudolph Cole. *Dispute Resolution*. 5th ed. New York: Wolters Kluwer, 2007.

Goldberg v. Kelly. 397 U.S. 254 (1970).

Gonstead, Mariana H. C. "A New Chapter in Natural Resource-Seeking Investment: Using Shared Decision System Design (SDSD) to Strengthen Investor-State and Community Relationships." *Cardozo Journal of Conflict Resolution* 18 (2017): 551–620.

———. "A New Dance on the Global Stage: Introducing a Cultural Value–Based Toolbox to Optimize Problem-Solving, Innovation, and Growth." *Ohio State Journal on Dispute Resolution* 34 (forthcoming).

Gough, Mark D. "Employment Lawyers and Mandatory Arbitration: Facilitating or Forestalling Access to Justice?" In *Managing and Resolving Workplace Conflict*, edited by David B. Lipsky, Ariel C. Avgar, and J. Ryan Lamare, 105–34. Bingley, UK: Emerald, 2016.

Gould, William B., IV. "Using an Independent Monitor to Resolve Union-Organizing Disputes Outside the NLRB: The FirstGroup Experience." *Dispute Resolution Journal* 66 (May–July 2011): 46–62.

Granite Rock Co. v. Teamsters. 561 U.S. 287 (2010).

Gray, Barbara. *Collaborating: Finding Common Ground for Multiparty Problems*. San Francisco, CA: Jossey-Bass, 1989.

Green, Michael Z. "Reconsidering Prejudice in Alternative Dispute Resolution for Black Work Matters." *SMU Law Review* 70, no. 3 (2017): 639–80.

Greenberg, Elayne E. "Fitting the Forum to the Pernicious Fuss: A Dispute System Design to Address Implicit Bias and 'Isms in the Workplace." *Cardozo Journal of Conflict Resolution* 75 (2015): 75–113.

Greenberg, Elayne E., and Noam Ebner. "What Dinosaurs Can Teach Lawyers About How to Avoid Extinction in the ODR Evolution." St. John's School of Law Legal Studies Research Paper No. 19-0004, January 17, 2019. https://papers.ssrn.com/sol3/papers.cfm ?abstract_id=3317567.

Greenberg, Jerald. "Everybody Talks About Organizational Justice, but Nobody Does

Anything About It." *Industrial and Organizational Psychology* 2 (2009): 181–95.

———. "Organizational Justice: Yesterday, Today, and Tomorrow." *Journal of Management* 16 (1990): 399–432.

———. "The Social Side of Fairness: Interpersonal and Informational Classes of Organizational Justice." In *Justice in the Workplace: Approaching Fairness in Human Resource Management*, edited by Russell Cropanzano, 79–94. Hillsdale, NJ: Lawrence Erlbaum, 1993.

———. "Using Socially Fair Treatment to Promote Acceptance of a Work Site Smoking Ban." *Journal of Applied Psychology* 79 (1994): 288–97.

Greenberg, Jonathan D., and Evan Darwin Winet. "International Investment Law and Dispute Resolution." In *Handbook on the Geopolitics of Business*, edited by Joseph Mark S. Munoz, 227–55. Northampton, MA: Edward Elgar, 2013.

"Greensboro Truth and Reconciliation Report: Executive Summary." May 25, 2006. http://www.greensborotrc.org/exec_summary.pdf.

Green Tree Finance Corp.-Ala. v. Randolph. 531 U.S. 79 (2000).

Grenfell, Laura. *Promoting the Rule of Law in Post-conflict States*. Cambridge: Cambridge University Press, 2013.

Gross, Jill. "Justice Scalia's Hat Trick and the Supreme Court's Flawed Understanding of Twenty-First Century Arbitration." *Brooklyn Law Review* 81, no. 1 (2015): 111–48.

Groton, James P., Robert A. Rubin, and Bettina Quintas. "Comparing Dispute Review Boards and Adjudication." In *American Arbitration Association Handbook on Construction Arbitration and ADR*, 3rd ed., 501–6. Huntington, NY: JurisNet, 2016.

Guidi, Nicholas. "Oil, Fire, Smoke and Mirrors: The Gulf Coast Claims Facility and Its Dangerous Precedent." *William and Mary Environmental Law and Policy Review* 39, no. 3 (2015): 739–64.

Guthrie, Chris. "Procedural Justice Research and the Paucity of Trials." *Journal of Dispute Resolution* 2002, no. 1 (2002): 127–30.

Hadfield, Gillian K. "Framing the Choice Between Cash and the Courthouse: Experiences with the 9/11 Victim Compensation Fund." *Law and Society Review* 42, no. 3 (2008): 645–82.

Haggard, Stephan, Andrew MacIntyre, and Lydia Tiede. "The Rule of Law and Economic Development." *Annual Review Political Science* 11 (2008): 205–34.

Haig, Robert L., ed. *Successful Partnering Between Inside and Outside Counsel*. 4 vols. Wilmington, DE: Potter, Anderson, Corroon, 2012.

Hajer, Maarten A., and Hendrik Wagenaar, eds. *Deliberative Policy Analysis: Understanding Governance in a Network Society*. Cambridge: Cambridge University Press, 2003.

Hall, Edward T. *Beyond Culture*. New York: Doubleday, 1976.

Halliday, Terence C. "The Fight for Basic Legal Freedoms: Mobilization by the Legal Complex." In *Global Perspectives on the Rule of Law*, edited by James J. Heckman, Robert L. Nelson, and Lee Cabatingan, 210–40. London: Routledge, 2010.

Hall Street Associates L.L.C. v. Mattel, Inc. 552 U.S. 576 (2008).

Hangzhou Internet Court. "The Operation Process." https://www.netcourt.gov.cn/portal/main/en/index.htm (accessed May 20, 2019).

Hanna, Kevin S., and D. Scott Slocombe, eds. *Fostering Integration: Concepts and Practice in Resource and Environmental Management*. Cambridge: Oxford University Press, 2005.

Hansmann, Henry. *The Ownership of Enter-prise.* Cambridge, MA: Belknap Press, 2000.

Harmon, Kathleen M. J. "Case Study as to the Effectiveness of Dispute Review Boards on the Central Artery/Tunnel Project." *Journal of Legal Affairs and Dispute Resolution in Engineering and Construction* 1, no. 1 (2009): 18–31.

Harrington, Christine B. *Shadow Justice: The Ideology and Institutionalization of Alternatives to Court.* Westport, CT: Greenwood Press, 1985.

Harter, Philip J. "Assessing the Assessors: The Actual Performance of Negotiated Rule-making." *New York University Environmental Law Journal* 9, no. 1 (2000–2001): 32–59.

Harvard Law School. "Harvard Negotiation and Mediation Clinical Program." http://hls.harvard.edu/dept/clinical/clinics/harvard-negotiation-and-mediation-clinic (accessed May 20, 2019).

Hatcher-Moore, Jessica. "Is the World's Highest Court Fit for Purpose?" *The Guardian,* April 5, 2017. https://www.theguardian.com/global-development-professionals-network/2017/apr/05/international-criminal-court-fit-purpose.

Haughney, Kathleen. "Florida Justice Shuts Down Foreclosure Mediation." *Orlando Sentinel,* December 20, 2011, p. A10.

Hayner, Priscilla B. *Unspeakable Truths: Transitional Justice and the Challenge of Truth Commissions.* New York: Routledge, 2011.

Hazard, Geoffrey C., Jr. "Reflections on Judge Weinstein's Ethical Dilemmas in Mass Tort Litigation." *Northwestern University Law Review* 88 (1994): 576–78.

Heckman, James J. "The Viability of the Welfare State." In *Global Perspectives on the Rule of Law,* edited by James J. Heckman, Robert L. Nelson, and Lee Cabatingan, 93–117. London: Routledge, 2010.

Heckman, James J., Robert L. Nelson, and Lee Cabatingan. *Global Perspectives on the Rule of Law.* London: Routledge, 2010.

Hedeen, Timothy. "The Evolution and Evaluation of Community Mediation: Limited Research Suggests Unlimited Progress." *Conflict Resolution Quarterly* 22, nos. 1–2 (2004): 101–33.

Hedeen, Timothy, and Patrick G. Coy. "Community Mediation and the Court System: The Ties That Bind." *Mediation Quarterly* 17, no. 4 (2000): 351–67.

Helfer, Laurence, and Anne-Marie Slaughter. "Toward a Theory of Effective Supranational Adjudication." *Yale Law Journal* 107 (1997): 273–391.

Hempel, Paul S., Zhi-Xue Zhang, and Dean Tjosvold. "Conflict Management Between and Within Teams for Trusting Relationships and Performance in China." *Journal of Organizational Behavior* 30 (2009): 41–65.

Henry Schein Inc. v. Archer and White Sales Inc. No. 17-1272 (U.S. Jan. 8, 2019).

Hensler, Deborah. "As Time Goes By: Asbestos Litigation After Amchem and Ortiz." *Texas Law Review* 80 (2002): 1899–924.

———. "Justice for the Masses? Aggregate Litigation and Its Alternatives." *Daedalus* 143 (Summer 2014): 73–82.

———. "The Private in Public, the Public in Private: The Blurring Boundary Between Public and Private Dispute Resolution." In *Formalisation and Flexibilisation in Dispute Resolution,* edited by Joachim Zekoll, Moritz Balz, and Iwo Amelung, 45–68. Leiden, Netherlands: Brill/Nijhoff, 2014.

———. "Resolving Mass Toxic Torts: Myths and Realities." *University of Illinois Law Review* 89, no. 91 (1989): 89–104.

———. "Suppose It's Not True: Challenging Mediation Ideology." *Journal of Dispute Resolution* 2002, no. 1 (2002): 81–99.

Hensler, Deborah, William L. F. Felstiner, Molly Selvin, and Patricia A. Ebener. *As-*

bestos in the Courts: *The Challenge of Mass Toxic Torts*. Santa Monica, CA: RAND, 1985.

Hensler, Deborah R., and Mark A. Peterson. "Understanding Mass Personal Injury Litigation: A Socio-legal Analysis." *Brooklyn Law Review* 59, no. 3 (1995): 961–1063.

Henton, Douglas, John Melville, Malka Kopell, and Terry Amsler. *Collaborative Governance: A Guide for Grantmakers*. Menlo Park, CA: William and Flora Hewlett Foundation, 2005.

Higgins, John E., Jr., ed. *The Developing Labor Law: The Board, the Courts, and the National Labor Relations Act*. 6th ed. Washington, DC: Bloomberg BNA, 2012.

Higgins, Paul, and Mitchell B. Mackinem. *Problem-Solving Courts: Justice for the Twenty-First Century*. Santa Barbara, CA: ABC-CLIO, 2009.

Hill, Marvin F., Jr., and Anthony V. Sinicropi. *Remedies in Arbitration*. 2nd ed. Washington, DC: Bloomberg BNA, 1991.

Hill, Marvin F., Jr., and James A. Wright. *Employee Lifestyle and Off-Duty Conduct Regulation*. Washington, DC: Bloomberg BNA, 1993.

Hinshaw, Art, and Timothy Burr. "Foreclosure Mediation in Arizona." *Arizona State Law Journal* 45 (2013): 749–80.

Hirschl, Ran. "The 'Design Sciences' and Constitutional 'Success.'" *Texas Law Review* 87 (2009): 1339–74.

Hirschman, Albert O. *Exit, Voice, and Loyalty: Responses to Decline in Firms, Organizations, and States*. Cambridge, MA: Harvard University Press, 1970.

Hirst, Megan. *Too Much Friendship, Too Little Truth: Monitoring Report on the Commission of Truth and Friendship in Indonesia and Timor-Leste*. New York: International Center for Transitional Justice, 2008.

Hocker, Joyce L., and William W. Wilmot. "Hocker-Wilmot Conflict Assessment Guide." In *Interpersonal Conflict*, 2nd ed., edited by Joyce L. Hocker and William W. Wilmot, 129–56. Dubuque, IA: William Brown, 1985.

———, eds. *Interpersonal Conflict*. 2nd ed. Dubuque, IA: William Brown, 1985.

Hoffman, Jan. "Looking for Someone to Clean Opioid Mess." *New York Times*, February 1, 2019, p. A21.

Hoffman, Sharona. "Mandatory Arbitration: Alternative Dispute Resolution or Coercive Dispute Suppression?" *Berkeley Journal of Employment and Labor Law* 17 (1996): 131–57.

Hoffmann, Elizabeth A. "Dispute Resolution in a Worker Cooperative: Formal Procedures and Procedural Justice." *Law and Society Review* 39 (2005): 51–82.

Hofstede, Geert. *Culture's Consequences: International Differences in Work-Related Values*. Thousand Oaks, CA: Sage, 1980.

Holder, Jane, Colm O'Cinneide, and Michael Freeman, eds. *Current Legal Problems*. Vol. 57. Oxford: Oxford University Press, 2004.

Honeyman, Christopher, James Coben, and Giuseppe De Palo, eds. *Rethinking Negotiation Teaching: Innovations for Context and Culture*. St. Paul, MN: DRI Press, 2009.

———, eds. *Venturing Beyond the Classroom*. St. Paul, MN: DRI Press, 2010.

Honeyman, Christopher, James Coben, and Andrew Wei-Min Lee, eds. *Educating Negotiators for a Connected World*. St. Paul, MN: DRI Press, 2013.

Honeyman, Christopher, and Andrea Kupfer Schneider, eds. *The Negotiator's Desk Reference*. 2 vols. Minneapolis, MN: DRI Press, 2017.

———. *The Negotiator's Fieldbook: The Desk Reference for the Experienced Negotiator*. Washington, DC: American Bar Association, 2006.

Hooters of America, Inc. v. Phillips. 173 F.3d 933 (4th Cir. 1999).

Horton, David. "Arbitration as Delegation."
    New York University Law Review 86 (2011):
    437–99.

Horton, David, and Andrea Cann Chan-
    drasekher. "After the Revolution: An
    Empirical Study of Consumer Arbitration."
    Georgetown Law Journal 104 (2015): 57–124.

———. "Employment Arbitration after the
    Revolution." *DePaul Law Review* 65 (2016):
    457–96.

Houk, Carole S., and Lauren M. Edelstein.
    "Beyond Apology to Early Non-judicial
    Resolution: The MedicOm Program as
    a Patient Safety–Focused Alternative to
    Malpractice Litigation." *Hamline Journal
    of Public Law and Policy* 29 (Spring 2008):
    411–22.

Howard, Charles L. *The Organizational
    Ombudsman: Origins, Roles, and Opera-
    tions—a Legal Guide.* Chicago: American
    Bar Association, 2010.

Howe, Amy. "Opinion Analysis: Court
    Strikes Down Public-Sector Union Fees."
    SCOTUSblog, June 27, 2018. http://www
    .scotusblog.com/2018/06/opinion-analysis
    -court-strikes-down-public-sector-union
    -fees.

Howsam v. Dean Witter Reynolds, Inc. 537
    U.S. 79 (2002).

Hresko, Tracy. "Restoration and Relief:
    Procedural Justice and the September 11th
    Victim Compensation Fund." *Gonzaga Law
    Review* 42 (2007): 95–131.

Human Rights Watch. *Selling Justice Short:
    Why Accountability Matters for Peace.* New
    York: Human Rights Watch, 2009.

Hyman, Chris Stern. "Mediation and Medical
    Malpractice: Why Plaintiffs, Hospitals and
    Physicians Should Be at the Table." *Dispute
    Resolution Journal* 66, no. 3 (2011): 32–37.

Hyman, Chris Stern, Carol B. Liebman, Clyde
    B. Schechter, and William Sage. "Interest-
    Based Mediation of Medical Malpractice
    Lawsuits: A Route to Improved Patient

Safety." *Journal of Health Politics, Policy,
    and Law* 35, no. 5 (2010): 797–828.

Hyman, Jonathan M. "Swimming in the Deep
    End: Dealing with Justice in Mediation."
    Cardozo Journal of Conflict Resolution 6,
    no. 1 (2004): 19–56.

ICANN (Internet Corporation for Assigned
    Names and Numbers). "Online Dispute
    Resolution: Standards of Practice." July
    2009. https://www.icann.org/ombudsman/
    odr-standards-of-practice-en.pdf.

Innes, Judith E. "Evaluating Consensus Build-
    ing." In *Consensus Building Handbook: A
    Comprehensive Guide to Reaching Agree-
    ment,* edited by Lawrence Susskind, Sarah
    McKearnan, and Jennifer Thomas-Larmer,
    631–75. Thousand Oaks, CA: Sage, 1999.

In re Atlantic Pipe Corp. 304 F.3d 135 (1st Cir.
    2002).

In re Final Report and Recommendation on
    Residential Mortgage Foreclosure Cases.
    No. AOSC09-54 (Fla., December 28, 2009).
    http://www.floridasupremecourt.org/clerk/
    adminorders/2009/AOSC09-54.pdf.

In re NLO, Inc. 5 F.3d 154, 157–58 (6th Cir. 1993).

In re Oil Spill by the Oil Rig "Deepwater Ho-
    rizon" in the Gulf of Mexico on April 20,
    2010. MDL no. 2179, 2011 WL 323866, at *8
    (E.D. La. February 2, 2011).

In re Pinochet (House of Lords, January 15,
    1999). https://www.publications.parliament
    .uk/pa/ld199899/ldjudgmt/jd990115/pin001
    .htm.

In re Waller. 573 A.2d 780 (D.C. App. 1990).

Interagency Alternative Dispute Resolution
    Working Group. "FAR Provisions Pertinent
    to ADR." In "Electronic Guide to Federal
    Procurement ADR." https://www.adr.gov/
    adrguide (accessed June 14, 2019).

———. "Federal ADR Programs and Con-
    tacts." https://adr.gov (accessed May 20,
    2019).

International Center for Transitional Justice.
    "Criminal Justice." https://www.ictj.org/our

-work/transitional-justice-issues/criminal
-justice (accessed June 21, 2019).

———. "U.S.A: Greensboro, NC." https://www
.ictj.org/our-work/regions-and-countries/
usa-greensboro-nc (accessed June 21,
2019).

International Centre for Settlement of Investment Disputes. "About ICSID." https://icsid
.worldbank.org/en/Pages/about/default
.aspx (accessed November 5, 2019).

International Council for Online Dispute
Resolution. "ICODR Standards." https://
icodr.org/standards (accessed November
5, 2019).

International Court of Justice. "Statute of the
International Court of Justice." https://www
.icj-cij.org/en/statute (accessed November
5, 2019).

International Criminal Court. "Rome Statute
of the International Criminal Court."
2011. http://www.icc-cpi.int/nr/rdonlyres/
ea9aeff7-5752-4f84-be94-0a655eb30e16/0/
rome_statute_english.pdf.

International Institute for Conflict Prevention and Resolution. "The CPR Corporate Counsel Manual for Cross-Border
Dispute Resolution." https://www.cpradr
.org/news-publications/store/corporate
-counsel-manual-for-cross-border-dispute
-resolution (accessed June 14, 2019).

———. "CPR Minitrial Procedure." https://
www.cpradr.org/resource-center/rules/
international-other/mediation/cpr
-minitrial-procedure (accessed May 20,
2019).

———. "A Guide to Self-Administered
ADR and CPR's Dispute Resolution
Services." https://www.yumpu.com/en/
document/read/29802392/cprs-guide-to
-self-administered-adr-cpr-institute-for
-dispute- (accessed June 14, 2019).

———. "Principles for ADR Provider Organizations: CPR-Georgetown Commission
on Ethics and Standards of Practice in

ADR." May 1, 2002. https://www.cpradr
.org/resource-center/protocols-guidelines/
ethics-codes/principles-for-adr-provider
-organizations.

———. "21st Century Pledge." https://www
.cpradr.org/resource-center/adr-pledges/
21st-century-pledge (accessed June 14,
2019).

International Mediation Institute. "Criteria
for Approving Programs to Qualify Mediators for IMI Inter-cultural Certification."
https://www.imimediation.org/wp-content/
uploads/2018/04/imi-intercultural-criteria
-and-cfa-final-draft-modified-.pdf (accessed
May 23, 2019).

International Ombudsman Association. "IOA
Best Practices: A Supplement to IOA's
Standards of Practice." October 13, 2009.
https://www.ombudsassociation.org/assets/
docs/IOA_Best_Practices_Version3_101309
_0.pdf.

———. "IOA Code of Ethics." January 2007.
https://www.ombudsassociation.org/assets/
IOA%20Code%20of%20Ethics.pdf.

———. "IOA Standards of Practice." October
2009. https://www.ombudsassociation.org/
assets/docs/IOA_Standards_of_Practice
_Oct09.pdf.

Issacharaoff, Samuel. *Civil Procedure*. 3rd ed.
New York: Foundation Press, 2012.

Isser, Deborah, ed. *Customary Justice and the
Rule of Law in War-Torn Societies*. Wash-
ington, DC: United States Institute of Peace
Press, 2011.

Isser, Deborah H., Stephen C. Lubkemann,
and Saah N'Tow. *Looking for Justice:
Liberian Experiences with and Perceptions
of Local Justice Options*. Washington, DC:
United States Institute of Peace Press, 2009.

"Jed D. Melnick Symposium: The Pound
Conferences; Where Do We Come From?
What Are We? Where Are We Going?"
Cardozo Journal of Dispute Resolution 18,
no. 3 (2017): 513–698.

Jenkins, Randall C., Gregory Firestone, Kari L. Aasheim, and Brian W. Boelens. "Mandatory Pre-suit Mediation for Medical Malpractice: Eight-Year Results and Future Innovations." *Conflict Resolution Quarterly* 35, no. 1 (2017): 73–88.

Jenness, Valerie, and Kitty Calavita. "'It Depends on the Outcome': Prisoners, Grievances, and Perceptions of Justice." *Law and Society Review* 52, no. 1 (2018): 41–72.

Jesner et al. v. Arab Bank, PLC. 584 U.S. ___, 138 S. Ct. 1386 (2018).

Joint Commission on Accreditation of Healthcare Organizations. "Health Care at the Crossroads: Strategies for Improving the Medical Liability System and Preventing Patient Injury." 2005. https://www.jointcommission.org/assets/1/18/Medical_Liability.pdf.

Jones, Tricia S., ed. "Conflict Resolution in the Field: Special Symposium." Special issue, *Conflict Resolution Quarterly* 22, nos. 1–2 (2004): 1–320.

Jones v. Halliburton Co. 583 F.3d 228 (5th Cir. 2009).

Judicial Arbitration and Mediation Services. "About Us: JAMS Mediation, Arbitration and ADR Services." https://www.jamsadr.com/about (accessed May 23, 2019).

———. "JAMS Foundation/NAFCM Minigrant Program." https://www.jamsadr.com/nafcm (accessed June 3, 2019).

Judicial Council of California. "California Rules of Court." https://www.courts.ca.gov/cms/rules/index.cfm?title=three&linkid=rule3_859 (accessed October 3, 2019).

Kagan, Robert A. *Adversarial Legalism: The American Way of Law*. Cambridge, MA: Harvard University Press, 2003.

Kahale, George, III. "Is Investor-State Arbitration Broken?" *Transnational Dispute Management*, October 2012. http://www.curtis.com/siteFiles/News/Is%20Investor-State%20Arbitration%20Broken.pdf.

Kaiser Arbitration Oversight Board. "Board Comments on the Annual Report for 2018." http://www.oia-kaiserarb.com/pdfs/AOB-Comments.pdf (accessed June 14, 2019).

Kaiser Arbitration Oversight Board. "Status of Blue Ribbon Panel Recommendations." December 31, 2018. http://www.oia-kaiserarb.com/pdfs/BRP-Status-Report.pdf (accessed February 23, 2019).

Kaiser Permanente Office of the Independent Administrator. "Annual Report of the Office of the Independent Administrator of the Kaiser Foundation Health Plan, Inc. Mandatory Arbitration System for Disputes with Health Plan Members, January 1, 2013–December 31, 2013." http://oia-kaiserarb.com/pdfs/2013-Annual-Report.pdf (accessed July 2, 2019).

———. "First Annual Report of the Office of the Independent Administrator of the Kaiser Foundation Health Plan, Inc. Mandatory Arbitration System for Disputes with Health Plan Members, March 29, 1999–March 28, 2000." http://www.oia-kaiserarb.com/pdfs/annrptyr1.pdf (accessed November 28, 2019).

———. "Report Summary." http://www.oia-kaiserarb.com/pdfs/Summary.pdf (accessed October 14, 2019).

———. "Rules for Kaiser Permanente Member Arbitrations." January 1, 2019. http://oia-kaiserarb.com/pdfs/Rules.pdf.

Kakalik, James S., Terence Dunworth, Laural A. Hill, Daniel McCaffrey, Marian Oshiro, Nicholas M. Pace, and Mary E. Vaiana. *An Evaluation of Mediation and Early Neutral Evaluation Under the Civil Justice Reform Act*. Santa Monica, CA: RAND Institute for Civil Justice, 1996.

———. *Just, Speedy, and Inexpensive? An Evaluation of Judicial Case Management Under the Civil Justice Reform Act*. Santa Monica, CA: RAND, 1997.

Kamminga, Y. P. "Towards Effective Governance Structures for Contractual Relations: Recommendations from Social Psychology, Economics, and Law for Improving Project Performance in Infrastructure Projects." PhD diss., Tilburg University, Netherlands, 2008.

Karatnycky, Adrian, and Peter Ackerman. "How Freedom Is Won: From Civic Resistance to Durable Democracy." 2005. https://freedomhouse.org/sites/default/files/How%20Freedom%20is%20Won.pdf.

Karl, Herman, and Lawrence Susskind. "Use of Joint Fact Finding in Science Intensive Policy Disputes, Part I: MIT; Joint Fact Finding in Science Intensive Policy Disputes (Lecture 2 of 2)." Academic Room. http://www.academicroom.com/video/use -joint-fact-finding-science-intensive-policy -disputes-part-i-mit-joint-fact-finding -science-intensive-policy-disputes-0 (accessed May 20, 2019).

Kaskell, Peter H., and Thomas J. Stipanowich. *Commercial Arbitration at Its Best: Successful Strategies for Business Users; A Report of the CPR Commission on the Future of Arbitration*. Chicago: CPR Institute for Dispute Resolution, 2001.

Katsh, Ethan, and Orna Rabinovich-Einy. *Digital Justice: Technology and the Internet of Disputes*. New York: Oxford University Press, 2017.

Katsh, Ethan, and Janet Rifkin. *Online Dispute Resolution: Resolving Conflicts in Cyberspace*. San Francisco, CA: Jossey-Bass, 2001.

Kellerman, Barbara. "When Should a Leader Apologize—and When Not?" *Harvard Business Review*, April 2006, https:// hbr.org/2006/04/when-should-a-leader -apologize-and-when-not.

Kessler, Amalia D. *A Revolution in Commerce: The Parisian Merchant Court and the Rise of Commercial Society in Eighteenth-*

Century France. New Haven, CT: Yale University Press, 2007.

Kiefer, John, and Robert Montjoy. "Incrementalism Before the Storm: Network Performance for the Evacuation of New Orleans." *Public Administration Review* 66 (2006): 122–30.

Kim, Nam, James A. Wall Jr., Dong-Won Sohn, and Jay S. Kim. "Community and Industrial Mediation in South Korea." *Journal of Conflict Resolution* 37 (1993): 361–82.

Kiobel v. Royal Dutch Petroleum Co. 569 U.S. 108 (2013).

Kleinfeld, Rachel. *Advancing the Rule of Law Abroad: Next Generation Reform*. Washington, DC: Carnegie Endowment for International Peace, 2012.

Knapp, Charles L. "Blowing the Whistle on Mandatory Arbitration: Unconscionability as a Signaling Device." *San Diego Law Review* 46 (2009): 610–28.

Kochan, Thomas, Brenda Lautsch, and Corinne Bendersky. "An Evaluation of the Massachusetts Commission Against Alternative Dispute Resolution Program." *Harvard Negotiation Law Review* 5 (2000): 233–74.

Kochan, Thomas A., and David B. Lipsky, eds. *Negotiations and Change: From the Workplace to Society*. Ithaca, NY: Cornell University Press, 2003.

Kochan, Thomas A., David B. Lipsky, Mary Newhart, and Alan Benson. "The Long-Haul Effects of Interest Arbitration: The Case of New York State's Taylor Law." *ILR Review* 63 (2010): 565–84.

Kolb, Deborah M. "Corporate Ombudsman and Organization Conflict Resolution." *Journal of Conflict Resolution* 31 no. 4 (1987): 673–91.

——. *When Talk Works: Profiles of Mediators*. San Francisco, CA: Jossey-Bass, 1994.

Konisky, David M. "Environmental Justice." In *Environmental Governance Reconsidered:*

Challenges, Choices and Opportunities, 2nd ed., edited by Robert F. Durant, Daniel J. Fiorino, and Rosemary O'Leary, 205–34. Cambridge, MA: MIT Press, 2017.

Koppell, Jonathan G. S. *The Politics of Quasi-government: Hybrid Organizations and the Dynamics of Bureaucratic Control.* Cambridge: Cambridge University Press, 2003.

Korobkin, Russell. *Negotiation: Theory and Strategy.* 2nd ed. Austin, TX: Wolters Kluwer, 2009.

———. "Psychological Impediments to Mediation Success: Theory and Practice." *Ohio State Journal on Dispute Resolution* 21 (2006): 281–338.

Korobkin, Russell B., and Thomas S. Ulen. "Law and Behavioral Science: Removing the Rationality Assumption from Law and Economics." *California Law Review* 88, no. 4 (2000): 1051–144.

Kovick, David. "The Hewlett Foundation's Conflict Resolution Program: Twenty Years of Field-Building, 1984–2004." May 2005. https://www.hewlett.org/wp-content/ uploads/2016/08/HewlettConflict ResolutionProgram.pdf.

Kramer, Larry. "Beyond Neoliberalism: Re-thinking Political Economy." April 26, 2018. https://hewlett.org/wp-content/uploads/ 2018/04/Beyond-Neoliberalism-Public -Board-Memo.pdf.

Kressel, Kenneth, Dean G. Pruitt, and associates. *Mediation Research: The Process and Effectiveness of Third-Party Intervention.* San Francisco, CA: Jossey-Bass, 1989.

Kritz, Neil. "Policy Implications of Empirical Research on Transitional Justice." In *Assessing the Impact of Transitional Justice: Challenges for Empirical Research*, edited by Hugo van der Merwe, Victoria Baxter, and Audrey R. Chapman, 13–21. Washington, DC: United States Institute of Peace Press, 2009.

Ku, Julian G. "Kiobel and the Surprising Death of Universal Jurisdiction Under the Alien Tort Statute." *American Journal of International Law* 107, no. 4 (2013): 835–41.

Kucsko-Stadlmayer, Gabriele. "The Legal Structures of Ombudsman-Institutions in Europe: Legal Comparative Analysis." In *European Ombudsman-Institutions: A Comparative Legal Analysis Regarding the Multifaceted Realization of an Idea*, 1–10. Vienna: Springer, 2008.

Kunreuther, Howard, and Mark V. Pauly. "Rules Rather than Discretion: Lessons from Hurricane Katrina." *Journal of Risk Uncertainty* 33, no. 1 (2006): 101–16.

Kunreuther, Howard, Lawrence Susskind, and Thomas D. Aarts. "The Facility Siting Credo: Guidelines for an Effective Facility Siting Process." 1991. http://web.mit.edu/ publicdisputes/practice/credo.pdf.

Lamare, J. Ryan, and David B. Lipsky. "Employment Arbitration in the Securities Industry: Lessons Drawn from Recent Empirical Research." *Berkeley Journal of Employment and Labor Law* 35 (2014): 113–33.

Lamparello, Adam. "Social Psychology, Legitimacy, and the Ethical Foundations of Judgment: Importing the Procedural Justice Model to Federal Sentencing." *Columbia Human Rights Law Review* 38 (2006): 115–50.

Lamps Plus, Inc. et al. v. Varela. 587 U.S. ___ (2019).

Lande, John. "Commentary: Focusing on Program Design Issues in Future Research on Court-Connected Mediation." *Conflict Resolution Quarterly* 22, nos. 1–2 (2004): 89–102.

———. "Failing Faith in Litigation? A Survey of Business Lawyers' and Executives' Opinions." *Harvard Negotiation Law Review* 3 (1998): 1–70.

———. *Lawyering with Planned Early Negotiation: How You Can Get Good Results for*

Clients and Make Money. Chicago: American Bar Association, 2011.

———. "Possibilities for Collaborative Law: Ethics and Practice of Lawyer Disqualification and Process Control in a New Model of Lawyering." *Ohio State Law Journal* 64, no. 5 (2003): 1315–84.

———. "Principles for Policymaking About Collaborative Law and Other ADR Processes." *Ohio State Journal on Dispute Resolution* 22, no. 3 (2007): 619–706.

Lande, John, and Peter Benner. "Why and How Businesses Use Planned Early Dispute Resolution." *University of St. Thomas Law Journal* 13 (2017): 248–96.

Lande, John, Kurt L. Dettman, and Catherine E. Shanks. "User Guide: Planned Early Dispute Resolution." 2016. http://www .americanbar.org/content/dam/aba/events/ dispute_resolution/committees/PEDR/ abadr_pedr_guide.authcheckdam.pdf.

Langsdale, Stacy, Allyson Beall, Elizabeth Bourget, Erik Hagen, Scott Kudlas, Richard Palmer, Diane Tate, and William Werick. "Collaborative Modeling for Decision Support in Water Resources: Principles and Best Practices." *Journal of the American Water Resources Association* 49, no. 3 (2013): 629–38.

La Plante, Lisa J. "Outlawing Amnesty: The Return of Criminal Justice in Transitional Justice Schemes." *Virginia Journal of International Law* 49, no. 15 (2009): 22–47.

Lappé, Frances Moore. *Diet for a Small Planet.* New York: Ballantine Books, 1971.

Lappé, Frances Moore, and Adam Eichen. *Daring Democracy: Igniting Power, Meaning, and Connection for the America We Want.* Boston, MA: Beacon Press, 2017.

"Large Morass: Dalkon Shield Trust, Hailed as Innovative, Stirs a Lot of Discord." *Wall Street Journal,* June 3, 1991, p. 1.

Latham, Michael. *Constructing the Team: Joint Review of Procurement and Contractual Arrangements in the United Kingdom Construction Industry.* London: HMSO, 1994.

Laue, James, and Gerald Cormick. "The Ethics of Intervention in Community Disputes." In *The Ethics of Social Intervention,* edited by Gordon Bermant, Herbert C. Kelman, and Donald P. Warwick, 205–32. New York: Halstead Press, 1978.

LaVan, Helen, Michael J. Jedel, and Robert Perkovich. "Vacating of Arbitration Awards as Diminishment of Conflict Resolution." *Negotiation and Conflict Management Research* 5 (2012): 29–48.

Lawler, Edward E., III. *High-Involvement Management.* San Francisco, CA: Jossey-Bass, 1986.

Laws, David. "Representation of Stakeholding Interests." In *Consensus Building Handbook: A Comprehensive Guide to Reaching Agreement,* edited by Lawrence Susskind, Sarah McKearnan, and Jennifer Thomas-Larmer, 241–85. Thousand Oaks, CA: Sage, 1999.

Lax, David, and James Sebenius. *The Manager as Negotiator: Bargaining for Cooperation and Competitive Gain.* New York: Free Press, 1986.

———. *3-D Negotiation: Bargaining for Cooperation and Competitive Gain.* Boston, MA: Harvard Business School Press, 2006.

Leach, William D. "Collaborative Public Management and Democracy: Evidence from Western Watershed Principles." *Public Administration Review* 68 (2006): 100–110.

———. "Watershed Partnerships in California and Washington: Final Report for the Watershed Partnerships Project." *SSRN,* February 2002. https://papers.ssrn.com/ sol3/papers.cfm?abstract_id=2268676.

Leach, William, and Paul Sabatier. "Facilitators, Coordinators, and Outcomes." In *Promise and Performance of Environmental Conflict Resolution,* edited by Rosemary O'Leary and Lisa Bingham, 148–71.

Washington, DC: Resources for the Future Press, 2003.

LeBaron, Michelle. "The Alchemy of Change: Cultural Fluency in Conflict Resolution." In *The Handbook of Conflict Resolution: Theory and Practice*, edited by Peter T. Coleman, Morton Deutsch, and Eric C. Marcus, 581–603. San Francisco, CA: Jossey-Bass, 2014.

Lederach, John Paul. *The Little Book of Conflict Transformation*. Intercourse, PA: Good Books, 2003.

Lee, Cynthia G., Fred L. Cheesman II, David B. Rottman, Rachel Swaner, Suvi Hynynen Lambson, Mike Rempel, and Ric Curtis. *A Community Court Grows in Brooklyn—a Final Report: A Comprehensive Evaluation of the Red Hook Community Justice Center*. Williamsburg, VA: National Center for State Courts, 2013.

Leithead, Alistair. "Rwanda Genocide: International Criminal Tribunal Closes." *BBC News*, December 14, 2015. https://www.bbc.com/news/world-africa-35070220.

Lerner, Josh. *Making Democracy Fun: How Game Design Can Empower Citizens and Transform Politics*. Cambridge, MA: MIT Press, 2014.

"Lessons Learned from the Media's Coverage of Boston Bombing." *National Public Radio*, April 20, 2013. http://www.npr.org/2013/0420/178090655/lessons-learned-from-the-medias-coverage-of-boston-bombing.

Levi, Margaret, and Brad Epperly. "Principled Principals in the Founding Moments of the Rule of Law." In *Global Perspectives on the Rule of Law*, edited by James J. Heckman, Robert L. Nelson, and Lee Cabatingan, 192–209. London: Routledge, 2010.

Levin, A. Leo, and Russell R. Wheeler, eds. *The Pound Conference: Perspectives on Justice in the Future*. St. Paul, MN: West, 1979.

Levine, Neil A. "Hands Up, Don't Shoot: A Case for the Community Relations Ser-

vice." Levine Strategies, August 25, 2104. https://www.levinestrategies.com/all-posts/2014/8/25/hands-up-dont-shoot-a-case-for-the-community-relations-service.

Lewicki, Roy J., Bruce Barry, and David M. Saunders. *Negotiation*. New York: McGraw Hill, 2005.

Lewicki, Roy J., Robert J. Bies, and Blair H. Sheppard. *Research on Negotiation in Organizations*. Newton, MA: JAI Press, 1986.

Lewicki, Roy J., David M. Saunders, and Bruce Barry. *Negotiation*. 7th ed. New York: McGraw-Hill, 2015.

Lewicki, Roy J., and Edward C. Tomlinson. "Trust, Trust Development, and Trust Repair." In *The Handbook of Conflict Resolution: Theory and Practice*, 3rd ed., edited by Peter T. Coleman, Morton Deutsch, and Eric C. Marcus, 104–36. San Francisco, CA: Jossey-Bass, 2014.

Lewin, David, and Richard B. Peterson. *The Modern Grievance Procedure in the United States*. Westport, CT: Greenwood Press, 1988.

Lewin, Kurt. *Group Decision and Social Change*. New York: Holt, Rinehart and Winston, 1952.

Liebman, Carol B. "Medical Malpractice Mediation: Benefits Gained, Opportunities Lost." *Law and Contemporary Problems* 74, no. 3 (2011): 135–49.

Liebman, Carol B., and Chris Stern Hyman. "Medical Error Disclosure, Mediation Skills, and Malpractice Litigation: A Demonstration Project in Pennsylvania." 2005. http://www.pewtrusts.org/-/media/legacy/uploadedfiles/wwwpewtrustsorg/reports/medical_liability/liebmanreport pdf.

Lien, Tracy. "Uber Stops Requiring Sexual Misconduct Victims to Quietly Use Arbitration Instead of Suing." *Los Angeles Times*, May 15, 2018. http://www.latimes

.com/business/technology/la-fi-tn-uber -misconduct-policy-20180515-story.html.

Lies, Mark A., II, ed. *Preventing and Managing Workplace Violence: Legal and Strategic Guidelines.* Chicago: American Bar Association, 2008.

Lind, E. Allan, Robert J. MacCoun, Patricia A. Ebener, William L. F. Felstiner, Deborah R. Hensler, Judith Resnik, and Tom R. Tyler. "In the Eye of the Beholder: Tort Litigants' Evaluations of Their Experiences in the Civil Justice System." *Law and Society Review* 24 (1990): 953–96.

Lind, E. Allan, and Tom R. Tyler. *The Social Psychology of Procedural Justice.* New York: Plenum, 1988.

Lipsky, David B., Ariel C. Avgar, and J. Ryan Lamare. *Managing and Resolving Workplace Conflict.* Bingley, UK: Emerald, 2016.

Lipsky, David, and Ronald L. Seeber. "In Search of Control: The Corporate Embrace of ADR." *University of Pennsylvania Journal of Labor and Employment Law* 1 (1998): 133–57.

Lipsky, David B., Ronald L. Seeber, and Richard D. Fincher. *Emerging Systems for Managing Workplace Conflict: Lessons from American Corporations for Managers and Dispute Resolution Professionals.* San Francisco, CA: Jossey-Bass, 2003.

Liptak, Adam. "Sent to Prison by a Software Program's Secret Algorithms." *New York Times,* May 1, 2017, p. A22.

Liu, Mingwei. "Conflict Resolution in China." In *The Oxford Handbook of Conflict Management in Organizations,* edited by William K. Roche, Paul Teague, and Alexander J. S. Colvin, 494–517. Oxford: Oxford University Press, 2014.

Lopez, Antoinette Sedillo. "Evolving Indigenous Law: Navajo Marriage—Cultural Traditions and Modern Challenges." *Arizona Journal of International and Comparative Law* 17 (2000): 283–307.

Lowe, Rebecca "Back to Basics." International Bar Association. January 23, 2014. https://www.ibanet.org/Article/Detail.aspx ?ArticleUid=2ce3cb9b-55a1-48e0-b6a7 -2db47771aa85.

Lukensmeyer, Carolyn J., and Steven Brigham. "Taking Democracy to Scale: Large Scale Re-interventions—for Citizens." *Journal of Applied Behavioral Science* 41, no. 1 (2005): 47–60.

Lukensmeyer, Carolyn J., Joe Goldman, and Steven Brigham. "A Town Meeting for the 21st Century." In *The Deliberative Democracy Handbook: Strategies for Effective Civic Engagement in the Twenty-First Century,* edited by John Gastil and Peter Levine, 154–63. San Francisco, CA: Jossey-Bass, 2005.

Luna, Erik. "Punishment Theory, Holism, and the Procedural Conception of Restorative Justice." *Utah Law Review* 2003 (2003): 205–302.

Luo, Yadong, John Hongxin Zhao, and Jianjun Du. "The Internationalization Speed of E-commerce Companies: An Empirical Analysis." *International Marketing Review* 22, no. 6 (2005): 693–709.

Lynch, Jennifer. "Beyond ADR: A Systems Approach to Conflict Management." *Negotiation Journal* 17, no. 3 (2001): 207–16.

MacCormick, Neil. *Institutions of Law: An Essay in Legal Theory.* Oxford: Oxford University Press, 2008.

MacCoun, Robert J. "Comparing Legal Factfinders: Real and Mock, Amateur and Professional." *Florida State University Law Review* 32, no. 2 (2005): 511–18.

———. "Unintended Consequences of Court Arbitration: A Cautionary Tale from New Jersey." *Justice System Journal* 14, no. 2 (1991): 229–43.

———. "Voice, Control, and Belonging: The Double-Edged Sword of Procedural Fairness." *Annual Review of Law and Society Science* 1 (2005): 171–201.

Macneil, Ian R. *American Arbitration Law*. Oxford: Oxford University Press, 1992.

Mahdi, Sajida A. "Gateway to Arbitration: Issues of Contract Formation Under the U.C.C. and the Enforceability of Arbitration Clauses Included in Standard Form Contracts Shipped with Goods." *Northwestern University Law Review* 96 (2001): 403–46.

Mahony, Douglas M., and Brian S. Klass. "HRM and Conflict Management." In *Oxford Handbook of Conflict Management in Organizations*, edited by William K. Roche, Paul Teague, and Alexander J. S. Colvin, 79–104. Oxford: Oxford University Press, 2014.

Malin, Martin H. "The Legislative Upheaval in Public-Sector Labor Law: A Search for Common Elements." *ABA Journal of Labor and Employment Law* 27 (2012): 149–64.

———. "The Paradox of Public Sector Labor Law." *Indiana Law Journal* 84 (2009): 1369–99.

———. "Public Employees' Right to Strike: Law and Experience." *University of Michigan Journal of Law Reform* 26 (1993): 313–402.

———. "Topic in Jurisprudence: The Distributive and Corrective Justice Concerns in the Debate over Employment-at-Will: Some Preliminary Thoughts." *Chicago-Kent Law Review* 68 (1992): 117–46.

———. "Two Models of Interest Arbitration." *Ohio State Journal on Dispute Resolution* 28 (2013): 144–69.

Malkin, Victoria. "Community Courts and the Process of Accountability: Consensus and Conflict at the Red Hook Community Justice Center." *American Criminal Law Review* 40 (2003): 1573–94.

———. "Problem-Solving in Community Courts: Who Decides the Problem?" In *Problem-Solving Courts: Justice for the Twenty-First Century*, edited by Paul Higgins and Mitchell B. Mackinem, 139–60. Santa Barbara, CA: ABC-CLIO, 2009.

Malloy, Brian J. "Binding Interest Arbitration in the Public Sector: A 'New' Proposal for California and Beyond." *Hastings Law Journal* 55, no. 1 (2003): 245–69.

"Managing the $30 million 'One Fund' to Aid Boston Victims." *National Public Radio*, May 16, 2013. http://www.npr.org/templates/story/story.php?storyId=184524656.

Mansbridge, Jane J. *Beyond Adversary Democracy*. Chicago: University of Chicago Press, 1983.

Mansbridge, Jane, Janette Hartz-Karp, Matthew Amengual, and John Gastil. "Norms of Deliberation: An Inductive Study." *Journal of Public Deliberation* 2, no. 1 (2006): 1–47.

Marine Science Institute. "MarineMap." http://msi.ucsb.edu/marinemap (accessed June 30, 2019).

Marrow, Paul B. "Determining If Mandatory Arbitration Is Fair: Asymmetrically Held Information and the Role of Mandatory Arbitration in Modulating Uninsurable Contract Risks." *New York Law School Law Review* 54, no. 1 (2009): 187–240.

Martinez, David. "Mediation Design in Bhutan." 2012. Unpublished fieldwork research notes in authors' possession.

Martinez, Janet, Esther Conrad, and Tara Moran. "Upstream, Midstream, and Downstream: Dispute System Design for Sustainable Groundwater Management." *University of St. Thomas Law Journal* 13, no. 2 (2017): 297–314.

Marvinney, Craig A. "Mediation in the United States Circuit Courts of Appeals: A Survey." *FDCC Quarterly* 64, no. 1 (2014): 53–67.

Maslow, A. H. "A Theory of Human Motivation." *Psychological Review* 50 (1943): 370–96.

Masucci, Deborah. "2016–2017 Global Pound Conference." *Dispute Resolution Section Magazine* 73 (Spring 2018): 6–8.

Masucci, Deborah, and Shravanthi Suresh. "Transforming Business Through Proactive Dispute Management." *Cardozo Journal of Conflict Resolution* 18, no. 3 (2017): 659–76.

Mather, Lynn. "Disputes, Social Construction and Transformation." In *International Encyclopedia of the Social and Behavioral Sciences*, edited by Neil J. Smelser and Paul B. Baltes, 3772–76. Amsterdam: Elsevier, 2001.

Mathews v. Eldridge. 424 U.S. 319 (1976).

Matias, J. Nathan, Amy Johnson, Whitney Erin Boesel, Brian Keegan, Jaclyn Friedman, and Charlie DeTar. "Reporting, Reviewing, and Responding to Harassment on Twitter." May 13, 2015. https://arxiv.org/ftp/arxiv/papers/1505/1505.03359.pdf.

May, Kenneth, Patrick M. Sanders, and Michelle T. Sullivan, eds. *Elkouri and Elkouri: How Arbitration Works.* 7th ed. Washington, DC: Bloomberg BNA, 2012.

Mayer, Bernard S. *Beyond Neutrality: Confronting the Crisis in Conflict Resolution.* San Francisco, CA: Jossey-Bass, 2004.

———. *The Dynamics of Conflict Resolution: A Practitioner's Guide.* San Francisco, CA: Jossey-Bass, 2000.

Mayer-Rieckh, Alexander, and Pablo de Greiff, eds. *Justice as Prevention: Vetting Public Employees in Transitional Societies.* New York: Social Science Research Council, 2007.

Mayes, Thomas A. "A Brief Model for Explaining Dispute Resolution Options in Special Education." *Ohio State Journal on Dispute Resolution* 34, no. 1 (2019): 153–70.

Maynard, Micheline. "An Apology from Toyota's Leader." *New York Times*, February 24, 2010. https://www.nytimes.com/2010/02/25/business/global/25toyota.html.

McAdoo, Bobbi, and Nancy A. Welsh. "Look Before You Leap and Keep on Looking: Lessons from the Institutionalization of Court-Connected Mediation." *Nevada Law Journal* 5 (2004–2005): 399–421.

McAdoo, Bobbi, Nancy A. Welsh, and Roselle L. Wissler. "Institutionalization: What Do Empirical Studies Tell Us About Court Mediation?" *Dispute Resolution Magazine* 9 (2003): 8–10.

McCabe, Douglas C. *Corporate Nonunion Complaint Procedures and Systems: A Strategic Human Resources Management Analysis.* New York: Praeger, 1988.

McDonell, Colin. "The Gulf Coast Claims Facility and the Deepwater Horizon Litigation: Judicial Regulation of Private Compensation Schemes." *Stanford Law Review* 64, no. 3 (2012): 765–96.

McEwen, Craig A., and Richard J. Maiman. "Mediation in Small Claims Court: Achieving Compliance Through Consent," *Law and Society Review* 18, no. 1 (1984): 11–50.

———. "Small Claims Mediation in Maine: An Empirical Assessment." *Maine Law Review* 33 (1981): 237–68.

McGillis, Daniel. *Community Mediation Programs: Developments and Challenges.* Washington, DC: National Institute of Justice, 1997.

McGovern, Francis E., ed. "Claims Resolution Facilities and the Mass Settlement of Mass Torts." Special issue, *Law and Contemporary Problems* 53, no. 4 (1990): 79–112.

———. "Resolving Mature Mass Tort Litigation." *Boston University Law Review* 69 (1989): 659–94.

———. "Second Generation Dispute System Design Issues in Managing Settlements." *Harvard Negotiation Law Review* 14 (Winter 2009): n.p.

———. "The Second Generation of Dispute System Design: Reoccurring Problems and

Potential Solutions." *Ohio State Journal on Dispute Resolution* 24 (2008): 53–80.

———. "The What and Why of Claims Resolution Facilities." *Stanford Law Review* 57 (2005): 1361–89.

McIlwrath, Michael, and John Savage. *International Arbitration and Mediation: A Practical Guide.* Dordrecht, Netherlands: Kluwer Law International 2010.

McKearnan, Sarah, and Patrick Field. "The Northern Oxford County Coalition." In *The Consensus Building Handbook: A Comprehensive Guide to Reaching Agreement*, edited by Lawrence Susskind, Sarah McKearnan, and Jennifer Thomas-Larmer, 711–41. Thousand Oaks, CA: Sage, 1999.

"Mediation in Civil and Commercial Matters." Eur-Lex, August 17, 2015. http://europa.eu/legislation_summaries/justice_freedom_security/judicial_cooperation_in_civil_matters/l33251_en.htm.

Mello, Michelle M., Richard Boothman, Timothy McDonald, Jeffrey Driver, Alan Lembitz, Darren Bouwmeester, Benjamin Dunlap, and Thomas Gallagher. "Communication-and-Resolution Programs: The Challenges and Lessons Learned from Six Early Adopters." *Health Affairs* 33, no. 1 (2014): 20–29.

Meltzer, Leah D. "The Federal Workplace Ombuds." *Ohio State Journal on Dispute Resolution* 13, no. 2 (1998): 549–609.

Menkel-Meadow, Carrie. "Are There Systemic Ethics Issues in Dispute System Design? And What We Should [Not] Do About It: Lessons from International and Domestic Fronts." *Harvard Negotiation Law Review* 14 (2009): 195–212.

———. *Dispute Processing and Conflict Resolution.* Burlington, VT: Ashgate and Dartmouth, 2003.

———. "Dispute Resolution." In *Oxford Handbook of Empirical Legal Research*, edited by Peter Cane and Herbert Kritzer, 596–624. Oxford: Oxford University Press, 2010.

———. "Do the 'Haves' Come Out Ahead in Alternative Justice Systems? Repeat Players in ADR." *Ohio State Journal on Dispute Resolution* 15 (1999): 19–61.

———. "Ethics and the Settlement of Mass Torts: When the Rules Meet the Road." *Cornell Law Review* 80 (1995): 1213–21.

———. "Ethics in ADR: The Many 'C's' of Professional Responsibility and Dispute Resolution." *Fordham Urban Law Journal* 28 (2001): 979–90.

———. "Is the Adversary System Really Dead? Dilemmas of Legal Ethics as Legal Institutions and Roles Evolve." In *Current Legal Problems*, vol. 57, edited by Jane Holder, Colm O'Cinneide, and Michael Freeman, 85–99. Oxford: Oxford University Press, 2004.

———. "The Lawyer's Role(s) in Deliberative Democracy." *Nevada Law Journal* 5 (2004–2005): 347–69.

———. "Mothers and Fathers of Invention: The Intellectual Founders of ADR." *Ohio State Journal on Dispute Resolution* 16 (2000): 1–37.

———. "Regulation of Dispute Resolution in the United States of America: From the Formal to the Informal to the 'Semi-formal.'" In *Regulating Dispute Resolution: ADR and Access to Justice at the Crossroads*, edited by Felix Steffek, Hannes Unberath, Hazel Genn, Reinhard Greger, and Carrie Menkel-Meadow, 419–54. Oxford: Hart, 2013.

———. "Roots and Inspirations: A Brief History of the Foundations of Dispute Resolution." In *The Handbook of Dispute Resolution*, edited by Michael Moffitt and Robert Bordone, 13–31. San Francisco, CA: Jossey-Bass, 2005.

———. "Taking the Mass out of Mass Torts: Reflections of a Dalkon Shield Arbitrator on Alternative Dispute Resolution, Judging, Neutrality, Gender, and Process." *Loyola Los Angeles Law Review* 31 (1997–1998): 513–50.

Menkel-Meadow, Carrie J., Lela Porter Love, Andrea Kupfer Schneider, and Michael Moffitt. *Dispute Resolution: Beyond the Adversarial Model.* 3rd ed. New York: Wolters Kluwer, 2019.

Menkel-Meadow, Carrie J., Lela Porter Love, Jean R. Sternlight, and Andrea Kupfer Schneider. *Dispute Resolution: Beyond the Adversarial Model.* 2nd ed. Danvers, MA: Wolters Kluwer, 2010.

Menkel-Meadow, Carrie, Andrea P. Schneider, and Lela K. Love. *Negotiation: Processes for Problem-Solving.* 2nd ed. Danvers, MA: Wolters Kluwer, 2014.

Menzel, Donald C., and Harvey L. White. *The State of Public Administration: Issues, Challenges, and Opportunities.* Armonk, NY: M. E. Sharpe, 2011.

Mernitz, Scott. *Mediation of Environmental Disputes: A Sourcebook.* New York: Praeger, 1980.

Merry, Sally Engle, and Neal Milner, eds. *The Possibility of Popular Justice.* Ann Arbor: University of Michigan Press, 1993.

Mesch, Debra J. "Arbitration and Gender: An Analysis of Cases Taken to Arbitration in the Public Sector." *Journal of Collective Negotiations in the Public Sector* 24 (1995): 207–18.

———. "Grievance Arbitration in the Public Sector: A Conceptual Framework and Empirical Analysis of Public and Private Sector Arbitration Cases." *Review of Public Personnel Administration* 15 (1995): 22–36.

Metropolitan Life Ins. Co. v. Glenn. 554 U.S. 105 (2008).

Meyerson, Bruce, and John M. Townsend. "Revised Code of Ethics for Commercial Arbitrators Explained." *Dispute Resolution Journal* 59, no. 1 (2004): 10–17.

Michel, James. "Alternative Dispute Resolution and the Rule of Law in International Development Cooperation." *Journal of Dispute Resolution* 2011, no. 1 (2011): 36–51.

Miller, Richard E., and Austin Sarat. "Grievances, Claims, and Disputes: Assessing the Adversary Culture." *Law and Society Review* 15, nos. 3–4 (1980–1981): 525–66.

Miller, Russell A. "Theoretical Approaches to International Indigenous Rights: Collective Discursive Democracy as the Indigenous Right to Self-Determination." *American Indian Law Review* 31 (2007): 341–73.

Minow, Martha. *Between Vengeance and Forgiveness: Facing History After Genocide and Mass Violence.* Boston, MA: Beacon Press, 1998.

Mistelis, Loukas A. "ADR in England and Wales: A Successful Case of Public Private Partnership." In *Global Trends in Mediation,* edited by Nadja Alexander, 139–80. Alphen aan den Rijn, Netherlands: Kluwer Law International, 2006.

Mnookin, Robert H. "Why Negotiations Fail: An Exploration of Barriers to the Resolution of Conflict." *Ohio State Journal on Dispute Resolution* 8, no. 2 (1993): 235–49.

Mnookin, Robert, Scott R. Peppet, and Andrew S. Tulumello. *Beyond Winning: Negotiating to Create Value in Deals and Disputes.* Cambridge, MA: Harvard University Press, 2000.

Moffitt, Michael L. "Schmediation and the Dimensions of Definition." *Harvard Negotiation Law Review* 10 (2005): 69–102.

Moffitt, Michael, and Robert Bordone, eds. *The Handbook of Dispute Resolution.* San Francisco, CA: Jossey-Bass, 2005.

Montijo, Mark, Kathleen Nelson, Mark Scafidi, Dave St. Pierre, Dorothy Tarrant, Jocelyne Vistan, and Maureen Whitemore. "Bridging Physician-Patient Perspectives Following an Adverse Medical Outcome." *Permanente Journal* 15, no. 4 (2011): 85–88.

Moon, Yuseok, and Lisa Blomgren Bingham. "Transformative Mediation at Work: Employee and Supervisor Perceptions on USPS REDRESS Program." *International Review of Public Administration* 11 (2007): 43–55.

Moore, Christopher W. *The Mediation Process: Practical Strategies for Resolving Conflict.* 3rd ed. San Francisco, CA: Jossey-Bass, 2003.

Moore, Christopher W. *The Mediation Process: Practical Strategies for Resolving Conflict.* 4th ed. San Francisco, CA: Jossey-Bass, 2014.

Moore, Jennifer, Marie Bismark, and Michelle Mello. "Patients' Experiences with Communication-and-Resolution Programs After Medical Injury." *JAMA Internal Medicine* 177, no. 11 (2017): 1595–603.

Moran, Michael, Martin Rein, and Robert E. Goodin, eds. *The Oxford Handbook of Public Policy.* Oxford: Oxford University Press, 2008.

Moreno, Guillermo Palao. "Cross-Border Consumer Redress After the ADR Directive and the ODR Regulation." In *The New Regulatory Framework for Consumer Dispute Resolution*, edited by Pablo Cortés, 393–406. Oxford: Oxford University Press, 2016.

Morgan, Glen, John L. Campbell, Colin Crouch, Ove Kaj Pedersen, and Richard Whitley. *The Oxford Handbook of Comparative Institutional Analysis.* Oxford: Oxford University Press, 2010.

Morrison, Alan B. "Can Mandatory Arbitration of Medical Malpractice Claims Be Fair? The Kaiser Permanente System." *Dispute Resolution Journal* 70, no. 3 (2015): 35–79.

Morrison and Foerster. "2017–2018 Southern California Wildfires, Mudslides, and Related Disasters Helping Handbook: A Resource for Individuals, Families, and Small Businesses." January 24, 2018. https://www.mofo.com/culture/community/2017-2018-southern-california-disasters.html.

Moskowitz, Eric. "Marathon Victim Payout Method Faulted." *Boston Globe*, July 4, 2013. http://www.bostonglobe.com/metro/2013/07/03/methodology-marathon-victim-payout-faulted-lawyer-group/sqxc7kjTz2OFpdxOTLT5VP/story.html.

Mullenix, Linda S. "Prometheus Unbound: The Gulf Coast Claims Facility as a Means for Resolving Mass Tort Claims—a Fund Too Far." *Louisiana Law Review* 71, no. 3 (2011): 819–916.

Mundlak, Guy. "Fifty Years of the National Insurance Law: The Celebrations Will Take Place in the Courtroom." *Social Security* 67 (2004): 83–108 (in Hebrew).

Munoz, Joseph Mark S., ed. *Handbook on the Geopolitics of Business.* Northampton, MA: Edward Elgar, 2013.

Murray v. United Food and Commercial Workers Int'l Union. 289 F.3d 297 (4th Cir. 2002).

Mutz, Kathryn M., Gray C. Bryner, and Douglas S. Kenney. *Justice and Natural Resources: Concepts, Strategies, and Applications.* Washington, DC: Island Press, 2002.

Nabatchi, Tina. "The Institutionalization of Alternative Dispute Resolution in the Federal Government." *Public Administration Review* 67, no. 4 (2007): 646–61.

———. "An Introduction to Deliberative Civic Engagement." In *Democracy in Motion: Evaluating the Practice and Impact of Deliberative Civic Engagement*, edited by Tina Nabatchi, John Gastil, Matt Leighninger, and G. Michael Weiksner, 3–17. New York: Oxford University Press, 2012.

———. "Putting the 'Public' Back in Public Values Research: Designing Participation to Identify and Respond to Values." *Public Administration Review* 72, no. 5 (2012): 699–708.

Nabatchi, Tina, and Lisa Blomgren Amsler. "Direct Public Engagement in Local Government." Supplement, *American Review of Public Administration* 44, no. S4 (2014): 63S–88S.

Nabatchi, Tina, John Gastil, Matt Leighninger, and G. Michael Weiksner, eds. *Democracy in Motion: Evaluating the Practice and Impact of Deliberative Civic Engagement*. New York: Oxford University Press, 2012.

Nabatchi, Tina, David H. Good, and Lisa Blomgren Bingham. "Organizational Justice and Workplace Mediation: A Six-Factor Model." *International Journal of Conflict Management* 18, no. 2 (2007): 148–74.

Najita, Joyce M., and James L. Stern. *Collective Bargaining in the Public Sector: The Experience of Eight States*. New York: Routledge, 2001.

Naoum, Shamil. "An Overview into the Concept of Partnering." *International Journal of Project Management* 21, no. 1 (2003): 71–76.

National Academy of Arbitrators. *National Academy of Arbitrators Annual Proceedings, 2010*. Edison, NJ: BNA Books, 2010.

———. "National Academy of Arbitrators Policy Statement on Employment Arbitration." May 20, 2009. https://naarb.org/ employment-arbitration-policy-and -guidelines.

National Academy of Arbitrators, American Arbitration Association, and Federal Mediation and Conciliation Service. "Code of Professional Responsibility for Arbitrators of Labor-Management Disputes." September 2007. https://www.adr.org/sites/ default/files/document_repository/Code %20of%20Professional%20Responsibility %20for%20Arbitrators%20of%20Labor -Management%20Disputes_0.pdf.

National Association for Community Mediation. "Purpose." https://www.nafcm.org/ page/Purpose? (accessed June 3, 2019).

National Center for State Courts. "Comparing State Courts." http://www.ncsc .org/information-and-resources/comparing -state-courts.aspx (accessed May 30, 2019).

National Center for Technology and Dispute Resolution. "Ethical Principles for ODR." 2016. http://odr.info/ethics-and-odr.

National Center for Victims of Crime. "National Compassion Fund." http://www .victimsofcrime.org/our-programs/national -compassion-fund (accessed June 3, 2019).

National Coalition for Dialogue and Deliberation. "Dialogue and Deliberation Methods." September 12, 2010. http://ncdd.org/rc/ item/4856.

———. "Resource Center." http://ncdd.org/rc (accessed September 6, 2019).

National Conference of Commissioners on Uniform State Laws. "Uniform Arbitration Act." December 13, 2000. https:// www.uniformlaws.org/HigherLogic/ System/DownloadDocumentFile.ashx ?DocumentFileKey=cf35cea8-4434-0d6b -408d-756f961489af&forceDialog=0.

———. "Uniform Mediation Act." August 2001. http://www.mediate.com/articles/ umafinalstyled.cfm.

———. "Uniform Mediation Act." December 10, 2003. https://www.uniformlaws .org/HigherLogic/System/Download DocumentFile.ashx?DocumentFileKey= 9b244b42-269c-769e-9f89-590ce048d0dd &forceDialog=0.

National Institute of Justice. "Drug Courts." August 23, 2018. https://www.nij.gov/ topics/courts/drug-courts/pages/welcome .aspx.

———. "Specialized Courts." May 30, 2018. https://www.nij.gov/topics/courts/pages/specialized-courts.aspx.

National Insurance Institute of Israel. "Hostile Action Casualties." https://www.btl.gov.il/English%20Homepage/Benefits/Benefits%20for%20Victims%20of%20Hostilities/Pages/default.aspx (accessed June 3, 2019).

Nduwimana, Françoise. "United Nations Security Council Resolution 1325 (2000) on Women, Peace and Security: Understanding the Implications, Fulfilling the Obligations." Available at http://www.un.org/womenwatch/osagi/cdrom/documents/Background_Paper_Africa.pdf (accessed June 21, 2019).

Needup, Pema. "Traditional Dispute Resolution System in Bhutan." November 10, 2011. Unpublished paper in authors' possession.

———. "Training and Consultation on ADR for Local Leaders: Taking Justice Closer to the People." 2012. Unpublished paper in authors' possession.

Neuman, Scott. "Social Media Helped Find Loved Ones After Marathon Bombing." *National Public Radio*, April 16, 2013. https://www.npr.org/sections/thetwo-way/2013/04/16/177443006/social-media-helped-find-loved-ones-after-marathon-bombing.

New Prime Inc. v. Oliveira. No. 17-340, 586 U.S. ___ (U.S. Jan. 15, 2019).

New York State Governor's Office of Employee Relations. "New York State Public Employees' Fair Employment Act—the Taylor Law." https://goer.ny.gov/new-york-state-public-employees-fair-employment-act-taylor-law (accessed October 12, 2019).

Nickel, Henry, William Anderson, Kenneth Feinberg, and Nicholas Yost. Panel discussion. *Environmental Law Reporter* 16, no. 8 (1986): 10216–19.

Nino, Carlos. "The Duty to Punish Past Abuses of Human Rights in Context: The Case of Argentina." *Yale Law Journal* 100 (1991): 2619–40.

NLRB v. Joseph Macaluso, Inc. 618 F.2d 51 (1980).

Nocera, Joe. "BP Makes Amends." *New York Times*, January 10, 2012, p. A21.

Nolan-Haley, Jacqueline. "Evolving Paths to Justice: Assessing the EU Directive on Mediation." In *Proceedings of the Sixth Annual Conference on International Arbitration and Mediation*, 2–5. Leiden, Netherlands: Brill-Nijhoff, 2012.

Nolan-Haley, Jacqueline, Ellen E. Deason, and Mariana Hernandez-Crespo Gonstead. *Global Issues in Mediation* (St. Paul, MN: West Academic, 2019).

Noveck, Beth Simone. *Smart Citizens, Smarter State: The Technologies of Expertise and the Future of Governing*. Cambridge, MA: Harvard University Press, 2015.

Nussbaum, Lydia. "ADR's Place in Foreclosure: Remedying the Flaws of a Securitized Housing Market." *Cardozo Law Review* 34 (2013): 1889–953.

Obama, Barack. "Transparency and Open Government: Memorandum for the Heads of Executive Departments and Agencies." *Federal Register* 74 (2009): 4685–86.

Office of the United Nations High Commissioner for Human Rights. *Rule-of-Law Tools for Post-conflict Nations: Amnesties*. New York: United Nations, 2009.

O'Hara O'Connor, Erin A., Kenneth J. Martin, and Randall S. Thomas. "Customizing Employment Arbitration." *Iowa Law Review* 98, no. 1 (2012): 133–82.

O'Hear, Michael M. "Plea Bargaining and Procedural Justice." *Georgia Law Review* 42 (2007): 407–69.

O'Hear, Michael M., and Andrea Kupfer. "Dispute Resolution in Criminal Law: An Introduction to Dispute Resolution in Criminal Law." *Marquette Law Review* 91 (2007): 1–8.

Olam v. Congress Mortgage Co. 68 F. Supp. 2d 1110 (N.D. Cal. 1999).

O'Leary, Rosemary, with Terry Amsler and Malka Kopell. *Environmental Conflict Resolution: Strategies for Environmental Grantmakers.* Menlo Park, CA: William and Flora Hewlett Foundation, 2005.

O'Leary, Rosemary, and Lisa Blomgren Bingham. *The Collaborative Public Manager.* Washington, DC: Georgetown University Press, 2009.

———, eds. *The Promise and Performance of Environmental Conflict Resolution.* Washington, DC: Resources for the Future Press, 2003.

O'Leary, Rosemary, Robert F. Durant, Daniel J. Fiorino, and Paul S. Weiland. *Managing for the Environment: Understanding the Legal, Organizational, and Policy Challenges.* San Francisco, CA: Jossey-Bass, 1999.

O'Leary, Rosemary, Tina Nabatchi, and Lisa Blomgren Bingham. "Assessing and Improving Conflict Resolution in Multiparty Environmental Negotiation." *International Journal of Organizational Theory and Behavior* 8, no. 2 (2005): 181–209.

Olson, Chester L. *Statistics: Making Sense of Data.* Boston, MA: Allyn and Bacon, 1987.

Online Dispute Resolution Advisory Group. "Online Dispute Resolution for Low Value Civil Claims." February 2015. https://www.judiciary.uk/wp-content/uploads/2015/02/Online-Dispute-Resolution-Final-Web-Version1.pdf.

Onwuamaegbu, Ucheora. "Limiting the Participation of Developed States: Impacts on Investor-State Arbitration." Investor-State Arbitration Series paper no. 11, September 2016. https://www.cigionline.org/sites/default/files/isa_paper_no.11_web.pdf.

Orentlicher, Diane F. "A Reply to Professor Nino." *Yale Law Journal* 100 (1991): 2641–44.

———. "Settling Accounts: The Duty to Punish Human Rights Violations of a Prior Regime." *Yale Law Journal* 100 (1991): 2537–615.

———. "'Settling Accounts' Revisited: Reconciling Global Norms with Local Agency." *International Journal of Transitional Justice* 1 (2007): 7–30.

Organization for Economic Cooperation and Development. "Conference on Empowering E-Consumers: Strengthening Consumer Protection in the Internet Economy; Background Report." December 2009. http://www.oecd.org/ict/econsumerconference/44047583.pdf.

———. "OECD Employment Outlook, 2017." June 13, 2017. http://dx.doi.org/10.1787/empl_outlook-2017-en.

———. "The Paris Declaration on Aid Effectiveness and the Accra Agenda for Action." http://www.oecd.org/dac/effectiveness/34428351.pdf (accessed June 21, 2019).

Ortega, Luisa Maria Dietrich. "Transitional Justice and Female Ex-Combatants: Lessons Learned from International Experience." In *Disarming the Past: Transitional Justice and Ex-Combatants*, edited by Ana Cutter Patel, Pablo de Grieff, and Lars Waldorf, 158–88. New York: Social Science Research Council, 2009.

Ortiz v. Fibreboard Corp. 527 U.S. 815 (1999).

Osi, Carlo. "Understanding Indigenous Dispute Resolution Processes and Western Alternative Dispute Resolution: Cultivating Culturally Appropriate Methods in Lieu of Litigation." *Cardozo Journal of Conflict Resolution* 10 (2008): 163–231.

Osmond, Michael, S. Airame, M. Caldwell, and J. Day. "Lessons for Marine Conservation Planning: A Comparison of Three Marine Protected Area Planning Processes." *Ocean and Coastal Management* 53 (2010): 41–51.

Ostrom, Elinor. "Collective Action and the Evolution of Social Norms." *Journal of Economic Perspectives* 14, no. 3 (2000): 137–58.

———. *Governing the Commons: The Evolution of Institutions for Collective Action.* Cambridge: Cambridge University Press, 1990.

———. *Understanding Institutional Diversity.* Princeton, NJ: Princeton University Press, 2005.

Pace University Elisabeth Haub School of Law. "Speaker Presentations." http://law.pace.edu/speaker-presentations (accessed June 23, 2019).

PacifiCare Health Systems, Inc. v. Book. 538 U.S. 401 (2003).

Palefsky, Cliff. "Mandatory Binding Arbitration: Is It Fair and Voluntary?" September 15, 2009. https://www.ca-employment-lawyers.com/Articles/MandatoryArbitrationTaskForce.NELA.Palefksy.pdf.

Panka, Brian. "Use of Neutral Fact-Finding to Preserve Exclusive Rights and Uphold the Disclosure Purpose of the Patent System." *Journal of Dispute Resolution* 2003, no. 2 (2003): 531–46.

Pardun, John. "How ADR Can Be Used to Resolve Mass Disaster and Insurance Claims." *International In-House Counsel Journal* 6, no. 23 (2013): 1–5.

Parker, Christine, and Vibeke Lehmann Nielsen, eds. *Explaining Compliance: Business Responses to Regulation.* Northampton, MA: Edward Elgar, 2011.

Parloff, Roger. "Steering Billions to Victims." *New York Times*, June 24, 2017, p. B1.

Parra, Antonio R. *The History of ICSID.* Oxford: Oxford University Press, 2017.

Partridge, Scott. "The Monsanto Case Study: A Practical Roadmap to Relationship-Based Conflict Resolution." Presentation to the International Institute for Conflict Prevention and Resolution, New York, February 15, 2016. https://slideplayer.com/slide/11714593.

Partridge, Scott, Jeremy Lack, and Debra Gerardi. "Session 2: Navigating, Building, and Strengthening Relationships." *Pepperdine Dispute Resolution Law Journal* 16, no. 2 (2016): 163–92.

Patel, Ana Cutter, Pablo de Grieff, and Lars Waldorf, eds. *Disarming the Past: Transitional Justice and Ex-Combatants.* New York: Social Science Research Council, 2009.

Penn, Ivan. "When Utilities Spark Wildfires." *New York Times*, June 15, 2018, p. B1.

Perry, James L. "Measuring Public Service Motivation: An Assessment of Construct Reliability and Validity." *Journal of Public Administration Research and Theory* 6 (1996): 1–28.

Peterson, Mark A. "Giving Away Money: Comparative Comments on Claims Resolution Facilities." *Law and Contemporary Problems* 53, no. 4 (1990): 113–36.

Pilkington, Ed. "Kenneth Feinberg Prepares to Put a Price on Trauma of Boston Bombings." *The Guardian*, April 26, 2013. https://www.theguardian.com/world/2013/apr/26/kenneth-feinberg-boston-bombings-trauma-compensation.

Pinter, Nicholas. "The New Flood Insurance Disaster." *New York Times*, August 29, 2013, p. A21.

Podziba, Susan. *Civic Fusion: Mediating Polarized Public Disputes.* Chicago: American Bar Association, 2012.

Posner, Richard A. *The Problems of Jurisprudence.* Cambridge, MA: Harvard University Press, 1990.

Press, Sharon. "Mortgage Foreclosure Mediation in Florida: Implementation Challenges for an Institutionalized Program." *Nevada Law Journal* 11, no. 2 (2011): 306–67.

Priest, George L. "The Problematic Structure of the September 11th Victim Compensation Fund." *DePaul Law Review* 53 (2003): 527–46.

Prima Paint Corp. v. Flood and Conklin Mfg. Co. 388 U.S. 395 (1967).

Primm, Edith. "The Neighbor Justice Center Movement." *Kentucky Law Journal* 81 (1993): 1067–83.

Pritzker, David M., and Deborah S. Dalton, eds. *The Negotiated Rulemaking Sourcebook.* Washington, DC: Administrative Conference of the United States, 1995.

Pruitt, Dean G. *Negotiation Behavior.* New York: Academic Press, 1981.

Pruitt, Dean G., and Peter J. Carnevale. *Negotiation in Social Conflict.* Ann Arbor, MI: Open University Press, 1993.

Pruitt, Dean G., Jeffrey Rubin, and Sung Hee Kim. *Social Conflict: Escalation, Stalemate, and Settlement.* 3rd ed. Boston, MA: McGraw-Hill, 2004.

Public Policy Lab. "About Us." http://public policylab.org/about-us (accessed May 20, 2019).

Purcell, Sheila. "Growing Mediation in Our Courts: Why and How One Court Made the Journey." *California Courts Review* 12 (Spring 2007): 12–19.

Quintanilla, Victor D. "Human-Centered Civil Justice Design." *Penn State Law Review* 121, no. 3 (2017): 745–806.

Quintanilla, Victor D., and Alexander B. Avtgis. "The Public Believes Predispute Binding Arbitration Clauses Are Unjust: Ethical Implications for Dispute-System Design in the Time of Vanishing Trials." *Fordham Law Review* 85 (2017): 2119–49.

Raab, Jonathan. "California Marine Life Protection Act: Evaluation of the Central Coast Regional Stakeholder Group Process." August 14, 2006. https://www.dfg.ca .gov/marine/pdfs/agenda_090606e.pdf.

———. "Report on Lessons Learned from the Marine Life Protection Act Initiative: North Central Coast Study Region." October 31, 2008. In the authors' possession.

———. *Using Consensus Building to Improve Utility Regulation.* Washington, DC: American Council for an Energy Efficient Economy, 1994.

Raab, Jonathan, and Lawrence Susskind. "New Approaches to Consensus Building and Speeding Up Large-Scale Energy Infrastructure Projects." Paper presented at Expansion of the German Transmission Grid, Gottingen University, Gottingen, Germany, June 23, 2009.

Rabin, Robert L. "Review of *What Is Life Worth? The Unprecedented Effort to Compensate the Victims of 9/11,* by Kenneth R. Feinberg." *Columbia Law Review* 106, no. 2 (2006): 479–82.

———. "The September 11th Victim Compensation Fund: A Circumscribed Response or an Auspicious Model?" *DePaul Law Review* 53, no. 2 (2003): 769–804.

———. "Some Thoughts on the Efficacy of a Mass Administrative Compensation Scheme." *Maryland Law Review* 52, no. 4 (1993): 951–82.

Rabinovich-Einy, Orna. "Escaping the Shadow of Malpractice Law." *Law and Contemporary Problems* 74 (Summer 2011): 241–78.

Rabinovich-Einy, Orna, and Ethan Katsh. "Blockchain and the Inevitability of Disputes: The Role for Online Dispute Resolution." *Journal of Dispute Resolution* 2019, no. 2 (2019): 47–75.

———. "A New Relationship Between Public and Private Dispute Resolution: Lessons from Online Dispute Resolution." *Ohio State Journal on Dispute Resolution* 32 (2017): 695–772.

Rackham, Neil, and John Carlisle. "The Effective Negotiator—Part I: The Behaviour of Successful Negotiators." *Journal of European Industrial Training* 2, no. 6 (1978): 6–11.

Rahim, M. Afzalur. *Managing Conflict in Organizations.* 4th ed. London: Routledge, 2017.

Raiffa, Howard. *The Art and Science of Negotiation.* Cambridge, MA: Belknap Press,
1982.

———. *Negotiation Analysis: The Science and
Art of Collaborative Decision Making.* Cambridge, MA: Belknap Press, 2007.

Rainey, Daniel. "Ethical Principles for ODR."
*International Journal of Online Dispute
Resolution* 4 (2017): 21–26.

Rawls, John. *A Theory of Justice.* Cambridge,
MA: Belknap Press, 1971.

Raz, Nicole. "Las Vegas Victims' Fund to
Distribute $31.4M to Victims in March."
Las Vegas Review-Journal, March 2, 2018.
https://www.reviewjournal.com/crime/
shootings/las-vegas-victims-fund-to
-distribute-31-4m-to-victims-in-march.

Reilly, Louise. "An Introduction to the Court
of Arbitration for Sport (CAS) and the Role
of National Courts in International Sports
Disputes." *Journal of Dispute Resolution* 63
(2012): 63–82.

Rent-a-Center, West, Inc. v. Jackson. 561 U.S.
63 (2010).

*The Report of the Iraq Inquiry: Report of a
Committee of Privy Counsellors.* London:
Her Majesty's Stationery Office, 2016.
http://webarchive.nationalarchives.gov.uk/
20171123122743/http://www.iraqinquiry.org
.uk/the-report.

Resnik, Judith. "The Contingency of Openness
in Courts: Changing the Experiences and
Logics of the Public's Role in Court-Based
ADR." *Nevada Law Journal* 15, no. 3 (2015):
1631–88.

———. "Diffusing Disputes: The Public in
the Private of Arbitration, the Private in
Courts, and the Erasure of Rights." *Yale
Law Journal* 124 (2015): 2804–939.

———. "Managerial Judges." *Harvard Law
Review* 96, no. 2 (1982): 374–448.

Reuben, Alan Miles, Frank Elkouri, and Edna
Asper Elkouri. *How Arbitration Works.*

Arlington, VA: Bureau of National Affairs,
2010.

Reuben, Richard C. "Process Purity and Innovation: Response to Professors Stempel,
Cole, and Drahozal." *Nevada Law Journal*
8, no. 1 (2007): 271–313.

Rhodes, Edwardo Lao. *Environmental Justice
in America: A New Paradigm.* Bloomington: Indiana University Press, 2003.

Richards, Kenneth, David Bach, and Robert K.
Fleming. "Golden Agri Resources and Sustainability." *Yale University Teaching Case
Study,* 2013. https://som.yale.edu/case/2013/
golden-agri-resources-and-sustainability.

Richards, Lara K., and Jason W. Burge.
"Analyzing the Applicability of Statutes of
Limitations in Arbitration." *Gonzaga Law
Review* 49, no. 2 (2013): 213–48.

Rinaker v. Superior Court. 62 Cal. App. 4th 155
(3d Dist. 1998).

Riskin, Leonard L. "Decision-Making in
Mediation: The Old Grid and the New Grid
System." *Notre Dame Law Review* 79, no. 1
(2003): 14–30.

———. "Understanding Mediators' Orientations, Strategies, and Techniques: A Grid
for the Perplexed." *Harvard Negotiation
Law Review* 7 (1996): 17–30.

Riskin, Leonard L., James E. Westbrook, Chris
Guthrie, Richard C. Reuben, Jennifer K.
Robbennolt, and Nancy A. Welsh. *Dispute
Resolution and Lawyers.* 4th ed. Eagan,
MN: West Academic, 2014.

Rittel, Horst W. J., and Melvin M. Webber.
"Dilemmas in General Theory of Plan-
ning." *Policy Sciences* 4, no. 2 (1973): 155–69.

Robbennolt, Jennifer K., and Jean R. Sternlight. *Psychology for Lawyers: Understanding the Human Factors in Negotiation,
Litigation, and Decision Making.* Chicago:
American Bar Association, 2012.

Robbins, Lee P., and William B. Deane. "The
Corporate Ombuds: A New Approach to

Conflict Management." *Negotiation Journal* 2, no. 2 (1986): 195–205.

Roberts, Nancy C., ed. *The Age of Direct Citizen Participation*. Armonk, NY: M. E. Sharpe, 2008.

Robertson, Campbell, and Clifford Krauss. "BP May Be Fined Up to $18 Billion for Spill in Gulf." *New York Times*, September 5, 2014, p. A1.

Roche, William K., Paul Teague, and Alexander J. S. Colvin, eds. *The Oxford Handbook of Conflict Management in Organizations*. Oxford: Oxford University Press, 2014.

Rodriguez, Daniel B., Mathew D. McCubbins, and Barry R. Weingast. "The Rule of Law Unplugged." *Emory Law Journal* 59 (2010): 1455–94.

Rogers, Catherine A. "Transparency in International Commercial Arbitration." *Kansas Law Review* 54 (2006): 1301–38.

Rogers, Nancy H. "When Conflicts Polarize Communities: Designing Localized Offices That Intervene Collaboratively." *Ohio State Journal on Dispute Resolution* 30, no. 2 (2015): 173–231.

Rogers, Nancy H., Robert C. Bordone, Frank E. A. Sander, and Craig A. McEwen. *Designing Systems and Processes for Managing Disputes*. 2nd ed. New York: Wolters Kluwer, 2019.

Rogers, Vikki. "Managing Disputes in the Online Global Marketplace." *Dispute Resolution Magazine* 19, no. 3 (2013): 20–24.

Rogge, Jacques. "IOC President Addresses Sports Ministers at First World Olympic Sport Convention." October 23, 2010. https://www.olympic.org/news/ioc -president-addresses-sports-ministers-at -first-world-olympic-sport-convention.

Roht-Arriaza, Naomi. "After Amnesties Are Gone: Latin American National Courts and the New Contours of the Fight Against Impunity." *Human Rights Quarterly* 37, no. 341 (2015): 341–82.

Roht-Arriaza, Naomi, and Javier Mariez-currena, eds. *Transitional Justice in the Twenty-First Century: Beyond Truth Versus Justice*. Cambridge: Cambridge University Press, 2006.

Rosenberg, Joshua D., and H. Jay Folberg. "Alternative Dispute Resolution: An Empirical Analysis." *Stanford Law Review* 46 (1994): 1487–551.

Rotberg, Robert I., and Dennis Thompson, eds. *Truth v. Justice: The Morality of Truth Commissions*. Princeton, NJ: Princeton University Press, 2000.

Rouillard-Labbe, Lindy. "Justice Among the Ashes: How Government Compensation Facilities Can Bring Justice to Disaster Victims." *Fordham International Law Journal* 38, no. 1 (2015): 245–97.

Rowe, Mary. "Dispute Resolution in the Non -union Environment: An Evolution Toward Integrated Systems for Conflict Management?" In *Workplace Dispute Resolution: Directions for the 21st Century*, edited by Sandra E. Gleason, 79–106. East Lansing: Michigan State University Press, 1997.

———. "Disputes and Conflicts Inside Organizations." *Negotiation Journal* 5, no. 2 (1989): 149–57.

———. "The Ombudsperson's Role in a Dispute Resolution System." *Negotiation Journal* 7 (1991): 353–72.

———. "An Organizational Ombuds Office in a System for Dealing with Conflict and Learning from Conflict." *Harvard Negotiation Law Review* 14 (2009): 279–89.

Rozdeiczer, Lukasz, and Alejandro Alvarez de la Campa. *Alternative Dispute Resolution Manual: Implementing Commercial Mediation*. Washington, DC: World Bank, 2006. http://documents.worldbank.org/ curated/en/922161468339057329/pdf/

384810ADR1Manu1l1Mediation01PUBLIC1
.pdf.

Rubin, Jeffrey, and Bert R. Brown. *The Social Psychology of Bargaining and Negotiation*. New York: Academic Press, 1975.

Rubin, Jeffrey, and Frank Sander. "Culture, Negotiation, and the Eye of the Beholder." *Negotiation Journal* 7 (1991): 249–63.

Rule, Colin. "Making Peace on eBay: Resolving Disputes in the World's Largest Marketplace." Speech to the Association for Conflict Resolution, Harvard Law School, Cambridge, MA, October 19, 2008.

———. *Online Dispute Resolution for Business: B2B, E-commerce, Consumer, Employment, Insurance, and Other Commercial Conflicts*. San Francisco, CA: Jossey-Bass, 2002.

Rule, Colin, Vikki Rogers, and Louis F. Del Duca. "Designing a Global Consumer Online Dispute Resolution (ODR) System for Cross-Border Small Value–High Volume Claims—OAS Developments." *Uniform Commercial Code Law Journal* 42, no. 3 (2010): 221–64.

Rule, Colin, and Mark Wilson. "Online Resolution and Citizen Empowerment: Property Tax Appeals in North America." In *Revolutionizing the Interaction Between State and Citizens Through Digital Communications*, edited by Sam B. Edwards III and Diogo Santos, 185–205. Hershey, PA: Information Science Reference, 2015.

Sabbeth, Kathryn A., and David C. Vladeck. "Contracting (out) Rights." *Fordham Urban Law Journal* 36, no. 4 (2009): 803–38.

Sager, Thomas L., and Richard L. Horwitz. "Early Case Assessment: DuPont's Experience." In *Successful Partnering Between Inside and Outside Counsel*, vol. 4, edited by Robert L. Haig, 19. Wilmington, DE: Potter, Anderson, Corroon, 2012.

Saipem S.p.A. v. The Peoples Republic of Bangladesh. ICSID case no. ARB/05/07, para 67 (March 21, 2007).

Salacuse, Jeswald. "The Emerging Global Regime for Investment." *Harvard International Law Journal* 51 (2010): 429–73.

———. *Making Global Deals*. New York: Random House, 1991.

Salamon, Lester, ed. *The Tools of Government: A Guide to the New Governance*. New York: Oxford University Press, 2002.

Salasky, Julia. "ODR Rulebook." Paper presented at 13th Annual Online Dispute Resolution Forum, Stanford Law School, Stanford, CA, June 26–28, 2014.

Salzwedel, Matthew R., and Devona Wells. "National Arbitration Forum Settlement with Minnesota Attorney General." *State AG Tracker* 1, no. 4 (2009). https://fedsoc-cms -public.s3.amazonaws.com/update/pdf/ RNhzz01Xy8MkGjKXRSlexfbd58K2EO0e9 LkJtwq5.pdf.

Sandel, Michael J. *Justice: What's the Right Thing to Do*. New York: Farrar, Straus and Giroux, 2009.

Sander, Frank E. A. "Varieties of Dispute Processing." In *The Pound Conference: Perspectives on Justice in the Future*, edited by A. Leo Levin and Russell R. Wheeler, 65–87. St. Paul, MN: West, 1979.

Sander, Frank, and Stephen Goldberg. "Fitting the Forum to the Fuss: A User-Friendly Guide to Selecting an ADR Procedure." *Negotiation Journal* 10 (1994): 49–68.

Sanders, Joseph, and Lee V. Hamilton, eds. *Handbook of Justice Research in Law*. Berlin: Springer, 2001.

Sandholtz, Wayne, and Mariana Rangel Padilla. "Law and Politics in the Inter-American System: The Amnesty Cases." *Journal of Law and Courts* 8, no. 1 (forthcoming).

Scanlon, Kathleen M., and International Institute for Conflict Prevention and Resolution. *Drafting Dispute Resolution Clauses: Better Solutions for Business*. Edited by Helena Tavares Erickson. New York: International Institute for Conflict Prevention and Resolution, 2006.

Schabas, William A. "The Sierra Leone Truth and Reconciliation Commission." In *Transitional Justice in the Twenty-First Century: Beyond Truth Versus Justice*, edited by Naomi Roht-Arriaza and Javier Mariezcurrena, 21–42. Cambridge: Cambridge University Press, 2006.

Schefer, Krista Nadakavukaren, ed. *Poverty and the International Economic Legal System*. Cambridge: Cambridge University Press, 2013.

Schelling, Thomas C. *The Strategy of Conflict*. Cambridge, MA: Harvard University Press, 1960.

Schmitz, Amy J., and Colin Rule. *The New Handshake: Online Dispute Resolution and the Future of Consumer Protection*. Chicago: ABA Press, 2017.

———. "Online Dispute Resolution for Smart Contracts." *Journal of Dispute Resolution* 2019, no. 2 (2019): 103–25.

Schneider, Andrea Kupfer. "How Does DSD Help Us Teach About Community Conflict (and How Can Community Conflict Help Illustrate DSD)?" *University of St. Thomas Law Journal* 13, no. 2 (2017): 370–80.

———. "The Intersection of Dispute Systems Design and Transitional Justice." *Harvard Negotiation Law Review* 14 (2009): 289–315.

———. "Shattering Negotiation Myths: Empirical Evidence on the Effectiveness of Negotiation Style." *Harvard Negotiation Law Review* 7 (2002): 143–233.

Schneider, Andrea Kupfer, and Natalie C. Fleury. "There's No Place Like Home: Applying Dispute Systems Design Theory to Create a Foreclosure Mediation System." *Nevada Law Journal* 11 (2011): 368–96.

Scholtz, John T., and Bruce Stiftel, eds. *Adaptive Governance and Water Conflict: New Institutions for Collaborative Planning*.

Washington, DC: Resources for the Future Press, 2005.

Schoonhoven, Ray J., ed. *Fairweather's Practice and Procedure in Labor Arbitration*. 3rd ed. Washington, DC: Bloomberg BNA, 1991.

Schroeder, Christopher H. "Corrective Justice and Liability for Increasing Risks." *University of California Los Angeles Law Review* 37 (1990): 439–78.

Schuck, Peter H. *Agent Orange on Trial: Mass Toxic Disasters in the Courts*. Cambridge, MA: Belknap Press, 1986.

———. "Mass Torts: An Institutional Evolutionist Perspective." *Cornell Law Review* 80, no. 4 (1995): 941–89.

Schwartz, David S. "State Judges as Guardians of Federalism: Resisting the Federal Arbitration Act's Encroachment on State Law." *Washington University Journal of Law and Policy* 16 (2004): 129–61.

Schwartz, Eric. "International Conciliation and the ICC." *ICSID Review—Foreign Investment Law Journal* 10, no. 1 (1995): 98–119.

Schwartz, John. "Man with $20 Billion to Disburse Finds No Shortage of Claims or Critics." *New York Times*, April 19, 2011, p. A1.

Schwartz, Roger M. *The Skilled Facilitator: A Comprehensive Resource for Consultants, Facilitators, Managers, Trainers, and Coaches*. 2nd ed. San Francisco, CA: Jossey-Bass, 2002.

Schwarz, Shalom H. *Beyond Individualism/Collectivism: New Cultural Dimension of Values*. Thousand Oaks, CA: Sage, 1994.

Schwebel, Stephen. "Is Mediation of Foreign Investment Disputes Plausible?" *ICSID Review—Foreign Investment Law Journal* 22 (2007): 237–41.

Scott, Robert E., and George G. Triantis. "Anticipating Litigation in Contract Design." *Yale Law Journal* 115 (2006): 814–79.

Scott-Clayton, Judith. "The Looming Student Loan Default Crisis Is Worse than We

Thought." Brookings, January 11, 2018. https://www.brookings.edu/research/the -looming-student-loan-default-crisis-is -worse-than-we-thought.

Scully, Patrick L., and Martha L. McCoy. "Study Circles: Local Deliberation as the Cornerstone of Deliberative Democracy." In *The Deliberative Democracy Handbook: Strategies for Effective Civic Engagement in the 21st Century*, edited by John Gastil and Peter Levine, 199–212. San Francisco, CA: Jossey-Bass, 2005.

"The Second Generation of Dispute System Design: Reoccurring Problems and Potential Solutions." Special issue, *Ohio State Journal on Dispute Resolution* 24 (2008).

Seils, Paul. "The Place of Reconciliation in Transitional Justice: Conceptions and Misconceptions." *ICTJ Briefing*, June 2017. https://www.ictj.org/sites/default/files/ICTJ -Briefing-Paper-Reconciliation-TJ-2017 .pdf.

Sela, Ayelet. "Can Computers Be Fair? How Automated and Human-Powered Online Dispute Resolution Affect Procedural Justice in Mediation and Arbitration." *Ohio State Journal on Dispute Resolution* 33 (2018): 91–148.

———. "The Effect of Online Technologies on Dispute Resolution System Design: Antecedents, Current Trends and Future Directions." *Lewis and Clark Law Review* 21 (2017): 635–83.

———. "e-Nudging Justice: The Role of Digital Choice Architecture in Online Courts." *Journal of Dispute Resolution* 2019, no. 2 (2019): 127–63.

Sen, Amartya. *The Idea of Justice*. Cambridge, MA: Belknap Press, 2009.

Seneca Nation of Indians. "Peacemaker's Court." https://sni.org/government/ peacemakers-court (accessed June 3, 2019).

Senge, Peter. *The Fifth Discipline: The Art and Practice of the Learning Organization*. New York: Doubleday, 1990.

Senger, Jeffrey M. *Federal Dispute Resolution: Using ADR with the United States Government*. San Francisco, CA: Jossey-Bass, 2003.

Shack, Jennifer, and Hanna Kaufman. "Promoting Access to Justice: Applying Lessons Learned from Foreclosure Mediation." *Dispute Resolution Magazine* 71 (Spring 2016): 16–20.

Shady Grove Orthopedic Assocs., P.A. v. Allstate Ins. Co. 130 S. Ct. 1431 (2010).

Shapiro, Debra L. "Reconciling Theoretical Differences among Procedural Justice Researchers by Re-evaluating What It Means to Have One's Views 'Considered': Implications for Third-Party Managers." In *Justice in the Workplace: Approaching Fairness in Human Resource Management*, edited by Russell Cropanzano, 51–78. Hillsdale, NJ: Lawrence Erlbaum, 1993.

Shapiro, Debra L., and Jeanne M. Brett. "Comparing Three Processes Underlying Judgments of Procedural Justice: A Field Study of Mediation and Arbitration." *Journal of Personality and Social Psychology* 65, no. 6 (1993): 1167–77.

Shapo, Marshall S. *Principles of Tort Law*. 3rd ed. St. Paul, MN: West Academic, 2010.

Shapo, Marshall S., and American Bar Association Special Committee on the Tort Liability System. *Towards a Jurisprudence of Injury: The Continuing Creation of a System of Substantive Justice in American Tort Law*. Chicago: American Bar Association, 1984.

Shariff, Khalil. "Designing Institutions to Manage Conflict: Principles for the Problem Solving Organization." *Harvard Negotiation Law Review* 8 (2003): 133–57.

Shaw, Rosalind, and Lars Waldorf, eds. *Localizing Transitional Justice: Interventions and*

Priorities after Mass Violence. Stanford, CA: Stanford University Press, 2010.

Shell, G. Richard. *Bargaining for Advantage.* 3rd ed. New York: Penguin, 2018.

Sheppard, Blair H., Roy J. Lewicki, and John W. Minton. *Organizational Justice: The Search for Fairness in the Workplace.* Lexington, MA: Lexington Press, 1992.

Shestowsky, Donna. "Disputants' Preferences for Court-Connected Dispute Resolution Procedures: Why We Should Care and Why We Know So Little." *Ohio State Journal on Dispute Resolution* 23 (2008): 549–626.

———. "How Litigants Evaluate the Characteristics of Legal Procedures: A Multi-court Empirical Study." *University of California Davis Law Review* 49 (2016): 793–841.

———. "Improving Summary Jury Trials: Insights from Psychology." *Ohio State Journal on Dispute Resolution* 18 (2003): 469–96.

———. "Inside the Mind of the Client: An Analysis of Litigants' Decision Criteria for Choosing Procedures." *Conflict Resolution Quarterly* 36, no. 1 (2018): 69–87.

———. "Misjudging: Implications for Dispute Resolution." *Nevada Law Journal* 7 (2007): 487–99.

———. "Procedural Preferences in Alternative Dispute Resolution: A Closer, Modern Look at an Old Idea." *Psychology, Public Policy, and Law* 10, no. 3 (2004): 211–43.

———. "The Psychology of Interpersonal Persuasion: Lessons for the Advanced Negotiator." In *The Negotiator's Fieldbook,* edited by Christopher Honeyman and Andrea Schneider, 361–70. Washington, DC: American Bar Association, 2006.

———. "The Psychology of Procedural Preference: How Litigants Evaluate Legal Procedures Ex Ante." *Iowa Law Review* 99 (2014): 637–710.

———. "When Ignorance Is Not Bliss: An Empirical Study of Litigants' Awareness of Court-Sponsored Alternative Dispute Resolution Programs." *Harvard Negotiation Law Review* 22 (Spring 2017): 189–239.

Shestowsky, Donna, and Jeanne M. Brett. "Disputants' Perceptions of Dispute Resolution Procedures: An Ex Ante and Ex Post Longitudinal Empirical Study." *Connecticut Law Review* 41 (2008): 63–107.

Shonholtz, Raymond. "Justice from Another Perspective: The Ideology and Developmental History of the Community Boards Program." In *The Possibility of Popular Justice,* edited by Sally Engle Merry and Neal Milner, 201–38. Ann Arbor: University of Michigan Press, 1993.

Shprintz, Janet. "John Schulman: Hollywood Law Impact Report." *Variety,* March 28, 2007, https://variety.com/2007/biz/markets-festivals/john-schulman-1117961951.

Sierra Martinez, Claudia. "Mexican Experience in Cases of International Child Abduction: Judicial Process vs Mediation." Paper presented at International Parental Child Abduction and Mediation in a Globalized World symposium, Stanford University, Stanford, CA, April 10, 2018.

Singapore International Arbitration Center. "The Singapore Arb-Med-Arb Clause." http://www.siac.org.sg/model-clauses/the-singapore-arb-med-arb-clause (accessed May 20, 2019).

Singh, Shilpa. "Analyzing Features of Investment Court System Under CETA and EUVIPA: Discussing Improvement in the System and Clarity to Clauses." *Kluwer Arbitration Blog,* February 8, 2019. http://arbitrationblog.kluwerarbitration.com/2019/02/08/analyzing-features-of-investment-court-system-under-ceta-and-euvipa-discussing-improvement-in-the-system-and-clarity-to-clauses.

Slaikeu, Karl, and Ralph H. Hasson. *Controlling the Costs of Conflict: How to Design a System for Your Organization*. San Francisco, CA: Jossey-Bass, 1998.

Smiley, Tavis, ed. *The Covenant with Black America: Ten Years Later*. Carlsbad, CA: SmileyBooks, 2016.

Smith, Stephanie E. "Comment: Trends and Challenges in Bringing Together ADR and Rule of Law." *Journal of Dispute Resolution* 2011, no. 1 (2011): 189–96.

Smith, Stephanie, and Janet Martinez. "An-alytic Framework for Dispute Systems Design." *Harvard Negotiation Law Review* 14 (Winter 2009): 123–69.

Society of Professionals in Dispute Resolution. "Designing Integrated Conflict Management Systems: Guidelines for Practitioners and Decision Makers in Organizations." January 1, 2001. http://digitalcommons.ilr.cornell.edu/icrpubs/2.

———. "Guidelines for the Design of Integrated Conflict Management Systems Within Organizations: Executive Summary." https://www.mediate.com/articles/spidrtrack1.cfm (accessed June 13, 2019).

Sohn, Dong-Won, and James A. Wall Jr. "Community Mediation in South Korea: A City-Village Comparison." *Journal of Conflict Resolution* 37 (1993): 536–43.

Solum, Lawrence B. "Procedural Justice." *Southern California Law Review* 78 (2004): 181–224.

Sperfeldt, Christoph. "Collective Reparations at the Extraordinary Chambers in the Courts of Cambodia." *International Criminal Law Review* 12 (2012): 457–72.

Stallworth, Lamont, Arup Varma, and John T. Delaney. "The NLRB's Unfair Labor Practice Settlement Program: An Empirical Analysis of Participant Satisfaction." *Dispute Resolution Journal* 59, no. 4 (2004–2005): 16–29.

Stanford Law School. "Community-Led System Design." https://law.stanford.edu/courses/community-led-system-design (accessed May 20, 2019).

St. Antoine, Theodore J., ed. *The Common Law of the Workplace: The Views of Arbitrators*. 2nd ed. Washington, DC: BNA, 2005.

State of Nevada Foreclosure Mediation Program. "Foreclosure Mediation Factsheet." https://www.scribd.com/document/46273434/Nevada-Foreclosure-Mediation-Program-Factsheet (accessed July 2, 2019).

Staton, Jeffrey K. "A Comment on the Rule of Law Unplugged." *Emory Law Journal* 59 (2010): 1495–514.

Stedman, Barbara Epstein. "A Multi-option System Helps Get to the Bottom of 'Big Dig' Conflicts." *Negotiation Journal* 15, no. 1 (1999): 5–10.

Steffek, Felix, Hannes Unberath, Hazel Genn, Reinhard Greger, and Carrie Menkel-Meadow, eds. *Regulating Dispute Resolution: ADR and Access to Justice at the Crossroads*. Oxford: Hart, 2013.

Steinberg, Robin, and Skylar Albertson. "Broken Windows Policing and Community Courts: An Unholy Alliance." *Cardozo Law Review* 37 (2016): 995–1024.

Stern, Alissa J., and Tim Hicks. *The Process of Business/Environmental Collaborations: Partnering for Sustainability*. Westport, CT: Quorum Books, 2000.

Sternlight, Jean R. "Is Alternative Dispute Resolution Consistent with the Rule of Law? Lessons from Abroad." *DePaul Law Review* 56 (2007): 569–84.

———. "Mandatory Arbitration Stymies Progress Towards Justice in Employment Law: Where to, #MeToo?" *Harvard Civil Rights–Civil Liberties Law Review* 54 (2019): 1–51.

Stewart, Richard B. "U.S. Administrative Law: A Model for Global Administrative Law?"

Law and Contemporary Problems 68, nos. 3–4 (2005): 63–108.

Stienstra, Donna. "ADR in the Federal District Courts: An Initial Report." Federal Judicial Center, November 16, 2011. https://www.fjc .gov/sites/default/files/2012/ADR2011.pdf.

Stienstra, Donna, Molly Johnson, and Patricia Lombard. "Report to the Judicial Conference Committee on Court Administration and Case Management: A Study of the Five Demonstration Programs Established Under the Civil Justice Report Act of 1990." January 24, 1997. https://www.fjc.gov/sites/ default/files/2012/0024.pdf.

Stiglitz, Joseph E. "Regulating Multinational Corporations: Towards Principles of Cross-Border Legal Frameworks in a Globalized World Balancing Rights with Responsibilities." *American University International Law Review* 23 (2008): 452–66.

Stipanowich, Thomas J. "Arbitration: The New Litigation." *University of Illinois Law Review* 2010, no. 1 (2010): 1–60.

———. "The Arbitration Fairness Index: Using a Public Rating System to Skirt the Legal Logjam and Promote Fairer and More Effective Arbitration of Employment and Consumer Disputes." *Kansas Law Review* 60 (2012): 985–1069.

———. "The Third Arbitration Trilogy: *Stolt-Nielsen, Rent-A-Center, Concepcion* and the Future of American Arbitration." *American Review of International Arbitration* 22 (2011): 323–434.

Stipanowich, Thomas J., and J. Ryan Lamare. "Living with ADR: Evolving Perceptions and Use of Mediation, Arbitration, and Conflict Management in Fortune 1000 Corporations." *Harvard Negotiation Law Review* 19, no. 1 (2014): 1–68.

Stover, Eric, and Harvey M. Weinstein. *My Neighbor, My Enemy: Justice and Community in the Aftermath of Mass Atrocity.*

Cambridge: Cambridge University Press, 2004.

Strandell v. Jackson County. 838 F.2d 884 (7th Cir. 1987).

Strasburg, Jenny. "Workers Fight Lawsuit Waiver; Justices Will Decide Whether Employers Can Force Mandatory Arbitration on Hires." *San Francisco Examiner*, May 31, 2000, p. C1.

Strassel, Kimberley A. "Mr. Fairness." *Wall Street Journal*, August 7, 2011, p. A11.

Strong, S. I. "Limits of Procedural Choice of Law." *Brooklyn Journal of International Law* 39, no. 3 (2014): 1027–122.

———. "The Role of Empirical Research and Dispute System Design in Proposing and Developing International Treaties: A Case Study of the Singapore Convention on Mediation." *Cardozo Journal of Conflict Resolution* 20 (forthcoming).

Strong, Suzanne M., Ramona R. Rantala, and Tracey Kyckelhahn. "Census of Problem-Solving Courts, 2012." *Bureau of Justice Statistics Bulletin*, September 2016. https:// www.bjs.gov/content/pub/pdf/cpsc12.pdf.

Studdert, David M., Michelle M. Mello, Atul A. Gawande, Tejal K. Gandhi, Allen Kachalia, Catherine Yoon, Ann Louise Puopolo, and Troyen A. Brennan. "Claims, Errors, and Compensation Payments in Medical Malpractice Litigation." *New England Journal of Medicine* 354, no. 19 (2006): 2014–33.

Stulberg, Joseph B. "Mediation and Justice: What Standards Govern?" *Cardozo Journal of Conflict Resolution* 6 (2005): 213–45.

———. "Procedural Justice, Legitimacy, and the Effective Rule of Law." *Crime and Justice* 30 (2003): 283–357.

———. "The Theory and Practice of Mediation: A Reply to Professor Susskind." *Vermont Law Review* 6, no. 1 (1981): 85–118.

Sugarman, Stephen D. *Doing Away with Personal Injury Law: New Compensation*

Mechanisms for Victims, Consumers, and Business. Westport, CT: Quorum Books, 1989.

Superior Court of California. "The Multi-option ADR Project: Evaluation Report, July 2007–July 2008." January 2009. https://www.sanmateocourt.org/documents/adr/2007_2008_evaluation_report.pdf.

Supreme Court of England and Wales County Courts. "The Civil Procedure Rules, 1998." March 12, 2014. http://www.wipo.int/edocs/lexdocs/laws/en/gb/gb317en.pdf.

Susskind, Lawrence. "Can Public Policy Dispute Resolution Meet the Challenges Set by Deliberative Democracy?" *Dispute Resolution Magazine* 12 (2006): 5–6.

———. "Deliberative Democracy and Dispute Resolution." *Ohio State Journal on Dispute Resolution* 24, no. 3 (2009): 395–406.

———. "Environmental Mediation and the Accountability Problem." *Vermont Law Review* 6, no. 1 (1981): 1–49.

———. "Make Compensatory Payments in the Gulf Coast NOW!" *Consensus Building Approach* (blog), June 2, 2010 http://theconsensusbuildingapproach.blogspot.com/search?q=gulf+coast+now.

———. *Using Assisted Negotiation to Settle Land Use Disputes: A Guidebook for Public Officials*. Cambridge, MA: Lincoln Institute of Land Policy, 1999.

Susskind, Lawrence, Alejandro E. Camacho, and Todd Schenk. "A Critical Assessment of Collaborative Adaptive Management in Practice." *Journal of Applied Ecology* 49, no. 1 (2011): 47–51.

Susskind, Lawrence S., and Jeffrey L. Cruik-shank. *Breaking Robert's Rules: The New Way to Run Your Meeting, Build Consensus, and Get Results*. New York: Oxford University Press, 2006.

Susskind, Lawrence, and Larry Crump. *Multiparty Negotiation*. Vol. 2, *Theory and*

Practice of Public Dispute Resolution. Los Angeles: Sage, 2008.

Susskind, Lawrence, and Michele Ferenz. "'Good Offices' in a War-Weary World: A Review of the Practice and Promise of Track One and a Half Diplomacy." Harvard Law School Program on Negotiation working paper 01-1, 2001.

Susskind, Lawrence, Patrick Field, and Mieke van der Wansem. "Integrating Scientific Information, Stakeholder Interests, and Political Concerns in Resource and Environmental Planning and Management." In *Fostering Integration: Concepts and Practiced in Resource and Environmental Management*, edited by Kevin S. Hanna and D. Scott Slocombe, 181–203. Cambridge: Oxford University Press, 2005.

Susskind, Lawrence, Sarah McKearnan, and Jennifer Thomas-Larmer. *The Consensus Building Handbook: A Comprehensive Guide to Reaching Agreement*. Thousand Oaks, CA: Sage, 1999.

Susskind, Lawrence, and Gerard McMahon. "The Theory and Practice of Negotiated Rulemaking." *Yale Journal on Regulation* 3, no. 1 (1985): 133–48.

Susskind, Noah G. "Wiggle Room: Rethinking Reservation Values in Negotiation." *Ohio State Journal on Dispute Resolution* 26, no. 1 (2011): 79–117.

Sviridoff, Michele, David B. Rottman, Brian Ostrom, and Richard Curtis. *Dispensing Justice Locally: The Implementation and Effects of the Midtown Community Court*. Amsterdam: Harwood Academic, 2000.

"Systems Design: Organizational Systems for Dealing with Conflict and Learning from Conflict Ideas." Special issue, *Harvard Negotiation Law Review* 14 (2009).

Szalai, Imre S. "A Constitutional Right to Discovery? Creating and Reinforcing Due Process Norms Through the Procedural

Laboratory of Arbitration." *Pepperdine Dispute Resolution Law Journal* 15 no. 2 (2015): 337–75.

———. "Exploring the Federal Arbitration Act Through the Lens of History." *Journal of Dispute Resolution* 2016, no. 1 (2016): 115–40.

———. *Outsourcing Justice: The Rise of Modern Arbitration Laws in America.* Durham, NC: Carolina Academic Press, 2016.

Szmania, Susan J., Addie M. Johnson, and Margaret Mulligan. "Alternative Dispute Resolution in Medical Malpractice: A Survey of Emerging Trends and Practices." *Conflict Resolution Quarterly* 26, no. 1 (2008): 71–96.

Talesh, Shauhin A. "How Dispute Resolution System Design Matters: An Organizational Analysis of Dispute Resolution Structures and Consumer Lemon Laws." *Law and Society Review* 46, no. 3 (2012): 463–96.

Tanaka, Yoshifumi. *The International Law of the Sea.* 2nd ed. Cambridge: Cambridge University Press, 2015.

Teitel, Ruti G. *Globalizing Transitional Justice: Contemporary Essays.* New York: Oxford University Press, 2014.

———. *Transitional Justice.* New York: Oxford University Press, 2000.

Thaler, Richard H., and Cass Sunstein. *Nudge: Improving Decisions About Health, Wealth, and Happiness.* New York: Penguin Books, 2009.

Thibaut, John W., and Laurens Walker. *Procedural Justice: A Psychological Analysis.* Mahwah, NJ: Lawrence Erlbaum, 1975.

———. "A Theory of Procedure." *California Law Review* 66 (1978): 541–67.

Thompson, Leigh L., and Brian J. Lucas. "Judgmental Biases in Conflict Resolution and How to Overcome Them." In *The Handbook of Conflict Resolution: Theory and Practice*, 3rd ed., edited by Peter T.

Coleman, Morton Deutsch, and Eric C. Marcus, 255–82. San Francisco: Jossey-Bass, 2014.

Thoms, Oskar N. T., James Ron, and Roland Paris. "State-Level Effects of Transitional Justice: What Do We Know?" *International Journal of Transitional Justice* 4 (2010): 329–54.

Tinsley, Catherine H. "Models of Conflict Resolution in Japanese, German, and American Cultures." *Journal of Applied Psychology* 83, no. 2 (1998): 316–23.

Tinsley, Catherine H., Jared Curhan, and Ro Sung Kwak. "Adopting a Dual Lens Approach for Examining the Dilemma of Differences in International Business Negotiations." *International Negotiations* 4, no. 1 (1999): 5–22.

Tjosvold, Dean. "The Conflict-Positive Organization: It Depends upon Us." *Journal of Organizational Behavior* 29, no. 1 (2008): 19–28.

Torres, Lars Hasselblad. *Deliberative Democracy: A Survey of the Field.* Washington, DC: AmericaSpeaks, 2003.

Trans Atlantic Consumer Dialogue. "Alternative Dispute Resolution in the Context of Electronic Commerce." February 2000. https://tacd.org/wp-content/uploads/2013/09/TACD-ECOM-12-00-Alternative-Dispute-Resolution-in-the-Context-of-Electronic-Commerce.pdf.

Traum, Lara, and Brian Farkas. "The History and Legacy of the Pound Conferences." *Cardozo Journal of Dispute Resolution* 18, no. 3 (2017): 677–98.

Travers, Timothy E. Annotation, "Arbiter's Power to Award Punitive Damages." 83 A.L.R.3d 1037 (1978).

Tribal Law and Policy Institute. "Tribal Healing to Wellness Courts: The Key Components." April 2003. https://www.ncjrs.gov/pdffiles1/bja/188154.pdf.

Tulis, Benjamin A. "Final-Offer 'Baseball' Arbitration: Context, Mechanics, and Applications." *Seton Hall Journal of Sports and Entertainment Law* 20, no. 1 (2010): 86–130.

Tyler, Tom R. "The Psychology of Legitimacy: A Relational Perspective on Voluntary Deference to Authorities." *Personality and Social Psychology Review* 1, no. 4 (1997): 323–45.

———. "The Psychology of Procedural Justice: A Test of the Group Value Model." *Journal of Personality and Social Psychology* 57 (1989): 830–38.

———. "The Quality of Dispute Resolution Processes and Outcome: Measurement Problems and Possibilities." *University of Denver Law Review* 66, no. 3 (1989): 419–36.

———. "What Is Procedural Justice? Criteria Used by Citizens to Assess the Fairness of Legal Procedures." *Law and Society Review* 22, no. 1 (1988): 128–42.

———. *Why People Obey the Law*. Princeton, NJ: Princeton University Press, 2006.

Tyler, Tom R., and Robert J. Bies. "Beyond Formal Procedures: The Interpersonal Context of Procedural Justice." In *Applied Social Psychology and Organizational Settings*, edited by John S. Carroll, 77–98. Hillsdale, NJ: Lawrence Erlbaum, 1990.

Tyler, Tom R., and E. Allan Lind. "Procedural Justice." In *Handbook of Justice Research in Law*, edited by Joseph Sanders and Lee V. Hamilton, 65–92. Berlin: Springer, 2001.

———. "A Relational Model of Authority in Groups." *Advances in Experimental Social Psychology* 25 (1992): 115–91.

Udall Foundation. "U.S. Institute for Environmental Conflict Resolution." http://www.udall.gov/OurPrograms/Institute/Institute.aspx (accessed June 30, 2019).

———. "U.S. Institute for Environmental Conflict Resolution: Find a Mediator or Facilitator." https://www.udall.gov/ OurPrograms/Institute/FindMediator Facilitator.aspx (accessed June 30, 2019).

Umbreit, Mark S. *The Handbook of Victim-Offender Mediation: An Essential Guide to Practice and Research*. San Francisco, CA: Jossey-Bass, 2000.

Umbreit, Mark S., Robert B. Coates, and Betty Vos. "Victim-Offender Mediation: Three Decades of Practice and Research." *Conflict Resolution Quarterly* 22, nos. 1–2 (2004): 279–304.

Uniform Law Commission. "Collaborative Law Act." 2010. https://www.uniformlaws.org/committees/community-home?CommunityKey=fdd1de2f-baea-42d3-bc16-a33d74438eaf.

Uniform Law Commission. "2001 Mediation Act." https://www.uniformlaws.org/committees/community-home?CommunityKey=45565a5f-0c57-4bba-bbab-fc7de9a59110 (accessed May 30, 2019).

Uniform Law Commission. "Uniform Mediation Act." 2003. https://www.uniformlaws.org/viewdocument/final-act-no-comments-45?CommunityKey=45565a5f-0c57-4bba-bbab-fc7de9a59110&tab=librarydocuments.

United Nations. "Guidance Note of the Secretary-General: United Nations Approach to Transitional Justice." March 2010. https://www.un.org/ruleoflaw/files/TJ_Guidance_Note_March_2010FINAL.pdf.

———. "Special Court for Sierra Leone Faces Funding Crisis, as Charles Taylor Trial Gets Under Way, Security Council Told Today in Briefing by Court's Senior Officials." June 8, 2007. https://www.un.org/press/en/2007/sc9037.doc.htm.

———. "UN Charter." October 24, 1945. https://www.un.org/en/sections/un-charter/un-charter-full-text.

United Nations Commission on International Trade Law. "Origin, Mandate and

Composition of UNCITRAL." http://www
.uncitral.org/uncitral/en/about/origin.html
(accessed June 23, 2019).

———. "UNCITRAL Technical Notes on
Online Dispute Resolution." April 2017.
http://www.uncitral.org/pdf/english/texts/
odr/V1700382_English_Technical_Notes
_on_ODR.pdf.

———. "United Nations Convention on International Settlement Agreements Resulting
from Mediation." http://www.uncitral
.org/pdf/english/commissionsessions/51st
-session/Annex_I.pdf (accessed June 23,
2019).

———. "United Nations Convention on Transparency in Treaty-Based Investor-State
Arbitrator." December 10, 2014. http://www
.uncitral.org/uncitral/en/uncitral_texts/
arbitration/2014Transparency_Convention
.html.

United Nations Commission on Trade and
Development. *Investor-State Disputes:
Prevention and Alternatives to Arbitration.*
New York: United Nations, 2010. http://
unctad.org/en/docs/diaeia200911_en.pdf.

———. "Most Recent IIAs." http://investment
policyhub.unctad.org/IIA (accessed June
22, 2019).

United Nations General Assembly. "Basic
Principles and Guidelines on the Right to
a Remedy and Reparation for Victims of
Gross Violations of International Human
Rights Law and Serious Violations of International Humanitarian Law." December 16,
2005. http://www.un.org/ga/search/view
_doc.asp?symbol=A/RES/60/147.

———. "Report of Working Group II (Dispute
Settlement) on the Work of Its Sixty-
Seventh Session (Vienna, 2–6 October
2017)." October 11, 2017. https://documents
-dds-ny.un.org/doc/UNDOC/GEN/V17/
072/79/PDF/V1707279.pdf?.

———. "Report of Working Group III (Online
Dispute Resolution) on the Work of Its

Thirty-Second Session (Vienna, 30 November–4 December 2015)." December 16, 2015.
https://documents-dds-ny.un.org/doc/
UNDOC/GEN/V15/089/16/PDF/V1508916
.pdf?OpenElement.

———. "Transforming Our World: The 2030
Agenda for Sustainable Development."
September 25, 2015. http://www.un.org/en/
development/desa/population/migration/
generalassembly/docs/globalcompact/A
_RES_70_1_E.pdf.

United Nations Security Council. "Resolution
1820." June 19, 2008. https://www.un.org/
ruleoflaw/files/women_peace_security
_resolution1820.pdf.

United States Courts. "Table C-4: U.S. District
Courts—Civil Cases Terminated, by Nature
of Suit and Action Taken, During the
12-Month Period Ending March 31, 2019."
2019. https://www.uscourts.gov/statistics/
table/c-4/federal-judicial-caseload
-statistics/2019/03/31.

United Steelworkers of Am. v. Am. Mfg. Co.
363 U.S. 564 (1960).

United Steelworkers of Am. v. Enter. Wheel
and Car Corp. 363 U.S. 593 (1960).

United Steelworkers v. Warrior and Gulf Navigation Co. 363 U.S. 574 (1960).

Ury, William. *Getting Past No: Negotiating
with Difficult People.* New York: Bantam
Books, 1991.

Ury, William L., Jeanne M. Brett, and Stephen
B. Goldberg. *Getting Disputes Resolved: De-
signing Systems to Cut the Costs of Conflict.*
San Francisco, CA: Jossey-Bass, 1988.

U.S. Department of Justice Community
Relations Service. "What We Do." February
14, 2017. https://www.justice.gov/crs/what
-we-do.

U.S. Department of State. "Chile 2017 Human
Rights Report." https://cl.usembassy
.gov/wp-content/uploads/sites/104/Chile
-Human-Rights-Report-2017.pdf (accessed
October 14, 2019).

———. "Post Conflict Reconstruction Essentials Tasks Matrix." April 1, 2005. http:// 2001-2009.state.gov/s/crs/rls/52959.htm.

U.S. District Court–Northern District of California. "ADR Local Rules." May 1, 2018. http://www.cand.uscourts.gov/localrules/ ADR.

———. "ADR Program Report: Fiscal Year 2018." https://www.cand.uscourts.gov/adr/ annualreports (accessed May 30, 2019).

———. "Alternative Dispute Resolution." https://www.cand.uscourts.gov/adr (accessed February 23, 2019).

———. "Alternative Dispute Resolution Procedures Handbook." May 2018. https://www .cand.uscourts.gov/adr/adr-handbook.

U.S. District Court–Northern District of Ohio. "In re National Prescription Opiate Litigation: Transcript of Proceedings." January 9, 2019. http://psych-history.weill.cornell.edu/ pdf/Polster%20Transcript.pdf.

U.S. General Accounting Office. "Equal Employment Opportunity: Complaint Caseloads Rising, with Effects of New Regulations on Future Trends Unclear." August 16, 1999. https://www.gao.gov/assets/230/ 227882.pdf.

———. "Equal Employment Opportunity: Rising Trends in EEO Complaint Caseloads in the Federal Sector." July 24, 1998. https:// www.gao.gov/archive/1998/gg98157b.pdf.

Vairo, Georgene M. "The Dalkon Shield Claimants Trust: Paradigm Lost (or Found)?" *Fordham Law Review* 61, no. 3 (1992): 617–60.

van de Merwe, Hugo, Victoria Baxter, and Audrey R. Chapman. *Assessing the Impact of Transitional Justice: Challenges for Empirical Research.* Washington, DC: United States Institute of Peace Press, 2009.

van den Bos, Kees. "Uncertainty Management: The Influence of Uncertainty Salience on Reactions to Perceived Procedural Fairness." *Journal of Personality and Social Psychology* 80 (2001): 931–41.

van den Bos, Kees, and Allan Lind. "Uncertainty Management by Means of Fairness Judgments." *Advances in Experimental Social Psychology* 34 (2002): 1–59.

van den Bos, Kees, Henk A. M. Wilke, E. Allan Lind, and Riel Vermunt. "Evaluating Outcomes by Means of the Fair Process Effect: Evidence for Different Processes in Fairness and Satisfaction Judgments." *Journal of Personality and Social Psychology* 74, no. 6 (1998): 1493–503.

van den Wyngaert, Christine. "Victims Before International Criminal Courts: Some Views and Concerns of an ICC Trial Judge." *Case Western Reserve Journal of International Law* 44 (2011): 475–96.

van der Meer, Frits M., Jos C. N. Raadschelders, and Theo A. J. Toonen, eds. *Comparative Civil Service Systems in the 21st Century.* 2nd ed. New York: Palgrave Macmillan, 2015.

Van Loo, Rory. "The Corporation as Courthouse." *Yale Journal on Regulation* 33 (2016): 547–602.

Van Soye, Scott C. "Illusory Ethics: Legal Barriers to an Ombudsman's Compliance with Accepted Ethical Standards." *Pepperdine Dispute Resolution Law Journal* 8 (2007): 117–46.

Ver Ploeg, Christine D. "Pay Equity in Interest Arbitration." *William Mitchell Law Review* 27, no. 2 (2000): 811–39.

Ver Steegh, Nancy, Gabrielle Davis, and Loretta Frederick. "Look Before You Leap: Court System Triage of Family Law Cases Involving Intimate Partner Violence." *Marquette Law Review* 95 (2012): 955–91.

Vidmar, Neil, and Jeffrey Rice. "Jury-Determined Settlements and Summary Jury Trials: Observations About Alternative Dispute Resolution in an Adversary Culture." *Florida State University Law Review* 19 (1991): 89–104.

Villarreal, P. D. "Unnecessary Litigation: A System Flaw—GE Launches Zero Defect Campaign." *Metropolitan Corporate Counsel Annual Index* 7, no. 8 (1999): 1–36.

von Bertalanffy, Ludwig. "An Outline of General Systems Theory." *British Journal for the Philosophy of Science* 1 (1950): 134–65.

von Neumann, John, and Oskar Morgenstern. *Theory of Games and Economic Behavior*. Princeton, NJ: Princeton University Press, 1944.

Wahab, Mohamed Abdel, Ethan Katsh, and Daniel Rainey, eds. *Online Dispute Resolution: Theory and Practice: A Treatise on Technology and Dispute Resolution*. The Hague: Eleven International, 2012.

Waldman, Ellen A. "The Evaluative-Facilitative Debate in Mediation: Applying the Lens of Therapeutic Jurisprudence." *Marquette Law Review* 82, no. 1 (1998): 155–70.

———. "Identifying the Role of Social Norms in Mediation: A Multiple Model Approach." *Hastings Law Journal* 48, no. 4 (1998): 703–69.

Waldorf, Lars. "'Like Jews Waiting for Jesus': Posthumous Justice in Post-genocide Rwanda." In *Localizing Transitional Justice: Interventions and Priorities After Mass Violence*, edited by Rosalind Shaw and Lars Waldorf, 183–202. Stanford, CA: Stanford University Press, 2010.

Walker, Tracey. "Advocacy with Compassion: Dorothy Tarrant's Role as Healthcare Ombudsman/Mediator Places Her at the Nexus of Patient-Provider Interaction." *Managed Health Care Executive*, June 1, 2006, pp. 34–36.

Wall, James A. "Community Mediation in China and Korea: Some Similarities and Differences." *Harvard Negotiation Journal* 9 (1993): 141–53.

Wall, James A., Jr., Michael Blum, Ronda Roberts Callister, Nam-Hyeon Kim, and Dong-Won Sohn. "Mediation in the USA, China, Japan and Korea." *Security Dialogue* 29 (1998): 235–48.

Wall, James A., Jr. and Ronda Roberts Callister. "Malaysian Community Mediation." *Journal of Conflict Resolution* 43 (1999): 343–65.

Wall, James A., Jr., John B. Stark, and Rhetta L. Standifer. "Mediation: A Current Review and Theory Development." *Journal of Conflict Resolution* 45, no. 3 (2001): 370–91.

Walton, Richard, and Robert McKersie. *A Behavioral Theory of Labor Negotiations: An Analysis of a Social Interaction System*. New York: McGraw-Hill, 1965.

Wardhaugh, Bruce. "Unveiling Fairness for the Consumer: The Law, Economics and Justice of Expanded Arbitration." *Loyola Consumer Law Review* 26 (2014): 42–69.

Ware, Stephen J. "Employment Arbitration and Voluntary Consent." *Hofstra Law Review* 25, no. 1 (1996): 83–163.

Warters, William C. *Mediation in the Campus Community: Designing and Managing Effective Programs*. San Francisco, CA: Jossey-Bass, 2000.

Washington State Department of Labor and Industries. "Workplace Violence." https://www.lni.wa.gov/Safety/Research/OccHealth/workVio/default.asp#Resources (accessed September 26, 2019).

Wehr, Paul. *Conflict Regulation*. Boulder, CO: Westview Press, 1979.

Weidenmaier, W. Mark C. "Customized Procedure in Theory and Reality." *Washington and Lee Law Review* 72, no. 4 (2015): 1865–946.

Weil, David. *The Fissured Workplace: Why Work Became So Bad for So Many and What Can Be Done to Improve It*. Cambridge, MA: Harvard University Press, 2014.

Weinstein, Jack B. *Individual Justice in Mass Tort Litigation.* Evanston, IL: Northwestern University Press, 1995.

Weir, Richard. "One Fund's Second Act 'Uncharted Territory.'" *Boston Herald,* September 12, 2013. http://bostonherald.com/news_opinion/local_coverage/2013/09/one_fund_s_second_act_uncharted_territory.

Weisbord, Marvin R. "Organizational Diagnosis: Six Places to Look for Trouble With or Without a Theory." *Group and Organization Studies* 1, no. 4 (1976): 430–47.

Weller, Christian E., ed. *Inequality, Uncertainty, and Opportunity: The Varied and Growing Role of Finance in Labor Relations.* Champaign, IL: Labor and Employment Relations Association, 2015.

Welsh, Nancy A. "Class Action–Barring Mandatory Pre-dispute Consumer Arbitration Clauses: An Example." *University of St. Thomas Law Journal* 13, no. 2 (2017): 381–433.

———. "The Current Transitional State of Court-Connected ADR." *Marquette Law Review* 95 (2012): 873–86.

———. "Dispute Resolution Neutrals' Ethical Obligation to Support Measured Transparency." *Oklahoma Law Review* 71, no. 3 (2019): 823–84.

———. "I Could Have Been a Contender: Summary Jury Trial as a Means to Overcome Iqbal's Negative Effects upon Pre-litigation Communication, Negotiation and Early, Consensual Dispute Resolution." *Penn State Law Review* 114 (2010): 1149–89.

———. "Magistrate Judges, Settlements, and Procedural Justice." *Nevada Law Journal* 16 (2016): 983–1060.

———. "Mandatory Predispute Consumer Arbitration, Structural Bias, and Incentivizing Procedural Safeguards." *Southwestern Law Review* 42 (2013): 187–228.

———. "Perceptions of Fairness." In *The Negotiator's Fieldbook: The Desk Reference for the Experienced Negotiator,* edited by Christopher Honeyman and Andrea Kupfer Schneider, 165–74. Washington, DC: American Bar Association, 2006.

———. "Stepping Back Through the Looking Glass: Real Conversations with Real Disputants About Institutionalized Mediation and Its Value." *Ohio State Journal on Dispute Resolution* 19, no. 2 (2004): 573–678.

———. "Theory and Reality in Regulating Dispute Resolution." *Dispute Resolution Magazine* 20, no. 4 (2014): 22–25.

———. "The Thinning Vision of Self-Determination in Court-Connected Mediation: The Inevitable Price of Institutionalization?" *Harvard Negotiation Law Review* 6, no. 1 (2001): 1–96.

Welsh, Nancy A., and Bobbi McAdoo. "Look Before You Leap and Keep on Looking: Lessons from the Institutionalization of Court-Connected Mediation." *Nevada Law Journal* 5 (2004–2005): 399–432.

West, Darrell M. *Billionaires: Reflections on the Upper Crust.* Washington, DC: Brookings Institution Press, 2014.

Weston, David C., and G. Edward Gibson Jr. "Partnering-Project Performance in U.S. Army Corps of Engineers." *Journal of Management Engineering* 9, no. 4 (1993): 410–25.

Wheeler, Michael A., and Gillian Morris. "GE's Early Dispute Resolution Initiative (A)." Harvard Business School case HBS 9801395-E, June 19, 2001.

Wholey, Joseph S., Harry P. Hatry, and Kathryn E. Newcomer. *The Handbook of Practical Program Evaluation.* San Francisco, CA: Jossey-Bass, 2004.

Williams, Preston M. "Comments on 'The Ethics of Intervention in Community Disputes.'" In *The Ethics of Social Intervention,* edited by Gordon Bermant, Herbert C. Kelman, and Donald P. Warwick, 233–42. New York: Halstead Press, 1978.

Williamson, Abigail, and Archon Fung. *Mapping Public Deliberation: A Report for the William and Flora Hewlett Foundation.* Cambridge, MA: John F. Kennedy School of Government, 2005.

Wilmet, Nicole. "Utah Small Claims Court Launches New Online Dispute Resolution Pilot Program." *Just Court ADR*, December 3, 2018. http://blog.aboutrsi.org/2018/pilot-program/utah-small-claims-court-launches-new-online-dispute-resolution-pilot-program.

Wilson, E. O. *Biophilia.* Cambridge, MA: Harvard University Press, 1984.

Wing, Leah. "Cyberbullying Hackathon Challenge Report." Presentation at 2014 ODR Forum, San Francisco/Palo Alto, CA, June 21–22, 2014.

———. "Ethical Principles for Online Dispute Resolution: A GPS Device for the Field." *International Journal of Online Dispute Resolution* 3 (2016): 12–29.

Winick, Bruce J. "Therapeutic Jurisprudence and Problem Solving Courts." *Fordham Urban Law Journal* 30, no. 3 (2003): 1055–103.

Winn, Maisha T. *Justice on Both Sides: Transforming Education Through Restorative Justice.* Cambridge, MA: Harvard Education Press, 2018.

Winslade, John, and Gerald D. Monk. *Narrative Mediation: A New Approach to Conflict Resolution.* San Francisco, CA: Jossey-Bass, 2000.

Winston, Kenneth I., ed. *The Principles of Social Order: Selected Essays of Lon L. Fuller.* Durham, NC: Duke University Press, 1981.

Wissler, Roselle L. "Court-Connected Settlement Procedures: Mediation and Judicial Settlement Conferences." *Ohio State Journal on Dispute Resolution* 26 (2011): 271–325.

———. "The Effectiveness of Court-Connected Dispute Resolution in Civil Cases." *Conflict Resolution Quarterly* 22, nos. 1–2 (2004): 55–72.

Woolf, Lord. *Access to Justice: Final Report to the Lord Chancellor on the Civil Justice System in England and Wales.* London: Her Majesty's Stationery Office, 1996.

———. *Access to Justice: Interim Report to the Lord Chancellor on the Civil Justice System in England and Wales.* London: Her Majesty's Stationery Office, 1995.

World Bank. "Worldwide Governance Indicators." http://info.worldbank.org/governance/wgi/#home (accessed June 30, 2019).

World Trade Organization. "The Doha Round Texts—Introduction." https://www.wto.org/english/tratop_e/dda_e/texts_intro_e.htm (accessed November 5, 2019).

———. "Negotiations to Improve Dispute Settlement Procedures." https://www.wto.org/english/tratop_e/dispu_e/dispu_negs_e.htm (accessed November 5, 2019).

———. "A Unique Contribution." https://www.wto.org/english/thewto_e/whatis_e/tif_e/disp1_e.htm (accessed November 5, 2019).

———. "WTO Analytical Index: WTO Agreement, Article IX." February 2018. https://www.wto.org/english/res_e/publications_e/ai17_e/wto_agree_art9_oth.pdf.

Wymbs, Cliff. "How E-commerce Is Transforming and Internationalizing Service Industries." *Journal of Services Marketing* 14, no. 6 (2000): 463–77.

Yang, Kaifeng, and Erik Bergrud, eds. *Civic Engagement in a Network Society.* Charlotte, NC: Information Age, 2008.

Yankelovich, Daniel. *The Magic of Dialogue: Transforming Conflict into Cooperation.* New York: Simon and Schuster, 1999.

Zack, Arnold M., and Michael T. Duffy. "ADR and Employment Discrimination: A Massachusetts Agency Leads the Way." *Dispute Resolution Journal* 29 (1996): 28–53.

Zartman, I. William. "The Elephant and the Holograph: Toward a Theoretical Synthesis and a Paradigm." In *International*

Multilateral Negotiation: Approaches to the Management of Complexity, edited by I. William Zartman, 213–22. San Francisco, CA: Jossey-Bass, 1994.

———, ed. *International Multilateral Negotiation: Approaches to the Management of Complexity*. San Francisco, CA: Jossey-Bass, 1994.

Zartman, I. William, and Maureen Berman. *The Practical Negotiator*. New Haven, CT: Yale University Press, 1982.

Zaslowsky, David. "What to Expect When Litigating Smart Contract Disputes." *Law360*, April 4, 2018. https://www.law360.com/articles/1028009/what-to-expect-when-litigating-smart-contract-disputes.

Zehr, Howard. "Commentary: Restorative Justice: Beyond Victim-Offender Mediation." *Conflict Resolution Quarterly* 22 (2004): 305–16.

Zekoll, Joachim, Moritz Balz, and Iwo Amelung, eds. *Formalisation and Flexibilisation in Dispute Resolution*. Leiden, Netherlands: Brill/Nijhoff, 2014.

Zelizer, Craig, and Robert A. Rubinstein, eds. *Building Peace: Practical Reflections from the Field*. Sterling, VA: Kumarian Press, 2009.

Zifcak, Spencer. "Restorative Justice in East Timor: An Evaluation of the Community Reconciliation Process of the CAVR." http://pdf.usaid.gov/pdf_docs/Pnado632.pdf (accessed June 21, 2019).

Zirhlioglu, Ersoy. "The Diamond Industry and the Industry's Dispute Resolution Mechanisms." *Arizona Journal of International and Comparative Law* 30, no. 3 (2013): 477–506.

Zoma, Jean-Baptiste. "Communication sur les interprofessions au Burkina Faso" [Communication on interprofessions in Burkina Faso]. October 2006. http://www.inter-reseaux.org/IMG/pdf/Burkina_Etatdeslieux_Interpro_PAF.pdf.

Zweigert, Konrad, and Hein Kotz. *An Introduction to Comparative Law*. Translated by Tony Weir. 3rd ed. Oxford: Oxford University Press, 1998.

Zywicki, Todd. "The Consumer Financial Protection Bureau: Savior or Menace?" *George Washington Law Review* 81 (2013): 856–928.

INDEX

Page numbers in italics indicate material in figures or tables.